The Chapel and Burial Ground
on St Ninian's Isle, Shetland:
Excavations past and present

by
Rachel C Barrowman

with contributions from
K Forsyth

and

P Ashmore, J Barrett, C S Barrowman, C E Batey, A Bayliss,
R Cerón-Carrasco, A Clydesdale, G Cook, M Donnelly, P Duffy, I Fisher,
R Gamble, L J Gidney, W Goodwin, A J Hall, J Henderson, R Hedges,
P G Johnson, R Jones, R Lewis, G McDonnell, A MacSween, J Meadows,
J Miller, W Murray, Z Outram, E Photos-Jones, S Ramsay, J Roberts, A Small and R Will

HISTORIC   ALBA
SCOTLAND   AOSMHOR

THE SOCIETY FOR MEDIEVAL ARCHAEOLOGY
MONOGRAPH 32

ISSN 0583-9106
ISBN 978-1-907975-46-2

Edited by Christopher Gerrard
Published by The Society for Medieval Archaeology, London
Printed and bound by Charlesworth Press, Wakefield, UK

This publication has been made possible by a grant from Historic Scotland

The Society for Medieval Archaeology
www.medievalarchaeology.org/publications

The Society for Medieval Archaeology Monographs are available from Maney Publishing, www.maney.co.uk

Barrowman, R C, 2011
The chapel and burial ground on St Ninian's Isle, Shetland: Excavations past and present,
The Society for Medieval Archaeology Monograph 32,
London

Cover: *View of tombolo and St Ninian's Isle from the mainland. Photograph: Christopher Gerrard*

CONTENTS

LIST OF FIGURES

COLOUR PLATES

SUMMARY

St Ninian's Isle in Shetland was brought to public attention when a magnificent hoard of 28 pieces of Pictish silverware was discovered there during excavations by Professor Andrew O'Dell of Aberdeen University in 1958. O'Dell had begun working on the Isle in 1955, to locate and excavate the medieval chapel. By the final excavation season in 1959 he had uncovered a remarkable archaeological site from under thick layers of sand, with evidence from the earliest years of Christianity in Shetland, lying above a short cist and cremation cemetery and the remains of Iron Age buildings and middens. However the finding of the treasure eclipsed all other aspects of the site, and although articles and a volume on the treasure were produced, the excavations remained largely unpublished. In 1999, as a response to erosion at the site and the need to re-examine the archaeology there, a small research project was initiated at Glasgow University, funded jointly by Historic Scotland, the Shetland Amenity Trust and Shetland Museum, to locate and re-assess the archive material from the 1950s and undertake small-scale excavations on the site. The results of the 1950s and recent work were ultimately combined and are presented in this volume.

At the base of the excavated sequence were found the remains of an Iron Age settlement consisting of cellular buildings that were rebuilt and re-used, and then abandoned in the 7th century AD, when the area became a burial ground. The first church was built on the site in the 8th century, and accompanied by a long cist cemetery with cross-incised stones and shrine sculpture. The church may have continued in use into the 9th or 10th centuries, and the recent work has confirmed that the famous hoard was buried within its walls. There was a degree of continuity between the pre-Christian and Christian burials, with evidence that the site was considered a special place for burial before the advent of Christianity. The burial assemblage also spans the native/Norse interface, with the Norse burials respecting the earlier short and long cists. Modelling of the radiocarbon dates confirmed that a group of infant burials, marked by headstones inscribed with crosses of Norse type, were buried in succession over a period of time in the 10th century. The infants also exhibit signs of malnutrition, which may reflect a period of hardship amongst the local population at this time. The end of this phase is marked by the burial of an adult male who died a violent death and was moved post-mortem to be buried on the site some time between the 11th and end of the 12th centuries, when the site was inundated with a thick layer of wind-blown sand. A new chapel with an accompanying long cist cemetery was then built above the earlier church, and a chancel with an apsidal east end housing a free-standing dry stone altar was added later. The associated graveyard continued in use until around 1840, long after the building was demolished. After this the ruined footings of the chapel walls remained buried in wind-blown sand and turf until Prof O'Dell's excavations began at the site over a hundred years later. The recent work incorporates specialist analyses of previously unpublished finds from the site, including a fantastic collection of glass beads, and a re-assessment of the ogham stone found on the site in 1876, and brings into the wider domain the findings from this extraordinary archaeological site.

RÉSUMÉ

L'île de Saint-Ninian dans les Shetland a été portée à l'attention du public lorsqu'en 1958 un magnifique trésor de 28 pièces d'argenterie picte fut découvert au cours des fouilles du Professeur Andrew O'Dell de l'Université d'Aberdeen. O'Dell commença à travailler sur l'île en 1955 pour localiser et fouiller la chapelle médiévale. A la dernière saison de fouilles en 1959, il avait découvert un remarquable site archéologique sous des couches épaisses de sable, avec des indices des premières années du christianisme dans les Shetland, au-dessus d'une petite ciste et d'un cimetière de crémation et les vestiges de constructions et de tertres de l'Age du Fer. Cependant, la découverte du trésor éclipsa tous les autres aspects du site, et bien que des articles et un volume sur le trésor furent produits, les fouilles restèrent largement non publiées. En 1999, en réponse à l'érosion du site et au besoin de réexaminer l'archéologie, un petit projet fut initié à l'Université de Glasgow, fondé conjointement avec l'Historic Scotland, le Shetland Amenity Trust et le Shetland Museum, pour localiser et réévaluer le matériel d'archives des années 1950 et entreprendre des fouilles à petite échelle sur le site. Les résultats des années 1950 et les travaux récents furent finalement combinés et sont présentés dans ce volume.

A la base de la séquence fouillée ont été trouvés les vestiges d'une implantation de l'Age du Fer consistant en des constructions cellulaires qui ont été reconstruites et réutilisées, puis abandonnées au VIIe siècle après J.C., quand la zone est devenue un cimetière. La première église fut construite sur le site au VIIIe siècle, accompagnée d'une longue ciste avec des pierres à croix incisée et une sculpture d'autel. L'église a probablement été utilisée aux IXe et Xe siècles, et l'étude récente a confirmé que le célèbre trésor avait été enterré sous le sol. Le site a connu une continuité d'inhumations préchrétiennes et chrétiennes. Il semblerait, comme l'attestent certains indices, que le site était considéré comme une place spéciale pour l'inhumation avant l'avènement du christianisme. L'assemblage des inhumations s'étend également à l'interface natifs/norvégiens, avec les inhumations norvégiennes respectant les petites et longues cistes antérieures. La modélisation des dates radiocarbone a confirmé qu'un groupe de sépultures d'enfants en bas âge, marquées par une pierre tombale inscrite de croix de type norois, furent inhumées les unes derrière les autres au cours du Xe siècle. Les enfants en bas âge montrent également des signes de malnutrition, ce qui peut refléter une période de privations au sein de la population locale à cette époque. La fin de cette phase est marquée par l'inhumation d'un adulte mâle qui a succombé d'une mort violente et a été déplacé post-mortem pour être inhumé sur le site entre le XIe et la fin du XIIe siècle, quand le site a été inondé par une épaisse couche de sable éolien. Une nouvelle chapelle accompagnée d'une longue ciste de cimetière a ensuite été construite au-dessus de l'ancienne église et un chœur absidal abritant un autel en pierres sèches sur pied a été ajouté ultérieurement. Le cimetière associé a utilisé jusqu'en 1840 environ, longtemps après la démolition de l'édifice. Les fondations en ruine de la chapelle sont restées enterrées dans le sable éolien et la tourbe, jusqu'au début des fouilles du site par le Professeur O'Dell's une centaine d'années plus tard. L'étude récente comprend les analyses de spécialistes des découvertes antérieures du site non-publiées, incluant une collection fantastique de perles en verre, une réévaluation de la pierre ogham découverte sur le site en 1876. Elle dévoile ainsi au grand public les découvertes de cet extraordinaire site archéologique.

RIASSUNTO

L'isola St Ninian appartenente all'archipelago dello Shetland è stato portata all'attenzione del pubblico quando, nel 1958, un ricco bottino formato da 28 pezzi di argenteria dei pitti fu scoperto durante gli scavi del Prof Andrew O'Dell dell' Università di Aberdeen. O'Dell incominciò a lavorare nell'isola nel 1955, per trovare e scavare la cappella medioevale. Alla fine della stagione di scavo del 1959 O'Dell portò alla luce un notevole sito archeologico sommerso da densi strati di sabbia, a testimonianza dei primi anni del Cristianesimo nello Shetland, situato su una piccola cista, un cimitero crematorio, i resti di costruzioni dell'età del ferro e rifiuti. Il ritrovamento del tesoro, tuttavia, pose in secondo piano gli altri aspetti del sito, e sebbene sono stati scritti articoli ed una monografia sul tesoro, gli scavi rimasero per la maggior parte non pubblicati. Nel 1999, a causa dell'erosione del sito e della necessità di riesaminarlo, un breve progetto di studio fu intrapreso dall' Università di Glaslow, finanziato da "Historic Scotland", "Shetland Amenity Trust" e il museo dello Shetland, per trovare e rivalutare i materiali d'archivio del 1950 e per intraprendere saggi di scavo del sito. Questo volume presenta i risultati degli scavi effettuati negli anni '50 e quelli della recente ricerca.

Alla base della seguenza stratigrafica dello scavo sono stati ritrovati resti di un insediamento dell' età del ferro costituito da abitazioni modulari ricostruite e riusate, e poi abbandonate nel settimo secolo dC, quando l'area diventò un cimitero. La prima chiesa fu costruita nel sito nell' ottavo secolo, con accanto un cimitero di lunghe ciste con croci incise su pietra e una scultura sacra. La chiesa probabilmente continuò ad essere usata nel nono e decimo secolo, e gli studi della recente ricerca hanno confermato che il famoso bottino era stato sepolto nel pavimento. Si può notare un certo grado di continuità tra le tombe pre-cristiane e cristiane, a testimonianza che il sito fu considerato un posto funebre particolare per la sepoltura prima dell'avvento del Cristianesimo. Il complesso funerario si estende anche nella fase di transizione tra la popolazione autoctona e dei Norse, con sepolture dei Norse rispettando le precedenti ciste piccole e lunghe. La datazione con il radiocarbonio ha confermato che un gruppo di sepolture infantili, contrassegnate da lapidi con croci del tipo di Norse, erano state sepolte in successione nel corso di un lasso di tempo nel decimo secolo. I resti umani dei neonati mostrano anche segni di malnutrizione, che probabilmente riflettono una fase di povertà in questo periodo tra la popolazione locale. La fine di quest'epoca è stata segnata dalla sepoltura di un adulto maschio che morì di una morte violenta, mosso post-mortem e sepolto nuovamente nel sito all'incirca tra l'undicesimo e fine del dodicesimo secolo, quando il sito fu inondato con uno strato spesso di sabbia trasportata dal vento. Una nuova cappella con accanto un cimitero di ciste lunghe fu poi costruita sopra una precedente chiesa e successivamente fu construito il coro, nella cui parte terminale orientale dell'apside si trova un altare di pietra a secco. Il cimitero adiacente alla cappella continuò ad essere in uso fino al 1840 circa, anche molto tempo dopo la demolizione della costruzione. Dopodiché il rovinato basamento delle mura della cappella è rimasto sepolto dalla torba e dalla sabbia portata dal vento finché il prof. O'Dell ha iniziato gli scavi presso il sito oltre un centinaio di anni più tardi. La recente ricerca include analisi specialistiche di ritrovamenti del sito non pubblicati precedentemente, una fantastica collezione di perline vitree e una rivalutazione dell' ogham di pietra trovato nel sito nel 1876, e colloca in un campo più vasto i ritrovamenti di questo straordinario sito archeologico.

ACKNOWLEDGEMENTS

A particular debt of gratitude is owed to the project funders: the Shetland Amenity Trust, Historic Scotland, Glasgow University and the Shetland Museum, and to Professor Christopher Morris, who initiated and was very supportive of the setting up of the project. I am also very grateful to the Budge family at Bigton Farm, especially Jim, Nancy, Owen and Bryden, and to the fieldwork team: Paul Johnson (survey and geophysics), Kevin Brady (excavation supervisor), Julie Roberts (human remains specialist), Aileen Maule (environmental supervisor), Chris Barrowman (logistics), and student volunteers: Alastair Becket, Kevin Kerrigan, Philomena Kennedy, Julie Madsen, Tracey Muir, Alison Parfitt, Laura Scott, Tracey Provan, Tracy Thomson, Lucy Bailey, Trevor Kelly, Amit Sarkar, Sandra Jack and Heather Blackie. Also to Laurie and Elma Johnson of Bigton, Biddy Simpson (Shetland Amenity Trust), Douglas Coutts, and to all those who visited the excavations and were kind enough to share their memories. Helpful suggestions and support were given by Val Turner (Shetland Archaeologist), Dr Sally Foster, Rod McCullagh, Dr Ann McSween and Dr Alan Rutherford (Historic Scotland), Dr Colleen Batey, Professor James Graham-Campbell and the late Dr Alan Small. The illustrations were produced by Lorraine McEwan and Gillian McSwan, Gary Tompsett processed the survey data and drawings. Mr Ian Scott donated a significant amount of his time to produce the drawings of the cross-incised stones. During the archive study many individuals were of great assistance. All photographs are by the author, unless otherwise credited.

A particular debt is owed to Helen Nisbet, who allowed me unrestricted access to her personal archives, and has been a constant source of help when studying the 1950s excavations. Moran taing Eilidh. My father's old Rolls-Royce Conversion Booklet: *Tables, Factors, Definitions and Basic Units* (10th edition), TSD publication 201, Derby, was extremely useful when converting all imperial measurements in the archive to metric. Professor Charles Thomas was kind enough to share his archive and thoughts on O'Dell's excavations, as was Dr James Coull. Brian Smith, Shetland Archivist, Tommy Watt, Shetland Museum curator, and Ian Tait, Museum Assistant, were of great assistance throughout the project. Professor Robert Hedges, Dr James Barrett and Dr Gordon Cook gave up their time to discuss aspects of the dating programme,

Tim Neighbour provided a draft copy of his report on Galson, Lewis, Mark Elliot photographed finds for the archive, Eileen Brooke-Freeman, Project Officer for the Shetland Place Names project, and Robert Leask, kindly provided and discussed place-name information. Finally I am particularly grateful to Dr Colleen Batey for her support throughout and comments on the final draft at very short notice, to Professor James Graham-Campbell who read and provided helpful comments on the text, and most of all to Chris Barrowman, fond counsellor and honest critic. The responsibility for the ideas presented here remains as ever solely with the author.

Dr Colleen Batey is most grateful for the advice and comments of a number of colleagues in the preparation of her note on the beads. Several people were consulted in her quest for parallels to the beads and she is most grateful to the late Margaret Guido, Professor Rosemary Cramp and Trevor Cowie in particular. She wishes to thank Professor Charles Thomas for his discussion about the site and the original excavations, and Professor James Graham-Campbell for making her aware of the beads in the first place and for his contribution to the revision of her paper. Others have read and commented on the text, particularly Christopher Morris, Rachel Barrowman and Hilary Cool, but any remaining inadequacies remain with the author.

Dr Richard Jones would like to thank Gert Petersen for the extraction steps and Jim Tweedie for the GC. This work benefited greatly from the practical assistance given to GP by Anna Mukherjee, at Professor Evershed's laboratory in Bristol, in October 2003. The writer is however responsible for the results presented here. Robert Will would like to thank George Haggarty who commented on the medieval pottery sherds.

Zoe Outram kindly re-modelled all the radiocarbon dates from St Ninian's Isle at the eleventh hour and at very short notice, five years after the first modelling was undertaken so as to take account of the new calibration curve which had been released in 2009.

Finally, it was with great sadness that just as the text was being submitted, the authors and contributors to this volume learnt that Tommy Watt, Shetland Museum curator and friend, passed away in May 2010 after a long battle with leukaemia. He will be greatly missed by all those who have ever had the fortune to work in Shetland's archaeology.

INTRODUCTION AND BACKGROUND

1.1 THE STRUCTURE AND SCOPE OF THIS PUBLICATION

St Ninian's Isle in Shetland is best known for being the find spot of the St Ninian's Isle treasure (Plate 1), a magnificent hoard of 28 pieces of Pictish silverware found in 1958 during excavations on the Isle by Professor Andrew C O'Dell of Aberdeen University. O'Dell had been attracted to the site by the local tradition that a medieval chapel dedicated to St Ninian lay below the sand on the east side of the Isle. O'Dell was to uncover and excavate the chapel in 1955–56, but when his excavations in succeeding summer seasons continued below and to the south of the chapel, he uncovered archaeological remains that spanned the late prehistoric to medieval periods.[1] In 1958 the 'treasure' was found during excavations below the chapel and by 1959, when O'Dell and his team returned to the Isle for the last time in an attempt to 'finish' the excavations and tidy up the site, they had uncovered an ever more complicated suite of archaeological features from below up to 6m of wind-blown sand, on what was clearly a nationally important site. Above the ruins of Iron Age stone structures, paving and middens, short cist burials and cremations, long cists and early incised crosses and cross slabs were excavated. An earlier church[2] building was found below the later medieval chapel, and a collection of early Christian shrine posts were discovered in a secondary position outside the SE corner of the chapel. Iron Age pottery, a bone and antler necklace, animal bone, worked stone and beads were also found in the Iron Age levels. At the end of the summer of 1959, the site was consolidated and turfed over, and arguments continued as to where the treasure should be housed: in Aberdeen, Shetland or Edinburgh (Smith 1973). Meanwhile the archaeological remains on the site received less attention, and compounded by the lack of published information or an excavation archive as we would understand it today, this has remained the case, with academic investigation since concentrating on the nature and art style of the hoard and the circumstances of its deposition (see below). This volume does not intend therefore to discuss the treasure in great depth, but rather the archaeological site that produced such a unique find. It describes the results of a small research project undertaken at Glasgow University between 1999 and 2004 with the aim of revisiting the archaeology at the site through a study of the archive material from the 1950s excavations, and renewed survey and excavation work on the Isle over two summer seasons. It was intended that the project should attempt to redress the balance between the archaeology in and around the chapel on St Ninian's Isle and the spectacular find that was to make it famous.

The discoveries from St Ninian's Isle are described and analysed in chronological order. Following an introduction to the site, outlining the archaeological, historical and geological background, Forsyth in Chapter 2 re-assesses the ogham stone found in the 19th century by the antiquarian Gilbert Goudie when he visited the Isle and attempted to locate the chapel. There then follows an assessment and analysis in Chapter 3 of the sources available to study the results of O'Dell's excavations on the Isle between 1955 and 1959, and specialist analyses and discussions on the new material found in the archives. Chapter 4 then moves on to the results of the excavations directed by the author in 1999 and 2000 in order to record and assess O'Dell's previous work at the site,[3] also with the specialist analyses and discussions of the artefactual, environmental and human bone assemblages, and radiocarbon dating of that material. The concluding Chapter 5 discusses the range and significance of the results of all the research described in this report, and what they can tell us about this remarkable archaeological site.

The publication of this research cannot claim to be a 'final excavation report' on the 1950s excavations, as we would understand it today. It does bring the archive material into the wider domain for discussion and analysis, however, and it has been possible to outline a chronological sequence of archaeological phases within which most of the excavated features can be located, and to outline and discuss how this impinges on the interpretation of the site as a whole, not least the treasure itself.

1.2 SITE LOCATION AND DESCRIPTION

St Ninian's Isle is in the Shetland Isles, the most northerly islands in the British Isles. From a modern, mainland UK perspective, the islands are often considered 'remote', being situated 180km (112 miles) north of mainland Britain and as far north as the southern tip of Greenland. Their position in the

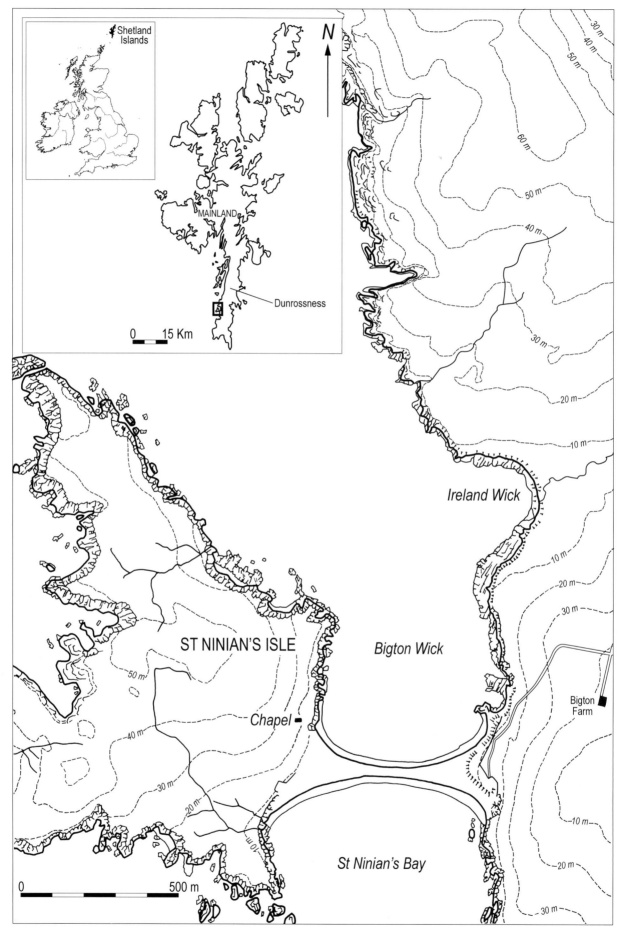

FIGURE 1.1
Location map. Drawing: L McEwan and G McSwan

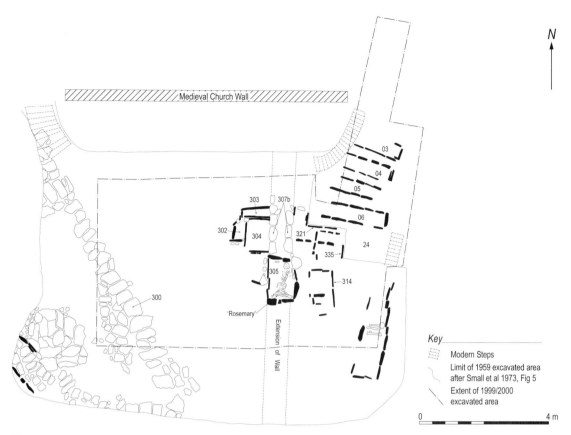

Figure 1.2

Excavations in the area to the south of the chapel (after Small et al 1973, fig 5), with additions showing extent of 2000 excavations and labelling of re-examined features. Re-drawn by L McEwan and G McSwan

centre of the seaways between the North Atlantic, Scandinavia, Europe and mainland Britain, equidistant between Bergen in Norway, and Aberdeen in mainland Scotland, has opened them up to contacts from far and wide.

The small, now uninhabited, island of St Ninian's Isle lies off the SW coast of Dunrossness, the most southerly district of mainland Shetland, to which it is joined by a sandy bar or tombolo (Figure 1.1). The Dunrossness peninsula comprises a central upland spine of heather moorland, peat bog and rough grazings which undulate downwards to the south, east and west before rising again towards the impressive cliffs at the SW coast. The presence of coastal sandy fertile areas of improved grassland and cultivated farmland has meant that Dunrossness has the largest coverage of fertile agricultural land in Shetland and has traditionally been an area of crofts and farms. St Ninian's Isle is in the Bigton township on the west coast of the peninsula and is part of the lands belonging to the old Bigton Farm, which is still worked today. The tombolo provides easy access to the Isle from Bigton at most times of the year (see cover plate), except during very high tides or strong north-westerly gales, and is one of Shetland's foremost beauty spots (PLATES 1 and 2).

A Site of Special Scientific Interest (SSSI) encompasses the tombolo, the east side of the Isle and the west side of the mainland (Nature Conservancy Council 1976). The SSSI also falls within the mainland sector of the Shetland National Scenic Area, and geomorphological interest in the site is high due to the presence of the sandy tombolo (tombolos composed of sand, as opposed to shingle or gravel, are unusual features on the national scale; Dargie 1998, vol 2, 1, 22). The sandy beach is thought to overlie a shingle ayre, some of the stones of which are occasionally exposed after severe combing down or scouring of the surface material by the sea (Mather and Smith 1974, 26–29). The tombolo itself is thought to have been formed by wave action on the sea-floor sand (Flinn 1997).

St Ninian's Isle rises to 50m above sea level at its highest point, with a gentle slope down to the sandy tombolo on the east side. Sand that has blown up from the tombolo covers the east side of the Isle, to a depth of at least 6m in places, and the marks of former turf layers in the sand suggest that the inundations were an intermittent process. Below the sand lies the clay subsoil, formed from the underlying grey schists. The archaeological site discussed in this report is located on this east side, 25m above sea level (NGR HU 3685 2090), and was excavated from a thick layer of wind-blown sand. Despite its position on a small offshore island, it should not be viewed in isolation but as part of a wider landscape, rich in archaeological sites, in particular the outstanding multi-period settlements excavated

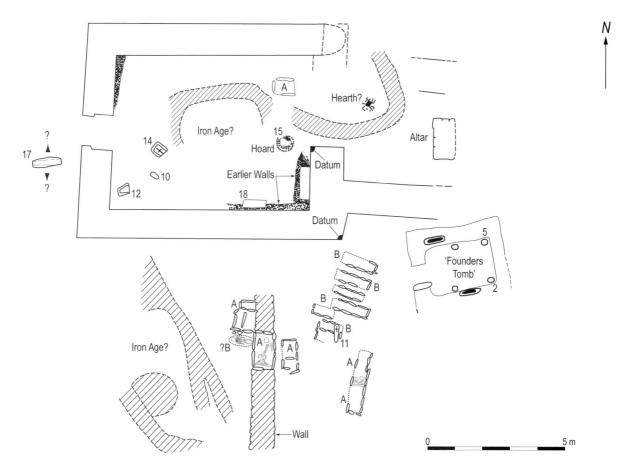

FIGURE 1.3

Reconstructed site plan (1967) showing probable positions of (numbered) sculptured stones, after Thomas 1973, fig 8. Re-drawn by L McEwan and G McSwan

at Jarlshof (Hamilton 1956) and Scatness (Nicholson and Dockrill 1998; Dockrill 2003), lie 11km (7 miles) south of St Ninian's Isle at Sumburgh Head.

1.3 ARCHAEOLOGICAL BACKGROUND

The 1955–59 excavations

Professor Andrew C O'Dell already had a keen interest in the historical geography of the Shetland Isles (O'Dell 1939) when, at the Viking Congress held in Lerwick in 1950, Dr W Douglas Simpson drew his attention to St Ninian's Isle, the Ninianic dedication and the local tradition of a chapel on the Isle (O'Dell 1959b, 241; 1960, 4). Five years later O'Dell, Geography Professor at Aberdeen University, began his fieldwork (O'Dell 1957), which involved the digging of test pits over the general area to locate the medieval chapel. In succeeding years, once the chapel was located, a huge depth of wind-blown sand and thousands of medieval and later burials were removed over an area roughly 16 x 16m, with a proportion being re-buried to the west of the chapel (Small 1973, 4). The interior of the medieval chapel was also excavated with the aid of timber shoring, and in the process, walling belonging

to an earlier, presumed church, building (O'Dell 1959b, 241–242) was uncovered. Cist burials were discovered within the church, lying up to 2m below the medieval chapel foundations, above layers of paving and walling which yielded Iron Age pottery (Small 1973, 5) and several sculptured stones were also found in and around the chapel, including four corner-posts, three median posts and two side- or end-panel fragments from either three, or two, each possibly double, early Christian shrines, and four later Norse carved and incised steatite crosses and a hogback grave cover (Thomas 1971, 153–160; 1973, 20–31; 1983; 1998). In 1959 excavations in the area to the south of the chapel were continued to a level below the chapel foundations and an array of stone paving and walling, with associated Iron Age pottery, were discovered from below several stone cists, one containing a crouched burial (O'Dell 1959c; Small 1973, 6–7). By far the most exciting discovery, for which St Ninian's Isle is renowned, was that of the 'Treasure', uncovered on 4 July 1958 by a Shetland schoolboy, Douglas Coutts, who had come to the site for the day to help out (O'Dell 1958; 1959a; 1959b; 1959c, 242–243; 1960). This hoard of Pictish silverware was found in the remains of a larch wood box, covered by a cross-marked slab at some depth below the floor of the medieval chapel, within the possible earlier church building. The hoard (PLATE 4) remains to this day one of the largest collections of Pictish silver ever to be discovered (Graham-Campbell 2003a).

Three short annual accounts of the excavations were published by O'Dell, in *Discovery and Excavation in Scotland* (O'Dell 1957; 1958; 1959c), followed by three articles concerning the treasure found in 1958 (O'Dell 1959a; 1959b; 1960). Only the short introductory parts of these papers described the excavations, however, and it was not until six years after the death of Professor O'Dell in 1967, that the findings of the 1955–59 excavations were published by Alan Small, then of Dundee University, who had supervised at the site as a student (Small *et al* 1973), with colleagues David Wilson and Charles Thomas reporting on the treasure and the sculptured stones respectively. Small faced an extremely difficult task as few site records, finds records or plans had been made at the time of the excavation. Instead he relied heavily on his own memory and notes, slides both he and other excavation members had taken, and personal recollections and diaries of members of the excavation team, especially the site diary of Helen Nisbet, a student who attended the dig in 1956, 1957 and 1959. The resulting final volume dealt primarily with the magnificent treasure and Small's account of the excavations themselves comprised only four pages, a site location plan, drawings of some of

the other finds from the site other than the treasure and a plan of the archaeological remains (Small 1973, 4–7, figs 1–6; fig 5 reproduced in this volume in Figure 1.2). Thomas added his own thoughts and a plan (reproduced in Figure 1.3) in the succeeding chapter on the sculptured stones and crosses (Thomas 1973, 11–14). The final chapter dealt with the law relating to the treasure (Smith 1973).

Not surprisingly, given the lack of excavation records, academic investigation has since concentrated on the nature and art style of the hoard and the circumstances of its deposition, rather than the wider archaeological site (O'Dell 1959b; McRoberts 1962; Wilson 1970; 1973; Graham-Campbell 1975, 43; 2003a, 21–23; forthcoming; Youngs 1989; Webster and Blackhouse 1991; Forsyth forthcoming b). Over and above discussions centred upon the nature of the treasure itself, there has also been some debate concerning the earlier, possible church, building identified below the medieval chapel, with, for example, Thomas proposing that it is an early Christian stone church, accompanied by long cist burials aligned E–W, a theory supported by the presence of the shrine components (Thomas 1971, 14–15; 1973, 11–13; 1983, 285–292), and Morris suggesting that 'it might be asked whether the stone building that Thomas has hypothesized below the later stone church ... could come from a later (i.e. Norse) period?' (Morris 1996b, 189). The sculpture, too, has been the subject of renewed discussion, particularly

FIGURE 1.4

The chapel on St Ninian's Isle in August 1999 from the NE. The concrete post in the centre marks the find spot of the treasure. Photograph: R Barrowman

FIGURE 1.5

The area to the south of the chapel on St Ninian's Isle in August 1999 from the SE. Photograph: R Barrowman

in relation to other examples (eg Stevenson 1981; Thomas 1983; Lamb 1995), and to the ogham inscribed stones found at the site by Goudie in 1876 (Goudie 1879; Forsyth 1996a; Chapter 2 below).

The 1999–2000 survey and excavations

Two small excavations were led by the author on St Ninian's Isle in 1999 and 2000 in tandem with a wider programme of survey and excavation on Shetland chapel sites by colleagues at Glasgow University (Morris and Brady with Johnson 1999; Morris and Barrowman 2008). The work was initiated in 1998 after the Shetland Archaeologist, Val Turner, had drawn attention to the dilapidated state of the site, and after gaining joint funding from Glasgow University, Historic Scotland and the Shetland Amenity Trust, the first season of fieldwork was completed in August 1999. Work concentrated on non-intrusive methods of research that were designed to assess the survival of the archaeological remains and to produce a set of recommendations for their management and consolidation within the scheduled area around the chapel. This covered a large area on the east side of the Isle, 120m E–W and 150m N–S, with the fenced-off chapel area located within it towards the south (Plate 2). The site of O'Dell's excavations had deteriorated considerably. Overgrown vegetation covered the site within

the fenced area (Figure 1.4), around the chapel there had been extensive rabbit burrowing (Figure 1.5), and to the east outside the fenced area, erosion had resulted in a threat of collapse of sandy deposits into the sea. Rabbit burrowing and subsequent destabilisation of areas of grassland outside the fenced area, to the west and south, and wind blow and stock movement on the subsequently denuded areas, was also having a drastic effect. The lack of any obvious management or presentation of the archaeology in the vicinity of the chapel enhanced the general feeling of neglect and had been noted by visitors to the site (Scheduling record contained in SMR, no. 707–SN767, 16).

The methodology for the 1999 season was straightforward. First a desktop study of O'Dell's previous work at the site consulted the ADS, NMRS, SMR, Shetland Museum, Shetland Archives, National Museum of Scotland, Ordnance Survey 1st edition and aerial photographs. Papers and photographs relating to O'Dell's excavations, which had been deposited in the Shetland Archives by the late Dr Alan Small in 1998 were also examined.

This was followed by fieldwork, which was split into three main elements: topographic survey, geophysical survey and limited trial trenching (Harry 2000). Topographic survey was a necessary starting point to record above-ground features (Plate 2), and the geophysical survey was then undertaken of the

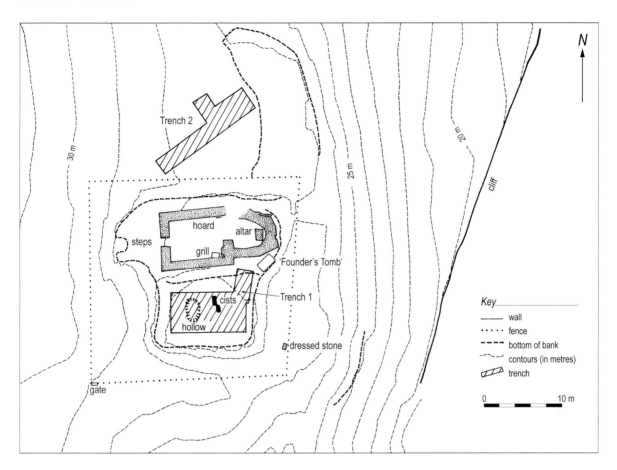

FIGURE 1.6

St Ninian's Isle trench location plan in 2000. Drawing: L McEwan

scheduled area to try and accurately define the limits of the site as it was clear that the archaeology must extend below ground beyond the limits of the fenced area around the chapel. It was also hoped that geophysical survey would be able to establish the nature of the subsurface archaeology, in particular the extent of the burial ground outside the fenced area, but also the position and extent of the 1950s trenches. Despite the scale of the survey and the intensity of the sampling density employed, however, relatively little of archaeological significance was detected (Johnson 2000). Whilst the gradiometer survey identified dipolar readings in a small area, resulting from near-surface ferrous material, possible coffin furniture, many of the larger anomalies detected in the survey were thought likely to be of geological or geomorphological origin. It was also difficult to interpret the results of the survey accurately in the knowledge that so much of the site had been badly affected by rabbit burrowing. The combination of dry, free-draining sand and a 'honeycomb' of rabbit burrows across the site precluded the success of the multiplexed resistivity survey, which had been undertaken to supplement the gradiometer results. The four small trial trenches opened to investigate the nature and extent of the archaeology proved more successful. Backfill and surviving archaeology left by O'Dell's excavations was found in Trial

Trench 1 (the results of which were incorporated later into Trench 1; see Chapter 4 below) and two extant post-medieval burials were found outside the fenced area to the north in Trial Trench 2 (later incorporated in Trench 2; Barrowman 2000, 32–39) in an area highlighted by the geophysics as potentially being a continuation of the medieval/post-medieval burial ground. Cultivated soils but no archaeological features were found in Trial Trench 3 at the north limit of the scheduled area, and spoil from O'Dell's excavations was found in Trial Trench 4 (Harry 2000, 42–44). A plan was also drawn of the chapel and a detailed photographic record made of the wall elevations so as to provide a record of the building for any future conservation work (now lodged with Historic Scotland).

On the completion of the 1999 fieldwork, ten recommendations were made suggesting ways in which the archaeological site could be managed in the future (Harry 2000, 45–53). These were designed to bring the site to a state whereby it could be cared for and/or consolidated by a responsible body or partnership. They included geomorphological advice as to the long-term risks to the site from natural erosion, archaeological recording through excavation of eroding deposits, especially those with visibly eroding human remains, a health and safety assessment, consolidation of the fabric of the chapel walls, improved interpretation, monitoring of visitor erosion and the initiation of a management group for the site. In response to eight of the recommendations, a further season of fieldwork was undertaken in July 2000 (Harry 2000, 48–53). The fieldwork included a site visit and geomorphological report (see below), and the excavation of areas to the south (Trench 1) and north (Trench 2) of the chapel (Figure 1.6), the completion of a health and safety assessment in advance of the fieldwork and a meeting of some of the members of the management group on an *ad hoc* basis, in order to address specific issues. The Shetland Archaeologist and the Historic Scotland Monument Warden for Shetland continued to monitor visitor erosion.

The excavation of Trial Trench 1 to the south of the chapel in 1999 had already shown that archaeology was being damaged, or at threat from being damaged, by rabbit burrowing, and in 2000 the trench was expanded (Trench 1) so as to record and partially excavate the archaeological deposits that had been left *in situ* by O'Dell in an attempt to define a stratigraphical sequence of features and deposits. This was especially desirable in advance of any consolidation or improved presentation of the site. To the north of the chapel outside the fenced area where the excavation of Trial Trench 2, in 1999, had confirmed that there were medieval and later burials, as indicated by the dipolar readings in the gradiometer survey (Johnson 2000, 33, feature 12), a larger area (Trench 2), was opened to assess the extent of the medieval and post-medieval graveyard on the north side of the chapel so that any further disturbance to the burial ground could be mitigated in the future.

Post-excavation and archive study

Following the 2000 fieldwork and a management meeting on site it was decided that the consolidation and interpretation of the site should not be addressed until the key management issue – that of who should manage the site, and how – was resolved. It was therefore decided to embark upon the post-excavation and publication of the results of those parts of the 1999–2000 excavations which investigated O'Dell's work (Trial Trench 1 and Trench 1), so that if the site were to be managed and improved in the future, interpretative text for presentation to visitors, and suggestions about which features should be consolidated and presented and which should be covered over and protected, could be made from the publication. The results from the small excavation areas, Trench 2 and Trial Trenches 2 and 3 that lay outwith the area of O'Dell's excavations and relate to the medieval and later history of the site were therefore reported separately (Harry 2000, 40–43; Barrowman 2000, 32–39). Trial Trench 4, which had located a spoil heap from the 1950s excavations and contained only sand and re-deposited disarticulated

human bone to a depth of 1.3m was also taken no further (Harry 2000, 43–44).

As the post-excavation project began in the winter of 2002/3, Mr Tommy Watt of the Shetland Museum drew the author's attention to a further group of material, which had been deposited in the Shetland Museum following Alan Small's death in 2000. A brief look at this material made it clear that a reassessment of the aims of the final publication was needed. The collection (hereafter called 'the Small collection') comprised over 1000 pieces of material, mainly pottery, most originating from O'Dell's trenches below and to the south of the chapel. Furthermore, most of the bags of finds contained a paper label identifying it to a particular 'pit', and whilst these pits are not mentioned in the published sources, they are described in a site notebook contained within Small's documentary archive in the Shetland Archives.

In discussion with Historic Scotland and the Shetland Museum, an assessment of the material showed that by taking the finds, labels and notebook together, it would be worth attempting to reconstruct the approximate position and depth of the finds and, possibly, of some of the pits and features that were associated with them. The 1950s material was therefore included in the post-excavation analysis of the 1999/2000 excavations, and it was attempted to pull all the material together into one broad, chronological framework. Many of the extant features on the site that were first uncovered to the south of the chapel in 1959 had been re-investigated in 2000, and the resulting stratigraphic sequence that was built up from the recent excavations could be combined with, and tested against, the 1950s material. The subsequent refinements made possible by radiocarbon dating and specialist analysis of both excavation assemblages meant that the suggestions put forward in an interim paper (Barrowman 2003) could be further investigated. There were no excavations in the area below the chapel in 1999 or 2000, as it had been filled in with gravel and concrete after the 1950s excavations, and would have been subject to considerable Health and Safety limitations. Through the study of the 'Small archive' however it was possible during post-excavation to combine the results of the 1950s excavations below the chapel with those from the area to the south of it from the 1950s and the 1999/2000 excavations. The final results of this research are presented and discussed in Chapters 3 to 6 below.

1.4 GEOLOGICAL BACKGROUND

Solid and drift geology
with Paul G Johnson

The bedrock of St Ninian's Isle is composed exclusively of metasedimentary rocks of the Whiteness Division. In general these consist of flaggy mi-

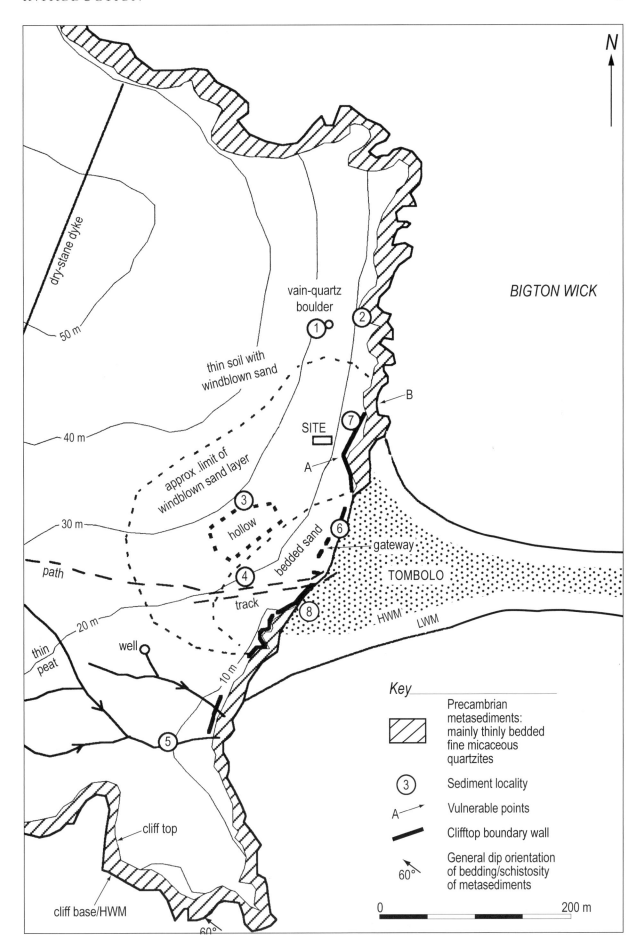

N

dry-stane dyke

50 m

vain-quartz
boulder

BIGTON WICK

①

②

thin soil with
windblown sand

40 m

B

SITE

⑦

A

approx .limit of
windblown sand layer

③

30 m

hollow

⑥

gateway

bedded sand

TOMBOLO

path

④

track

⑧

HWM

LWM

20 m

thin
peat

well

10 m

⑤

Key

Precambrian
metasediments:
mainly thinly bedded
fine micaceous
quartzites

③ Sediment locality

A⟶ Vulnerable points

Clifftop boundary wall

60° General dip orientation
of bedding/schistosity
of metasediments

cliff top

cliff base/HWM

60°

0   200 m

FIGURE 1.7

Schematic map showing main geomorphological features on the east side of St Ninian's Isle. Drawing: A J Hall

caceous quartz-feldspar-granulite containing bands
of crystalline limestone. Specifically, the rocks of
St Ninian's Isle belong to the Colla Firth group of
minerals, formed by Permeation metamorphism, after the regional Tectonising and Porphyroblast metamorphism had taken place, but whilst the thermal
gradients arising from these earlier events were still
in place. The materials subjected to metamorphosis
were essentially limestones and the degree of meta-
morphisation was relatively slight resulting in crystalline limestones, and in the western extremity of
the Isle, East Burra Pelite. Interestingly, the majority
of the Colla Firth group of minerals in Shetland as a
whole lie to the west of the Nesting Fault, St Ninian's Isle lies to the east sandwiched between it and
the Bigton Grit Complex of the Clift Hills Phyllitic
group (Johnson 2000, 25; Mykura 1976). There are
some recorded intrusions into the metasediments
of St Ninian's Isle. In the western Pelite deposits,
gneisses and other vein complexes are known and
there is no reason to doubt that minor intrusions of
similar material exist elsewhere on the Isle.

In common with the whole of Shetland, and indeed Scotland, St Ninian's Isle was subjected to the
effects of all four glacial episodes of the Pleistocene
period. A thin, irregular deposit of stony till covers a
proportion of the archipelago, the matrix and content of which depend on local bedrock conditions.
There is no reason to suspect that St Ninian's Isle
does not possess similar deposits, but the most obvious surface deposits on the Isle are post glacial and
consist of large quantities of wind-blown sand. The
lack of wind-blown sand found in the excavation
trenches below a certain level in the 1950s (Small
et al 1973, 1) and in 1999/2000 (Harry 2000; Barrowman 2000) suggests that in the Iron Age the Isle
may have been a true island approachable only by
boat. The origins and development of the tombolo
are far from clear. In a recent sand dune vegetation
survey of Shetland, the dunes at St Ninian's Isle were
classed as being 'mobile' (Dargie 1998, vol 2, 1, 22),
and it seems that the tombolo itself is a transient feature, growing and declining with the movement of
the seabed and rise and fall of sea levels (Flinn 1997).

Geomorphology
Allan J Hall

Active erosion

A geomorphological study of the area around the
chapel was undertaken in 2000 specifically to investigate the stability of the site (Hall 2000). The site
is vulnerable 'geologically' due to its proximity to
an actively eroding precipitous coastline, with the
two most vulnerable points at A to the NE of the
site, and B, to the NE at a greater distance of c50m
(Figure 1.7).

Point A presents the greatest risk as it is close to
the site. The near vertical cliffs that form more than
90% of the boundary of the island are migrating
inland, forming small irregular coves with features
such as caves and natural arches. Eventually the cliff
will reach the archaeological site, and although it is
difficult to estimate how long it will take before the
cliff line reaches the site, it is probably in the order of
500–1000 years. It is likely that erosion takes place
sporadically during major storms. Point A is at the
back of a small cove that lies above the intertidal
zone, the cove lies on the relatively sheltered ENE
side of the island, and erosion is therefore likely to
be less severe than around the rest of the cliff line.
All the cliffs are probably postglacial, hence less than
10,000 years old, and are developing in response to
regional subsidence and marine transgression over
a post-glacial landscape. The fact that the cliff-top
boundary wall projects into space over the cliff at
locality 7 (Figure 1.7) confirms significant erosion
in recent times. The cliff line does not need to reach
the site to influence it. As it approaches the site, the
risk of subsidence and landslip increases.

Point B presents a lesser risk as it is further from
the site (Figure 1.7). The small cove to the NE of
the site appears to be actively extending inland. The
cliff-top boundary wall projects northwards into this
cove and appears to have been removed by coastal
erosion. Sands are thin here inland of the cliff, probably less than 1m, but thicken SW towards the site.
The slope from the site to the cliff top is relatively
gentle. Risk from erosion here is long term (hundreds to thousands of years to impact on site).

The geological setting of the site focusing on the wind-blown sands

Most of the island is covered with grass and there are
relatively few rock exposures. Examination of exposures in the SE area of the island provided information for some limited observations however and the
main geological features are presented on Figure 1.7.
Soil profiles were examined at a number of key localities and small samples taken for laboratory examination at the localities marked on Figure 1.7. The
results of field observations and the examination of
each sample using binocular microscopy (Hall 2000
39–46, 77–79) are summarised below.

The wind-blown sands are clearly concentrated
on the eastern slopes of the island close to the tombolo. The fine sands consist of a mixture of mineral
sand (dominated by quartz) and shell sand. The sand
is a mixture of quartz-rich sand from rock erosion
and shell sand. There is no potential source of wind-
blown sand on St Ninian's Isle or within a reasonable distance on the mainland of Shetland, and it
seems inevitable therefore that sand has been blown
from the tombolo to accumulate on the Isle when
the wind comes from the east and on the mainland
when the wind comes from the west.

The youngest sands are thinly layered with dark
organic-rich layers (presumably former soils) sepa-

rated by light brown sandy layers, sometimes of coarser sand, up to 100mm thick, that represent thick accumulations from occasional special events (sandstorms). These bedded sands overlie a cliff-top boundary wall which was constructed around 1744 (see below), at a time when the chapel was still exposed because stones from it were used to construct the wall and only extend up to c100m west from the tombolo. The exact stratigraphic sequence and thickness of sediments at the site are unknown, but it is evident that the site is vulnerable to landslip/subsidence should the cliff-top boundary wall near the SE corner of the site collapse.

On the island, away from the area of the tombolo, exposures near cliff tops and in streams demonstrate that there is a thin layer of schistose rock debris; this is a basal sedimentary breccia, or 'scree', developed on the steeply dipping metasediments of schistose quartzite. The basement rock and the scree are only slightly weathered in places. There is silty alluvial sediment in the breccia in places, indicative of some transport by water. The breccia deposit is probably immediately post-glacial and about 10,000 years old. There is a thin soil (up to 100mm) developed on the scree which is exposed around the cliff tops. A thin peat has developed in the SE of the island. The thin schistose breccia and silty alluvial sediments are likely to be present over much of the island, under the area of wind-blown sands, including the area of the archaeological site. Observation of thin soils around the site (Hall 2000) confirms that degraded weathered schist and wind-blown sand are the two sources of inorganic material for the soils on the Isle.

1.5   HISTORICAL BACKGROUND

The first half of Small's chapter in the 1973 volume is dedicated to the history of the Isle (Small 1973, 1–4). This reflects O'Dell's own keen interest in the historical geography of Shetland (O'Dell 1939; 1962) and the following account relies heavily on his and Small's own research.

As with many other chapel sites in the Northern and Western Isles there is a lack of documentary evidence for the chapel on St Ninian's Isle. According to Alan Small, local tradition had it that the chapel was built by shipwrecked mariners, but as he states, this is a common tradition in the Northern Isles and can be dismissed. There was also the strong local tradition that this site is the Mother Church in Shetland, but there is a lack of references to it in the immediate post-Reformation period. The chapel is not included in the list of Shetland churches submitted to the General Assembly of the Church of Scotland in 1586 by the Lord Clerk of the Register (Peterkin 1839, 304). McEwan, whom Small consulted when writing the 1973 volume, was of the opinion that the chapel was disused at least since the Reformation, and that the parishes of Dunrossness and Fair Isle were united by the end of the 16th century, with

the parishes of Sandwick and Cunningsburgh added to Dunrossness around 1600 (Shetland Archives: 1/359/2/23. Letter to Small from Professor James S McEwen, Department of Church History, King's College, Aberdeen, dated 21/1/69).

Small cites the earliest references to St Ninian's Isle as being in legal documents. In 1576 Arthur Sinclair declared that he possessed the heritable title to St Ninian's Isle (Goudie 1904, 204–205) and in 1588 Laurence Sinclair of Houss had a disposition from Robert, Earl of Orkney, of the lands of St Ninian's Isle in Dunrossness (Grant 1893, 289). The Isle is mentioned as 'Sancttrinyeanis Yle' in the Court Book of Shetland for 1 August 1603, in a case dealing with the fishings off the Isle (Donaldson 1954, 106). There is however no reference to the chapel in any of these documents.

Although O'Dell was of the opinion that the style and size of the chapel on the Isle was proof enough that it was once a 'head church', comparable to that on the Brough of Birsay, in Orkney, Cant has more plausibly suggested that: 'Relatively ambitious as it was in design, it does not seem to have been a 'head church' in the parochial system developed in Shetland from the 12th century onwards' (Cant 1975, 9; 1973). Brian Smith (pers comm) also draws attention to a document (Ballantyne and Smith 1994, no. 120), which is dated at 'Irland *in parish of St Neneain* in Dunrosness' (3 July 1560, my italics), an unusual description in this context. The description of 'Irland in *parish* of St Neneain in Dunrossness' does not dedicate the church in Ireland to St Ninian, but the parish itself. This suggests that the church on the Isle had been of prime significance to the parish, but we cannot presume that it was still in use at the time of the document in 1560. The 'walls and steeple of an old kirk' still stood at Ireland, opposite the Isle in 1711 (Sibbald 1711, 15). The Ireland church may have belonged to the 12th-century group of round-towered churches (RCAHMS 1946, no. 1186), and could therefore be contemporary with the chapel on the Isle. Local tradition however records that the steeple from St Ninian's Isle was taken and used for the church at Ireland (see below; and O'Dell 1959b, 242, fig 1). Nothing can now be seen of this church in Ireland today although when a house was being built on the site in 1947 a worked stone with a beaded corner from the side of a doorway was found, which is now housed in the Shetland Museum (Shetland Amenity Trust: Historic Buildings, Sites and Monuments Record, SMR no. 705, SN765).

Although Pont's c1608 map of the Shetland Isles, published in Blaeu's atlas of 1654, depicts a church on St Ninian's Isle no indication is given of whether the building was in use. Pont's map also shows a settlement or house near to the church to the SW, which Goudie suggests may have been the dwelling of a resident priest (Goudie 1879, 21), and interestingly, the tombolo is not depicted. The Isle is named 'S.Tronons Yle', which Small suggests may be 'St Ronon's Yle' or indeed 'St Tronon's Isle' (Small 1973, 3–4). James Kay writing in 1680 mentions a church on the Isle but gives no further information (Kay 1908, 31). He also notes the difficulty in access to the Isle in north-westerly gales, suggesting that the tombolo was in use at this time. The Rev John Brand visited St Ninian's Isle in 1700 and wrote in 1701: 'To the northwest of the Nwess lyes St Ninian's Isle, very pleasant; wherein there is a chapel and ane altar in it, whereon some superstitious people do burn candles to this day. Some take this Isle rather to be a kind of Peninsula, joined to the Main by a Bank of Sand, by which in an Ebb People may go into the Isle, tho' sometimes not without danger' (Brand 1701, 84). Later writers copy this description almost verbatim.

Goudie outlines the history of the ownership of St Ninian's Isle from the mid-17th century, when it was mortgaged to Laurence Stewart of Bigtown in 1667 by James Sinclair of Scalloway, with consent of Arthur Sinclair, his eldest son, and Grizel Sinclair, heiress of Houss (Goudie 1879, 21). By 1744 the Laird, John Bruce Stewart, obtained the property by marriage to Clementina Stewart, and demolished the remains of the chapel to build the retaining wall which can still be seen today along the east side of the Isle (see Point A, in Figure 1.7). When Rev George Low inspected the site in 1774 he noted that the remains of the chapel could be seen, and that 'the lower storey of the kirk may be distinctly traced, which having once been vaulted, is supposed to have served for a burying place' (Low 1879). Here Low refers to the local tradition that the building was barrel vaulted, and the steeple for it was across the bay at Ireland (Ayreland).

Within 100 years of Low's visit, when Thomas S Muir visited the site, the ruins of the chapel had disappeared, covered over by sand, and Muir comments on the barenness of the Isle, as did Hibbert in his own account (Muir 1861, 127; Hibbert 1822). Small suggests that the ruined chapel was probably covered over in the late 18th century, when there was a period of extremely stormy conditions in northern Scotland (Small 1973, 3). The sand inundation at this time was periodic, and sand could be blown away from the site as well as over it, so briefly revealing and then covering features within short periods of time. Small records local stories of the altar of the chapel being visible within the lifetime of people who died twenty or 30 years previous to the 1950s. Similarly, local inhabitants who visited the site during the 1999 fieldwork told childhood stories of burials over the area of the chapel being uncovered by wind blow, and of children daring each other to go up to the Isle and spend the night there. When Shetland antiquarian Gilbert Goudie visited the site shortly after Muir, in July 1875, he failed to find the chapel, but he did find an ogham-inscribed stone, which he deposited in the Society of Antiquaries of Scotland in Edinburgh (Small 1973, 4; Goudie 1904; see Chapter 2 below). Goudie found two further inscribed stones during his visit, but left them on the site and they have never been (re-) located (Chapter 2 below). Goudie wrote:

> All was desolation and silence except for the moaning of the waves, the screeching of the sea-fowl, and the bellowing of the cattle … Indeed there was some difficulty in prosecuting a search on the site, the cattle contesting possession of the ground, and tossing the skulls and trampling the bones which are strewn about the sand-blown surface, or protrude from beneath'
>
> (Goudie 1912, cited in Small 1973, 4)

When the Ordnance Survey visited the Isle at around the same time as Goudie, whilst gathering information for the First Edition map of Shetland (1878), they recorded the site of the ancient kirk and burial ground: 'The only remains now are bones and pieces of coffins the ancient building having totally disappeared through the atmospheric action and drifting sand. The Burial Ground is now disused' (OS Name Book 10, 7). Mr Robert Leask, a local historian brought up in Bigton, visited the 1999 excavations and confirmed that burial took place in the graveyard on the Isle until about 1840, when the laird insisted that burying stopped because old burials were being revealed when the sand blew. It was at this time that a new graveyard was created at Ireland across the bay. Even then an exception was made for 'an old goy wo wanted to be buried with "da auld fokk"': he had been a servant at Bigton, and the laird's wife interceded for him. Mr Leask also remembered there being three inscribed gravestones in the graveyard when he was a boy, in particular a gravestone dated 1832, dedicated to Marsha Goudie, who was the last person buried on the Isle (Robert Leask pers comm).

The Isle had been depopulated in the last few decades of the 18th century, when Shetland's rural population was being affected by great changes (Smith 1984). Small is tempted however to connect the depopulation of St Ninian's Isle to the difficulty of access to the Isle in the more stormy conditions of the period. Locally it is also believed that this, and the wind-blown sand, was the reason for the abandonment of the Isle. The last recorded child born on the Isle was James Sinclair in 1771, to William Sinclair and his wife Ursula Leask, and George Low, when visiting the Isle in 1774, says that there was one family living there (Low 1879). A year later, in 1775, the same John Bruce Stewart of Symbister who demolished the chapel entered into a contract with his brother that 'the farm called the Hall-last of Bigtoun, consisting of sixteen merk land, with the Isle of St Ninian's, shall be kept and reserved to the parties themselves, and be managed by the said William Bruce, the said Isle to be used for grasing of slaughter cattle, milk cows and sheep, and the said sixteen merk land to be kept and used as a farm' (Smith 2000, 23; Shetland Archives GD.144/118/16). The agricultural value of St Ninian's Isle was by no means negligible, being valued as a 'last of land' – 18 merks of land – and a large settlement by Shetland standards (Brian Smith pers comm). It also lay in one of the most fertile areas of Shetland at that time. In the First Statistical Account the parish of Dunrossness is described as 'comparatively the most fertile district in the Zetland Isles … The lands are reckoned by a peculiar measurement, by what are called merks-land. Each merk-land ought to contain 1600 square fathoms. To each one cow is allotted; and the parish contains 2000 of these merk-lands, and consequently as many cows' (Statistical Account of Scotland 1791–99, vol 7, 393). By the time of the Second Statistical Account of 1845, St Ninian's Isle is grazed solely by cattle after an imported English ram spread the disease of scab to the flocks in the area to catastrophic affect (Statistical Account of Scotland 1845, 94).

The place-name evidence for the Isle is, as discussed in the context of Pont's map above, uncertain, being equally ascribed to St Neneain in 1560, and to St Tronon, or St Ronon, on Pont's map in c1608. The Shetland Place Names project, initiated by the Shetland Amenity Trust (Brooke-Freeman 2005), has identified many names for the natural geos and stacs around the Isle, but has not yet discovered any further information on the St Ninian's Isle place-name itself. Robert Leask, who grew up in Bigton, has recorded all local names associated with the Isle, including *Botherl* on the east side of the Isle, just north of the chapel site. This place-name is thought most likely to originate from two words: *botr* and *houl*, which probably relate to past tenants of the Isle keeping their small boats here. A shingle beach on the north side of the houl, or prominence, would have served this purpose well (Robert Leask pers comm). Stewart, in his book Shetland Place Names, lists 'sent niniens ail, Rinansey, Sanct Ninian's Yle, Sanct trinyeanis yle, Sanctrinheanes yle, St Tronan's yle and St Ringans Isle' amongst his examples (Stewart 1987). One thing is extremely unlikely, however, and that is that St Ninian himself founded the chapel on the Isle, even an earlier chapel

building than the ruinous walls seen today at the site. W Douglas Simpson's enthusiasm for a Ninianiac mission that could be traced via the location of sites with a Ninian dedication in the north and west of Scotland (Simpson 1940) had inspired O'Dell to begin searching for the chapel on St Ninian's Isle in 1955 (O'Dell's notes in Shetland Archives D1/359/7/1), but this was subsequently thought extremely unlikely (Thomas 1973, 14; Thomson 2007, 522–525). Instead the most likely scenario is that the present ruinous chapel on the site was dedicated to St Ninian in the 12th century at the earliest, being what Thomson calls an 'antiquarian dedication' (Thomson 2007, 523), and it is from this building that the Isle got its name. The adjacent mainland settlements today all have Norse names, being called Ireland, from Old Norse *eyrr* or *øyrr*: sand or gravel bank, Rerwick, from ON *røyrr*: reed or rush, and *vík*: inlet or small bay and Bigton, from ON *bygg*: barley, and *tún*: a fenced plot, farmyard, homefield belonging to a farm (Stewart 1987; Jakobsen 1993).

Notes

[1]   The terms Late Iron Age, and Norse, are used in this volume for the periods from the 3rd to the 8th or 9th centuries AD, and the 9th to the 13th centuries AD respectively (Foster 1990, 143). Late Iron Age is used in preference to Early Historic, or Early Medieval, as it is felt that Late Iron Age is a more accurate term for what is essentially in Shetland still a pre-Historic period. 'Pictish' is used as a cultural term where appropriate.

[2]   The term 'church' rather than 'chapel' is used by Professor O'Dell and Dr Alan Small in the archives. The upstanding remains of the medieval building on the site have caused it however to be considered a 'chapel-site', i.e. not a main parish church, and so in this report the medieval building is termed the 'chapel', and the earlier building below is named the 'church', or 'earlier church building'. The arguments for this earlier building being a church are outlined in Chapter 3 and discussed further in Chapter 5. 'Church' is also used throughout the report as a general term.

[3]   In other words, those parts of the excavation directly relevant to the assessment of O'Dell's previous work at the site. Other limited, and small-scale, excavations were undertaken at the site and are reported at an interim stage (Harry 2000; Barrowman 2000).

2

AN OGHAM-INSCRIBED SLAB
FROM ST NINIAN'S ISLE, FOUND IN 1876

Katherine Forsyth

2.1 DISCOVERY

The Shetland antiquarian Gilbert Goudie[1] visited St Ninian's Isle in July 1876, in the company of the Rev J C Roger,[2] 'in the hope of being able to trace some portions of the foundation of the chapel, and possibly of finding some relic of early times' (Goudie 1879, 23). Goudie's careful search was rewarded with the discovery of an ogham-inscribed slab 'embedded in the sand' (Goudie 1879). He presented it to the Society of Antiquaries of Scotland the following year and it is now in the National Museums of Scotland (Anon 1878; NMAS Cat 1892, IB 112).[3] Later that day, soon after the original discovery, Goudie found '[t]wo other stones, similarly inscribed, … fragments, somewhat defaced by exposure'. Unfortunately he gives no indication of the size or nature of these two fragments, nor is it clear from his description whether he was of the opinion that these were fragments of the same monument or of one or more separate monuments. The two fragments were left on site and by December of that year had disappeared. Goudie's hope that he would be able to recover them has remained thwarted (Goudie 1879, 24; Moar 1952, 94). Small reports that 'diligent search in modern times' had failed to recover the missing oghams (1973, 4). There have been more recent, unconfirmed reports that one or more of these stones survives, built into the wall which divides the island, beside the gate, but initial investigation has failed to uncover them (Brian Smith pers comm).

2.2 DESCRIPTION

The extant stone is a thin, oblong slab of lightly coloured micaceous sandstone, 760mm long by 265mm broad and 45mm thick (Figure 2.1). According to Dr Suzanne Miller, Keeper of Natural Sciences, National Museums of Scotland:[4]

> It shows bedding parallel lamination with, possibly, some ripple marks. It is entirely consistent with the outcrop of Old Red Sandstone (ORS; Devonian Sandstone) in Shetland. St Ninian's Isle is composed of Dalradian schist and gneiss and is not the source of the slab. However, there is an extensive outcrop of ORS on the East side of the Southern Shetland Peninsula, from Sandwick to Sumburgh Head … The traces of a white substance visible in several places on the surface of

the slab are almost certainly biological in origin and fully in keeping with its being buried in sand. It is likely to be calcium carbonate, possibly from barnacles (or similar creature).

The original form and function of the slab are not clear, nor is it clear whether it was formerly recumbent or stood upright, and, if the latter, whether it stood vertically on its narrow end or lay (F) on its side as a component of a cist. The two broad faces have suffered extensive de-lamination and large patches of the surface have been lost. As Dr Miller notes:

> De-lamination is a natural feature of finely laminated sandstone as the laminae are planes of natural weakness along which pore water can percolate. Freeze-thaw, dissolution of natural cement or expansion/contraction of clay minerals can then produce de-lamination. The 'top' surface, which shows the most weathering, looks like it may have lost up to 8–10mm over some parts of the surface. However, I can see no evidence of carving on the broad surfaces where there appears to be less de-lamination. The only other possibility is that a complete layer weathered off at some point – but there is really no way of knowing this for sure.
>
> (pers comm, July 2006)

What may be a portion of the original surface survives at the 'lower'/left end of the 'upper' surface (B).[5] This portion is L-shaped, widening from approximately one-sixth of the face, to one-third. It is devoid of any trace of carving. At the opposite end of the same face there is a thin linear discolouration which traces a half-circle of diameter 140mm, centred on the narrow edge of the stone. It is tempting to see this as the very bottom of a groove which formed, say, the ring of an incised cross. However, the same discolouration is found in the matching position on the opposite face (D) and on the sides. In Dr Miller's opinion it 'appears to be entirely natural'.

The two narrow ends of the slab are different in appearance (Figure 2.1). The 'top' (E) is uneven and weathered and may be the original edge of the slab. The 'lower' end (F), in contrast, presents a clean break, smooth and even. There are no traces of tool marks and the sharp break may be natural, i.e. along a jointing plane. It does appear to have occurred after carving. Both short ends are parallel to each other but not quite perpendicular to the long sides,

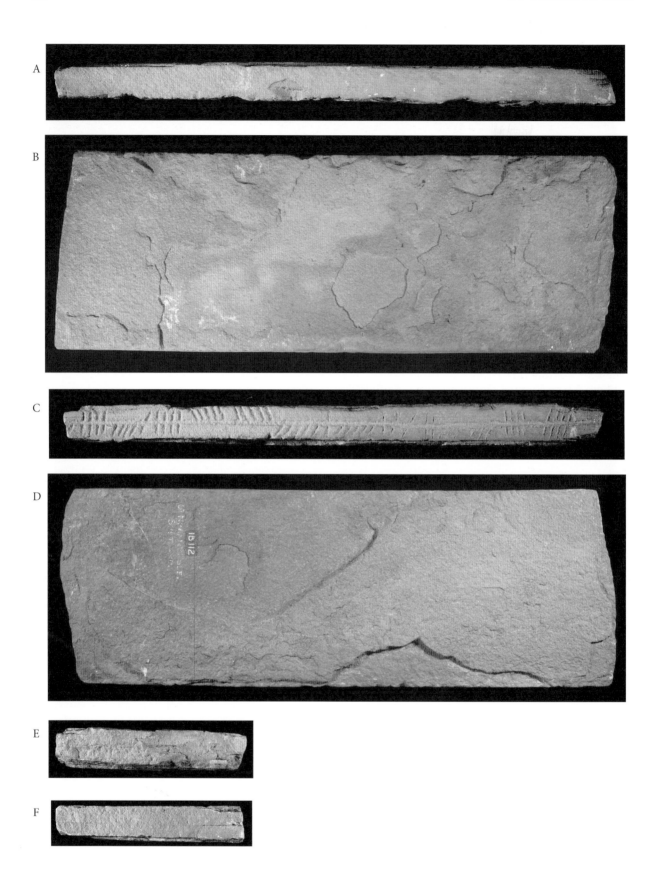

FIGURE 2.1

Six faces, (A) plain edge, (B) 'upper' surface, (C) inscribed edge, (D) 'lower' surface, (E) 'top', (F) 'bottom' ,of the ogham-inscribed slab from St Ninian's Isle, found in 1876 (National Museums of Scotland)

FIGURE 2.2
Detail of ogham inscription (National Museums of Scotland)

and it may be that all four sides have used natural weakness along jointing planes (Suzanne Miller pers comm). Whether the stone snapped through deliberate human action or accident, it is clear that the inscription is incomplete at this end (the beginning). The inscription occupies the whole of one long edge (C). Apart from the loss of a portion of unspecified length from the beginning, it is otherwise well-preserved. It is a well-carved, formal, monumental inscription, not a casual graffito (Figure 2.2).

The position of the inscription on the long narrow face of a slab is paralleled on several Scottish ogham stones[6]: Birsay 1–3, Inchyra, Altyre and Bressay. The three ogham-inscribed Orkney flag-stones from Birsay may have been building slabs, although this is far from certain as two out of the three have been lost since the early 1970s and are recorded only by photographs of rubbings (Forsyth 1996a, 69–92). The Birsay stones are undecorated except for the inscriptions, and the ogham lettering on them is informally set-out. Thus they may be graffiti, perhaps carved on the exposed surface of a stone built into a wall. Other examples of ogham on narrow faces are limited to stones which have some other carving on their broad faces. Ogham is carved on three of the narrow faces of the slab from Inchyra, Perthshire, which has Pictish symbols on both broad faces (Forsyth 1996a, 332–359; Stevenson 1959; Wainwright 1961). When found this stone was acting as the lid of an inhumation grave, though this appears to have been a secondary position and the stone may have stood upright at one time. In fact the carving on this complex monument may reflect three phases of re-use as it bears three separate ogham inscriptions in different hands, each linked to a different pair of Pictish symbols. The upright cross-slabs from Altyre, Morayshire, and Bressay, Shetland, both have ogham inscriptions on their long narrow faces and crosses on their broad faces (Forsyth 1996a, 23–40, 117–38; Calder and Jackson 1957; Stevenson 1981). Elsewhere in Scotland, ogham inscriptions on slabs (as opposed to pillars) are typically placed across the broad face of the slab, with the exception of Golspie, Sutherland where, uniquely, it is written without a stem-line on an arris (Close-Brooks 1989). Allowing for the missing portion, the St Ninian's Isle slab is of similar size to the Bressay slab (1150mm x 400–300mm x

50mm) and, like it, may once have stood upright.

There is ambitious Christian sculpture from St Ninian's Isle in the form of the remains of at least two corner-post shrines of possibly 8th-century date (Thomas 1973, 12; 1983; Scott and Ritchie 2010, 4–6, 20–25); however, the *complete* lack of any trace of carving on the broad faces of the ogham-inscribed slab makes it an unlikely candidate for a cross-slab, however eroded. An alternative, and perhaps more plausible, explanation is that the ogham-inscribed slab was part of a cist grave, like Inchyra. At just 265mm across, the St Ninian's Isle slab seems rather narrow to have been a grave lintel – Inchyra is 310–430mm across (by 1600mm (5'3") and 70–90mm thick) – and is perhaps more likely to have been a side panel. It might seem perverse to inscribe a stone which was going to be buried, but, in addition to the Inchyra example itself, comparison may be made with a series of inscribed slabs from composite cist graves at various sites in eastern Brittany (Davies *et al* 2000, 259–297). Some of these were found *in situ* as side panels, others appear to have been smaller slabs placed within a stone-lined grave. The inscriptions – simple personal names, or the statement 'here lies N' – were certainly not visible when the graves were in use. Their significance may have related to funerary rites or the preparation of the grave, or, perhaps more likely, they were intended to be read on the Day of Judgement when the dead will arise from their graves.

As noted above, the St Ninian's Isle slab was 'embedded in the sand' when found by Goudie, and already fractured. It may have formed part of a cist grave that had become partially exposed; Goudie comments on the disruption to the graves of the cattle who grazed on the island (1879, 23–24). If this were the case, however, it would not account for the break, unless the use in the cist was secondary. Alternatively the stone might formerly have stood upright, but have toppled, or been blown over (in which case the break might have been on impact with the ground). If it had been deliberately struck, and thereby fractured near the base, the stub might have been left in the ground. Either way, the upper fragment could then have been swallowed up over time by wind-blown sand. A third possibility is that the stone had been deliberately trimmed for re-use, either in a cist or as building stone, the latter fate being very familiar from early medieval church sites elsewhere in Scotland (Allen and Anderson 1903, vol 3, *passim*). As noted by Miller, however, there is no trace of obvious tool-marks on the (sharply) broken edge of the St Ninian's Isle slab so if it had been deliberately trimmed, this edge has been 'cleaned off'. It is perhaps more likely that a break has occurred naturally along a jointing plane.

2.3 THE INSCRIPTION

The ogham is arranged along one narrow long edge of the stone with the medial stem-line, around which the letters are arranged, running right to both ends (Figure 2.2). Oghams read from left-to-right, but with a (now) portable object such as the St Ninian's Isle slab there may be uncertainty as to the inscription's orientation. Because of the nature of the ogham script, inversion would affect not only the order of the letters, but, in many cases, the actual identification of individual letters. In our case, the M, the s^T, and the vowels, which are all symmetrical, would be unaffected by a change in orientation, but the consonants could represent different letters depending on which way up they lie: eg the five stroke letter is either ('Q') or ('N'), and the four-stroke letter, either ('s') or ('C'). There is no physical indication as to the original orientation of the slab, but, fortunately, there is an internal clue as to the direction of reading, namely the forward slope of the 'short stroke' consonants (i.e. the b- and h-groups, or *aicmi*).

The earliest ogham inscriptions, including all those in Ireland, have b- and h-consonant strokes – respectively, above and below the stem – which are perpendicular to the stem. There are, however, numerous later inscriptions from various parts of Scotland which feature b- and h-consonants which consistently lie at an angle to it. In every instance where the direction of reading can be established, the slope of these consonants is consistently with the proximal end (i.e. the end closest to the stem) forward of the distal end, relative to the direction of reading (i.e. a B and H together would form an arrow pointing to the right) (Forsyth 1996a, xlvi–xlvii). This is a clear indication that the St Ninian's Isle inscription begins with a b-*aicme* letter and ends with an m-*aicme* letter.

The inscription appears to begin in mid-letter and it is clear that a portion, possibly substantial, has been lost from the beginning. It is possible that one or both of the fragments found by Goudie may have been the missing part of this slab, although he does not suggest this himself and his wording seems to imply that they are not. It appears that the other end of the inscription is intact. The stem-line continues beyond the final letter for a further 30mm to the very edge of the slab, but there are no traces of any further strokes in this area. As Padel says, the inscription 'gives the impression of stopping at this point' (1972a, 140), a view shared by most commentators

since Ferguson (cited in Goudie 1879; Ferguson 1887, 134).

The ogham has been carved using the familiar pock-and-smooth technique. Little attention has been given to smoothing and the pocks are still clearly visible. The strokes are well-defined but not deep, they have rounded ends and a curved cross-section. The inscription is very neat and regular, the letters are clearly differentiated by size, slope, and spacing, hence the almost total consensus among previous writers regarding the reading.

The only real uncertainty concerning the *reading* (as opposed to the transliteration) is the identity of the first character. The first clear stroke is a single b-*aicme* stroke. Before this the stem-line is visible for approximately 25mm but the area below the stem, where any further b-*aicme* strokes would be, is very worn. Macalister claims to have seen an additional stroke. This is possible but not certain. The area above the stem is better preserved and devoid of any ogham strokes. Thus if there are any preceding strokes they can only have been of the b-*aicme*. The first letter is thus B, or any subsequent member of the b-*aicme* (L, V, S, or N), indicated in the following discussion by 'B⁺'.

Southesk (1884, 205), Rhŷs (1892, 296), and Allen and Anderson (1903, 18) read the twelfth and thirteenth characters together as a single letter ⟨#⟩, G, but Padel (1972a, 139–140) correctly points out that the careful spacing between the two strokes means they must be read as separate letters ⟨//⟩, MM. The distance between the two M strokes is 20–25mm in contrast to the distance between the two component strokes of the following letter O, which are about 10mm apart. There is a small, natural flaw in the stone above the stem at the point where it intersects with *13*. Macalister (1940, 206) was misled in thinking that it was a corrected superfluous A.

The inscription can therefore be read with confidence as:

Using the standard transliteration key, which gives conventional values to each ogham letter (McManus 1988; Sims-Williams 1993), gives the following reading:[7]

[B+] E S M E Q Q N A N N A M M O V V E ST

2.4 TRANSLITERATION

Assigning sound values to ogham graphemes is not straightforward, especially in Scotland, and there are several problems concerning transliteration.

The value of 'Q'

If the ogham alphabet was adopted in Scotland during the Primitive Irish period, then the value of the character Q at that time would have been /kʷ/. McManus has explained that its letter name, Old Irish

Cert, was originally ★kʷerkʷ-, cognate with Latin *quercus* (ultimately from the root ★perkʷ-), cf Welsh *perth* 'bush' (1991, 37; cf McManus 1986, 15, 29); the Pictish cognate is reflected in Scottish place-names in *pert*, such as Perth and Logiepert (Watson 1926, 356–357). If the borrowing of the alphabet was sufficiently early, it is possible that this fourth member of the h-*aicme* was assigned the value /p/ in Pictland, either because that is what the borrowers heard as the initial of ★kʷerkʷ-, or because they were able to recognize the cognate word in their own language. If however, the alphabet was adopted at a date later than the 6th century, Primitive Irish /kʷ/ would have fallen together with /k/, for which there were now two symbols, ⿲ Q and ⿲ C. The correspondence between Irish *mac* and Welsh *map* was not lost on the Irish compiler of Cormac's Glossary,[8] *c*900 (O'Donovan 1868, 111–112). It may also have been obvious to Pictish oghamists a few centuries earlier. McManus has shown how the creation of the ogham alphabet 'was accompanied by a careful analysis of the sounds of ... (the target) language' (1991, 31). One wonders if the adoption of the alphabet by non-Gaels might not have been accompanied by a similarly careful analysis of the mis-match between donor alphabet and target language? 'The creative input into Ogam was', he says, 'quite considerable' (1991, 39). If the oghamists of Scotland were both as linguistically aware and creative as the original framers of the alphabet, they may well have been able to take the redundant symbol 'Q' and assign to it the new and useful value /p/.

Although there was no /p/ sound in Irish at the time of the invention of the ogham script, as early as the 5th century Irish-speakers began to need a symbol for /p/, both to accommodate the growing number of borrowings from British Latin and for the new /p/ sound being generated in their own language through the loss of medial syllables between *b* and *h* (Sims-Williams 1992, 39). As Sims-Williams points out, most of the names on Irish ogham pillars are native and few show syncope (loss of medial syllables), so it is no surprise that there is only one candidate for a P symbol: an ×-shape hanging from the stem-line on a pillar from Valencia Island, Co. Kerry (CIIC 231). As Sims-Williams explains, this is two superimposed Bs, an understandable creation given the phonetic relation between /p/ and /b/ (Sims-Williams 1992, 40–42).

The same character appears in Wales on the 6th-century dual-script inscription at Crickhowell, Breconshire (CIIC 327).[9] The interpretation of the Valencia Island inscription is disputed, but the Crickhowell one is unambiguous because the ogham character corresponds to a P in the roman alphabet text (Sims-Williams 1992, 40–41). Clearly, this early P symbol had more than local currency at the time, but it vanishes thereafter. It did not make it into the canon of supplementary letters (*forfeda*) and does not occur again, either epigraphically or in

manuscripts. It is not attested in Scotland.

In the 9th century, an entirely different strategy for representing *P* was adopted by the probably Irish scribe of the ogham alphabet and syllabary in Bern, Burgerbibliothek, MS 207, fol 257r. In this text Latin *P* is twice rendered in ogham with a y-like character which is not attested elsewhere (Sims-Williams 1992, 38, 42). The 12th-century ogham alphabet with Latin key in Bibliotheca Apostolica Vaticana MS Ref. Lat. 1308, fol. 62v, includes a single supplementary character labeled 'p'. It hangs down from the stem and is clearly based on the Latin character, being no more than an angular, inverted *p* (i.e. *b*) (McManus 1991, 137, 143). Although this character is never found in 'practical' use, it gained currency in the learned tradition and features in exemplary manuscript alphabets, for instance, in the text *In Lebor Ogaim* 'the Book of Ogham', as found in the Book of Ballymote (Calder 1917, line 5465ff). Neither of these three *p* symbols occurs in Scotland, yet there surely would have been a need for some kind of /p/ symbol. There are numerous supplementary characters on Scottish oghams, some of which are unique and many which have not been satisfactorily explained. Several are clearly vowels and of the remainder, none are obvious candidates for /p/. Tellingly, the Q-character appears in Scotland only in the formula word MAQQ/MEQQ[10] which tells against it having been adopted wholesale to represent /p/. So what, then, was the value of the fourth member of the h-*aicme* in Scottish ogham inscriptions, /kʷ/, /k/, or /p/? The texts are surely all too late for /kʷ/, and /k/ is already catered for by C. Since we thus have no independent check on the value, we cannot know if in Pictland MAQQ might actually have meant /map/.

The value of v

Sims-Williams concedes that 'no transcription ... is wholly satisfactory in all circumstances' (1993, 142). The Primitive Irish value of the third member of the b-*aicme*, *fern* (<★*wern*-) 'alder-tree', is /w/ (transliterated v) (McManus 1991, 37–38; Sims-Williams 1993, 140–143). By the Old Irish period this sound had developed into /f/, hence the later manuscript ogham transliteration F. By the 8th century, the Welsh reflex of /w/ had become /gʷ/. There was already an ogham character for this sound, the third member of the m-*aicme*, ⧻ *gétal*, but in Irish that sound had long since fallen together with its non-labialized counterpart /g/ and ⧻ *gétal* never appears on oghams of the early period (up to the 7th century) and only very rarely in practical use after that. That the later manuscripts accord *gétal* the unhistorical value NG indicates that its original value had been forgotten and this would certainly have happened before the need for it became apparent in Welsh. There are no Welsh ogham inscriptions as late as the 8th century in any case. Names such as *Uurad*

(Irish *Ferad*) and *Uurguist* (Irish *Forcus*) imply Pictish retained original /w/ (Jackson 1955, 163). Thus the transliteration of *fern* in Scotland is problematic. In a Gaelic context /w/ would be appropriate up to about the 7th century and thereafter /f/. In a Pictish context the value /w/ should perhaps be preferred regardless of date. The transliteration v is retained, however, to preclude prejudging the language of a text and, where the text is thought to be Pictish, to maintain a consonant/vowel distinction between ogham v = /w/ =? manuscript *uu*, and ogham U = /u/ = manuscript *u*.

The value of s^T

Whatever its original value, the fourth member of the m-*aicme*, #, had become linguistically redundant by the time of the earliest ogham pillars and does not appear in any Irish inscription. It features at the appropriate point in the sequence in an ogham alphabet carved on a 12th-century stone from the Isle of Man (Kermode 1907, 72–74, 100–102). St Ninian's Isle is thus the only epigraphic example of the character in practical use. Patrick Sims-Williams has discussed possible values for this letter in almost exhaustive detail, but concluded that the original value, perhaps /ˈs/, perhaps /sw/, cannot be recovered (1993, 151–162). Since this original value was forgotten at such an early stage, however, it is probably irrelevant to the St Ninian's Isle text. In the later medieval bardic tradition, which utilized the traditional names of the ogham characters, this character was called *s(t)raif* and its standard value was /st/, 'where *s* stands before *d*, it is *straiph* that is to be written there' (Calder 1917, lines 443–444, quoted by Sims-Williams 1993, 161). Sims-Williams explains how this would have arisen through a reinterpretation of the old letter-name, an equation with Latin Z – as in the 12th-century Vatican manuscript Reg. lat. 1308 (1993, 151) – and finally its (orthographically redundant) assignment to the sound /st/ (1993, 161; cf McManus 1991, 38; Sims-Williams 1992, 35). The ogham alphabet in the 9th-century manuscript Bern, Burgerbibliothek, MS 207, fol 257r has a grid-like character which appears in the position of Latin Z. It consists of four horizontal strokes superimposed on four vertical strokes below the stem and is labeled *ss*. As Sims-Williams points out, this is 'two superimposed versions of the fourteenth ogam letter *Sraif*' (1992, 38) and implies that the undoubled version of *Sraif* had not yet been given the value 'Z', i.e. /st/. Sims-Williams over-looks the St Ninian's Isle ogham in claiming there are no epigraphic instances of the character apart from the late and linguistically undiagnostic example from Man. While the Shetland inscription is impossible to date closely, it is unlikely to be as late as the 12th century and thus contains what is the earliest extant example of this character and still the only instance of it in practical use, rather than simply in an exemplary alphabet. The character ℼ (s) occurs earlier in the inscription making it unlikely that z represents simply /s/. As discussed below, the value /st/ is the most plausible explanation of the character in context.

Other issues

McManus has discussed the 'remarkable extravagance' among Irish ogham inscriptions of the 'capricious' and 'apparently meaningless duplication of consonants' (1991, 124). Gemination of consonants is even more common in Scottish inscriptions, occurring on a higher proportion of inscriptions, and where it does occur, doing so in greater quantity (up to a dozen times in a single inscription). There are even two instances of *triplication* (of N). The phonetic significance of this duplication remains opaque, though a number of patterns may be observed. In Ireland it is equally common among early as among late inscriptions. In Scotland, however, it is rarer on portable objects and on stones with an archaeological claim to be early, and more common on later and more ambitious sculpture. In Scotland the letters affected are those of the h-*aicme* (H, D, T, C, Q), the b-*aicme* (B, L, V, S, N), and M and R of the m-*aicme*. This tallies with the Irish evidence, with the exception of doubled G which occurs in Ireland but has not yet been found in Scotland. As McManus discusses, it has been suggested that duplication was a device to indicate lenition. This however has been questioned by Harvey (1987, 65). What Harvey has shown, however, is that gemination is usually avoided in word-initial position. He explains this convincingly as the result of Latin influence, there being no geminate symbols in word-initial position in Latin (1987, 4–6). It appears that this convention was followed in Scotland too. There are no examples of inscription-initial geminate symbols and where word-division is indicated, or can be deduced from, say, the location of the formula word MAQQ/MEQQ, geminate symbols appear to be avoided in word-initial position even more conscientiously than in Ireland.

2.5 INTERPRETATION

Word-division is indicated only very rarely on ogham inscriptions, so the apparently general rule that geminate consonants are avoided in word-initial position is a great boon. In the case of the St Ninian's Isle inscription it would suggest that the sequence following MEQQ is a single word and should not be subdivided. The Irish corpus does, however, contain, a number of exceptions to the rule, and due notice should be taken of these, and of the obvious danger of circularity. Nonetheless, it seems likely that we should divide the St Ninian's Isle inscription into three words:

--*[b$^+$]es meqq nannammovves^t*

The letters 4–7: MEQQ

The Primitive Irish word MAQQI (genitive of ★MAQQAS 'son') is ubiquitous in early Irish ogham inscriptions in the formula X MAQQI Y ('of X, son of Y'), and it is tempting to see St Ninian's Isle's MEQQ as a form of this word. But how to account for the spelling? The Gaelic language underwent a series of profound changes during and after the period of the early Irish ogham pillars. Final syllables were lost in a change known as apocope, which had occurred by the beginning of the 6th century (McManus 1991, 88–89). Less dramatically, the sound Q lost its labial element, i.e. /kʷ/ > /k/. There are a number of examples from towards the end of the main Irish ogham sequence, i.e. the 7th century, in which MAQQI is written as MACI, although, as McManus points out the retention of I (which would already have been lost in pronunciation by this stage due to apocope) shows that this is an artificial spelling which reflects 'the tenacity of the orthographical convention of writing final i in this formula word' (1991, 90). Remarkably, the spelling MACCI occurs, uniquely, on the earliest roman alphabet inscription in Ireland, that from Inchagoill, Co. Galway (CIIC 1) (Thurneysen 1946, 137). There are a further four or so ogham pillars from the very end of the main Irish tradition which have MAC, a spelling closer to contemporary pronunciation (CIIC 83, 90, 127, 256).

A third linguistic change of relevance which was occurring in Gaelic around this time is the palatalization of consonants (McManus 1991, 90–91). This occurred in circumstances where a front vowel (*i* or *e*) followed a consonant, as it does in MAQQI. In anticipation of the palatal quality of the following vowel, the consonant itself became invested with palatal quality, even when the following syllable was lost to apocope. Thus ogham MAQQI became manuscript *mai(c)c*, with the *i* indicating the palatal quality of the *c*. The opposition palatal/non-palatal came to play a key role in the inflection of nouns, thus in Old Gaelic *ma(c)c* (nominative singular) was opposed to *mai(c)c* (genitive singular), from earlier MAQQAS/ MAQQI. Palatalization is not indicated in ogham orthography.[11] The standard manuscript spelling of the genitive singular of *ma(c)c* in the Old Irish period (8th and 9th centuries) and in the early Middle Irish period (10th–11th century) was *mai(c)c*, later *meic(c)*. In the later Middle Irish period (11th–12th century) and Modern Irish period (12th century onwards), there is also *mec* and later *mic* (*DIL* s.v.).

There are about a dozen or so ogham inscriptions from Scotland which appear to contain the formula word which appears in Ireland as MAQQI, etc. This identification can be made on the grounds that the sequence regularly appears between what seem to be two personal names, even if these cannot often be readily or fully interpreted: eg Latheron's DUNNODNNAT MAQQ NET(U⁺)[–. The most common form is MAQQ, of which there are at least four examples, all on substantial cross-slabs of the 8th to 10th century: Altyre (Morayshire), Dyce (Aberdeenshire), Formaston (Aberdeenshire), and probably Golspie (Sutherland), although in the latter the vowel is very worn and there is a *possibility* that it might be the remains of an x-shaped E. Birsay 3 is probably a sixth example of MAQQ but the second character is worn. There are two examples of MAQ: on the inscribed bone handle from Bac Mhic Connain, North Uist, and the early pillar on Gigha. There are only two examples of MEQQ, both from Shetland: Bressay and St Ninian's Isle. The recently discovered inscribed bone plaque from Bornais, South Uist, may contain the single example of MEQ but this is not certain (Forsyth 2007). The newly discovered ogham inscription from Dyce, Aberdeenshire (RCAHMS 2007, 126–127), has M★QQ with an unusual s-shaped character where the vowel would be. This is exactly how it appears on Latheron. The s-shaped character occurs also at Lunnasting in the sequence –TT★NNN. As an s-shape is, in sense, a curved version of a single stroke then perhaps it is some kind of A, although quite what distinction is being made is not clear.

If MAQQ is Gaelic then the spelling is unhistorical. As outlined above, the labial quality of Q was being lost in the 6th century, a process reflected in ogham spelling before the end of the main Irish ogham tradition in the 7th century. This would imply that the roots of the ogham orthographic system in Scotland reach back at least to the 6th century to the period when, in the Irish home of ogham, the formula word was still spelled with Q. It also implies that Scottish ogham spelling was highly conservative, preserving the traditional spelling for centuries after a Gaelic speaker would more naturally have spelled it with C. It is significant that, as already noted, the character Q does not occur in Scotland except in this formula word. The MAQQ spellings would also be conservative in failing to indicate palatalization (in line with traditional Irish practice), while the two Shetlandic examples with MEQQ would be innovative, influenced by the manuscript spelling of the late Old Gaelic genitive *meicc*, as Jackson suggested (1955, 140). The lengthy inscription on the elaborate Pictish cross-slab at Brodie, Morayshire, may contain the sequence –]MECC[– but the inscription is so damaged as to be almost illegible.

The letters 1–3: [–] (b⁺)ES

If MEQQ is indeed 'of the son', then we would expect the preceding segment to be a male personal name in the genitive. Unfortunately, too little survives to indicate what that might have been. Both -*nes* and -*les* are possible final syllables for personal names in Gaelic. *Nes* was an Irish male personal name in its own right, but if this were really Gaelic we would expect it to appear in the genitive (*Neissi*) (see Sims-Williams 2003, 303), unless we are quite mistaken about the MEQQ standing for genitive *meicc*. Although there are numerous examples among the 6th- and 7th-century inscriptions in western Britain of non-agreement between the case of the personal name of the word for son (eg CIIC 344, 352A, 357, 375), these have 'son' in the nominative and the name in an ungrammatical genitive, under the influence of standard Irish ogham formulae which have the personal name in the genitive. Pictish appears to have lacked declension (Koch 1983, 214–220) and so the ending is perhaps more plausibly interpreted as Pictish; although the corpus of Pictish personal names is very small, -nes, and -les are also possible final syllables for personal names in Brittonic languages. Note also Bressay's *Bennises meqq*. Padel drew a parallel between the texts of St Ninian's Isle and Altyre, pointing out that on both, the 'son' word came 'very near to the start of the legend, and is followed by a very long series of letters' (1972a, 140). The Altyre text, however, is intact, whereas the St Ninian's Isle ogham is clearly missing strokes, if not several letters, from its beginning.

The letters 8–19: NANNAMMOVVES[T]

If gemination was indeed avoided in word-initial position, this could be a single word. Note, however, that one line of the Bressay ogham reads MEQQDDROANN(–) which would appear to contradict the 'rule', unless MEQQ is the first part of a compound name such as *Mac-bethad, Mac-Dara, Mac-draignin* (see index to O'Brien 1962 for numerous Irish examples of names in Mac-). The name of the father of '-(b⁺)es', *Nannammovvest* is probably to be transcribed /nanamowest/ or /nanamogwest/, with the proviso that the orthographic significance, if any, of the doubling of consonants remains opaque. At four syllables this is long for a single name and further segmentation may be required, perhaps NANN AMMOVVES[T].

It is tempting to explain the final syllable (?/-west/, ?/-gwest/) as a form of Pictish *-(g)uist* (< Celtic *gustos* 'choice'), which appears in such names as Pictish *Onuist* (< *Oinogustos*), cf Irish *Oengus*; Pictish *Uurguist* (< *Worgustos*), cf Irish *Forggus*, Welsh *Gorwst, Gwrwst* (<*Gworwst*) (Jackson 1955, 163). Celtic *-st* became *s* in Gaelic, whereas in Brittonic it either remained *st* or gave *s*; in Pictish it appears never to have become *s* (Jackson 1955, 165). If this identification is correct then the name is Pictish rather than Gaelic, especially since it appears to lack the expected Irish genitive ending *-guso*. As stated, Koch has argued that Pictish lacked declension (1983, 214–220) and Pictish *-(g)uist* appears in written sources in both nominative and genitive position (Jackson 1955, 165). AMMO- may be compared with the first element in AMMECATI, which appears on the ogham pillar from the Isle of Man, CIIC 500 (cf Gaulish *Ambicatus*). *Emchat* is the name of a northern Briton baptized by Columba in Glen Urquhart in an episode in Adomnán's *Life of Columba*.

This is the same name in a partially Gaelicised form, cf Irish *Imchath* (Jackson 1955, 142). The element *ammo-* from *ambi-* means 'around' but is used here as an intensifying suffix (Uhlich 1993, 265). To pursue such an interpretation, however, leaves the somewhat puzzling O. One would have expected E or I as the composition vowel, if indeed one could expect one at all. Such syllables were lost in Brittonic in the first half of the 6th century 'and in Gaelic slightly later' (Jackson 1955, 166). Bede's *Meilochon* (*HE* III.4) (< *Maglocunos*, later *Mailgun, Maelgwn*), written at the beginning of the 8th century of a Pict living in the third quarter of the 6th, though apparently drawing on contemporary written sources, implies that syncope was later in Pictish, perhaps in the second half of the 6th century (Jackson 1955, 166). This seems rather early for a monument such as the St Ninian's Isle slab; moreover, such an interpretation leaves NANN unexplained.

What then of /nanamo-/? A favourite Gaulish onomastic element was *namo-*, which Evans interprets as deriving from perhaps more than one root: (1) **nem-* 'allot', 'take', (2) **nem-* 'bend', 'glade', 'sacred grove', cf Irish *neimed* 'sanctuary', Middle Welsh *nyuet*; possibly Welsh *naf* 'lord' (Evans 1967, 234–235). The form most commonly found in composition has the old Celtic t-suffix, *namanto-*; Evans refutes, however, the argument that *namo-* is an abbreviated form, asserting instead that it is an independent o-stem (Evans 1967, 234–235). Perhaps St Ninian's Isle's *Nanamo-* is a reduplicated form of Celtic *Namo-*. Evans makes the link with Welsh/Cornish/Breton *nam* 'defect, blemish, fault, vice' (Evans 1967, 369), but rejects the comparison with Middle Irish *náma(e)* 'enemy', preferring O'Brien's explanation of *am* 'love' + *ne-*, negative prefix (Evans 1967, 234). The latter word is unlikely to be relevant here since it is a t-stem, and St Ninian's Isle lacks a dental. If the ogham NA- could be a negative prefix (with E > A through vowel harmony?), might the St Ninian's Isle name mean 'unblemished choice'? The name *Náeingus* appears in a Ciarraige genealogy preserved in the Books of Ballymote and Lecan (O'Brien 1976, no. 160 a 26), but this appears to be for *Nóemgus*, 'sacred choice', from *noíb* (var. *naeb*) 'holy, sacred' (*DIL*). The question of the composition vowel applies to this interpretation too. An alternative explanation is presented by Lindeman's new analysis of Celtic **namant-*, as deriving from an adjective **namo-* 'afraid, frightened' (2006). The form *nanamo-* might then be interpreted as this root preceded by a negative particle, 'not afraid'. The resulting name would be the appropriately heroic 'fearless choice one'.

2.6 PALAEOGRAPHY

The St Ninian's Isle ogham is written on a stem-line, with long, straight vowel-strokes, and consistently sloping B- and H-*aicme* consonants. It entirely lacks 'developed' features such as any of the supplementary letters (*forfeda*), bind-strokes, or word-division, which are the defining characteristics of the latest Scottish oghams. The St Ninian's Isle ogham cannot, however, be readily labeled 'early' because it exhibits two features not found on the earliest Scottish oghams, namely generous spacing between its letters, and consistently sloping B- and H-*aicme* consonants. In spacing, proportions and general aspect, St Ninian's Isle ogham more closely resembles 'later' Scottish examples, despite the lack of 'developed' features.

If one is trying to place the script of the St Ninian's Isle ogham in relation to ogham scripts elsewhere in Scotland, one distinctive attribute worth noting is that both vowel and M-*aicme* (sloping consonant) strokes occupy only the middle three-quarters of the 'ogham-band' defined by the outer tips of the B- and H-*aicme* (straight consonant) strokes. This is unusual. Inscriptions in which M-*aicme* consonants do not reach the full width of the band usually have very short 'notched' vowel strokes, and when vowel and M-*aicme* strokes are the same width, this is usually the full width of the band. An exception is Brandsbutt, Aberdeenshire (Forsyth 1996a, 102–116; Allen and Anderson 1903, 506–507), which is similar to St Ninian's Isle, except that it has only the slightest of slope on its B- and H-*aicme* letters and has no clear spacing between letters. Similarly, Scoonie, Fife (Forsyth 1996a, 480–494; Allen and Anderson 1903, 347) is perhaps closer to the script of St Ninian's Isle, but this also lacks a consistent slope on its B- and H-*aicme* consonants. Inchyra B is also similar to St Ninian's Isle in general appearance (though again, without the consistent slope), and perhaps significantly, only the final part of its text has bound letters, suggesting that this feature was not always universally applied even when available. For all its simplicity, however, it would be hard to believe the St Ninian's Isle ogham is particularly early. It shares with Lunnasting and Cunningsburgh (see below) a certain squatness which suggests they are not as far apart as their initial appearance might suggest. Perhaps St Ninian's lack of *forfeda* is due simply to the coincidence that the text did not happen to require any. The complexity of the St Ninian's Isle ogham's palaeographical affinities underlines the difficulty of attempting to construct a comprehensive script typology and, *a fortiori*, of trying to use this for purposes of absolute dating.

2.7 DISCUSSION

The St Ninian's Isle ogham is one of eight lapidary oghams from Shetland (Scott and Ritchie 2010, 6–7, 26–28).[12] These constitute a diverse collection in several respects. The upright pillar from Lunnasting, which is undecorated apart from the ogham, was found in the depths of a peat-bog, far from any known settlements. It may have been a boundary stone or way-marker. The others were all found in or near churchyards. Stylistically, the ogham-inscribed cross-slabs from Bressay and Whiteness (of which only a small fragment survives) appear to date from about the 10th century, i.e. within the Norse period. Both are/were elaborate and ambitious monuments. Both feature bind-oghams,[13] a late feature. The Whiteness fragment has only five characters remaining, but the lengthy Bressay ogham features numerous supplementary letters. Four small fragments were recovered in and around the churchyard at Cunningsburgh, although one of these was lost without further record. The three extant fragments are very different from each other. One, from a sculpted monument, perhaps a cross-slab, features bind-oghams. The others are undecorated apart from the lettering, which is palaeographically quite simple, although in both cases the layout of the stem-line is unusual if not idiosyncratic. Bressay, Cunningsburgh 3 and Lunnasting all use double dots astride the stem-line to indicate word-division, an effect not seen elsewhere in the ogham corpus. Experiments in word-division are seen in the Irish ogham corpus from about the 9th century and the double-dot device in Shetland may be a local invention. It may, however, have been influenced by the widespread use of double-dots to indicate word-division in the Norse runic tradition, as seen in Shetland at Papil (Forsyth 1996a, lix–lx). Given the well-documented interest in ogham in Norse cultural contexts in Ireland, Man and Western Scotland (Forsyth 2007), it is quite possible that all of these inscriptions date from the Norse period,[14] although the Lunnasting and Cunningsburgh examples need not.

The use of double dots for word-division is a feature which is unique to Shetland, but in other respects, the Shetland oghams are part of the Scottish mainstream. The fundamental unity of the Scottish ogham tradition is underlined by the fact that certain palaeographical innovations, such as bind-oghams and unusual supplementary letters are found throughout Scotland.[15] The preponderance of these in Shetland may be due simply to the comparatively late date being proposed for many of the Shetlandic examples, rather than any regional or dialectal distinctiveness. The archaeological and palaeographical diversity of the Shetland oghams shows that they were not the product of an isolated burst of ogham carving activity: even the three extant examples from the single site of Cunningsburgh are very different from one another and clearly the work of different 'hands'. Instead, the impression is of on-going participation in the Scottish ogham tradition over a potentially extended period, with a possible emphasis in the 10th century.

That Shetland oghamists should still be part of the common tradition after the Norse *adventus* is perhaps surprising, yet it appears to be borne out by the numerous parallels between Shetland oghams and the ogham from Dyce, Aberdeenshire, which probably dates to the 10th century. In addition to more general similarities, such as the use of bind-strokes and the 'hammer-head' A, Dyce exhibits one character otherwise attested only on the Bressay slab, and one found elsewhere only on Cuningsburgh 2. These shared innovations suggest that at least the Church in 10th-century Shetland was not cut off from contemporary developments in non-Norse Scotland.

The absence of 'late', i.e. developed, palaeographic features on a Scottish ogham does not necessarily rule out a date later than, say, the 9th century as the majority of Irish ogham inscriptions which can be dated to this period are palaeographically simple. Thus, the form of the script used on the St Ninian's Isle slab is not a clear indicator of date. If the text is correctly interpreted as preserving a composition vowel in the second name then the ogham can scarcely be later than the 7th century (unless we posit a remarkably strong and long-lived early orthographical tradition). This is remarkably early and does not sit well with the general aspect of the script, which is quite different from the earliest Scottish examples (eg Gigha and Pool, Orkney) and from 7th-century Irish examples. The linguistic interpretation of the text is very uncertain, however.

On the face of it, MEQQ appears to be the Gaelic word for 'son', implying Irish was being spoken. The unhistorical spelling, however, indicates that this is being treated as a formula word and so this can bear little weight. More telling, perhaps, is the ending of the final word which appears to be a form of the Pictish −(g)uist. Ogham was invented in Ireland, its use in Western Britain is an Irish trait and, at least in its initial phases in the 6th and 7th centuries, ogham carving in Scotland is an indication of Irish influence and perhaps of Irish settlement. Over the centuries, however, the practice appears to have been adopted with enthusiasm by the local population and integrated into Pictish sculptural practice. It is a moot point, therefore, whether by, say, the ninth or tenth centuries the use of ogham still retained any specifically Irish or Gaelic associations.

The choice of ogham over roman script is a striking one. The curved forms of the roman alphabet are, indeed, harder to render in stone than the straight lines of ogham, but would not have been beyond the capabilities of the carvers of such ambitious monuments as Bressay and Whiteness, or of the St Ninian's Isle corner-post shrines. The cultural reasons behind the choice of script in Shetland, as in Scotland as a whole, remain opaque. Nor is it a question of 'access' to roman alphabet literacy. Major ecclesiastical centres such as St Ninian's Isle and Papil would certainly have housed literate clerics. Indeed, clerics carrying book-satchels are depicted in stone on the Papil and Bressay slabs (Scott and Ritchie 2010, 18–19; Forsyth 1998, 40–41). Although the majority are demonstrably Pictish, there is no certainty that the various items in the St Ninian's Isle hoard of silver were manufactured in Shetland. Nonetheless, the presence

of a roman alphabet inscription on one of the sword chapes (NMS cat. no. FC 282) indicates, at the very least, some contact with a centre of Latin literacy, and not merely one where there was knowledge of how to write, but one where manuscripts were produced. As J Brown points out (1993), the choice of uncial script for the lettering on one side of the chape and minuscule script for the other reflects familiarity with the hierarchy of scripts employed in the monastic scriptorium. The chape is well-illustrated in Youngs (1989, pl 103), and by Henderson and Henderson (2004, 113), where it is subjected to art-historical analysis, and by Graham-Campbell (2003a, 28–32). The inscription has been discussed by Jackson (1973a), Okasha (1985, 57–59), Brown (1993) and M P Brown (1989), and most recently, Forsyth (forthcoming b). On one side, in uncial letters, is the text INNOMINEDS, interpreted as *in nomine D(ei) S(ummi)*, 'in the name of God the Highest', or, if the minuscule s is a slip based on a misreading of a horizontal suspension mark above an I, simply as *in nomine D(e)i* 'in the name of God'. On the other side, in minuscule, is RESADFILISPUSSCIO. Previous interpretations include *Resad fili Spusscio* 'Resad son of Spusscio' (Jackson), or *res ad Fili Sp(irit)us S(an)c(t) io*, 'property of the Holy Spirit' (Brown 1989). *Resad* has been recently confirmed as a likely Pictish male personal name cognate with well-known Brittonic names based on *Res/Ris* (> Welsh *Rhys*) (Forsyth forthcoming b). The very close parallel with the Latin inscription on the contemporary Anglo-Saxon helmet from Coppergate, York (Tweddle 1992, 1134–35; Okasha 1992), suggests that the two sides of the chape should be taken together as a single text in which the name of the chape's owner, Resad, is embedded in a protective invocation of the Trinity. Comparison with the Coppergate text, and with contemporary Gaelic liturgy suggests that, depending on how the final *o* is interpreted, the full text might be something like: *in nomine D(ei) S(ummi) (et) Fili (et) Sp(irit)us S(an)c(t)i (et) o(mnes dicimus, Amen)*, or *in nomine D(ei) S(ummi) (et) Fili (et) Sp(irit)us S(an)c(t)i (et) o(mnium sanctorum)*, 'in the name of God the Highest (and) of the Son (and) of the Holy Spirit, to/with all (we say Amen)' or 'in the name of God the Highest (and) of the Son (and) of the Holy Spirit, (and) of All (Saints)' (see Forsyth forthcoming b for detailed discussion).

2.8 PREVIOUS READINGS

Goudie, Brash, Southesk	−ESMEQQNANAGOFFES[T]
Ferguson	−ESMEQQNAN AMMOFFES[T]
Rhŷs	BESMEQQNANAMMOVVEF
Nicholson	LESMEQQNANAMMOVVES[T]
Allen and Anderson	BESMEQQNANAMMOVVEF
Macalister	L)ESMEQQNANAMMOVVESZ
Padel	−B)ESMEQQNANAMMOVVEZ

Notes

1   At the time of the discovery Goudie was a Fellow of the Society of Antiquaries of Scotland; he later went on to be the Society's Treasurer and his portrait appears in the bottom left-hand corner of the stained-glass window made to commemorate the opening of the National Museum of Antiquities in Edinburgh in 1891 (Clarke 1990, 206, illus 26).

2   Subsequent finder of the Lunnasting ogham, discussed below.

3   At the time of writing (2007) the slab was on loan to Shetland Museum.

4   Pers comm July 2006. I am most grateful to Dr Miller for examining the slab and providing her expert opinion on various aspects of its geology.

5   As discussed below, the ogham lettering gives a clue as to orientation.

6   A hand-list of the Ogham Inscriptions of Scotland by Katherine Forsyth:

Abernethy, Perthshire: Forsyth 1996a, 2–10;

Ackergill, Caithness: Forsyth 1996a, 11–22; Close-Brooks and Stevenson 1982, 27;

Altyre, Moray: Forsyth 1996a, 23–40; Calder and Jackson 1957;

Auquhollie, Kincardineshire: Forsyth 1996a, 41–54; Allen and Anderson 1903, 203–204;

Bac Mhic Connain, North Uist: Forsyth 1996a, 55–68; Hallén 1994, 219;

Birsay, Orkney: Forsyth 1996a, 69–92; Radford 1959, 5 (1); Radford 1962, 174 (2); Morris 1996c, 54–55 (3);

Blackwaterfoot, Arran: Forsyth 1996a, 93–101; Fisher 2001, 61–69; Jackson 1973b;

Bornais, South Uist: Forsyth 2007;

Brandsbutt, Aberdeenshire: Forsyth 1996a, 102–116; RCAHMS 2007, 135;

Bressay, Shetland: Forsyth 1996a, 117–138; Close-Brooks and Stevenson 1982, 35;

Brodie, Moray: Forsyth 1996a, 139–159; Allen and Anderson 1903, 132–135;

Buckquoy, Orkney: Forsyth 1996b;

Burrian, North Ronaldsay, Orkney: Forsyth 1996a, 187–205; MacGregor 1976, 96–97; Forsyth forthcoming a;

Cunningsburgh, Shetland: Forsyth 1996a, 206–226; RCAHMS 1946, no. 1136;

Dunadd, Argyll: Forsyth 2001;

Dupplin, Perthshire: Forsyth 1996a, 243–260;

Dyce, Aberdeenshire: RCAHMS 2007, 134;

Formaston, Aberdeenshire: Forsyth 1996a, 261–287; Simpson 1944, 101–103;

Gigha: Forsyth 1996a, 288–298; RCAHMS 1971, 96–97;

Golspie, Sutherland: Forsyth 1996a, 299–320; Close-Brooks 1989, 14, 16;

Gurness, Orkney: Forsyth 1996a, 321–332; Hedges 1987, 213, no. 252;

Inchyra, Angus: Forsyth 1996a, 333–359; RCAHMS 1994, 95; Stevenson 1959;

Latheron, Sutherland: Forsyth 1996a, 360–373; Anderson 1904, 76;

Lochgoilhead, Argyll: Forsyth 1996a, 374–384; Fisher 2001, 151;

Logie Elphinstone, Aberdeenshire: Forsyth 1996a, 385–401; RCAHMS 2007, 128;

Lunnasting, Shetland: Forsyth 1996a, 402–419; RCAHMS 1946, 81–82;

Mains of Afforsk, Aberdeenshire: RCAHMS 2007, 126–127;

Newton, Aberdeenshire: Forsyth 1996a, 420–442; Okasha 1985, 54–56;

Poltalloch, Argyll: Forsyth 1996a, 443–455; Fisher 2001, 151;

Pool, Sanday, Orkney: Forsyth 1996a, 456–466; Hunter 1985;

Scoonie, Fife: Forsyth 1996a, 480–494; Allen and Anderson 1903, 347;

St Ninian's Isle, Shetland: This volume, Chapter 2;

St Vigeans, Angus: Borland 2005, 212;

Whiteness, Shetland: Forsyth 1996a, 495–502; Stevenson 1981, 285–287.

7   For the record, if oriented in the opposite direction, the reading would be: s^{t}ETTOMMQAQNNEMCED.

8   *Dind map Lethain i tírib Bretan Corn .i. Dun Maic Liathain, ar is mac indní is map isin Bretnais*, 'Dind map Lethain in the lands of the Cornish Britons, i.e. 'the fort of the sons of Liathan', because *mac* is *map* in British.

9   A further elaborated version of this character may appear on the damaged dual-script inscription from Eglwys Nynnid, Margam, Glamorgan CIIC 409, discussed by Sims-Williams (1992, 42, 44).

10   The third character of the Gigha ogham is virtually illegible and could be C or Q (VI*ULA) (Forsyth 1996a, 292).

11   Macalister claimed, albeit with hesitation, a unique example of the spelling MAIC on CIIC 83, but this is not confirmed by McManus (1991, 66), even when it would have been present in pronunciation; for instance, the MAQ at Arraglen, Co. Kerry (CIIC 145) is genitive (McManus 1991, 91).

12   I have been able to confirm that the carvings on a small 'amulet' (actually a spindle whorl) from Vaivoe, Whalsay (Forsyth 1996b, 529), now in the Shetland Museum are not, as had once been suggested, ogham inscribed.

13   'Bind-oghams' feature an additional stroke, parallel with the stem, joining the distal tips of letter strokes. This aid to legibility 'binds' the component strokes of individual letters together into bundles clearly differentiated from the strokes of neighbouring letters.

14   The site at Cunningsburgh was of great commercial and political importance in the Norse period and three runic inscriptions have also been recovered there.

15   Bind-oghams are found elsewhere in the north at Birsay and Burrian, Orkney, in the east at Dyce, Aberdeenshire, and in the south at Abernethy and Inchyra, Perthshire.

AN ASSESSMENT OF THE 1955 TO 1959 EXCAVATIONS

3.1 THE AVAILABLE SOURCES

Professor A C O'Dell's own published accounts

O'Dell submitted three reports to *Discovery and Excavation in Scotland*, in 1957, 1958 and 1959. The 1957 entry (O'Dell 1957) describes the results of a culmination of three seasons work, in 1955, 1956 and 1957 (see below), including clearing of the interior of the medieval chapel, excavation of the 'Founder's Tomb', and the excavation of a large pit within the nave. The following year's entry (O'Dell 1958) describes the location of some of the trenches excavated around the area of the chapel in 1958, as well as a deep trench within it and the finding of Iron Age levels and the silver hoard (see below). The 1959 entry (O'Dell 1959c) describes the further excavation of the nave, and the excavation of a large area to the south of the chapel (see below).

Following the finding of the treasure in 1958, O'Dell also published an article in the *Scottish Geographical Magazine* published in 1959 (O'Dell 1959a), the 'Introduction' to an article in *Antiquity*, also published in 1959 (O'Dell 1959b), and two pages of 'notes' in a volume of photographs by Alexander Cain, published in the Aberdeen University Studies Series (O'Dell and Cain 1960). The parts of these articles covering the excavations are all based on an unpublished typescript written by O'Dell in 1958 entitled *Preliminary Report of excavations at St Ninian's Isle, 1955–8*, several versions of which are held in the Shetland Archives (see below).[1]

The *Scottish Geographical Magazine* article outlines how O'Dell first came to be working at the site and his own enthusiasm to prove a link between the Isle, St Ninian and his *Candida Casa* at Whithorn, an enthusiasm which was to lead him to associate the plastered chapel walls on the Isle with a Ninianic foundation (O'Dell 1959a, 41–42). The article is clearly based on the same typescript as an article written by James R Coull, one of the excavation supervisors, which was published in *Scotland's Magazine* in 1958 (D/1/359/14/7 in the Shetland Archives). O'Dell's introduction to the *Antiquity* article covers only two pages, including a location plan and plan of the chapel, with the remainder of the article by Stevenson, Brown, Plenderleith and Bruce-Mitford dealing solely with the treasure. Finally, the

O'Dell and Cain volume contains two pages of text by O'Dell, who reconstructs the story of the site, beginning with the excavations to the south of the chapel. This adds some further information to what is already published, although much of it is contained in the 1959 *DES* entry.

St Ninian's Isle and its treasure: Small, Thomas and Wilson 1973

This publication is in two volumes, the first containing the text, the second the illustrations. The dust jacket describes it as 'the definitive account of the 1958 St Ninian's Isle excavation, begun by the late Professor A C O'Dell, and of the treasure discovered'.

There are four parts to the volume. The first is by Alan Small, excavation supervisor, who writes about the site, its history and excavation. The second is by Charles Thomas, who in the main discusses the sculptured stones and crosses from St Ninian's Isle and Papil in Shetland, but also adds his own thoughts on the excavations (pp 11–14), with the benefit of extra information from O'Dell himself and discussions with Alan Small. The third and most extensive part is by David M Wilson, who describes and discusses the magnificent treasure in detail, including a full catalogue and comparisons with material from Britain and further afield. The accompanying illustrations in the second volume are mainly concerned with this section, and there are drawings and photographs of comparative material from elsewhere, as well as of the St Ninian's Isle treasure itself. To conclude, the final part written by T B Smith discusses the law relating to the treasure, and the appendices by Kenneth Jackson and Hugh McKerrell describe the inscriptions and chemical analyses of the silver objects respectively.

Small outlines the difficult task he was faced with in attempting to write up O'Dell's excavations, and the three pages of description and two plans that resulted from five seasons of excavations testify to this. As Graham-Campbell writes in his recent reappraisal of the treasure, Small 'was the first to admit that it was a sorry affair, given that he had had to cobble it together, as best he might, from the most meagre scraps of information' (Graham-Campbell 2003a, 14). In the volume Small writes:

There is no master grid for the site, and small finds are frequently recorded by the name of the excavator rather than by their specific location; it is thus impossible to relate them to specific horizons. No site diary can be found nor a comprehensive finds record, with the result that most of the prehistoric account in this volume is based on the recollections of the author and his former fellow students who have kindly lent him notes, photographs, and personal diaries.

(Small 1973, 5).

The National Monuments Record of Scotland and the National Museums of Scotland

The NMRS collection contains five aerial photographs taken before the excavations began: two from 1944 (Sortie 106G/DY 24, frames 60007 and 60006), and three from 1950 (Sortie 540/A/466, frames 3142, 3143 and 3144). There are also three from 1967 and six from 1971 (Sortie S/67/152, frames 2716, 2717 and 2718; NMRS numbers SH/1449, SH/1448, SH/1805 and SH/1806) which clearly show the grassed-over spoil heaps and the hollow left by the excavations. There are also news cuttings from 1958 in the archive, covering the discovery of the silver hoard, and photographs of drawings of the hoard. In addition, there are news cuttings and a piece of prose about the treasure in the F T Wainwright collection (MO/746/110).

A full copy-set of the slide collection of Helen Nisbet, a student at Glasgow University who attended the excavations in 1956, 1957 and 1959 and kept a personal diary of the findings, is also housed in the NMRS. The original slide collection was kindly donated by Ms Nisbet to Glasgow University Archaeology Department in 2000.

The National Museum holds the St Ninian's Isle treasure and the porpoise jawbone found with it. The only other material from the Isle held by the Museum comprises a box of disarticulated human bone that originates from the spoil heaps at the site and was donated after the excavations (Helen Nisbet and Natasha Powers pers comm).

The Shetland Archives

Four boxes of documents deposited by Dr Alan Small in 1998, and a later collection of slides deposited after his death in September 1999, are held in the Shetland Archives (the slides accompanied finds which were donated to the Shetland Museum, and they are now available to view on the Shetland Museum website).

The documents concern the excavations, the discovery of the treasure, the publication of a report on the treasure, and the arguments about where it should be housed. There is a mixture of correspondence to and from O'Dell, but also Small's own papers and so it is not always possible to identify the author of some of the un-named typescripts. All the papers date from between 1955 and the early 1970s and comprise:

— D/1/359/1–5. Two boxes of correspondence by, and addressed to, Professor A C O'Dell, 1956–61.

— D/1/359/1/11/24. Typescript, written by O'Dell, entitled *St Ninian's Isle: Preliminary Report*, with letter returning said typescript, from Bruce-Mitford at the BM, dated 14 April 1959 (Bruce-Mitford was working on an article which was submitted to the *Scientific American* magazine and published November 1960).

— D/1/359/6. A site notebook, only partially filled, probably written by O'Dell or Alan Small with notes on the 1958 excavation.

— D/1/359/7. Draft typescripts and duplicates for an article and/or lectures by O'Dell on *St Ninian's Isle excavations 1955–58*. Written in 1958–59.[2]

— D/1/359/8. Draft typescripts and duplicated typescripts of articles, lectures and reports by O'Dell on the St Ninian's Isle excavations and treasure, late 1950s–1961.

— D/1/359/9. Typescripts, such as a *Report to Session 1958*, and British Museum typescript press release concerning finding of treasure.

— D/1/359/10. Comments on the typescript concerning the finding of the treasure.

— D/1/359/11. Miscellaneous papers (rough notes, etc) from the St Ninian's Isle excavations, late 1950s, eg D/1/359/11/6. List of levels taken on site, D/1/359/11/8. Sketch of NE of nave, D/1/359/11/7. Sketch of section of south face of wall.

— D/1/359/12. Statement concerning where the hoard will be disposed.

— D/1/359/13. Press cuttings covering the finding of the treasure.

— D/1/359/14. Magazine articles.

— D/1/359/15. Miscellaneous photographs of the St Ninian's Isle excavations; no dates but some from 1958, including photographs X15, X6 and X10, which were originally in Helen Nisbet's notebook, but were removed for use when Small compiled the 1973 volume.

The draft typescripts held in the Shetland Archives (D/1/359/7) are the most important documents in the collection. There are several versions of a typewritten draft of a Preliminary Report of excavations at St Ninian's Isle, 1955–8 (hereafter PDR), written by O'Dell after the 1958 season. When the different drafts are combined, it is possible to produce a more detailed account of the excavations than has otherwise been published. All subsequent accounts published by O'Dell (1959a; 1959b; 1960) were based on this preliminary report. Other typescripts and short reports contained in D/1/359/8 and 9 are also useful for additional small details.

The small number of photographs in the collection that were taken during the excavation, some originating from Helen Nisbet's personal diary (see

FIGURE 3.1

Excavation in the 'Founder's Tomb'. Photograph: H Nisbet from her diary (Shetland Archives, D.1/359/15/15)

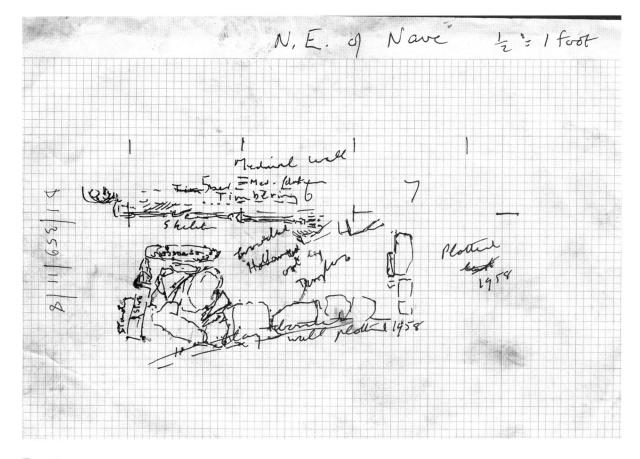

FIGURE 3.2

Sketch of NE of nave from O'Dell's excavations (reproduced with permission of the Shetland Archives, D.1/359/11/8)

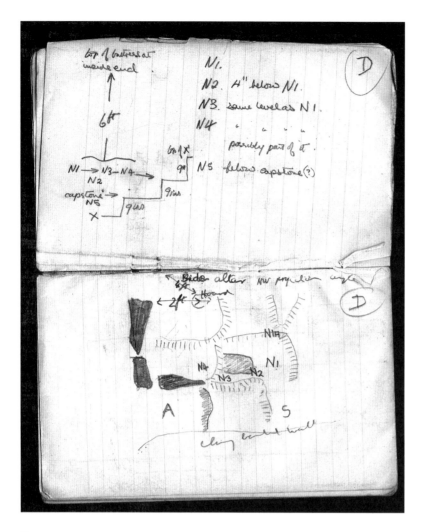

FIGURE 3.3
Sketches from site notebook (reproduced with permission of the Shetland Archives, D.1/359/6)

below), include a photograph of the excavation hole in the so-called 'Founder's Tomb' (Figure 3.1) and other parts of the 1957 excavations in the nave. The archive also contains loose sheets of paper with rough sketches from the excavations (eg Figure 3.2).

The site notebook (D/1/359/6), hereafter *SN*, contains rough notes and sketches (eg Figure 3.3), all from the 1958 excavations within the chapel. The first half of the notebook has been ripped out, and only part of the second half has notes on it. These include sketches of the position of the excavation 'pits', sketches of cists and burials, rough descriptions and locations of artefacts and positioning of timber shoring. The sketches are very rough, however, with no scale, direction or dimensions and are consequently difficult to locate. They, and the descriptions, are more likely to be tied to the name of an excavator than to a location or depth within the excavations.

The correspondence held in the archives is useful when passing references are made to the ongoing work. For instance, letters to the engineering contractor in Lerwick, who provided shoring for the team in 1958 and 1959, locate the areas of ex-

cavation in these years (D/1/359/1/12/22). O'Dell also describes in letters (D/1/359/1/8/15, dated 9/12/58) how attempts at level-taking were ruined by the presence of so many later burials, and how the Iron Age levels were 5ft (1.52m) below the medieval walls.

The Shetland Museum

The Shetland Museum holds all the inscribed and worked stone recovered from O'Dell's excavations, including the fragment of porphyry, and also an iron padlock and the bone and antler beads, deposited by Small in the early 1970s after the completion of the 1973 volume. The stone, porphyry and beads are all published in the 1973 volume (Small *et al* 1973, 5, 7, fig 6; Thomas 1973, figs 9–11, pls III–XI). The padlock is, however, only mentioned in the O'Dell and Cain volume, where it is described as a 'much corroded barrel-lock of Romano-British type' (O'Dell 1960, 4).

In addition to this, three boxes of mainly pottery finds (Items 379, 797 and 798), and one box of bones (Item 379) from O'Dell's excavations were deposited in the museum in 1998 and 2000. Only the box of bones was labelled: 'From O'Dell Chattels. Part of skeleton. From St Ninian's Isle. No date or provenance. ? Re-bury'. The box of 16 finds deposited by Alan Small, in 1998 (Item 397), contains those that were of particular note to the excavator at the time, such as decorated pottery, worked stone and a spindle whorl. Only half of these finds have labels with them, and only one can be identified in the 1973 volume (pottery sherd A19.1998.11; illustrated in Small et al 1973, fig 3).

Most of the bags of finds in the remaining two boxes (Items 797 and 798) have small scraps of paper inside the bag annotated with either a person's name, or a letter code reference to a particular pit dug on the site. There are 174 bags in total, many of which contain more than one type of material and only 12 of which do not contain a label. The majority of the collection comprises pottery, which numbers around 840 sherds. Only 34 bags in the entire collection can definitely be attributed to a particular year of the excavation (1959) from their labels, but most appear to have originated from excavations inside and below the chapel, probably in 1958 or 1959.

Fragments of a 13th-century Limoges enamel crucifix, including a gilt copper-alloy figural mount, were also contained amongst O'Dell's papers deposited by Small in 1998. Unfortunately the fragments were identified too late in the post-excavation programme to be analysed further, but they were conserved by William Murray, Artefacts and Preventative Conservator, Scottish Conservation Studio, prior to being displayed in the new Shetland Museum, and his description is included in 3.4 below. The fragments are mentioned only once in O'Dell's papers, in a typescript (D1/359/8/4) in the Shetland Archives of a lecture that he was to give/or gave at some time during or after the 1956 season, but definitely before the 1957 season (there is no mention at all of digging below the chapel), when he lists amongst his finds: 'a) A late 17th century coin, b) a small brass religious figurine. These were both in crevices of the high altar and may be part of Brand's superstitious offerings.'

Although the coin is mentioned in all O'Dell's subsequent typescripts for lectures and articles, mention of the figurine is dropped, perhaps because it was deemed too fragmentary. As described above, a collection of slides was also deposited in the Museum by Small in 1998. Many of the slides are duplicated in the Helen Nisbet collection, and are all catalogued and available on the Shetland Museum website.

The Marischal Museum, Aberdeen

During the excavations in 1957, 1958 and 1959, bones were sent to the Department of Anatomy, Marischal College, at Aberdeen University, for identification and analysis by Professor R D Lockhart. Horse bones were sent in 1957 for a nitrogen test (letter dated 23/7/57), and notes in *SN* refer to bones from an extended E–W burial being removed for examination in 1958. A burial in a 'disarticulated and perhaps broken condition' was also uncovered in the Founder's Tomb in 1957 (see below), but it is not known whether the bones were removed from the site. In 1959 O'Dell describes in correspondence two groups of bones, code-named 'Robert' and 'Elizabeth', which were sent to the Aberdeen Anatomy Department (D/1/359/1/14/2, dated 21/8/59). 'Robert' is described as 'Dark Age' and from a wooden coffin, with some of the bones being of a peculiar shape. 'Elizabeth' however was a small group of bones, judged to be Iron Age, and 'all the bones which were in the grave were collected but the body had been buried or translated from an earlier burial with the thigh bones touching the skull'.

A visit to the Marischal Museum in February 2002 by the author and Julie Roberts identified three corresponding groups of bones from the 1959 excavations, code-named 'Rosemary', 'Robert' and 'Hubert' (given accession numbers ABDUA 14269, 14270 and 14254 respectively). These remains were studied in the museum, and samples from each group were later submitted for radiocarbon dating (see below).[3] However, it seems that the bones from 'Elizabeth' were not in the end sent to the Aberdeen University Anatomy department with other material in 1959 as no record of their arrival there could be found. For a long time it was assumed they were lost until the box of bones that Small deposited in the Shetland Museum in 1998 was analysed (A26.1998, Item 379). This box contained long bones and pieces of skull, amongst other skeletal elements (see Duffy, Figure 3.32 below), and it is possible that these correspond to 'Elizabeth'.

The Natural History Museum, London

A group of mixed disarticulated bones that were visibly eroding from the old excavation spoil heaps were removed from the site by visitors in the 1960s and subsequently sent to the Natural History Museum. The material comprises 70 boxes of cranial material and 131 boxes of post-cranial material, and has been housed in the Natural History Museum since as least 1964.[4]

Personal archives and recollections

Professor Charles Thomas' papers

After the 1958 excavation season at St Ninian's Isle, Professor Charles Thomas was invited to present a radio programme on the St Ninian's Hoard for the BBC to be broadcast on Network 3 on Tuesday 4 November 1958. Thomas had never visited the excavations in progress, and so as part of his research he

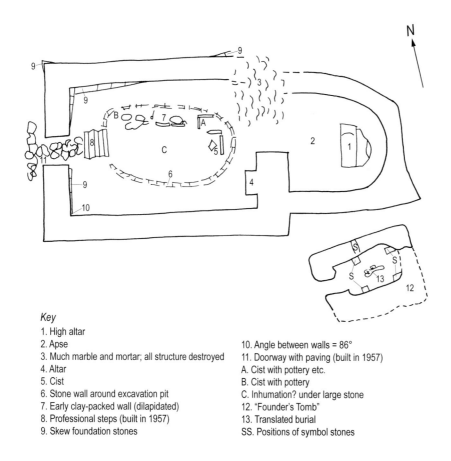

Key
1. High altar
2. Apse
3. Much marble and mortar; all structure destroyed
4. Altar
5. Cist
6. Stone wall around excavation pit
7. Early clay-packed wall (dilapidated)
8. Professional steps (built in 1957)
9. Skew foundation stones

10. Angle between walls = 86°
11. Doorway with paving (built in 1957)
A. Cist with pottery etc.
B. Cist with pottery
C. Inhumation? under large stone
12. "Founder's Tomb"
13. Translated burial
SS. Positions of symbol stones

FIGURE 3.4

Sketch plan of 1957 excavations from H Nisbet's diary. Re-drawn by Gillian McSwan

travelled to Aberdeen on 16 October 1958 to interview O'Dell about his findings. Nine years later, after O'Dell's death, Thomas was asked by Small to report on the sculptured stone assemblage for the volume on St Ninian's Isle and its treasure, and in 1967 he visited St Ninian's Isle and Papil, and made plans of both sites, as well as visiting the Shetland museum to look at and record all the stonework from them.[5] The site on the Isle had by this time been backfilled and consolidated so Thomas could only record what he could observe above ground. However, contained in his archive are notes and sketches, letters and other papers concerned with the BBC broadcast and seven black-and-white prints of the excavation. Also, some time after the 1958 interview Thomas met up with Alan Small and from Small's notes they drew out a ground plan (Thomas pers comm), which Thomas later annotated and re-drew for the 1973 volume (Figure 1.3).

From the available information, Thomas and Small were able to reconstruct two phases of walling in the nave pit, with a third dry-stone wall built by the excavators themselves in 1957 as revetment for the excavation pit at that time. Thomas' sketch plan was to form the basis of the reconstructed plan published in the 1973 volume, and the Iron Age walling below the chapel shown therein (Thomas 1973,

fig 8; Figure 1.3). There are depth measurements on Thomas' original sketch plan and notes taken from O'Dell. The remainder of Thomas' notes concern the shrine posts and are worked into his report on the sculpture in the 1973 volume (Thomas 1973, 14–20).

In 1988 Professor Graham-Campbell discovered two tobacco tins containing glass beads in a filing cabinet in University College London that had previously belonged to David Wilson. The beads were originally accompanied by a letter, now held in Thomas' archive, which had been sent to Thomas by Small in 1967 and describes from whereabouts on the excavation the beads came. The beads and the letter were subsequently passed to Dr Colleen E Batey, then lecturer at the Medieval Archaeology Department at University College London, who reports on them below.

Helen Nisbet's archive

Helen Nisbet, who at the time was a Geography student at Glasgow University, visited the site with the Scottish Summer School of Archaeology in August 1956, and subsequently attended the excavations as a student in 1957 and 1959. In 1957 she made a detailed site diary of the excavation, drew a sketch plan

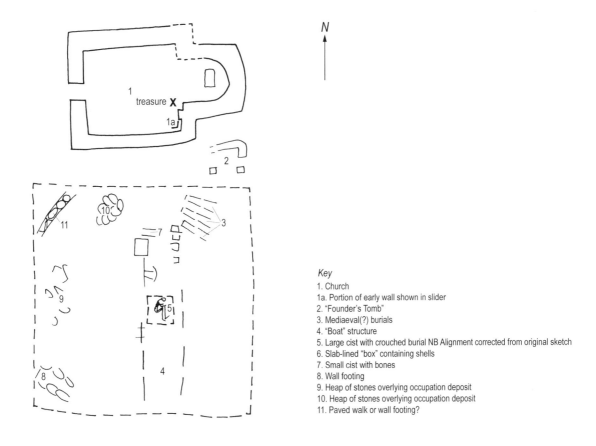

Key
1. Church
1a. Portion of early wall shown in slider
2. "Founder's Tomb"
3. Mediaeval(?) burials
4. "Boat" structure
5. Large cist with crouched burial NB Alignment corrected from original sketch
6. Slab-lined "box" containing shells
7. Small cist with bones
8. Wall footing
9. Heap of stones overlying occupation deposit
10. Heap of stones overlying occupation deposit
11. Paved walk or wall footing?

FIGURE 3.5

Sketch plan of 1959 excavations from H Nisbet's diary. Re-drawn by Gillian McSwan

(Figure 3.4) and took many slides and black-and-white photographs. Her records of the 1959 excavation are less detailed although she again drew a sketch plan of the excavation (Figure 3.5) and jotted down her recollections afterwards. Both Alan Small and Charles Thomas made considerable use of typewritten extracts and photographs provided by Miss Nisbet when compiling the 1973 volume.

In 2003, Miss Nisbet was kind enough to make her original site diary, notes, letters and photographs available to the author and these have proved invaluable, especially when studied in conjunction with the notebook and notes from the O'Dell and Small archives.

Other than the slides now held by GUAD, the Nisbet archive includes four black-and-white print photographs from 1956 and 26 from 1957, all with captions, that were originally stuck into her site diary (eg Figures 3.1, 3.6 and 3.7). It also includes, one black-and-white postcard from 1958 (Figure 3.8), eleven items of various correspondence and thirteen sheets of typewritten notes, some taken from the 1957 site diary, with notes interleaved on yellow paper of comments added by Miss Nisbet at a later date. These notes include lists of slides taken each year, and the two sketch plans, each with a key to features, for the years 1957 and 1959 (Figures 3.4 and 3.5).

The site diary of the June 1957 excavations is most detailed and includes thirteen black-and-white print photographs mainly relating to the social aspects of the excavation, sketch plans of the 1957 and 1959 excavations identical to those included with typewritten notes, notes taken for a talk in 1959 on the excavations, newspaper cuttings, duplicate prints and oddments and a packet of rubbings of crosses found in 1959.

Personal recollections

During excavations in August 1999, many Shetlanders shared their memories of their part in and experience of O'Dell's excavations.[6] Mr Douglas Coutts, who found the St Ninian's Isle treasure as a 16-year-old schoolboy, and Mr Robert Leask, a local historian born and brought up in Bigton, were especially helpful when they visited the Open Day at the site. In particular Douglas Coutts pointed out the whereabouts of the 1950s spoil heaps, many of which could now be mistaken for archaeological features. Mr Coutts confirmed that the dry-stone walling eroding out from the slope to the east of the chapel was revetment for one of the 1950s spoil heaps, not an eroding Iron Age structure, as had been suggested by the author in an interview on the

FIGURE 3.6
End of season 1956. Photograph: H Nisbet

FIGURE 3.7
Excavation in progress in 1957. Photograph: H R Mackenzie (from H Nisbet 1957 diary)

BBC Radio Shetland news the previous morning! He also identified the linear bank to the north of the site as a spoil heap, with revetment walling along the edge, not an enclosure bank, for which it could easily be mistaken (cf Fojut 1993, 62). Shortly after his visit, the identification of both banks as spoil heaps was verified by results from Trial Trenches 2 and 4, where depths of up to 1.3m of sand, spoil and disarticulated human remains were uncovered (PLATE 5; Barrowman 2000). Mr Coutts also recollected that some human skeletal material was reburied in pits to the west of the chapel and around the inner edge of the fenced area, but these areas were not excavated in 1999/2000.

After the fieldwork, Dr James R Coull of Aberdeen University, who helped with Alan Small to supervise the excavations, was kind enough to share his memories of the excavations and was also helpful with suggestions as to the whereabouts of material from them (James Coull pers comm), as well as discussing various points on the landscape around the Isle (Coull 2003).

3.2 THE EXCAVATIONS 1955–1959

The 1955 excavation

During the Viking Congress in Lerwick in 1951 Dr W Douglas Simpson drew O'Dell's attention to similarities, in his view, between St Ninian's Isle and Whithorn (Simpson 1954; 1940; O'Dell 1959b, 241). O'Dell was suitably intrigued and in June 1955 began a field project at the site, attended by students from Aberdeen University Geographical and Archaeological societies. O'Dell describes in his *PDR* how: 'On arriving there for the first time there was nothing to betray the site of the church. Under our feet was smooth green turf, unbroken except for one or two projecting boulders which later proved of no significance'. The team attempted to first locate the site using stereoscopic examination of aerial photos, and then by sinking an auger in an effort to reveal the stratigraphy of the site. However, 'this was so easily foiled by the smallest pebble that it was soon abandoned'. Instead, the excavators dug small 'trial trenches', or pits, over the general area in the hope of striking what was left of the old walls.

Despite knowing the approximate position of the chapel, the team was unsuccessful for nearly a week until they dug a test pit where burials had clearly taken place and found films of mortar dust but no structure. They then dug test pits radiating out to the north and found a layer of rubble – broken stone and mortar – and followed its top surface upslope in the hope that it was banked against a wall. In this way, O'Dell's team discovered the east end of the chapel wall, and, moving westwards, dumping the spoil beyond the east end, the excavation pit was enlarged up the slope and the NE corner of the chapel wall was located. Subsequently, the curved chancel,

or apse[7] and high altar were also found and O'Dell notes that lime plaster survived in places on the inside wall. Dr Coull confirmed (pers comm) that in 1955 the east end of the chapel was uncovered with the excavation continuing westwards into the hillside, uncovering the rest of the chapel in 1956 and 1957.

Although the site was extremely complex due to the insertion of many interlocking burials during the post-medieval period, it was not until the team reached the chapel foundations that 'trowelling replaced spade work' (PDR).

The 1956 excavation

The south half of the nave was cleared in 1956 (Figure 3.6), although there are few details other than finds mentioned from that year in the *PDR*. These include a late 17th-century copper coin, found wedged in the altar, and brown and blue glass beads said to be from post-Reformation interments (although see Batey below). Medieval finds are described as including fragments of 'igneous slabs' into which had been hewn crosses, fragments of green and brown glazed pottery (see Will below) and a boat-shaped grave covering. The stone crosses and grave covering are nos 12–14 and 17 in Thomas' catalogue (Thomas 1973, pls IX and XI). An inscribed cross (no. 18) attributed to the 12th century was also found in 1956, within the nave of the chapel, and was re-erected in the local church at Bigton. This stone was found over a burial and had mortar adhering to it, suggesting that it was originally used in the medieval chapel building (Thomas 1973, 38, no. 18, pl XII). A small brass religious figurine and brass fragments were also found, 'in crevices in the high altar' (D1/359/8/4), and have recently been identified and conserved as part of a Limoges cross (PLATE 15).

Small (1973, 4) states that 'structures were the only significant feature on the excavation' and that thousands of medieval and later interments were 'removed rapidly without record and reburied to the west of the church'. This is confirmed on slides taken at the end of the 1956 and 1957 season (now in the Nisbet and Shetland Museum collections), showing that a huge amount of spoil was removed from the site and barrowed eastwards over the edge (eg Slide R03544). It was also confirmed in Trial Trench 4, excavated in 1999 down the slope to the east of the chapel (PLATE 5), which contained only sandy spoil and disarticulated bone to a depth of 1.3m (Barrowman 2000, 43–44). O'Dell refers in his *PDR* to problems of discerning the *in situ* remains of the original chapel and the complex of Iron Age stone walls from the tumbled stones around them. The huge amount of rubble that was removed from the area of the chapel during the excavations can be clearly seen from slides in the archives, and it must have been hard for the excavators to discern features

ST. NINIAN'S ISLE. SHETLAND

FIGURE 3.8

End of season, September 1958. Postcard reproduced with permission of Shetland Times Ltd

in amongst the complexity of collapsed stonework.

There are references in the *PDR* to surveying by plane table and finds plotted by offsets and angle measurements from the well-preserved south wall, with a datum for vertical measurement on the foundation stone at the NW corner (this is a misprint and should be SW corner) of the 'chancel arch'. It is certain that a datum on a foundation stone at the SW corner of the chancel 'arch' was used, as it is also referred to by Helen Nisbet, who writes in her diary of days spent surveying the site with a plane table. However, in a letter (D/1/359/1/8/15) dated 9/12/58, O'Dell refers to level-taking as being impossible due to the intrusion of the later burials, and unfortunately to date, no records of any levels, or of plans, survive in the archives for this, or subsequent years of the excavation.

The 1957 excavation

In 1957 (O'Dell 1957; *PDR*; Small *et al* 1973, 5–6) the rest of the nave and along the outside north and west walls were cleared (Figure 3.7). Trial pits were sunk in both 1957 and 1958, both inside and outside the chapel walls. The first indication of what Small later called 'pre-Christian' occupation came during this, the third season of excavation, when a small area of some 2 x 2m was excavated in the centre of the nave to ascertain whether the medieval chapel

had had a crypt, and whether there had been an earlier church on the same site. At the east end of the nave, where O'Dell postulated the destroyed north part of the chancel arch, was a considerable mass of boulders with voids between them. O'Dell firmly believed this was evidence of a crypt below the chapel (the voids) and a barrel-vaulted roof above the chancel arch (the rubble), as suggested by the Rev Low's description in 1774 of 'the remains of an old chapel is still to be seen ... The lower storey of the kirk may be distinctly traced, which having once been vaulted, is supposed to have served for a burying place' (Low 1879, cited by Small 1973, 3).

The test trench however revealed the top of an 'Iron Age complex' of walling at some 5ft (1.52m) below the medieval foundation, as well as cists, calcined bone and pottery, and a thin peat layer. In the 1973 volume Small describes 'an extensive complex of fragments of paving and walls some two metres below the medieval foundations' and how 'most of the structural evidence had been completely destroyed by the intrusion of later pre-Christian and Christian burials and also by the several periods of re-building in the pre-Christian phases'. At least two short stone cists were discovered below the church, both containing fragments of 'Broch period' urns, and Small describes how one of these cists 'also contained numerous small well-rounded quartz pebbles apparently set in a clay floor, and both cists contained burnt and calcined bone, suggesting cremation burials', and that they were set into earlier 'confused domestic remains' (Small 1973, 5–6).

Thomas' description, written after his interview with O'Dell and Small, is similar and refers to:

> Bedrock, overlain by a thin layer of peat ... encountered some seven feet below the level of the wall footings. Immediately above this peat ... crude stone walls, with rubble collapses, paved areas, and occupational debris, appeared to indicate (pre-Christian) secular occupation.
>
> (Thomas 1973, 11).

On the other hand, Nisbet's diary entry for 22 June 1957 describes a different order of layers and features in relation to the peat: 'Stewart in his trench found a layer of peat apparently over the old foundations and under the wall ... and finally some apparently built stones about eleven feet below the original surface'.

These and Nisbet's reference to the layer of peat 'apparently over the old foundations and under the wall' differ to those of Thomas (above), and it may be that what was encountered were two or more different old ground surfaces, or periods of abandonment, between structural phases. Thomas' interpretation may refer to a thin layer of an old ground surface of peaty soil lying immediately over bedrock, whilst the thicker layer described by O'Dell and Nisbet is more reminiscent of midden, or soil build-up, between the Iron Age cists and structures, and the early church building below the medieval chapel. A soil sample was taken from the thin peat layer and a letter in the Shetland Archives (D/1/359/1/1/4, dated 20/1/58), from the Macaulay Institute of Soil Research refers to the soil sample as having a 'very low pollen count', given that only 'two tree pollen grains (both birch) were recorded along with low counts for non-arboreal pollen'. In his reply, O'Dell writes:

> I hope that this season we will be able to get the proper section of peat. As I told you, this sample was from a very thin layer indeed which lapped over the top of the cist level below the chapel, and it is possible that it had been a local hollow with peat forming conditions and that it is not a period of widespread peat formation.
>
> (Shetland Archives D/1/359/1/1/5).

O'Dell (1957) describes the pit in the east end of the nave as revealing cist burials *under peat* (my italics) about 4ft (1.22m) below the foundation level of the medieval chapel, and in her diary entry for the last day of the excavation in 1957 (5/7/57) Helen Nisbet describes how O'Dell instructed that samples should be taken from this peaty layer, which resulted in her 'pulling out handfuls of sticky black stuff'.

On Thomas' sketch plan in his archive, the oldest, curved walling is show as being at 5ft (1.52m) below the medieval chapel foundations, a wall across the east of the nave, where it meets the chancel, or apse, is shown at 4ft (1.22m), and the 'clay-bonded

wall', mentioned elsewhere in O'Dell's draft report, correspondence and Nisbet's diary, is shown at 3ft (0.91m). Thomas describes these walls as 'some stone walls below chancel and nave: these define an at least two-period hut complex on the OLS, with pots and a hearth'. The old land surface described here by Thomas is clearly different to the peaty layer which lapped over the level of the cists.

Finds mentioned from 1957 include a 'wealth of Iron Age pottery' and in the area of the postulated chancel arch in the 'confusion of rubble and burials' above the foundation level, a polished fragment of porphyry was found which Thomas suggests may have been on the site in the medieval period and have originated from a shrine or portable reliquary (Thomas 1973, 31–32, 38; Stone 21). Immediately to the SE of the chancel, a small dry-stone enclosure was also excavated, which (in correspondence) C A Ralegh Radford likened to a 'Founder's Tomb', drawing on similar Irish examples. Within the Founder's Tomb, as it then became known, were seven grooved stones found 'in secondary positions'. Charles Thomas and Ralegh Radford later identified these stones as shrine posts (Thomas 1973, pls III–VII), although the excavators did not recognise them as such at the time.

The chapel, when uncovered, measured 50ft (15.24m) by 23ft (7.01m) overall, and consisted of a nearly rectangular nave for two-thirds of its length, with an internally curved chancel or apse. The walls averaged 3ft 2in (0.97m), being thicker, up to 5ft 4in (1.63m), at the east angles of the chancel. Parts of the medieval walls stood to 4ft (1.22m) and were constructed with lime and mortar from burnt shells, O'Dell noting by this time lime plaster inside and out. He records that the walls of the chapel were too low to preserve the windows and were built from diverse masonry, mostly from the beach.

By the end of the 1957 season most of the excavation pits had been filled in, apart from the large one in the centre of the nave, which O'Dell buttressed round with blocks that had fallen from the chapel (Prof's wall: see also D/1/359/1/1/11, dated 14/6/58). Helen Nisbet, in her site diary, also refers to the building of turf and stone dykes around areas in which to dump spoil, as well as the construction of a dry-stone path through the entrance and centre of the nave.

The 1958 excavation

In the 1958 DES entry O'Dell records that:

> Excavation was carried out on a number of points outwith the walls of the medieval chapel. To the north a wall parallel to the chapel was traced over a length of 30 feet. It may have been a garth wall. A test pit was sunk north of the apse and this was found to have at a depth of 6 feet below the medieval chapel two non-Christian burials. A test pit was sunk south of the apse and a cist burial was

found at about this same depth. To the south east of the chapel on the flank of the hillside a pit was sunk to a depth 14 feet below the foundation of the chapel, and this pit revealed a succession of features; a long extended burial, long cist burials and what appears to be iron ore and iron slag. Within the area of these pits it was not possible to obtain much information about structures.

(O'Dell 1858, 34).

The remainder of the account describes the trench opened in the nave, where 'the ground was opened out to a depth of about 6 feet [1.83m] and there has been found abundant evidence of Iron Age occupation with a great number of pot fragments', and the finding of the hoard 'between the Iron Age occupation zone with its structure (?wheel-house) and the medieval chapel'.

The *PDR*, letters and slides in the archive show that in 1958 the hole in the nave was widened and shored, and shoring was also put in place in a new pit in the chancel, around 10ft (3.05m) in length (this can be seen in Figure 3.8). Evidence of Iron Age occupation was found over the whole area in the bottom of this pit, below the chapel foundations, and it was also traced in test pits to the east. O'Dell refers to the bones and teeth of a horse, found 'below the Celtic Christian zone' and to almost countless fragments of coarse pottery. As outlined in O'Dell's *DES* account, excavation was also carried on at a number of points outwith the walls of the medieval chapel, as in the previous season, including to the north where the garth wall was found, and to the south and east of the chapel. It is not known how large the test pit to the south of the chapel was although the archive sources suggest that the majority of the area was excavated a year later, in 1959.

Trowelling within the nave had been in progress for some weeks in 1958 before the hoard was found, and O'Dell refers to the finding of four distinct layers of pot fragments above it. To the NW of the side altar a buttress of material had been left to give support and provide the datum and when this buttress was trowelled down on 4 July a slab and then below that the treasure was found at about 4ft (1.22m) below the medieval wall foundations. The slab was 15 x 10½in (381 x 267mm) and was subsequently washed and found to have a lightly inscribed cross of which part had broken off long prior to the excavation. O'Dell describes in his *PDR* that there were fragments of rotted wood and metal with the familiar bright green of weathering copper in contact with the stone (see below). He concludes from this that the appearance was of a box of material hurriedly packed.[8] In his *PDR* he also describes a flake of larch which was in contact with the stone and how elsewhere the wood was only recognisable as a darker stain in the brown soil.[9] He concludes that perhaps it was a church treasure buried for safety, even though all the objects could not be identified as ecclesiastical, and he suggests that the inscribed

cross on the covering slab implies concealment by a Christian. 'What Viking would have bothered to bury a porpoise bone with metalware and what pagan would have placed it for safety under the sign of the cross?' (*PDR* D/1/359.1/11/24).

O'Dell's description in the *PDR* of the thin flag lying immediately above the metalware, with the *top surface* lightly inscribed with a cross (my italics) was, however, never to make it to print. Instead, in the 1973 volume, Charles Thomas describes how the slab was found 'face downwards covering the hoard or treasure of silver objects' (Thomas 1973, 37). This was to remain uncorrected until Graham-Campbell's recent re-appraisal, which studies the slide of the slab when the treasure was found (slide SL05166 in the Shetland Museum collection, reproduced here as PLATE 9), and letters and articles written at the time, as well as the staining on the slab itself, and comes to the conclusion, also subsequently accepted by Thomas, that the slab was indeed face up (Graham-Campbell 2003a, 14–17). This slide also shows the fragments of wood of the box, which was not to survive being excavated (apart from the aforementioned flake), and also the position of the treasure in a thick layer of black soil below sand seen in the sides of the excavation pit.

O'Dell's *PDR* also contains incidental details for this year, such as who attended the excavations, and these can be used to date and identify some of the trial trenches and features, which were often related to the names of the excavators, rather than the site itself. O'Dell writes in his PDR, version D1/359/7/6:

> It is noticeable too, how the reference names of various features in the site developed ... many things were christened after the students themselves: thus we had 'Eric's wall', 'Johnnie's cist', 'Alan's hole', etc. The students themselves have represented a good few from England, and even one from British Guiana, while members of the Engineering, Chemistry and Zoology departments have been attracted into our midst, as well as a geology student from Glasgow. There have been few dull moments in our team of 10 to 15 on the 'dig'.

Professor O'Dell was in the first instance a historical geographer, rather than an archaeologist, and there are also notes in the archive relating to the topography and geology of the site. Prior to the excavations O'Dell noted the progressive increase in the depth of the humus layer down from the brow of the slope to the west and NW of the site, suggestive of downhill creep, and the uniformity of the layer from long-continued cultivation before the inhabitants left the island in the late 18th century. One of the geography students on the excavation, a Mr A Stewart-Fraser, also examined the soils and O'Dell notes his opinions in his *PDR*. He found the smooth slope SE from the site of the medieval chapel foundations from the trial pits to be a modern development from a skin of blown sand. He also noted the sand cover at the lip of a concealed cliff to about 4ft 6in (1.37m) deep, resting directly on a weathered schistose with the upper profile completely immature and showing traces of sand movement after short periods of fixation by vegetation. Also, he notes that on the east side of the island the cliff face was eroding where the schist has been shattered, stating that 'in four years it has been a matter of interest to see changes of cliff profile immediately below the chapel'. These observations were all noted and confirmed by geomorphological observations and trial trench excavations in 1999 (see Hall above; Hall 2000, 45; Harry 2000, 43).

The 1959 excavation

Each year fieldwork had lasted for between four and six weeks, but in this final season some members of the team stayed for longer to clear up, backfill and cover the site with turf. O'Dell records in his *PDR* that a plane-table survey of the excavations was undertaken and that finds were plotted by offsets and angle measurement from the well-preserved south wall of the chapel. Although this survey has yet to be located, there is evidence from 1959 of a nominal finds-recording system. On one of Nisbet's slides of the excavation in 1959, the letters W, X and Y can be seen painted on the shoring timbers at the east end of the nave, and the numbers 3–7 on the shoring timbers along the south side of the nave, against the south wall (PLATE 6). A slide in the Shetland Museum collection similarly shows the letters H–L painted on stones along the edge of the trench to the south of the chapel in 1959 (Slide SLO5141). There is no evidence that this recording system was used in previous years, and all of the finds in the Shetland Museum which can be attributed to a particular year, and which display a letter/number code, originate from the 1959 excavation.

Work continued below the chapel during this year, with special attention paid to attempts to locate an earlier phase of church building. In the correspondence in the Shetland Archives O'Dell refers to evidence of the 'early pre-Norse church' in 1959, 3ft (0.91m) below the level of the medieval chapel, and writes that the walls were well plastered on the inner face (D1/359/1/14/3), this time referring to the earlier church building, whereas before he had described plastering as being on the inside and outside of the *medieval* chapel walls (in a draft article in the Shetland Archives, D1/359/7/7, written by O'Dell in 1958). Nisbet describes in notes made in her diary after the 1959 excavation: 'During the 1959 season timbering was erected in the nave and the whole interior was excavated down to pre-Christian level. We found … underlying Iron Age domestic structures. There were a few Christian burials well under the medieval walls'.

In his 1959 DES account O'Dell describes 'The lower courses of the Pre-Norse church at 3ft 2ins [0.97m] below the medieval foundation' found in the south end of the nave. Also 'a complex of Iron Age structures immediately below the pre-Norse church level' resting on 'gley at a depth of about 6ft [1.83m] below the medieval foundations' (O'Dell 1959c). To the south of the chapel, O'Dell describes the finding of 'four graves with kerb stones and foot stones but no head stones … at the same level as the pre-Norse church', and also to the west and south 'a group of Iron Age graves which centred on a crouched burial of late Bronze Age type. The whole is resting on a midden which contains a great quantity of whelks, dog whelks, limpets, a few oyster shells and a considerable number of white quartz pebbles'.

This same description is found in the 1960 volume with Cain, this time including mention of animal bones, and describing the midden 'as yet unexcavated' and O'Dell also describes extended burials within cist structures on 'the flanks of the Late Bronze Age crouched burial. At the edge of the cist stones were a set of antler rings and knife hafts and a much corroded barrel-lock of Romano-British type' (O'Dell 1960, 4). The antler rings and knife hafts were published as the bone and antler bead necklace in the 1973 volume (PLATE 14). The barrel-lock is now in the Shetland Museum,[10] recorded as being 'recovered from the near vicinity of the chapel during the University excavation in 1958'. Unfortunately, there is no other information on this find and so its exact find spot will never be known. This type of padlock has a long history, being common up to the end of the medieval period, although it is very similar to an example from Scalloway, which Campbell assigns to a 7th-century or later date in the post-Roman period (Campbell 1998b, 166, fig 107; E Campbell pers comm).

The most detailed account of the excavations south of the chapel is given in Small's account in the 1973 volume, over ten years later. This describes the excavation as being *c*12 x 8m and requiring the removal of a huge quantity of wind-blown sand, later burials and loose rubble and stones (Figures 3.9 and 3.10). It is possible that several phases of archaeology were removed here, and what was left to be shown on the final plan that was reproduced in the 1973 volume was fortuitously what lay at a level across the site (Figure 1.2). The features shown on this plan include an area of paving and structures along the west edge of the trench, a blank central area and along the east side of the trench a wall and several stone cists. Small refers to there being no stratigraphical link between the structures in the east and west parts of the area (Small 1973, 6). The dominant feature on the east side is a wall, 1.2m wide, extending beyond the limits of the excavation at both ends. The short cist described by O'Dell in 1960 as containing an adult skeleton in a crouched position is described in the 1973 volume as being dug into the top of this

FIGURE 3.9
Excavations to the south of the chapel 1959. Slide taken by H Nisbet (RCAHMS no. 695152)

FIGURE 3.10
Excavations to the south of the chapel 1959. Slide taken by H Nisbet (RCHAMS no. 695148)

wall (Small 1973, 7). Three other cists were found close to this latter cist, one containing 'only charred human bones', one filled with shells and the third with human bones (Small 1973, 7). The area to the east of the wall was not completely excavated, but Small's plan shows indications of stone box-like structures. Several finds of pottery were recovered, as was a bone and antler necklace (presumably the antler rings and knife hafts noted by O'Dell 1960, above). Some of the pottery and the necklace are illustrated in the 1973 volume (and held in the Shetland Museum; PLATE 14).

In the NE corner of the area south of the chapel 'early Christian graves … separated from the earlier structures by a clear stratigraphical break' (Small 1973, 7) were excavated, described by O'Dell (1960,4) as 'four extended burials in sand with the grave edges marked by thin stone slabs with edge and foot stones but no headstones'. Small and O'Dell's hypothesis at the end of 1959 was that, except for these four burials, all the structures and cists shown on the published plan belonged to the Iron Age, as attested by the pottery assemblage, with the exception of the crouched burial which was believed to be Bronze Age. Small also notes that 'in the lower levels of the site the earlier structures are set on a gleyed soil with no evidence of sand in the profile. Sand does not in fact appear until the barren horizon below the dark-age graves. This points to St Ninian's Isle being a complete island at this time, the formation of the tombolo coming later' (Small 1973, 7).

Nisbet and Small's slide collections are particularly relevant in the study of the 1959 excavation because most of the slides were taken in 1959 at the end of the final season. The differences between the area to the south of the church as depicted on slides taken at the end of the excavation, when the area had been tidied up and re-turfed (PLATE 7) and those taken during the excavation (PLATE 8) are particularly interesting. These alert us to possible reasons for discrepancies between the final plan in the 1973 volume (Figure 1.2), the complexity of what was actually excavated in 1959, and the site as it first re-appeared when the turf was taken off in 2000. On PLATE 8, for instance, there are more head stones visible in the area of the long cists than are shown on the final plan, and indeed there seem to be further cists below the wheelbarrow in the NE corner of the trench. There is also a large hole, in the area where the Founder's Tomb is located by Thomas (Figure 1.3), but unfortunately outwith the edge of the final plan. A large cist side-slab can be see leaning against the north side of the trench, partially covered with sand, and the large pile of rubble in the centre of the trench, together with the smaller pile to the left, make one wonder what complex features might have been contained therein, as do the rubble piles seen to the north of the chapel and on the top edges of the trench. In comparison, PLATE 7 shows a neat wall across the centre of the trench, south of

the large cists (shown filled with sand) as found in Trench 1 in 2000, when the turf was first taken off the area.

3.3 EXCAVATED FEATURES

Introduction

The following account gathers together from all available sources the information relating to each specific feature or 'pit' identified and excavated during the 1950s excavations. At first it was intended, during the research into O'Dell's excavations for this report, to reconstruct a rough site plan of all features, with locations and levels. This increasingly frustrating task proved impossible in the end, however, and instead, one has to content oneself with viewing the various sources in the same manner as they were originally recorded, i.e. by excavator and date, rather than necessarily by location or record. In this way, all the small pieces of information relating to each feature can be gathered into one place, and from this a 'best guess' based on circumstantial evidence can be hazarded as to the location and depth of each feature, its extent and nature, and the finds from it. During the archive analysis, such incidental information as who was digging where for instance proved to be just as useful as the sketches and rough measurements made at the time.

All the finds and the labels from the finds deposited in the Shetland Museum by Alan Small have been catalogued (Appendix 1) and, when this evidence was put together with information from the site notebook (SN: D1/359/6 in the Shetland Archives) to form a table (Appendix 2), a pattern became clear. This pattern of recording however is different depending on the year. In 1958 (in SN), it seems to have involved groups of finds from a particular location or individual archaeological feature, such as a cist or a wall, being given an alphabetical letter which sometimes, in the case of finds, was then subdivided to a lower case letter eg all finds from Cist A are called Aa, Ab, Ac, etc. But, in 1959 the upper case letter is then given a number and sometimes then subdivided to a lower case letter (eg K.11.g, or Y.4.h). These codes relate to the site grid that was initiated in 1959 (see below). Other than these codes there are some records of depths in relation to the medieval chapel wall foundations, but otherwise the grid can only give a very rough location for the 1959 finds.

The medieval chapel

In a typescript in the Shetland Archives (D1/359/8/3), presumably written by O'Dell, he describes the chapel building as:

> a rectangular nave, measuring about 23 x 17ft internally, with an apsidal quire some 12ft 6ins wide by about 15ft long … The substantial character of

the quire walls – 3ft 6ins to 3ft 9ins. thick – and of the dividing wall between the nave and quire – 4ft thick – suggest that the quire was vaulted. This is borne out by the irregular buttresses added to the outer curve of the apse, which imply a strengthening against impending collapse. These buttresses give the appearance of a polygonal east end, but their character as additions and the original curve of the outer face are both clear.

Shetland Archives (D1/359/8/3)

When the chapel walls were surveyed 50 years later by plane table in 1999 (Figure 3.11), the rectangular nave was measured at 7 x 5.1m internally and the rounded chancel at 3.8m wide by 4.5m long. The walls were found still upstanding to c1.25m, although due to small repairs made to the walls during the 1950s excavations, and to the presence of mortar and vegetation covering many of the joints, it remained the case that it was still 'extremely hard to make much of the visible church' (Thomas 1973, 12). The rounded chancel or apse walls survived only to a height of up to 0.8m at the most on the south side, but the odd shape of the external face of the chancel could still be made out at the east end when small portions of turf were stripped to locate the plan of the chancel on the ground. Two small strips of turf were cut in this area to trace the foundations of the wall where they disappeared below the ground surface, and the two small sections of wall uncovered appeared to splay out at an angle towards the east end of the nave wall (Figure 3.11). The elevations of the church walls were photographed using scales and overlapping shots from which drawings could be made if required, and the slides are held in the NMRS.

Nisbet's slide of the chapel from the east, taken at the end of the 1957 season (Figure 3.12), as well as showing the steps and dry-stone wall that were built around the excavation pit in the nave at the end of the 1957 season, also shows the east end of the north wall broken down and the ground surface in the resulting gap between it and the chancel paved for a barrow run through the gap in the wall to the spoil heap east of the chapel, down the seaward slope. The east end of the south nave wall opposite is, however, a well-built butt end and set adjacent to the north of it is the roughly circular chancel, or apse as it was called at this point in the excavation. A block of dry-stone masonry, also showing in the slide, outside and parallel to the SE corner of the chancel is presumably related to the Founder's Tomb, which was excavated in 1957, and may be an attempt to consolidate and tidy up after the excavation of that feature.

The first published plan of the chapel on St Ninian's Isle is O'Dell's own plan in his account of the finding of the treasure in *Antiquity* (O'Dell 1959b, 242, fig 1). This shows the junction of the nave, chancel arch and chancel walls on the north side of the church as missing, and also describes a side altar in the SE interior corner of the nave, and the spring for a chancel arch adjacent to it at the east end of the nave. Nisbet's diary records that, as the north wall was being cleared inside the chapel, there was nothing but stone tumble all the way down where the nave joined the chancel writing on 20 June 1957: 'I was shovelling mostly inside the church. A great deal of rubble and tumbled stones, in places with mortar'. She also annotates on her 1957 sketch plan 'much marble and mortar' at the junction of the nave and

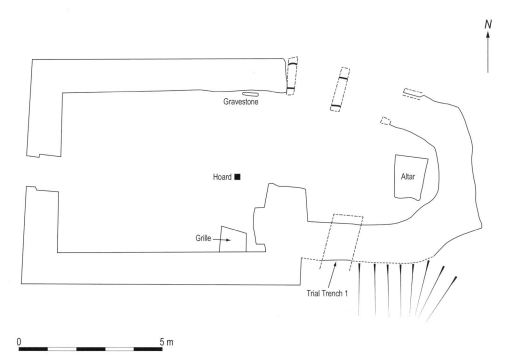

0   5 m

FIGURE 3.11
Plane table survey of the chapel 1999. Re-drawn by L McEwan

FIGURE 3.12
Chapel from the east at end of 1957 season. Slide taken by H Nisbet (RCHAMS no. 696418)

chancel at the NE interior corner of the nave (Figure 3.4). The *SN* records, however, that there was a wall at the junction of the nave and the chancel, across the nave, separating it from chancel. This is also depicted on one of Thomas' sketch plans in his archive (as is a blocked window on the south wall at the west end, and five late inserted burials over the west side of the north wall of the chapel). None of these features are shown on the published plan (Figure 1.3).

Typescript D1/359/8/3 also contains a detailed description of two altars in the chapel. O'Dell describes the altar, or so-called leacht, in the chancel as: 'The highest point stands 1ft 8 ins [1.72m]. The stones are water worn or weathered, quite unlike the sharp edges of the quarried stones used in the chapel; they are set in a shelly clay and I could see no trace of lime mortar. The structure appears to stand on the same level as the church', but he also describes a side altar contemporary with the medieval chapel, and mirrored possibly by another side altar in the same position on the north side of the opening to the 'quire'. In *PDR*, version D.1/359/1/11/24 he describes traces of a medieval floor adjacent to the side altar as:

> The only signs of the medieval floor were fragments of thin schist at floor level behind the altar, this schist had almost completely rotted to a stiff yellow clay, and a thickening of the plaster in the

gap between the side altar and the south wall. This plaster bulged at the foot and stopped abruptly as if it had flowed down to a hard earth or stone floor.

If O'Dell's identification was correct, this was presumably the only part of the medieval floor that remained undisturbed by the insertion of later burials into the sand over the ruined medieval chapel.

These differing descriptions of the area between the nave and the chancel are difficult to unravel, but it seems most likely that there was once a wall at the east end of the nave which was then broken through and a chancel arch constructed for an opening into the chancel, and that this arch subsequently collapsed, together with the east end of the north nave wall, and resulted in the pile of rubble found at the NE and east edges of the nave within the chapel.

O'Dell in *PDR*, D.1/359/1/11/24 was of the view that: 'Except for the buttresses strengthening the apse the whole structure is of one date.' However, in another typescript for a lecture, which can be dated from its content to 1956 or 1957, he states conversely that the 'church is obviously of mediaeval pattern with a chancel end which seems to have been built later with its foundations resting on blown sand' (D/1/359/8/4). Thomas concluded, after visiting the site in 1967, that there were two phases to the chapel (1973, 12), and from the archive evidence this seems the most likely interpretation of the chapel's construction. Although the *SN* records that on the south side of the interior, the chancel was bonded onto the nave wall, Thomas observed that 'the medieval church was apparently refaced, in parts even rebuilt, in the medieval period, and some restoration was undertaken in the course of the excavation'. He argues that:

> the western half, Professor O'Dell's 'nave', was in origin a rectangular unicameral chapel, with a central west doorway and internal dimensions of the order of 16 ft 6 in by 22 ft 6 in (or longer). This was remodelled, when the east wall was broken, giving access (through a chancel arch, or a simple opening) into an internally rounded chancel.

(Thomas 1973, 12).

Thomas described the 'side-altar' as being of poor construction, and 'not, as previously published plans might imply, bonded into the wall at all', and could not make out the 'odd external shape' of the chancel. He described it as an 'internally rounded chancel' (1973, 12), and does not include the east end of the chapel at all on his plan in the same volume (Thomas 1973, fig 8), perhaps suggesting that he too had consulted O'Dell's notes and come to no definitive conclusion. An internally, but not externally, rounded east end was recorded by the plane table survey of the upstanding walls in 1999 (Figure 3.11), and is also shown on O'Dell's published plans (1959b, fig 1; 1960, 2), and whilst the rounded internal dimensions are similar to the church on the Brough of Birsay, to which it is often compared (see eg Cant 1975, 12, fig 2 and discussed in Fawcett forthcoming), the two are quite different. The St Ninian's Isle chancel east end external face is not rounded, although depicted as such in comparison plans, and there is little space between the altar and the rounded inner wall. The thickness of the curved wall at the east end of the chancel, and the odd external shape, can in fact be traced on the ground, and it is possible that the external shape may have resulted from the need for extra support for vaulting of the apse/curved east end of the chancel, which certainly seems to be suggested by the large quantity of rubble described by Nisbet, and by O'Dell himself who described buttresses strengthening the apse.

Thomas was also the first to ascribe in print a date for the first phase of the single-roomed medieval chapel as 'a reflection of Norse Christianity, unlikely to be older than the 12th century', with a date suggested sometime after 1200 for its enlargement (there are letters concerning this in the archive from Ralegh Radford, whom Thomas cites: 1973, 13). He also identified six 'Christian Norse and Medieval monuments', all of steatite, in his catalogue of the sculptured stone from the Isle (1973, 30). Similar cross-incised slabs, Stones 12–14, argued by Thomas to be recumbent slabs, and Stone 16, a small standing cross, are all suggested by him to date no earlier than the mid-11th century, whilst Stone 16 has parallels

on earlier sites (1973, 36–37). Stone 17, a steatite hogback grave cover, was found at the doorway of the chapel, and is dated by Thomas to the late 11th or 12th century (1973, 31, 37), but by Lang to the 11th (1974, 231).

Finds from within the chapel included a small incised cross with crosslets, on red sandstone, found lying face downwards somewhere in the SW quarter of the nave, not very deep. However, this is cross-incised Stone 10 in Thomas' catalogue (1973, 36, fig 8, pl 8), found in 1959 and described by Nisbet in her diary, is considered by him to be a primary cross-slab and may therefore have been dug up during the interment of later burials on the site. A further cross-incised slab was found in 1956, face downwards, against the inner face of the south wall of the chapel, 5ft (1.52m) west of the inner SE angle of the nave (1973, 38, fig 8, pl 12). Thomas ascribed this to the 12th century or later and perhaps assignable to a burial within the (enlarged) church (1973, 31). A further find is mentioned in a newspaper article (Dumfries and Galloway Standard and Advertiser, 21 November 1959): 'There was, in addition to the medieval crosses and the altar, a curious blackish stone near the altar which could be either a stoup or a pivot stone for a door …'. This may be the broken stone with hollow (?cresset-lamp), identified by Thomas in his catalogue (1973, 38–39, Stone 22, pl 11), and was probably contemporary with the use of the medieval chapel building.

The earlier church building

There are different, often confusing, notes in the archives that relate to the earlier walling below and at the east and west ends of the medieval chapel. This confusion is reflected in the contradictory published and archive accounts. [11] Earlier walling is shown under the west end wall of the medieval chapel on Thomas' plan published in the 1973 volume (Figure 1.3), but not to as great an extent as on his field plan, or on O'Dell's published site plan in Antiquity (1959b, 242). In these latter two plans, walling is shown at the west end wall of the medieval nave, from the NW almost right down to the SW interior corners.

The earlier walling shown in the NW corner of the nave on Thomas' published plan is not labelled as earlier walling, but exactly mirrors that shown on Nisbet's own sketch plan, made at the time of the excavation in 1957 (Figure 3.4) and identified as 'skew foundation stones'. In her diary for 20 June 1957 Nisbet writes 'I was shovelling mostly inside the church. A great deal of rubble and tumbled stones, in places with mortar. At the west end there were projecting stones of peculiar aspect, foundation stones I suppose, and beneath that apparently sand.' Then, on 22 June, she records 'a layer of peat under the medieval wall but apparently over 'the old foundations' in the west end of the nave pit'. Later, on 1

FIGURE 3.13

Early church walling in SE corner of nave in 1959. Slide taken by H Nisbet (RCHAMS no. 695130) whose caption reads 'Close-up of early chapel, note: white plastering, angle of wall c75° although it doesn't look like it here. Pseudo-corbelled sloping-walled type. I think.'

July, Nisbet describes a 'lower wall', and then on 5 July 1957: 'We … exposed a bit more of the lower dry-built wall, finding it to be standing at least three courses high'. These four entries all refer to the same dry-built wall of rough stones at the west end of and below the medieval nave (H Nisbet pers comm).

Further evidence for this west wall is contained in the 1957 list of levels (D1/359/11/6) which records skewed stones at the NW corner of the chapel as projecting 6in (0.15m) outside to 1ft (0.31m) inside at the corner, and are shown as continuing *outside* the nave at the NE corner, as described in her diary (Figure 3.4).

On Thomas' published plan (1973, fig 8; see Figure 1.3), earlier walling is also shown in the SE corner of the nave. In 1959 Nisbet (who did not attend the excavations in 1958; see Nisbet 1958; Nisbet and Gailey 1962), took a photograph of this earlier walling on the SE side of the nave (Figure 3.13) and has annotated her 1959 sketch plan '1a' to show the location of the walling photographed (Figure 3.5). O'Dell's plan in *Antiquity* does not show this wall, but this is simply because it was not uncovered until after the 1958 season. O'Dell does refer to it in the 1960 volume as 'the foundations of a 3 feet thick dry-stone wall, with plastering on the inner face, which is formed of rectangular blocks'. He

also describes how this foundation underlies 'very closely the south-east angle of the medieval nave', continuing 'for the greater part of the length of the south wall of the nave. There is little doubt that it is the pre-Norse church' (O'Dell 1960, 5). As far as Nisbet remembers no relationship was established between the two stretches of early walling at the west side and SE corner of the nave, although she writes 'the second one certainly seemed to indicate an earlier church underlying the 12th cent. building' (H Nisbet pers comm). Thomas archive plan shows sketchy walling at the east end of the nave, annotated as four feet below the medieval chapel foundations. This walling is also noted in *SN* (Figure 3.16) and is possibly the east wall of the earlier church building, added by Thomas to his plan after discussions with Small (see above).

There is little other information available concerning the depth of the earlier walling beyond O'Dell's 1959 *DES* account: 'The lower courses of the Pre-Norse church at 3ft 2 in below the mediaeval foundation. This was found in the south end of the nave'. A sketch in the Shetland Archives of a 'Section on south face of wall' shows the exterior south face on the other side of the medieval chapel wall from the early walling on the west side of the nave, covered with plaster and standing up

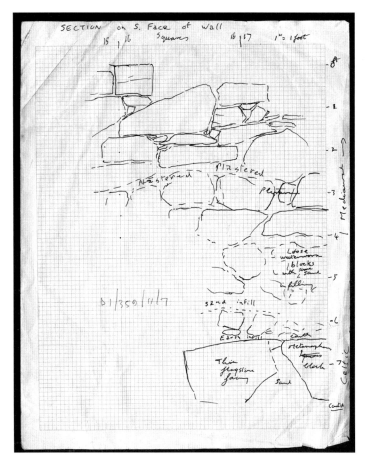

FIGURE 3.14
*Section on south face of wall. Sketch from O'Dell's excavations (reproduced
with permission of the Shetland Archives, D.1/359/11/7)*

to 4ft (1.22m) high (D/1/359/11/7; Figure 3.14),
with a gap shown below the medieval foundations
of around 2ft (0.61m). This gap comprises 'Loose
water-worn blocks with some sand infilling' immediately below the medieval church wall, and then six
inches of 'Earth infill' and stones below that. Below
this in turn, at a depth of 2ft 6in (0.76m) below
the medieval wall foundations, there are shown two
large blocks described as 'thin flagstone facing' and
'metamorphous black', and labelled as 'Celtic', with
sand below them. This 'section' can be located by
reference to a slide taken in 1959 (PLATE 8) which
shows the same stones as those drawn in the section
(Figure 3.14) in the outer face of the SW corner of
the chapel wall (seen at the top left hand corner of
the slide). The stones drawn below this on the lower
half of the section are still covered by wind-blown
sand in the slide, suggesting that the section was
drawn after the slide was taken, i.e. towards the end
of the 1959 season, the sand was cleared away from
below part of the outer chapel wall so as to try and
record the outer face of the earlier walling below
it. This sketch section may show a period of disuse
and collapse between the 'Celtic' horizon, and the
later medieval one 2ft 6in (0.76m) above, but does
not tally with the descriptions of the two buildings

as excavated in the pit inside the chapel, where the
medieval foundations were found to directly overlie
the earlier church walls.

If Nisbet's skew foundation stones at the west end
of the nave are taken to be the footings of walls from
the same earlier building as that evidenced in 1959
in the SE corner of the nave, the different archive
sources outlined above, when taken together, suggest that up to three of the lowest courses of walling from an earlier, small, dry-stone building were
found surviving, on a slightly different alignment,
but roughly the same internal measurements, as the
later medieval chapel nave above. Given its situation
directly below the medieval nave, its dimensions,
alignment and its location on a site with cist burials, there seems little doubt that this building was an
earlier church.

O'Dell was keen to keep the earlier walling
visible at the end of his excavations, and so when
the site was consolidated a hole at the SE corner of
the nave interior was left open, lined with concrete
sides, and covered with an iron grille through which
a part of it could be seen. In 1999, this grille was
opened and a level was taken on the top of the
earlier wall and directly below the medieval chapel
foundations, which measured 25.88m above sea

level. The depth of some of the finds in the Shetland Museum collection is recorded in relation to the medieval foundations, and so this information has proved extremely useful.

Other archaeological features below the chapel

Site grid and finds U–Z/1–6

Forty-four finds in the Shetland Museum collection are labelled with letter/number codes U–Z and 1–6 and almost all have a level recorded below the 'medieval horizon' or 'foundation', presumably the bottom of the medieval chapel wall. Levels taken in 1999 measured the medieval wall foundations at 26.6m above sea level (see above).

The finds letter codes U–Z can be related to a site grid that was used in 1959 and can be seen in one of the Nisbet slides showing excavations inside the chapel that year (PLATE 6).

It was possible from this information to gain a rough idea of where the finds were located within the nave. When the U–Z/1–6 grid was plotted over a plan of the nave it showed that the finds were distributed around the edges of the nave pit, with a blank in the middle. This is because the nave pit had already been excavated to a considerable depth in 1957, with the edges of the pit buttressed with stone blocks from the fallen masonry of the chapel (= 'Prof's wall', just visible in Figure 3.12 around pit in centre of nave). The sand along the edges of the chapel walls could not be excavated until shoring had been organised through a local construction team working in Lerwick harbour in 1958 (see letter from O'Dell to Brown, D/1/359/1/1/11, and the reply, D/1/359/1/1/14). O'Dell had planned to excavate the entirety of the nave in 1958, but it was actually only the east end of the nave and the chancel, that was shored in 1958, the entire nave not being shored until 1959 (see letter to Brown from O'Dell in 1959, D/1/359/1/12/22). All of the finds located by the U–Z/1–6 grid were excavated at a depth of 5–7ft below the medieval foundations (24–25m above sea level), a considerable depth, comparable to Cist A (see above), and lower than all of the cists excavated to the south of the chapel in 1959.

Two cists labelled X and Y do not relate to the U–Z site grid, and were located *outside* the nave on the north side of the chapel (see below). These can be distinguished from X and Y finds from within the chapel by other means, however, eg only finds from within the chapel are given a depth relative to the medieval foundations. Finds recorded with a Y prefix would all seem to relate to the 1959 UVS-XY/123456 grid used within the nave. They include LIA pot sherds A21.2000.2 (3 rims, one of which is slightly everted, and 5 Fabric 1 body sherds, labelled with a drawing as being from 'Y1' from outside lower of two box kerbstone edges in peat ash, 69in be-

low kerbstone'(1.75m), LIA pot sherds A21.2000.6 (base and body smoothed Fabric 1 sherds), labelled as 'Y.3.h, 54in below medieval foundation' (1.37m, i.e. c25.23m below sea level) to south of large kerbstone, and pot sherds and a yellow/brown glass bead (A21.2000.21), found in 'Y.1 65in' (1.65m) below the medieval foundation (c24.95m above sea level). These finds are at the same level as the Iron Age structures and cists below the chapel.

Cists

Cist A

This cist is one of the two short stone cists described by Small:

> From Miss H Nisbet's personal diary it is clear that at least two short stone cists were unearthed in this area: no dimensions are recorded, but both contained fragments of two urns. One grave also contained numerous small well-rounded quartz pebbles apparently set on a clay floor, and both cists contained burnt and calcined bone, suggesting cremation burials.
>
> (Small 1973, 5–6).

Cist A was found when digging deep in the trench in the nave and is the first cist recorded by Nisbet in her diary as she excavated it herself so there is a good description of the contents: 'a mess of sticky peat, humus and yellow clay ... bits of pot and some chips of calcined bone … a considerable number of very smooth little quartz pebbles and some wood charcoal.' Nisbet records that there were the fragments of at least two pots with a large rim diameter of c10in (0.25m), and a rolled rim. The pot was associated with 'greasy carbonaceous material and … burned bone' and seemed likely to be an urn.

The position of Cist A is shown on Nisbet's sketch plan (Figure 3.4) and Thomas' plan in his archive, and it is undoubtedly the cist described by Small as having numerous quartz pebbles set into a clay floor. The pit containing Cist A was later enlarged to the west and became the nave excavation pit by the end of the 1957 season, as shown on Nisbet's sketch.

A level for the bottom of Cist A is given in the list of levels (D1 held in the Shetland /359/11/6) which was probably written in 1957 as it includes Cist A and the Founder's Tomb, both of which were only excavated that year. The level for the bottom of Cist A is given as 7ft 6in (2.29m) below the sill of the west door of the chapel, which is recorded as being around 72ft (21.95m) above high-water mark. Ground level at the west door on the turf above the sill was recorded as exactly 27m (88ft 6in) above sea-level in 1999, a difference of around 16ft (4.88m) from the earlier level readings, possibly due to their measurement in relation to the high-water mark in 1959 rather than mean sea level. A re-calculation, using the mean sea level and the 1999 measurement for the doorsill, still puts the base of Cist A

FIGURE 3.15
Cist A 1957. Photograph: H Nisbet

very deep down on the site at approximately 24.7m or 81ft above sea level. No features of comparable depth were excavated in either 1999 or 2000, and a photograph of Cist A (Figure 3.15) taken by Nisbet in 1957 which includes a 6ft (1.83m) ranging rod, suggests that the Cist A excavation pit was at 5–6ft (1.52–1.83m) below the level of the foot of the medieval walls. This would place Cist A at 82–3ft above sea level (or 25–25.3m) if the 1999 mean sea level measurements were used. This is comparable in depth to the short cists excavated from below the sand in the area to the south of the church.

Either way, Cist A appears to have been well into the Iron Age levels of the site, and contained quartz pebbles as well as what appears to be pieces of cremated bone and a broken pottery vessel. It is not known what happened to this pottery, but it was found at a comparable depth to finds recorded from within the nave in 1959 (see U, V, W, X and Y below). There are finds in the Small collection in the Shetland Museum with a letter 'A' prefix, labelled Aa to Ar (see Appendix 2), but these originate from various places in the nave, not just the area of Cist A. They include pot sherds from under the hoard (Aq) mentioned in the site notebook, but not present in the Shetland Museum collection. Three LIA body sherds (A21.2000.36) are labelled 'A', however, and may be assigned to Cist A.

Cist B

Cist B was located at the west end of the nave pit on Nisbet's 1957 sketch (Figure 3.4), and may be

identified as the second cist referred to by Small in the 1973 volume as containing fragments of urn and calcined bone (Small 1973, 5; see above). On 26 June, Nisbet records '… another cist, apparently with two pots, in the big hole inside the church.', and this is presumably Cist B.

Earlier in her diary, on 21/6/57, she records: 'In the west end of the chapel a deep pit was sunk to get complete stratification. There was a burial complete with a great headstone and remains of a wooden coffin right below where the original foundations must have been'. However, this is not Cist B, the second short cist. Also, in a later note that Nisbet has added to her diary entry she writes 'I wonder if this could be a mistake for east, in view of what follows about a burial, and destruction of the wall. There was indeed a small trench made at the west end … but I don't recollect any burial there' (undated note added by Nisbet to her diary entry).

There is nothing more in the archives to shed light on the contents of Cist B. There are fifteen finds labelled with a 'B' prefix (Ba to Bo; see Appendix 2), but all originate from the excavations two years later in 1959 and relate to a 'stone pavement' or 'platform' in the Iron Age levels excavated in the SE of the nave.

Cist C

Cist C is shown on a rough sketch at the beginning of SN (1958), but then gets no further mention. It was located in the centre of the nave, to the south of the 'clay bonded wall' and Cist S (see below). Nisbet notes a 'trough-like structure built of stones, not slabbed' in her diary, in the last week of the excavation in 1957, and it is possible that this is Cist C, which is then described at the beginning of the following year in the 1958 SN.

In addition to this, find A19.1998.7 (a LIA rolled rim sherd), which was found in front of the altar in 1959, contained with it a page torn out of *SN* from 1958. On one side of this page is a sketch of a line section annotated H; and on the other, the complex of D North pits, Cist A and a clay-bonded wall are drawn (although the latter two are not annotated). Adjacent to these features is annotated 'Site of Cist C'. Another sheet of paper in the Shetland Archives, which also describes features D, E, F and H and a thick black clay layer (see F below), describes C as 'a continuance of the DN (i) layer underneath position of stone C. Inferred to be associated with it' (D/1/359/11/4). This is rather more confusing until one refers to Nisbet's 1957 sketch (Figure 3.4) which shows C in the centre of the nave as 'inhumation under a large stone'. The sketches in the archives mentioned above clearly show Cist C as being over a foot above a thick black clay layer F (see below) and therefore above the Iron Age structures below the church.

If these sketchy descriptions are taken together they suggest that Cist C was probably not a short cist, like cists A and B, but possibly a long cist built from upright stones, covered by a large stone slab similar to a lintel grave, and containing an inhumation. Five sherds of pottery and a piece of charcoal

in the Shetland Museum collection have a 'C' prefix (A21.2000.3: 3 LIA base sherds; A21.2000.52 and A21.2000.69b: LIA body sherds; A21.2000.124: LIA incised flat base sherd with angled side (Figure 3.24) and A21.2000.69a: Abies (Fir) charcoal), and may have been found in Cist C.

Cist H: 'John and Evie's cist'

Upright stones at right angles to each other shown on Nisbet's 1957 plan as a cist numbered '5' (Figure 3.4) was probably excavated a year later in 1958, as it is also drawn on a sketch in *SN*. The cist was adjacent to Cist A, at the junction of the nave and chancel.[12] On the sketch in the *SN* the hoard is located immediately adjacent to this Cist or feature H to the W, and the holes 1–5, dug within Pit D North, are situated also immediately west of H, with N4 possibly within it. 'Broad diagonal wall' is written on two of the finds labels from H, and this wall is mentioned elsewhere in relation to other finds in this area of the chancel, and find Hh (A21.2000.47: base and body sherds of Fabric 1) is from 'John and Evie's pit' (described in *SN* as a cist; Figure 3.16). A sketch in the Shetland Archives (D/1/359/11/4) annotates H as 'Red pot in rubble beside Prof's wall. No particular level.' Also that 'All pot in thick black clay layer except H (in wet black clay, probably same stuff but wetter nearer Prof's wall in rubble)'.

'John and Evie's cist' is described in *SN* as:

> Cist under cracked slab. Cist interior 27" x 18". Bones extended burial E–W removed for examination by John McKenzie. Fragments of pot.

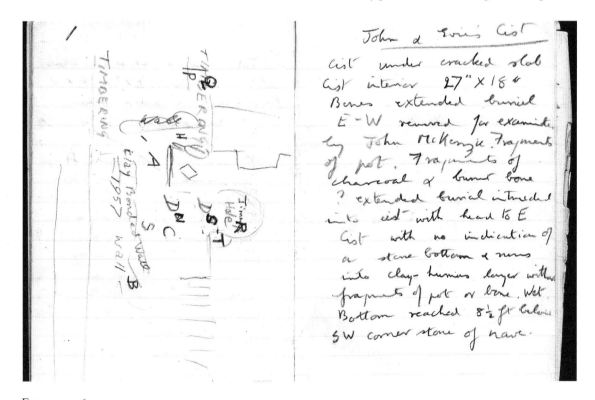

FIGURE 3.16

Sketch and description of John and Evie's cist from site notebook (reproduced with permission of the Shetland Archives, D.1/359/6)

Fragments of charcoal and burnt bone. ?Extended burial intruded into cist with head to E. Cist with no indication of a stone bottom runs into clay humus layer with fragments of pot and bone. Wet. Bottom reached 8½ feet below SW corner stone of nave.

This pit could not have been situated in the SW corner of the nave however because the west half of the nave was not dug in 1958. Instead, the sketch in the 1958 *SN* suggests that it is situated in the SW corner of the shored excavation pit in the area at the nave/chancel junction (Figure 3.8), rather than in the nave itself. The description of 'John and Evie's cist' in Figure 3.16 in *SN* is adjacent to a sketch showing one of the cist stones of H circled. From this description, Cist H was a short cist under an extended inhumation covered by a slab. It is possible, but difficult to say with any certainty (given the confused descriptions), that the extended inhumation is Cist C (above). Cist H certainly belonged to the earlier group of cists, being either set into or covered by the 'clay humus layer', and from the description of fragments of charcoal and burnt bone, possibly contained a cremation.

Nisbet, in notes in her diary, made in relation to slides to accompany a talk she was to give in the 1959 season, states 'In 1957 we dug a trnch [sic] through the mass of rubble in the nave and found no sign of an early church. We did find 3 cists with burnt bones and Iron Age A pottery …'. Cists A and B are two of these cists, it is likely that H is the third given its record on Nisbet's 1957 site plan.

Only one find of twenty conjoining sherds of Fabric 1, including conjoining sherds of a LIA burnished rolled rim (A21.2000.34; Figure 3.24) is labelled as being from feature H. Seven other finds were given the letter H prefix (H14, H14e, H15 x 2, H15n, H18 and Hh) but only one (Hh:A21.2000.47: 2 LIA body sherds and a base), can definitely be assigned to 'John and Evie's cist' (Appendix 2). It is more likely that the remaining six finds are from the area to the south of the chapel, which in 1959 was given a nominal site grid, confusingly using the letters F–L (see below).

Cists P and Q

An archive sketch locates Cists P and Q to the south side of the chancel. Cist P is described in SN as 'Edge of cist – south side left white quartzite pebbles and 1 piece of pot - ?medieval pot', and finds recorded from Cist P include pottery sherd, A21.2000.59 (LIA burnished Fabric 1 body sherd) and possibly A21.2000.99 (10 LIA Fabric 3 body sherds and 1 flat base sherd with angled sides) which are annotated 'P1'. Cist Q is described in SN as 'Cist under edge of timbering. Excavated from side. 2 small bits of pot, animal teeth and part jaw, burnt bone'. A21.2000.43 (LIA burnished Fabric 1 body sherd, and sheep/goat, cow and indet animal bone frags and teeth) is recorded as being from 'P and Q'.

No mention is made of the shape or dimensions of these cists, but from the finds it seems most likely that they were both cut into 'thick black layer' F (see below). The description of white pebbles accords with both long and short cists excavated from below the chapel.

Cist R = Pit D South

Cist R is not mentioned anywhere in *SN* or on finds labels, but only on a sketch showing R as being positioned in the same place as 'Jimmy's Hole' and D South (see Pit D South, below).

Cist S

Finds labels record this cist as being north of Cist C. *SN* describes: 'At foot of clay bonded wall. 2 lots of pot broken on schist slab paving floor. White chunks stone. Fragments of ?bark jammed against western patch of pot. 2 large bits of pot lying immediately above the easterly patch. 2 sections removed in plasticine?'. Finds from Cist S include Late Iron Age (LIA) pottery: A21.2000.4 (plain, slightly inverted, rim and 3 Fabric 1 smoothed body sherds: Figure 3.24); A21.2000.150 (Fabric 1 body sherd); A21.2000.153 (18 Fabric 1 body sherds, 3 rim and 5 frags and water-rounded pumice); and A21.2000.169 (Fabric 1 body sherd with coil junction) which is recorded from 6in (152mm) above Cist S. A find of three pieces of pottery and teeth is described as 'Ss Higher level than Cist S and to west towards 4th step' in *SN*, but cannot be assigned to any particular find in Shetland Museum's Small collection.

The lack of inhumations suggests a short cist, possibly with a paved floor and white stones. The identification of bark, if correct, suggests a good degree of preservation in the damper contexts deep below the church.

Cist T

Cist T in *SN* is described as 'Cist T. Fiona's pot. Large conglomeration of pot in angle between Ian's pot and Jimmy's hole (= R) at approx same level as Ian's pot. Nail marked rim', but there is no mention of any remains other than the pot. It is shown on a sketch in *SN* as being located in the centre of the nave, to the west of 'Jimmy's hole', R and D South. Despite the description of the decoration on the pot, it is not illustrated in the 1973 volume. The description of Cist T as 'Fiona's pot' may mean that LIA pottery find Ah (A21.2000.145; Figure 3.24), which is described in SN as 'Fiona. Coarse pot in base of angle between 4th step and south side of pit as 1st enlargement. Adjoining 4 pieces of finer pot', may thus refer to Cist T, despite having an A prefix. The step described is one of those built by O'Dell down into the nave excavation pit (visible on Figure 3.12) in 1957 (also shown on Nisbet's sketch; Figure 3.4). He also constructed stone paving here that can still be seen at the doorway in the west wall of the chapel.

Pits

Pit D North

There are three sketches of this pit on finds labels, labelled 'D North 1' and 'D North 2 (about 4in below DN1)'. Two of the LIA ceramic finds are also labelled 'Ian's pot': A21.2000.155 (11 Fabric 1 smoothed rim and body sherds, including an everted rim) and A21.2000.156 (2 Fabric 1 smoothed base and body sherds). A21.2000.63 (3 smoothed base and body sherds of Fabrics 1 and 2) is also labelled '?E about 1ft above Ian's pot'.

Pit D is shown in *SN* as being in the nave, and adjacent to Cists A, C and S and west of 'H' and the site of the hoard (Figure 3.16). On the following page in the notebook there is a detailed sketch of Pit D North, showing that it is subdivided into five separate holes or areas, labelled N1, N1A, N2, N3 and N4 (Figure 3.3). A sketch of a section of DN in *SN* implies that Pit D was excavated in 9in (229mm) spits from a surface 6ft (1.83m) below the 'top of buttress inside end', and an attempt at the stratigraphical relationships between DN1–5 is made. A capstone is also mentioned and shown on the sketch, but there is no further mention of it, or the D North pits, in the notebook.

The 'buttress' is referring to a lump of sand and soil that had been left unexcavated at the north corner of the side altar to provide a datum for taking levels. The 'inside end' presumably means the NW corner of this lump, furthest towards the interior of the nave. The hoard was found when this lump was removed, '5ft below buttress foundation'. Pit D North is therefore adjacent to the burial of the hoard, and excavated to around the same depth. It could be postulated that the capstone mentioned is the cross-incised stone that covered the hoard. The position of the hoard however is clearly shown as being to the south of this capstone, and it is also mentioned elsewhere in O'Dell's *PDR* that the hoard was found when the buttress of material was trowelled away, whereas the capstone is shown in the notebook as being uncovered whilst the buttress was still in existence.

As discussed above, Cist C adjacent to Pit D is described as an 'inhumation under a large stone' and it is possible that this is the capstone referred to. Cist H was also 'under a cracked slab' but in a deeper level, being in wet layers at up to 8½ft (2.59m) below the medieval chapel. Both D and C are shown as being above the thick black layer F (see below).

Pit D South = R = 'Jimmy's hole'

There is a finds label sketch of this pit, locating it in the SE corner of the nave, next to Pit D North. There is also a sketch in SN showing 'Jimmy's hole' as being in the same place as 'R' and DS. There are two descriptions in SN of 'DS1 Top zone – bit of pot and small fragment of copper', an interesting description when it is taken into account that

this pit was, like D North to the north, adjacent to the hoard find spot. Find A21.2000.127, four LIA smoothed body sherds of Fabrics 1, 2 and 3, and one burnished vessel neck sherd, is also labelled as being from D S edge of Jimmy's hole, top layer. Also labelled as being from DS2 is A21.2000.103, one base and two body sherds of LIA Fabric 2 and iron coffin nails. Other LIA ceramic finds from this area include A21.2000.118 (5 burnished and smoothed sherds of Fabrics 1 and 2), A21.2000.83 (2 smoothed Fabric 1 body sherds) and A21.2000.29 (2 burnished Fabric 2 body sherds).

Pit G

There is no mention of a feature associated with 'G', only finds, one described as being from 'Alan's midden pit'.

Layers

E: rubble

A large area of rubble was uncovered during the 1958 and 1959 excavations at the north end of the nave/chancel junction. This area was excavated in the east end of the shored nave pit in 1958, and in the west end of the shored chancel pit in 1959. The rubble appears to be given letter 'E' in SN, and finds allocated the letter 'E' were recovered, being described there as:

> Ek Aco large Reddish pot – thick and firm curve to rim. Found as Ej under pile of boulders continuing approx line of Prof's wall. At least three large white quartz boulders in pile of stones above pot. Stones continue under timbering on north side. Pot had sand (blown) underneath. Pieces of charcoal about pot and in stones and to east decayed bone.

The 'Prof's wall' is the revetment wall built around the excavation pit in the nave at the end of the 1957 season. There is also a note about 'numerous fragments of pot and charcoal fragments under fallen stones to north end of Prof's Wall …'. This rubble and the Garth wall are both described as overlying the 'stone platform' which is noted from this part of the site in *SN*, and the thick black layer F (see below).

There are several finds attributed to the letter E in the Small collection (Appendices 1 and 2) and those that had a finds label accompanying them can be located to the east end of the nave, at the junction with the chancel, or just to the west of it. They comprise LIA ceramic body sherds: A21.2000.5, A21.2000.25, A21.2000.27, A21.2000.32, A21.2000.33, A21.2000.46, A21.2000.51, A21.2000.54; base sherds: A21.2000.22b, A21.2000.111, A21.2000.146; rim sherds: A19.1998.8a, A21.2000.146; peat fragments: A21.2000.61; corroded iron fragments, possibly part of a nail: A21.2000.51; and a pebble gaming piece: A21.2000.22b.

F: The 'thick black layer'

F is described as: 'A layer of broken pot associated with rotted bone in crushed layer below rubble'. Below this an annotation states 'all pot in a thick black clay layer...' and includes a small sketch showing the black clay below rubble and sand in the nave. This layer may extend to the west side, where a 'clay humus layer with fragments of pot and bone' was excavated in a deep hole up to 8ft 6in (2.59m) below the cornerstone (ground level) of the nave (at 24.41m above sea level).

A clue to the whereabouts of F is given on a finds label describing: 'Site F below D North Ian's pot'. Other finds that include 'F' in their code are described as being from the 'top layer of occupation layer' and these, rather confusingly, refer to the site grid F–L used in the excavations to the south of the chapel in 1959 (see below). On a sheet of paper in the Shetland archives, a sketch (D/1/359/11/4) shows F below C, D and E. If taken with a page in *SN* showing a plan of these pits, all in the central and east parts of the nave pit (Figure 3.16), the sketch section implies that features E and F are below C, which is to the east of D North and D South. Feature or Cist H is to the east of this.

Many of the nominal short cists described in the archives that are from deep down in the damp layers on the site and contain bone fragments, pottery and preserved wood (eg Cists A, H and S) are most likely to be cut into the 'thick black layer F', which is probably on occupation or midden layer. Nisbet describes in 1957, a thin black layer lapping over the cists, however, as does O'Dell (1957) but the confusion caused by later burials cutting into earlier deposits and cists makes it entirely possible that the occupation layer F did pre-date the cists, but was churned up and re-deposited by the insertion of so many burials.

What is clear from an overview of all the evidence is that Layer F provides a vital stratigraphical marker within the chapel because it underlies the medieval chapel, the rubble and sand, but overlies the Iron Age domestic remains.[13]

The hoard

O'Dell (and Thomas after him) records the location of the hoard towards the east end of the nave (O'Dell 1959b, fig 1; 1960; Thomas 1973, fig 8). This is confirmed on a sketch in the *SN* (Figure 3.16) which shows the hoard at the point of intersection 2ft (0.61m) to the west of an upright stone of feature H, and 4ft (1.22m) NW of the NW angle of the side altar (Figure 3.3), and by Nisbet's 1959 sketch (Figure 3.5), which shows the buttress of sand which was left at the north corner of the side altar at the south side of the nave; the hoard was found when this lump was removed, '5 ft [1.52m] below buttress foundation'. The depth of the buttress foundation is unknown, but Thomas notes in his own archive

notes made after meeting up with O'Dell, that the hoard was at about 3ft (0.91m) to 3ft 6ins (1.07m) below the datum 'X', which was at the base of the chancel arch. Survey in 1999 measured this point (X) at 26.6m above sea level, so 3ft to 3ft 6in below that would place the hoard at *c*25.53–25.69m. As outlined above, the base of the possible earlier church walling is recorded by O'Dell as 3ft 2in below the medieval foundations, i.e. at 25.63m, so putting the hoard at up to 100mm below the base of the earlier church walling. There is thus no reason to doubt O'Dell's statement that the hoard was found at the level of the base of the earlier church wall (O'Dell 1960, 5).

A photograph taken at the time of the discovery of the hoard (see PLATE 9) has already been studied by Graham-Campbell and as described above, he demonstrates that the cross-incised slab over the hoard was face up not face down (Stone 15; Thomas 1973, 37, pl VIII). In a letter (D/1/359/1/2/15) O'Dell writes: 'When the stone with a cross was lifted and we saw the bright green weathering of bronze, we thought the base of an upturned bowl was a helmet'. This can clearly be seen on the photograph. There is no mention here of the box that contained the treasure, although in a later letter, O'Dell states 'there were fragments of timber where it had been jammed against the stone, it was impossible to get any details as to the exact size and structure of the box and the rest had decayed completely' (D/1/359/1/12/4). Graham-Campbell has, however, suggested that given the dimensions of the slab over the hoard, and the extent shown on the photograph, the box was oblong and measured approximately 24 x 18cm. O'Dell describes in his *PDR* (D/1/359.1/11/24; see above), how 'the bowls were upside down in a nest, the hemispherical was uppermost while entangled on the east side and below the bowls were the other items including the porpoise bone. Earth had penetrated but slightly between the objects and there were many voids'. It is the burial of the bowls upside-down that led O'Dell to state in the *PDR*: 'The appearance was of a box of material hurriedly packed and buried upside-down otherwise to have so fitted in the bowls would have been difficult'.

A partial description of the hoard on a page in *SN* suggests that O'Dell carried out a preliminary examination of the objects before sending them down to Bruce-Mitford in London, despite Bruce-Mitford's statement to the contrary (Graham-Campbell 2003a, 19; Bruce-Mitford 1960, 157). O'Dell describes:

Found by Douglas Coutts 5ft below buttress fda-
tion. Fragment of red pot above. Wood fragments
– ? box – remains round it.
6 simple bowls 7" diameter and c. 2 " deep
1 bowl 'double' with 3 rings
2 (sketch) 'handles'
1 bone copper stained ?reliquary
3 'pepper pots' (and sketch of same)
2 'pins'

1 (sketch here of the possible strap end)
12 'brooches' (sketch of a penannular brooch)
Cross inscribed by thin stone slab covering hoard.

There is also a sketch of the 'lettering' on one of the 'handles' (i.e. the inscribed sword chape).

There are no further clues as to the position of the hoard in relation to other features on the site. However, in a newspaper report of a lecture given by O'Dell is described 'a curious lozenge-stone near which the treasure was later found. It may have been a marker for the treasure' (The *DGSA*, 21 November 1959, in Nisbet's archive). This stone was evidently uncovered in the 1957 season but excavated in 1958, and it is referred to in the description of a find location at the beginning of the *SN* (i.e. the beginning of the 1958 season): 'Em. Douglas. Under wall to east of lozenge'. It could be said that a marker stone was not needed because the treasure was marked by the cross-incised slab that covered it. However, the association by O'Dell of a lozenge-shaped stone with the treasure is an interesting one in view of the lozenge-shaped hogback grave cover that was found during the 1957 excavation (Stone 17; Thomas 1973, 37, pl XI). No lozenge-shaped stone, other than the hogback, is found in the Shetland Museum's collection of worked stone from the excavations. However, if Thomas' record of the hogback as having been found outside the west wall of the chapel nave is correct (1973, 37, fig 8; see Figure 1.3), it cannot be the lozenge-shaped stone that was found inside the nave at the east end near the hoard.

The clay-bonded wall

The first wall to be excavated in the nave pit was the clay-bonded wall, which is shown on Nisbet's 1957 plan (Figure 3.4; see also Figure 3.2), so it seems likely that it is 'the beautifully built wall' she refers to. It is situated along the north edge of the 1957 pit, within the area defined by 'Prof's wall', the retaining wall O'Dell built around the excavation pit at the end of the 1957 season, and roughly parallel to and south of the north wall of the nave. The locations of Cists C and S were defined in relation to the clay-bonded wall, but there is very little information on this wall itself. Later in Nisbet's diary, and also from a sketch plan by Thomas, we learn that the clay-bonded wall is later than, and on top of an earlier Iron Age structure, and Thomas' sketch plan clearly shows two phases of walling along the north side of the nave – the later of which is shown as 3ft (0.91m) deep (i.e. 3ft below point X1 at the base of the chancel arch), the earlier as 5ft (1.52m) deep. There is also a reference in a newspaper article (*DGSA*, 21 November 1959, in Nisbet's archive) to two levels of wall. The later clay-bonded wall does not make it onto Thomas' published plan in the 1973 volume (Figure 1.3), however, whereas the earlier walling is shown as part of the Iron Age structures below the nave. No attempt is made to interpret the later

clay-bonded wall in the archives or in print. This is frustrating because it is situated stratigraphically above the Iron Age structures, but below the medieval foundations at roughly the same depth as the 'Celtic' levels recorded outside the chapel adjacent to the south wall (Figure 3.14).

Stone platform or pavement and Iron Age walling

Small records that 'O'Dell's notes suggest that he identified at least four phases of occupation, but on extant evidence this cannot be confirmed or refuted' (Small 1973, 6). After having studied the archive material now available, one must concur with Small's conclusion. It is probable that Small is referring here to O'Dell's identification, both in his *PDR* and articles, that in 1958: 'Trowelling within the nave had been in progress for some weeks … during which time four distinct layers of pot fragments had been found'. Thomas describes 'both inside and outside (to the south of) the church, crude stone walls, with rubble collapses, paved areas, and occupation debris, appeared to indicate (pre-Christian) secular occupation', and on his archive sketch plan, made after interviewing O'Dell and Small, on which his published site plan is based (Figure 1.3), he shows curved walling at 5ft (1.52m) below the medieval chapel and describes these walls as 'some stone walls below chancel and nave: these define an at least two-period hut complex on the OLS, with pots and a hearth' (see above).

Otherwise there are occasional references in the archives to the Iron Age 'domestic' remains below the cists. Nisbet describes 'Iron Age domestic structures' in notes in her diary for 1959, when the whole of the chapel nave interior was excavated down to 'pre-Christian level'. There are notes in *SN* referring to a stone platform and also a stone pavement, set in clay, below rubble and sand in the east end of the nave, and a sketch of part of the paving is shown with 'yellow ashes' referred to under the paving (presumably the hearth shown on Figure 1.3 at the east end of the nave). There are also finds recorded in relation to these features, and those pavement finds which can be located are assigned to 'X6', which according to the 1959 grid, was in the SE corner of the nave. LIA pottery finds include sherd Bl (smoothed Fabric 1 sherd: A21.2000.62) found 'about 4–6in above "stone pavement" between crevices of smallish fallen pieces', and Bm (burnished Fabric 2 body sherd: A21.2000.114) '3in below Bl and therefore close to 'stone pavement''. Find Bo (find unlocated) is described as a 'Stone ring. Close to Bn. Immediately above stone pavement under protecting stone' and is possibly one of the two stone beads or whorls discussed below by Batey, in 3.4.3 (A19.1998.8b or A19.1998.10; Figure 3.20). Bk (5 body sherds of Fabrics 1 and 2: A21.2000.23a/b) are also recorded as 'pot pieces found below Bd at level immediately above stones ?stone platform'. The label from A19.1998.5 also describes 'whalebone and fish from above east end of "stone platform"'.

In *SN*, under 'Er', a 'knocking stone' is described, from the '2nd layer slightly above platform' and a sketch below the description shows a stone broken into two pieces, 20in (0.51m) long overall and 4¼in (110mm) wide at each end, widening in the centre, of grey granite and described above the sketch as '?stone coffin'. This stone was found adjacent to the lozenge-shaped stone, but unfortunately, like that stone, cannot now be located (see *The hoard*, above).[14]

The label for LIA pottery A21.2000.55 (2 smoothed Fabric 1 body sherds) records that the finds were just above the pavement, set on 'glay'?hut circle, and A21.2000.137 (2 smoothed Fabric 1 body sherds) is described as 'X6 77in above pavement on gley'. This latter label refers to 77in (1.96m) *below* the medieval foundations, but *above* the pavement. These brief descriptions indicate a paved surface set onto clay (i.e. below the wind-blown sand), into which is also set a circular, stone-built structure (the 'hut circle'), over 6ft (1.83m) below the medieval foundations, i.e. at 24.64m above sea level, roughly the same level as Cist A and finds from 1959 (see U–Z/1–6 above).

The finds which were excavated in 1959 and recorded in relation to the medieval foundations vary in depth between 71in (1.8m) and 48in (1.22m) below these foundations (i.e. between 24.8m and 25.38m above sea level) and mostly therefore well into the Iron Age levels. There is only one exception, where the depth is 27in (0.69m) below the medieval foundations. These finds include mainly LIA pot sherds, but also charcoal (A21.2000.101b, *Picea/Abies/Larix* charcoal; 70in below; 1.78m), a gaming piece (A21.200.123b; 71in below; 1.80m), human bone frags (A21.2000.16b; 59in below; (1.50m) and a worked schist object (A21.2000.17b; 54in below; 1.37m). Figure 3.14, although showing a section outside the chapel, marks the 'Celtic' horizon as extending from 2ft 6in to 4ft (0.76–1.22m, i.e. 25.38–25.84m above sea level) below the medieval foundations on the outer face of the medieval chapel south wall, with sand still present at this depth. This suggests that the Iron Age levels were below this, in the clay subsoil at 25.4–24.80m above sea level. The depths given for the stone pavement finds from X6 are at the base of the Iron Age levels, at 70-80ins below the medieval foundations, i.e. 24.85–24.60m above sea level.

Pits outside the chapel

Pit Y

A sketch in *SN* shows Pit Y to the north of the apse and describes: 'Small skull 5in below foundation of apse, large skull about 3in lower. With small skull a few rib bones ?where rest. Over small skull 2 small capstones and a larger single block over large skull. Large slab appears to be to north about 1ft below small skull ?significance'.[15] This pit is also described in the 1958 *DES* entry as a test pit to the north of the apse, sunk up to 6ft (1.83m) below the medieval chapel, containing two non-Christian burials. It is possibly the alignment of the burials that caused O'Dell to describe them as non-Christian, and perhaps the depth at which they were found (the skulls and ribs were apparent, protruding from beneath the medieval church walls).

All the finds with a Y prefix held in the Shetland Museum collection relate to the 1959 site grid used within the nave.

Pit Z

This is the trial pit excavated south of the chapel in 1958. It is described in *SN* as: 'Bones of skull Z and odd bones removed. Piece of pot found in Z near top of spine. Skeleton has curved spine ?due to slipped stones. Skull crushed by slipped block. Extended burial. Right leg over left. Front teeth misplaced. At foot of grave another skull (Za) and ?by other foot. Horse tooth at Zc. 2 mouse skulls and land shells. Skulls Za and Zc – facing E. Cist Z floored small stones and clay.' There is a sketch of Z on the finds label for LIA burnished Fabric 1 body sherd A21.2000.24, described as 'Alan's pit enlarged by Ian Patterson'. O'Dell's *Report to session 1958* (D/1/359/9/6) describes: 'A test pit was sunk south of the apse and a cist burial was found' and this test pit was later extended in 1959 to cover the area to the south of the chapel (Figure 1.3). A site grid of sorts using the letters F–L was set up in this area and there are finds in the archives that were recorded by Ian and Alan, and use the letter K prefix, suggesting that Pit Z was located south of the chapel.

The description of the extended burial in the cist suggests it was a long cist, with possibly a second burial, with both set into the midden deposit below.

X1 and the SE Pit (X1–X4)

A pit is located in *SN* at 32ft (9.75m) from the SE angle of the chancel, and 42ft (12.8m) from the corner of the 'south east buttress' (i.e. the external SE corner of the nave). This places the pit around 2m north of Trial Trench 4 excavated in 1999 (PLATE 5). There is also a description: 'Earth 10ft [3.05m] below top of altar'. In the 1958 *DES* account, this pit is described as being 'on the flank of the hillside', 14ft (4.27m) deep, and as revealing a 'succession of features'. These include an extended burial, long-cist burials and iron ore and slag. Dry stone walls were built around this pit and as a revetment on the flank of the hill at the end of the 1958 season.

In *SN* there is sketch of the 'S E Pit', showing X1–X4. X1 is described as 'Pot + skeleton – crouched', X4 as 'Pot + skeleton bones' and X3 as 'Base of pot'. In the Shetland Museum Small collection there are many finds from X1–4, but some are dated to 1959, not 1958, and originate from within the nave (see U–Z/1–6 above). Those undated include A21.2000.13: 'Below X1' (slag and cow bone and teeth frags), LIA pottery A21.2000.76: 'below X1' (4 body sherds and 1 base sherd) and A21.2000.41: 'Alan's pit Below X1' (3 body sherds and one Fabric 1 flat base; although this may relate to Alan's pit Z, south of the chancel). Also 'X3': A21.2000.50 (3 burnished Fabric 2 body sherds) and 'X4 north end': A21.2000.106 (2 Fabric 1 base and body sherds and a peat fragment). There are four small sketches of X1 in *SN* showing a cist, 5ft (1.52m) in length, 18in (0.46m) wide at the top, 12in (0.31m) wide at the bottom, and partially covered by a capstone and other stones. It is possible that this is a lintel grave and may be similar to Cist C excavated in 1957–58 within the chapel.

A table describing the 'Section below X1' is also included at this point in *SN*, but it is not the same X1 used to describe the datum within the nave at the base of the chancel arch. X1 is shown in a layer 1ft 9in (0.53m) thick, on the same level as a 'wall', and 'crouch burials (three in cist), various burials, some flint' and at the boundary with the layer below, an 'extended burial'. Above X1 is shown 8ft 3in (2.52m) of blown sand containing 'Recent Christian burials', and below it a 2ft 6in (0.76m) 'Black layer' containing 'Thick black clay widespread with peaty patches' and 'considerable shells'. Four pieces of pot, bog iron ore and animal bones are also noted from this layer. Below this a layer of blown sand, 2ft (0.61m) thick is shown. This table confirms that the 'black occupation layer' is above sand and must therefore post-date all the other Iron Age features at the site, but pre-date the medieval chapel. The black layer in the SE pit may be the same black clay layer as layer F within the nave (see above), but thickened down the slope to the east of the site, although layer F seems to have pre-dated all the sand.

There are finds and labels from the following year (1959) that are also labelled 'X' but none relate to the SE pit. Rather they conform to the recording system used in 1959 in the nave and evidenced by the numbers 3–7 and letters W, X and Y painted on to the timber shoring seen in one of Nisbet's 1959 slides (PLATE 6). In line with the grid mentioned above, X1 would be situated at the SW end of the nave, for instance, and X2–X4 further to the east. A sketch on a torn-out page of *SN* which was included with a rim sherd in the Shetland Museum collection (A19.1998.7; Figure 3.24) shows one of the stones of a right-angled stone setting of upright stones adjacent to Cist A as 'X1'. In this case, however, X1 refers to the other end of the section (the west end being annotated X) drawn to show how all the different pits at D relate to one another; it does not relate to the SE pit.

NW Pit: charnel pit

From a sketch (*SN*), this pit is at roughly 30ft (9.14m) NW of the NW outer angle of the nave. A sketch section shows the top of the pit at 2ft (0.61m) above the NW angle, and the bottom at 8ft 3ins (2.52m). The top part of the section is shown as being 5¾ft (1.75m), the bottom part is labelled 'Humus and rotted schist'. This pit is well away from the excavation of the chapel walls and is probably the charnel pit mentioned by Small in relation to the medieval and later burials reburied to the west of the chapel (confirmed by Helen Nisbet pers comm). No other references to this pit could be found and it is not depicted on any photographs or slides, or mentioned in the 1958 *DES* account.

The 'Founder's Tomb'

The so-called 'Founder's Tomb' was excavated at the external SE corner of the apse in 1957. A dry-stone structure can be seen on the left-hand side of a slide taken of the east end of the church at the end of the 1957 season (Figure 3.12) which shows a stump of dry stone walling in the area where the Founder's Tomb was excavated. There are no clues in the archive as to what this stump of walling is, although the fact that it has been covered in turf, in a similar fashion to the wall footings of the chapel, suggests that it is a 'real' feature and not simply a well-stacked stone spoil heap, for instance. Since the area to the south of the chapel was excavated and the site consolidated in 1959, this feature now lies under the sand.

Nisbet in her site diary notes that a 'nice big flagstone' was found in the Founder's Tomb, and that the excavators digging there 'eventually came upon quite an old skeleton in a most odd position, doubled up and lying on its side' (Figure 3.1). However, in a note she added later before sending extracts from the diary to Alan Small: 'I now feel sure that this is an incorrect description, and that the bones represent a re-burial, in a disarticulated and perhaps broken condition.' O'Dell refers in his *PDR* to the Founder's Tomb, and how between 'the Pictish Christian symbol stones' (i.e. the shrine posts), found in 1957, was a pagan interment with knees bent up to the chin, but above and below which were found extended burials. Nisbet, in her diary, is strongly of the opinion that the interment was a translated burial as the bones were in poor condition and appeared to have originated in a wetter environment than the burials excavated from the free-draining sand.

On 26 June 1957 Nisbet describes how the Founder's Grave had to be filled in, and there is no reference to it being re-excavated in later years. Find A21.2000.151 (a burnished later Iron Age Fabric 3 body sherd, indeterminate animal bone and a ?seal tooth, and natural quartz chunks) is from the Founder's Tomb pit. In a letter (D/1/359/1/13/29), dated 19 August 1959, O'Dell describes that to the north of the nave, rising above the level of the 'Celtic Church', was a grave structure with several stones standing above the level of the early chapel. He suggests that it is 'part of the pagan interlude between *c*820 and re-conversion in the 11th century'. This feature is not mentioned anywhere else, but it seems almost certain that this is the Founder's Tomb on the *south* side of the chapel that O'Dell is referring to here, and Helen Nisbet has kindly confirmed this to the author, writing: 'As far as I can remember the rising ground on the north side was featureless, and no digging was done there, apart from the charnel pit'.

The list of levels (D1/359/11/6), when converted as described above in relation to Cist A, record that the shrine posts in the Founder's Tomb were found at 3.3ft below the top of the wall of the tomb at *c*26m above sea level (with the top of the wall at 26.95m). These levels suggest that the shrine posts were inserted at a later date than the burials predating the medieval chapel and so support O'Dell's (1957) observation that they were undoubtedly in a secondary position. Thomas agreed, writing 'The seven shrine posts were all found within, or on the walls of, a curious little unroofed structure (Founder's Tomb) lying just south of the apsidal chancel. This was stratigraphically high and late, and is probably no older than the medieval period' (Thomas 1973, 12).

In his own unpublished notes, Thomas suggests that the shrine(s) from which the shrine posts originally came may have been removed from the east end of the present 'nave', between the two altars, when the 'apsidal chancel' was added in the 10th or 11th centuries. He also points out that, at the time of the excavation, O'Dell and his team were not aware of the identification of the carved stones as shrine posts and so did not know to look for side or end panels. Nisbet's reference in her site diary (above) to 'a nice big flagstone' is intriguing in this regard, and one wonders if this may have been part of the shrine structure.

The 'Garth' wall

In his 1958 *DES* account O'Dell describes a 'Garth wall' situated to the north of the chapel and parallel to it, 30ft (9.14m) of which was traced. In the *DGSA* the following description is given:

> Towards the end of the 1958 season a great accumulation of peat ash was found, and an energetic student clearing a dry-stone wall which extended the whole length of the chapel, and is probably the garth wall of the pre-Norman chapel, also found a hearth which is still to be fully excavated. An angle of this garth wall extended under the medieval wall.

> *DGSA*, 21 Nov 1959.

The 'Garth' wall is described in *SN* as being constructed from coarse water-worn blocks, 3–4 cours-

es (22in) high at the east end only, where it ran under a tip. O'Dell also records that the wall is built onto blown sand. It is possible that the 'tip' referred to is one of the 1950s spoil heaps north or east of the chapel, but the description of 'a tip' rather than 'the tip' would suggest that the feature in question is more likely to be the collapse of rubble that was uncovered at the north end of the nave/chancel junction (see below).

Wall footings and pavements on the west side of the area south of the chapel

Nisbet describes in her diary that the western half of the excavated area south of the chapel 'contained domestic occupation under some very heavy tumbled stones (remember difficulty in moving some of these)'. She also describes that there were wall footings running diagonally across the SW corner, and a paved pathway or 'pavement' curving toward it from the north. These are both shown in the SW corner of Small's plan of the area to the south of the chapel (Figure 1.2), on Nisbet's sketch of the 1959 excavations (Figure 3.5) and on two poor-quality slides in the Shetland Museum (SL05156 and SL05125) that were taken at the end of the excavation that year.

Small's description of the features on the west side of the area is as follows:

> In the western section of this area there is an extensive paved area as shown in the plan (fig. 5); large flat stones are carefully laid on a clay base, and the interstices between the stones packed with clay. From the north-eastern corner of this paved area a narrow flagged path rises north-westwards with the natural ground slope towards another paved section which continues beyond the excavated zone. From the large quantity of pottery sherds recorded from this area it is clear that these are the fragmentary floors of at least one and possibly two huts; the pottery suggests a Broch period or Wheelhouse date (figs. 3,4). Overlying these structures in the south west corner, with a clear stratigraphical break, is a later kerbed and flagged pathway some 1.3m wide rising steeply to the north-west; since only 3m of its length was excavated no conclusions can be drawn as to its purpose.

> (Small 1973, 6).

Most interestingly, Small's description of two phases of structures on the west side of the area: two possible huts with occupation layers and a path connecting them; and then above these, a kerbed pathway in the SW corner of the trench, opens up the possibility that the kerbed pathway belonged to a later phase and therefore may have fulfilled a function associated with burials on the site. This kerbed pathway can be seen on a slide taken by Helen Nisbet (RCAHMS no. 701028, in the Nisbet slide collection), and has more the appearance of a long cist with a paved base than a pathway, and the pavements to the north of it may just as easily have been wall footings, as pavements. Small does not expand as to what the clear stratigraphical break between the other 'pathways' and the kerbed pathway was, although it is possible that it was the occupation layer that covered the floors of the huts. Unfortunately, there is little stratigraphic information in the archives to investigate this further, exacerbated by the 'gap' seen on the final plan between the cists on the east side of the south area, and the paths and wall footings on the west (see Figure 1.2).

One of the sherds described as coming from the floor of these huts, and illustrated in figs 3 and 4 in the 1973 volume, can be matched to a sherd in the Shetland Museum collection (Iron Age finger-decorated body sherd: A19.1998.11). The sherd does not have a label accompanying it, but there is a '21' written onto the sherd, which relates to a list of pottery sherds, with drawings, that was written by Small and is held in the Shetland Archives (D.1/359/11/11). This annotates sherd '21' as 'nave', which suggests it was recovered from the huts below the chapel, not to the south of it, despite the description in the 1973 volume.

Finds labels in the Shetland Museum collection refer to an 'occupation surface' or 'layer', possibly a midden layer located south of the chapel, eg LIA pottery smoothed Fabric 1 body sherds (A21.2000.95) and Fabric 2 body sherds (A21.2000.142) are both described as being from 'F13 top layer top of occupation layer'; burnished body and plain rim Fabric 1 sherds (A21.2000.98) and smoothed fabric base and body sherds (A21.2000.130) are labelled as being from 'H14 below occupation layer'; and burnished Fabric 1 body sherd (A21.2000.134) is labelled as 'H15 9–18in below occupation layer'. There are also references to a 'broad diagonal wall', eg burnished Fabric 1 sherds and a bird bone (A21.2000.128a) and smoothed base angle Fabric 1 sherd (A21.2000.152) are described as 'H 15 6in below level of broad diagonal wall'. Fabric 1 body sherd (A21.2000.157) and Fabric 2 body sherd (A21.2000.170) are labelled 'I.14 below level of broad diagonal wall'. Smoothed Fabric 1 LIA body sherds and rims (one of which is beaded), and one smoothed base angle sherd, (A21.2000.73; Figure 3.24) are labelled as 'J below occupation surface'. Burnished LIA Fabric 1 body sherds and base angle sherds, and perforated stone (A21.2000.1) are labelled 'Ian and Alan K15h (peat ash) bde associated with structure. 12in below. Iron Age level (pavement)'. There are also finds located only to these features, with no letter codes (Appendix 2).

A slide in the Shetland Museum collection (SLO5141) also confirms that the letters, H–L were used as a 'site grid' south of the chapel in 1959 (although the annotation of *Pits* F and H associated with Iron Age features below the chapel can lead to some confusion; see above). The slide records the completion of a dry-stone revetment wall built around the site at the end of the excavation, to pre-

vent the sides the hollow that had been dug into the sand from collapsing inwards, and the neat re-turfing of the banks above it. Still in place is a line of stones at the edge of the SW corner of the trench, each a yard apart (0.91m), with the letters H, I, J, K or L painted on them in red paint. Presumably the letters F and G were further east towards the other corner of the trench.

The twelve finds labelled H, I and J and associated with the 'broad diagonal wall', 'occupation surface' or 'occupation level' are certainly from the Iron Age levels south of the chapel as they are not mentioned at all in the *SN*, which records the excavations below the chapel. Also, although smoothed Fabric 2 body sherds of LIA pottery (A21.2000.89; labelled 'I14') are recorded at a depth below the medieval foundation, find 'I14' is most likely to have been found in the NW corner of the trench to the south of the chapel, where the exterior face of the medieval chapel wall was showing in the trench edge, so allowing a depth measurement in relation to the medieval foundations (this outer face and section below it is recorded on a sketch held in the archives, reproduced in Figure 3.14).

The wall, 'cairn' and short cists on the east side of the area south of the chapel

After his description of the features on the west side of the area, Small states:

> There is no clear stratigraphical link between these structures and those in the eastern part of the area, where the dominating feature is a dry-stone wall running north and south across the area. This wall, 1.2m wide, and constructed of two facing walls and rubble core, extends beyond the limits of excavation at both ends, and was badly collapsed in the south … The most important find recorded from this area is a necklace of seventeen bone-and-antler beads (fig 6); this was discovered below the north/south wall, and consequently may belong to the earliest period of occupation of the area.

(Small 1973, 6–7).

In addition to this, though not mentioned in Small's account, Nisbet shows on her 1959 sketch plan (Figure 3.5, no. 4) a 'boat structure' at the south end of the wall across the site, described as a 'cairn' on finds labels in the Shetland Museum collection, including A19.1998.1, labelled 'Iron object found in debris from east edge of "cairn" at southern section of it'. LIA pottery base and three Fabrics 1 and 2 body sherds and burnt bone fragments (A21.2000.100), found 'Close together at the edge of 'cairn' about 1½ to 2 ft below occupation surface. L. 16. hdi M.17.a', originate from this feature. In addition to these finds, an empty envelope labelled 'I.17.g 'Beads' at edge of cairn' under lip of stone', probably refers to the bone and antler beads found in 1959 and illustrated by Small in the 1973 volume.

Slides of the excavation show the cairn as a large linear pile of rubble across the area (PLATE 8; SL05128 and SL05120) are unfortunately too poor in quality to reproduce here). These slides and Nisbet's descriptions demonstrate that the archaeology in this area was considerably more complex than the final plan (Figure 1.2) suggests. In her diary Nisbet further describes the cairn:

> Running N–S was a long cairn-like structure which was referred to as a 'boat grave' but on getting the stones off it there was revealed a complex system of stone cists and boxes with queer burials. This complex comprised shell-boxes, cists with child burials, Iron Age pottery, a pecked cross-slab★ and a crouched burial of Early Bronze Age type. There were, I believe more burials 18 ins below this lot, but I left before they were investigated, and do not know what they were like.
>
> ★Small cross-slab of flaky micaceous metaquartzite, with sides on natural cleavages. The top of this was below the level of the side slabs of the medieval (?) graves. It appeared to be associated with cists on east flank of the 'boat' structure, but was 2 ft. from south edge of the most southerly grave. The open-armed pecked cross faced west. Its position can be seen on slides indicated ★, but I have a feeling that it had fallen down and been set up again.

The slides indicated ★ by Nisbet have been reproduced here as PLATE 7 and Figure 3.13. PLATE 7 (given no. CH81 by Nisbet) is described by her as 'Looking NE Medieval (?) graves refilled and turfed over. Most of "boat" complex seen. Shell-box refilled with shells. Crouched burial removed and its cist filled with clean sand. Position of small cross slab★ well seen'. Figure 3.13 (given no. CH85 by Nisbet) however shows the original position of the cross slab, and on another of her slides (given no. CH82 by Nisbet; reproduced here as PLATE 8) showing the ongoing cairn excavation, the stone has been removed, confirming her observation that the stone was re-positioned during consolidation at the end of the excavation in 1959. Nisbet's description is of Cross 11 in Thomas' catalogue (1973, 36, fig 8, pl 8). It was found in 1959 in association with a group of early long cists, but is shown in a different place on Thomas' (1973) fig 8 (Figure 1.3 and 4.2.3; long cists below), which was drawn by Thomas when he was researching the excavations and visited the site in 1967, after it had been reconstructed and filled in.

O'Dell himself describes the findings from this part of the site:

> on top of a midden of shells of limpets, dogwhelks and animal bones (as yet unexcavated) is a Late Bronze Age type of crouched burial in a cist and on the flanks of this are extended burials within cist structures. At the edge of the cist stones were a set of antler rings and knife hafts and a much corroded barrel-lock of Romano-British type. To the north-east of the Late Bronze Age burial was a simple cross poorly cut in a small slab, 2 feet

> above this cross, and to the north, are four extended burials in sand with the grave edges marked by thin stone slabs with edge and foot stones but no headstones …

(O'Dell 1960, 4–5).

The 1959 *DES* entry adds a reference to a considerable number of small white quartz pebbles in the midden below the cist burials. The Museum entry record (no. 4860) for the bone and antler necklace (PLATE 14) also locates the necklace 'at an early level and in association with a crouched burial'. This record was made in 1972, when the finds were donated to the museum by Dundee University (Alan Small) and so we can assume that the reference to their association with the crouched burial came from him (Andrew Williamson pers comm).

Small adds description of the cists and stone boxes in the east part the area in the 1973 volume (Figure 1.2). Dug into the top of this wall, and (according to the 1973 account), clearly post-dating it, was the short cist containing an adult skeleton in a crouched position, but no grave goods, described by O'Dell as Bronze Age. Both ends of this grave consisted of two large parallelopiped stones set on end, with the sides being of thinner slabs set on edge. The skeletal remains from this burial are mentioned in a letter in the Shetland Archives (see above), from the Anatomy Department at Aberdeen University, acknowledging the safe arrival of the crouched burial 'Rosemary' (ABDUA 14269) in 1959. Helen Nisbet and/or Alan Small took photographs of the short cist with the crouched burial *in situ* (Figure 3.17), and general shots of the excavations to the south of the chapel, in 1959, show the excavation of this feature (Figure 3.9). The museum card for this burial adds only the suggestion of '?Late Bronze Age'.

Three other cists are noted next to the large short cist with the adult crouched burial. One of these had thin stone slabs forming three of its sides, while the wall formed the fourth: this contained only charred human bones. Another lay to the south of this cist, against the wall, with thin stone slabs forming the remaining three sides of the box, and was filled with shells. To the west of this a further small cist of similar construction was in a somewhat ruinous state, but contained human bones. The area to the east of the wall was not completely excavated, but Small notes that the only available site plan (Figure 1.2) shows a number of box-like structures formed by stones set on edge, suggesting further burials (Small 1973, 6–7). Thomas adds a reference to the possibility that the human bones in one of the short cists were perhaps those of a mother and child (Thomas 1973, 11–12). This may be from Nisbet's diary. In her 1959 list of slides with captions, she notes for slide CH85 (Figure 3.13) 'Beyond this north end of "boat" complex – large square box containing shells, may [sic] of which have been taken out. I think the small cist adjoining its north end contained bones of a child'. A collection of bones deposited by Small in

FIGURE 3.17

'Rosemary' in situ (original image blurred). Slide taken by Alan Small (Shetland Museum collection, no. SL05113)

the Shetland Museum in 1998 (A26.1998) and identified by Duffy below, contains a minimum of one adult and one juvenile, and so could possibly be the burial that Thomas recalls. 'Elizabeth', a burial that was excavated and subsequently lost, might also be identified as A26.1998 (see above), however because O'Dell describes 'Elizabeth' as having been translated from another burial and re-buried with the thigh bones touching the skull and the collection of bones A26.1998 is identified by Duffy as consisting largely of thigh and skull bones, although others are present, a cist shown in the SE corner of the trench on the 1959 final plan (Figure 1.2) also shows thigh bones and a skull and may be 'Elizabeth'. Ultimately there is frustratingly too little information in the archives or with the skeletal material to confirm any of these theories.

O'Dell describes the 'Bronze Age' cist burial to the south of the chapel as being *c*60ft (18.28m) above sea level (O'Dell 1960, 5), although there is again a discrepancy here between the 1959 reading and the modern readings, given that high water mark was used when recording the levels in 1959, rather than mean sea level. A separate level measurement taken on the base of this same cist in 2000 confirms that it

is at 25.52m (83ft 9in) above sea level. This is comparable in depth to the cists excavated below the chapel, which were found in the thick black layer F, below the earlier church wall (25.88m), and to that of the hoard (25.53–25.69m), but is above the Iron Age domestic remains excavated below the nave in 1959, at 24–25m above sea level (see above).

The long cists SE of the chapel

In her diary Nisbet describes:

> Toward the east end of this area was a number (3) of slab-sided graves, dug into clean sand with no trace of a turf-line. Of the two we examined, one had the stain of a wooden coffin, with iron nails; the other had none. O'Dell thinks these are Dark Age, but stratigraphically they might just as well be medieval, though they seem rather 'low' relative to the chapel...

In addition, Small describes 'the early Christian graves in the north-east corner of the excavated area, which are separated from the earlier structures by a clear stratigraphical break' (Small 1973, 7). Thomas, who marks these burials as B on his plan (Figure 1.3) and describes them as 'the first Christian interments', adds:

> These oriented long cists were, stratigraphically, from two to three feet higher than the short cists (those marked A). Normally one would expect them to lie east, or south-east, of a contemporary chapel or oratory, in this part of the world most likely to be stone-walled; I take this to be represented by the 'Earlier Walls' said to have been noticed below the footings of the medieval church
>
> (Thomas 1973, 12).

In a letter to Ralegh Radford (D/1/359/1/13/29, dated 19/8/59), and also in the O'Dell and Cain volume (1960, 4–5) O'Dell writes that the putative earlier chapel wall was the same depth below the medieval chapel wall foundations as the long cist graves, two of which had large upstanding foot-stones (he suggests that the headstones had already been robbed). At about 2ft below these graves, O'Dell also describes how he found a Christian burial with a 'rather small, but charming' cross (this is Stone 11 in Thomas' catalogue; 1973, 36). O'Dell's description implies two groups of graves: those with the upstanding foot stones, and those 2ft below them.

Another letter in the archives, this time written to O'Dell (D/1/359/1/13/17), acknowledges the safe receipt by the Anatomy Department at Aberdeen University, of 'Hubert' (ABDUA 14254), a long-cist burial and O'Dell was 'certain that the bones came from a Dark Age grave before 820 AD'. Fortunately, Helen Nisbet and/or Alan Small took a photograph of the long cist with the burial *in situ* (Figure 3.18) and this shows 'Hubert' deep in a hole in the bank of sand left in the NE corner of the 1959 excavation trench in the area of the long cists. Nisbet's slide is annotated 'Slab-graves, including Hubert, H's side

FIGURE 3.18

'Hubert' in situ in 'Dark Age' grave. Slide taken by H Nisbet (RCHAMS no. 696428), whose caption for this slide read 'Slab-graves, including Hubert. H's side slabs have been removed … Small cross-slab is seen on left. Beyond this is north end of 'boat' complex. Large square box containing shells, many of which have been taken out. I think the cist adjoining its north end contained bones of a child.'

slabs have been removed' in notes Nisbet made in her diary for slides to accompany a talk she was to give in 1959. A second burial 'Robert' was also received by the Anatomy Department in 1959. 'Robert' (AB-DUA 14270) is also now located in the Marischal Museum with 'Hubert', and the museum cards for ABDUA 14270 and 14254 both contain the same description: 'An extended burial found in sand with grave edges marked by thin stone slabs with edge and foot stones but no head stone. Believed to be contemporary with a pre-Norse Church and, if so, is a Dark Age grave'. As we have already seen however, Nisbet describes 'a wooden coffin with iron nails' associated with one of the burials and this tallies with O'Dell's description of 'Robert', contained in a letter to the Anatomy Department in 1959, in which he describes 'Robert' as originating from a wooden coffin (D/1/359/1/14/2, dated 21/8/59). Nisbet's slide however confirms her observation that 'Hubert' was buried deep down in the sandy bank and the descriptions in the archive, and of Christian sculpture below the sandy bank, suggests there were two different groups of long cist burial in this part of the site, one group above the sand, and one group below.

3.4 ARTEFACTS DEPOSITED BY ALAN SMALL IN THE SHETLAND MUSEUM

Introduction

The Shetland Museum catalogue numbers for the two groups of artefacts deposited by Alan Small have been used in this report so as to avoid confusion with the finds assemblage recovered during the 1999/2000 excavations. A third digit has also been added so that each find has a unique number, with an 'a' or 'b' where bags have been subdivided by material type. The ARC.2002 numbers have been allocated by the Shetland Museum.

As described above, many of the old finds were accompanied by labels, usually in pencil and written on scraps of paper, the backs of old cigarette packets, etc, with a letter code for the find, or a description of the feature from which the find came. These labels had the potential to be more important than some of the finds themselves, given that the information written on them, in conjunction with *SN* especially, and also Nisbet's archive, could be used to try and roughly locate excavated features below the chapel. Consequently, before any of the finds were sent out to the relevant specialists, they were all listed with a note being made of each label; this was then bagged separately and given the same number as the find so that the two could be re-united once specialist work was completed. Specialist identifications of the finds were then added to the listing when the material was returned. This listing is included in Appendix 1.

The majority of the finds assemblage held in the Shetland Museum comprises coarse pottery. Small assemblages of other materials are also present however: medieval and post-medieval glazed pottery, iron, worked bone and antler, steatite, worked stone, pumice, glass and industrial waste. The first box, deposited by Alan Small in 1998, had clearly been 'processed' to some extent after the 1959 excavations because this collection contained the most intriguing finds, such as large sherds of decorated pottery and a glass bead. Prior to the collection being donated to the Shetland Museum, some of the pieces of pottery had been stuck back together, and the metal objects covered in waxoyl to prevent them from rusting. Also, some groups of pottery sherds that were clearly from one vessel were bagged together. For these reasons conservation work was undertaken in 2003 on a selection of the most vulnerable finds at the Conservation Unit at AOC, and a short synopsis of this work is included with the specialist reports below.

Some 137 out of the total assemblage of 190 finds have been located to a specific feature on the site (Appendices 1 and 2) and 115 of these date from the Iron Age. Of the non-pottery finds, those that are situated particularly deep in the Iron Age levels, below the chapel, are a stone pebble gaming piece (A21.2000.123b), water-rounded pumice (A21.2000.153b) from Cist S, a trimmed schist fragment (A21.2000.17b; Figure 3.20) from below the chapel, and a perforated stone (A21.2000.1b; Figure 3.20) from the SW corner of the area to the south of the chapel.

Conservation summary
Amanda Clydesdale and Rob Lewis

Ceramics

Although standard practice with the reconstruction of ceramics is to construct only a profile, from which the form of the vessel can be interpreted and an illustration drawn, it was not possible to do this with these accessions (Figure 3.19). While each accession consisted of a number of sherds, none of them included an entire profile and it was therefore decided to reconstruct all the sherds that could be securely matched up in order to allow the form of the vessel to be interpreted from those sections. Unnecessary reconstruction was avoided for various reasons, notably the difficulties in packaging a fully reconstructed ceramic vessel, and the dangers that reconstruction can present, particularly for less well-fired ceramics.

Some sherds had been adhered before arriving for conservation with an unknown adhesive and some of them were further supported with what appeared to be plasticine. Regrettably, the plasticine was often placed on the inside wall of the vessel, where organic traces often remain. It should be remembered that plasticine (composed principally of hydrocarbons) can leach material into the substrate, so that any future analysis of such a vessel must bear in mind the possible presence of contaminants; the dryness of the remaining plasticine does suggest that oils, etc, had been lost into the body of the ceramic. The plasticine was removed with hand-tools under the microscope and a sample being retained for future analysis; although it was not always possible to remove all of its traces.

It was not always possible to remove all of the former adhesive because some of the closer joins proved resistant to softening by immersion in acetone. It was considered possible that exerting too much physical pressure would, given the fragility of the body, cause the ceramic to fail rather than the adhesive. Such joins usually appeared to be accurate, and so it was not considered problematic in terms of interpretation (and preferable in terms of preservation of the vessel) to leave these joins in tact.

Copper alloy

The one copper-alloy find (A21.2000.127b) was lightly cleaned using a scalpel and glass bristle brush under the binocular microscope, using the x-radiograph as a guide to any possible features (Figure 3.19). None showed, and the object proved itself to be totally mineralised. The presence of iron corrosion products on one side of the larger fragment raised queries over the efficiency of benzotriazole in this case, and this factor, coupled with the absence of any metallic copper, led to the decision not to treat with a corrosion inhibitor.

Accession No.	Description	X-ray	Notes
A19.1998.1	Iron object in 2 pieces	6, 7, 9, 10	Covered in ?Waxoyl
A21.2000.103b	Iron nails (3)	6, 7, 9, 10	–
A21.2000.127b	Copper-alloy fragments	8, 10	–
A21.2000.135b	Iron object	6, 7, 9, 10	–
A21.2000.144	Pottery	–	Some sherds held with red material
A21.2000.30	Pottery	–	–
A21.2000.4	Pottery, 2 pieces	–	Red material over tacky adhesive
A21.2000.5	Pottery	–	–
A21.2000.51a	Iron object	8, 9, 10	–
A21.2000.77b	Iron object	6, 7, 9, 10	–
A21.2000.91e	Pottery sherds, glazed	–	–
A21.2000.9a	Pottery sherds	–	–

FIGURE 3.19

Conserved artefacts from the Shetland Museum (Small) collection

Iron

The iron finds were X-rayed at several different exposure values to reveal any pertinent information; this demonstrated that there was little information that could be gained by cleaning any of the artefacts, particularly those which are heavily mineralised, with no sound core. One find (A21.2000.51a) was very lightly cleaned by air-abrasion to remove the loosely adhering dirt and soil. One side of A19.1998.1 was cleaned to allow a better interpretation of its form, with the fragments being rejoined using araldite epoxy.

Worked stone
Colleen E Batey

Steatite

—A19.1998.9 (ARC.2002.111), one piece labelled '722' (Figure 3.20). Two conjoining fragments of a thin and shallow steatite vessel. Perforated lug handle with triangular end at one edge, set slightly below rim. Slight variation in discoloration could indicate different burial environments, and the smaller, handled fragment retains traces of burnt deposit particularly on the inner face, which may be food debris. The tapering and slightly flattened rim is intact in some sections. Overall dia c105 x 53 x 4mm; handle 20 x 17mm.

This small food vessel is of remarkably fine workmanship, with careful working of all faces, only on the inner face are there traces of knife markings, but these are due to scraping clean the surface rather than to the manufacturing process. Its incomplete nature allows only for the presence of a single lug handle, although this could have been matched by another on the other side. Finding close parallels for this item is hard, although a miniature steatite vessel of the same fine quality is reported from Phase III at Jarlshof, from the 'Lower Slope Communal Peat Ash Midden', dated to the 10th century, and Hamilton cites examples for the type in Norway (Hamilton 1956, 143, pl XXXI). Examples from more dispersed contexts include one of similar form, but with a single decorated lug handle, from Austmannadal in the Western Settlement of Greenland (Fitzhugh and Ward 2000, 292, illus 21.10). On the other hand, such fine workmanship cannot be paralleled in the large Norwegian assemblage from the Viking period town of Kaupang, where there is evidence for the completion of half-finished vessels quarried from inland sites (Irene Baug pers comm). It is clear that the quality of the workmanship of this piece is relatively rare in this medium in the Viking world.[16]

Gaming pieces

— A21.2000.20b (Figure 3.20). (i) Polished black stone disc, with eliptical section and chamfered edges. Dia 22 x Th 10mm. (ii) Water-worn quartzite pebble, with slightly flattened lower surface. Dia 16 x Th 9mm.

— A21.2000.22b. Water-worn quatzite pebble, slightly flattened and smooth on one face. Dia 22 x Th 9mm.

— A21.2000.123b. Water-worn pebble of spotted stone, similar to a serpentinite, possible a greisen or metadiorite, with smoothed and lower flattish face. Dia 25 x Th 12mm max.

As with the two examples recorded from the Barrowman excavations (see below), both probably originally from Phase II, these four 'gaming' pieces conform to the type perhaps to be described as 'counters', which fall within the common size range of 25mm diameter and which have commonly been found on Iron Age sites (Clarke 1998b, 178; Wilson 1998, 180). The polished black stone disc (one of A21.2000.20b) is closely comparable to SF 392 from Phase II in the Barrowman excavations which is noted as being similar to an example from The Howe, in Orkney (Ballin Smith with Collins 1994, 188, illus 106). A similar example, with grozed edge but of lighter stone, was recovered from a Viking period pagan grave in Norway, at Asak, Skedsmok, Akerhus, and dated to the 10th century (H Gjøstein Resi pers comm). It is clearly the case therefore that such well-executed artefacts are not confined to Iron Age contexts, although the context of this excavated example strongly suggests the earlier dating.

Pumice

— A21.2000.6b. Water-rounded black pumice. 35 x 26 x 20mm.

— A21.2000.7 (Figure 3.20). Water-rounded black pumice, with simple incised cross on one flat face. 60 x 46 x 25mm.

— A21.2000.8b. Water-rounded black pumice with two flattened faces, smoothed by use. 52 x 41 x 28mm.

— A21.2000.9b. Water-rounded black pumice with broad faces smoothed by use. 43 x 30 x 15mm.

— A21.2000.11. Large irregular black pumice block with very large vessicles. Potentially industrial in nature? 121 x 93 x 60mm.

— A21.2000.18b. Water-rounded black pumice with one smoothed face. 28 x 18 x 12mm.

— A21.2000.19b. Water-rounded black pumice. 34 x 23 x 18mm.

— A21.2000.23b. Water-rounded black pumice with one smoothed face. 30 x 25 x 16mm.

— A21.2000.153b. Water-rounded black pumice. 28 x 21 x 19mm.

These nine finds of black pumice include four which appear to have been used for smoothing purposes, possibly pottery or skins (Batey and Newton 2009). The largest piece (A21.2000.11) is however of different character and may in fact not be pumice, as it is relatively heavy. Of particular significance is find A21.2000.7 which has a simple incised cross on one flat face. This is an interesting example which is difficult to date specifically and it could even be a more recent deposition by a pious visitor to this chapel site, in the manner of votives deposited at the Brough of Deerness, in Orkney (Morris with Emery 1986a, 366–367), and, indeed, at St Ninian's Isle (see above). In common with all the finds from

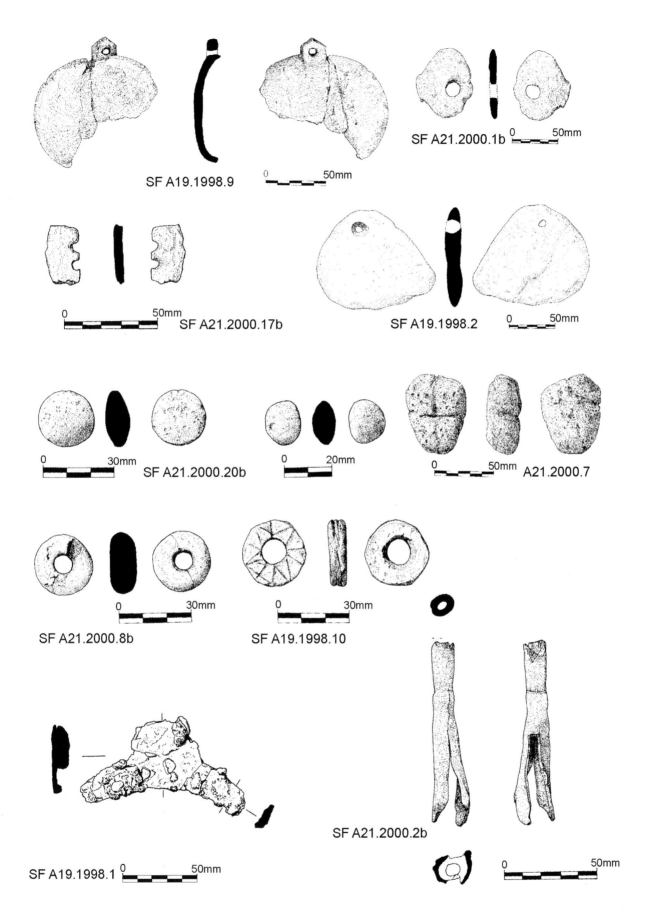

SF A19.1998.9

SF A21.2000.1b

SF A21.2000.17b

SF A19.1998.2

SF A21.2000.20b

SF A21.2000.7

SF A21.2000.8b

SF A19.1998.10

SF A21.2000.2b

SF A19.1998.1

FIGURE 3.20
Iron, stone and bone finds from the Shetland Museum (Small) collection. Drawings: A Braby and A Sperr

the 'Small collection', detailed contextual information is lacking.

Weights and whorls

— A19.1998.2 (ARC.2002.111) (Figure 3.20). Labelled in pencil 'S of south Wall east end (or cut?) 2 (feet) Below Wall Top'. Flat beach pebble, roughly triangular, with probably a natural perforation of tapering form at one corner. 108 x 125 x 11mm max; perforation 15–5mm.

— A21.2000.1b (Figure 3.20). Incomplete flat piece of schistose stone, with large smoothed perforation. 71 x 58 x 5mm; perforation Dia 15mm.

— A19.1998.8b (ARC. 2002.111, also labelled '25') (Figure 3.20). Recently repaired stone whorl or bead, circular with central drilled perforation, with one part of its outer face missing, of roughly even thickness and curved edges. Dia 23 x Th 9mm; perforation Dia 8mm.

— A19.1998.10 (ARC.2002.111) (Figure 3.20). Spindle whorl of fine grained, light coloured stone, possibly steatite. Flat sectioned and incised mid groove around circumference. Upper face has incised radial line decoration with possible simple cross at one point. Dia 26 x Th 7mm: perforation Dia 11mm.

A19.1998.2 is a roughly triangular stone weight, with probably a natural perforation, which can be closely paralleled in a find from Area 2, Brough Road, Birsay in Orkney; this (SF 246) is identified as a sinker of a ubiquitous nature, and has been discussed with reference to several other similar pieces from sites such as Jarlshof and Underhoull in Shetland, and Freswick Links in Caithness (Batey 1989, illus 155, 193, 202, 211–212).

The two whorls, one of roughly globular form and the other flattened, have perforations of 8 and 11mm, which fall within the standard size range cited by Sharman (1998c, 150–152) in discussion of the types from Scalloway in Shetland. The different types encompass contexts cited elsewhere (eg Clickhimin, Jarlshof and Kebister in Shetland, and Buckquoy, Orkney) from the Iron Age to the Viking period. The globular example from St Ninian's Isle (A19.1998.9b) is very carefully made and, although it could be a whorl, it might equally have functioned as a bead. On the other hand, A19.1998.10, of flattened form, is decorated on one surface, presumably the upper, and would not therefore have been suitable for use as a bead as only the edge (which has a medial incised line) would then have been visible. A small number of spindle whorls have radial lines, including the well publicised Pictish example from Buckquoy, which has an ogham inscription (Jackson 1977, 221–222; Forsyth 1995). Despite best efforts with this example, it does not seem possible to identify these incised lines as ogham/runic, and indeed the possible incised cross element at one part of the design may simply be crossed lines.

Miscellaneous stone

— A21.2000.17b (Figure 3.20). Trimmed schist fragment, flat with two cut denticulations on one edge. 30 x 18 x 4mm. The function of this item remains unclear.

Lithics
Chris Barrowman

The majority of the finds in the small assemblage of lithics in the Small collection are of natural origin, with one potentially worked piece.

They are six unworked chips of flint waste, natural unworked fragments and natural quartz flakes.

— A19.1998.4. Grey flint. 19 x 17 x 10mm. This abraded chunk of flint has steep retouch down parallel sides, with similarities to a plano-convex knife in section; its ventral face is flat to slightly convex, with the dorsal having retouch intended to blunt the edges. It could, however, have been any form of scraper. Much natural wear and flaking from crushing on ventral surface.

— A21.2000.103c. Orange and black banded flint. 19 x 12 x 9mm.

— A21.2000.26. Two chips of flint: a: orange, 10 x 5 x 3mm, b: brown, 19 x 8 x 7mm.

— A21.2000.22c. Quartz. 18 x 12 x 7mm.

— A21.2000.151c. Quartz. a: 42. x 20 x 12mm, b: 21 x 11 x 3mm.

Metals
Colleen E Batey

Iron

— A19.1998.1 (Figure 3.20). Two pieces of highly corroded iron plate, with two remaining rivet projections and a third one possibly missing. Each projection has possible traces of rivets for attachment or support, possibly for an organic surface, such as a wooden bucket or a leather strap, or they could possibly be fragments from the repair of a patched iron vessel. c110 x 45 x 10mm.

— A21.2000.51a. Very corroded iron fragments, conjoining, which seem to be the remains of a nail or spike, with traces of expansion at one end; otherwise indeterminate. c60 x 23 x 16mm.

— A21.2000.77b. Worn iron fragment of nail or rivet head. 13 x 15 x 7mm.

— A21.2000.103b. Three iron fragments; two are nail shanks, one of which is bent, and another (c) has a flat expanded head, which appears metal-rich on X-ray (probable coffin fittings of indeterminate date). a: 40 x 38 x 5mm; b: 43 x 25 x 10mm; c: 28 x 28 x 11mm.

—A21.2000.135b. Triangular sheet iron fragment, indeterminate form. 30 x 16 x 2mm.

As these are essentially unstratified finds, the significance of the small iron assemblage is limited; however, it can be sub-divided into two groups. Group One comprises three finds units of nails of varying types, possibly representing coffin fittings, with A21.2000.51a being the most substantial and possibly representing a re-used piece of structural wood. Group Two comprises two finds units of metal sheet (A19.1998.1 and A21.2000.135b) and could be parts of a repaired iron vessel or a vessel patch, which may indicate recovery from a midden deposit following discard.

Copper

— A21.2000.127b. Three small fragments of copper sheet. Two are probably conjoining and form a piece of sheet, with rivet (a and b); c) is a thinner sheet metal fragment. a: 20 x 18 x 1mm; b: 13 x 11 x 3mm; c: 15 x 9 x 2mm.

These are probably pieces of a copper vessel, possibly a cauldron of general medieval date, but its precise form is unclear from such small fragments.

Metalworking debris
Effie Photos-Jones

— A21.2000.60. Six conjoining fragments of silaceous slag. Reddish on underside from contact with soil, suggesting that this is a smithing hearth bottom.

— A21.2000.90b. One lump of ferruginous smithing or smelting slag.

— A21.2000.91c. One lump of vitrified fuel ash from metalworking. Not highly ferruginous and may possibly be from the burning of driftwood rather than peat as fuel for the metalworking process.

— A21.2000.13a. One lump of silicate ferruginous smithing or smelting slag.

This is a very small assemblage of metalworking debris, and little more than an identification of each piece is appropriate. No analysis was undertaken as the assemblage is so small and all of the pieces are unstratified.

The 'Limoges' cross fragments
William Murray

The following description is taken from the initial conservation report, completed in 1998, and from subsequent observations made during the conservation of the object (ARC 2002 111; A19.1998), which was completed in 2005 (PLATE 15). It is hoped that there will be specialist analysis and reporting of this object in the future.

The mount is made up of four main parts:
— A flat plate of copper alloy, c44 x 60 x 3mm, with four nails, a plain back, and a decorated front. The decoration appears to show a bird, indicated by incised lines and less corrosion due to the presence of a layer of gilt, and defined by fields of enamel. The nails are bent at the tips, indicating that the plate was fastened to a support with a thickness of c8mm.
— A flat plate of copper alloy, c56 x 60 x 1mm, with three small tacks, a plain back, and a gilt front which once held a human figure. There are two large circular perforations in the upper corners. The tacks are 7mm long, and are not bent at the tips. The plate now consists of one large and four or five smaller fragments.
— A human figure, 68 x 22 x 6mm, with a large nail which passes through the chest, and another nail hole 11mm from the base. The figure is portrayed as wearing robes, and the arms and legs are not distinct. The eyes are made of a translucent grey material,

possibly glass, but only the right survives. The body is hollowed at the back, but the head is solid. The nail protrudes c10mm beyond the back of the figure and it is bent over at the tip. The presence of gilt and enamel is indicated.
— A plate with sides bent up to form a shallow tray section. This part of the object is now in three or four fragments, the largest of which measures 33 x 10 x 3mm. One of these fragments contains a small piece of preserved wood. At least part of the surface is gilt.

Preliminary research has located a close parallel to the mount amongst pieces held by private collectors and published in 1995 (Bertrand 1995, cat. no. 40), and also to pieces exhibited in the same year in the Louvre, Paris (Metropolitan Museum of Art 1996, 184–185, 232–235, 327). A Limoges enamel held by the Musée d'Art religieux et d'Art mosan, in Liège, is also closely comparable (Toussaint 1996, 75, no. 36), and this has been used as the model for the mount to hold the St Ninian's Isle cross fragments in the new Shetland Museum.

Glass beads
Colleen E Batey, with contributions from Julian Henderson, Rachel Barrowman and the late Alan Small

The circumstances of the recovery of the two groups of glass beads discussed here are far from clear, although information in the archives confirms that they are indeed from O'Dell's St Ninian's Isle excavations, even if they were omitted from the 'definitive' publication. Twenty-nine of the beads came to light in the 1980s in two tobacco tins (as originally sent by Alan Small to Charles Thomas in 1967) in a filing cabinet in University College London that had previously belonged to David M Wilson, whilst in 2003 an additional bead of Group Two, Type 9, was discovered amongst a group of material in the St Ninian's Isle archive of the late Alan Small which had been deposited with the Shetland Museum Service (A21.2000.21b). This final bead is added to the total of beads in this discussion, but is not on the illustrations of the original groups. It is identical in all ways to the rest of the Group Two assemblage, and although it is possible that this bead was recovered from a different context, it is included in that group. The total assemblage is therefore 30 beads in all (see also Batey 2008).

The 29 glass beads were originally sent to Thomas by Alan Small in 1967, whilst the 1973 volume was being prepared. The letter that accompanied the beads describes:

> I enclose two boxes which contain parts of separate necklaces. Box 1 contains brown beads which had the following note with them –ie inside the nave. Unfortunately, there is no depth given and from the structures which exist on the site they could belong to practically any period from the Iron Age upwards … The second tin contains a

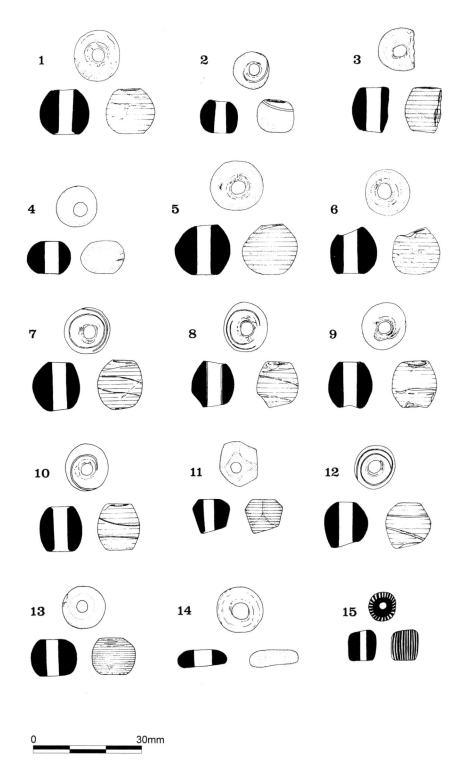

0   30mm

FIGURE 3.21

Group One beads nos 1–15. Drawing: N Emery

mixture of blue, white, black and brown beads which carried a note – 'beads from grave c3' south-east of nave from the south-east angle', this brings them close to the location of the so-called Founder's Tomb

(Letter from Alan Small, held in Thomas' archive, dated14 July 1967)

Small's quote '6in west of side altar, 4ft north of wall' is taken from a description under 'Brown beads',

found in O'Dell's site notebook (D/1/359/6).

Two further pieces of archive information can be brought to bear on the original find spot of the beads. O'Dell's, in one of his versions of a typed 'Preliminary Draft Report' (D/1/359/7/1) describes in relation to finds from excavations inside the nave in 1956: 'Relics found include a late 17th century copper coin wedged in the high altar, *and brown and blue glass beads from post-Reformation interments*' (my italics). In addition to this, a label included with a brown glass bead A21.2000.21 from the Shetland Museum's Small collection, identical in all respects to those brown beads in Small's 'Box 1', is labelled as being from 'Y.1 65in', i.e. in the Iron Age levels within the nave, 65in (1.65m) below the medieval chapel foundations (see U–Z/1–6, above).

For the purposes of this report the beads have been separated into Group 1 (the second tin of blue, white, black and brown beads) and Group 2 (the first tin, Box 1, of brown beads, and the stray bead A21.2000.21).

The archaeological context

The archaeological contexts for both groups of beads are obscure, and as seen above, there are conflicting accounts as to their provenance. Only one of the groups was accompanied by a label. The tin containing the 21 blue and brown glass beads of Group One was labelled 'St. Ninian's Isle, Shetland (Nos 1–21; Figures 3.21 and 3.22, PLATES 10–11). Beads from 'grave ca 3ft SE of SE nave center angle (sic)', with bead Nos 1–6; and 7–15 threaded onto pipe-cleaners, and the rest loose. I am most grateful to Alan Small who subsequently confirmed that this (the larger) group of beads was indeed found in one of the long cists situated to the south of the apse of the medieval chapel, so refuting O'Dell's reference to post-Reformation interments within the nave. These long cists lie stratigraphically above a complex Iron Age horizon (Small *et al* 1973, fig 8) and, clearly, almost 1m below the foundations of the medieval chapel. Thomas (1973, 12) regards these graves as representing the earliest of up to four Christian phases on the island. The recent excavations however, have confirmed that in this part of the site there are *two* levels of cist graves, the lower being the Late Iron Age (Pictish) phase (see above).

The association of a group of beads with human remains is also recalled by one of the diggers (Helen Adamson pers comm) during the later years of the excavation, but in the area noted in the publication as a 'small area excavation about 12m x 8m ... attempted on the south side of the church ..., which revealed an extensive complex of prehistoric walls, pavements, and graves; all the structures extend beyond the limits of the excavated area ...' (Small *et al* 1973, 5). The artefacts recovered from this area included sherds of pottery (so-called 'Broch type'; Small *et al* 1973, figs 3 and 4), as well as the necklace of bone and antler 'beads'(Small *et al* 1973, fig 6) found underlying the N–S wall shown on Figure 1.2, and taken to be from the earliest occupation of the site (Small *et al* 1973, 7).

Group Two (Nos 22–29; Figure 3.22 and PLATE 11) beads, which are of a different character to those in the other group, may have come from a second grave. A label included with the brown glass bead A21.2000.21 (PLATE 12) found in 2003 in the Shet-

land Museum collection locates it deep in the Iron Age levels below the nave/chancel of the chapel excavated in 1959, and it is possible that the rest of the brown beads are from the same area, although this cannot be confirmed from the archive.

Discussion

Despite the varying bead types and colours in this assemblage (subdivided below), it has proved rather difficult to discover parallels for them. I am particularly grateful for the assistance in this matter of the late Mrs Margaret Guido, who confirmed this problem. Examination of other Scottish assemblages, which are generally smaller in scale, with the exception of groups from pagan Viking graves, such as Cnip which produced 44 beads of predominantly segmented form (Welander *et al* 1987, 163–165, illus 9), has failed to produce any close parallels. There are a limited number of examples of long cists which have produced groups of beads, such as Dalmeny Park, South Queensferry (Baldwin Brown 1915, 332–338; Proudfoot and Aliaga-Kelly 1996, 5) and Morham Church, East Lothian (Donations 1928; Proudfoot and Aliaga-Kelly 1996, 5–6), the latter of which provides close similarities of both form and colour in different beads, with a suggested date in the 7th century. Ongoing excavations at Old Scatness broch in southern Shetland have produced, amongst an extensive artefact record, two beads which are also close parallels for Group One: Find 2845, from context 2008 is a 'black' glass bead and Find 7857, from context 1674, a dark blue one; unfortunately both are from later mixed contexts (J Bond and S Dockrill pers comm). A number of assumed broadly contemporary bead assemblages have also been considered, such as amber and polychrome beads from the Croy hoard, Perthshire (NMAS Cat. 1892, 203, FC 16–22), amber beads from the Burgar hoard, Orkney (Graham-Campbell 1985, 6–7), and a brief survey of examples from the NE Scotland which includes a number of beads (eg Ralston and Inglis 1984, nos 15, 44 and 17, 45). All, however, are of a different character to those from St Ninian's Isle.

The St Ninian's Isle beads can be subdivided into nine types, and these are considered below, although Group Two consists exclusively of Type 9, which is not present in Group One.

Group One

— *Bead Type 1*: Opaque blue, generally barrel shaped (Nos 1, 3, 5–10, 12, 17). This is the most numerous bead type in Group One, with ten examples. Although there are slight differences within the type, for example nos 1 and 17 are a slightly deeper blue, they form a coherent grouping. Some of the pieces, such as 6, 10 and 12 show more clearly the method of manufacture by winding the glass around a core. At this stage no precise parallels can be found for

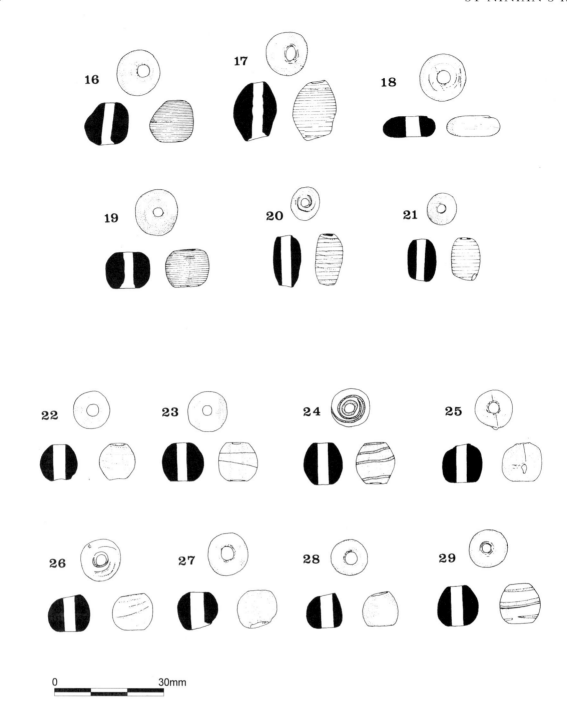

FIGURE 3.22

Group One beads nos 16–21 and Group Two nos 22–29. Drawing: N Emery

this bead type, although a 'light blue drop-shaped bead, quite different from the others' was recorded from Lagore Crannog in Ireland (Hencken 1950, 134, fig 65A) and may be somewhat similar. A single unprovenanced find from the Monach Islands, North Uist, in the collections of Glasgow Museums, is clearly similar, (GAGM A6116).

— *Bead Type 2*: Dark blue, angular (No. 11). The nearest parallel for this bead has been noted from an unstratified context in Orkney (Batey with Freeman 1986, no. 12, illus 9), from the site of Lavacroon, Orphir. Although the colour is described rather dif-

ferently, this is somewhat mis-leading as there is in fact little difference in either colour or form of these beads. Although in the case of the Lavacroon example dating was also problematic, a suggestion of a 6th-century AD date was put forward by comparison with an example from Ipswich (Batey with Freeman 1986, 298). The significance of such a parallel may be disputed, but an additional Northern Isles example is more useful.

— *Bead Type 3*: Translucent amber-coloured, annular (No. 14). Examples of this bead type have been recorded from Clickhimin, Shetland, in an Iron Age context (Hamilton 1968, 90, nos 177–179, fig 41), although these are slightly smaller. Examples were also found from the period of broch usage and on into the occupation of the wheelhouse at this site (Hamilton 1968, 133, 80). It is difficult to ascribe a particularly close date range to the type, but it would seem likely to be Iron Age.

At this stage no precise parallels can be found for any of the following types of beads:

— *Bead Type 4*: Almost black, flattened sphere (Nos 13, 16, 19).

— *Bead Type 5*: Opaque off-white, flattened sphere (Nos 2, 4).

— *Bead Type 6*: Very dark blue, irregular (Nos 20, 21).

— *Bead Type 7*: Banded decoration, cylindrical (No. 15).

— *Bead Type 8*: Opaque off-white, annular (No. 18).

Group Two

— *Bead Type 9:* Amber coloured, generally spherical (Nos 22–30). Although yellow beads have been recorded at other sites, the translucent amber colour of these nine Group Two beads is harder to parallel. Hamilton noted several yellow beads of similar form, but smaller, from Iron Age contexts at Clickhimin Broch, Shetland (Hamilton 1968, 90). These are most commonly a more opaque and bright yellow in contrast to the amber of this group, but these do appear to be glass rather than amber. Of particular interest is the discovery that some of the beads, which have dense white patination, do in fact have linear decoration in the form of a clearer sinuous band, applied over the apparent patination. Thus in those cases (beads 22, 24, 26, 29 and possibly 23) the surface finish would have appeared different to the rest of the group, providing perhaps a single string of yellow and white beads. This does not, however, assist in the search for parallels.

Scientific analysis

Preliminary results of scientific analysis of some of these bead types by Professor Julian Henderson, of Nottingham University, using electron-probe microanalysis are at this stage of little help. Bead Types 4 and 5 have been examined so far, and it is intended to examine Bead Type 1 at some stage. Bead 4 (of Type 5), a pale opaque white, and Bead 13 (of Type 4) which is virtually black, both appear to have an unusual composition. The white one is composed of a potassium-rich mixture of wood ash, silica and lime, with the opaque colour being formed by the presence of arsenic. This is highly unusual at such a potentially early date, but the archaeological context is as secure as we can make it at this remove. The black bead, probably to be described as brown as there is apparently no such thing as black glass, is of different composition with high alumina, tita-nia and iron levels, which would be more consistent with an accidentally made glass associated with fuel-ash slag from iron production. Results of the analysis of the largest group of opaque blue glass beads (Type 1) are awaited.

Conclusion

The data available suggest that the Group One beads were probably found in the group of long cists, of Early Christian date, which were probably associated with a chapel beneath the extant 12th-century one, and conceivably related to the original context of the Pictish hoard, dated to the 8th to 9th centuries. A single bead of Type 9 was found in the Shetland Museum collection, having been recovered from Iron Age levels below the nave in 1959; it may by implication place Group Two in these levels below the nave.

These two groups of beads are clearly significant discoveries in this context, although a scarcity of contemporary parallels for this artefact type makes cultural identification somewhat problematic, although it seems probable that they are of different dates. In order to confirm a Pictish origin for the Group One beads (with the possible exception of Type 3, which may in fact be an antique inclusion), it will be necessary to compare the glass compositions of some of them with datable and culturally diagnostic material, such as the glass studs on the penannular brooches in the hoard, which include blue glass amongst others (Small *et al* 1973, 98). It is to be hoped that this work might be undertaken through the National Museums of Scotland, who hold the St Ninian's Isle hoard. It is, however, certain that these beads, which have eluded publication since their discovery over forty years ago, will provide more information under modern academic and scientific scrutiny.

Catalogue of the beads

Group One (21 beads)

— 1. Opaque blue, flattened sphere is pitted around central perforation. Winding lines slightly visible. Scratched on surface and perforation. Type 1. 13 x 12mm. Perforation dia 4–5mm.

— 2. Opaque off-white, flattened sphere lightly pitted around the central perforation. Surface damaged by pitting and small surface scratches. Winding line partially visible. Type 5. 10 x 9mm. Perforation dia 3mm.

— 3. Opaque blue, cylindrical tapering towards each end. Broken along one side revealing light grey core. Slight surface scratches. Winding lines visible. Type 1. 9 x 12mm. Perforation dia 4–5mm.

— 4. Opaque off-white, flattened sphere. Slightly eccentric perforation, chip at lower edge (Sampled 30.1.91). Type 5. 11 x 9mm. Perforation dia 4mm.

— 5. Opaque blue, flattened sphere. Slightly eccentric perforation. Winding lines visible, some scratching of smooth surface. Type 1. 14–15 x 13mm. Perforation dia 5mm.

— 6. Opaque grey/blue with damage at upper edge, grey core. Central perforation and slight pitting. Winding lines visible. Type 1. 12 x 11–12mm. Perforation dia 4mm.

— 7. Opaque blue, elongated sphere flattened at both ends. Slightly damaged and scratched. Winding lines visible and two particularly distinctive. Slightly eccentric perforation. Type 1. 11 x 13mm. Perforation dia 4mm.

— 8. Variable opaque blue, uneven flattened sphere. Damaged at the central perforation. Winding lines visible and perforation appears to be lined with lighter material. Type 1. 11 x 12mm. Perforation dia 5mm.

— 9. Opaque blue, barrel-shaped. Damaged around central perforation revealing lighter material as in No. 8. Type 1. 12 x 12mm. Perforation dia 4mm.

— 10. Darker opaque blue, barrel-shaped, damaged at perforation. Winding lines visible. Type 1. 11 x 12–13mm. Perforation dia 4mm.

— 11. Dark blue angular bead, unique in group. Facetted, slightly eccentric perforation. Slightly scratched. Type 2. 10–11 x 10mm. Perforation dia 3mm.

— 12. Opaque blue, barrel-shaped, damaged at both ends around slightly eccentric perforation revealing core. Winding lines clearly highlighted. Type 1. 11–12 x 12mm. Perforation dia 5mm.

— 13. Almost black, flattened sphere. Slightly eccentric perforation, pitted surface (sampled 30.1.91). Type 4. 10 x 12mm. Perforation dia 3–4mm.

— 14. Translucent amber-coloured, annular with slightly eccentric perforation. Scratched surface. Winding lines visible. Type 3. 12 x 4mm. Perforation dia 4mm.

— 15. Very dark blue core with applied smoothed vertical bands of grey/white decoration. Clear surface covering noted by Ewan Campbell. Tapering cylinder with central perforation and severe cracking of outer surface. Type 7. 7–8 x 8mm. Perforation dia 2mm.

— 16. Almost black, irregular sphere with central perforation. Slight scratching and patches of wear. Traces of winding lines. Type 4. 12 x 11mm. Perforation dia 3mm.

— 17. Bright opaque blue, barrel-shaped with flattened ends. Damage around the oval perforation, indicating grey core and substantial chip removed. Slight winding lines. Type 1. 12 x 13–14mm. Perforation dia 4mm.

— 18. Opaque off-white, annular with a slightly eccentric perforation. Slight scratching and winding lines. Type 8. 12 x 5mm. Perforation dia 4mm.

— 19. Almost black, flattened sphere with central perforation. Slight scratching around perforation and traces of winding lines. Type 4. 11–12 x 10mm. Perforation dia 2mm.

— 20. Very dark blue, cylindrical and tapering towards the slightly eccentric perforation, which is slightly scratched. Winding lines visible. Perforation obstructed. Type 6. 8 x 13mm. Perforation dia 2mm.

— 21. Very dark blue, irregular shape with ends flattened. Striations around beads body can be seen. Central perforation is blocked (as No. 20), and has small surface scratches. Type 6. 8 x 11mm. Perforation dia 2mm.

Group Two (9 beads)

— 22. Amber coloured glass, with mottled patina, spherical with ends slightly flattened. Slightly eccentric central perforation. Traces of sinuous linear bands over the patina. Slightly damaged surface. Type 9. 10 x 9mm. Perforation dia 3mm.

— 23. Amber coloured glass, as No. 22. Possible sinuous linear band decoration over patina. Type 9. 11 x 10mm. Perforation dia 3mm.

— 24. Amber coloured glass, as No. 22. Winding lines visible. Central perforation, slightly damaged. Possible sinous linear band decoration over dense white patina. Type 9. 10 x 11mm. Perforation dia 3mm.

— 25. Amber coloured glass, as No. 22. Cracked in two and slightly scratched. Patchy opalescent patina, also to be seen along fracture. One end slightly raised? Type 9. 10 x 9mm. Perforation dia 3mm.

— 26. Amber coloured glass, as No. 22. Possible winding lines. Chipping and scratches around the perforation. Traces of sinuous linear band decoration over patina. Type 9. 10–11 x 9mm. Perforation dia 3mm.

— 27. Amber coloured glass, as No. 22. Uneven end. Type 9. 11 x 9mm. Perforation dia 3–4mm.

— 28. Amber coloured glass, as No. 22. Eccentric perforation, flattened ends. Slight scratching. Type 9. 9 x 8–9mm. Perforation dia 3–4mm.

— 29. Amber coloured glass, slightly barrel-shaped. Flattened around the slightly eccentric perforation, slightly chipped. Traces of sinuous linear band decoration over patina. Type 9. 10 x 10mm. Perforation dia 2–3mm.

— 30. Small archive: A21.2000.21b. Amber coloured glass, as No. 22. Slightly eccentric perforation, flattened ends, complete and very slightly patinated. Type 9. 10 x 10mm. Perforation dia 4mm.

Worked bone and antler
Colleen E Batey

— A19.1998.3 (ARC. 2002.111). Lower part of a very fine bone pin shaft, point intact but head lacking. Slightly polished. L 38 x Dia 2mm.

— A21.2000.2b (Figure 3.20). Worked sheep/goat tibia. Expanded and fractured at one end and possibly trimmed at narrow end, possibly to take tang. Traces of having been turned at mid-point, possibly decorative or as raw material for making a bead? 93 x 20 x 13mm max.

Two further bone pin fragments have been noted from the material excavated by Barrowman (SF 539 of Phase II, and SF 399 from Phase III, Chapter 4). This example is particularly slender and although it is partially polished, it is not fully circular in section, exhibiting squared areas where it has been worked with the knife. It is akin to the type described by Hamilton in relation to the Clickhimin examples as a 'sliver point' (Hamilton 1968, 41), but more carefully finished. The lack of its full length and head in particular does not allow fuller comment, although it might be of more recent date than the other two examples in the assemblage. The ubiquitous nature of simple bone points has been commented on in relation to the material from Scalloway (Campbell and Smith 1998, 150), and it is clear that such items are not chronologically sensitive or indeed function specific.

The shock-absorbing qualities of bone make it ideal for handles, although the worked sheep/goat tibia was presumably broken in manufacture. There are bone beads from St Ninian's Isle, although made of much larger sections of bone. Excavations at Scalloway have also produced beads of worked bone of varying sizes (Sharman and Smith 1998).

Coarse ceramics

Ann MacSween

The assemblage from the 1955–59 excavations was deposited in the Shetland Museum following the death of Allan Small. It comprises around 850 sherds and most of the vessels are represented by one or two sherds. In cataloguing the assemblage, a range of attributes was recorded and the resulting data are presented as a spreadsheet catalogue (Appendix 3).

Almost all the sherds are small, undiagnostic body sherds. The majority are sooted on either one or both surfaces and are probably derived from cooking vessels (Figure 3.23).

Rim forms (Figure 3.24) include plain (eg A21.2000.92b), rolled (eg A19.1998.7), flat (eg A19.1998.11), everted (eg A21.2000.104a.1), inverted (eg A21.2000.4) and beaded (eg A21.2000.73.1). Several vessels were decorated (Figure 3.24): a deep groove below the lip of the vessel (eg A19.1998.16.4); an applied finger-impressed neckband below a flat rim (A19.1998.11); and incised chevrons, above the shoulder of one vessel (A19.1998.12), and above the base of another (A21.2000.124). Most of the bases represented are flat bases with straight or slightly angled sides, although there are a couple of examples of more finely made 'dished' bases (eg A21.2000.15a).

A range of clays was used (sandy, fine sandy, fine and steatitic, sometimes with rock fragments) and five fabric types were identified: (1) sandy clay; (2) fine sandy clay; (3) fine clay; (4) steatitic clay; (5) sandy steatitic clay (Figure 3.23). Usually the percentage of rock fragments was fairly low at around 10%, but occasionally a 20–30% addition was noted. The most common fabric types were sandy clays (Fabric 1) and fine sandy clays (Fabric 2). Where method of manufacture could be determined this was by hand building, using coil-construction, with 17% of the vessels finished by burnishing and the surface of 42% of the vessels with a wet hand smoothing.

Most of the vessels are of medium thickness (6–10mm) with very few more than 10mm thick. Some examples of vessels with wall thicknesses less than 6mm thick were noted, eg a plain rim 5mm thick (A21.2000.120a.4) and an everted rim (A21.2000.75.7) also 5mm thick. Walls of 5mm or less thick are very fine for handthrown pottery.

Discussion

As the assemblage was in effect unstratified, the main aims of the analysis were, firstly, to produce a catalogue and, secondly, to provide a comment on the chronological range represented in the assemblage.

As with the assemblage from Barrowman's excavations (see Chapter 4), a date in the later part of the Iron Age date or later, is most likely for most of the material represented. The discussion of that assemblage notes that there are none of the coarser fabrics of the Shetland earlier Iron Age as seen, for example at Jarlshof (Hamilton 1956, 46–47) and Clickhimin (Hamilton 1968, 121–123). The present assemblage, however, has some examples of everted rims, and of applied finger-impressed neckbands, which either indicates a date in the earlier Iron Age for some of the material, or the continued use of earlier decorative forms into the LIA. A very thick (23mm) but abraded, heavily steatite-tempered vessel (A19.1998.13) is completely different in character from the rest of the assemblage (Figure 3.25) and indicates pre-Iron Age settlement in the vicinity of the site. Parallels indicating a Late Bronze Age or Early Iron Age date for this pottery were found at Scalloway, Jarlshof, Kebister and Clickhimin (Sharples 1998, 132–133, 135 and refs therein) and also as stray finds held in the Shetland Museum from Sandwick and Norwick in Unst (ARC.2002.288; ARC.2002.291; Ian Tait pers comm), and Broch of Cuppister, Yell (ARC.1999.8), although it has yet to turn up in a secure, well-dated context.

Overall, the assemblage has more in common with the LIA assemblages of Upper Scalloway Phase 3 (MacSween 1998a, 135) and Kebister (Dalland and MacSween 1999, 187) than with earlier Iron Age, 'broch'-related assemblages. These LIA assemblages are characterised by: a general lack of decoration, although there is occasional incised decoration, usually in bands; a preference for untempered sandy fabrics or sandy fabrics with a low percentage of rock fragments; and the use of burnishing and polishing. The pottery with an incised groove under the rim may also date to the LIA – there are examples from Clickhimin (Hamilton 1968, fig 65, 47–50). Dished bases, similar to those noted in the St Ninian's Isle assemblage were also noted at Kebister (Dalland and

Context	Vessels	Smoothed	Burnished	Polished	Combed	Wiped
A19.1998	12	4	–	1	–	–
A21.2000	323	141	57	1	–	5
		42%	17%			

Context	Fabric 1	1+10%	1+20%	1+30%	2	2+10%	3	3+20%	4	4+20%	4+20%	4+30%
A19.1998	2	1	–	–	2	–	–	2(st)	–	4(st)	1(st)	1(st)
A21.2000	115	86	3	4	24	49	9	4	9	3	–	–

Fabrics 1: Sandy clay 2: Fine sandy clay 3: Fine clay 4: Steatitic clay

(A21 also has 2x2+30%; 1x2+40%; 2x10%st; 1x3+20%; 1x3+20%st; 1x10%st; 1xcoarse sand; 1xcoarse sand+10%st; 1x4+50%st)

FIGURE 3.23

Coarse pottery from the Shetland Museum (Small) collection

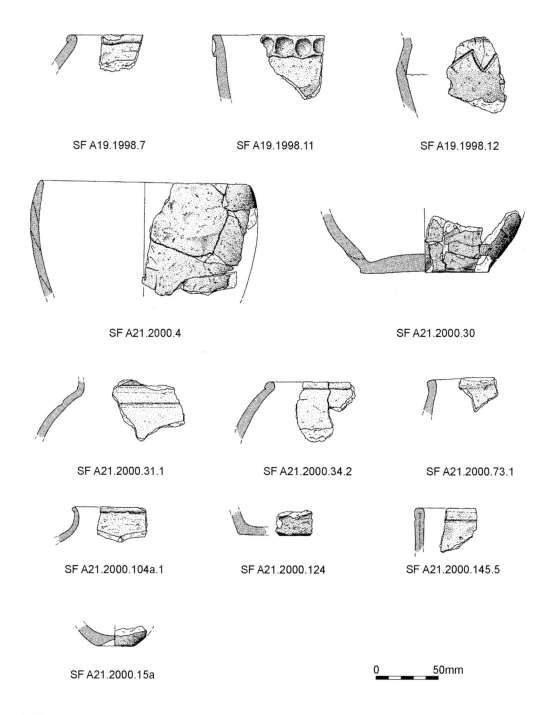

FIGURE 3.24

Coarse pottery from the Shetland Museum (Small) collection. Drawings: A Braby

MacSween 1999, illus 163.1 and 163.5) and Upper Scalloway (MacSween 1998a, 136, fig 84.1).

At Old Scatness settlement, preliminary analysis indicated that the latest of the pre-crofting styles, which included midden infill of a Pictish building, is fine thin-walled pottery with little temper and plain rims. It is possible that this type of pottery continued in use from the LIA/'Pictish' period through the Norse period and into the medieval period (MacSween 1998b, 87). It probably equates with that termed 'Late Wheelhouse' at Clickhimin (Hamilton 1968, 159, fig 71).

Catalogue of illustrated sherds (Figure 3.24)

— A19.1998.7. Rolled rim. Fabric 1, with c10% of rock fragments. Both surfaces are sooted. Th 8mm; Wt 12g.

— A19.1998.11. Flat rim with a finger-impressed band just below the lip of the vessel. The exterior surface is smoothed. Fabric 1. Both surfaces are sooted. Th 8mm; Wt 22g.

— A19.1998.12. Body sherd from the shoulder of a vessel. The exterior surface is smoothed and just above the shoulder is decorated with a band of incised chevron. Fabric 4, with c10% of steatite fragments. The exterior surface is sooted and there is a residue on the interior surface. Th 7mm; Wt 26g.

FIGURE 3.25

Coarse pottery sherd A19.1998.13, from the Shetland Museum (Small) collection. Photograph: M Elliot/Shetland Museum

— A21.2000.4. Plain rim from a vessel with a slightly inverted profile. The exterior surface is smoothed. Fabric 1, with *c*10% of rock fragments. The exterior surface is sooted and there is residue in the interior. Th 8mm; Dia 140mm; Wt 104g.

— A21.2000.15a. Five body sherds and a base with a concave underside. The exterior surface is burnished. Fabric 1, with *c*10% of rock fragments. The exterior surface is sooted. Th 9mm; Wt 36g.

— A21.2000.30. Flat base with angled sides (reconstructed). Fabric 1, with *c*10% of angular rock fragments. Both surfaces are sooted. Th 7mm; Dia 120mm; Wt 433g.

— A21.2000.31.1. Decorated body sherd with parallel incised grooves below the neck. The exterior surface is burnished. Fabric 1. The exterior surface is sooted. Th 6mm; Wt 27g.

— A21.2000.34.2. Rolled rim. The exterior surface is burnished. Fabric 1. Both surfaces are sooted. Th 9mm; Wt 24g.

— A21.2000.73.1. Beaded rim. The exterior surface is smoothed. Fabric 1. Both surfaces are sooted. Th 8mm; Wt 11g.

— A21.2000.104a.1. Everted rim. The exterior surface is burnished. Fabric 1. Sooted exterior surface. Th 5mm; Wt 12g.

— A21.2000.124. Sherd from a flat base with slightly angled sides. The exterior surface is smoothed and has incised chevron

decoration 12mm above the base. Fabric 1. Both surfaces are sooted. Th 8mm; Wt 10g.

— A21.2000.145.5. Rim with a shallow groove 9mm below the lip. Fabric 1, with *c*10% of rock fragments. Both surfaces are sooted. Th 7mm; Wt 8g.

Medieval and glazed ceramics
Robert Will

This small assemblage of 22 sherds, weighing 440g, is an interesting mixture of fabrics and dates (Figure 3.26). The largest group consists of fifteen body sherds probably from the same vessel and recovered from the same context (A21.2000.91e; Figure 3.27). The sherds are from a Yorkshire jug that would date from the mid-13th to mid-14th century. Several potteries were operating in the Yorkshire area in the period 1250–1350, the best known being the group of kilns from Scarborough. The potteries were producing a similar range of vessels most typically decorated jugs which an all over green glaze. These Yorkshire wares were being traded quite widely along the east coast of Britain and are often the largest group of imported wares recovered from medieval excavations in Scotland. The sherds from St Ninian's Isle have a green/brown glaze with vertical ribbing on the shoulder with impressed 'dot' decoration.

Two sherds from another decorated green glaze jug (A21.2000.91d) were also recovered. These are from a Low Countries Highly Decorated Ware jug. This red fabric is quite distinctive as there is often a thin layer of white slip between the main fabric and the surface green glaze (the underlying colour of the fabric does effect the final colour of the glaze). Low Countries Highly Decorated Wares were thought to have been made at Aardeburg in southern Holland, but it is now thought that they were being made at several sites in and around Brugge in the period 1250–1325 (Verhaeghe 1983). These wares have been recovered from several excavations on the east coast of Scotland, including Aberdeen (Murray 1982) and St Andrews (Will and Haggarty 1996). The two sherds from St Ninian's Isle have an impressed chevron design which may have been applied by rouletting or a stamp.

Three redware sherds were recovered, consisting

Context	Fabric	Rim	Base	Handle	Body sherds	Weight (g)	Description
Pottery							
A21.2000.91b	Local	–	–	1	–	24	Hand-made rod handle, coarse fabric
A21.2000.91e	Yorkshire	–	–	–	15	276	Highly decorated jug with ribbed decoration
A21.2000.91e	N European	–	–	1	–	36	Hollow rod handle, 16th/17th century
A21.2000.91d	LHDW	–	–	–	2	8	Green glaze with incised chevron decoration
A21.2000.116	N European	1	–	–	–	52	Large fragment pipkin with handle scar
A21.2000.125b	N European	–	–	1	–	44	Pipkin foot
Total		*1*	*0*	*3*	*17*	*440*	
Tile							
A21.2000.91a	Tile	–	–	–	1	64	Corner sherd, red/brown fabric

FIGURE 3.26

Medieval and post-medieval pottery from the Shetland Museum (Small) collection

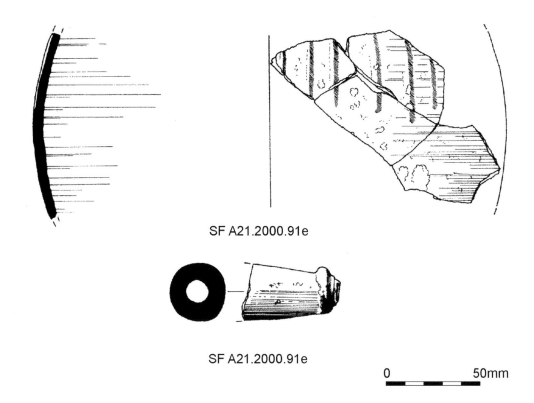

SF A21.2000.91e

SF A21.2000.91e

0 _____ 50mm

FIGURE 3.27
Medieval ceramics from the Shetland Museum (Small) collection. Drawings: A Braby

of a hollow tubular handle (A21.2000.91e; Figure 3.27), a tripod foot (A21.2000.125b) and a large rim sherd (A21.2000.116) with pronounced rilling marks. The rim and foot sherds are both glazed on their internal surface with a clear glaze, although the rim sherd is quite abraded. The rim sherd also has a handle scar on the external surface. These sherds belong to a group of fabrics known as North European earthenwares and are probably from the same vessel, a tripod cooking pot. These vessels tend to date from the post-medieval period (16th to 17th centuries) and one of the largest assemblage in Scotland was recovered from the excavations at Papa Stour on Shetland (Crawford and Ballin Smith 1999).

One handle sherd of probably locally made red-ware was also recovered (A21.2000.91b); in the absence of any earlier parallels from Shetland, it is thought to be medieval in date.

In addition to the pottery there was one corner fragment of a tile (A21.2000.91a), possibly a floor or wall tile rather than a roof tile in a smooth red/brown fabric. This probably dates to the post-medieval period.

Conclusions

Although this is a very small assemblage of pottery, it does highlight strong trading links with Britain and mainland Europe. The three different fabrics have been found on excavations along the east coast of Scotland, and Yorkshire wares and North European wares have been found in Shetland from the excavations at Papa Stour (Crawford and Ballin Smith 1999) and Scalloway Castle (Hall and Lindsay 1983). Intriguingly, these fabrics have also been recovered from excavations in Trondheim, Norway (Reed 1990), and it is likely that this trade could have been coming through Shetland.

3.5 ENVIRONMENTAL ASSEMBLAGE DEPOSITED BY ALAN SMALL IN THE SHETLAND MUSEUM

Hand-collected animal bones
Louisa J Gidney

A very small assemblage of animal bones was retained from the early investigations at St Ninian's Isle (Appendix 1). There is little information to correlate these finds with the more recent excavations.

Preservation was generally good but two of the cattle bones were in noticeably poor condition and several cattle teeth were reduced to fragments of enamel. This suggests either exposure to surface weathering or re-deposition. It can be seen from the table of species identified (Figure 3.28) that cattle bones were most commonly identified. This

Species present	Fragments	Accession no.
Cattle	17	A21.2000.8a, 10c, 12a, 13b, 15b, 43b, 49b, 56, 120b, 138a, 154b
Sheep/goat	4	A21.2000.2b, 8a, 43b, 92a
Pig	1	A21.2000.131
Cattle size	2	A21.2000.13b
Bird sp.	1	A21.2000.128b
Carnivore sp.	1	A21.2000.131
Seal?	1	A21.2000.151b
Whale	2	A21.2000.122a

FIGURE 3.28

Animal bone species identified from Shetland Museum (Small) collection

contrasts with the more recent finds (see Chapter 4), where sheep bones are as numerous, or more abundant, than those of cattle. Recovery of animal bones may not have been as rigorous as during the modern excavations. The cattle bones include examples from infant calves, as was also observed in the more recent collection. Sheep and pig are represented in this collection but there are too few bones for further comment. Bones of rabbit are, surprisingly, absent, given their ubiquity in the recent finds. Either bones from topsoil deposits were not retained from the earlier excavation, or the rabbit has become more common subsequently. Bird is represented by one fragment, not identifiable to species. One tooth is almost certainly from a seal and a further tooth is certainly from a carnivore, but not a domestic cat or dog. Seal, again, seems most probable. Whale is represented by two, or three, small fragments of cancellous bone.

Hand-collected fish bone
Rachel Gamble and James Barrett

A small number of un-phased bones from the 1950s excavations have been identified. They are listed here for identification purposes (Figure 3.29), but are not otherwise discussed as they are unprovenanced. For discussion of the species represented, see Gamble and Barrett in Chapter 4.

Botanical material
Jennifer Miller and Susan Ramsay

Seven small samples, termed Box A21.2000, were recovered and are described in Figure 3.30; they include 61, 69a, 70a, 74a, 101b and 106b relating to '2000 item 798', and 87b relating to '2000 item 797'. They are all either single finds or small collections of material. The samples were examined and identified but to date are without any definite context information, meaning that the information able to be drawn from them at this stage is limited. Nevertheless, some interpretation is possible.

Many of the finds were fragments of peat, from highly humified, richly organic sources, implying they had come from true peat bog sources rather than from minerogenic heathland turf. Some of the fragments were incompletely carbonised. Bog peat is not commonly used for construction in the same way that minerogenic heather turf can be, but is the fuel source of choice in areas where woodland resources are limited, such as on Shetland. Since most of the peat was burned, albeit some fragments incompletely, it is likely the material was collected for fuel. Peat fuel is particularly good for cereal parching and for banking a fire overnight, although on Shetland it is likely to have been utilised more indiscriminately. Unfortunately, it is not possible from these samples alone to determine what age of deposits they may have come from, since site records are scant and peat does not make a good radiocarbon dating medium.

Although carbonised peat fragments were the main discovery from this small collection, three samples were charcoal spot finds. All three finds (69a, 87b, 101b) were from coniferous charcoal, none of which were from species native to Scotland. Sample 69a in particular was interesting, in that it was a single, large fragment of fir (*Abies*) charcoal, from a tree more than 40 years old. The internal anatomy of the charcoal was identified with close reference to Schweingruber (1990) and was separated from closely similar taxa such as spruce (*Picea*) and larch (*Larix*) by the absence of any resin canals on the well-preserved fragment. Several species of fir are found in continental Europe, although only silver

Provenance	Species	Element	No.
A19.1998.5 (ARC 2002.111 inside bag)	Unidentified	Unidentified	62
A19.1998.5 (ARC 2002.111 inside bag)	Saithe	Abdominal vertebra	19
A19.1998.5 (ARC 2002.111 inside bag)	Saithe	Caudal vertebra	21
A19.1998.6 (ARC.2002.111 inside bag)	Unidentified	Unidentified	9
A21.2000.74c	Unidentified	Unidentified	2
A21.2000.74c	Gurnard	Dentary	1
A21.2000.90a	Unidentified	Unidentified	30
A21.2000.90a	Gurnard	Parasphenoid	1
A21.2000.90a	Gurnard	Opercular	1

FIGURE 3.29

Hand-collected fish bone from the Shetland Museum (Small) collection

No.	Taxon	Common name	No. (weight)	Description
A21.2000.61	Peat	Peat	4 (5.6g)	Incompletely carbonised. Very humified, black organic peat
A21.2000.69a	Abies	Fir	1 (3.2g)	Large fragment from major tree. > 40 year rings visible. Good preservation and no resin canals so not *Picea* (spruce)
A21.2000.70a	Peat	Peat	5 (12.1g)	Incompletely carbonised. Very humified, black organic peat
A21.2000.74a	Peat	Peat	2 (8.8g)	Very humified, black organic peat. Glassy appearance
A21.2000.106b	Peat	Peat	1 (2.95g)	Very humified, black organic peat
A21.2000.101b	*Picea/Abies/Larix*	Spruce/fir/larch	4 (1.0g)	No resin canals visible, but fragments small and cannot be identified further on basis of wood anatomy
A21.2000.87b	*Picea/Abies/Larix*	Spruce/fir/larch	20 (5.1g)	Fragments of various sizes. Preservation various, resin canals unseen but cannot be discounted. Cannot be identified further

FIGURE 3.30

Botanical material from the Shetland Museum (Small) collection

fir (*Abies alba*) is also recorded from Scandinavia. The fragment discovered in 69a is too large to be from coffin wood, but may have come from silver fir driftwood or harvested timber, originally from Scandinavia, utilised for whatever purpose. A further possibility is that it had been a traded or imported artefact.

Samples 87b and 101b were identifiable only as fir/spruce/larch, since they were either not sufficiently large or not well enough preserved to state with any confidence whether they had originally possessed resin canals. Suggestions for the original provenance of spruce and larch charcoal on this site are discussed below, and include driftwood from North America and Scandinavia, traded items and coffin wood. Some fragments from these samples could have come from coffin wood, but others are considered somewhat large to have been used in this manner, and are perhaps more likely to have come from driftwood or traded items.

Although it was not feasible to draw extensive conclusions from the carbonised remains from this limited collection, it is possible to indicate the burning of peat from bog-land resources, and to suggest the use of driftwood or harvested/traded timber from Scandinavia, whether for construction, fabrication of artefacts (including, but not necessarily, coffins) or fuel.

3.6 HUMAN REMAINS FROM THE 1955–1959 EXCAVATIONS

Articulated skeletons held in the Marischal Museum, Aberdeen
Julie Roberts

Preservation

The three skeletons, which were excavated from the site in 1959, are held in the Marischal Museum, Aberdeen, where they were analysed in 2003. They comprise two adults and one immature individual (Figure 3.31). Two of the skeletons, 'Hubert' (AB-DUA 14254) and 'Robert' (ABDUA 14270), were in a good state of preservation, and the condition of

the third, 'Rosemary' (ABDUA 14269), was fair, her bones being more eroded and fragmented. Unfortunately, all three individuals had been subjected to over-zealous reconstruction work. The pelvic girdle of 'Hubert' had been glued into articulation, 'Rosemary's' teeth had been glued into occlusion, and all the epiphyses of 'Robert' had been glued onto the ends of the bones. Overall, however, the state of preservation of the remains allowed a comprehensive osteological analysis to be undertaken.

Slides taken of 'Rosemary' whilst still *in situ* in the cist show that the burial was in an unusual position (Figure 3.17) lying prone, with both hips and knees tightly flexed. The head was twisted round to face left, and the feet were pointing left and covered by a stone. The left arm was entirely missing, although the left shoulder and the left hand bones and fingers were intact. There was no evidence of dismemberment to indicate that the arm had been removed at the time of burial, but it was not present in the excavation slides, nor was it found amongst the rest of the remains that were stored in the museum.

Sex

ABDUA 14270 ('Robert') could not be identified as male or female due to its immature status. Of the two adults, one was male ('Hubert', ABDUA 14254) and the other was female ('Rosemary', ABDUA 14269). In ABDUA 14254, the sex was unambiguous: all the sexually dimorphic features of the pelvis were male as were most of the cranial features, the two exceptions being the shape of the zygomatic bones and the temporal ridges. The sex of ABDUA 14269 was less clear-cut as there were many masculine traits of the cranium and a number of features on the pelvis that appeared to be more male than female. In addition, the post-cranial bones were large and robust, and much of the metric data relating to them fell within the male range. The overall shape of the pelvis was, however, female, particularly with regard to the sub-pubic angle and pelvic inlet shape. As the pelvis is accepted as being the most accurate indicator of sex, it was concluded that ABDUA 14269 was probably female.

Skeleton ref	Preservation	Elements present Cranial	Elements present Post-cranial	Age at death	Sex	Pathology
'Rosemary' ABDUA 14269	Fair. C. 70% complete. Mod surface erosion and fragmentation. Some reconstruction of cranium and long bones. Upper and lower teeth glued into occlusion.	R and L mandible, frontal, parietal, occipital, temporal, R sphenoid, L and R zygoma, maxilla, palatine, and nasal bones, ethmoid, hyoid, all dentition except L mandibular 8 (absent)	R and L scapula, L clavicle, R humerus, radius, and ulna, R and L ilium, ischium, pubis, femur, patella, tibia, fibula, 3 R ribs, L and R lunate, triquetrum, L pisiform, trapezium, L and R capitate and hamate, 1st, 2nd, 3rd, 4th and 5th metacarpals, 15 hand phalanges, R and L talus, calcaneus, cuboid, navicular, 1st, 2nd and 3rd cunei-forms, 1st, 2nd, 3rd, 4th and 5th meta-tarsals, 11 foot phalanges, 5 cervical, 12 thoracic, 5 lumbar and 5 sacral vertebrae	18–25 years	F	Mild porotic hyperostosis, healed periostitis
'Hubert' ABDUA 14254	Very good. 95% complete, minimal surface erosion. Pelvic girdle glued together	Fully intact cranium, all adult dentition except both maxillary incisors (lost PM) and R and L mandibular 7 and 8's, R and L maxillary central inci-sors, 6's and 5's and R maxillary 4 (lost AM)	Sternum and all R and L post cranial remains with exception of R patella, 7 cervical, 12 thoracic, 5 lumbar and 5 sacral vertebrae	35–50 years	M	Dental disease, compression fractures of T10, T11, L2, and L3 slight DJD, en-thesopathy right clavicle and right tibia
'Robert' ABDUA 14270	Good. 70% com-plete, moderate surface erosion. All epiphyses glued to ends of bones	R and L mandible, all mandibular adult den-tition exc. Unerupted 8's R maxillary 1, 2, 4, L maxillary 1, 2, 3, 4, 5	R and L scapula, clavicle, humerus, radius, ulna, ilium, ischium, pubis, femur, patella, tibia (proximal epiphyses only, scaphoid, lunate, trapezium, hamate, 1st, 2nd, 3rd, 4th and 5th metacarpals, right triquetrum, and capitate, 12 R and 12 L ribs, 7 cervical, 12 thoracic, 5 lumbar and 4 sacral vertebrae	11–14 years	M	Dental disease, DEH

FIGURE 3.31

Articulated skeletons from St Ninian's Isle held in the Marischal Museum, Aberdeen

Age at death

The dental development of ABDUA 14270 was consistent with that of a child aged 12 years ± 36 months. The epiphyses of the long bones and the pelvis indicated an age of less than 13–15 years, and the length of the long bones suggested an age of 11–12 years. Based on the above, an overall age range of 11–14 years was assigned.

ABDUA 14269 was aged 18–25 years at death. This age range was based on the state of fusion of the first and second sacral vertebrae, the epiphysis at the medial end of the clavicle, and the appearance of pubic symphysis.

Dental development and epiphyseal fusion was complete in ABDUA 14254. The pubic symphyses could be seen despite the glueing together of the pelvic girdle, and these were consistent with late stage IV/early stage V (Brooks and Suchey 1990). The sternal end of the right 4th rib indicated an age of 33–42 at death, but the tooth attrition was heavier than might be expected in an individual of this age. There were also some severe degenerative changes in the spine, although there was little evi-dence of degenerative joint disease elsewhere. On balance, it is safe to conclude that ABDUA 14254 was probably over 40 years of age at death.

Stature and body build

ABDUA 14269 measured 166.979 ± 3.72cm (5ft 4in) in height, and ABDUA 14254 had a living stature of 175.65 ± 3.27cm (5ft 8in). Both these heights are tall for pre-modern individuals (Brown and Roberts 2000) suggesting that they were suffi-ciently well nourished to fulfil their growth poten-tial. There was a possibility that ABDUA 14269 was contemporary with the infant skeletons recovered from the Barrowman excavations (see 4.5, below). If this had proved to be the case, her higher than average stature for a pre-medieval female is in di-rect contrast to those of the infants who were sickly and had, almost without exception, failed to thrive. The results of the radiocarbon dating programme modelling suggest, however, that the infants died at a later date than ABDUA 14269 (see Chapter 5).

In addition to being tall, ABDUA 14269 was also robust, with pronounced muscle attachment sites on her arms and her legs. There was also a discrep-ancy between the shape, and indeed the lengths of her right and left femur. The right femur was some 22mm shorter than the left, and was notice-ably broader in the region of the upper shaft and greater trochanter. There did not appear to be any evidence of traumatic injury, or congenital deform-ity associated with the differences in length or shape. It is possible that the difference in the shape of the proximal third of the right femur, were related to the mechanical stresses incurred as a result of that leg being shorter. The discrepancy in the lengths of the legs may simply have been a mild congenital defect.

ABDUA 14254 is likely to have had pronounced musculature of his lower limbs. In particular, on the right and left tibia the muscle attachment sites for *soleus*, the calf muscle used extensively in walking, were well developed.

	Element	Side	Sex	Age	Comments
A21.2000.10b	Femur	L		I	Small, proximal and distal ends broken PM
A21.2000.12b	?Mandible				3 highly eroded fragments
A21.2000.16b	5th Metacarpal	R			Unfused distal end, erosion damage distal end
A26.1998	Tibia	L	?M	A	2 pieces, broken PM, well developed popliteal line, pitting around proximal joint surface
unbagged	Femur	R	?M	A	2 pieces, broken PM, well developed linea aspea, pitting around P and D joint surfaces, noticeable Anterior, posterior bowing at proximal end, head diam 49.7mm, AP32.7mm, MD25.4mm, BC n/o
	Femur	L	?M	A	5 pieces broken PM, P and Mid only, well developed lesser trochanter and linea aspera, head diam n/o, AP32.8, ML24.1,
	Talus	R		A	Some PM erosion
	Illium	L		A	Fragment of L illium body
	Rib	L		A	Fragment of typical rib body
A26.1998 Bag no. 1	Cranium				Refitting pieces of cranium consisting of 12 parietal (L and R), 6 occipital including well developed external occipital protuberance, all show same pronounced thickening as Tex 859 elements (same skull?)
	Maxilla	R		A	1pm, 2pm, 3, 4, 5pm. Heavy calculus 3,4 lingual aspect, moderate wear, periodontal disease, external tori
	Maxilla	L		A	Same as above, 1pm, 2, 3pm, periodontal disease
	Maxilla	L		A	6pm, external tori, periodontal disease
	6u	R		A	Heavy wear, calculus lingual aspect
	6u	L		A	Heavy wear, calculus lingual aspect
	6u	R		A	Heavy wear, calculus lingual aspect
	3l	L		A	Calculus distal aspect
	5u	R		A	Heavy wear
	4u	L		A	Moderate wear
	Frontal			A	2 pieces, pronounced thickening of diploe
	Cranium				25 undiagnostic fragments
	Ethmoid				3 fragments
A26.1998	Rib	R			11th rib
Bag no. 2	Phalange				Hand, prox
	Phalange				Hand, mid
	Vertebrae				Thoracic spinous process
	Sacrum				Fragment of 1st sacral vertebra
	Clavicle	L		A	Medial end
	Sacrum				Sacral vert fragment
A26.1998	Longbone				23 undiagnostic fragments
Bag no. 3	Ulna	U			2 pieces midshaft
	Radius	U			Midshaft
	Radius	U			Midshaft
	Animal bone				1 piece
A26.1998	Cranium			I	14 pieces infant skull
Bag no. 4	Temporal	R		I	Petrous portion
	Temporal	L		I	Petrous portion
	Ishium	R		I	Fragment of acetabulum and body
	Vertebra			A	Fragment of spinous process
	Pars Lateralis	L		I	Fragment of occipital condyle
	Longbone			I	Fragment
	Rib			I	2 shaft fragments
	Rib	L		I	Fragment of 1st rib
	Vertebra			I	Body
	Sacrum			I	Body
	Vertebra			I	Neural arch fragment
	Illium			I	2 body fragments
	Rib			A	Body fragment
	Longbone			A	Undiagnostic fragment
A26.1998	Temporal	L	M	A	Mastoid Process 21.7mm, Zygomatic process, Petrous portion intact
Unmarked bag	Femur	L		A	2 pieces, 9 fragments, condyles only, fragmentary medial condyle
	Temporal	R	?M	A	Petrous portion and zygomatic process intact - Mastoid process pm break, poss same as l temporal
	Frontal		?M	A	Five refitting pieces of frontal (main body), thickened diploe, thickened appearance of skull, unfused frontal suture
	Sphenoid				L greater wing and body
	Occipital			A	R occipital condyle and foramen magnum border
	Occipital			A	L occipital condyle
	Zygomatic	L		A	L zygomatic
	Sphenoid				3 fragments of sphenoid body
	Incus	?L			

FIGURE 3.32

Disarticulated bone from the Shetland Museum (Small) collection

Health and disease

ABDUA 14270 showed no evidence of skeletal pathology.

ABDUA 14269 had slight periostitis of the right and left tibiae, but this was healed and the bone had almost completely remodelled. She had slight pitting of the right and left parietal bones and moderate pitting of the occipital, which was characteristic of mild *porotic hyperostosis*, indicating iron deficiency anaemia. In addition, there were small Schmorls Nodes on the 6th, 7th, 8th and 12th thoracic vertebrae.

ABDUA 14254 suffered from degenerative joint disease, particularly affecting the spine, and dental disease. Although there are many factors involved in the aetiology of degenerative joint disease, the primary causes are age and repeated stress to a joint (Roberts and Manchester 1997). The disease is characterised by porosity of the joint surfaces, caused by erosion of the cartilage between the bones and the formation of sub-chondral cysts, and osteophyte formation (extra bone production around the margins of the joints formed in an attempt to increase its surface area in response to extra stress). Eburnation, polishing of the joint surface, also occurs in more severe cases. 'Hubert' showed degenerative changes in all his vertebrae, although these were only slight in the cervical region, with the exception of C2 (characterisation after Sagar 1969). The most severe manifestations of the disease were seen in the mid to lower thoracic vertebrae, and the first three lumbar vertebrae. The changes were associated with large compression fractures in the 9th and 10th thoracic, and 2nd and 3rd lumbar vertebrae. As with SK 3 (see below), it is unlikely that the fractures themselves would have caused any neurological deficit, but the secondary arthritis (and the primary arthritis throughout the rest of the spine) would almost certainly have caused some pain and restricted mobility. ABDUA 14254 showed only slight degenerative changes elsewhere in his skeleton, in the right and left shoulder joints and at the right wrist and elbow.

The teeth of ABUDA 14254 were very heavily worn, indicating his advanced age as well as a relatively coarse diet. In addition to excessive tooth wear, he had also lost both his second and third mandibular molars, both his maxillary first molars and 2nd premolars and central inciors, and his right maxillary 1st premolar, before death. Ante-mortem tooth loss generally occurs as a result of periodontal disease, from which ABDUA 14254 suffered also. Periodontal disease is a term used to describe the inflammatory changes that can occur in the soft tissues and bone around a tooth in response to plaque.

As the disease progresses resorption of the alveolar bone of the maxilla and mandible may occur and if the periodontal ligament becomes affected then the result can be loss of one or more teeth. Poor oral hygiene is a primary cause. In addition to this, 'Hubert' had four dental abscesses (two medium and two large) and two carious lesions. Two of the dental abscess were associated with the carious teeth, the left mandibular and maxillary 2nd molars, and two were in the region of the right and left maxillary premolars. Caries is an infectious progressive disease that occurs when oral bacteria metabolise any fermentable carbohydrates present on a tooth. The tooth becomes de-mineralised and carious lesions form. Dental abscesses can ensue as toxic products are formed which diffuse out of the apex of the tooth and into the periodontal ligament. Localised resorption of the bone around the tooth root then occurs, which is eventually followed by the formation of a draining sinus (a hole through which pus escapes). All in all, this individual must have been in a considerable amount of pain and discomfort.

Discussion

Unlike the infant burials excavated from the site in 2000 (see below), juvenile skeleton ABDUA 14270 'Robert' showed no evidence of nutritional disease and he was the correct height for his age.

The burial position of ABDUA 14269 'Rosemary' was unusual, as was the fact that her left arm was missing, and a possible explanation for this is hard to find.

Disarticulated human bone deposited by Alan Small in the Shetland Museum
Paul Duffy

This material contained a minimum of one adult male individual, and one juvenile (Figure 3.32), finds A21.2000.10b, 12b, 16b, and a large box of disarticulated bones A26.1998, identified as possibly relating to a burial 'Elizabeth' excavated in 1959 (see above). Pathology was noted on the adult remains in the form of a pronounced thickening of the diploe of the frontal, parietal and occipital bones of the cranium, potentially indicative of iron deficiency anaemia. Periodontal disease was noted on the maxilla, as was external bony outgrowths known as tori. Heavy calculus and significant wear was also noted on the maxillary and mandibular teeth and moderate to heavy wear were noted on all teeth.

3.7 RADIOCARBON DATING OF THE MARISCHAL MUSEUM COLLECTION OF HUMAN SKELETAL MATERIAL
Patrick Ashmore, Rachel Barrowman and Gordon Cook

Methodology

Three radiocarbon determinations by the Scottish Universities Environmental Research Centre, East Kilbride were made on human skeletons held in the Aberdeen University Marischal Museum that

Laboratory no.	Sample reference	Sample description	Radiocarbon Age (BP)	δ13C (‰)	δ15N (‰)	Calibrated date range (95% confidence)
SUERC-5440	'Hubert' ABDUA 14254	Femur	1245±35	−18.8	11.1	cal AD 680–890
SUERC-5441	'Robert' ABDUA 14270	Femur	1125±35	−19.4	10.0	cal AD 780–1000
SUERC-5442	'Rosemary' ABDUA 14269	Femur	1305±35	−20.0	10.0	cal AD 660–780

FIGURE 3.33

Radiocarbon ages, calibrated age ranges and stable isotope values for the three skeletons from the 1959 excavation

originated from O'Dell's excavations in 1959. Collagen samples were prepared in East Kilbride using the method outlined in Longin (1971). The collagen was combusted in sealed quartz tubes using copper oxide as the oxidant, and the CO_2 converted to graphite by the method of Slota *et al* (1987) and measured by the University of Arizona AMS Facility. Both laboratories maintain continual programmes of quality assurance procedures, in addition to participation in international inter-comparisons (Scott *et al* 1998). These tests indicate no laboratory offsets and demonstrate the validity of the precision quoted. ^{13}C analyses were carried out using a VG Isotech Sira 10 mass spectrometer. ^{15}N analyses were carried out using a Finnigan Tracer MAT mass spectrometer coupled to a Carlo Erba NA 1500 N/C/S Analyser.

The ^{14}C measurements were then undertaken using the SUERC AMS facility. The results are given in Figure 3.33.

Archaeological background

The three skeletons were given the names 'Rosemary', 'Robert' and 'Hubert' during the 1959 excavations, but when moved from Aberdeen University Anatomy Department to the Marischal Museum in 1973, they were given the accession numbers ABDUA 14269, 14270 and 14254 respectively. 'Hubert' (ABDUA 14254) and 'Robert' (ABDUA 14270) are described in the archives as extended burials in long cists outside the SE corner of the church (see above), and 'Rosemary' (ABDUA 14269) as an unusually positioned, crouched burial in the largest short cist on the site.

In 2003 the three skeletons were studied by Julie Roberts in the Marischal Museum (see above). O'Dell records also that whilst 'Rosemary' was located below the wind-blown sand, 'Hubert' and 'Robert' were from the long cist burials set into the sand at the SE corner of the chapel. However, the results of the study of the 1950s archive suggest that there were two phases of long cist in this corner: one earlier group below, or at the bottom of, the wind-blown sand, and one later, higher up in the sand. There is a slide showing 'Hubert' *in situ* on the site but unfortunately there is less evidence for 'Robert's original location, and there are conflicting descriptions of the burial as either being cut into the

sand in a wooden coffin, or as being from one of the earliest long cists on the site.

An age range of 11–14 years at death has been assigned to juvenile 'Robert' whose sex could not be determined, 'Rosemary' is a robustly built adult female, aged 18–25 years at death, and 'Hubert' is an adult male, with an age at death of over 40.

Results

The ^{14}C results (Figure 3.33) appear to confirm an early medieval date for ABDUA 14254 and 14270, the long cist burials 'Hubert' and 'Robert'. The results of the stable isotope analyses are in the main consistent with a largely terrestrial diet, although 'Hubert' (ABDUA 14254) has $\delta^{15}N$ and $\delta^{13}C$ values that would tend to indicate a larger marine component. This is discussed in more detail in Chapter 4. The results are consistent with the archaeological evidence that there are two phases of long cist burial and that 'Rosemary' (ABDUA 14269) is not Bronze Age, but is the earliest of the three dated burials. The dating of these burials in relation to further burials dated from the 2000 excavations is discussed below in Chapter 4, Figure 4.73.

3.8 SUMMARY AND ANALYSIS OF THE EXCAVATED FEATURES

Investigation and analysis of the available archive material and published accounts has made possible a relative sequence of archaeological features (Figure 3.34), which is summarized below. This sequence can then be combined with the results of the recent re-evaluation excavations on the site (see Chapter 4). The results of both campaigns of work are pulled together and discussed in Chapter 5.

The medieval chapel, burials and 'Founder's Tomb'

Neither the most recent survey of the chapel in 1999, nor the subsequent archive study, produced any evidence to refute the earlier suggestion that the medieval chapel was originally what is now the nave: a rectangular chapel, with a central west doorway, to which an internally rounded chancel was added (Thomas 1973, 12). Similar church plans

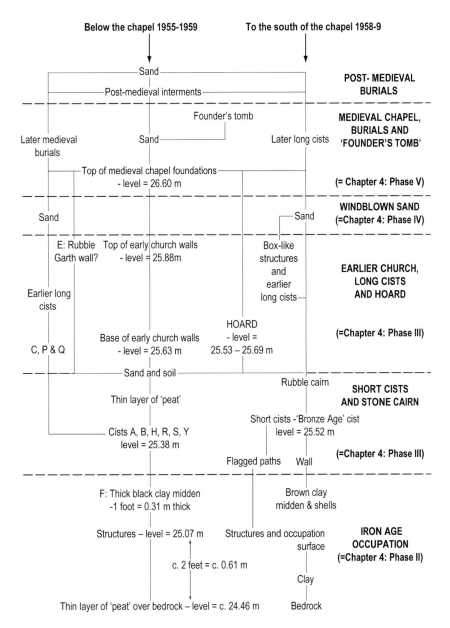

FIGURE 3.34

Reconstructed excavation sequence for the 1955–59 excavations

with a curved chancel, or apse as it was labelled at the time, were unsuccessfully sought in Scotland and Norway by O'Dell at the time of the excavation, and it was Ralegh Radford who suggested a late 12th-century date and drew attention to the plan of the chapel on the Brough of Birsay, Orkney (cited by Thomas in 1973, 13; letter in Shetland Archives, D1/359/1/12/27). The outer walls of the east end of the chancel on St Ninian's Isle however are not curved but of irregular shape, suggested by O'Dell to be buttressing. Thomas splits the dating further ascribing a 12th-century date to the earliest phase of the medieval chapel, with a date sometime after 1200 for the addition of the chancel. Thomas' sequence is possibly corroborated by the position of two long cists (P and Q), containing white quartz pebbles and a medieval pot sherd, and excavated

from the south side of the chancel. The cists extended under the timber shoring (and therefore the chancel wall), and may therefore have been associated with the first phase of the medieval chapel. The mention of white quartz pebbles, and the depth of the cists, may suggest however that at least one of them belongs to an earlier phase of church building.

Few of the original features of the medieval chapel, other than the altar in the chancel, were found surviving. O'Dell notes lime plaster on the inner and outer faces of the walls, in addition to lime and burnt shell mortar between the stonework. He describes a side altar in the SE corner of the nave, and suggests that there may have been another side altar in the same position on the north side, although there is no evidence of this. He also suggests there was a chancel arch between the nave and the chancel, and notes and sketches in the archive support this, with Nisbet in particular describing a mass of rubble, mortar and marble at the north side of the east end of the nave. This may also support O'Dell's suggestion that the curved chancel/apse was vaulted. O'Dell refers to the remains of a medieval floor of schist fragments surviving *in situ* behind the altar, with a thick bulge of slumped mortar at the base of the south wall (see above). A blocked window on the south side of the nave is also recorded, but there no evidence for a roof. A possible cresset lamp (Stone 22; Thomas 1973, 38, pl XI) and a large slab with an inscribed cross (Stone 18; Thomas 1973, 31, 38, pl XII) found over a burial in the nave, may date to when the chapel was in use; Thomas dates the slab with mortar adhering to it to the 12th century or later, and so it is possible that it may originally have been incorporated into the wall of the chapel building and then re-used to mark the position of a burial into the medieval chapel floor.

A small polished fragment of porphyry (Stone 21, Thomas 1973, 38) was found in the rubble on the north side of the nave in 1957 (O'Dell 1957; O'Dell and Cain 1960, 5), and Thomas suggests that 'imported fragments of this kind were circulating in the Middle Ages', although it is equally possible that the fragment may have originated as a later post-medieval votive offering, as seen in the Limoges enamel fragments and coin recovered by O'Dell's team from the altar in the medieval chapel in 1956. Fragments of porphyry have been found in earlier contexts elsewhere however, and it is still possible that the St Ninian's Isle fragment belongs to the phase of earlier church building on the site (Owen 1999).

The 'Founder's Tomb', despite its name, was a secondary feature and was probably associated with the medieval chapel rather than the earlier church below it. It is described as a 'curious little unroofed structure' (Thomas 1973, 12) and lay just south of the east end of the chapel. It contained extended burials both above and below a burial 'with knees bent up to the chin', which was subsequently considered to be a disarticulated, translated burial. It became known as the 'Founder's Grave', or 'Founder's Tomb', due to the recovery of the early Christian shrine posts from the pit within the structure. Thomas suggests that the shrine posts were re-located here from their original position, possibly within the presumed earlier church, when the chancel was added in the 12th century or later. From his own research into the 1950s excavations he concluded that the shrine posts were not originally housed in the 'Founder's Tomb', writing that 'Nor can the 'Founder's Tomb' at St Ninian's Isle be used to support the idea of an external position, since this is no more than a muddled, and probably very late, repositioning of corner-posts from two distinct shrines.' He suggests instead that the shrines would have stood within the earlier church on the site, probably against a wall (Thomas 1973, 20; 1998, 87–88). Ni-

sbet records that the bones originated in a different burial environment than that in which they were found, suggesting that they were moved into this secondary structure, with the shrine posts.

In total nine shrine stones were found, identified by Thomas (1973, 20–26, 33–35, pls III–VII) as belonging to one double shrine 'A' (Stones 1–7 and 20; including 3 corner-posts, 2 median posts and 2 panel and lid fragments; Thomas 1973, fig 10), and a second, also possibly double, shrine 'B' (Stones 8–9; Thomas 1973, fig 11). Thomas concluded that single shrines belong to the early or middle 8th century, whilst double shrines, such as the St Ninian's Isle example, date to the middle or later 8th century. He suggested that 'If the art be predominantly Pictish, the shrines are an innovation from Pictish Christianity under Northumbrian influence, and on this last ground none may actually be earlier than circa 725 or so' (Thomas 1973, 20).[17]

There is very little material in the archives relating to the medieval burials on the site, mainly because these were removed rapidly and without record. Four long cists were excavated from outside the SE corner of the chapel in 1959, and Thomas describes them as 'the first Christian interments' (Thomas 1973, 12). Small describes how they are separated from the earlier short cists by a clear stratigraphical break (the thick layer of wind-blown sand) (Small 1973, 7). However, there was some confusion over what appear to have been two different groups of cists. In her diary, Nisbet records the stains of a wooden coffin and nails in the sand associated with one of these graves that were 'dug into clean sand with no trace of a turf line', but there were evidently long cist burials earlier (i.e. lower down in the sand) than these four cists. O'Dell describes in a letter (see above) that 'about 2 feet below the long cist graves, cut into the sand', he found 'a Christian burial with a rather small, but charming, cross' (see O'Dell 1960, 4; and Thomas 1973, 36, Stone 11, fig 8, pl VIII). Small's plan (Figure 1.2) also shows uprights of further long cists outside, and therefore *below*, the sand left unexcavated outside the SE corner of the chapel. His plan is confirmed by Nisbet's slides of the 1959 excavation (PLATE 8) and subsequent consolidation (PLATE 7), which show the end of a cist (three upright stones at a right angle) poking out from below the sand at the west edge of the sandy bank (labelled '321' on Figure 1.2). In addition to this, her slides of the excavations in progress (Figures 3.9 and 3.18) show 'Hubert', a long cist burial, deep down in a hole in the sand, below the level of cist and foot stones set into the sand nearby.

These pieces of evidence all combine to confirm O'Dell's reference to there being two groups of long cist burials here: an earlier group at the south end of, and below, the sandy bank, and a later group with coffin stains and nails, higher up in the sand at the north end. It is the former group that are the earliest Christian interments described by Small, and probably contemporary with the early church building, the latter group may belong to the first phase of the medieval chapel above (the simple nave without the chancel). The radiocarbon dating programme has shed some light on this. The results for 'Hubert' (ABDUA 14254), found deep down in the sand, confirm an early medieval date (680–890 cal AD), the dating for 'Robert' (ABDUA 14270), is (780–1000 cal AD), less conclusive, as there is no other archive material to locate from where he was excavated other than the description as a 'long cist burial' which is recorded as having been accompanied by a wooden coffin. Modelling of the radiocarbon dates was carried out in tandem with the dates from burials excavated from the site in 2000 to test the hypothesis that 'Robert' was interred only shortly after 'Hubert', and hence into the same phase of long cists and this is reported in Chapter 4.

A hint at activity at this time on the site is also given by the carved stone assemblage from the site, studied by Thomas. Three broken slab grave-markers of steatite with incised crosses (Stones 12–14 and 16; Thomas 1973, 36–37, pl IX–X) and a hogbacked grave cover (Stone 17; Thomas 1973, 37, pl XI), which were all found in the upper, sandy layer on the site in 1956, are dated by Thomas to the Norse period (10th to 11th centuries), and the hogback stone to the late 11th or 12th centuries (Thomas 1973, 30). It is possible that these grave markers are contemporary with the first phase of the medieval chapel and the four narrow long cists that were excavated in the upper part of the wind-blown sand.

The earlier church building, long cists and hoard

By 1959 the south and west sides, possibly half of the east side, and a small portion of the north side, of an earlier building below the chapel had been uncovered. This building lay directly below the medieval chapel, and only the lower courses of the walls survived, the stone from the earlier building presumably having been used to build the chapel above. The walls were dry-stone and of roughly the same alignment and internal measurements as the nave of the chapel above. According to O'Dell (1960, 5), they were also plastered on the inner face. No trace of a floor was found. Sketches show a wall across the east end of the nave, 4ft (1.22m) below the medieval foundations, and this might be the east wall of the earlier building. O'Dell also notes rubble 'E' at the east end across the nave, below the medieval chapel but above sand (Figure 3.34), although it is not clear whether this belongs to the east wall of the earlier church, or has fallen from the later chapel. There is no definitive evidence for the nature of the earlier building, but given the circumstantial evidence – namely its situation directly below the medieval chapel and on the same alignment, the presence on the site of an early phase of long cists below the sand

(i.e. earlier than the medieval period), and the existence of the shrine posts (only circumstantial evidence as there is as yet no archaeological evidence for their original location) – it seems most likely that this earlier building functioned as a small church.[18]

A 'Garth wall', recorded as situated north of, and parallel to, the chapel and traced for 30ft (9.14m) (i.e. the length of the chapel nave) before turning south at an angle *under* the medieval wall, was built onto sand and is therefore situated stratigraphically above the Iron Age levels, but below the medieval chapel and may well therefore belong to the same phase as the earlier probable church building.

Three long cists, C, P and Q, may be associated with this earlier church. Cist C, found within the nave and described as an inhumation under a large stone, was situated in sand 12in (0.31m) above the thick black layer F and earlier cist H, and was probably a long cist covered by a stone lintel. Cists P and Q on the south side of the chancel, are discussed above, and they possibly belong to the group of earlier long cists and a cross-marked stone (Stone 11; Thomas 1973, 36) marked 'B' on Thomas' plan (Figure 1.3) uncovered to the south of the chancel wall, below the sandy bank. Long cists and 'Christian burials' were also found in X1-4, a pit dug down around 10m SE of the chapel, on the sandy slope to the east of the site, which suggests that the long cist cemetery associated with the first small church building, and later chapel above it, was considerably larger than is indicated by the three or four remaining long cists recorded on the published plans of the site (Figures 1.2 and 1.3).

Sculptured stones that may have been associated with the earlier church building and long cists include a broken cross-incised sandstone slab (Stone 10; Thomas 1973, 36, fig 8, pl VIII) found face downwards in the SW part of the nave of the medieval chapel in 1959, but which Thomas dates to the 8th century or a little earlier (Thomas 1973, 28), the composite shrines discussed above, and the ogham-inscribed stone found in the 19th century (Stone 19; Thomas 1973, 38; Chapter 2, above), and possibly the small fragment of porphyry (Stone 21; Thomas 1973, 38) found during O'Dell's excavations in the nave pit in the church, although this may be a later introduction to the site. The Group One glass beads, reported by Batey above and cautiously dated by her to the 8th/9th centuries, may also have originated from long cists at the SE corner of the church, but cannot in themselves be used to date or confirm an earlier church building. This may also be said of the hoard, which was described by O'Dell as having been found in the floor of the earlier church, but O'Dell (1960, 5) describes that: 'No definitive traces of floor could be seen but at the horizon of this, as given by the lower edge of plastering on the wall, the hoard was found on the fourth of July 1958'. The archive confirms that the hoard was found between the Iron Age levels and the medieval chapel foundations however. The slide showing the treasure as it was found, correctly reproduced adds further clues. It is fortunate that it is a colour slide and therefore shows clearly fragments of wood around the upturned bowls, and the green copper staining that O'Dell describes, as well as the broken cross-incised slab that covered the treasure. But just as importantly, soil can be seen at the level of the hoard, differentiated from the sand above it at the sides of the excavation pit and this confirms the hoard's position below sand and therefore the medieval foundations, but above the Iron Age structural levels (Figure 3.34). Analysis of the levels on the site has shown that the hoard was found at a depth of between 10cm below to 6cm above, the base of the early walling, and it is therefore feasible that it was buried into the floor of the earlier church, although the stratigraphic relationship is far from clear. O'Dell himself records that no definitive traces of the floor could be seen at the time, and the position of the hoard is therefore recorded only in relation to the base of the wall of the earlier church building. This does not therefore confirm that the hoard was deposited whilst the earlier church building was in use, and this may have implications for the dating of its deposition (discussed further in Chapter 5).

The short cists and stone cairn

Several cists were found below the chapel cut into the midden layer F, and post-dating the Iron Age structures below it. Eight cists are specifically mentioned in the archives, but three of these (C, P and Q) were probably long cists. Of the remaining five, Cists A and B contained possible cremation urns and burnt bone: Cist A contained a cremation and well-rounded quartz pebbles set into a clay floor, and was set deeply into the disused Iron Age structures below. Cist H comprised upright stones at right angles to each other and was immediately adjacent to Cist A, at the junction of the nave and chancel, and set into the thick black clay layer F below it. Cist R is also mentioned, but with no other details as to its form, contents or depth, other than its find spot in the nave, near to a pit D (near cists A and H). Cist S was probably a short cist, possibly with a paved floor, containing pottery and white stones, on the north side of the nave interior. Cist T also contained pottery.

A further eight cists are mentioned outwith the chapel, and consist of a range of types and probably therefore dates. To the north of the apse, outside the chapel wall, two burials were excavated, incorporated in the description of Cist Y. They lay 5ft (1.52m) below the medieval chapel, at the base of the cist zone (Figure 3.34). A small skull and a large skull were excavated, but a few rib bones were also uncovered and the presence of the small skull suggests that there was more to the burial. Two small capstones were found over the small skull, and a larger

single block over the larger skull, suggesting the use of stone 'head boxes'. O'Dell describes these burials as pre-Christian due to the depth at which they were found.

In addition to this, when the area to the south of the chapel was excavated in 1959, a group of 'Iron Age graves' (centred on a crouched burial of 'Bronze Age type' in a large short stone cist), was uncovered: all situated over a midden and a considerable number of white quartz pebbles. Three cists, other than the crouched burial, are described: one contained charred human bones, with another lying to the south of this cist being filled with shells. To the west of this, a further small cist of similar construction was in a ruinous state but contained human bone. The area to the east of the wall was not completely excavated, but a number of box-like structures, formed by stones set on edge and suggestive of further burials, was noted, set into the edge of a rubble cairn (see below). Thomas also suggests the possibility that one of the short cists contained the bones of a mother and child (Thomas 1973, 12). In the SE corner of the area a 'double' cist is shown on the final plan (Figure 1.2), one compartment of which contains a skull and long bones. These may be identified as 'Elizabeth', a burial recorded as being 'from an earlier burial with the thigh bones touching the skull'. The same description is given for the translated burial in the Founder's Tomb, but this cannot be 'Elizabeth' as the Tomb was excavated in 1957 and Elizabeth in 1959.

The dominant burial outwith the chapel was, however, the large cist containing a crouched burial of 'Bronze Age type'. Roberts' study of the slide of the burial ('Rosemary') shown *in situ* (Figure 3.17) has shown that it was lying prone with both legs tightly flexed at the hips and knees, and the head twisted round to face left. She also concludes that the burial is female, aged 18–25, and tall and robust in stature. According to the published final plan (Figure 1.2) this large cist burial was set into a wall that extended beyond the limits of the excavated area at its north and south ends, and O'Dell's accounts describe how all the short cist burials were set into midden. The latter observation accords well with the stratigraphic sequence observed adjacent below the chapel, where the cists are set into a thick black midden layer, above the remains of Iron Age structures, except that the midden layer recorded to the south of the church was not black, but brown clay. The nature of the 'wall' into which this burial was set was however clearly different when first uncovered (Figure 3.9 and PLATE 8) from how it is described in these accounts. During the excavations Nisbet described it as a cairn-like structure, and marked it as a 'boat structure' on her plan (Figure 3.5). It is also mentioned on contemporary finds labels as a 'cairn'. Nisbet described how, once the stones of this cairn were removed, a complex system of stone cists and boxes was revealed, one of which had an associated cross-incised stone. O'Dell, on the other hand, does not mention either the N–S wall or the cairn in either his *DES* 1959 account or the O'Dell and Cain (1960) volume. This throws a different light on the 'wall' and its relationship to the large cist (i.e. that the cist was 'set into' the wall).

The radiocarbon dating results from 'Rosemary' (ABDUA 14269) confirm that this was the earliest of the three burials excavated from the site in 1959 and now held in the Marischal Museum, but is not Bronze Age. Instead the radiocarbon date (660–780 cal AD) places the burial in the Late Iron Age (Pictish) period. This has implications for the associated cairn and other cist burials ranged around this large central cist, and these are discussed further in Chapter 5.

A pit dug down the slope SE from the chapel is described as containing crouched cist burials, as well as long-cist burials and extended burials, all cut into a two-foot thick black clay layer. These cists are shown together in a notebook as being at a greater depth below the ground surface than the burials within and immediately to the south of the chapel, yet they are still shown as being above sand, which may suggest that sand accumulated against this east facing slope earlier than the rest of the site further inland.

Iron Age occupation

Below the chapel, a thick black clay midden layer F, containing broken pot and burnt and rotted bone, was excavated from below rubble at the east side of the nave. The layer may have extended to the west side of the nave, where a 'clay humus layer with fragments of pot and bone' was excavated in a deep hole up to 8ft 6in (2.59m) below the cornerstone (ground level) of the nave. Stratigraphically this midden layer was situated between the earlier church building and the Iron Age structures below it.

A thick black layer is also recorded in pit excavated on the side of the sandy cliff to the SE of the chapel, where cist burials are shown within a black layer up to 2ft (0.61m) thick. The black layer excavated in this pit was at a greater depth than layer F below the church and, unlike layer F, had sand below it. As suggested above, it is possible that the layer sequence here on the east side of the sandy slope reflects a situation in which the sand built up first at the seaward edges of the site during the Iron Age.

Small refers to 'several periods of re-building in the pre-Christian phases' below the nave (1973, 5) and notes O'Dell's suggestion of four phases of occupation there. As discussed above this is probably taken from O'Dell's mention of four layers of pottery encountered when trowelling within the nave, rather than from four distinct structural phases. Thomas describes a hut complex with pots and a hearth (Thomas 1973, 11, 13, fig 8), and there are

sparse references within the archives of Iron Age 'domestic' remains below the cists under the nave. These include references to a stone platform or a stone pavement and ashes, set in the clay subsoil below rubble and sand in the east end of the nave, with finds of pottery, possibly a stone whorl or bead, discussed by Batey above, and whale and fish bone. The structural remains were situated below the black occupation layer F, into which the cists were set, and evidently pre-dated the use of the site for burial. The black layer is testament to the presence of other Iron Age buildings (as dated by the artefactual content of the layer) out with the excavation area, and may be evidence of a subsequent settlement shift after the buildings below the chapel went out of use.

In the area to the south of the chapel the picture is a little more confused. The published plan shows an E–W divide. On the east side of the area are the group of cist burials (which were once covered by a large rubble cairn, although this is not shown on the plan, which shows instead a wall). On the west side, the floors of two structures, or huts, were uncovered, joined by a paved pathway, from below a tumble of large stones. The amount of stone and rubble removed from across the whole area before the plan was drawn (eg see Figure 3.9) makes it possible that features may have gone unrecorded, and indeed the complexity of the features being excavated may not have been appreciated. Small suggests that above the floors of two huts there was a later pathway (shown in the SW corner of the trench, Figure 1.2; Small 1973, 6), which was separated from them by a clear stratigraphical break.

Ultimately, O'Dell's intention to link the structural remains to the south of the chapel, with those found below it, was thwarted when excavations ceased after the 1959 season. Notes and sketches in the archive suggest that both areas of structures, those below, and those to the south of, the chapel, were set onto clay subsoil, and were overlaid by midden deposits, into which cists were then laid, but in the area south of the chapel there appear to be two phases of occupation. Small's description of one of the pathways south of the chapel as being *above* the Iron Age structures suggests that within this group of features excavated on the west side of the area there were at least two phases of use, with the uppermost being situated above the huts and occupation layer, and therefore possibly contemporary with the use of the site for burial, rather than settlement. This was further investigated during the 2000 excavations (see Chapter 4).

The artefactual assemblage

The boxes of miscellaneous finds from the Shetland Museum Small archive (A19.1998, A21.2000) and the two tins of glass beads found in a filing cabinet can be added to the finds that are already reported from the site; namely the famous hoard, the ogham-inscribed stone (Chapter 2), the carved stone assemblage and bone and antler necklace and pottery published in the 1973 volume (Thomas 1973; Wilson 1973; Small 1973, figs 3, 4, 6), and an iron padlock and fragments of Limoges enamel held in the Shetland Museum (ARC 2002.111; A19.1998).

Research into the Small collection of finds deposited into the Shetland Museum in 1998 and 2000 has provided an original location for 16 out of the 20 bags containing non-pottery finds. Many of the non-pottery finds can be located to Iron Age levels deep below the chapel, including a stone weight (A19.1998.2) described by Batey above as ubiquitous in nature, and pumice. Batey identifies the group of weights and whorls as having parallels on other Iron Age to Viking period sites, such as Scalloway, Clickhimmin, Jarlshof and Kebister in Shetland, and Buckquoy in Orkney. Of these, stone bead/whorl A19.1998.8b was found in Iron Age levels below the chapel, but a flattened, decorated spindle whorl, with similarities to the Pictish example from Buckquoy (although with no ogham inscription) remains unlocated. The pebble gaming pieces are all from Iron Age levels, as are two examples of bone identified by Batey, as similar to other Late Iron Age examples. A small, finely made, steatite food vessel reported above, does not sit so comfortably in a Late Iron Age context, and Batey discusses parallels in a miniature vessel from Jarlshof, dated to the 10th century.

The largest group of non-ceramic finds recovered comprises the collection of glass beads discussed by Batey. Although the archive references to the archaeological context of the beads are confusing, she is concludes that the Group One beads were probably excavated from the long cists to the SE of the chapel and that they conceivably belong to the late 8th to early 9th centuries. There are also conflicting accounts as to where the Group Two beads were found, but a label with a single bead confirms that it was recovered from the Iron Age levels and so may imply an earlier date for this group. Other non-ceramic finds include the Limoges cross fragments described by Murray, which were found pushed into the stones of the altar inside the medieval chapel. They were probably placed there as a votive offering after the chapel had gone out of use in the 16th century, as the pieces were already fragmentary and worn when deposited.

The coarse ceramics identified by MacSween as predominantly later Iron Age are found scattered through most of the features and pits. Almost all the sherds are small, undiagnostic body sherds, but she identifies examples of rolled, everted, inverted and beaded rims, as well as several decorated vessels, and notes that the majority of sherds are sooted on one or both surfaces, so probably deriving from cooking vessels. MacSween prefers a later Iron Age date for most of the material, although some everted rims and applied finger-impressed neck-

bands may belong to the earlier Iron Age. One sherd is highlighted as an exception to this: a very thick, heavily steatite-tempered, sherd completely different from the rest of the assemblage and indicative of a Later Bronze Age or Early Iron Age date.

The medieval and post-medieval glazed ceramics discussed by Will reflect trading contacts with mainland Britain and Europe: the remains of a 1250–1350 Yorkshire jug and a Low Countries Highly Decorated Ware jug, dating from 1250–1325. He also identifies sherds of 16th- to 17th-century North European earthenware, found elsewhere in Shetland. None of the bags of finds of medieval and post-medieval glazed ceramics contain a label so nothing can be said as to their location on the site. Little is known of the late medieval/post-medieval layers on the site, which were all removed without record, however it is possible that this pottery may have derived from trial pits that were dug all over the general area of the site in 1955–56, and a study of the history of the Isle shows that it was inhabited at this time, eg the depiction of a house or settlement to the SW of the chapel on Pont's (1608) map.

The environmental assemblage

There is a very small assemblage of ecofactual material in the archives. Gidney reports on the very small and fragmentary assemblage of animal and bird bones that were found scattered throughout the site, almost all of which were bagged with pottery. The animal bones included cattle, sheep and pig, but were recovered in such small numbers as to preclude any further comment. Bird, seal and whale are also represented. In addition, Gamble and Barrett were able to identify a very small number of saithe or gurnard amongst the tiny fish-bone assemblage. Seven small finds of botanical material have been identified by Miller and Ramsay as mainly peat, together with three examples of coniferous charcoal. They conclude that the presence of this charcoal suggests 'the use of driftwood or harvested/traded timber from Scandinavia, whether for construction, fabrication of artefacts (including, but not necessarily, coffins) or fuel'.

The human skeletal material

The assemblage of human remains comprises two groups of material. The disarticulated human bone reported on by Duffy contained a minimum of one adult male individual and one juvenile; the three skeletons now held in the Marischal Museum in Aberdeen were analysed by Roberts. 'Rosemary' was female, aged 18–25 years at death and 5ft 4in tall. 'Hubert' was male, aged over 40 at death and 5ft 8in tall. Both heights are tall for pre-modern individuals. 'Robert' was juvenile, aged 11–14 years at death, and is considered to be of correct height for that age. Samples were taken from these individuals for radiocarbon dating, which when calibrated, suggest that 'Hubert' could be described as 'Dark Age' as O'Dell suggested (680–890 cal AD), although together with 'Robert' which was dated to 780–1000 cal AD, both long cist burials could equally date to the time of the Norse incursions into Shetland. The prone and semi-crouched burial, 'Rosemary', excavated from the large cist, was confirmed at the earliest of the three, but does not date to the Bronze Age, dating to between the late 7th and late 8th centuries AD (660–780 cal AD).

Fortunately, the results of the further excavation of a large part of the area to the south of the chapel in 2000 have enabled more research to be carried out into some of the features discussed above, and this is reported in the next chapter.

Notes

1 *PDR*: D1/359/7/1–7, D1/359/8/2 and D1/359/1/11/24 in the Shetland Archives.

2 Although the articles are not dated, circumstantial evidence locates them to 1958 (see [9] below).

3 I am indebted to Dr James Coull and Mr Tommy Watt who first drew my attention to this collection.

4 Dr J Barrett came across this assemblage whilst searching in the stores for other material and kindly alerted me to its existence. Dr Tickell (formerly of the Nature Conservancy Council, Shetland) and Ms V Turner (Shetland Amenity Trust) provided further information on the circumstances of the recovery of the material, and Professor D Brothwell and Dr L Humphrey (Natural History Museum) kindly gave me information on the contents of the assemblage, on which Professor Brothwell has undertaken a small amount of work.

5 I am grateful to Professor Thomas, who kindly made all of his archive available for study.

6 Mr Brian Smith, the Shetland archivist, and Mrs Elma Johnson, a resident of Bigton, kindly assisted with suggestions regarding Shetlanders with local knowledge of the work.

7 The chancel is variously described as a 'chancel' or an 'apse' in the archives. See discussion below.

8 This description of the finding of the treasure is found in the *PDR*, version D/1/359.1/11/24, in the Shetland Archives.

9 The typescripts of *PDR* D1/359/7/2–D1/359/7/5 are all identical, but D1/359/7/2 only is annotated by hand as 'Dec' and pre-dates the identification of the wood fragments of the box holding the treasure as larch because it describes 'fragments of rotted wood'. D1/359/7/1 however describes the same, but 'wood' is crossed out and 'larch' is annotated by hand above, suggesting that the annotation has occurred after

Nov/Dec 1958, when the wood was identified as larch by Metcalfe at Kew (discussed in detail by Graham-Campbell 2003a, 25–26). I am grateful to James Graham-Campbell who drew my attention to the significance of the timing of the identification of the larch wood. D1/359/7/6 and D1/359/7/7 do not mention the wood fragments at all but the contents suggest they were written for a Shetland audience shortly after the treasure was found, and presumably date to the summer of 1958 when O'Dell was in Shetland.

10 ARC 74200, donated by the University of Aberdeen in 1974.

11 See also Graham-Campbell 2003a, 16–18.

12 Confirmed by Helen Nisbet pers comm, as another cist that had been disturbed by later burials.

13 Another sketch section of a pit in *SN*, excavated down the slope to the SE of the chapel (see below), is described as 'Section below X1' and shows a 2½ft (0.76m) thick black clay layer with many shells below 8ft (2.44m) of sand (up to the ground level) beneath a wall and X1. It is possible that the black clay layer is the continuance of Layer F, from below the (later) chapel eastwards down the slope. However, the section shows wind-blown sand shown below the black layer, whereas F was found the sand, and so they may not be the same layer.

14 The hogback, now held in the Shetland Museum and published in the 1973 volume, cannot be the cover for this '?stone coffin' as the measurements are significantly different, the hogback measuring 3ft 11in (1.19m) long overall, and 11in (0.28m) wide across its centre, 5½in (140mm) wide at the ends (Thomas 1973, 37, pl XI). However, the 'knocking stone' or '?stone coffin' *was* found adjacent to the lozenge-shaped stone.

15 The stones described in *SN* either side of one of the skulls, and over the other skull, were probably 'head boxes', upright stones set either side of the skull, and found throughout Scotland and elsewhere in Britain, on Late Iron Age to late medieval sites, including now St Ninian's Isle itself; see Chapter 4 and discussion in Chapter 5.

16 See also spindle whorl A19.1998.10 (below) for a further possible steatite artefact.

17 Stevenson subsequently suggested a date later in the 9th century (Stevenson 1981, 287–288), although Thomas has since re-iterated his late 8th century dates for composite shrines from Shetland, with 'a limited but undatable diffusion to Iona; and more such shrines during the 9th century' (1998, 95), and suggesting that Shrine B could comprise two separate shrines (Thomas 1983, 285; 1998, 96; see Chapter 5).

18 The plastering recorded on the earlier walling also lends weight to it being of an earlier church, and indeed was cited by O'Dell as evidence of such. However, there is also some confusion as to the presence of plastering, which is first recorded as being on the inside and outside of the medieval chapel walls by O'Dell in 1958, and then as being on the inner face of the earlier chapel wall in 1959.

EXCAVATIONS TO THE SOUTH OF THE CHAPEL
IN 1999 AND 2000

4.1 INTRODUCTION AND METHODOLOGY

As part of the initial assessment in August 1999 excavations within the small area of Trial Trench 1, south of the chapel (PLATE 5), demonstrated that the archaeology uncovered in 1959 was largely *in situ* and intact (Harry 2000, 38–41), but was in the process of being damaged or at threat of being damaged by rabbit burrowing. The need for a larger excavation (Trench 1) was identified, with the emphasis being on the assessment of the previous, 1950s, excavations.

On the published plans of the 1959 excavation area to the south of the chapel (Figures 1.2 and 1.3) the trench covers 13 x 9m (Small *et al* 1973; 6, 11 and figs 5 and 8). Small trial pits had been opened in 1958, but in 1959 up to 6m of sand was dug away by hand from the entire area to reveal 'an extensive complex of prehistoric walls, pavements and graves; all … extending beyond the limits of the excavated area'. When the area was re-investigated in Trench 1 in July 2000, a smaller trench was opened, 9 x 5m, due to more rigorous health and safety regulations than in the past (mainly relating to the proximity of excavations to sections cut through wind-blown sand).

The aim of the new excavation was to fully record and excavate the archaeological deposits below turf, topsoil and backfill to such a point as to characterise the site and establish a stratigraphical sequence for the extant features, particularly those already excavated or uncovered in 1959. Environmental samples were taken from all undisturbed contexts for environmental flotation using a SIRAF tank set up at Bigton Farm. The treatment of human remains on the site was guided by the *Historic Scotland Operational Policy Paper 5: The Treatment of Human Remains in Archaeology*, and standard archaeological procedures were followed whereby all human remains that were fully exposed within the trench were excavated, but those that could not be entirely excavated were partially uncovered, and analysed in the ground.

The majority of the features that had been uncovered in 1959 were re-investigated in 2000, although due to the smaller size of the later trench, areas of paving and possible structures at the west side of the 1959 excavation area, and a group of small cists shown on the east side of the trench, were not exposed (Figure 1.2). Many of the features (mainly cists) examined in 2000 had been fully excavated in 1959 and their fills removed. In some cases, the features themselves had been partially rebuilt prior to backfilling at the end of the 1959 excavation. During the post-excavation analysis the letters 'a' and 'b' were added to some context numbers to allow differentiation between original (a) and reconstructed or re-excavated features (b).

The site sequence below identifies the broad phases of activity evidenced at the site, from the earliest to the latest. It builds on the interim account published prior to the completion of the post-excavation analysis and archive study (Barrowman 2003). At the end of each phase the relevant finds and environmental data are summarised, with a figure providing an overview of the material, and the full specialist reports follow at the end of the chapter. This roughly follows the mode of presentation used for other, more extensive, sites where previous excavations have been re-assessed (eg see Harry and Morris 1997; Barrowman *et al* 2007). There are also appendices of some of the more pertinent listings of data (Appendices 4–9). A full archive of all original records, illustrations, specialist reports and archive listings is deposited in the NMRS.

4.2 SITE SEQUENCE

Phase I: Bedrock

A large hollow was found in the centre of the trench, which had been cut through the site during the 1959 excavations in an attempt to find the bedrock and to verify that the pre-Christian horizons all lay on clay soil formed from the underlying grey schist (350). This pit was emptied in 2000 (Figure 4.20, Phase VI), and revealed clay to a depth of 1m above the schist bedrock at the bottom of the pit.

Phase II: Remains of Iron Age occupation and midden deposits (Figure 4.1)

The earliest feature uncovered in the trench in 2000 was the footings of an ephemeral wall (301), comprising an inner and outer face of large stones with a core of clay and small stones (320), aligned N–S cross the centre of the trench. The wall was adjacent to a pit that had been dug in 1959, where it seems that the

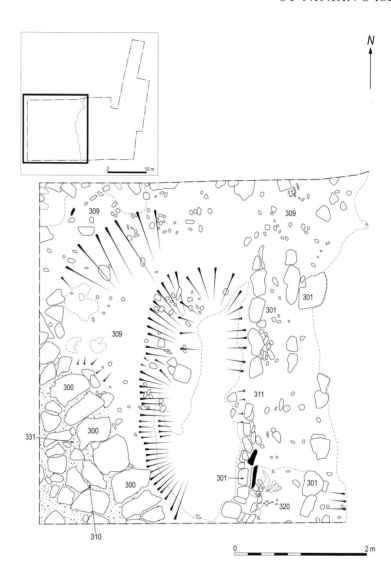

N

FIGURE 4.1

Phase II: Remains of Iron Age occupation and midden deposits. Drawing: Lorraine McEwan and Gillian McSwan

excavators followed the edges of the wall when digging down to find bedrock. The wall footings were covered by a layer of compact dark yellowish-brown silty sandy clay (309/311) which contained frequent inclusions of patches of red and orange ash, flecks of charcoal, shells, quartz pebbles and burnt stones, and finds of pottery and bone. This deposit is the midden layer that was uncovered by O'Dell in 1959 and is described by him in published accounts (O'Dell 1959c, 35; 1960, 4). In 2000 the top of this thick layer was cleaned, and then the upper 100–200mm excavated. Finds of occasional human bone indicated that the use of the site for burial in later phases had disturbed the surface of the layer, as had the trampling and digging in 1959. Furthermore, post-1959 rabbit burrowing was evident in the NW corner of the trench, where the resulting sandy patches and shallow 'runs' of the burrows could be seen. The artefactual assemblage recovered included over 80 sherds of pottery, pieces of charcoal, burnt bone, animal bone, slag, seven flakes of quartz, five possible worked stones, three pieces of steatite, a lump of whalebone and half a gaming counter (Figure 4.2).

In the SW corner of the trench, an area of flat

sandstone paving stones was excavated. The stones had been laid on a level deposit of cobbles, pebbles and gravel (310), which in turn had been set onto a mixed reddish brown and grey clay (331) on the surface of the midden. This small area of stones was part of a paved pathway joining the floors of two structures that were first uncovered in 1959 and are shown on the west side of the final plan published in 1973 (Figure 1.2; described by Small 1973, 5). The small area of paving stones (300) that were totally excavated in 2000 included a broken, well-used saddle quern (SF 376) and two further, possibly worked, stones (SF 377 and 378). Two of the paving stones were also found to have been marked with red paint by the 1959 excavators, denoting that they had been removed and then re-placed at the end of the excavation (J Coull pers comm). The clay layer below (331) contained 160 undecorated sherds and 29 fragments of pottery (SF 390; Figure 4.33), some conjoining, and fragments of bone (SF 464).

These paving stones are rather a mystery. No relationship between them and the features on the east side of the trench could be determined as all layers above and to the east were removed in 1959 (this

Context	Description	Worked stone and steatite	Quartz lithics	Coarse pottery	Worked bone	Cinder and industrial waste	Carbonised plant	Disarticulated human bone	Animal bone	Fish bone	Marine shell	Land snails
300	Paving	Broken saddle quern	–	–	–	–	–	–	–	–	–	–
301	Remnant wall	Stone pounder	–	–	–	–	–	–	–	–	–	–
309	Midden (same as 311)	Slate disc, gaming piece, stone pounder, stone pot lid	4 quartz flakes, quartz core and blade	80 body sherds, 1 rim	Whalbone spike or stake and chopping block, whittled cattle long bone shaft frag	4 burnt soil/cinder, 4 slag	23 heather family, 1 birch, 1 apple type, 16 spruce/larch, 1cf larch, 9 six-row barley, 11 cf six-row barley, 1 dock, 2 chickweed	1 juvenile rib body, 1 adult lateral cuneiform, mandible, rib, 5th metatarsal, proximal hand phalange	9 frags indet burnt bone, 16 cow, 22 sheep/goat, 9 pig, 5 small and 2 large ungulate, 4 indet frags, 1 bird sp, whale frag, 1 cat, 1 auk sp	7 saithe, 19 turbot family, 1 unident	83 periwinkle, 8 limpet, 2 oyster	Cochlicopa lubricella C. lubrica Aegopinella pura A. nitidula Discus rotundatus
310	Cobbles and gravel below paving	–	–	1 body and 1 rim sherd	–	–	9 heather family, 4 spruce/larch, 1 hulled six-row barley, 4 six-row barley	–	1 sheep/goat, 2 indet, 1 bird sp	1 cod, 1 ling, 9 unident	97 periwinkle, 24 limpet,	Cochlicopa lubricella C. lubrica
311	Midden (same as 309)	2 lumps and 1 broken weight of steatite	1 quartz flake	26 body sherds	–	3 cinder, 1 slag	1cf spruce, 1 oak, 1 conifer, 4 heather family, 1 peat fragment, 1 spruce/larch, 5 hulled six-row barley, 6 six-row barley, 2 cf six-row barley, 2 indet cereal	1 adult rib body, metacarpal heads, coxygeal vertebrae, skull fragment, lower 1st incisor	1 indet frag burnt bone, 16 sheep/goat, 2 thrush sp, 3 pig, 5 indet frags, 4 cow, 2 small, ungulate, 1 gull sp, 1 gannet, 1 bird sp, 1 small mammal	1 Atlantic mackerel, 2 cod, 17 cod family, 13 cod/saithe/pollack, 30 saithe, 5 saithe/pollack, 82 unident	1854 periwinkle, 159 limpet, 45 dog whelk, 12 common cockle, 10 spiny cockle, 5 Arctica islandica	Cochlicopa lubricella C. lubrica
320	Fill between stones of 301	–	–	–	–	1 cinder	–	–	3 cow	–	1 periwinkle	–
331	Dump of pot sherds and ash	–	–	160+ rim, base and body sherds	–	–	1 six-row barley	–	1 cattle	–	–	–

FIGURE 4.2

Material identified from Phase II: small finds, general finds and samples

area is shown blank on the final published plan; Figure 1.2). Slides in the archive show that the paving (including 300) was excavated from below wind-blown sand, and the 2000 excavation confirmed that (300) and the bedding surfaces 310 and 331 below it, were set on top of the clayey midden layer 309/311, which contained an artefactual assemblage datable to the Late Iron Age (see below). This suggests that the paving (300) at least, if not the whole of the stone features excavated from the west side of the trench in 1959, post-date the Iron Age occupation on the site. And that although this paving and the other features were considered by the excavators to be the remains of Iron Age hut floors and paths, there must have been at least two phases of structures. Small does describe a later kerbed and flagged pathway that lay in the SW corner of the trench, above the other features and separated from them by a 'clear stratigraphical break' (Small 1973, 6; Figure 1.2), although he does not expand on what is meant by a clear stratigraphical break.

Given that such a small area of the paving and hut floors was re-examined in 2000, and that typologically it fits with the structure elements in the trench, paving 300 is included in Phase II (remains of Iron Age occupation) for the purposes of this analysis. Clearly the features on the west side of the trench uncovered in 1959 however were more complicated than is indicated in the 1973 volume. There is in fact the distinct possibility that the areas of paving, if not structures, that were uncovered on the west side of the trench post-dated the abandoned Iron Age structures and accumulated midden layers elsewhere on the site, and were actually associated with the later use of the site for burial (Phase III) rather than domestic occupation. This possibility has been highlighted elsewhere (Barrowman forthcoming) and is discussed further in Chapter 5.

Artefactual and ecofactual summary for middens (Figure 4.2)

The worked finds and ecofactual material from this phase almost all derive from the midden 309/311 and indicate a range of domestic activities. Finds include a whalebone chopping block (SF 514; Figure 4.31), a whalebone stake or spike (SF 348; Figure 4.31), a whittled bone peg, a stone pot lid (SF 370; Figure 4.24), two stone pounders and a broken saddle quern. Three pieces of steatite – two unworked pieces and one identified by Batey (4.3.2) as a broken perforated weight, probably used in fishing (SF 372; Figure 4.24), were also found. Donnelly identifies below eight finds of worked quartz, including five flakes, one of which showed signs of utilisation (SF 333), another signs of retouch (SF 316), and a blade. One polished broken gaming piece (SF 392) was recovered (Figure 4.24) and is identical to another example (SF 573) found in the disturbed upper layers of the site. The counters are directly com-

parable to examples that have been found elsewhere on Iron Age sites (see Batey below). More than 260 sherds of coarse pottery were recovered from this phase (Figure 4.32), including 160+ from one vessel, SF390 found in 331, and are identified by Mac-Sween as representing 89 vessels of general later Iron Age or later date.

Carbonised plant remains and spot finds (small finds) of charcoal were recovered from midden layer 309/311 and paving bedding layers 310 and 331. Species identified by Miller and Ramsay below include: apple type, birch, oak, Scot's pine and both spruce and larch (identified separately, rather than as non-specific spruce/larch type charcoal). Contexts 309, 310 and 311 contained heather family and spruce/larch charcoal and carbonised six-row barley grains, context 331 contained only one example of six-row barley. Of the small assemblage of animal bone from this phase, the majority is identified by Gidney as cattle and sheep, with sheep being marginally more numerous than cattle, although there are examples of pig and cat, and bird species, including thrush. Marine animals appear not to have been exploited for food, an observation which is borne out by the small fish bone assemblage. The worked objects of whalebone may imply that this species was seen more as a raw material for craft work. In contrast, although maritime birds were taken (Auk sp. and Gannet sp.), no domestic birds appear to have been kept. Gidney suggests that infant lamb bones and sea bird bones may suggest a seasonal component within the midden, deriving from spring lambing time and the breeding sea-bird colonies. The fish bone assemblage recovered is small, despite good bone preservation at the site and flotation of environmental samples. However, the sample from midden layer 311 has markedly more fish bone in it than either of the other two layers. The bones recovered from this phase indicate mainly shore-based fishing, with Gamble and Barrett identifying cod, saithe, pollack and ling, with single examples of Atlantic mackerel and turbot family. In addition, Cerón-Carrasco identifies small quantities of marine shellfish from all layers, again apart from 311, which contained large numbers of periwinkle and limpet, together with smaller numbers of whelk and common and spiny cockle, oyster and *Artica islandica*. Land snails recovered from this phase included those associated with dry habitats of limestone grassland and calcareous sand dunes (*Cochlicopa lubricella* and *Cochlicopa lubrica*), and the common *Discus rotundatus*.

Burials and dating summary

This phase can be given a Late Iron Age date from the coarse pottery, and radiocarbon dating of Phase III burials excavated from above midden 309/311 (see below). The earliest of these dated burials, 'Rosemary' (ABDUA 14269), a short cist inhumation excavated from the site in 1959 (see Chapter

3) that has been dated to 660–780 cal AD at 95.4%, and SK 7, a juvenile burial cut into the midden and excavated in 2000 (see Phase III, below), dated to 670–890 cal AD at 95.4%, give a *terminus ante quem* for Phase II of the late 7th to mid 8th centuries AD at the latest, allowing for the midden to accumulate, although this date can be refined. The Phase II midden layer itself was not dated. Although finds of charcoal and animal bone were recovered from 309/311 and 331, they were not acceptable for dating as they were in a secondary context.

The only finds of steatite from the excavations originate from this phase, and it should not surprise us that Shetland's natural steatite sources may have been utilised in the Late Iron Age on this site, although the broken steatite fishing weight is described by Batey, below, as having similarities to a 'hogback' fishing weight that would conventionally be dated somewhat later. The small assemblage of stray human bone recovered from Phase II, rather than indicating burial in this phase, comprises small bones and fragments, such as rib fragments, metatarsal and metacarpal bones, that were missed or overlooked by the excavators in 1959 when excavating the many later burials from the sand covering the site. Indeed the likelihood of such a bias affecting the numbers of smaller bones found scattered across the site in general is studied by Duffy below.

Phase III: Late Iron Age to Late Norse burials and related features (Figure 4.3)

The short cists, wall base, rubble cairn and paving (Figure 4.4)

O'Dell's excavations in 1959 uncovered at least four short cists grouped in the centre of the area south of the chapel (Figure 1.2), although further cists are indicated in the SE corner by lines of upright stones and a skull and long bones. In addition to this two small possible cremation cists were found in the north side of the trench in 2000, in an area shown as blank on the 1959 plan. The four cists in the centre of the area were found still *in situ* below the turf and topsoil when Trench 1 was opened in 2000, and were numbered 302–305. Small (1973, 7) had described cist 303 as containing 'only charred human bones', cist 304 as 'filled with shells' and cist 302 as 'in a somewhat ruinous state but contained human bones'. The fourth cist, 305, shown on the plan as set into a wall in the centre of the 1959 trench, contained an unaccompanied, N–S aligned, crouched inhumation ('Rosemary', ABDUA 14269); this was analysed and radiocarbon dated with other elements of the 1959 excavation assemblage (see Chapter 3).

The excavations in 2000 were able to establish some stratigraphical relationships between the cists and showed them to have been entirely emptied and partially reconstructed following the 1959 excavation. Cist 302 on the west side of the group was aligned with its longer axis N–S. It comprised three upright slabs of sandstone on the west, east and south sides, each measuring 0.45–0.65m long, and 0.13–0.31m deep. A large veined lump of quartz formed the north end, and the corners were filled with small packing stones. Overall an area 0.4m E–W and 0.5m N–S was enclosed by the cist stones. The east stone of the cist formed the west side of adjacent cist 304. Occasional bone and shell inclusions were recovered from the topsoil within the cist, but they cannot be attributed to its fill. The construction of the cist stones suggests that cist 302 was built onto, and therefore after, cist 304, although the possibility that it was completely reconstructed after the 1959 excavations cannot be ruled out.

Cist 304 adjacent was also aligned N–S, and comprised three vertical upright slabs of sandstone, 0.62–0.65m long and up to 0.31m deep, on its north, south and west sides (the latter being shared with cist 302). The east side of this cist abutted a feature shown as a wall aligned N–S across the site on the published plans (Figures 1.2 and 1.3), and its north side lay adjacent to cist 303. The north and south side slabs of this cist were overlain by the top course of stones of the wall feature, although investigation in 2000 showed that some degree of reconstruction of the wall had taken place in 1959 and it is very likely that this was not the original position of the stones when they were first uncovered. The internal dimensions of cist 304 were 1.02m N–S and 0.65m E–W and it had been backfilled in 1959 with the hundreds of periwinkle shells, occasional oyster and limpet shells and the bone fragments that had originally filled it (Figures 3.9 and 4.4, the former showing 304 under excavation, with a pile of shells adjacent mixed with topsoil).

Cist 303 was of a different shape and alignment to the other short cists, being narrower and longer and aligned E–W. It was formed from three narrow vertical uprights, set immediately adjacent to and abutting 304 to the south. To the north was an area of paving (313; see below), with cists 303 and 304 both built into or against it. Gaps at the corners of the cist were filled by small stones and white quartz pebbles. Prior to the excavation of wall feature 307 the cist side slabs enclosed an area 0.85m E–W and 0.2–0.35m N–S. Removal of the upper courses of the wall demonstrated however that the cist extended further to the east below the reconstructed upper course of the wall.

In 2000 it was found that cist 303 had been filled with topsoil and 1959 excavation backfill (consisting mainly of excavated midden layer 325, see below). Below this no specific basal layer was found, other than sandy soil, and there was no sign of the charred human bones attributed to this cist by Small (1973, 7). Only a few centimetres below the 1959 backfill, however, long bones, pelvis and a skull were uncovered from a burial (SK 5) situated within cist 303 (Figure 4.5). Cist 303 was dismantled to enable the

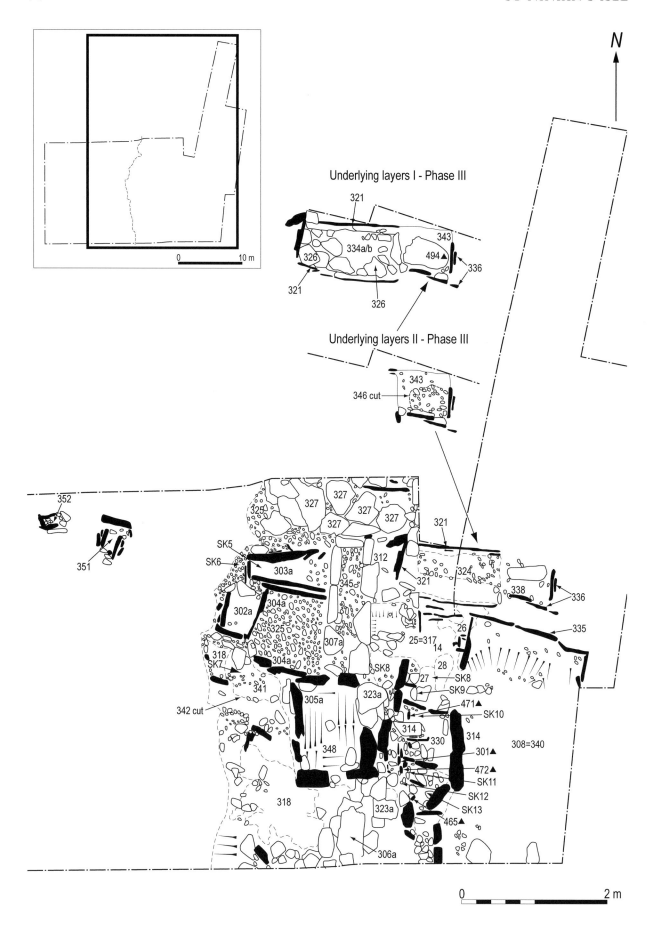

FIGURE 4.3

Phase III: Late Iron Age to Late Norse burials and related features. Drawing: L McEwan and G McSwan

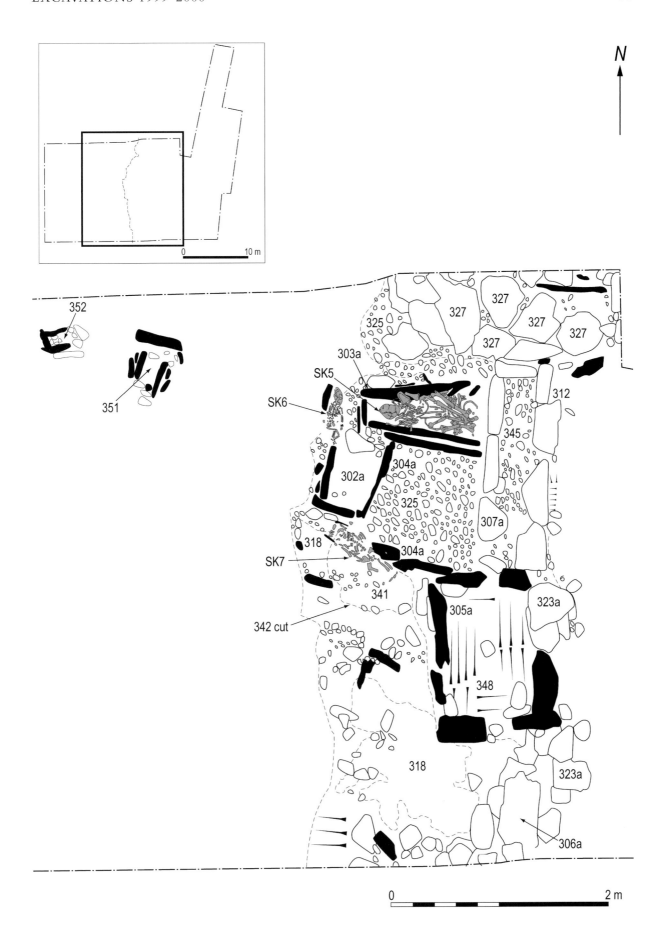

FIGURE 4.4

Phase III: Short cists, wall base, rubble cairn and paving. Drawing: G McSwan

investigation of SK 5, which once fully excavated was revealed as being extremely flexed and partially articulated (Figure 4.6). It had the appearance of having been squashed up and then inserted into the short, narrow cist, at a depth slightly below the base of the cist stones. A small iron knife (SF 497), with traces of mineral-preserved wood on the tang, was excavated from the left side of the burial, possibly inserted as a token burial gift (Figure 4.4 and PLATE 13). The remains were aligned E–W, and only the femur, parts of the spine and part of the pelvis were articulated. The spine was present but had been broken into two sections of articulated vertebrae, with the second then re-interred upside-down. Many other disarticulated skeletal elements were present, originating from the same burial.

The fourth cist (305) was also partially excavated in 1959, although the cist slabs and basal layer (348) were found still in tact in 2000. Basal layer (348) had been compacted by trample in 1959 and small specks of red paint were found that had become impressed into its surface. This cist was aligned N–S, with maximum internal measurements of 1.12m N–S, and 0.8m E–W, and comprised five upright stones, supported by smaller stones; two slabs on the north side and two on the south, each measuring some 0.5 x 0.2m thick, and standing to 0.7m, and one large slab on the west side, 0.8m long and up to 0.7m deep. It is probable that there were once two slabs on the west side, as suggested by the gap in the SW corner, and that the second was removed in 1959. The schist and 'parallelepiped' side slabs described by Small (1973, 7) were noted during the excavations in 2000, glinting silver in sunlight. These caused the cist to stand out from its surroundings. As with cist 304, the east side of cist 305 was defined by a line of flat stones, which had been excavated and then re-placed after the 1959 excavation of the rubble mound to the south and east of the large cist in 1959. When the trampled clay base (348) had been removed from this cist, it was found to overlie the Phase II midden layer 309=311.

In addition to these four cists, at the north side of the trench two empty square stone settings (351 and 352), not unlike small cists, each measuring some 350 x 350 x 150mm, were found. These were simply described as stone settings during the excavations as they were devoid of any fill (Barrowman 2000, 40). Subsequent study of the archives however found a 1959 excavation slide that shows a small mound of large slabs and stones over the areas where they were found (see left-hand side of PLATE 8), which has been excavated in later slides (see PLATE 7), and by comparison with other similar features found below the chapel, it seems most likely that they were cists belonging to Phase III, and possibly once contained cremation deposits.

On the plan in the 1973 volume (Figure 1.2), a

FIGURE 4.5

Cists 302, 303 and 304 from the east, partially excavated, with burial SK 6 to the west of cist 303

FIGURE 4.6
Burial SK 5 after removal of cist stones 303 from around it, from the north

FIGURE 4.7
Wall base 307a, paving 327 and cists, with skeletons SK 5 and SK 6 under excavation, July 2000, from the north

stone wall up to 2m long, is shown north of cist 305. The line of the wall is projected as extending across the trench to the north and south of this, to the trench edges, with a dashed line. Small describes:

> ... the eastern part of the area, where the dominating feature is a dry-stone wall running north and south across the area. This wall, 1.2m wide, and constructed of two facing walls and rubble core, extends beyond the limits of excavation at both ends, and was badly collapsed in the south. Dug into the top of this wall and clearly post-dating it was a short cist containing an adult skeleton ...

(Small *et al* 1973, 6).

The remnants of this wall were re-investigated in 2000 and slides and archive descriptions from the 1959 excavation were studied to try and determine the appearance of the wall when first excavated. Two slides in particular showed a marked difference between the wall as reconstructed at the end of the excavations (PLATE 7) and its appearance when first uncovered (PLATE 8). In fact, the wall is never described as such in the 1959 excavation archive notes and sketches. Instead it is referred to as a 'mound' or 'cairn'. These observations were confirmed by the excavations in 2000. The wall was found to comprise two phases; an upper, later layer of loose, roughly placed, flat slabs (307b) that had been reconstructed at the end of the 1959 excavations (Phase VI, below), and a lower short, well-built, dry-stone double wall base (307a), and the partially excavated remains of rubble (323a/306a) to the east and south of the large cist (305) (Figure 4.4).

Earlier wall phase (307a) was a discrete rectangular feature, akin to a low stone base, rather than a wall (Figure 4.7). It was constructed as a double wall of schist and sandstone boulders, sub-rectangular in shape, with an inner core of sandy soil, shell and quartz pebbles (345). To the south of stone base 307a, and forming the east of cist 305, the remains of a roughly-built low rubble wall or mound (323a), was excavated, extending to the south edge of the trench where it was given the feature number 306a. This curving rubble feature was of an entirely different construction to the well-built dry-stone wall 307a. Although the suggestion on the final plan published in the 1973 volume (Figure 1.2) is that a wall extended south of cist 305 into the south section of the 1959 trench, no trace of a wall was found during the 2000 excavation, and the area to the south of cist 305 also looks quite different to Figure 1.2 on slides of the ongoing excavation in this area (eg see PLATE 8). These slides also show that a rubble mound, described during the 1959 excavations as a 'boat-shaped cairn' covered the area around and to the south of the short cists when they were first excavated from the sand (Figure 3.9). This cairn was mostly removed by the excavators in 1959, and the disturbance evident in the upper layers of the cairn rubble when excavated in 2000 (306b of Phase VI) attests to this. The environmental and artefactual as-

semblages from this upper layer were also relatively rich and are an indication of the archaeological potential of the cairn that has unfortunately been lost.

From the final plan published in the 1973 volume it is understandable that Small interpreted the sequence as he did – namely that the large short cist (305) was dug into the top of the wall. The re-investigations of these features in 2000 however confirmed what is already suggested in the archive notes and slides: the 'wall' when first discovered was in fact a large, oval-shaped mound of rubble found around and to the south of the large cist. When this was removed, the discrete 'wall base' (307a) was found underneath, adjacent to and butted against cist 305, suggesting that the two were contemporary in construction. Also, the wall base 307a, which measured 1.8 x 0.6m, stopped a metre short of the north edge of the 2000 trench, and between its north end and the trench edge, a paved surface was uncovered (327), very similar to the Phase II paving (300) excavated in the SW corner of the trench. It was covered by a further course of paving (313, Phase VI), which had been excavated and then re-placed in 1959.

Artefactual and ecofactual summary for the short cists, wall base, rubble cairn and paving (Figure 4.8)

The contents of the short cists had already been removed in 1959 and so very few finds were recovered from them in 2000. A small iron knife (SF 497) was found beside burial SK 5 in cist 303, and five body sherds of coarse pottery were found in the basal layer (348) of short cist 305. Following conservation, the iron knife was shown to have a single-edged, convex blade, triangular in cross-section, with a concave back *c*2.5mm thick (PLATE 13). The only artefact recovered from the wall was a possible rubber stone from the layer 345 in the basal core.

A small assemblage of ecofactual material was recovered, including carbonised plant remains from the basal cist layer (348) of heather family and conifer type charcoal, six-row barley grains and indeterminate cereal (an assemblage common to many of the contexts from this site). Four animal bones were also recovered and eighteen fish bones identified as mainly cod, saithe, pollack and hake. Edible periwinkle was the most numerous marine shell identified. Cist 304, to the north of 305, contained hundreds of edible periwinkle shells when it was first excavated in 1959, and slides of the excavation at the time give an indication of the huge amount of shell removed (Figure 3.9). In addition to this the short cists were all surrounded by a spread of periwinkle shell midden (325, see below), and there is evidence from this phase that the periwinkle shells, and to a lesser extent, limpet, whether first used as a food source or not, were certainly of ritual or decorative significance and associated with the cist burials. Samples from 345 were analysed for charred plant macrofossils, but none were recovered, although

Context	Description	Burials	Worked stone	Coarse pottery	Metal	Carbonised plant	Animal bone	Fish bone	Marine shell	Land snails
302a	Short cist	None	–	–	–	–	–	–	–	–
303a	Short cist	SK5. Burnt bone frags removed in 1959	–	–	Iron knife	–	–	–	–	–
304a	Short cist containing shells	None	–	–	–	–	–	–	–	–
305a	Short cist	'Rosemary'= ABDUA 14269	–	–	–	–	–	–	–	–
306a	Rubble mound = 323a	–	–	–	–	–	–	–	–	–
307a	Stone wall 'base'	–	–	–	–	–	–	2 unidentified	–	–
323a	Remains of rubble mound	–	–	–	–	–	–	–	–	–
327	Paving to north of wall 307	–	–	–	–	–	–	–	–	–
345	Basal layer of wall 307a	–	Possible rubber stone	–	–	–	2 cow 1 sheep/goat Indet frags	1 cod family 1 saithe 4 unident	780 periwinkle 96 limpet 8 spiny cockle 6 Arctica islandica	
348	Clay inside cist 305	–	–	5 body sherds	–	1 conifer 4 heather 8 hulled six-row barley 6 six-row barley 13 indet cereal 1 chickweed	1 cow 2 sheep/ goat 1 indet frags	2 cod, 2 cod family, 1 hake, 2 saithe, 2 saithe/ pollack, 9 unident	390 periwinkle 48 limpet 4 spiny cockle 3 Arctica islandica	Cochlicopa lubrica Lauria cylindracea Oxychillus cellarius Discus rotundatus
351	Small square cist	–	–	–	–	–	–	–	–	–
352	Small square cist	–	–	–	–	–	–	–	–	–

FIGURE 4.8

Material identified from Phase III short cists, wall base, rubble cairn and paving: small finds, general finds and samples three animal bones and fragments and six fish bones, identified to cod family and saithe, were recovered. Edible periwinkle was once again the most numerous marine shell identified, and to a lesser extent, limpet. The base of the wall feature, and also the short cists, were placed on or cut into a thick layer of shells and midden (see midden layer 325, below), and it is from this layer that most of the ecofactual material in the basal wall fill originates. Land snails recovered from the short cists include those associated with dry habitats of limestone grassland and calcareous sand dunes (*Cochlicopa lubricella*), in moderately damp places (*Cochlicopa lubrica, Trichia hispida, Punctum pygmaeum, Aegopinella pura* and *Aegopinella nitidula*), stone walls or under rocks (*Lauria cylindracea* and *Oxychillus celarius*) and the common *Discus rotundatus*.

Burials and dating summary

The crouched burial excavated from the largest cist (305) in 1959, code-named 'Rosemary' was analysed by Julie Roberts in 2002 (see Chapter 3). A sample from her skeleton (ABDUA 14269) has been radiocarbon dated and calibrated to 660–780 cal AD at 95.4% probability, which places her in the Late Iron Age, or 'Pictish' period. A δC13 measurement of -20.0‰ suggests that she had a mainly terrestrial diet, low in marine foodstuffs.

The burial (SK 5) found in cist 303 is identified by Roberts below as an adult male, aged 25–36 years at death. He had suffered a violent death, been buried, dug up and then interred on the site in cist 303 after a period of decomposition. A radiocarbon date taken on a sample from the right femur has been calibrated to 1020–1240 cal AD at 95.4% probability, a later date than expected for a burial in a short cist, suggesting re-use of this area after the Late Iron Age.

Sandy clay, shells and re-deposited midden layers

Below the short wall 307a and the remains of the rubble cairn (323a and 306a), a sandy clay midden layer (318/319) was excavated, from a semi-circular area to the west side of the short cists. This layer overlay the clayey Phase II middens, and probably contained earlier midden material, which had been dug into during the construction of the short cists and the insertion of later burials. The semi-circular area had once been covered in rubble, which was removed during the 1959 excavations, as seen by comparing, for instance, PLATES 7 and 8.

A layer of compact silty sand and shells (325), with occasional small round quartz pebbles, bone, charcoal and other midden inclusions, was also excavated from a discrete area around the short cists and wall 307a. The short cists were all surrounded by this layer, and probably set into it, although it was impossible to confirm whether they pre- or post-dated it

due to the disturbance and removal of stratigraphical relationships by the previous excavations. Shells had been used to block gaps between the uprights at the base of some of the cists, and this suggested that the shell layer may have been thicker when first excavated in 1959. Many small finds were recovered from layer 325, including coarse pottery, burnt bone, worked bone, slag, a quartz flake and charcoal. The marine mollusc shells were clearly connected with the short cists, perhaps being used for decoration or delineation of a special place, as they were confined to the area around the burials and the paving 327 to the north of them.

Several contexts of sandy soil containing midden inclusions, pebbles and shells (25–28, 308, 312 and 317) were also identified to the east, and subsequently shown to be the same as sandy midden layer 340, found in the SE corner of the trench. This layer remained largely unexcavated in 2000.

To the west of cists 303 and 304, two burials were excavated: SK 7, a NW–SE aligned extended juvenile burial aged 4–5 years, and SK 6, a N–S aligned, semi-flexed, infant burial aged 0–2 months (see Roberts below). These two burials cut into and then re-covered by layer 325. At first sight during excavation, the burials appeared to have been interred with no associated cist or formal setting (see Barrowman 2003, 57). SK 7 however had a small upright stone on either side of the head, and an upright stone found to the south of the burial and parallel to the south edge of cist 302, may be the remnants of a cist. Upright stones were also found on the east and west sides of burial SK 6, and an upright stone extending west at right angles to cist 305 to the south is also shown on Small's final plan of the 1959 excavation (Figure 1.2). Taken together these remnants suggest that SK 6 and SK 7 were originally buried in cists that were then either dismantled/disturbed by the insertion of later burials above, or perhaps removed by the 1950s excavators during the removal of rubble from above.

Artefactual and ecofactual summary for the sandy clay, shells and re-deposited midden layers (Figure 4.9)

The worked finds and ecofactual assemblage from these layers all derived from occupation material from Phase II deposits that was subsequently mixed with Phase III layers during the use of the area for burial. Finds from 325 include charcoal, and also a worked cancellous whalebone with a central drilled perforation (SF 432; Figure 4.31), which may have served as a fishing float or mallet, and a simple bone point. Two lumps of pumice were found in layer 25.

Two bone beads (worked cattle metatarsal shaft sections SF 460 and 512; Figure 4.31), identical to some of those found during the 1959 excavations (PLATE 14; Small *et al* 1973, fig 6), were also found, in layer 318 below the area of re-deposited rubble (306b, Phase VI) from which an identical antler bead was found. Although the seventeen bone-and-antler beads found in 1959 are described in 1973 as having been 'discovered below the north/south wall' (Small *et al* 1973, 7), an empty envelope in the Small collection in the Shetland Museum describes their location as 'at the edge of cairn, under lip of stone' (see Chapter 3 above), referring to the stone or 'rubble' cairn that was partially excavated in 1959, and the remains excavated as 323a and 306a in 2000.

The top part of a wire-wound shroud pin, although found in soil overlying burial SK 7, is more likely to have been intrusive from a later medieval or post-medieval burial interred in the sand above. A small assemblage of 38 sherds of coarse pottery was recovered from the sandy midden layers, representing 30 vessels in total of Fabrics 1–4, and four examples of worked quartz, including a flake and a blade.

The sandy clay middens contained one of the more diverse assemblages of botanical material from the site. The carbonised assemblage from 340 contained heather family (Ericaceae), spruce/larch (*Picea/Larix*) and oak (*Quercus*) charcoal, and carbonised six-row barley grains (*Hordeum vulgare* var *vulgare*). A similar range of species is present in the midden layers 028, 312 and 341, re-deposited sandy midden above SK 7. Layer 325 also contained examples of Scots pine charcoal, as well as poorly preserved cereal grains. Context 318 included similar carbonised material to 306 (the rubble cairn) above it, although with the addition of Scots pine type.

Of the remaining ecofactual assemblage, cow and sheep/goat were the most numerous animal bones identified, with examples of pig, dog, and charred fragments. Bird bones included gull species and puffin bones. A larger assemblage of fish bone was recovered from these layers than from other Phase III layers, and included cod, saithe and Pollack, all indicative of shore-based fishing. Edible periwinkle was once again the most numerous marine shell identified in the bulk samples and, to a lesser extent, limpet, with examples also of dogwhelk, whelk, spiny cockle, oyster, *Artica islandica* and rough periwinkle. Land snails recovered are the same species as present at the base of wall 307a above: those associated with dry habitats of limestone grassland and calcareous sand dunes, and moderately damp places and stone walls or under rocks. The common *Discus rotundus* was also recovered.

Burials and dating summary

Radiocarbon measurements for SK 7 of 680–860 cal AD at 95.4% place it with 'Rosemary' as one of the earliest burials known from the site. However, more surprising were the radiocarbon measurements for SK 6, which produced a date range of 1020–1160 cal AD @ 95.4%, much later than anticipated. It may be of note that burial SK 6 was interred next to SK 5, also dated to between the 11th and early 13th centuries AD (1020–1240 cal AD at 95.4%). As with

SK 5, above, these radiocarbon measurements reveal that the area of short cists was re-used after the Late Iron Age, with later burials being added into the sides of the area. This is discussed further below.

Consistent with the findings from the earlier Phase II middens, little disarticulated human bone was recovered from the Phase III sandy midden contexts, with seven adult and one juvenile bone or fragments of bone recovered from 318 and 325. A small assemblage of infant hand bones and teeth were recovered from the fill of SK 7, representing a minimum of two individuals. Whereas SK 7 was aged 4–5 years at death, the infant hand bones and teeth are calculated as being slightly younger, at 6–12 months and 12–24 months old (see Roberts below for full discussion). Whilst it is possible that this reflects a specific use of this part of the site for infant burial, it is also likely that the infant bones are intrusive from the insertion of later burials from above, and that the predominance of infant bones is a result of recovery bias from the previous excavations, with adult bones, or larger skeletal elements, being easier to 'spot' and remove (Duffy below).

Finds from the midden layers re-deposited in and around the burials, including those from shell layer 325 which seems to be specifically associated with the short cist burials, all provide a date generally later than the Late Iron Age, in keeping with the radiocarbon measurements for SK 7 (and 'Rosemary', ABDUA 14269), of between the late 7th and late 9th centuries AD.

Long cists

As discussed in 3.8 (above), the 1973 published plans depict six (Small 1973, fig 5), or seven (Thomas 1973, fig 8), long cists in the NE corner of the trench, but there seems to have been some confusion between what were actually two different phases of long cist burials. Small refers to the 'early Christian graves in the NE corner of the excavated area, which are separated from the earlier structures by a clear stratigraphical break' and shows this relationship on his site plan (Figure 1.2), which has a dotted line delineating the edge of the excavated sand below four narrow long cists in the NE corner (Small 1973, 7, fig 5). Thomas labels the cists 'B' on his plan (Figure 1.3) and describes them as 'stratigraphically, from two to three feet higher than the short cists', with the furthest south having a cross-incised stone (no. 11) at its east end (Thomas 1973, 12, fig 8). O'Dell's own description in 1959 seems to imply two groups of Christian graves, one 2ft (0.61m) above the other (see O'Dell 1960, 4–5) and the archive analysis described in Chapter 3, above, concluded that there were in fact probably two different groups of long cists in this part of the trench.

Excavations in 2000 demonstrated that the long cists in the NE corner of the trench were indeed divided into two distinct groups, both quite different

Context	Description	Quartz lithics	Coarse pottery	Worked bone	Cinder and industrial waste	Iron/ Cu alloy	Carbonised plant	Disarticulated human bone	Animal bone	Fish bone	Marine shell	Land snails
025	Midden deposit = 028 = 317 = 308 = 312	–	8 body sherds	–	2 lumps ?pumice	–	24 heather family, 3 spruce/larch, 1 oak, 10 six-row barley, 4 cf six-row barley	Unid frag, 2 adult thoracic vertebrae, juvenile left scapula	2 sheep/goat, Gull sp, 1 dog, Indet frags	–	<5 limpet, 2 oyster, 1 common cockle	–
026	Unexcavated – patches of sand within 025	–	–	–	–	–	–	–	–	–	–	–
027	Unexcavated – patches of sand within 025	–	1 body sherd	–	–	–	–	–	–	–	–	–
028	Midden and shells (same as 025)	–	–	–	–	–	–	–	Indet frags	–	130 periwinkle, 45 rough periwinkle, 95 limpet, < 5 oyster	Cochlicopa lubricella, Lauria cylindracea, Aegopinella pura, A. nitidula, Oxychillus alliarius, Arianta arbustorum
308	Unexcavated. Probably = 312, 217 and 025	–	–	–	–	–	–	–	–	–	–	–
312	Layer of sandy shell midden, same as 25 and 317 = 308 below cists 314 and wall 307a	1 flake, 1 core, 1 blade	–	–	–	–	1 conifer, 1 hulled six-row barley, 1 six-row barley, 3 indet cereal	–	Seal, indet frags, 2 sheep/goat, 2 large ungulate	1 cod family, 3 cod/ saithe/ pollack, 5 saithe, 25 unid	97 periwinkle 24 limpet	Cochlicopa lubricella, C. lubrica, Aegopinella pura, Oxychillus cellarius, Arianta arbustorum, Trichia hispida, Discus rotundus
317	Same as 25 and 312 = 308 (sandy midden deposit)	–	–	–	–	–	–	–	2 sheep/goat, 1 gull sp, 1 pig, indet frags	–	396 periwinkle, 76 limpet, 19 dogwhelk, 4 whelk, 4 oyster, 5 common cockle, 1 Artica islandica	–

FIGURE 4.9A

Material identified from Phase III sandy clay and shell middens: small finds, general finds and samples

Context	Description	Quartz lithics	Coarse pottery	Worked bone	Cinder and industrial waste	Iron/ Cu alloy	Carbonised plant	Disarticulated human bone	Animal bone	Fish bone	Marine shell	Land snails
318/319	Sandy midden around cists 302, 304 and 305	1 poss flake	20 body sherds	2 beads	–	–	2 conifer 16 heather family, 2 spruce/larch, 1 Scots pine type, 6 hulled six-row barley, 8 six-row barley, 3 cf six-row barley	3 adult distal hand phalanges, fragment adult metacarpal head, unid adult long-bone	3 indet charred, 10 cow, 11 sheep/goat, 1 large ungulat, 1 pig, 1 bird indet frags	1 cod family, 2 saithe, 2 saithe/ pollack, 1 unid	346 periwinkle, 12 rough peri-winkle, 79 limpet, 2 dogwhelk, 5 whelk, 2 oyster	Cochlicopa lubrica Aegopinella pura A. nitidula Oxychillus cellarius Arianta arbustorum
325	Layer of sandy shell midden, overlying 309 in west of trench, around all cists and wall 307	–	–	Bone point, whale-bone with drilled central hole	–	1 indet frag	21 Scots pine, 3 indet cereal	Adult rib body, adult distal fibula, juvenile neural arch fragment	3 cow, 6 sheep/goat, 3 small ungulate, 1 pig, indet frags	1 cod, 1 cod family, 1 cod/saithe/ pollack, 4 saithe, 1 saithe/pollack, 18 unid	780 periwinkle, 96 limpet, 8 Spiny cockle, 6 Artica islandica	Cochlicopa lubricella C. lubrica Lauria cylindracea Aegopinella pura A. nitidula Oxychillus cellarius Discus rotundatus
340	Same as 308, sand and stones in SE corner of trench. Largely unexcavated	–	7 body sherds, 1 rim sherd	–	1 indet cinder	1 object, 1 nail shank	9 Heather family, 3 spruce/larch, 1 oak, 1 monocot stem, 10 hulled six-row barley 6 six-row barley, 8 indet cereal, 1 chickweed	–	4 cow, 3 sheep/goat, 1 small ungulate, 2 pig, 1 bird, 1 cf puffin, indet frags	1 cod, 1 saithe, 5 unid	610 periwinkle, 90 limpet, 3 Dogwhelk, 4 Spiny cockle 1 oyster, 3 Artica islandica 2 mussel	Cochlicopa lubricella C. lubrica Lauria cylindracea Aegopinella pura A. nitidula Oxychillus cellarius Arianta arbustorum Discus rotundatus
341	Re-deposited sandy midden over SK 7	–	–	–	–	Part of shroud pin	1 alder, 10 heather family, 1 spruce/larch, 6 hulled six-row barley, 4 six-row barley, 6 indet cereal, 1 chickweed	Juvenile 2 incisors, 1st molar crown, premolar crown, 16 vertebrae bodies, R lunate, distal hand phal-ange, proximal hand phalange	Indet frags, 2 unid burnt bone frags	1 cod/saithe/ pollack, 2 saithe, 8 unid	<5 periwinkle, <5 limpet	Cochlicopa lubricella C. lubrica Lauria cylindracea Aegopinella pura A. nitidula Oxychillus cellarius Trichia hispida Discus rotundatus
342	Cut for SK 7, aligned NW-SE	–	–	–	–	–	–	Cut for SK 7	–	–	–	–

FIGURE 4.9B

Material identified from Phase III sandy clay and shell middens: small finds, general finds and samples

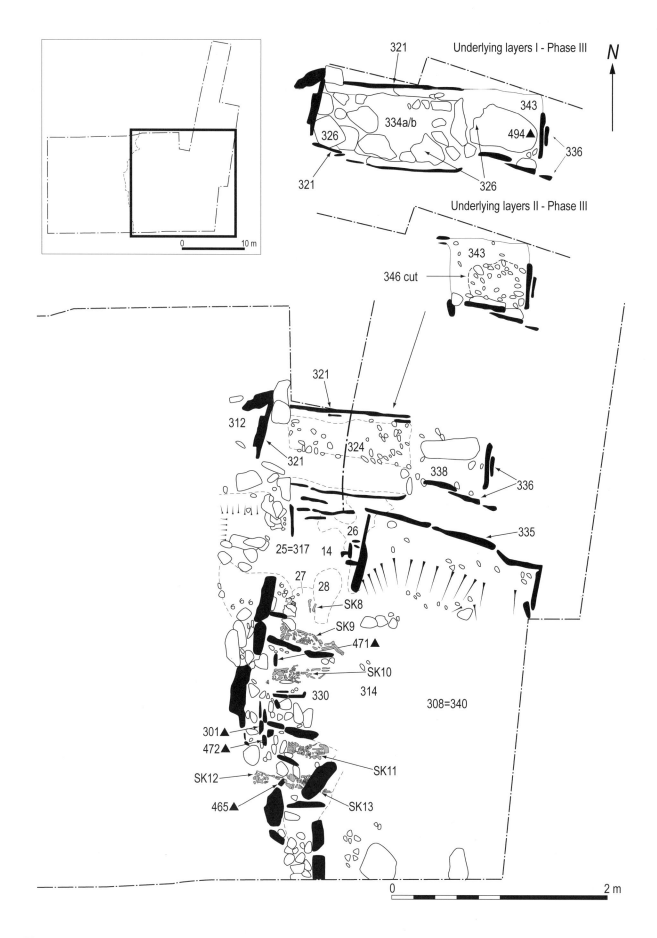

FIGURE 4.10

Phase III: Long cists and infant burial complex. Drawing: G McSwan

in their construction and stratigraphical position: two earlier and wider cists (Phase III), and four later and narrower cists (Phase V). The latter four cists, were found cut into a thick layer of wind-blown sand, *c*1m deep (layer 024a); a small remnant of the thick layer of wind-blown sand that had originally covered the whole site. Below the sand in the NE corner, two earlier long cists were found of a different form to the Phase V cists above, being wider, shorter and constructed from larger slabs. The edges of these earlier, wider long cists can actually be seen on Small's plan (labelled 321 and 335 on Figure 1.2).

On excavation in 2000, the two earlier long cists (321 and 335) and an 'extension' (336), attached to the end of the northern cist 321, and possibly part of it (Figures 4.10 and 4.11), were found aligned E–W at the bottom of the sand. Both cists were 0.65m wide, narrowing to 0.5m at the east end (and the box-like extension). Cist 321/336 was largely intact, although the contents of both cists had been removed in 1959, and cist (335) had been partially dismantled and then backfilled, with steps built back up to the chapel from this corner of the site, which had been used as a barrow run out of the trench (PLATE 7).

Cist 321 measured 1.4 x 0.65m in plan and was up to 0.35m deep; it had three sides upstanding: west, north and south. The sides were constructed from large sandstone slabs, the north from one large rectangular slab (1.3 x 0.32 x 0.05m), the south from two, measuring 0.84 and 0.51m long, respectively, and the west from one 0.49m long. The base of the cist consisted of a layer of dark brown sand with pebbles and shells (334). Layer 334 contained some100 human bone and tooth fragments, a small lump of mortar, and limpet shells containing silty soil with roots, which are presumably intrusive. The presence of these finds strongly suggested that the cist was dug into in 1959 and partially backfilled. For the purposes of specialist analysis, therefore, layer 334 and subsequent layers were given the dual designation of a/b to indicate that there was evidence during excavation in 2000 that they had previously been disturbed, if not totally excavated and reinstated by the 1959 excavators. The basal layer 334a/b was partially covered by loosely set flat stones (326a/b), up to 0.4 x 0.2 x 0.02m in size, with smaller stones in the gaps between. The stones were then covered with a further layer of mixed sand and mainly quartz pebbles (324a/b). Pebbles with a whitish mortar-like residue on them were recovered from this cist (SF 466 from layer 334) and thought possibly to indicate re-use from a mortared wall. This residue was found on pebbles elsewhere on the site, eg from layer 338; SF 483 in cist 336, and interestingly, also on the ogham stone found in the 19th century. Analysis has shown however that this residue is not mortar, and derives instead from a natural biological organism (see Hall below). The environmental assemblage recovered by flotation of samples from the layers infilling cists 321

and 336 (see below) are also strongly indicative of later disturbance.

Where the east end stone of cist 321 had fallen, there was adjacent to it an 'extension' 336, which measured 0.8 x 0.5m and had only its south and east sides upstanding. The east slab measured 0.48m and, behind it, was a smaller slab, possibly used to hold the other upright. Two overlapping slabs made up the south side, 0.33 and 0.42m respectively. A flat stone on the north side of this cist may have been the north side slab which had fallen. The bases of the side slabs of 336 were at the same level as those of the adjacent cist, and there were no indications that 336 cut cist 321, or *vice versa*, suggesting that the two were contemporary and that 336 was part of 321. The cist 'extension' 336 was fully excavated. It had been set onto a layer of silty sand with pebbles (343), which contained stones, midden inclusions and some fragments of human bone. Small fragments of uncarbonised coffin wood indicate disturbance from above during later phases of burial. No paving was found to indicate a base to this cist, but a cut (346) was found within 336, roughly subrectangular in shape, and cut into layer 343 below, mirroring the extent of the cist and containing a fill of silty sand with pebbles (75% quartz, 25% schist and sandstone), shells and occasional human bone fragments (344). This was covered by a large cross-incised schist slab 0.55 x 0.23 x up to 0.07m thick (SF 494; Figure 4.12). The whole was then topped by a further layer of loose yellowish-brown mixed sand and occasional pebbles (338), very similar to layer 324 at the top of cist 321 to the west. Above these layers of mixed sand and pebbles, a thick layer of wind-blown sand covered the cists.

This evidence for partial, mixed disturbance with fallen side slabs and the cross-slab (SF 494) still present, suggest that the cist 321/336 was not fully exposed in 1959, but only partially and inconsistently dug into. The slide of 'Hubert' *in situ* (Figure 3.18), although nominally depicting one of the four later, narrower, long cists from the top of the sand, may in fact be showing us the burial from an earlier cist directly below it, i.e., the burial in cist 321/336, which was situated directly below later cist 06 (Figure 1.2). This is further suggested by a slide of the ongoing excavation (Figure 3.9), which appears to show 'Hubert', but in a grave that is on a slightly different alignment to the long cists above, as indicated by a footstone, and is in the same location exactly as cist 321/336. Presumably the cross-incised slab SF 494 was once set upright at the foot of cist 321/336, but fell over into 336, possibly as a result of the excavations and removal of 'Hubert'.

To the south of cist 321/336, and parallel to it, a second long cist (335) was excavated of the same shape but shorter, without an east 'extension'. The west end stone upright of this cist can be seen at the edge of the revetted sandbank on Small's plan. In 2000, the north, east and west sides of this cist were

Figure 4.11

Long cists 321/336 and 335 from the east. Photograph: K Brady

found remaining, but otherwise the cist had been completely emptied and the south side had been replaced by a small revetment wall built in 1959. The overall length of this cist was 1.56m, with three upright stones forming the north side; its width was up to 0.65m, narrowing to 0.5m at the east end, as seen with cist 321/336 to the north. The west side was a single upright slab, 0.69m long, and the east side consisted of two smaller slabs extending under the 2000 trench edge. The cist had been re-filled, with layer 337, during the construction of the revetment wall 328/10 in Phase VI. The only Phase III layer surviving was a sandy midden layer (340) below the cists. A second burial of a juvenile, 'Robert' (ABD-UA 14270), excavated in 1959, may have originated from this shorter cist, but unlike 'Hubert', there is no slide of the burial *in situ* to confirm this.

At the west end of cist 335, a small stone post setting (14) was excavated in 1999 (see west end of cist 335 on Figure 4.10). No stone post or cross slab was found in 2000 associated with this setting; however in the 1973 volume, Thomas publishes a tall, thin slab of micaceous metaquartzite with pocked cross (Stone 11), described as having been 'found in 1959, outside the south wall of the medieval chapel, associated with the long cist graves' (Thomas 1973, 36). This cross slab (11) is shown on Thomas' site plan (Figure 1.3) as being at the east end of the southernmost of two adjacent long cists in Group 'B' (Thomas 1973, fig 8). Small's plan (1973, fig 5; reproduced

here as Figure 1.2) shows Thomas' two adjacent cists as a cross-shaped alignment of upright stones, and the east end of the south part of this alignment there is an upright stone at the west edge of the bank of sand. This is marked '335' on Figure 1.2 as it corresponds to the west end stone of long cist 335, which was found under the sand in 2000. The pocked cross (11) could therefore have been associated with long cist 335, and have been the headstone at the west end of the cist, where the post-setting (14) was identified. The setting measured 100 x 150mm at its narrowest internal measurement, and the base of Stone 11, according to Thomas, narrows 'to a 3-in [78mm] 'tang', and varies in thickness from 2⅛in [53mm] either end' (Thomas 1973, 36), meaning that it would have fitted into this post-setting, with room for small packing stones to hold it upright.

This confusion of earlier and later long cists and head and foot stones can be seen in the top right hand corner of PLATE 8 where upright slabs and grave markers are clearly seen at the edge of the rubble mound, below the bank of sand, and further cist stones and head stones can be seen sest into the top of the sand adjacent to the wheelbarrow.

Artefactual and ecofactual summary for long cists

The artefactual and ecofactual assemblages associated with the long cists (Figure 4.13) were small and derived principally from earlier midden layers that were disturbed by the Phase III burials. Of the few worked finds associated with the long cists only a cross-incised slab (SF 494; Figure 4.23) found at the east end 336 of long cist 321 was *in situ*, rather than re-deposited from earlier Phase II midden deposits. The slab comprised a large piece of crudely shaped schist (630 x 370 x 23mm) with a simple cross incised mid-way up on the slightly smoother face. The remaining finds from the long cists included an apparently deliberately shaped whalebone vertebral centrum (SF 488; Figure 4.31), which has no obvious function, although it was complete, and fragments of cinder and daub. Examples of worked quartz, including probable waste material, five flakes and a blade chip, and a fragment of mortar, were also found in context 334, and two water-worn pebbles with residue (SF 466 and 483) were found in layers 334 and 338 respectively.

Twenty sherds (including a small fragment) of Late Iron Age coarse pottery were recovered from the long cists (see SF 526; Figure 4.33), and probably derived from the earlier midden layers. They are identified by MacSween (below) as representing 17 vessels, spread between contexts 334, 338 and 343, with Fabrics 1 and 2 (sandy clays) being the most commonly represented.

The two environmental samples taken from context 334 ([316] and [329]) contained indeterminate coniferous (*coniferales*) and heather family charcoal, as well as six-row barley grains, some hulled, and some weed seeds, suggesting that the cists were con-

FIGURE 4.12
Inscribed cross slab SF 494 in cist 336, from the east. Photograph: K Brady

structed over earlier occupation layers. The layer of pebbles (324) that overlay pebble layer 334 in the long cists was also sampled but no botanical remains other than modern intrusive material was recovered from the sample examined. The basal layer (343) of silty sand and pebbles in cist 336 contained charcoal of heather type, spruce/larch and willow (*Salix*), with cereals and weed seeds, together with uncarbonised wood of indeterminate conifer type. Context 344 below slab SF 494 and the uppermost context (338) contained a somewhat similar, albeit reduced, carbonised assemblage.

A small assemblage of animal bones (31 finds) was recovered from the long cists and associated deposits, and again, these probably derived from earlier disturbed midden layers cut by the cists and insertion of burials. As with the Phase II layers, sheep/goat bones were the most commonly identified remains. The assemblage is too small for any meaningful analysis. The slight variations seen between the phases may be more a product of the small numbers of identified fragments from each phase rather than genuine differences in the composition of the bones originally deposited. The bone of one auk species (cf puffin) was present, and may have been utilised for food.

The small assemblage of fish bone recovered from the long cists undoubtedly derived from the midden layers of Phase II. Cod, saithe, pollack and ling were all represented and indicate shore-based fishing. There was also considerable evidence for marine shellfish exploitation from deposits associated with the long cists. Periwinkle and limpet were recovered from contexts 324 and 338, as well as the occasional rough periwinkle, whelk, spiny and common cockles. However, by far the largest numbers of periwinkle and limpet (as well as occasional rough periwinkle, dog whelk, common and spiny cockle and *Artica islandica*) were recovered from 334, the basal layer of sand and pebbles below the paving in cist 321. The layer of quartz pebbles and mixed midden below the incised cross slab SF 494 also contained numerous periwinkle and limpets (120 and 43 respectively), as well as fragments of oyster shell and examples of rough periwinkle, common and spiny cockle.

As with the other Phase III features, land snails recovered from the long cists included those associated with dry habitats of limestone grassland and calcareous sand dunes, those found on stone walls or under rocks, and moist places, including among rocks. However, species associated with humanly disturbed habitats (*Aegopinella nitidula*), walls, rocks and meadows (*Arianta arbustorum*), and moist and well-vegetated places (*Punctum pygmaeum*) were also identified.

Context	Description	Worked stone	Quartz lithics	Coarse pottery	Worked bone	Cinder and industrial waste	Mortar	Carbonised plant	Burials and disarticulated human bone	Animal bone	Fish bone	Marine shell	Land snails
14	Post setting?	–	–	–	–	–	–	–	–	–	–	–	–
321	Long cist partially excavated in 1959	–	–	–	–	–	–	–	?'Hubert' = ABDUA 14254	–	–	–	–
324a/b	Quartz pebbles within cist 321	–	–	–	–	–	–	None in sample	Adult proximal hand phalange	–	1 cod, 1 cod/saithe/pollack, 7 unident	79 periwinkle, 55 limpet, 2 whelk, 1 spiny cockle	Cochlicopa lubricella Cochlicopa lubrica Lauria cylindracea Aegopinella pura Oxychillus cellarius Arianta arbustorum Discus rotundatus Punctum pygmaeum
326a/b	Flat stones at the bottom of cist 321	–	–	–	–	–	–	–	–	–	–	–	–
334a/b	Sand and pebbles below paving in cist 321	Pebble with residue	3 waste, 2 flakes, 1 blade	6 body sherds	–	1 frag, 1 indet cinder	1 frag	3 conifer, 12 heather family, 9 hulled six-row barley, 6 six-row barley, 11 cf six-row barley, 5 indet cereal, 1 dock, 2 chickweed	>55 adult bones and frags and 3 adult teeth, and 24 juvenile bones and 2 teeth (see archive report for full identifications), 6 young juvenile and 8 neonate bones	4 indet frags, 3 cow, 1 sheep/goat, 4 pig	4 cod, 4 cod family, 1 ling, 10 saithe, 1 saithe/pollack, 25 unident	904 periwinkle, 18 rough, periwinkle, 159 limpet, 19 dog whelk, 3 Arctica islandica	Cochlicopa lubricella Cochlicopa lubrica Aegopinella nitidula Oxychillus cellarius Discus rotundatus
335	Rectangular cist totally excavated in 1959	–	–	–	–	–	–	–	?'Robert' = ABDUA 14270	–	–	–	–

FIGURE 4.13A

Material identified from Phase III long cists: small finds, general finds and samples

Context	Description	Worked stone	Quartz lithics	Coarse pottery	Worked bone	Cinder and industrial waste	Mortar	Carbonised plant	Burials and disarticulated human bone	Animal bone	Fish bone	Marine shell	Land snails
336	Partial cist or extension at E end of cist 321 with S and E stones only remaining	Cross-inscribed schist slab	–	–	–	–	–	–	Calcaneus frag, rib body, radius, adult lunate and 1st metatarsal head, juvenile distal humerus and proximal femur	1 indet frags	–	–	–
338	Sand and quartz pebbles over cross-slab SF 494	Pebble with residue	–	2 body sherds	Shaped whale-bone centrum	2 indet cinder	–	4 heather family	Adult metacarpal head and juvenile premolar crown	1 cow, 1 sheep/goat, 1 indet, 1 auk sp cf puffin	8 unident	96 periwinkle, 23 rough periwinkle, 56 limpet, 14 common cockle, 3 spiny cockle	Cochlicopa lubricella, Cochlicopa lubrica, Aegopinella nitidula, Oxychillus cellarius, Discus rotundatus
343	Sand, stones and midden below cross-slab and cist 336	–	1 flake	10 body and rim sherds	–	?daub frag 1 indet cinder	–	17 heather family, 5 spruce/larch, 2 salix 1 conifer wood frag, 8 hulled six-row barley 6 six-row barley, 4 indet cereal, 1 dock 4 chickweed	10 adult bones and frags, Juvenile femoral head and ishium	5 cow, 1 sheep/goat, 2 indet frags	1 cod, 3 cod family, 2 cod/ saithe/ pollack, 1 ling, 1 rockling, 17 saithe, 14 unident	–	Cochlicopa lubrica, Lauria cylindracea, Oxychillus cellarius, Discus rotundatus
344	Layer of quartz and other pebbles below SF 494.	–	2 flakes	1 body sherd, 1 frag	–	–	–	2 heather family, 1 monocot stem, 3 six-row barley	Adult lower 1st pre-molar, occipital frag and skull frags. Young juvenile ishium, neural arch and femur frag, 4 unid frags	1 cow, 2 sheep/goat, 1 indet frags	1 cod family, 2 unident	120 periwinkle, 15 rough periwinkle, 43 limpet, oyster frags, 6 common cockle, 3 spiny cockle	Cochlicopa lubricella, Oxychillus cellarius, Arianta arbustorum, Trichia hispida
346	Irregular cut within 336, filled by pebbles 344	–	–	–	–	–	–	–	–	–	–	–	–

FIGURE 4.13B

Material identified from Phase III long cists: small finds, general finds and samples

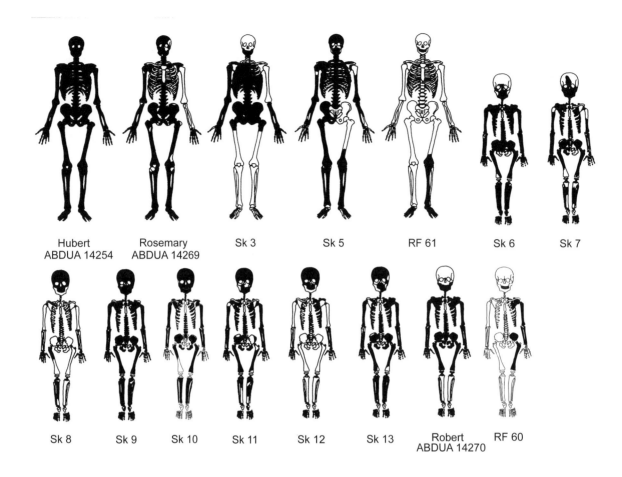

Hubert
ABDUA 14254

FIGURE 4.14

Preservation of burials from 1999 and 2000. Drawing: L McEwan

Burials and dating summary

No material suitable for radiocarbon dating was recovered from the long cists. Although carbonised plant material and disarticulated human bone were recovered, none of it could be confidently linked to the long cists or the burials that had once been placed in them. Typological dating of the simple cross slab is debatable (see Fisher below), it being as likely to be Norse (9th–11th centuries) as early medieval (7th–9th). Once again, the pottery gives only a general Late Iron Age or later date.

Although the two long cists excavated in this group were found to be empty in 2000, a large assemblage of disarticulated human bones and fragments was found scattered through all the contexts associated with the cists, in contrast with re-deposited midden layers from this phase which contained only occasional intrusive stray bones (see below). Context 334, infilling cist 321, contained the largest assemblage, with over 100 bones of adult, juvenile and neonate bones representing a minimum of two adults and two juveniles, with at least one male and one possible female identified. Age at death for two individuals was calculated at 35–45 years old,

and 0–6 months old. The cist extension (336) contained both adult and juvenile bone fragments, as did the cist fills 338, 343 and 344, suggesting considerable disturbance of these cists, probably during the 1959 excavations; coffin wood found in basal cist layer 343 also suggests disturbance in the medieval period or later.

As we have seen in discussions above, it is possible that burial 'Hubert' (ABDUA 14254), recorded by O'Dell as having been excavated from one of the long cists in this corner of the site in 1959, was excavated from cist 321. Radiocarbon dating of samples from 'Hubert' (ABDUA 14254) has produced a range of 680–890 cal AD at 95.4%, and this confirms that the burial originated from one of the earlier long cists at the base of the sand, rather than from one of the later cists above it. The radiocarbon dating for 'Robert' (ABDUA 14270) has a wider range of 780–1000 cal AD at 95.4%, but this still places it in Phase III. Although this burial is recorded as having originated from a long cist with the outline of a wooden coffin (i.e. a medieval burial) in 1959, the circumstantial evidence of the second empty long cist 335, and the radiocarbon date, places 'Robert' in Phase III.

The infant burial complex

To the east of the remains of the rubble mound (323a and 306a) and short cist (305) an unusual linear complex of small stone uprights (314) was excavated (Figure 4.3 and 4.10), aligned N–S, to the east of cist 305. It was divided internally by upright stones, into six small, E–W aligned, compartments (Figure 4.15), each measuring *c*400 x 800mm and filled with stones and quartz pebbles (330). Four of the compartments were marked at the west end by small headstones, two plain (SF 471 and 472) and two of incised with unusual crosses, one on the east face (SF 465; Figure 4.23) and one on the west (SF 301; Figure 4.23). The two crosses were of the same unusual form but SF 465 is a shallower and more unfinished incision than SF 301.

This low compartmentalised cairn had been partially uncovered in 1959, where it can be seen as a pile of stones in archive slides (Plate 8), and a series of uprights on the final plan in the 1973 volume (see 314 as marked on Figure 1.2). Small stated afterwards that 'the area to the east of the wall was not completely excavated, but the only available site-plan shows a number of box-like structures formed by stones set on edge which suggest further burials' (1973, 7; fig 5). On this figure a cross-shaped arrangement of uprights is also shown to the north of the complex, and Thomas (1973, fig 8) interprets

this arrangement as two long cists (Figure 1.3). It can be seen however that the stone boxes suggested by the cross-shaped arrangement on Small's plan are comparable in size and alignment with the compartments of the stone complex excavated to the south in 2000, suggesting that prior to the 1959 excavations the complex extended further to the north.

When the stone complex (314) and headstones were excavated, six infant burials were found below five of the six compartments. They had been shallowly interred and covered with a thin layer of soil, before being covered with the stone boxes filled with pebbles. Four of the infant skeletons (SK 9–11 and 13) were well preserved, whereas two, SK 8 and SK 12, had been truncated, the latter by SK 13 (Figures 4.10 and 4.14). The age at death of each infant has been estimated as being between birth and up to 2 years 4 months at the most (see Roberts below). Of the well-preserved burials, SK 10 and SK 11 were supine and extended, whilst SK 9 and SK 13 were semi-flexed. Small upright stones were set about the skulls of burials SK 8–11, to form a 'head box'. Each burial was aligned E–W below the compartments of the complex above, with the exception of one compartment, below which no remains were found, and at the south end where two burials were found below the same compartment (SK 12 and 13, with SK 13 cutting SK 12). The cross-incised head-stone (SF 301) was placed over a compartment that

Figure 4.15

The central four 'compartments' of the small kerbed cairn over the infant burials SK 8 to SK 13, from the east

had no burial beneath it, whereas the second incised headstone (SF 465) was placed over the compartment covering two burials (SK 12 and SK 13). The two unworked headstones (SF 471 and 472) were placed at the west end of the compartments covering burials SK 10 and SK 11 respectively on either side of the empty compartment.

Artefactual and ecofactual summary for the infant burial complex (Figure 4.16)

The artefactual assemblage associated with the infant burials includes a small water-worn flat quartz beach pebble recovered from the mouth of infant burial SK 12, and a deliberately shaped hexagonal flat stone or smoother (SF 510; Figure 4.24) found associated with SK 9. The two cross-incised headstones are discussed by Fisher below (Figure 4.23). SF 301, a flat schist pebble, displays a relatively deeply incised double cross with a curl at the base. The second (SF 465) is a schist stone with a lightly incised double cross. The remaining two headstones (SF 471 and 472) are un-worked.

The remaining artefactual and ecofactual assemblage derives from the midden deposits below the complex, which were dug into and re-deposited during the interment of the infants. Nine sherds of coarse pottery were found in 330, and one in feature 314, with eight vessels are represented in total. Samples from layer 330, and from sand around SK 9 and SK 10 contained the same combination of heather family and conifer charcoal and barley grains found elsewhere on the site in contexts indicative of midden. Cow and sheep/goat were the most numerous animal bones identified. Bird bones were also identified, including gull species, puffin, gannet and cf species guillemot, and are all probably indicative of the occasional exploitation of sea birds for food. Two rabbit bones recovered from context 314 of Phase III were probably intrusive from the topsoil and sandy backfill layers above, where rabbit bones were a ubiquitous find. A fish bone assemblage of mainly cod, saithe, pollack and ling was recovered, with one example of Atlantic herring identified. Edible periwinkle and limpet were the most numerous marine shells found in the bulk samples, together with examples of spiny cockle and oyster, and the instance of the limpet shell placed in the mouth of one of the infant burials (SK 9). The same species of land snails were recovered as from elsewhere on the site, i.e. those associated with either dry habitats of limestone grassland and calcareous sand dunes, or damper places such as stone walls or under rocks.

Burials and dating summary

Radiocarbon measurement of samples taken from the six infant burials produced interesting results (see below). Three of the burials (SK 8, 9 and 13) produced similar date ranges between the late 7th and late 10th centuries (SK 8 cal AD 770–990, SK 9

cal AD 690–990 and SK 13 cal AD 770–1000; all at 95.4% confidence). This places the infants at the end of the Late Iron Age, or 'Pictish' period, at the time of the Viking incursions into Shetland. However, the remaining three infants (SK 10, 11 and 12), adjacent to each other at the centre of the row of six infant burials, are placed in a later date range (SK 10 cal AD 890–1040, SK 11 cal AD 900–1160, and SK 12 cal AD 890–1030; all at 95.4% confidence). When it is taken into account that the two burials under the compartment at the south end of the complex (SK 12 and 13), are intercutting (SK 13 cutting SK 12), Bayesian analysis by Bayliss and Outram below can be used to narrow the date range further, to possibly sometime in the 10th century for all six burials. Following osteological analysis, Roberts (see below) has suggested that once the infants were ex-utero, being aged neonate to 32 months at death, and had used up the nutrients stored from the placenta, they simply 'failed to thrive and grow'. She identifies that rickets is indicated, suggesting a lack of vitamin D, which would normally at this age be derived from the breast milk of the mother, and concludes that this also has implications for the mothers' health. Routine samples were taken from the immediate area of each infant, but were found to be identical to layer 330, the midden layer below them, with which the results are included in Figure 4.16. However, whereas the samples from SK 8, 11 and 12/13 contained no bone at all, and SK 9 contained only one juvenile pre-molar crown, the sample from the area of SK 10 produced over 100 disarticulated infant bones and fragments, including the long bones from the left-hand side of the body and radius and ulna fragments. No element duplication or adult bone was identified, other than a fragment of burnt bone, and Duffy concludes that a minimum of one juvenile individual was present in the sample (see below). Subsequent comparison with the burial catalogue for SK 10 suggested that the sample elements represented a second individual within the burial area. There is thus the distinct possibility that the area adjacent and partially overlapped by the area of SK 10 had previously held another burial, which was subsequently cut and partially disinterred when SK 10 was buried (this is seen elsewhere in the complex, where SK 12 was cut by the later burial of SK 13). The area of this possible earlier burial corresponds with the supposedly 'empty' compartment with a cross-incised headstone above it, between skeletons SK 10 and SK 11, and these three burials are all evidence that the infants were not all interred at the same time, but over several years or generations. This is also borne out by the modeling of the radiocarbon dates, below.

Phase IV: Wind-blown sand

This phase of undisturbed (i.e. unexcavated) wind-blown sand was only seen in section in the 2000 excavations. When O'Dell's team first began exca-

Context	330	314
Description	Sandy shell, stones and midden between 314 and burials SK 8–13 below; material from SK 8–13 samples included	Low cairn of upright stones and pebbles over infant burials SKs 8-13
Quartz lithics	1 prob flake, 1 flake	–
Coarse pottery	9 body sherds	1 body sherd
Worked stone	2 unworked headstones smoothed, hexagonal stone assoc with SK 9; quartz pebble assoc with SK 12	2 cross-incised stones
Carbonised plant	12 heather family, 1 spruce/larch, 3 Scots pine type, 10 hulled six-row barley, 10 six-row barley, 10 indet cereal	–
Burials and disarticulated human bone	1 premolar crown from SK 9 samples; 130 neonate/infant bones and frags from SK 10 sample SK 8–13 found below 330	–
Animal bone	13 cow, 13 sheep /goat, 1 puffin, 1 gannet, 1 cf guillemot, 2 bird, 1 small mammal, 1 small bird, indet frags	1 sheep/goat, 1 cow, 2 rabbit, fish frags, indet frags
Fish bone	1 Atlantic herring, 1 cod, 4 cod family, 2 cod/saithe/pollack, 1 ling, 4 saithe, saithe/ pollack, 12 unident and 1 unident from SK 10	1 cod, 1 unident
Marine shell	140 periwinkle, 96 limpet, 4 Spiny cockle 1 limpet in mouth of SK 9	424 periwinkle, 11 limpet, 2 oyster
Land snails	*Cochlicopa lubricella, C. lubrica, Lauria cylindracea, Aegopinella pura, A. nitidula, Oxychillus cellarius, Arianta arbustorum, Trichia hispida, Discus rotundus*	–

FIGURE 4.16

Material identified from Phase III infant burial complex: small finds, general finds and samples

vating south of the chapel the area was covered in a thick layer of wind-blown sand, up to 6m deep in places. This was entirely removed by hand during the summer of 1959, and the huge extent of this task can be seen on the slides taken at the time (Figures 3.9 and 3.10). Thousands of medieval interments were removed with the sand, and also a large amount of rubble below that (see Chapter 3). In July 2000 only a small part of this wind-blown sand was found remaining *in situ* in a step in the NE corner of the area where four long cists had been excavated in

1959, and even here, the sand had been at least partially excavated and re-deposited afterwards when the long cists were consolidated, and so was included in Phase VI. In particular, sand was removed from the fills of the later long cists and then put back at the edge of the southernmost one (06), when steps were built up the slope in the NE corner of the trench as part of the reconsolidation work undertaken at the end of the 1959 season. Slides show that this corner of the site was used as a barrow run for the excavations in order to get spoil in and out of the trench (Figure 3.10) and, after the excavations were completed, the area was banked up and revetted by a low stone wall and steps. A slide taken at the end of the excavation (PLATE 7) shows the bank of sand reinstated, the long cists present and the turf back on the trench between the uprights. This reinstated upper part of the wind-blown sand bank was identified as such in 2000, labelled 024b, and included in Phase VI.

During the 2000 excavations, the southernmost long cist (06) was removed to allow examination of the earlier long cists below. Inspection of the wind-blown sand (024a) below long cist 06 showed it to be uniform throughout (Figures 4.17 and 4.18), with very few finds or inclusions, other than disarticulated bone from the many later burials. A study of the eroding sandy sections in and around the cliff edge adjacent to the site in 2000 (see above) demonstrated that the wind-blown sand was a gradual accumulation over a long period of time, and excavations on site confirmed that sand was first found in the first burials of Phase III that were buried into midden above the clay subsoil. However, the thickest sand inundation seems to have occurred after the first phase of long cists and before the medieval chapel was built.

Phase V: Medieval chapel and medieval/post-medieval burials

This phase includes the medieval chapel and altar, and associated medieval and post-medieval burials. The chapel was uncovered and investigated in 1956–59, and almost all of the medieval and later burials removed from above it and from the area to the south (see Chapter 3). Out with the ruined chapel therefore, little evidence for this period remained unexcavated in 2000. However, the south wall of the chapel was partially re-examined in Trial Trench 1 in 1999, and the partial remains of two medieval or later burials were uncovered. In Trench 1 in 2000, a third partially surviving medieval or later burial was uncovered, and the upper layer of long cist burials in the sandy 'step' in the NE corner of the trench were also re-examined and shown to be contemporary with the medieval chapel, rather than the earlier church below it.

Four long cists (03, 04, 05 and 06) were uncovered above the sand in 1999, and of these 06 was fully excavated in 2000. All four cists were narrower than the earlier long cists excavated from below the sand in Phase III. They were aligned E–W, built from long, flat slabs of sandstone, and each cist was set into sand (24), but with no fill or associated cuts visible (Figure 4.19). Initially, separate context numbers (18–23) were given to the areas of sand inside each cist in 1999, anticipating that each cist would have its own fill. On excavation however they were shown to all contain the same wind-blown sand that had been re-deposited in and around the cists at the

end of the 1959 excavation. It was clear that the southernmost cist, 06a, had been totally excavated in 1959, with the side slabs and sand removed and partially replaced (06b) during the consolidation and re-turfing of the site at the end of the excavation.

Small and Thomas describe these long cists as Early Christian graves (Small 1973, 4; Thomas 1973, 12), but these long cists were not the *earliest* Christian interments on the site because there were earlier long cists, as well as infant burials marked with incised crosses, below them in Phase III at the base of the wind-blown sand. The descriptions in the archives of wooden coffins and iron nails being found in these later long cists also suggests that they were more likely to be of Late Norse/medieval date.

Excavations in Trial Trench 1, in 1999, demonstrated that the medieval chapel south chancel wall (02) was built onto the wind-blown sand 024 (Figure 4.17) and therefore post-dated all the cist burials to the south of the chapel, other than possibly the four narrow long cists in the sand in the NE corner.

Burials and dating summary

The chapel on St Ninian's Isle has been dated to the 12th century by analogy with other sites, particularly the Brough of Birsay. Excavations in 1999 confirmed that the chapel was set *into* the wind-blown sand, and was therefore later than all the radiocarbon-dated burials that were excavated from *below* the sand. The latest of these, SK 5 and SK 6, have been dated to between the 11th and 13th centuries, which allows for the chapel to have been built sometime after the latter half of the 11th century.

The four narrow long cists excavated from the sand outside the SE corner of the chapel in 1959 were probably contemporary with the use of the chapel. Two groups of bones, code-named 'Robert' and 'Hubert' (ABDUA 14270 and 14254), were supposedly excavated from these cists in 1959, but the study of archive material described in Chapter 3, and the re-excavation of the cists 06 (Phase V), and 321 and 335 (Phase III) in 2000, have shown that 'Hubert' may have been excavated from cist 321 of Phase III, directly below cist 06, and the radiocarbon date for this burial (680–890 cal AD at 95.4%) supports this. No archive slides could be located to verify from which long cist 'Robert' was excavated, although radiocarbon dating has produced a similar date range of 780–1000 cal AD at 95.4% for this burial.

Three later (post-medieval) burials from this phase were also excavated in 1999 and 2000. An articulated burial SK 3 (Figure 4.20) was partially excavated from within the thick deposit of sand at the eastern of the trench in 2000. No cut or coffin was identified for this burial, which was aligned E–W and had been buried at a later date than any of the other burials in the trench. Burrowing had damaged the burial, and further disarticulated remains, from

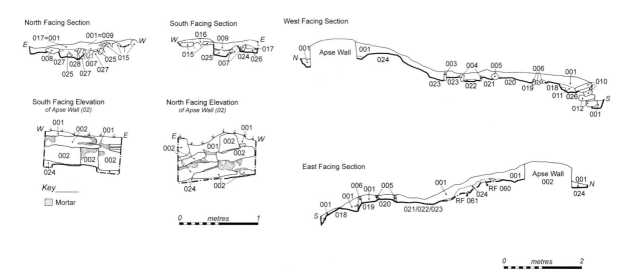

FIGURE 4.17

Trial Trench 1 (1999) elevations and sections. Drawing: L McEwan

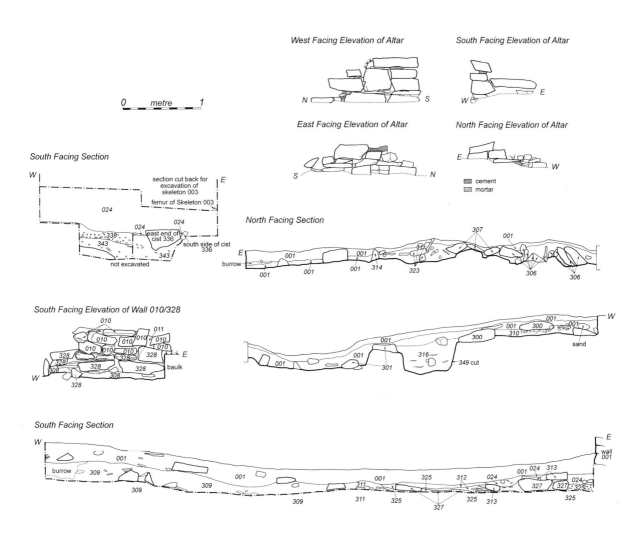

FIGURE 4.18

Trench 1 (2000) sections and elevations of chapel altar. Drawing: L McEwan

FIGURE 4.19
Long cists 03 to 06 when first uncovered in July 2000, from the north

additional burials, were recovered from burrows to the south and west. The skull was completely missing and it is possible that the burial was partially excavated in 1959.

Two further undisturbed post-medieval burials were partially uncovered and analysed *in situ* during the 1999 excavation of Trial Trench 1, between the chancel and the long cists. These had been interred into the sand, at a level post-dating the disuse of the chapel, and included part of an adult burial (SF 61) and an almost complete neonate infant burial (SF 60; Figures 4.14 and 4.20). The latter was possibly an un-baptised infant, as it had been interred very close to the wall of the ruined chapel. The adult burial was truncated by a later burial indicated only by a cut in the west section of the trench. The presence of three burials, in the small remaining area of wind-blown sand in the NE corner of the trench, is an indication of the density of medieval and post-medieval burials which once existed over the entire area of the site prior to the 1950s excavation.

Phase VI: 1959 backfill and reconstructed features (Figure 4.20)

All the features shown on the final published plan of the area in the 1973 volume which fell within the smaller confines of the July 2000 trench were

found to be extant. It became clear that many of these features had been partially, if not fully, excavated in 1959 and then put back or reconstructed at the end of the 1959 season.

In the NE corner, long cists 03b, 04b and 05b had been partially excavated, and 06b had been totally excavated and then rebuilt. All were backfilled with re-deposited sand (18–23). In 2000, following the removal of the turf and topsoil, an E–W section was taken across the sand in the NE corner, to the south of long cist 05 (Figures 4.18 and 4.20) to allow the re-excavation of cist (06) and to provide a vertical record of the relationship of the wind-blown sand (24) to the cists and layers below. It became clear from this section and the mixed assemblage of finds that was recovered that the wind-blown sand had been partially re-deposited (24b) on top of the earlier Phase III long cists 321 and 335. This section also showed that the sand 24b and southernmost long cist (06) were re-instated at the end of the 1959 season after the total excavation and then backfilling (337) of cist 335, and the area of sand in the NE corner then revetted with a low stone wall (328/10/11/12) with steps built in to the side. A dry-stone revetment wall was also built around the base of the entire excavation area south of the chapel to prevent the sand from collapsing inwards from the sloping banks around it.

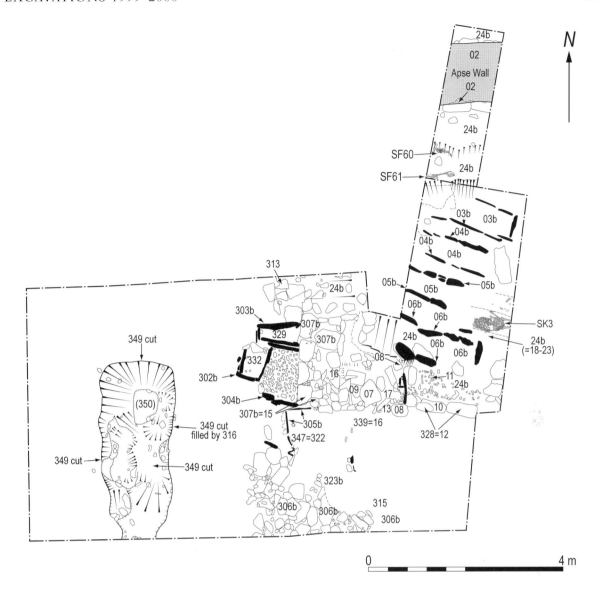

FIGURE 4.20

Phase VI: 1959 backfill and reconstructed features. Drawing: L McEwan

To the SW of this area, the four short cists had all been emptied, excavated and reconstructed (302b, 303b, 304b and 305b) in 1959. The stones of the largest cist, 305, had been left intact, and a thin layer of sandy backfill dumped into it (layer 322/347), whilst some of the stone uprights of the other three cists (302, 303 and 304) had been removed and then replaced, as evidenced by pockets of topsoil around them. Both cists 303 and 304 appeared to be set into, or possibly truncated by, wall 307 to the east, but excavation in 2000 demonstrated that the upper courses of 307 were not in their original position, having been excavated and replaced in 1959 at the same time as the cists. Large, water-worn stones and flat schist and sandstone boulders had been used to reconstruct the upper course of the wall (307b/15) and to the east of cist 305, the wall had been enhanced by the addition of further stones (323b) above the east side of cist 305. The short cists were back-filled with re-deposited sand,

pebbles and shells (339, 332 and 329/16), or the remains of the original fill, mixed with topsoil (333) in cist 304. These layers all contained flecks of the red paint used by O'Dell's team to mark a rough grid on some of the stones and to denote reconstructed features for anyone examining the site in the future (J Coull pers comm).

An upper layer of paving 313 overlying a lower, unexcavated layer 327 at the north end of wall 307, was set into topsoil and had clearly also been reconstructed after the 1959 excavation. Stone rubble and backfill 306b, 07–09, 13 and 17, had been replaced around wall 307. The rubble at the south end of the wall had patches of topsoil mixed with midden (315) between the stones and contained three stones marked with the red paint.

On the west side of the area re-deposited midden deposits, mixed with backfill and topsoil (316) were excavated from a large hollow (349) over 1m deep that had been cut right through all the layers of the

Context	Description	Quartz lithics	Coarse pottery	Worked bone	Worked stone	Metal/ misc	Carbonised plant	Human bone	Animal bone	Fish bone	Marine shell	Land snails
03 –06	Long cists	–	–	–	–	–	–	–	–	––	–	–
07 – 09, 13, 16–17	1959 backfill and topsoil	–	–	–	–	–	–	–	–	–	–	–
10	Revetment wall	–	–	–	–	–	–	–	–	–	–	–
18-23	Wind-blown sand = 024	–	–	–	–	–	–	–	Indet frags	–	–	–
24b	Wind-blown sand	2 flakes	1 body sherd	–	Pebble with residue	Frag of aluminium foil 3 lumps mortar	Coffin wood, mineral-ised coni-fer wood	98 adult bones and frags, 3 adult teeth, 55 juvenile bones and frags, 26 unident frags	1 cow 1 pig 1 sheep/goat 1 gull sp 1 indet	1 saithe, 1 saithe/ pollack	216 periwinkle 39 limpet 1 dogwhelk 4 whelk 6 oyster 3 spiny cockle 2 Artica islandia	Cochlicopa lubricella C. lubrica Lauria cylindracea Aegopinella pura A. nitidula, Oxychillus cellarius, Arianta arbustorum, Discus rotundus
302b-304b	Reconstructed short cists	–	–	–	–	–	–	–	–	–	–	–
306b	Tumble of stones S of cist 305	4 flakes blade, 2 waste	2 body sherds	Worked bone and broken antler bead	–	Nail, knife tang?, part of a ?key ?slag	1 birch, 5 heather family, 2 spruce/ larch, 3 six-row barley, 2 cf six-row barley	2 adult rib frags, 2 juvenile rib frags, juvenile neural arch frag and femur	6 cow, 57sheep/ goat, 1 puffin, 1 bird, 1 small un-gulate, 1 indet	1 Atlantic herring, 1 cod, 1 cod fam-ily, 4 cod/ saithe/ pollack, 4 saithe, 16 unident	28 periwinkle, 7 limpet, 4 oyster	Cochlicopa lubricella, C. lubrica, Aegopinella pura, A. nitidula, Oxychillus cellarius, Arianta arbustorum, Trichia hispida, Discus rotundus
315	Backfill	–	–	–	–	–	–	–	1 cow, 1 pig, 5 sheep /goat, 5 indet	2 cod, 1 cod/ saithe/ pollack, 1 pollack, 7 unident	<5 periwinkle, <5 limpet	Cochlicopa lubricella, C. lubrica, Lauria cylindricea, Aegopinella nitidula, Oxychillus cellarius, Arianta arbustorum, Trichia hispida, Discus rotundus
316	Backfill into hollow cut 349	–	5 body sherds	–	–	Nail	3 alder, 1 heather family, 2 peat/turf, 3 hulled six-row barley 1 cf six-row barley, 2 indet cereal, 1 blinks, 1 ribwort plantain, 1 redshanks, 2 chickweed	46 adult bones and frags, 3 adult teeth, 68 juvenile bones and frags, 2 juvenile teeth	6 cow, 21 indet	2 unident	1 oyster	Cochlicopa lubricella, C. lubrica, Oxychillus cellarius, Arianta arbustorum, Discus rotundus

FIGURE 4.21A

Material identified from Phase VI: small finds, general finds and samples

Context	Description	Quartz lithics	Coarse pottery	Worked bone	Worked stone	Metal/ misc	Carbonised plant	Human bone	Animal bone	Fish bone	Marine shell	Land snails
322 = 347	Backfill in cist 305	–	–	–	–	–	–	–	–	–	–	–
323	Rubble wall to E of cist 305	–	–	–	–	–	–	–	2 cow, 1 sheep/goat, 1 bird, 1 small ungulate, 2 indet frags	2 unident	120 periwinkle, 9 limpet	–
328 = 12	Mortared E–W revetment wall	–	–	–	–	–	–	–	–	–	–	–
329	Sandy backfill in cist 303	–	–	–	–	–	2 heather family, 1 Scot's pine type, 1 hulled six-row barley, 3 six-row barley	Adult sacrum frag, lumbar vertebra frag, and hand phalange, juvenile tooth	Indet frags, 1 sheep/goat	1 Atlantic herring, 2 saithe, 15 unident	396 periwinkle, 35 limpet, 3 rough periwinkle, 4 limpet, 1 oyster	Cochlicopa lubricella, C. lubrica, Discus rotundus
332	Mixed sandy midden backfill, in 302	–	–	–	–	–	1 conifer, 1 heather family, 1 six-row barley, 1 indet cereal	Adult cervical vertebra and navicular	5 cow, 2 pig, 1 sheep/goat, 1 small ungulate, 1 bird, 1 indet frags	–	1420 periwinkle, 141 limpet, 8 spiny cockle, 6 Artica islandica	Cochlicopa lubricella, C. lubrica, Lauria cylindracea, Aegopinella pura, Discus rotundus
333	Backfill in cist 304	–	6 body sherds	–	Grooved pebble, incised cross stone	Unid frag; frag plastic 2 frags mortar	–	–	6 rabbit, 8 cow, 1 pig, sheep/goat, 1 pig, 1 large ungulate, 1 small ungulate, 6 bird, 2 ?thrush sp, 11 rabbit, 100 indet frags, indet charred	3 cod, 10 / 3 cod, 6 unident	1560 periwinkle, 192 limpet, 16 spiny cockle, 12 Artica islandica	Cochlicopa lubricella, C. lubrica, Oxychillus cellarius, Trichia hispida, Discus rotundus
335	Excavated long cist	–	–	–	–	–	–	–	–	–	–	–
337	Sand and pebbles	Poss core	1 body sherd	–	Pebble with residue	–	Spruce/larch 3 hulled six-row barley	15 adult bones and frags; juvenile rib and humeral metaphysis	1 sheep/goat, 1 large ungulate, 4 indet frags	3 unid	272 periwinkle, 103 limpet, 7 dogwhelk, 5 oyster, 2 common cockle, 4 thick trough shell	Cochlicopa lubricella, C. lubrica, Lauria cylindracea, Aegopinella pura, Oxychillus cellarius, Trichia hispida, Discus rotundus, Punctum pygmaeum
339	Backfill between stones of wall 307b	Flake, 2 waste	1 body sherd	–	–	–	1 birch	–	5 cow, 1 pig, 1 sheep/goat, 2 small ungulate, 2 puffin, 26 indet frags	1 Atlantic herring, 3 cod, 4 cod family, 1 ling, 2 rockling, 4 saithe, 1 sea scorpion family	196 periwinkle, 24 limpet, 2 spiny cockle, 1 Artica islandica	Cochlicopa lubricella, C. lubrica, Aegopinella pura, A. nitidula, Oxychillus cellarius, Trichia hispida, Discus rotundus

FIGURE 4.21B

Material identified from Phase VI: small finds, general finds and samples

site and down to bedrock in 1959. This part of the trench is shown devoid of any features in the centre of Small's (1973) plan (Figure 1.2).

Artefactual and ecofactual summary for 1959 backfill and reconstructed features (Figure 4.21)

As might be expected, a mixed assemblage was recovered from this phase, with the re-deposited stone cairn rubble (306b) being particularly artefact rich. Flaked quartz was recovered from backfill, wind-blown sand and the largest number from the stone tumble (306b). A small assemblage of sixteen body sherds of coarse pottery was scattered through all the contexts. Iron finds included nails recovered from 316 and 306b, and a possible knife tang and a piece of a key, the latter found to conjoin with another piece (SF 551) found in the topsoil (Figure 4.29).

Three conjoining pieces of hollowed out antler tine, externally smoothed and worked into a bead, were found in two different deposits: two pieces in 306b and one in 315 (SF 515 and 538). This incomplete bead (Figure 4.31), and a second, found in 2000 in Phase III (SF 460 and 512; see above), are of the same type as those of the 'bone and antler necklace' found in the 1959 excavations (PLATE 14). Two pieces of worked bone were also recovered from 306b: a cattle metatarsal (SF 540) with a hole made in the proximal end, which Batey suggests (below) may have been used as an awl or the handle for a tool, and a sheep/goat metacarpal (SF 541; Figure 4.31) with the proximal end worked and polished.

Stone finds included a grooved, possibly worked pebble, from backfill layer 333, and an unusual schist stone with lightly incised simple cross with possible traces of a partial enclosing circle and a foot (SF 433; Figure 4.23). Pebbles were also recovered with a whitish residue adhering, probably of a natural, biological origin (see Hall, below). Evidence of disturbance from burials and the 1959 excavations included a section of plastic wire and fragments of mortar in 333, and fragments of coffin wood, aluminium foil and mortar in the wind-blown sand (24b).

A considerable assemblage of disarticulated human bone was excavated from the 1959 backfill deposits and other re-deposited contexts. Bone representing a minimum of one adult was retrieved from wall fill 11, surrounding the bank of wind-blown sand in the NE corner of the site. A minimum of five adults and three juveniles was represented in the assemblage from the wind-blown sand contexts 23 and 24, the juveniles aged 7–11 years, and 1 year 4 months to 2 years 8 months respectively. Disarticulated adult and juvenile bone were also found scattered through the wall tumble 306b, backfill deposits 316, 329 and 332, and modern wall fill 337.

No identifiable botanical remains were recovered from 024 other than modern material. Context 337 contained several grains of hulled six-row barley and a large fragment of spruce/larch charcoal

(SF 476), and the carbonised remains from contexts 329, 332, 333 and 339 backfilled into the three short cists included only tiny charcoal fragments of birch (*Betula*), Scots pine (*Pinus sylvestris* type) and heather family, together with a few grains of six-row barley (*Hordeum vulgare sl*). Carbonised botanical remains from 306b included very small fragments of birch, heather family and spruce/larch charcoal, together with several grains of six-row barley although midden material 315, mixed between the stones of 306, contained no botanical evidence to further the interpretation of the area. Context 316, re-deposited dark sand used to infill the large hollow cut into the site in 1959 contained mixed carbonised remains, such as alder (*Alnus*) and heather family charcoal, burnt peat/turf, carbonised cereal grains and weed seeds.

Rabbit bones were ubiquitous in these (and topsoil) deposits, equalling the domestic farm animals in numbers of fragments, if not in bulk. Puffin and gull species bones were also present, and also an example of cat. The fish bone assemblage included mainly cod, saithe, pollack and ling with two rockling, three Atlantic herring and one sea scorpion bone also represented. Edible periwinkle and limpet were the most common marine shells present, with particular concentrations in the backfill layers from short cists 302 and 304. Other marine shell species were present, the non-edible species probably having been brought in with seaweed (eg rough periwinkle, trough shell). The same range of land snail species is seen in this phase as others at the site.

Phase VII: topsoil and turf

A varied artefactual assemblage was recovered from the topsoil (01) across the site due to disturbance from rabbit burrowing and the previous excavations.

Artefactual and ecofactual summary from the topsoil and turf (Figure 4.22)

Worked finds from the topsoil included an elongated iron piece with rounded shaft at one end, bent and incomplete, which conjoins with SF 558 in Phase III (Figure 4.29), and is interpreted as part of an iron key. Other iron finds included a collection of nine nails, probably originating from Phase V burials, and roves with broken shanks attached, which may well have been removed from boat timbers. Stone finds included a pot lid of crudely chipped schist, two possible hones, a pebble hammerstone and two pieces of pumice, one with obvious smoothing that could have been used for burnishing pottery or cleaning skins (SF 567; Figure 4.24). A gaming piece (SF 573; Figure 4.24) that probably originated from Phase II (see Batey below) was also found. Five flakes and a core of quartz and 20 sherds of pottery were also found, but were mixed with an otherwise relatively modern assemblage of finds, including a fragment

Description	Topsoil and turf context 01, and topsoil and turf stripped from wall 02 of chapel
Quartz lithics	5 flakes, 1 core
Coarse pottery	20 body sherds
Glass/plastic	5 sherds modern green glass; 1 frag 35mm film
Worked stone	2 poss hones; pot lid; 2 poss worked pebbles; 2 pumice; ?perf quartz object gaming piece
Metal/misc	2 bog ore, 1 1957 half-penny, 9 iron roves/ nails, 1 frag aluminium foil, 1 iron frag iron key? 94 mortar frags
Carbonised plant	1 birch, 1 Scots pine type, 1 pine family, 1 indet coffin wood
Human bone	60 adult bones and frags; 22 juvenile bones and frags; 1 neonate rib
Animal bone	59 cow, 2 horse, 1 large ungulate, 68 sheep/ goat, 6 small ungulate, 1 dog, 23 pig, 1 seal, 15 gull sp, 1 wader sp, 9 bird sp, 3 whale frag, 110 rabbit, indt frags
Fish bone	1 grey gurnard, 1 saithe, 1 unident
Marine shell	1702 periwinkle, 39 rough periwinkle, 301 limpet, 27 dogwhelk, 27 whelk, 63 oyster, 11 common cockle, 7 spiny cockle, 2 *Artica islandica*, <5 mussel, <5 razor shell

FIGURE 4.22

Material identified from Phase VII: small finds, general finds and samples

of plastic 35mm film, aluminium foil, five sherds of modern glass, 94 fragments of mortar and a 1957 halfpenny.

A considerable assemblage of disarticulated human bone was found in the topsoil, representing a minimum number of four adults and two juveniles. One male and one female could be identified. The ages of two of the adults were identified as being between 17–25 and 35–45 years at death, and one juvenile as 2–4 years at death.

Botanical materials examined from the turf and topsoil consisted of spot finds of uncarbonised wood and metal fittings. The wood was either birch (*Betula*) or pine (*Pinaceae*), and it is highly likely that these wood fragments and metalwork are residual from coffins, probably of post-medieval date. The animal bone assemblage was very mixed. Horse was only represented in this phase, and single examples of dog and seal were found in this phase and in Phase III. Gull bones from one skeleton were found and were probably of comparatively recent origin. Rabbit bones were very common, and the disturbed remains of several virtually complete bodies are noted by Gidney (below), together with dispersed body parts. Only three fish bones were recovered, two being identified to grey gurnard and saithe.

4.3   THE ARTEFACTUAL ASSEMBLAGE (see Appendix 5)

The carved stones (Figure 4.23)
Ian Fisher

— SF 301, Context 314. Phase III. A thin water-worn slab of silvery-grey micaceous schist, with smooth rounded edges. It measures 245 x 104mm in maximum width near the top, and 22mm in maximum thickness. The lower part tapers obliquely, probably naturally, to a rounded foot at the right. The right edge swells out slightly c65mm above this, and again c60mm below the gently rounded top. At the centre of face (a) there is an elongated cross of plaited bands with two transoms, neatly incised with a sharp point. It is 93mm high and the shaft, divided into two bands by a central incision, varies from 11 to 13mm in width. The upper transom is 33mm in span and 13mm high, and it opens into the top arm of the cross, which is only 9mm high. This disrupts the even flow of the plaiting in the cross-head, which is developed round a horizontal incision cutting the long vertical divider to form a central crosslet. A continuous band plaited through the shaft, set 25mm above the base forms a rectangular lower transom, 28 x 11mm. The foot may have been intended to form a triquetra knot, a frequent termination in plaited crosses (Fisher 2001, fig 35P; 2002, fig 3.10) but the visible incisions form two small angular loops, the reconstruction of which is uncertain. On the back (face b) there are two slight vertical grooves and a horizontal one above them, but all are very faint and there is no other evidence of carving on this face.

— SF 465, Context 314. Phase III. A slab of micaceous schist similar to that used for 301, but with less regular edges. It measures 207 x 63mm in maximum width, near the top, and 18mm in maximum thickness. The lower part tapers obliquely to a naturally pointed foot at the left, and in the right edge, from c70–100mm above this, there is a shallow notch showing signs of rough shaping or damage. The upper part has slightly irregular but parallel edges rising to a top which slopes gently down to the right. At the back this part tapers in thickness to a sharp top edge. The surface of the front (face a) is irregular, with vertical striations which in some cases affect the identification of the light sharp incisions. Towards the right edge there is some exfoliation which has affected the right terminals of the plaited cross. This is similar to but slightly smaller than that on SF 301, and is carved in a similar position. It is 74mm high, with a lower transom 24mm across and 10-13mm high, set 20mm above the pointed foot. The upper transom, 8mm from the top, measures 26 x 10mm. Interpretation of the plaiting of both transoms is confused by natural grooves, but the cruciform centres at both junctions are distinct. The upper transom appears to be correctly interlaced with the shaft, which continues into the top arm in contrast to SF 301. Very little detail is visible at the foot, and it may be unfinished. The back is rough and uncarved.

— SF 494, Context 336. Phase III. An irregular slab of micaceous schist, measuring 0.63 x 0.35m and 40mm thick. The lower part tapers, especially at the right, to a rounded butt. A sharp-edged break at the top right is the only part that appears to have broken off since the slab was carved, but the whole surface is corrugated and heavily worn. The foliation of the schist has produced an alternation of vertical striations and heavily damaged softer layers, and the whole lower right part has flaked off. In the upper part there was a linear Latin cross, formed by channelled grooves up to 3mm deep and 4mm deep in the left arm. The apparent width of 6mm in the right side-arm is due to flaking both above and below, and the top arm and shaft have similarly lost much of their right edges. The terminals of the top and left arms are also lost, but the span was *c*95mm and the height 130mm, with the transom *c*55mm below the top. The back of the slab is convex in cross-section and worn smooth except for one flake.

— SF 433, Context 333. Phase VI. A slab of micaceous schist, worn smooth on the face but flaked at the back and at the bottom right edge. It measures 197 x 74mm and is 12mm in maximum thickness. The right edge swells out 60mm above the foot, while there is a small notch in the same edge below the peaked top. Filling most of the front is a Latin cross, scratched with light and irregular grooves. Its upper arm begins *c*30mm below the top of the slab, and the shaft extends to the damaged bottom edge. The span is 48mm, and slightly curving lines run from the shaft, 35mm below the crossing, to the ends of the arms, forming the lower half of an elongated 'ring' *c*60mm high. There are very slight traces of the upper left quadrant, but the area right of the top arm is worn away in concentric curves and no incision survives.

The stone bearing a linear cross (SF 494) is a small but not unusual example of a type of upright grave-marker which was widely distributed through Britain and Ireland during the early medieval period. The cross itself belongs to the simplest version of the Christian symbol and is one of the commonest ones in western Ireland and Scotland. In the West Highlands and Islands, for example, there are almost 80 stones bearing plain equal-armed or Latin incised crosses, often with repeated examples on the same carving. About 20 other crosses of this type are carved in a sunken technique, with flat grooves somewhat wider than those of this carving (Fisher 2001, 12–13, 28–29, 31–32). Some of the smaller examples on Iona, and at sites such as Ardnadam (Cowal) and Ellary (Mid Argyll), are close to the St Ninian's Isle example in scale, but differ in their incised or pecked carving-technique. This is also true of the linear crosses previously recorded on the Isle itself (Small *et al* 1973, nos 10, 13, 14).

Dating of these simple crosses is often impossible, especially when they are in such damaged condition. Although the 7th-9th century bracket favoured by Nash-Williams (1950, 17) is often quoted, and the group at Ellary has been attributed by the writer to this period, although the type continues much later. A significant occurrence is at Kiloran Bay, Colonsay, where irregular crosses were incised on two of the side-slabs enclosing a rich late 9th-century Norse burial (Fisher 2001, 28, 136; Graham-Campbell and

Batey 1998, 118–122). Central crosslets, plain or with pitted terminals, are found in Norway in the heads of free-standing crosses in the Stavanger area, including the large one bearing a runic inscription to Erling Skjalgsson (d 1028) (Birkeli 1973, 151–156). Some of the cruciform stones with similar crosslets in burial-grounds on the Shetland islands of Unst and Yell, and at Kilbar on Barra (Fisher 2001, 107), may have been influenced by the crosses of western Norway. Research is in progress to distinguish these elements from the older Irish tradition that is prominently represented in the Hebrides on Iona and North Rona, and in western Ireland particularly at Skellig Michael (Fisher 2001, 17, 56–57; 2002, 55–57; 2005). A rare Norwegian example of an unaccompanied plain cross is incised on a *bauta* or pillar-stone at Akre in Rendalen, in the eastern province of Hedmark (Birkeli 1973, 86–87). This and the other Norwegian parallels show that a date in the Norse period is perfectly credible for this slab on St Ninian's Isle.

The three other stones are unusually small, flakes of schist rather than slabs. They are comparable with motif-pieces rather than normal grave-markers, and the carving on SF 433 is of lightly scratched graffito style. However, the tapering or curving in of the lower parts of all three stones suggests that they were indeed intended to be set upright as miniature grave-markers rather than being recumbent or placed in the graves. Two other small stones (SF 471–472), of similar character but without ornament, obviously served the same purpose, as well as some rather larger slabs. The thinly scratched stone (SF 433) shows a Latin cross with a distorted ring, now incomplete in the upper parts, enclosing the cross-head. This motif, developed from the encircled equal-armed cross of early Christian Mediterranean art, probably antedates the free-standing ringed cross by centuries. Examples are found in Argyll, on Iona and Tiree, and in Aberdeenshire at Monymusk, as well as on Skellig Michael and at other sites in south Kerry (Fisher 2001, 22, 28; O'Sullivan and Sheehan 1996, 251, 258, 281). All of these have regular circles, but the irregular oval of the St Ninian's Isle carving can be matched in what is probably the largest example of the type, from Skuvøy in the Faroes. Described by the writer as 'uniquely coarse', this belongs to a group of stones whose date is controversial and are the subject of ongoing research. Most are of Hebridean/Irish character, but they come from a site which in medieval tradition was the principal base for the Norse conversion of the Faroe Islands at the end of the 10th century (Kermode 1930, 374; Fisher 2005, 162–164; Fisher and Scott 2007). Due to its lack of an archaeological context, the Shetland stone cannot contribute to this debate, but it is likely to belong to the Norse period with the other miniature carvings.

In contrast to the cross on SF 433, those on SF 301 and 465 were carefully designed and executed,

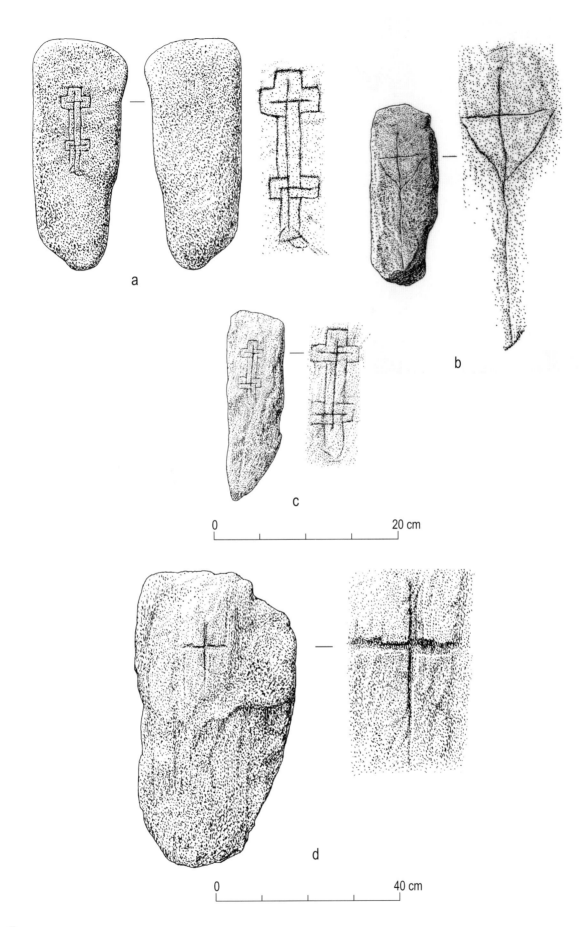

FIGURE 4.23

Cross-inscribed stones from 2000 excavation: SF 301 (a), SF 433 (b), SF 465 (c) and SF 494 (d). Drawings: I Scott, reproduced with permission of the Royal Commission on Ancient and Historical Monuments of Scotland, Edinburgh

although the surface of the latter was less regular and is heavily worn. Crosses with two or three transoms, thought to represent Christ's rood with its foot-rest and inscription-panel, are common in the Byzantine tradition. Simplified forms are found both in Argyll and Kerry, and in the Seljaland caves in south Iceland. Large and coarse examples, perhaps of 10th or 11th-century date, are found at Gleann na Gaoith' (Islay) and Clachan (Kintyre) (Fisher 2001, 29H, 33S, 37S, 39CC, 42D; O'Sullivan and Sheehan 1996, 253; Ahronson 2002, 114).

Crosses of two bands with square plaiting at the centre are found in Scotland and Ireland, but there is no compelling reason to date the type earlier than the 10th century (Fisher 2001, 42A; O'Sullivan and Sheehan 1996, 315–316). A close parallel for the square plaiting on the St Ninian's Isle stones is the fragment from Papil where the bands interlace within a double ring in the cross-head (Fisher 2002, 53–54). In other respects the Papil slab compares with others on Iona and at Glendalough in Ireland, all probably of the late 10th or early 11th century, although their bands curve into the adjacent arms rather than passing through the centre (Fisher 2001, 45B–C, 22A). Square plaiting at junctions appears to have been particularly favoured by Scandinavian patrons, whether in interlocking two-band oval or rectangular loops or in larger compositions as found in the cross-heads of several Manx slabs (Kermode 1907, 47 and passim). Less formal treatments are found on some motif-pieces, and one example from the monastic site of Nendrum (Co. Down) resembles a crude version of the St Ninian's Isle type, but with the transoms extended to the left to enclose a square (O'Meadhra 1979, no. 135A). The motif remained popular in Scandinavia, and simple rectangular links are found on Swedish runestones and on two runestones on Bornholm (Lager 2002, 65A6; Jacobsen and Moltke 1941, 1, 454, 463; 2, figs 962–963, 992–993). A more elaborate version with two transoms is found on a runestone from Holm (Halland, Sweden), now in the Stockholm Museum (Jacobsen and Moltke 1941, 1, 395; 2, figs 808–809). This may be of the 12th century, like the soapstone cross, built above the north doorway of the nave of Kinsarvik church (Hordaland, Norway). This has a two-band cross, plaited within rings at the centre and terminals, and the side-arms extend beyond the top and bottom circles to make a triple cross (Christie and Svarstad 1963, 7–8). One other plaited cross with triple bars is found on Iona, on a graveslab from Reilig Odhràin (RCAHMS 1982, 220–221, no. 227). This has a central ringed cross, and although the slab is no earlier than the 14th century, bearing a boat and sword, it may be based on a much older model. These elaborate compositions mark the culmination of a development in which the small stones from St Ninian's Isle stand near the beginning.

Other worked stone
Colleen E Batey

Discs

— SF 370 (Figure 4.24), Context 309. Phase II. Irregularly trimmed slate disc with irregular lines on upper surface, probable natural markings. 142 x 109 x 4mm.

— SF 570, Context 01. Phase VII. Crudely chipped schist disc. ?Pot lid. 98 x 118 x 17mm.

These two examples of stone discs were found one in Phase II, which is presumed to be its original context, and the other in the turf and topsoil of Phase VII. Their simple form would suggest identification as lids for ceramic vessels, and the type is ubiquitous in Scotland. Several of similar sizes were noted from The Howe in Orkney (Ballin Smith with Collins 1994, 204 and illus 119), as well as Scalloway in Shetland, for example (discussed in Clarke 1998a, 144–146). At Scalloway the size range is 45–240mm, with most falling within the range 50–90mm; the two from St Ninian's Isle fall within this wide range. Clarke (1998a) discusses the possibility of differing function between the larger and smaller discs, with the larger ones most likely to be associated with covering storage vessels.

Pebbles and coarse stone tools

— SF 300, Context 301. Phase II. Broken elongated pebble, with stone loss at possible work end. 126 x 76 x 28mm.

— SF 350, Context 309. Phase II. Ellipse-shaped pebble, with one edge damaged and chipped; could be natural damage through percussion. 111 x 64 x 28mm.

— SF 360, Context 311. Phase II. Quartzite beach pebble, possibly selected. 19 x 15 x 12mm.

— SF 509, SK 12. Phase III. Water-worn flat quartz beach pebble, not worked. 46 x 40 x 8mm.

— SF 510 (Figure 4.24), Context 330. Phase III. Hexagonal flat stone, mica rich with flat upper and lower surfaces. Deliberately shaped, possibly through use as a smoother. 53 x 50 x 9mm.

— SF 575, Context 345, Sample 328. Phase III. Pebble with one short edge slightly smoothed. Possible rubber. 120 x 70 x 30mm.

— SF 566, Context 333, Sample 314. Phase VI. Small pebble with two grooves on one face, possibly man-made. 24 x 21 x 4mm.

— SF 568, Context 01. Phase VII. Broken shaped quartz fragment, possible traces of perforation at one edge. 25 x 18 x 9mm.

— SF 569, Context 01. Phase VII. Water-worn pebble with one face very smoothed. Possible hone? 83 x 26 x 15mm.

— SF 571, Context 01. Phase VII. Quartzite pebble with rose patch, possibly selected. 67 x 60 x 32mm.

— SF 572, Context 01. Phase VII. Elliptical pebble, possibly utilised at both ends. 100 x 62 x 18mm.

— SF 574, Context 01. Phase VII. Long pebble with two long faces smoothed. Possible hone? 95 x 25 x 20mm.

This group of stone tools comprises pounders (SF 300 and SF 350) and two possible smoothers or rubbers

PLATE 1
General view of St Ninian's Isle

PLATE 2
A tombolo of white sand joins mainland Shetland with St Ninian's Isle. Photograph: Christopher Gerrard

PLATE 3
The chapel in August 1999, from the west

PLATE 4

The St Ninian's Isle treasure. Photograph: National Museums of Scotland

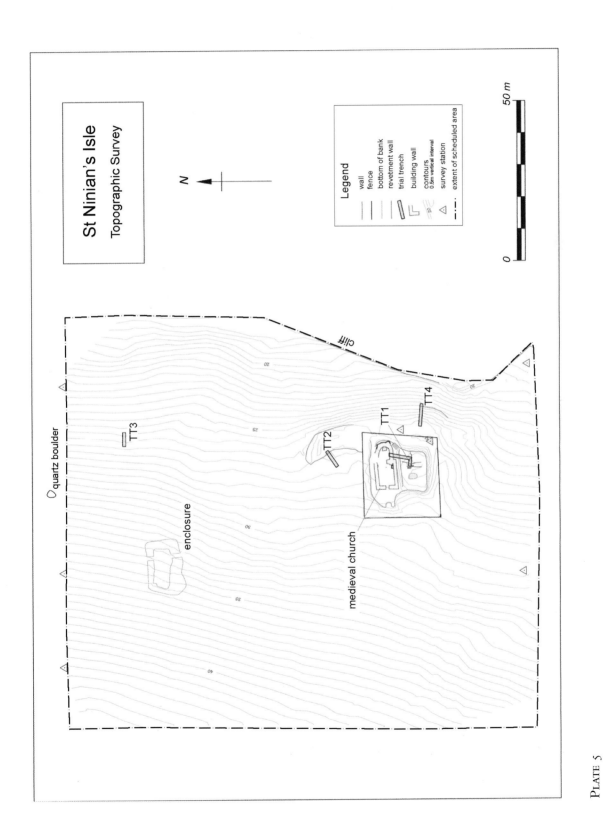

St Ninian's Isle
Topographic Survey

N

Legend

	wall
	fence
	bottom of bank
	revetment wall
	trial trench
	building wall
	contours 0.5m vertical interval
△	survey station
–··–	extent of scheduled area

0   50 m

quartz boulder

enclosure

TT3

TT2

medieval church

TT1

TT4

cliff

20

25

30

35

40

20

PLATE 5

Topographic survey of scheduled area 1999 (Harry 2000)

PLATE 6
Excavations below the church in 1959

PLATE 7
Consolidation south of the chapel 1959

PLATE 8
Excavations south of the chapel 1959

PLATE 9
The St Ninian's Isle hoard in the ground, showing weathering copper in contact with the stone

PLATE 11
Group One (nos 16–21) and Group Two (nos 22–29)

PLATE 12
Brown glass bead A21.2000.21b from the Shetland Museum (Small) collection

PLATE 10
Group One beads (nos 1–15)

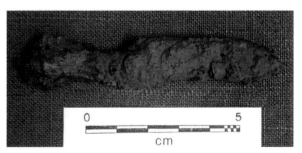

PLATE 13
Iron Knife SF 497 found beside cist burial SK 5

PLATE 14
Bone and antler bead necklace from the area south of the chapel 1959

PLATE 15
Limoges enamel cross fragments from the Shetland Museum (Small) collection, after conservation

PLATE 16
The east end of the chapel, with altar in the foreground, August 2000

PLATE 17
Cleaning the site after removal of turf and topsoil in July 2000

PLATE 18
Remains of rubble cairn and paving around short cists after removal of topsoil in July 2000, from the north

PLATE 19
Half section through long cist, from the east, with excavation in the background, July 2000

PLATE 20
Planning on site in July 2000, infant burials in situ in foreground

PLATE 21
Infant burials in situ, July 2000

PLATE 22
The chapel in 2008. Photograph: Christopher Gerrard

PLATE 23
The chapel in 2008. Photograph: Christopher Gerrard

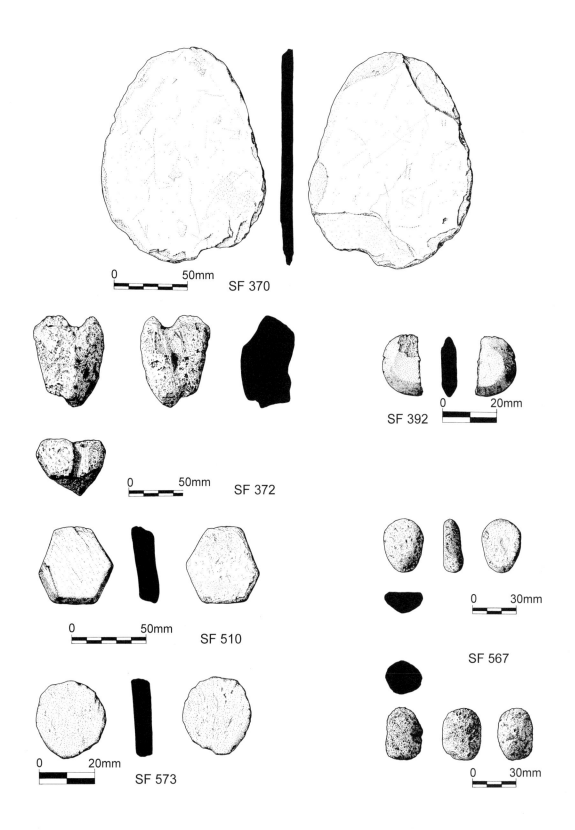

0 50mm SF 370

SF 392 0 20mm

0 50mm SF 372

0 50mm SF 510

0 30mm

SF 567

0 20mm SF 573

0 30mm

FIGURE 4.24

Stone and pumice finds from 2000 excavation: SF 370, SF 372, SF 392, SF 510, SF 567 and SF 573. Drawings: A Sperr

(SF 510 and 575) in Phase II, as well as a possible utilised grooved pebble in Phase III (SF 566); two finds in Phase VII may have been used as hones (SF 569 and 574) together with a pebble used as a hammerstone (SF 572). In all cases, the material is local and utilisation opportunistic. Several Iron Age sites provide comparable material, for example Scalloway, where beach pebbles were used as hones and other pebbles (or cobbles) were used as percussive tools (Clarke 1998a, 140–143, 147, fig 91). There is a similar situation at Clickhimin, where beach pebbles were used in a similar manner (Hamilton 1968, fig 58) during the wheelhouse phase of activity.

There are a few quartzite pebbles in this assemblage (Phase II SF 360, Phase III SF 509 and Phase VII SF 571). It is likely that they were selected and brought to the site, particularly so in the case of SF 509, from Phase III, which was found with SK 12. The association of quartz pebbles with burials has long been established, both as shroud weights (eg Birsay Brough Road, Orkney; Morris 1989, illus 40), as well as for use to form cairns over Pictish burials, as at Sandwick, Unst, in Shetland (Bigelow 1984, 115). The numbers in this assemblage are too small to support the latter identification, and the single find from the grave suggests a token gift rather than a set of shroud weights.

Steatite

— SF 372 (Figure 4.24), Context 311. Phase II. Heavily worked steatite piece with traces of two broken perforations, one at each end. Perhaps originally a weight. 55 x 44 x 30mm.

— SF 374, Context 311. Phase II. Indeterminate chunk of un-worked steatite. 65 x 40 x 18mm.

— SF 407, Context 311. Phase II. Irregular lump of talc-rich soft stone, could be un-worked steatite. 110 x 105 x 20mm.

All three pieces of steatite are from an early phase (Phase II) and from an undisturbed context (311). Two of these are un-worked pieces, raw steatite brought to the site, probably from one of the nearest mainland sources at Cunningsburgh. SF 372 however er is a well-worked piece, although broken and presumably discarded in the midden deposits of Phase II; this was originally a perforated weight, probably used in fishing. It has similarities to the type known as a hogback fishing weight, although such would conventionally be dated later than Phase II, falling more readily into Phase III (the type is discussed extensively by Clarke and Sharman 1998, 149, fig 95, no. 4). Steatite is a local commodity which is easily worked and, although it was massively exploited in the Viking and Late Norse periods, its earlier use has been recorded.

Gaming pieces

— SF 392 (Figure 4.24), Context 309. Phase II. Polished and heavily worked black stone disc with chamfered edges, incomplete. ?Gaming piece. 22 x 13 x 5mm.

— SF 573 (Figure 4.24), Context 01. Phase VII. Complete flat disc with ground edges. Gaming piece. 26 x 24 x 6mm.

Both these items have been carefully manufactured with ground edges, and it is most likely that Phase II is the original context for both of them, although SF 573 was recovered from the disturbed upper layers of the site. At Scalloway, this simple type was also represented alongside a number of spectacular gaming pieces. The use of selected small pebbles for game playing was also highlighted (Clarke 1998b, 180). This type of gaming piece from St Ninian's Isle might more accurately be described as counters. The diameter of *c*25mm appears to be a standard unit, as commonly found on Iron Age sites (Clarke 1998b, 178; Wilson 1998, 180). It is worth making a special mention of the fine quality of the pieces from St Ninian's Isle, with the grozed edges of SF 392 being paralleled at The Howe (no. 4047) which is similar in form to this example (Ballin Smith with Collins 1994, 188, illus 106).

Pumice

— SF 567 (Figure 4.24), Context 01. Phase VII. Two water-worn pieces of pumice, one (a) highly smoothed on one face. a) 35 x 25 x 11mm; b) 32 x 25 x 20mm.

The two pieces of pumice from Phase VII are presumed to have been disturbed from elsewhere, and the one with obvious smoothing could have been used for burnishing pottery or cleaning skins. This is a ubiquitous find on sites in Northern Scotland (discussed by Batey and Newton 2009, in relation to Brei Holm, Shetland).

Quernstone

— SF 376, Context 300. Phase II. Substantial beach boulder with modern peripheral breakage. One flat surface highly smoother through use as quernstone. 440 x 350 x 100mm.

This saddle quern (as opposed to rotary quern) has been well-used. Although the edge at one side is broken away, the overall form seems to have been sub-rectangular and its pronounced working hollow suggests that it had been an efficient tool. The type is discussed in relation to comparable finds from The Howe in Orkney (Ballin Smith with Collins 1994, 204 and illus 121), where a variety of forms is described from the Iron Age.

Flaked quartz
Michael Donnelly

Methodology

The pieces within the assemblage were analysed with the naked eye and with the aid of a x10–20 hand lens under a constant lighting source. Categories analysed include raw material, removal ascendancy (primary, secondary or inner), type (blade, core, flake, etc), sub-type (bladelet, multi-platformed core, decortical flake, etc), bulb type, platform preparation, terminal type, flaking pattern, retouch and location, utilisation and location and, finally, macroscopic evidence such as damage or burning (Appendix 6).

Within this analysis, all pieces less than 10mm in maximum linear dimension, which were neither snapped blade segments, flake segments of obvious sub-type nor tool types, were categorised as angular waste; as a result this category contains a large number of pieces usually identified as irregular flakes. Further levels of analysis were applied to selective elements within the assemblage. This included a study of blades and the more regular forms of flakes (regular, core trimming, core rejuvenation), looking at platform, terminal and bulbar characteristics not covered in the basic analysis (such as platform width and depth, presence of platform abrasion and/or isolation, etc).

Results

Raw materials

The assemblage from St Ninian's Isle consists entirely of quartz, with such commonly knapped materials as flint being absent. The majority of the quartz represents unequivocal examples of knapped material (Figure 4.25); however, some pieces are suspect. The major factors affecting the analysis of quartz are outlined below. The analysis adopted the classification scheme utilised by the author during the investigation of a number of quartz based assemblages from the central Highlands of Scotland (Atkinson *et al* 2000). This separates the material into four main categories;

— genuine: piece displays enough characteristics to appear real,
— probable: piece displays some characteristics that could be associated with knapping,

Removal ascendancy	Nos	%
Primary	8	16
Secondary	19	38
Tertiary/Inner	17	34
Natural	6	12
Total	**50**	

FIGURE 4.25

Numbers of worked material in the quartz assemblage

	Nos	%
Genuine	20	40
Probable	15	30
Possible	9	18
Natural	6	12
Total	**50**	

FIGURE 4.26

Numbers of genuine material in the quartz assemblage

— possible: piece gives some indication that it may relate to knapping activities,
— natural:[1] piece clearly not related to knapping activities and has not been retained.

Within the assemblage (Figure 4.26), genuine examples were most common (40%) and these together with probable examples (30%) dominate the total group (70%). Possible examples (18%) were rare for such a quartz-based assemblage, as were natural examples (12%), but this is due to on-site filtering of more suspect examples undertaken by the excavators.

Quartz-dominated assemblages are known elsewhere from Shetland, which does not have a ready supply of quality flint or chert. The quartz appears as two main forms: pebble quartz and vein quartz. Some of the void examples consist of small unknapped pebbles, while others appear to represent thin platy pieces of quartzite found in schist.

Removal ascendancy

All pieces examined were defined as being primary (90–100% cortex), secondary (less than 90% cortex) or inner/tertiary (free of cortex) removals (Figure 4.25). Quartz assemblages can present difficulties in determining removal ascendancy because this material can often exhibit outer surfaces similar in appearance to natural internal fractures. In other cases, such as pebble quartz, a definite outer surface can be identified.

Eight of the lithics (16%) were defined as primary. Secondary material was far more common with 19 examples (38%), whereas inner material accounted for 17 examples (34%). In addition, there were six natural pieces of quartz that were not classified.

The spread of material recovered would appear to suggest that the full range of quartz reduction occurred at St Ninian's Isle (Figure 4.27). This included the initial stages of reduction from nodules to prepared cores through to core exhaustion.

Assemblage composition

All data pertaining to assemblage composition should bear in mind the approach utilised by the analyst, stressing that all non-tools, snapped blades and snapped regular flakes, which are less than 10mm in maximum linear dimension (MLD), be treated as knapping waste products (as opposed to irregular flakes). This approach is not new but is not one often applied to Scottish assemblages, resulting in a disproportionately high incidence of flakes being recorded.

Waste (as defined above) accounted for only 16% of the St Ninian's Isle assemblage, while cores appeared to be more common than is usual with four examples (8%). Flakes were very common with 28 examples (56%), one of which was a snapped tool. Blades were less common with four examples (8%) although this figure is quite high for a quartz-based

Removal ascendancy	Nos	%
Natural	6	12
Waste	8	16
Cores	4	8
(Core tools)	(0)	
Flake	28	56
(Flake tools)	(1)	
Blade	4	8
(Blade tools)	(0)	
Total	**50**	

FIGURE 4.27

Numbers of removal ascendancy in the quartz assemblage

assemblage (see below). In addition to these arte-facts, there were six natural unworked pieces of quartz, accounting for 12% of the assemblage. Their recovery from the same layers as knapped quartz and/or from grave deposits may imply that they had some significance of their own and were not simply naturally occurring pebbles in the soil.

The assemblage from St Ninian's Isle is small and therefore care should be taken in reading too much into assemblage composition. However, a couple of pertinent facts regarding it can be outlined. Firstly, the assemblage contained material from all main classificatory types and secondly, it appeared to represent the full range of reduction stages (including prepared platform and bipolar cores, blade forms, decortical, preparatory and utilised flakes, etc.).

Core technologies

Four cores were recovered from St Ninian's Isle, amounting to 8% of the total assemblage. Two of these were genuine, with one probable and one possible example. The cores averaged 27.25 x 20.25 x 11.5mm, taking length as reflecting primary flaking direction and not the longest side. The often extreme thinness of the cores represents the heavy use of a bipolar reduction strategy and the level of exhaustion of the platform cores.

Only one of the cores had been worked unifacially (worked on one face partially around the core's circumference), and the remaining three had been worked bifacially (worked through two or more faces). Two of the cores (both of the definite examples) were bipolar, indicating the prominence of this technique at St Ninian's Isle. The number of bipolar cores is a more useful indicator of this practice than the presence of bipolar flakes. This is because many bipolar removals do not display enough indicators of this technique to be characterised as such.

The solitary single platform example was by far the most problematic. At first impression it resembled more an oddly angled flake with a very large bulbar scar, yet the flaking platform required for this to be the case would be obtuse and thus highly improbable. The vagaries of quartz knapping necessi-

tated a degree of caution in dealing with such an example. This core was so unlike the other three examples that when all these factors were taken into account a 'possible' tag was the only one that could be applied to it.

The cores displayed only flake removals, although this did not mean that they may not have been utilised for blade production at an earlier stage in their reduction sequences. Their heavily exhausted nature could lead to an oversimplified impression of the assemblage variability in blank production.

Flake component

Flakes dominated the assemblage with 28 examples accounting for 56% of the total. Of these, 15 were rated as genuine, 10 as probable and 3 as possible. There were 11 regular, 10 irregular and 7 decortical examples. The decortical examples, along with 4 core-preparation flakes (2 regular and 2 irregular), indicate that the quartz pebbles/nodules were prepared on or near to the site.

Three of the flakes were retouched (SF 316, cat. 1; SF 428.1, cat. 12; SF 454, cat. 19), with a fourth possible example also identified (SF 402, cat. 8). Of these, only one (SF 454, cat. 19) represented a formal tool type, in this case a snapped side scraper. A further two flakes displayed signs of possible utilisation in the form of edge damage/abrasion (SF 333, cat. 1; SF 362.1, cat. 4).

The solitary flake tool represented the only formal tool type in the assemblage, in the form of a large side scraper on regular flake. Due to its snapped status, it was impossible to understand its true complexity. Simple side scrapers are a feature of assemblages from nearly every period of known lithic use and, as such, it cannot help to date the assemblage.

Blade component

Although there were only four blade forms in the assemblage (8%), this still represents a significant proportion of the assemblage (anything over 10% is usually seen as being indicative of a blade-related assemblage). However, the small size of the overall assemblage means that the relative quantities of blades present cannot be seen as being truly significant (indeed, the recovery of a representative quantity of waste material would reduce the contribution of blades in the assemblage to $c1-3\%$).

None of these appeared to be bipolar in nature (narrow bladelets are often produced by the bipolar technique, particularly when small cylindrical cores are being knapped). Two of the four blade forms were blades (greater than 8mm width), one a bladelet (4–8mm width) and the fourth a chip (narrow blade-like waste form indicative of blade production). Three of the four blade forms were definite examples while one blade was a probable example. None of these blades displayed any signs of retouch or use.

Waste products

Material classified here as waste included many non-utilised blanks less than 10mm in MLD, usually termed *debitage*. Here, waste accounted for only 8 of the 50 lithics (16%). The waste was identified as falling into three of six main sub-types. These consisted of chunks (1 example), shatter >10mm (3 examples non flake or blade that does not fall into any of the above waste sub-types) and shatter <10mm (4 examples). Absent from the assemblage were split pebbles (pre-core testers), spalls and fragments (retouched unclassified broken tool).

The waste products were categorised as probable on three occasions and possible on five occasions. The less formal shapes associated with waste and the small size of these pieces probably account for much of the ambiguity surrounding them. Certainly, an assemblage containing a number of cores, blanks and utilised flakes should contain significant amounts of waste and, if genuine, the small amount identified is not nearly sufficient. Much of this may relate to the excavation strategy and to the inherent problems in identifying fine quartz waste products. It is also possible that knapping may not have occurred on site (explaining the lack of waste products) with the assemblage relating rather to selective deposition of lithic material.

Discussion

Technology

Before attempting to assess the assemblage as a chronological entity, it would appear prudent to attempt to identify the key technological properties of the assemblage. Overall, the assemblage appears to be a relatively compact technological unit heavily dependent on bipolar technology. This is particularly true of Phase II, the earliest phase to contain lithics. Elsewhere the assemblage contains a mix of bipolar and prepared platform removals, including two prepared platform cores recovered from Phase VI. Whereas these two groupings might seem to be at odds with each other, this is not necessarily the case. Bipolar technology is often used in association with a prepared platform technology, and bipolar removals can follow on from an initial core-use related to prepared platform removals. It is possible under this technique for small nodules/pebbles to be worked only by bipolar knapping, while some cores will only be worked by the prepared method, as would appear to be the case here.

The assemblage appears to contain a significant number of blade forms, although (as pointed out earlier), this may be more apparent than real. In any case, the appearance of blade forms does not necessarily equate to an early prehistoric date as many would usually suggest, given that a small number of blades would be perfectly at home in assemblages of later prehistoric date. Often these blades are a

product of core shape coupled with bipolar knapping, rather than a determined blade production strategy although it is uncertain if that is the case here (at least two of the blades are true blade forms).

The lack of formal tool types and the techniques associated with their production greatly reduces the possibility of refining the date of the period(s) in which this assemblage was produced.

Chronology

The assemblage has been categorised as consisting of a mixture of bipolar and prepared platform removals. Unfortunately, such assemblages are quite common, particularly dating from the Late Mesolithic to the Early Bronze Age. Assemblages of later periods are less well studied and it is difficult to determine whether or not these were bipolar in nature. Often such assemblages have been seen as residual without any real evidence for this assumption. In Shetland the lack of good flint and the preponderance of quartz as the raw material of choice has created a situation in which assemblages can be seen as highly undiagnostic. Moreover, many of the later prehistoric sites on Shetland (and Orkney) were investigated in the early parts of last century when the excavators do not appear to have been aware of the widescale use of quartz or of the problems inherent in identifying such material. This can readily be seen at Jarlshof where quartz was very common in the earliest Bronze Age layers dating up to the Late Bronze Age (Hamilton 1956) but was absent from all later levels. The assemblage is described as consisting of many hundreds of scrapers and cores, and the lack of flakes, blades and other waste products shows that the full range of lithics were not recovered. Despite this wealth of quartz material in the earliest layers, and despite the recovery of other residual material such as pot, there are no recorded examples of quartz tools in the later layers dating from the end of the Bronze Age through to the Norse Period. This is not to say that stone tools are absent; slate and steatite tools are common, as are tools of bone that may have supplemented or complimented tools of quartz. A similarly complex site at Clickhimin produced a near identical situation to Jarlshof in terms of the types of raw materials recovered, and in particular, an absence of quartz (Hamilton 1968). Furthermore, the initial excavations at St Ninian's Isle make no mention of any quartz artefacts being recovered (Small *et al* 1973), and it would appear that the excavators must have ignored many lithics.

More recent excavations of complex multi-period sites on Shetland have produced lithic materials from many phases, as opposed to having quartz in only the earliest layers, eg Scourd of Brouster (Whittle 1986), Kebister (Clarke 1999) and Sumburgh Airport (Lamb and Downes 2000). The assemblage at Kebister in particular mirrored that of St Ninian's Isle in that it contained a mix of prepared platform

 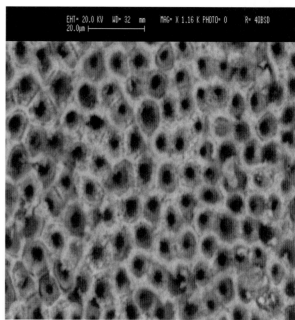

FIGURE 4.28
SEM/XRD analysis of pebble SF 479 with white encrustation. Photograph: A Hall

and bipolar reduction strategies, often working consecutively on some cores (Clarke 1999, 164). The lithics were also identified as dating from the Neolithic until the Iron Age and it was pointed out that there was almost no chronological variability in the assemblage indicating that quartz knapping techniques had altered little over a considerable period of time (Clarke 1999, 166). Similarly at Sumburgh Airport, an assemblage was identified that represents a near perfect match in technological terms to that from St Ninian's Isle. Although the assemblage was considerably larger than that from St Ninian's Isle, amounting to some 340 lithics, the heavy use of bipolar technology and levels of retouch on this site (10%) were very similar to that for St Ninian's Isle (8%). The analyst suggested a Late Neolithic-Early Bronze Age date (Finlayson 2000, 107) although large quantities of the lithics were recovered from the final phases that dated to the Early Iron Age. These lithics were technologically identical to the material recovered from the basal layers (Finlayson 2000, 109). While it is perfectly reasonable to suggest an early date for this assemblage, some emphasis should be made of the possibility that quartz knapping and bipolar technology continued at Sumburgh well into the Iron Age.

Bearing this in mind, it would seem prudent to suggest that the lithics recovered from the earliest layers at St Ninian's Isle relate to quartz use in the Iron Age. However, the possibility that the material relates to a much earlier site dating to the end of the Neolithic or the Bronze Age should also be considered, particularly when one considers the relative commonness of sites from Shetland displaying such a temporal depth of occupation. The alternative possi-

bility that some of the quartz use represents material worked in the early medieval/Norse periods should also be considered as there have been many examples, particularly from recent excavations, of lithics being identified on sites dating to these periods, and lithic specialist are displaying an increasing readiness to consider them as non-residual. However, the material recovered from later phases on this site most likely derives from re-deposited earlier layers, which makes a later use unlikely.

Examination of mortar
Allan J Hall

Four fragments of material from Phase VI (SF 444 and 446 from context 024, SF 576 from 333 and SF 577 from 334b) were submitted for identification and confirmed as shell mortar in various stages of weathering. Four pebbles were also submitted for examination, to identify a whitish residue thought to possibly be mortar (two from Phase VI; a general find from 024, and SF 479 from 337, and two from Phase III; SF 438 from 338 and SF 406 from 334). All pebbles were similar in appearance. SF 479 was examined further using XRD/SEM.

XRD SEM examination of SF 479 from context 337

This is flat greenish pebble coated in dull pinkish crust. The white material is in thin layers, as if painted all over the pebble. The layers 'rise up' in places becoming slightly botryoidal. The surface looks pitted in places, perhaps due to the release of small quartz grains trapped in the material, and was investigated using SEM. XRD analysis was then undertaken of a sample scraped from the surface, demonstrating that the sample was major calcite, with no significant impurities. The SEM confirmed that the surface of the layers were empty pits (Figure 4.28), the quartz grains being superficial, trapped in some of the pits. At high magnification the pits are seen to be holes in the centres of close-packed hexagons $c5$ microns across. The calcite coating consists of many layers of this porous calcite, each layer consisting of close packed, approximately hexagonal shapes, with the walls consisting of calcite, and holes in the centre of each hexagon. This has the appearance of a microscopic coral. The remaining three pebbles all have a similar sort of coating in places, with SF 466 being almost totally covered.

It seems most likely that these coatings are biological, akin to a type of bryozoa (McKinney and Jackson 1989[2]). The type observed on the St Ninian's Isle pebbles appears to be an 'encrusting multiserial colony', i.e. sheets of colonies. In general, the zooids that live in the little pits form colonies of 'tens to millions'. Each zoid is typically <1mm.

Metals
Colleen E Batey

Nickel

— SF 554, Context 01. Phase VII. Half penny of 1957. Light corrosion. D25mm.

This coin, dated 1957 was presumably dropped by O'Dell's field crew at the time of excavation.

Copper alloy

— SF 560, Context 341, Sample 327. Phase III. Top part of wire-wound pin. ?Shroud pin. 15 x 2 x 2mm.

This type of pin is very common between the mid-14th and the 18th centuries and its simple functionality has ensured little typological development through that period. Examples have been recorded from a variety of sites, including King's Lynn (Geddes and Carter 1977, fig 130, no. 19), where they were dated to 1350–1500, and at York where an 18th-century date is suggested (Addyman and Priestley 1977, fig 11, 141 and 142). Unstratified examples from Scottish sites include Freswick Links, Caithness (Batey 1987, eg 4.8.25–4.8.65) and Culbin Sands, Elgin (Black 1891, 508). They are an ubiquitous find from many eras, but are perhaps be more likely to be from Phase V of this site than from an earlier phase.

Iron

Key?

— SF 558 (Figure 4.29), Context 306b. Phase VI. Rod with twisted shaft and one end broken; the other ending in a looped terminal (joins with SF 551, Phase VII). The terminal of the rod seems a little elaborated on the X-ray. 43 x 10 x 5mm.

— SF 551 (Figure 4.29), Context 01. Phase VII. Iron rod with twisted shaft and U-shaped section at one end (incomplete circumference?). Bent and incomplete but joins with SF 558, Phase III (above). 42 x 10 x 8mm.

These two items were found in different contexts and consecutive phases, but were discovered during conservation to be conjoining. It is difficult to be sure of either function or period, but X-ray examination indicates that considerable care has been taken in the manufacture of the piece. SF 558 has a twisted shaft and a looped terminal with turned back end. Its other end (SF 551) is a U-shaped section of metal resembling a gouge, but where the drop of a key could originally have been located. In terms of function, this is inconclusive, but it may have been a key with a looped terminal to the handle and circular working end which has been broken (eg the hollow-stemmed type, illustrated by Ottaway 1992, 3614 and 3617, common in the 8th–11th centuries). The overall length of this complete item would have been $c80$–85mm which falls within the range identified in Ottaway's study (141–52mm) (1992, 668). These are a common find on sites throughout Europe, and identification as a key is consistent with the scale of this object, and would account for the slight decorative form of the handle and its terminal loop. An alternative identification, although less plausible, is that of an auger used in wood working. The piece, however, is probably too small and delicate for such a function.

Knives and blades

— SF 497, associated with SK 5 (PLATE 13). Phase III. Knife blade and most of tang, with traces of wooden haft remaining in corrosion The blade is single-edged, of triangular cross-section, and has a concave back and convex edge. It has no metal core; it retains its original outline, but the blade thickness has been distorted as a result of corrosion and lamination. 90 x 21 x 10mm.

— SF 559, Context 306b. Phase VI. Flat piece of iron, expanded at one end and broken at the other; possible knife tang or part of a tool. 50 x 17 x 2mm.

These two possible knife parts have suffered severely from corrosion. X-ray of both pieces has indicated a general form resembling a knife blade, although SF 599 lacks its complete length and indications of the blade edge. The more significant piece (SF 497) was found in situ associated with SK 5, of Phase III, which is of particular interest in view of both its Late Norse date and evidence of trauma (see below). It cannot be claimed however that this blade was the instrument of death for this individual, but its inclusion in the grave could have been a token burial gift. This might be similar, for example, to the bead and stone pendant buried with the child at Cnip in Lewis (Cowie et al 1993, 169–170). The knife seems to be similar to type C in the York assemblage, where the blade may be remodelled through use (Ottaway 1992, fig 231, nos 2827 and 2832). Ottaway does not, however, speculate as to whether the form was a specialised one. A knife of similar

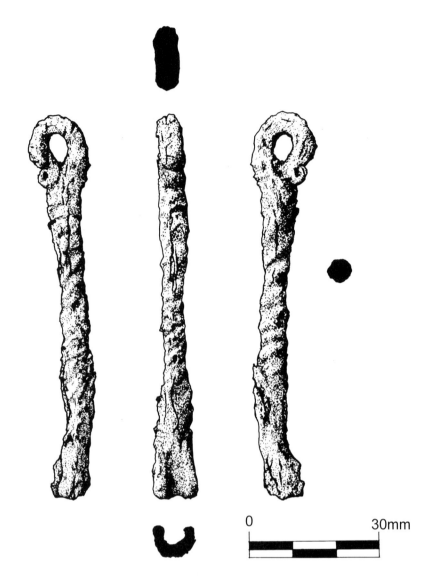

FIGURE 4.29

Iron key from the 2000 excavation (SF 551 and SF 558). Drawing: A Sperr

form was identified in the Scalloway assemblage being 'common Late Iron Age types with a wide chronological and cultural distribution' (Campbell 1998a, 159–160). Earlier examples of this knife type have also been noted, as for example from Monro's excavation at Buiston crannog in Ayrshire, although again no specific function is offered (Crone 2000, 144, eg 228 and 230). In general, the type conforms to Laing's Type 1, to which he assigns an Early Iron Age to Early Christian date range (Laing 1975, 288).

SF 599 is from a disturbed context. X-ray seems to suggest that this may have been a knife blade with part of the tang remaining; further detail is not clear from the surviving remains. It is conceivable that it may have originally been from another grave context disturbed by O'Dell's excavations, because it was found in the back-fill from the earlier work, although a settlement context would perhaps be more usual.

Nails and roves

— SF 555, Context 340. Phase III. Iron nail shank, very badly corroded. 32 x 8 x 8mm.

— SF 550, Context 316. Phase VI. Complete nail with round head and broken shank. 36 x 11 x 7mm.

— SF 557, Context 306b. Phase VI. Nail with narrow flat head and bent shank at lower end. 30 x 5 x 5mm.

— SF 542, Context 01. Phase VII. Flat topped nail with small head. 51 x 6 x 5mm.

— SF 543, Context 01. Phase VII. Rove, with part of shank. 34 x 24 x 19mm.

— SF 544, Context 01. Phase VII. Rove, broken and incomplete. 19 x 17 x 8mm.

— SF 545, Context 01. Phase VII. Rove, broken and incomplete. 21 x 14 x 11mm.

— SF 546, Context 01. Phase VII. Large round headed nail with short shank. 25 x 23 x 22mm.

— SF 547, Context 01. Phase VII. Complete small nail, highly corroded. 18 x 7 x 4mm.

— SF 548, Context 01. Phase VII. Long nail with broken shank, head expanded and corroded. Complete. 48 x 17 x 12mm.

— SF 552, Context 01. Phase VII. Broken nail shank, square section. Expanding towards the head. Overall c38 x 10 x 5mm.

— SF 553, Context 01. Phase VII. Quantity of shattered iron fragments, originally a nail. No dimensions available.

The collection of iron nails and roves is spread across three phases, a single example from Phase III (SF 555), two from Phase VI (SF 550 and 557) and nine from Phase VII. Eleven are from disturbed contexts; the turf and topsoil as well as O'Dell's backfill. The variety of forms, including nails with long and short shanks (where a complete length is available, 18–48mm), and simple flat topped nails, as well as bulky roves with traces of incomplete shanks, suggests different origins for the items. The nails with less distinct heads and of variable lengths could have been from the disturbed medieval burials of Phase V, whereas the simple nail shank from Phase III, presumably in its original context could have served any function, including a box fitting or a residual piece from re-cycled wood. Ottaway has discussed the variety of nails recovered from the excavations in York, spanning the 9th–11th centuries (Ottaway 1992, 613); in general he concludes that without the exact context for the nail, it is very difficult to be specific about the function of any individual items. The roves, from Phase VII (SF 543, 544 and 555), which have broken shanks attached to them, may well have been removed from doors (as clenched bolts; Goodall and Carter 1977; Dulley 1967) or boat timbers, with the breakage having resulted from their removal through use of perhaps a claw hammer (discussed in Ottaway 1992, 615–618). They were found in the disturbed horizon of Phase VII, and are hardly period specific.

Indeterminate pieces

— SF 491, Context 340. Phase III. Flat-sectioned piece of highly corroded iron; indeterminate on X-ray. 45 x 20 x 10mm.

— SF 556, Context 325. Phase III. Indeterminate fragment of corroded iron, flat; nothing further discernible on X-ray. 35 x 25 x 4mm.

— SF 549, Context 01. Phase VII. Small fragment with traces of wood in corrosion. 16 x 14 x 5mm.

Given the surviving condition of these items, even following X-ray investigation, nothing more can be said about their identification.

Assessment report on metalworking debris
Gerry McDonnell

A small quantity of material classified as industrial waste was sent for examination (Figure 4.30). The material was visually examined only, and no analysis was undertaken. The assemblage comprised small fragments, none exceeding 50g in weight. No context contained more than four fragments (Context 309). Due to the small size of the fragments they are difficult to identify with certainty. The identification and weight of the samples is given in Figure 4.30 below. The majority of the samples was identified as either bog ore or ferruginous concretion, i.e. naturally occurring iron-rich concretion. These may have formed over 'geological time' or after the occupation of the site, as part of site formation processes. Some of these ferruginous nodules may contain a remnant metallic iron object. X-radiography may be worthwhile to try to assess whether they do contain such vestiges. These fragments may also have developed naturally during site formation processes, effectively the development of a bog ore from the corrosion of metallic iron artefacts and subsequent re-deposition as nodules of the mobile corroding iron minerals.

Classification types

Smithing slag lumps?

Smithing slag lumps (SSL) are the irregularly shaped pieces of slag that develop in the hearth during smithing. The presence of the question mark with these fragments indicates that there is some doubt about the identification without further analyses. However, unless the confirmation of these slags is essential then further analyses to confirm the presence of a few fragments of smithing slags is not worthwhile. If they are not smithing slag, they are further examples of 'bog ore'.

Bog ore

Naturally occurring iron rich minerals that may have formed over 'geological' time or archaeological time. In the former case they may have formed elsewhere and have been imported into the site, for example for use as a pigment. In the latter case they may have formed during or after the occupation of the site, during site formation processes, in particular, the corrosion of iron artefacts and the subsequent re-deposition of the iron minerals.

Worked bone and antler
Colleen E Batey, with species identification by Louisa Gidney

Whalebone

— SF 348 (Figure 4.31), Context 309. Phase II. Three conjoining fragments of a worked whalebone spike or stake, rectangular in section and expanded at the head where it is slightly damaged, but partially cut; point in tact, slightly curved. It has two relatively smooth surfaces, at the 'front' and 'back'; the two sides are far more irregular and rough. The tip is present, and the end appears to have been partly hacked off; two cuts are visible. There does not appear to be any of the original bone surface present. 258 x 21 x 11mm.

	Finds Number	Context	Phase	Description	Count	Weight (g)
Trench TT1	54	25	3	Pumice? very light	1	15
	56	25	3	Pumice? very light	1	8
Trench 1	310	309	2	Ferruginous concretion/ex Fe obj?	1	20
	361	309	2	SSL?	1	15
	365	309	2	SSL?	1	8
	400	325	3	Natural manganese?	1	5
	413	309	2	SSL? very liquid	1	20
	563	305		SSL?	1	5
	561	1		Bog ore	1	5
	562	1		Bog ore/ex Fe obj?	1	8
	564	306		Bog ore	1	30
General finds						
	Date	Context	Phase	Description	Count	Weight
	14/7	311	-	SSL?	1	3
	19/7	318	-	Bog ore?	1	25
	17/7	311	-	Fe metal?	1	25
Trench 1 finds from flotation samples						
	Sample	Context	Phase	Description	Count	Weight
	330	316	6	Slag	4	1
	327	341	3	FAS	1	2

FIGURE 4.30

Classification of industrial residues, by trench and finds number (SSL: simithing slag lump; FAS: fuel ash slag)

— SF 514 (Figure 4.31), Context 309. Phase II. Chopped block of whalebone, shaped with traces of parallel cut marks on smooth upper surface. 150 x 115 x 50mm.

— SF 432 (Figure 4.31), Context 325. Phase III. Worked cancellous whalebone with large drilled central perforation. 110 x 90 x 30mm.

— SF 488 (Figure 4.31), Context 338. Phase III. Shaped whalebone vertebral centrum. 108 x 76 x 65mm.

This small group of whalebone finds is from three undisturbed contexts in Phases II and III and includes large pieces of whalebone that have been slightly modified for use. SF 514 was a chopping block, and similar examples have been recorded from The Howe in Orkney (Ballin Smith with Constantine 1994, 181–182), as also from Clickhimin (Hamilton 1968) and Scalloway, both in Shetland (Smith 1998, fig 98, 3985, 153). The remaining items served obscure functions: the whalebone spike (SF 348) from Phase II could perhaps have been used to secure a thatched roof, or even to hold down a fishing net; whereas the apparently deliberately shaped vertebral centrum of (SF 488) in Phase III, lacks an obvious function, although it is complete. SF 432 of Phase III is a perforated piece of whalebone which may have served as a fishing float, although the central perforation is somewhat large for that purpose and could have been for a wooden handle, the whole perhaps acting as a mallet.

Beads

— SF 460 (Figure 4.31), Context 318. Phase III. Cattle metatarsal shaft section, edges chipped and broken of off the main bone, forming a bead (larger than SF 512). 52 x 25 x 23mm.

— SF 512 (Figure 4.31), Context 318. Phase III. Cattle metatarsal shaft section, crudely chipped around both ends to make a bead (cf SF 460, 515, 538). 40 x 24 x 21mm.

— SF 515 (Figure 4.31), Context 306b, Sample 302; SF 538, Context 315. Phase VI. Three conjoining pieces of hollowed out antler tine, externally smoothed and very carefully worked into a bead (of better quality than SF 460 or 512), conjoined with single section SF 538 of Context 315; incomplete. Overall 44 x 25 x 20mm.

The two bone cylindrical beads from Phase III and broken antler one from Phase VI are comparable to the seventeen bone and antler beads reported from the original excavations (PLATE 14). The initial group was discovered beneath the N–S wall, and Small was of the opinion that they 'may belong to the earliest period of occupation of the area' (Small *et al* 1973, 7, fig 6).

Where there is detail on Small's illustration, it appears that the same method of manufacture was employed; that is, delimiting a section of bone and then chipping away beyond it, prior to snapping off to enable a cylinder to be formed. This can be clearly seen in SF 460 and 512 from Phase III. In two cases, the 1950s necklace includes metapodial sections which have been suggested in the reconstruction as amulets or similar. The broken bead from Phase VI is of well-finished antler and clearly this was disturbed by O'Dell's excavations; it is likely that this was originally from the same context as those published in 1973. The conjoining fragments of SF 515 and 538 indicate different burial conditions, as SF 538 is darker in appearance, but it is quite possible that they were shattered during the 1959 excavations. The 1950s necklace includes smaller beads which would appear to have been made of antler, in some cases distinguished by the careful shaping achieved.

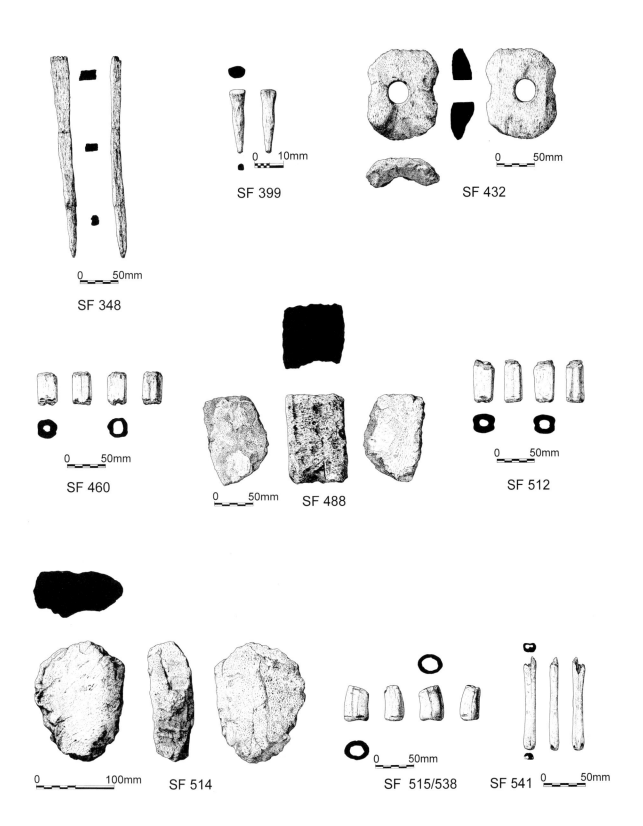

FIGURE 4.31

Bone and antler finds from the 2000 excavation: SF 348, SF 399, SF 432, SF 460, SF 488, SF 512, SF 514, SF 515, SF538 and SF 541. Drawings: A Sperr

The two beads are stratified in Iron Age midden that has been re-deposited in layers dated to the Late Iron Age/Norse period onwards. Comparable material from other sites includes several small bone cylinders recovered from Clickhimin in Shetland, of Iron Age date (Hamilton 1968, fig 38, nos 14–17 and fig 60, nos 9–10). Where indicated on the published drawing, it is clear that some are made in the same fashion as the two from Phase III at St Ninian's Isle, and others are more carefully finished, perhaps indicating that they are made of antler. They are termed cylinders or collars at Clickhimin. There are also six abraded examples from Scalloway which Smith considered to be complete artefacts rather than manufacturing debris, although identification as to function is dubious, including suggested use as toggles, ferrules or beads (Smith 1998, 155, fig 99). Certainly one and perhaps two of the illustrated examples (fig 99, no. 8, and less obviously no. 7) were made in the same way as those from Phase III at St Ninian's Isle. An illustrated example from The Howe, Orkney, is described as a toggle (Ballin Smith with Constantine 1994, illus 92, no. 2680). These comparable examples would support a date in the Iron Age for these items and, in terms of function, the large group from St Ninian's Isle may well have served as a necklace, as Small suggested, and it is not unlikely that they were originally associated with a burial.

Bone points

— SF 539, Context 309. Phase II. Fragment of whittled animal long bone shaft; possible peg, expanded slightly at mid-point. 41 x 5 x 5mm.

— SF 399 (Figure 4.31), Context 325. Phase III. Fragment of long bone shaft formed into small peg, tip missing. 22 x 5 x 4mm.

These two simple bone points were recovered from undisturbed contexts and represent activity on the site before the main Pictish and Norse floruit. An Iron Age date is indicated by the contexts, although the form of object is ubiquitous to all periods. Smith, writing of similar finds from Scalloway broch

in Shetland, underlines the variety of functions they could have served (Smith 1998, 150). Hamilton writing on finds from the Clickhimin Iron Age farmstead describes these as 'sliver points' (Hamilton 1968, 41).

Miscellaneous worked bone

— SF 540, Context 306b. Cattle metatarsal with hole made in proximal end, shaft fractured. 60 x 34 x 34mm.

— SF 541 (Figure 4.31), Context 306b. Sheep/goat metacarpal, proximal end is worked and polished; opposite end is broken. 104 x 10 x 11mm.

These further two items from the backfill of the earlier excavations would seem to derive from the Iron Age horizons. The worked cattle metatarsal with deliberate perforation in the joint end (SF 540) could perhaps have served as an awl (Ballin Smith with Constantine 1994, 172–174), although the terminal is now broken preventing confirmation; an alternative identification of function could be as a handle for a tool.

Conservation summary
Amanda Clydesdale

The artefacts selected for conservation are shown in Figure 4.32.

Condition

The bone and antler are in moderately good condition, although the surfaces and edges are rather friable; some edges have been lost on the bead (which was recovered from a sample), so the fit is not good. The iron has suffered extensive corrosion: although the surface is preserved on several items, there is very rarely a metal core (eg on the knife, lamination and swelling have occurred as a result of corrosion). Wood had been preserved by corrosion products on several items, notably the knife (SF 497) but also nails (SF 545, 549). Conservation of iron finds comprised cleaning with 53μ aluminium oxide in an air-abrasive machine. No protective coating was applied.

SF	Context	Phase	No. of items	Material	Description	X-ray no.
348	309	II	3	Whalebone	Whalebone stake in 3 pieces	n/a
491	340	III	1	Iron	Unidentified piece of very corroded iron ?sheet	2,4, 5
497	SK 5	III	1	Iron	Possible knife/blade	3, 4, 5
515	306	VI	3	Antler	Part of bead, SF 538	n/a
538	315	VI	1	Antler	Part of bead, SF 515	n/a
551	01	VII	1	Iron	Possible projectile point: part of SF 558	2, 4, 5
556	325	III	1	Iron	Small fragment of iron sheet	1
558	306b	VI	1	Iron	Iron rod: one end looped, other broken off. Part of SF 551	1, 4, 5
559	306b	VI	1	Iron	Flat piece of iron, unidentified	1, 4, 5

FIGURE 4.32

Artefacts from 2000 excavations selected for conservation

Coarse ceramics
Ann MacSween

The assemblage from St Ninian's Isle comprises some 360 sherds. Apart from one vessel (SF 390) which is represented by 160 sherds, most of the vessels are represented by one or two sherds. In cataloguing the assemblage, a range of attributes was recorded and the resulting data are presented as a spreadsheet catalogue (Appendix 7).

Almost all the sherds are small, undiagnostic body sherds, many badly abraded. The majority are sooted on either one or both surfaces and are probably derived from cooking vessels. Examples of plain (SF 526), flat (SF 390) and beaded (SF 409) rims were recorded (Figure 4.33). Only one example of decoration was noted, with incised herringbone or chevrons (SF 303). A range of clays was used: sandy, fine sandy, fine and steatitic, sometimes with rock fragments added. Usually the percentage of rock fragments added was fairly low at around 10%, but occasionally 20–30% addition was noted.

Most of the vessels are of medium thickness (6–10mm), with very few more than 10mm thick. Some examples of vessels with wall thicknesses less than 6mm thick were noted, eg SF 355 which is 4mm thick with a burnished surface. Walls of 5mm or less thick are very fine for hand-thrown pottery.

Fabric types

The fabrics identified in the figure below refer to: 1) sandy clay; 2) fine sandy clay; 3) fine clay; and 4) steatitic clay, as identified from the 1950s, excavation assemblage (see Chapter 3).

The numbers per fabric group are so small that only the general observation can be made that the most common fabric types are sandy clays (Fabric 1) or fine sandy clays (Fabric 2), either untempered or with 10% of inclusions (Figure 4.34). Inclusions at this level could indicate materials natural to the clay rather than deliberate addition. Although no thin section petrology was carried out, it is probable that production was local, with a range of clays being used throughout the life of the site.

Manufacture

The sherds are generally small but where method of manufacture could be determined this was by hand-building, using coil-construction. 13–20% of the vessels were finished by burnishing (Figure 4.35). The surface of many of the vessels had been given a wet hand smoothing.

Discussion

About 260 of the sherds from the excavations, including SF 390 which comprises 160 sherds, are from Phase II contexts, with some 70 sherds from Phase III contexts. The remaining sherds are from disturbed contexts. As discussed above, the assemblage comprises mainly undiagnostic body sherds and there is no obvious difference in terms of fabric or surface finish between the pottery from Phase II and that from Phase III, although Phase II has a higher incidence of very fine sherds (4–5mm thick).

As discussed above in relation to the material from O'Dell's excavation (see Chapter 3), it is difficult to attribute a date to an assemblage such as this, although, from comparisons with other sites, a date in the later part of the Iron Age or later is most likely. Within the St Ninian's Isle 1999–2000 excavated assemblage, for example, there are none of the everted rims and coarser fabrics of the Shetland earlier Iron Age as seen, for example at Jarlshof (Hamilton 1956, 46–47) and Clickhimin (Hamilton 1968, 121–123). Instead, the assemblage has more in common with the later Iron Age assemblages of Upper Scalloway Phase 3 (MacSween 1998a, 135) and Kebister (Dalland and MacSween 1999, 187), which are characterised by a general lack of decoration and a preference for untempered or low-tempered pottery. The exterior surfaces of the vessels are often burnished, sometimes to a polish. At Old Scatness settlement, however, preliminary analysis indicated that the latest of the pre-crofting styles, which included midden infill of a Pictish building, is fine, thin-walled pottery with little temper and plain rims. It is possible that this type of pottery continued in use from the Late Iron Age/ 'Pictish' period throughout the Norse period and into the late medieval period (MacSween 1998b, 87).

Dating the St Ninian's Isle assemblage more precisely within the 'Late Iron Age or later' has to depend on ^{14}C dates from the site. The burials which are cut into the Phase II middens have been dated to the 7th to 13th centuries AD, so the middens will predate this, although by how long is not certain. As the burials were dug into the Phase II midden, the presence of at least some Phase II pottery in Phase III contexts might be expected.

Recently there have been calls for more work to be carried out to characterise the later hand-made pottery from the Western Isles, in particular in the dating of assemblages which, through their lack of diagnostic features, are assumed to be Late Iron Age in date (MacSween 2002). There is a similar lack of clarity within the Shetland sequence. The St Ninian's Isle pottery, while undiagnostic, provides an opportunity, through ^{14}C dating, to add another marker to Shetland's pottery sequence.

Illustrated sherds (Figure 4.33)

— SF 303 Context 309. One body sherd. The exterior surface is burnished and there are faint traces of linear and herringbone decoration. The fabric is (1) sandy clay and the interior surface is sooted. Th 9mm; Wt 5g.

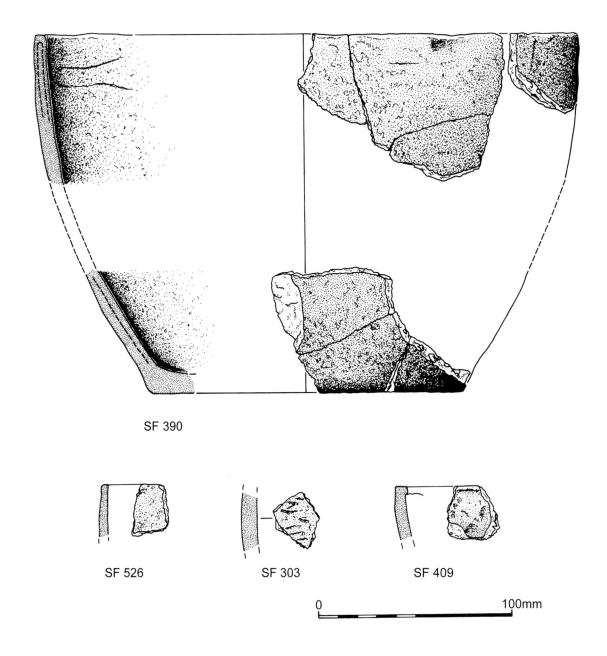

SF 390

SF 526   SF 303   SF 409

0   100mm

FIGURE 4.33
Coarse pottery from the 2000 excavations: SF 303, SF 390, SF 409 and SF 526. Drawings: A Braby

— SF 390 Context 331. 160 sherds and fragments, including four rim sherds and four basal sherds. The vessel is flat-based with angled walls and the rim is flat. The fabric is (1) sandy clay, the exterior surface is burnished and both surfaces are sooted. Th 6–8mm; Wt 889g.

— SF 409 Context 309. Rim, beaded to the interior. The fabric is (2) fine sandy clay and the exterior surface is sooted. Th 7mm; Wt 6g.

— SF 526 Context 334. Plain rim. The fabric is (1) sandy clay. Th 6mm; Wt 3g.

Pottery analysis

Marine isotope analysis
Robert Hedges

The aim of the analysis was to see if carbonaceous residues scraped from the inside of cooking pot-sherds might present any isotopic signature indicating a marine source. The hope was that, if marine signals were present, ^{14}C dating might confirm them

Context	1	1+10%	1+20%	1+30%	2	2+10%	3	3+10%	4	4+10%	4+20%	4+30%
				Fabrics								
Phase 2												
309	19	16	1	–	11	4	2	2	–	2	2	1(st)
311	8	1	–	–	9	2	1	1	–	–	–	–
331	1	2	–	–	–	–	–	–	–	–	–	–
Phase 3												
25	–	1	–	–	2	–	1	–	–	1	1	–
27	1	–	–	–	–	–	–	–	–	–	–	–
314	1	–	–	–	–	–	–	–	–	–	–	–
318	8	–	–	–	4	–	–	–	–	–	–	–
330	2	–	–	–	5	–	–	–	–	1	–	–
334	1	–	–	–	–	1	1	–	–	–	–	–
338	2	–	–	–	–	–	–	–	–	–	–	–
340	3	–	–	–	1	–	–	–	–	–	–	–
341	–	1	–	–	–	–	–	–	–	–	–	–
343	3	2	–	–	3	2	–	–	–	–	–	–
344	–	–	–	–	–	1	–	–	–	–	–	–
348	–	–	–	–	5	–	–	–	–	–	–	–
Phase 6												
1	5	1	–	–	8	–	–	–	–	–	–	–
24	–	2	–	–	–	–	–	–	–	–	–	–
316	1	1	–	–	2	–	–	–	–	–	–	–
333	2	1	–	–	1	–	1	–	–	–	–	–
306	–	–	–	–	–	2	–	–	–	–	–	–

FIGURE 4.34

Coarse pottery: numbers of vessels of each fabric for each context

Context	Vessels	Smoothed	Burnished	Combed
Phase 2				
309	64	6	11	1
311	22	–	3	–
331	3	–	1	–
		7%	17%	
Phase 3				
25	6	1	1	–
27	1	–	–	–
314	1	–	–	–
318	16	2	4	–
330	8	2	2	–
334	3	2	–	–
338	2	–	–	–
340	4	1	–	–
341	1	–	1	–
343	10	1	1	–
344	1	1	–	–
348	5	1	–	–
		19%	16%	
Phase 6				
1	14	2	2	–
24	2	1	1	–
316	4	1	1	–
333	5	–	1	–
306	2	1	–	–
		19%	19%	

FIGURE 4.35

Coarse pottery: numbers of vessels for each context

with a measured reservoir effect (i.e. marine-based carbon is usually several hundred years older, in ^{14}C terms, than contemporary terrestrial sources), and also, with such positive confirmation, encourage the application of intensive residue analysis to detect specific molecular structures diagnostic of fish, etc.

A few milligrams from the whole solid residue, after mechanical detachment, was washed in dilute HCl, rinsed in water and dried, and then combusted in a continuous flow CHN analyser interfaced to a continuous flow stable isotope ratio mass spectrometer.

The outcome was that the carbonaceous residues were all well within what is expected from terrestrial sources (Figure 4.36). This does not rule out the presence of fish in the pots, though it makes it less likely. Carbonaceous residues are more likely to be from, for example, charred carbohydrates than the high protein + oils from fish, but they certainly discourage further work along the lines of the original aims. The C/N values are of interest however, being relatively high values for the residues, and may warrant further work in the future (Figure 4.36).

The $\delta^{13}C$ values are fairly typical of terrestrial food in pot residues (though there are more negative values, perhaps due to greater lipid representation). There is, however, no clear signal of a heavier component, although a 2‰ (for example) increase in $\delta^{13}C$ due to marine diet is not likely to be detected.

The $\delta^{15}N$ is characteristic of plant food (or perhaps soil nitrogen); it indicates an absence of residual animal protein (and even more strongly, an absence of residual marine protein, for which the N15 value would be closer to 10–15‰).

Organic residue analysis
Richard Jones

Fifteen sherds from the midden areas uncovered in Trench 1 in 2000 were selected for organic residue analysis (Figure 4.37). They were small (40 x 50mm) body sherds, typologically uniform and had a dark fabric.

Method

The protocol for lipid extraction developed at the Organic Geochemistry Unit at Bristol University (Evershed et al 2002) was employed. A fragment (weighing c2 g) from each sherd was taken and its

Pot sherd find no.	Context	Residue (mg)	Samples	%C	C/N	δ13C	δ15N
437	309	118.4	309_437	3.72	12.82	–27.16	2.14
438	309	59.8	309_438	7.26	13.54	–26.62	4.74
439	309	44.4	309_439	8.88	13.77	–26.79	3.81
451	318	17.1	318_451	9.88	9.88	–26.36	4.53
461	318	16	318_461	18.16	10.09	–26.5	4.71
358	309	12.9					
448	309	6.2					
452	318	20.8					
455	318	14.6					

FIGURE 4.36

Results of marine isotope analysis of coarse pottery sherds

Context	SF	Main peaks in Gas Chromatograms (mins)	Relative yield
27	63	14.7, 15.8, 17.4, 17.6, 19.2, 20.7	Medium high
309	325	14.7, 15.7, 16.4, 17.4, 17.6, 18.3, 20.6	Low
309	329	11.9, 13.7, 15.8, 16.5, 17.4, 17.65, 19.2, 20.7, 20.8	High
309	387	13.3, 13.7, 14.6, 15.7, 17.3, 17.7, 19.1, 20.7	Medium high
309	517	14.3, 15.8, 17.0, 17.6, 18.8, 20.7 and some spurious peaks	High
330	504	13.0, 14.1, 14.7, 15.7, 15.8, 16.5, 17.4, 18.3, 20.6	Medium
331	390	17.4, 17.7, 20.7	Very low
331	390 1a	15.7, 16.4, 17.4, 17.7, 18.3, 20.7	Medium low
331	390 2a	14.7, 16.6, 18.3, 21.2, 22.65	High
331	390 3a	16.6, 17.4, 18.3, 20.7	Very low
331	390 1b	14.7, 16.5, 17.3, 17.7, 18.3, 20.7	Low
331	390 2b	15.7, 16.5, 17.3, 18.3, 20.8	Low
331	390 3b	14.7, 15.7, 16.6, 18.35, 20.7, 22.0, 22.6	Low
343	529	14.3, 15.8, 16.3, 17.0, 17.7, 19.4, 20.9 and several spurious peaks	Medium

FIGURE 4.37

Organic residue analysis of coarse pottery sherds: results of gas chromatography

Peak (minutes)	Identity
14.3	C 14 fatty acid
15.8	C 16 fatty acid
17.3	C 18:1 fatty acid
17.7	C 18:0 fatty acid
20.7	C 34 internal standard

FIGURE 4.38

Organic residue analysis of coarse pottery sherds: peak identifications

surface cleaned thoroughly with a drill head. It was ground to powder in an agate mortar and then sonicated in a chloroform/methanol (2:1 vol/vol) solvent; the internal standard added to each sample was C-34 alkane. The lipid extract was obtained by evaporating off the solvent with nitrogen, and the extract was subsequently silylated with N,O-bis(trimethylsilyl) trifluoroacetamide. After blowing down, a small volume was taken up in chloroform/methanol solvent and then injected into the GC.

Two GC systems in the Chemistry Department of Glasgow University were used: a Hewlett Packard 6890 instrument with (a) a fused Silica 25MXO.32MM ID coating CP-SIL 5CB column, and (b) a CP SIL8 CB MS column linked directly to a Jeol JMS 700 dual sector high resolution mass spectrometer.

Identification of the peaks in the chromatograms was mainly done with reference to two multiple fatty acid standards. All the samples and one blank were run as a single batch.

Results

Figure 4.37 shows the elution times (in minutes) of the main peaks identified in the gas chromatograms. The gas chromatograms (obtained from system (b) above) of the majority of samples are presented in Appendix 8. With reference to Figure 4.38 the most common constituents are the fatty acids, stearic and palmitic (C18 and C16 respectively). The peak at 18.3 minutes may be a monoacyl glyceride. Among the remaining peaks, at least one should be associated with plasticisers (resulting from storing the sherds in plastic bags prior to sampling). The yields of fatty acids and probable monoacyl glyceride vary from sample to sample which should cause little surprise as the sherds will have come from different pots and, just as important, different parts of the pot.

Comment

The results are clear cut: the majority of the sherds have residue which is clearly indicative of degraded animal fat. Two sherds (SF 390 and 3a 390, context 331; see Figure 4.37) have too little residue to say anything. SF 517, context 309 and SF 529, context 343) have a number of spurious, unidentified peaks, perhaps caused by some contamination. There is no

indication of fish oil residues because the fatty acids characteristic of fish oils, such as eicosapentanoic (C 20:5), elupadonic (C 22:5) and docosohexanoic (C 22:6) acids, are not apparently present.

It is gratifying to find satisfactory yields of lipid extract in these sherds, as has also been the case in Iron Age pottery from Scatness Broch on Shetland (Challinor *et al* 1998).

4.4 THE ECOFACTUAL ASSEMBLAGE

Archaeobotanical material
Jennifer Miller and Susan Ramsay

Background

During the fieldwork on St Ninian's Isle in 1999 and 2000, a programme of environmental sampling was followed whereby a 28 litre sample was taken from every undisturbed deposit for archaeobotanical analysis. Where particularly rich contexts were encountered, a further 28 litre sample was taken. It was anticipated that the study of these samples would reveal much information regarding the past utilisation of plant resources during the occupation of the site, in the form of fuel and food plants. It was also expected that this work would indicate samples suitable for AMS radiocarbon dating, should this technique be required at a later date.

Method

The samples for botanical analysis were from free-draining contexts in which uncarbonised ancient plant remains were unlikely to have been preserved. Consequently, samples intended for archaeobotanical analyses were processed using a flotation machine and the resultant flots and retents dried. Following this, laboratory examination and preliminary identification were undertaken using low power microscopy at variable magnifications between x4 and x45. The anatomical characteristics of charcoal were observed at x200 using the reflected light of a Zenith metallurgical microscope. Identification of seeds was initially by reference to the texts of Beijerinck (1947) and the extensive reference collection of Glasgow University. Charcoal was identified using the text and photographs in Schweingruber (1990). Vascular plant nomenclature follows Stace (1997) other than cereals, which follow Zohary and Hopf (2000).

Results

Results are shown by phase in Figures 4.39 and 4.40.

Phase VII

Botanical materials examined from turf and topsoil layer 01 in Phase VII consisted of spot finds of uncarbonised wood and metal fittings. Wood was either birch (*Betula*) or pine (Pinaceae), and it is highly likely that these wood fragments and metalwork are residual from coffins, possibly of relatively recent date.

Phase VI

Context 024 comprised a layer of sand surrounding long cists 03–06 in the NE corner of Trench 1. No identifiable botanical remains were recovered from this context other than modern material, concurring with the theory that this sand is of wind-blown origin.

Context 337 was a layer of sand and pebbles around a wall (328) which excavation indicated had been built after the 1959 excavations. Context 337 is likely to represent re-deposited material of unknown origin and contained several grains of hulled six-row barley that are not diagnostic of any particular time period. A large fragment of spruce/larch charcoal (SF 476), within 337, is evidence of the utilisation of driftwood or imported timber, probably as fuel.

Contexts 329, 332, 333 and 339 represent the re-deposited backfills of the three short cists excavated in 1959. Carbonised remains from these four fills were scant in comparison to the quantities of modern material observed; they included tiny charcoal fragments of birch (*Betula*), Scots pine (*Pinus sylvestris* type) and heather family, together with a few grains of six-row barley (*Hordeum vulgare sl*). These remains are consistent with re-deposited material from general occupation detritus.

Context 306 consisted of a rubble layer to the south of wall 307. Carbonised botanical remains from this context included very small fragments of birch, heather family and spruce/larch charcoal, together with several grains of six-row barley and a seed of chickweed (*Stellaria media*). Modern roots and earthworm eggs were however abundant, suggesting that the deposit was disturbed and contaminated. Midden material (315) was mixed between the stones of 306; 315 contained no botanical evidence to further the interpretation of the area.

Context 316 consisted of re-deposited dark sand used to infill a large hollow cut into the site during O'Dell's attempt to locate bedrock. Carbonised remains from 316 were varied, concurring with both the supposition of re-deposition and the theory of domestic occupation in the locality. Charcoal of alder (*Alnus*) and heather family, together with burnt peat/turf and carbonised cereal grains and weed seeds, implies the burning of heathy turf on a domestic hearth, perhaps in association with cereal processing. Given the re-deposited nature of the sample, however, this supposition cannot be confirmed since it is not possible to say whether or not the assemblage results from one or a series of burning episodes.

Phase III

Context 028 represented the only material solely from Trial Trench 1 presented for examination. Carbonised remains from 028 consisted of charcoal of the heather family (Ericaceae) and spruce/larch (*Picea/Larix*), together with a few grains of hulled six-row barley (*Hordeum vulgare* var *vulgare*). This concurs with the interpretation of this context as midden material.

A layer of pebbles (324) overlay pebble layer 334 in the long cists, but no botanical remains other than modern intrusive material were recovered from the sample examined. Two samples from context 334 were examined as being from Phases III/VI. Context 334 represented the pebble layer covering the base of the long cists to the NE corner of Trench 1 that may have been disturbed by the 1959 excavation. Both samples examined, [316] and [329], contained indeterminate coniferous (coniferales) and heather family charcoal, as well as six-row barley grains, some hulled, and some weed seeds, suggesting domestic origins. It is possible that the cists were constructed over earlier occupation layers, given that the excavators consider these deposits secure.

The basal layer (343) of silty sand and pebbles in cist 336 contained charcoal of heather type, spruce/larch and willow (*Salix*), with cereals and weed seeds, together with uncarbonised wood of indeterminate conifer type. The most likely explanation for this assemblage is that the cist was cut into midden material. The wood found may represent the remains of a wooden coffin or an associated grave item. Context 344 was cut into 343 and contained a somewhat similar, albeit reduced, carbonised assemblage. Uppermost context 338 had only scant botanical remains, although in keeping with the general trend.

A second long cist (335), to the south of the others, had been built over pre-existing midden material (340). The carbonised assemblage from 340 was one of the most diverse from the site, including remnants of fuel of local origins, including heather family charcoal, together with driftwood or imported timber in the form of spruce/larch and oak (*Quercus*), and some six-row barley grains. This assemblage is representative of midden deposits, confirming the interpretation given during excavation.

To the south of the long cists, a group of small kerbed cairns (314) overlay a group of E–W aligned infant burials. Sandy shell and midden layer 330 overlay the burials, and contained the same combination of heather family and conifer charcoal and barley grains as found elsewhere on the site in contexts indicative of midden. This would imply that 330 had a similar origin. Samples from sand around SK 9 and SK 10 contained carbonised botanical remains also suggestive of re-deposited domestic midden.

The basal layer (348) of short cist 305 was studied for botanical remains and contained heather fam-

Bulk samples		T1	T1	T1	T1	T1	T1	T1	TT1	TT1	T1	T1	T1	T1
Trench:														
Context:		309	309	310	311	311	311	331	025	028	312	318	324	325
Sample:		304	307	303	Sk 5	Sk5	305	313	3	7	306	309	308	310
Phase:		II	II	II	II	II	II	II	III	III	III	III	III	III
Total carbonised veg:		5ml	15ml	5ml	5ml	<5ml	5ml	<5ml	25ml	5ml	5ml	15ml	<5ml	10ml
Single entity AMS option:		N	Y	N	Y	N	N	N	N	N	N	N	N	N
Taxon	**Common name**													
Charcoal														
Alnus	Alder	–	–	–	–	–	–	–	–	–	–	–	–	–
Betula	Birch	–	–	–	–	–	–	–	–	–	–	–	–	–
Coniferales	Conifer	–	–	–	–	–	1 (<0.05g)	–	–	–	1 (<0.05g)	2 (0.05g)	–	–
Ericaceae	Heather family	–	23 (0.4g)	9 (0.05g)	1 (0.1)	1 (<0.05g)	2 (<0.05g)	–	24 (0.1g)	6 (0.05g)	–	16 (0.1g)	–	–
Picea/Larix	Spruce/larch	–	14 (0.1g)	4 (0.05g)	–	–	1 (<0.05g)	–	3 (<0.05g)	1 (<0.05g)	–	2 (<0.05g)	–	–
Pinus sylvestris type	Scots pine type	–	–	–	–	–	–	–	–	–	–	1 (<0.05g)	–	20 (0.2g)
Quercus	Oak	–	–	–	–	–	–	–	1 (<0.05g)	–	–	–	–	–
Salix	Willow	–	–	–	–	–	–	–	–	–	–	–	–	–
Indet charcoal		–	–	–	–	–	–	–	–	1 (<0.05g)	–	–	–	–
Monocot stem		–	–	–	–	–	–	–	–	–	–	–	–	–
Peat/turf		–	–	–	1 (0.1g)	–	–	–	–	–	–	–	–	–
Indet cinder		–	–	–	–	–	–	–	–	–	–	1 (0.9g)	–	–
Wood														
Coniferales	Conifer	–	–	–	–	–	–	–	–	–	–	–	–	–
Cereals														
Hordeum vulgare var *vulgare*	Hulled six-row barley	–	1	2	1	1	3	–	–	–	1	6	–	–
Hordeum vulgare sl	Six-row barley	2	7	5	–	–	6	1	10	1	1	8	–	–
cf Hordeum vulgare sl	cf six-row barley	4	7	–	2	–	–	–	4	3	–	–	–	–
Indet cereal		–	–	–	2	–	–	–	–	–	3	3	–	3
Carb seeds														
Montia fontana	Blinks	–	–	–	–	–	–	–	–	–	–	–	–	–
Plantago lanceolata	Ribwort plantain	–	–	–	–	–	–	–	–	–	–	–	–	–
Persicaria maculosa	Redshanks	–	–	–	–	–	–	–	–	–	–	–	–	–
Rumex sp	Dock	1	–	–	–	–	–	–	–	–	–	–	–	–
Stellaria media	Chickweed	–	2	1	–	–	–	–	–	–	–	–	–	–
Modern seeds														
Chenopodium album	Fat hen	–	–	–	–	–	–	–	–	–	–	–	–	–
Poaceae	Grass	1	–	–	–	–	–	–	–	–	–	–	–	–
Rumex sp	Dock	1	–	–	–	–	–	–	–	–	–	–	–	–
Stellaria media	Chickweed	16	1	–	–	–	–	–	–	–	–	–	–	–
Misc														
Modern veg		+++	+++	+++	–	++	+++	+++	+	+	+++	+++	+++	+++
Invertebrates		+	+	+	–	–	+	+	++	+	+	+	+	+
Earthworm eggs		>25	>25	3	–	–	1	–	>100	1	–	–	2	1
Shell		++	+	+	–	+	+	–	+	+	+++	+	+++	+
Bone		0.95g	–	0.1g	–	<0.05g	0.2g	–	2.2g	0.05g	–	0.2g	0.2g	<0.05g
Rabbit droppings		–	–	–	–	–	–	–	–	–	–	–	–	–
Metallic waste		–	–	–	–	–	–	–	0.55g	–	–	–	–	–

FIGURE 4.39A

Carbonised plant macrofossils identified from bulk samples

Bulk samples — Carbonised plant macrofossils identified from bulk samples

	Common name	T1 330 312 III	T1 338 320 III	T1 340 350 III	T1 341 327 Sk7 III	T1 343 332 III	T1 344 326 III	T1 345 328 III	T1 348 331 III	T1 Sk9 Sk9 III	T1 Sk10 Sk10 III	T1 334 316 III/VI	T1 334 329 III/VI	T1 024 301 VI
Total carbonised veg		10ml	5ml	15ml	10ml	15ml	5ml	<5ml	10ml	10ml	5ml	5ml	10ml	<5ml
Single entity AMS option		N	N	Y	N	Y	N	N	N	N	Y	N	Y	N
Taxon														
Charcoal														
Alnus	Alder	–	–	–	1 (<0.05g)	–	–	–	–	–	–	–	–	–
Betula	Birch	–	–	–	–	–	–	–	–	–	–	–	–	–
Coniferales	Conifer	–	–	–	–	–	–	–	1 (<0.05g)	–	–	1 (<0.05g)	2 (<0.05g)	–
Ericaceae	Heather family	11 (0.05g)	4 (0.05g)	9 (0.15g)	10 (0.05g)	17 (0.1g)	2 (0.05g)	–	4 (0.05g)	2 (0.05g)	4 (0.05g)	1 (<0.05g)	11 (0.1g)	–
Picea/Larix	Spruce/larch	1 (<0.05g)	–	3 (<0.05g)	1 (<0.05g)	5 (0.05g)	–	–	–	1 (<0.05g)	–	–	–	–
Pinus sylvestris type	Scots pine type	2 (<0.05g)	–	–	–	–	–	–	–	–	–	–	–	–
Quercus	Oak	–	–	1 (<0.05g)	–	–	–	–	–	–	–	–	–	–
Salix	Willow	–	–	–	–	2 (0.05g)	–	–	–	–	–	–	–	–
Indet charcoal		–	–	–	–	–	–	–	–	–	–	–	–	–
Monocot stem		–	–	1 (<0.05g)	–	–	1 (<0.05g)	–	–	–	–	–	–	–
Peat/turf		–	–	–	–	–	–	–	–	–	1	–	–	–
Indet cinder		–	2 (0.05g)	1 (0.3g)	–	1 (0.1g)	–	–	–	1 (0.7g)	–	1 (0.2g)	–	–
Wood														
Coniferales	Conifer	–	–	–	–	1 (0.2g)	–	–	–	–	–	–	–	–
Cereals														
Hordeum vulgare var *vulgare*	Hulled six-row barley	9	–	10	6	8	–	–	8	1	–	2	7	–
Hordeum vulgare sl	Six-row barley	8	–	7	4	6	3	–	6	7	3	2	6	–
cf *Hordeum vulgare* sl	cf six-row barley	–	–	–	–	–	–	2	–	–	1	–	11	–
Indet cereal		6	–	8	6	4	–	8	13	–	1	5	–	–
Carb seeds														
Montia fontana	Blinks	–	–	–	–	–	–	–	–	–	–	–	–	–
Plantago lanceolata	Ribwort plantain	–	–	–	–	–	–	–	–	–	–	–	–	–
Persicaria maculosa	Redshanks	–	–	–	–	–	–	–	–	–	–	–	–	–
Rumex sp	Dock	–	–	–	–	1	–	–	–	–	–	–	1	–
Stellaria media	Chickweed	–	–	1	1	4	–	–	1	3	2	–	2	–
Modern seeds														
Chenopodium album	Fat hen	–	–	–	–	–	–	–	–	–	–	–	–	–
Poaceae	Grass	–	–	–	–	–	–	–	–	–	–	–	–	–
Rumex sp	Dock	–	–	–	–	–	–	–	–	–	–	–	–	–
Stellaria media	Chickweed	–	–	–	–	1	–	–	–	–	–	–	–	–
Misc														
Modern veg		+++	++	+++	+++	+++	++	++	+++	–	+++	++	++	+++
Invertebrates		+	+	+	+	+	+	+	++	–	+++	+	+	+
Earthworm eggs		3	–	–	–	–	2	2	–	–	–	–	–	1
Shell		++	++	++	++	+	+++	+++	+	–	++	++	++	++
Bone		1.4g	–	0.1g	0.1g	<0.05g	–	–	0.1g	–	–	<0.05g	<0.05g	1.0g
Rabbit droppings		–	–	–	–	–	–	4	–	–	1	–	–	1
Metallic waste		–	–	–	–	–	–	–	–	–	–	–	–	–

FIGURE 4.39B

Carbonised plant macrofossils identified from bulk samples

Taxon	Common name	T1 330 312 III 10ml N	T1 338 320 III 5ml N	T1 340 350 III 15ml Y	T1 341 327 Sk 7 III 10ml N	T1 343 332 III 15ml Y	T1 344 326 III 5ml N	T1 345 328 III <5ml N	T1 348 331 III 10ml N	T1 Sk 9 III 10ml N	T1 Sk 10 III 5ml Y	T1 334 316 III / VI 5ml N	T1 334 329 III / VI 10ml Y	T1 024 301 VI <5ml N
Charcoal														
Alnus	Alder	-	-	-	1 (<0.05g)	-	-	-	-	-	-	-	-	-
Betula	Birch	-	-	-	-	-	-	-	-	-	-	-	-	-
Coniferales	Conifer	-	-	-	-	-	-	-	1 (<0.05g)	-	-	1 (<0.05g)	2 (<0.05g)	-
Ericaceae	Heather family	11 (0.05g)	4 (0.05g)	9 (0.15g)	10 (0.05g)	17 (0.1g)	2 (0.05g)	-	4 (0.05g)	2 (0.05g)	4 (0.05g)	1 (<0.05g)	11 (0.1g)	-
Picea/Larix	Spruce/larch	1 (<0.05g)	-	3 (<0.05g)	1 (<0.05g)	5 (0.05g)	-	-	-	1 (<0.05g)	-	-	-	-
Pinus sylvestris type	Scots pine type	2 (<0.05g)	-	-	-	-	-	-	-	-	-	-	-	-
Quercus	Oak	-	-	1 (<0.05g)	-	-	-	-	-	-	-	-	-	-
Salix	Willow	-	-	-	-	2 (0.05g)	-	-	-	-	-	-	-	-
Indet charcoal		-	-	-	-	-	-	-	-	-	-	-	-	-
Monocot stem		-	-	1 (<0.05g)	-	-	1 (<0.05g)	-	-	-	-	-	-	-
Peat/turf		-	-	-	-	-	-	-	-	-	1	-	-	-
Indet cinder		-	2 (0.05g)	1 (0.3g)	-	1 (0.1g)	-	-	-	1 (0.7g)	-	1 (0.2g)	-	-
Wood														
Coniferales	Conifer	-	-	-	-	1 (0.2g)	-	-	-	-	-	-	-	-
Cereals														
Hordeum vulgare var *vulgare*	Hulled six-row barley	9	-	10	6	8	-	-	8	1	-	2	7	-
Hordeum vulgare sl	Six-row barley	8	-	7	4	6	3	-	6	7	3	2	6	-
cf *Hordeum vulgare sl*	cf six-row barley	-	-	-	-	-	-	-	-	-	1	-	11	-
Indet cereal		6	-	8	6	4	-	-	13	-	1	5	-	-
Carb seeds														
Montia fontana	Blinks	-	-	-	-	-	-	-	-	-	-	-	-	-
Plantago lanceolata	Ribwort plantain	-	-	-	-	-	-	-	-	-	-	-	-	-
Persicaria maculosa	Redshanks	-	-	-	-	-	-	-	-	-	-	-	-	-
Rumex sp	Dock	-	-	-	1	1	-	-	-	-	-	-	1	-
Stellaria media	Chickweed	-	-	1	1	4	-	-	1	3	2	-	2	-
Modern seeds														
Chenopodium album	Fat hen	-	-	-	-	-	-	-	-	-	-	-	-	-
Poaceae	Grass	-	-	-	-	-	-	-	-	-	-	-	-	-
Rumex sp	Dock	-	-	-	-	-	-	-	-	-	-	-	-	-
Stellaria media	Chickweed	-	-	-	-	1	-	-	-	-	-	-	-	-
Misc														
Modern veg		+++	++	+++	+++	+++	++	++	+++	-	+++	++	++[f]	+++
Invertebrates		+	+	+	+	+	+	+	++	-	+	+	+	+
Earthworm eggs		3	-	-	-	-	2	2	+	-	-	-	-	1
Shell		++	++	++	++	+	+++	+++	+	-	++	++	++	++
Bone		1.4g	-	0.1g	0.1g	<0.05g	-	-	0.1g	-	-	<0.05g	<0.05g	1.0g
Rabbit droppings		-	-	-	-	-	-	4	-	-	1	-	-	1
Metallic waste		-	-	-	-	-	-	-	-	-	-	-	-	1

FIGURE 4.39C

Carbonised plant macrofossils identified from bulk samples

			Betula	cf Larix	cf Picea	Picea/Larix	Pinus sylvestris type	Pinus sylvestris type	Pinaceae	Quercus	Maloideae	Indet	Coffin	Burnt soil	Pot?
Taxon:			Birch	cf larch	cf spruce	Spruce/larch	Scots pine type	Scots pine type	Pine family	Oak	Apple type	Mineral-ised	Fittings		/Cinder
Common name:															
Context	SF	Phase	wood	charcoal	charcoal	charcoal	wood	charcoal	wood	charcoal	charcoal	wood	metal		
309		II	1 (3.5 g)	–	–	–	–	–	–	–	–	–	–	–	–
309	304	II	–	–	–	–	–	–	–	–	1 (1.6 g)	–	–	–	–
309	305	II	–	–	–	–	–	–	–	4 (0.8 g)	–	–	–	–	–
309	330	II	–	–	–	–	–	–	–	–	–	–	–	1 (3.3 g)	1 (2.3 g)
309	354	II	–	1 (1.2 g)	–	–	–	–	–	–	–	–	–	–	–
309	380	II	–	–	–	1 (0.9 g)	–	–	–	–	–	–	–	–	–
309	411	II	–	–	–	–	–	–	–	–	–	–	–	1 (2.5 g)	–
309	412	II	–	–	–	–	–	–	–	–	–	–	–	–	1 (3.5 g)
309	416	II	–	–	–	–	–	–	–	–	–	–	–	1 (8.0 g)	–
309	458	II	–	–	–	1 (0.6 g)	–	–	–	–	–	–	–	–	–
311	306	II	–	–	1 (1.0 g)	–	–	–	–	–	–	–	–	–	–
311	389	II	–	–	–	–	–	–	–	–	–	–	–	1 (0.9 g)	–
311	398	II	–	–	–	–	–	–	1 (0.2 g)	–	–	–	–	3 (3.1 g)	–
311	503	II	–	–	–	–	–	1 (0.1 g)	–	–	–	–	–	–	–
320	459	II	–	–	–	–	–	–	–	–	–	–	–	1 (1.8 g)	–
331 (309)	457	II	–	–	–	–	–	–	–	–	–	–	–	1 (0.4 g)	–
334	502	III/VI	–	–	–	–	–	–	–	–	–	–	–	1 (2.1 g)	–
337	476	VI	–	–	–	1 (0.6 g)	–	–	–	–	–	–	–	–	–
001		VII	1 (0.7 g)	–	–	–	–	–	1 (1.8 g)	–	–	–	–	–	–
001		VII	–	–	–	–	1 (3.3 g)	–	–	–	–	–	–	–	–
001		VII	–	–	–	–	–	–	–	–	–	–	2 (10.3 g)	–	–
001		VII	–	–	–	–	–	–	–	–	–	1 (0.6 g)	–	–	–

FIGURE 4.40

Botanical small finds

ily and conifer type charcoal, together with six-row barley grains and a chickweed seed, an assemblage common to many of the contexts from this site. Wall core 345, to the north of 348, contained no carbonised remains of any sort, but was set into a layer of silty sand midden (318), which contained one of the more diverse assemblages from this site. Context 318 was below Phase VI context 306, and contained similar carbonised material, although with the addition of Scots pine type, suggesting that these two contexts are of related origin. Layer 325 constituted the general midden layer underneath midden layer 318; its botanical macrofossils consisted of Scots pine charcoal and poorly preserved cereal grains.

Context 312 represents midden material, also defined elsewhere as 340 and 025. Carbonised remains were scant, including tiny coniferous charcoal and a few cereal grains, and so cannot add much to the interpretation.

Fill 341 surrounding SK 7 was characterised as re-deposited sandy midden and contained no botanical evidence to refute this hypothesis, including the same mixed charcoal assemblage and barley grains that were found throughout the site.

Phase II

Contexts 309–311 represented spreads of midden material. Findings were entirely in keeping with midden from the rest of the site, with heather family and spruce/larch, and six-row barley present in each context examined. The spot finds from contexts 309 and 311 have a greater diversity of charcoal types including apple type (Maloideae), birch (*Betula*), oak

and Scots pine. The spot finds also indicate that both spruce and larch were available for use rather than just as spruce/larch type of charcoal.

Context 331 produced large quantities of Iron Age pottery, and it was suggested that it might have been the remains of kiln waste, although no charcoal, and only a single grain of six-row barley, was recovered from this context. The botanical results cannot confirm that this context contains the remains of wastage from a kiln.

Discussion

The carbonised plant macrofossil assemblages from Trench 1 and Trial Trench 1 show no significant difference, either spatial or temporal. All phases other than the most modern, Phase VII, showed consistencies in terms of both charcoal types and cereal grains present, with the differences observed likely being due to random chance and the small quantities of material present. Many of the contexts examined were interpreted on site as midden material, and the carbonised botanical remains support this theory. Heather family (Ericaceae) and spruce/larch (*Picea/Larix*) charcoal were the most frequently encountered types on the site. The very small diameter of the heather type twigs (mostly 1–3 years old) meant that it was difficult to identify them to genus, although the majority had the outward morphology of heather (*Calluna vulgaris*). Furthermore, the twigs had the general appearance of 'above ground' stems rather than the more gnarled basal or subterranean stems often found in burnt peat deposits. This would suggest that the heather had been intentionally cut for domestic purposes, rather than being incorporated accidentally with peat fuel.

The recurrence of fragments of spruce/larch charcoal indicates the value put upon this important resource. Due to the small size and flaked nature of the fragments, it was impossible to be confident in the anatomical separation of these two closely similar genera other than two small finds of larger pieces of charcoal identified to cf larch (*cf larix*; SF 354, from Phase II midden 309) and cf Picea (*cf Spruce*; SF 306, from Phase II midden 311). Neither spruce nor larch is native to Scotland, however, and the charcoal is most likely to have come from North American driftwood, although in the case of spruce, timber could also have been harvested or traded from southern Scandinavia. Both spruce and larch charcoal have been identified from many archaeological sites in the Northern Isles, including Papa Stour (Dickson 1992), and interpreted as North American driftwood.

Other types of wood, including alder (*Alnus*), birch (*Betula*), Scots pine (*Pinus sylvestris* type), willow (*Salix*), apple type (Maloideae) and oak (*Quercus*), were utilised as fuel to a much lesser extent. However, it is not possible to say with confidence whether these types were growing fairly locally or whether they were collected as driftwood.

The only identifiable cereal present in the samples examined was six-row barley (*Hordeum vulgare sl*), some of which was well enough preserved to be confidently identifiable as the hulled variety (*Hordeum vulgare* var *vulgare*). Hulled barley has always been the most commonly encountered cereal in mainland Scotland and is also recorded from Scottish island contexts throughout the last several thousand years (Dickson and Dickson 2000). Consequently, it is not unexpected that hulled six-row barley is recorded from midden material thought possibly to have resulted from Iron Age occupation on St Ninian's Isle. No chaff was present in any of the contexts examined and very few weed seeds; this could be an indication of cleaned crops, or be due to the poor preservation conditions for plant remains and the re-deposited nature of the material within the sandy soil.

Animal bone
Louisa J Gidney

During the 1999–2000 excavations a small collection of animal bones was recovered, the majority of which were from poorly stratified contexts: the topsoil (Phase VII) and the backfill of previous excavations (Phase VI). Animal bones were also found in, possibly, more securely stratified contexts in Phase III. These deposits span the Late Iron Age to Late Norse burials and therefore some, at least, of the animal bones may have been disturbed and re-deposited, as suggested by the presence of human bones among them. The preceding Phase II midden also produced animal bones; however, the use of the site for human burial appeared to have disturbed even Phase II deposits, as several pieces of human bone were also recovered among the animal bones from this phase.

It can be seen that the nature of the archaeological deposits examined precludes detailed study and comparisons between phases and limit the possible analyses and interpretation of the faunal economy at this site.

Preservation

Preservation was generally excellent with good representation of bones from very young animals. It was noticeable in many contexts however that bones from adult cattle were in relatively poor condition whereas bones of infant calves in the same context were in pristine condition. It would appear that a proportion of the larger bones had been exposed to subaerial weathering before final burial, whereas the infant bones were rapidly incorporated into the archaeological deposits.

Methods

Fragments were identified using the author's personal reference collection. To reduce over-recording of the more robust bones from the larger species, only those fragments of cattle, sheep/goat and pig bones with 'zones' were catalogued. The zones used are those defined by Rackham (1987). All the identifiable fragments of the other species present were recorded. In brief, a zone is a diagnostic feature on an element and is only recorded if at least half of the feature is present. This procedure gives a truer indication of the relative abundance of the species exploited for food.

Besides 'zones', whole or partial mandibles and maxillae with any teeth present were recorded. The teeth are used to estimate the age structure of the slaughter population (Silver 1969). Loose cheek teeth were catalogued, but not incisors. The latter are readily lost from the jaw *post mortem* and do not add to the ageing information gathered from the cheek teeth. Teeth which were too damaged to be assigned a wear stage were not catalogued.

For the sake of convenience vertebrae fragments with a zone or proximal ribs with the capitulum were assigned to the categories of cattle size or sheep size. Pig vertebrae are generally distinctive and no other species comparable in size to either cattle or sheep are represented by more than a few fragments. Therefore, for some statements, the cattle and sheep size categories will be considered with the cattle and sheep/goat bones respectively.

An approximate record was made of the number of unidentified fragments for each context in the archive catalogue. In general, these data were not thought to enhance the information gained from the identified fragments and have not been presented in the data tables. Finds from Phase VII topsoil deposits were recorded and the species present listed in Figure 4.41. More detailed work on this group was not deemed worthwhile.

Measurements were taken where possible but there are too few data for analysis.

Species

The assemblage is dominated by bones of the domestic species cattle, sheep/goat and pig. Butchery marks were apparent on many of the larger, adult, bones, suggesting that domestic household refuse is a major component of the group. The presence of highly comminuted unidentifiable fragments of bone together with larger, identifiable, fragments with acid-etched surfaces indicates that dog faecal material may be the origin of much of the smaller component of this assemblage. A third source of the animal bones recovered appears to have been the disposal of corpses of newborn farm animals. It is not clear whether these were buried as intact bodies, which were subsequently disturbed, or whether the meat was utilised. These bones had certainly not been made available to dogs or they would not have survived.

Figure 4.42 examines the proportions of the domestic species. It can be seen in all phases that sheep/goat bones are generally the most commonly identi-

fied remains, with cattle bones slightly less abundant. Elements of pig are sparse in comparison. The slight variations seen between the phases may be more a product of the small numbers of identified fragments from each phase than genuine differences in the composition of the bones originally deposited.

Information on the skeletal elements present was recorded, but the assemblage is too small for any meaningful analysis of these data.

Cattle

The cattle bones derive from animals of small stature, though no complete long bones were recovered from which an estimate of withers height might be made. Analysis of ageing data has been confined to the, hopefully, better stratified deposits from Phases II and III. It can be seen from the tooth wear data in Figure 4.43, and epiphysial fusion data in Figure 4.44 that remains of immature animals are well represented. As noted previously, this is in part a reflection of the generally good preservational conditions for animal bone on this site. These immature animals include a high proportion of perinatal deaths, some 15% of all the cattle and cattle-sized bones from Phases II and III were noted as infants. In the sample retents, the proportion rises to over a third of the cattle bones deriving from infant calves. These are higher proportions than might be expected from routine natural mortalities and may suggest deliberate slaughter of newborn calves to liberate the dams for milking and to provide rennet for cheesemak-

		Hand-recovered general finds				Worked small finds			Unworked small finds		Retents		
Trench	TT1	Trench 1				VI	III	II	III	II	VI	III	II
Phases	VII	VII	VI	III	II	VI	III	II	III	II	VI	III	II
Cattle	9	44	29	29	21	–	2	1	–	3	7	13	1
Sheep/goat	6	60	21	36	36	–	–	–	1	5	10	11	2
Pig	–	20	5	10	12	–	–	–	–	–	3	–	–
Horse	–	2	–	–	–	–	–	–	–	–	–	–	–
Dog	1	–	–	–	–	–	–	–	–	–	–	–	–
Cat	–	–	1	–	1	–	–	–	–	–	–	–	–
Deer sp	–	–	1	–	–	1	–	–	–	–	–	–	–
Cattle size	–	1	2	3	2	–	–	–	–	–	–	–	–
Sheep size	–	6	6	5	7	–	–	–	–	–	1	–	–
Seal	–	1	–	–	–	–	–	–	–	–	–	1	–
Whale	1	2	–	–	1	–	2	2	–	–	–	–	–
Rabbit	25	119	27	2	–	–	–	–	–	–	11	–	–
Small mammal	–	–	–	–	–	–	–	–	–	–	3	2	1
Gull sp	–	1	2	1	1	–	–	–	1	–	–	–	–
Puffin	–	–	1	1	–	–	–	–	–	–	2	–	–
Auk sp	–	–	–	–	1	–	–	–	–	–	–	3	–
Gannet	–	–	–	1	1	–	–	–	–	–	–	–	–
Wader sp	1	–	–	–	–	–	–	–	–	–	–	1	–
Thrush sp	–	–	–	–	2	–	–	–	–	–	–	–	–
Bird sp	1	9	9	3	1	–	–	–	–	–	3	4	2
Totals	44	265	104	91	86	1	4	3	2	8	40	35	6

FIGURE 4.41

Animal and bird bone fragment counts for the species present

Phases	Hand-recovered finds				Retents	
	VII	VI	III	II	VI	III
Cattle and	45	31	32	23	7	13
Cattle size	34%	49%	42%	29%	39%	54%
Sheep/goat and	66	27	34	43	8	11
sheep/goat size	50%	43%	45%	55%	44%	46%
Pig	20	5	10	12	3	
	15%	8%	13%	15%	17%	
Totals	**131**	**63**	**76**	**78**	**18**	**24**

FIGURE 4.42

Animal bone: relative proportions of the domestic species from Trench 1

	Phases II and III		
	U	S/W	H/W
Cattle			
M1 5–6m	–	1	4
M2 15–18m	–	1	2
P2 24–30m	2	–	1
P3 18–30m	2	–	3
M3 24–30m	–	–	3
P4 28–36m	2	1	2
Sheep/Goat			
M1 3–5m	–	3	7
M2 9–12m	–	3	–
P2 21–24m	1	–	–
P3 21–24m	6	–	–
M3 18–24m	1	1	1
P4 21–24m	3	4	1
Pig			
M1 4–6m	–	–	2
M2 7–13m	–	3	–
P2 12–16m	–	–	–
P3 12–16m	–	2	–
P4 12–16m	–	2	–
M3 17–22m	1	1	–

m = months, U = unerupted/deciduous
S/W = slight wear, H/W = heavy wear

FIGURE 4.43

Animal teeth in approximate order of eruption (ages of fusion after Silver 1969)

ing. In a later age, Gervase Markham recommended to the housewife: 'Of the cheeselip bag or rennet, which is the stomach bag of a young suckling calf, which never tasted other food than milk, where the curd lieth undigested. Of these bags you shall in the beginning of the year provide yourself good store' (Best 1986, 175). Butter may also have been an important product of the dairy, as suggested by various finds of wooden kegs containing 'bog butter' from waterlogged sites in Scotland (Earwood 1993, 108–111).

Bone marrow is another useful source of fat. The chop marks clearly visible on the bones from adult animals indicate that marrow was routinely extracted from the shafts of limb bones.

Sheep/goat

While the term sheep/goat is used to cover the possibility that goat might be present, all the bones in this category appear to derive from sheep.

Figures 4.43 and 4.44 again demonstrate the presence of elements from animals in the younger age groups. Infant lamb bones are less common than those of calves, with two examples, probably from one animal, in Phase II, context 311. Infant lamb bones are strong indicators of seasonal deposition in spring, whereas calves can be born at any time of year. The slight peak of fused bones in the second age group in Figure 4.44 may suggest that animals were over-wintered at least once before selection for slaughter.

There were no complete bones from which to estimate the withers heights of the sheep. The visual impression is of gracile stock akin to the modern North Ronaldsay type.

Pig

There were so few pig bones found that little can be said about them. There is, however, a noticeable dearth of pig remains from the sample retents for Phase III; this is hard to interpret given that pig is reasonably well represented among the hand-recovered finds for this phase.

Elements from juvenile animals predominate once again, though only one bone from an infant piglet was recovered, from Phase II, context 311. The tooth wear data in Figure 4.43 suggest that animals may not have been slaughtered until over a year old, which would have produced a larger carcase for curing as bacon.

Horse

Horse was represented only in Phase VII. The two identified finds comprise one tooth and one bone.

Dog

Dog is represented by one positively identified element from Trial Trench 1, Phase VII. A further tooth, possibly of dog, was recovered from a Phase III context, also in TT1. Evidence for the presence of dog throughout the occupation of the site was provided not only by characteristic gnawing marks of dog on bones of other species (observed in Phases II, III and VI, most common in Phase III), but also by the suggestion of faecal deposition of bone.

Cat

The presence of cat is indicated by finds of single bones in Phases VI and II.

Deer

Deer is represented only in Phase VI. This is a worked section of antler tine, in three pieces (see

		U	JF	F
Cattle	by 18 months			
	Scap tub	-	-	1
	Acet symph	-	-	-
	Prox rad	-	-	5
	Dist hum	2	-	2
	Prox Ph 2	3	-	2
	Prox Ph 1	1	-	-
	by 2–3 years			
	Dist tib	1	-	1
	Dist mc	-	-	1
	Dist mt	1	-	1
	by 3.5–4 years			
	Prox cal	-	-	-
	Prox fem	2	-	-
	Dist rad	1	-	-
	Prox hum	2	-	-
	Prox tib	1	-	1
	Dist fem	2	-	-
	P and D uln	1	-	-
	by >5 years			
	Ant vert ep	2	-	2
	Post vert ep	2	-	-
Sheep/goat	by 1 year			
	Dist hum	2	-	1
	Prox rad	-	-	-
	Scap tub	-	-	-
	Acet symph	1	-	-
	by 1–2 years			
	Prox Ph 2	-	-	2
	Prox Ph 1	1	-	3
	Dist tib	-	-	2
	Dist mc	1	-	1
	Dist mt	1	-	1
	by 2.5–3.5 years			
	Prox fem	1	-	-
	Prox cal	-	-	1
	Dist fem	1	-	-
	Prox tib	-	-	1
	Dist rad	-	-	-
	Prox hum	-	-	-
	P and D uln	-	-	-
	by >5 years			
	Ant vert ep	8	-	-
	Post vert ep	8	-	-
Pig	by 1 year			
	Acet symph	-	-	-
	Scap tub	-	-	-
	Prox rad	-	-	-
	Dist hum	-	-	-
	Prox Ph 2	-	1	-
	by 2–2.5 years			
	Prox Ph 1	1	-	-
	Dist mc	2	-	-
	Dist tib	-	-	-
	Dist mt	-	-	-
	Prox cal	-	-	-
	by 2.5–3.5 years			
	Prox uln	-	-	-
	Prox tib	-	-	-
	Prox hum	1	-	-
	Dist rad	-	-	-
	Prox fem	1	-	-
	Dist fem	-	-	-
	by >5 years			
	Ant vert ep	2	-	-
	Post vert ep	2	-	-

F = Fused, JF = Just Fused, U = Unfused

FIGURE 4.44

Epiphyses in approximate order of fusion for animal bone from Phases II and III (ages of fusion after Silver 1969)

Batey above), hollowed out and incised at the edges on one face. It seems highly probable that this bead was brought onto site as a ready made artefact (SF 515 and SF 538). While this section of tine is too small for positive identification, it is probable that it derives from red deer.

Seal

Remains of seal are sparse with one element from Phase VII and a small phalanx, thought to be seal, from the Phase III sample retents.

Whale

Like deer antler, whalebone appears to have been valued more as a material for the production of arte-facts, rather than for food. Over half the few finds of whale are worked objects, recovered from Phases II and III, with amorphous lumps of whalebone found in Phases II and VII.

Rabbit

Rabbit bones were ubiquitous in the topsoil depos-its, equalling the domestic farm animals in numbers of fragments, if not in bulk. The disturbed remains of several virtually complete bodies are certainly pre-sent, together with general dispersed body parts. The two rabbit bones from Phase III would appear to be intrusive.

Bird species

In contrast to the mammal bones, where wild spe-cies are sparsely represented, the bird bones consist entirely of wild species with no positive evidence for domestic poultry, even in the recent topsoil de-posits. Only the obvious gull bones from Phase VII were identified, the remaining finds did not warrant the necessary resources for identification.

Gull species are represented in all four phases producing faunal remains. That from Phase VII is a largely complete skeleton, which may be of com-paratively recent origin. Most of the gull bones are of large birds, approaching the size of the Greater Black Back gull. At least one smaller variety is also represented. Several of the gulls are commensal spe-cies, living in association with humans, so natural mortalities might be expected.

Puffin is certainly present in Phases III and VI. The finds from the sample retents suggest that this species may have been of greater economic impor-tance than the hand-recovered finds indicate. The auk family bones include one possible example of a Great Auk tibia from Phase II, context 309. This bone exhibits the characteristics of the auk family, but is the size of the Great Auk specimen illustrated by Cohen and Serjeantson (1986, 70). The remain-ing auk bones from the Phase III retents comprise two more probable puffin bones and one possibly from a guillemot.

Gannet is represented in Phases II and III. Serjeantson (1998, 24) notes that the breeding season in late spring/summer is the most effective period for the capture of birds, such as the auks (including puffins) and gannet, which normally live out at sea and only come onto land to breed. Like the infant lamb bones, these seabird bones may also be indicators of seasonality of deposition. Certainly the auks and gannet have been exploited for food until the recent past in Shetland.

Wader species, despite their general edibility, are not well represented, with single examples only from Phase VII in TT1 and the retents from Phase III.

Bones from birds of the thrush family were found in Phase II deposits; again, these can be commensals but have also been regarded as food in the past. The unidentified bird bones from the Phase II sample retents include one probably from a member of the sparrow family.

Summary

The small assemblage of animal and bird bone from St Ninian's Isle derives principally from Late Iron Age to Late Norse midden material, disturbed to a greater or lesser extent by human burials. The majority of the finds derive from cattle or sheep. Sheep bones are marginally more numerous than those of cattle. Given the relative size of the two animals, beef was a more substantial item of diet than lamb or mutton. Both species may have been equally important for other products: wool from the sheep, cheese and butter from the cattle. The use of cattle for the dairy is strongly implied by the relatively high proportion of bones from infant calves that were recovered. Pigs were also kept. No evidence was found for the presence of horse in the earlier phases. The companion animals, dog and cat, were known. The paucity of remains from the companion, rather than food, animals suggests that the midden principally received household waste and that carrion carcases were disposed of elsewhere. Marine mammals appear not to have been exploited for food. Rather, the worked objects made of whalebone imply that this species was seen as a source of raw material for craftwork. In contrast, a range of maritime birds was taken, though no domestic birds appear to have been kept. The infant lamb bones and seabird bones suggest a seasonal component within the midden, deriving from spring lambing time and the breeding sea bird colonies.

Fish bone
Rachel Gamble and James Barrett

This report presents an analysis of fish bone from the 2000 excavation, from 28 contexts, together with one context excavated in 1999. Four of the site's seven phases produced fish bone (Phases II, III, VI and VII). It is likely that much of the sediment from Phase III, and to a lesser degree also later phases, was predominately re-deposited material from Phase II, broadly dated to the Iron Age, based on ceramics. This pottery, and presumably also the fish bone with which it is associated, is then found as residual material in later phases.

Recovery and methods

The majority of samples analysed contained fish material extracted during flotation and recovered with a 1mm mesh. The remaining material was hand-collected during excavation. Due to the small quantity of hand-collected bone, the subsequent analysis combines the results from these two fractions.

Recording followed the York protocol (Harland *et al* 2003), which uses a system of quantification codes (QC) to distinguish between diagnostic and non-diagnostic elements (Appendix 9). Under the York system, 18 diagnostic (QC1) elements are routinely recorded in detail, including species, texture, estimation of fish size and completeness. Vertebrae (QC2 elements) are identified to species or family level (as possible) and all other (QC0) elements are recorded as unidentified. Gadidae vertebrae are further identified to eight groups, according to their place along the vertebral column (as defined in Barrett 1997). All bone fragments were counted and weighed.

Preservation

A total of 571 fish bones was examined, of which a subset of 105 diagnostic elements (QC1) were analysed in detail. Preservation of these diagnostic elements was generally good (Figure 4.45).

Taxonomic abundance

The majority of the taxa identified belong to the cod family (Gadidae), including cod, saithe, pollack, ling and rockling (Figure 4.46). Of these, saithe is the most abundant with ling and rockling only represented by a few specimens. Non-gadid taxa are represented by single specimens of herring, hake, scorpion fish family (Cottidae), grey gurnard, Atlantic mackerel and most interestingly (because

York system texture	Description	Count
Excellent	Majority of surface fresh or even slightly glossy; very localised flaky or powdery patches	30
Good	Lacks fresh appearance but solid; very localised flaky or powdery patches	66
Fair	Surface solid in some places, but flaky or powdery on up to 49% of specimen	9
Total		**105**

FIGURE 4.45

Fish bone texture of QC1 elements from all phases

of the presence of cut marks) a vertebrae of the turbot family (Bothidae). This narrow taxonomic range is consistent with other broadly contemporary assemblages from Shetland, such as Upper Scalloway (Cerón-Carrasco 1993; 1998), Old Scatness (Nicholson 1998) and Sandwick North (Barrett and Oltmann 1998).

Size

The sample sizes from all the phases are small and only in Phases II and III are these deposits undisturbed by recent activity. The majority of elements in these two phases are from fish of 150–500mm estimated total length (Figure 4.47). Virtually all of these are gadids, mostly saithe, which can reach a far greater size. Saithe have a shoaling habit and groups of small fish of 150–550mm are typically caught near the shore in the first few years of their life (Barrett *et al* 1999, with refs). A general pattern seen in early historic fish assemblages from the Northern Isles is the presence of two fisheries, one shore-based, with fish either caught from the shore or from boats near the shore, and one exploiting deeper waters (Barrett *et al* 1999, 364). The size distribution of gadid elements represented in Phases II and III suggests that the St Ninian's Isle fishery was predominantly shore-based. The single Bothidae vertebrae does, however, indicate that some deep-water fishing could also have taken place at the site during Phase II, if the vertebrae is from a species such as megrim which is found to depths of *c*400m (Whitehead *et al* 1986, 1288).

Element representation

Element representation can be assessed based on the 105 QC1 elements and 117 QC2 elements identified. Due to the small sample sizes and the disturbed nature of Phases VI and VII, discussion is qualitative and limited to Phases II and III. Whole fish are represented by cranial elements and vertebrae in both of these phases (Figure 4.48). In Phase II however the majority of elements are cranial whilst in phase III vertebrae are more common (Figure 4.49). This pattern could be due to a difference in fish processing, but is more likely to be a result of small sample sizes.

If fish were processed for drying and then removed from the site, a lack of caudal vertebrae and appendicular elements such as the cleithrum would be expected in the archaeological record (Barrett 1997). The converse would be expected if fish were processed elsewhere and then imported to the site. The increase in caudal vertebrae at St Ninian's Isle in Phase III is not, however, accompanied by a corresponding increase in appendicular elements. In fact, gadid cleithra and supracleithra are absent from the site. Thus, it seems unlikely that the increase in posterior elements in Phase III is due to the transport of processed fish.

Taxon/Phase:	II	III	?III/VI	VI	VII	Total
Herring *Clupea harengus*	–	1	1	2	–	4
Cod *Gadus morhua*	2	8	5	7	–	22
Saithe *Pollachius virens*	37	38	13	8	1	97
Pollack *Pollachius pollachius*	–	–	–	1	–	1
Saithe/pollack *Pollachius*	5	7	1	1	–	14
Cod/saithe/pollack *Gadus/Pollachius*	13	10	4	1	–	28
Ling *Molva molva*	1	2	1	1	–	5
Rockling sp *Ciliata/Gaidropsarus*	–	2	–	2	–	4
Cod family *Gadidae*	17	14	5	6	–	42
Hake *Merluccius merluccius*	–	1	–	–	–	1
Scorpion fish family *Cottidae*	–	–	–	1	–	1
Grey gurnard *Eutrigla gurnardus*	–	–	–	–	1	1
Atlantic mackerel *Scomber scombrus*	1	–	–	–	–	1
Turbot family *Bothidae*	1	–	–	–	–	1
Total identified (QC1 and QC2)	77	83	30	30	2	222
Unidentified (QC0 and QC4)	110	115	38	85	1	349
Total	**187**	**198**	**68**	**115**	**3**	**571**

FIGURE 4.46

Fish bone number of identified specimens

Taxon	Size category*	II	III	?III/VI	VI	VII
Cod	small	1	1	–		–
	large	–	1	–	–	–
Saithe	tiny	7	–	–	–	–
	small	13	6	5	2	–
	medium	8	6	3	1	–
Saithe/pollack	small	3	1	–	–	–
	medium	–	3	–	1	–
Cod/saithe/pollack	tiny	2	–	–	–	–
	small	9	3	2	–	–
	medium	2	1	–	–	–
Ling	small	–	–	–	1	–
Cod family	tiny	2	1	–	–	–
	small	8	1	1	–	–
	medium	3	–	–	1	–
	large	–	1	–	–	–
	extra large	2	1	–	–	–
Grey gurnard	large	–	–	–	–	1

FIGURE 4.47

*Fish bone: size of QC1 elements by species and phase (*Estimated length of fish: tiny <150mm; small 151–300mm; medium 301–500mm; large 501–800mm; very large 801–1000mm)*

Taxon		Element	II	III	?III/VI	VI	VII
Herring	vertebrae	av	–	–	–	1	–
		cv	–	1	1	–	–
Cod		ceratohyal	1	–	–	–	–
		dentary	–	1	–	–	–
		premaxilla	–	1	–	–	–
	vertebrae	av1	–	–	1	–	–
		av2	–	1	1	1	–
		av3	–	1	2	2	–
		cv1	–	2	1	4	–
		cv2	1	2	–	–	–
Saithe		articular	5	–	–	–	–
		basioccipital	1	1	1	–	–
		ceratohyal	–	–	–	2	–
		dentary	2	–	–	1	–
		hyomandibular	2	–	–	–	–
		infrapharyngeal	–	–	1	–	–
		maxilla	5	–	–	–	–
		opercular	1	–	1	–	–
		parasphenoid	1	–	–	–	–
		preopercular	–	1	1	–	–
		posttemporal	3	2	3	–	–
		premaxilla	6	2	2	–	–
		quadrate	1	1	1	–	–
		vomer	1	–	2	–	–
	vertebrae	fv	1	2	–	–	–
		av1	1	1	–	1	–
		av2	–	2	–	1	–
		av3	4	10	4	1	–
		cv	1	–	–	–	–
		cv1	2	9	1	2	1
		cv2	–	2	–	–	–
Saithe/Pollack		articular	–	1	–	–	–
		maxilla	2	1	–	1	–
		palatine	–	1	–	–	–
		vomer	1	1	–	–	–
	vertebrae	av1	–	1	–	–	–
		av3	2	2	1	–	–
Cod/Saithe/Pollack		articular	2	–	–	–	–
		basioccipital	–	1	–	–	–
		ceratohyal	4	–	–	–	–
		dentary	–	2	–	–	–
		hyomandibular	1	–	–	–	–
		infrapharyngeal	1	–	–	–	–
		maxilla	1	–	–	–	–
		parasphenoid	2	–	–	–	–
		preopercular	–	1	–	–	–
		quadrate	2	–	–	–	–
	vertebrae	av	–	1	–	–	–
		av1	–	–	–	1	–
		av3	–	2	2	–	–
		cv1	–	1	–	–	–
		cv2	–	2	–	–	–
Ling		dentary	–	–	–	1	–
	vertebrae	cv1	1	2	1	–	–
Rockling	vertebrae	av	–	–	–	2	–
		av3	–	1	–	–	–
		cv	–	1	–	–	–
Cod family		articular	3	–	–	–	–
		ceratohyal	3	1	–	–	–
		dentary	2	1	–	–	–
		infrapharyngeal	–	–	–	–	–
		maxilla	4	–	–	–	–
		opercular	–	1	–	–	–
		parasphenoid	–	–	1	–	–
		preopercular	1	–	–	–	–
		posttemporal	–	1	–	–	–
		premaxilla	1	–	–	–	–
		quadrate	1	1	–	–	–
	vertebrae	av	–	2	–	1	–
		av1	1	–	1	3	–
		av3	1	1	1	1	–
		cv	–	2	–	–	–
		cv1	–	1	2	–	–
		cv2	–	1	–	–	–
		v	–	2	–	–	–
Hake	vertebrae	av3	–	1	–	–	–
Sea scorpion fish family	vertebrae	fv	–	–	–	1	–
Atlantic mackerel	vertebrae	cv	1	–	–	–	–
Turbot family	vertebrae	cv2	1	–	–	–	–
Grey gurnard		cleithrum	–	–	–	–	1
Total QC1			60	27	11	6	1
Total QC2			17	56	19	24	1

FIGURE 4.48

Fish bone: QC1 and QC2 element representation by species and phase (see Appendix 9 for definitions of vertebrae groupings)

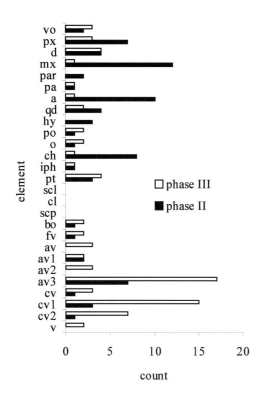

FIGURE 4.49

Combined cod family QC1 and QC2 element distribution

Bone modification

Modification was found on four of the 222 QC1 and QC2 elements analysed (Figure 4.50). The cut marks on the bothid vertebrae are interesting as, in the Northern Isles, butchery marks are typically associated with large gadid remains. The marks in question are most consistent with filleting.

Discussion

The broad phasing from the site and the small amount of fish material recovered makes meaningful interpretation of the St Ninian's Isle assemblage problematic. Phase II of the site is broadly Iron Age and Phase III spans the transition from the Late Iron Age (Pictish) to the Middle Ages (Late Norse). Moreover, the bone from Phase III may

largely derive from re-deposited Phase II sediments. In comparative perspective, the pattern of small gadid fish seen in both phases can be observed in the Late Iron Age (when it is the dominant pattern) and (more rarely) in the Viking Age and the Middle Ages. In the latter periods, this pattern has been tentatively associated with low-status settlement, as at Sandwick North (Barrett and Oltmann 1998) and Beachview, Orkney (Rackham *et al* 1996; Barrett 1995, 120).

In conclusion, the St Ninian's Isle fish assemblage from Phases II and III can be interpreted as representing a predominantly shore-based fishery focused on small gadids. It is unclear, however, whether this is a typical Late Iron Age assemblage or an example of a more specialised (possibly low status) Viking Age or medieval assemblage. If originally derived predominately from Phase II contexts, the former interpretation would be the stronger of the two.

Marine shell and land snails
Ruby Cerón-Carrasco

Methods

The marine shells from the 1999–2000 excavations derived from a variety of deposits some of which represent layers disturbed during the excavations carried out in the 1950s. Because of the complex history of the excavations at the site, there was no sampling strategy for the collection of molluscs; this analysis therefore deals mainly with species identification and description of their habitats to give an indication of how these molluscs may have been deposited at the site.

For the marine shells, species count was done to give an idea of main species representation. The land snails recovered at St Ninian's Isle were all carefully scanned for identification using a binocular microscope. The species were then quantified in terms of their relative frequency within each sample. This frequency was recorded as:

★ = rare: present, but in very low quantities (<5)
★★ = present: present in low quantities compared to main species (<10)
★★★ = common: present in large quantities similar to other species within a sample
★★★★ = present in large quantities: predominant species within a sample.

Bone ID no.	Phase	Taxon	Element description	Modification
736	VI	Saithe/pollack	Medium maxilla	Root etching
738	II	Turbot family	Extra large caudal vertebrae	3 fine cut marks across lateral aspect of neural arch, consistent with filleting action
741	II	Saithe	Medium maxilla	Carnivore gnawing
803	II	Cod family	Medium articular	Root etching

FIGURE 4.50

Fish bone modifications (for size estimate definitions see Figure 4.47)

Results

The results are given in Figures 4.51 and 4.52. Figure 4.51 gives the summary of marine mollusca species represented per context and by phase, Figure 4.52 gives the summary of land snail species represented per context.

The marine molluscs

A variety of contexts from Phases VI, III and II contained large quantities of marine molluscs and had a similar species representation: edible periwinkles and limpets were the most common species present as well as a variety of other edible molluscs and other non-edible marine molluscs. Phase VI also contained lumps of mortar, this was noted since one of its components would have involved the use of marine shells.

Only one context from Phase VII (turf and topsoil) was found with marine shells. These consisted mainly of edible periwinkles and limpets; lumps of mortar were also noticed with these remains.

The commonest species present was the edible periwinkle (*Littorina littorea*). These are found on rocks, stones and seaweed on the middle and lower shores. Its shell may be up to 25mm high. Although it has been demonstrated that a variety of environmental factors can influence the shells of certain other molluscs, studies done by Hylleberg and Christensen (1977) on edible periwinkles suggest that there are no significant allometric differences in *Littorina littorea* shells attributable to their recovery from different environments.

The limpet *Patella vulgata* was also common and is found throughout the Scottish coast on all rocky shores; it is a species of major importance in quantitative terms on most littoral shores and in shallow waters (Branch 1985). It is present on all rocky shores from the most sheltered ones dominated by the algae *Ascophyllum nosodum* L. to the most exposed, mussel and barnacle dominated types (Campbell 1989).

Other edible species included the common whelk (*Buccinum undatum*) found on sand and mud from shallow water down to c100m, common mussel (*Mytilus edulis*) found on rocks in estuaries and on rocks in exposed shores often in extensive beds, and the common oyster (*Ostrea edulis*) also found in shallow waters, as well as specimens of the common cockle (*Cerastoderma edule*), which are found on the lower shore burrowed in sand, mud or gravel. Fragments of the spiny cockle (*Acanthocardia aculeata*) and *Arctica islandica* and razor shells (*Ensis* sp.) were also recovered.

It is likely that these molluscs were originally gathered as foodstuff; from historical accounts, it appears that coastal dwellers consumed shellfish not as a rule of preference but as a necessity, particularly in times of hardship (Fenton 1984). Shellfish of various types were used as food, and there is considerable regional variation in this use of shellfish throughout the Scottish islands, including Shetland. Here mussel, limpets, whelks, pecten (razor shell), cockles and oysters have been used as food. The ethnographic accounts may therefore indicate that the farther back in time, the more dependence there was on shellfish, and the archaeological evidence may suggest that this may, indeed, have been the case (Pollard 1994), though perhaps not for every type of shellfish.

It is also important to note that shellfish, such as edible periwinkles, limpets and mussel, has also been traditionally used as fishing bait and thus fishing has depended largely on the seasonal variation in the type of bait (Fenton 1978; 1984).

Other species recovered and classified as non-edible were specimens of rough periwinkle (*Littorina littoralis*), found on seaweed (*Focus vesiculatus* and *Ascophyllum nosodum*), the flat periwinkle (*Littorina saxatilis*), and remains of the dogwhelk (*Nucella lapillus*). This species is found in a variety of habitats, including rocky shores, because the extent to which it is capable of adapting the shape and weight of its shell enables it to occupy a wide ecological niche (Kitching 1985). *Nucella lapillus,* like the limpet (*Patella vulgata*), covers a wide range of environmental conditions to which it is locally adapted.

Some of the non-edible molluscs may have been introduced with seaweed. The two species of seaweed which flourish well in Shetland are the intertidal *Ascophyllum nosodum*, found mainly in sheltered areas, and *Laminaria hyperborea* which grows all around the islands but particularly in coasts with extensive shallow subtidal rocky areas. For many centuries these species have been used extensively in the Northern Isles as an important organic fertiliser. The intertidal weeds are cut and gathered directly, and the subtidal weeds (*Laminaria* sp.) are collected as drift on the beaches after storms, particularly during the autumn, winter and spring. These large brown seaweeds grow luxuriantly in the Northern Isles and have been used there by man as a fertiliser of the thin soil, and as a source of certain chemicals (Fenton 1978; 1986).

The marine molluscan assemblage at St Ninian's Isle is similar to that found in other archaeological sites in Shetland. At Bayanne, in Yell, species representation resembles the St Ninian's Isle assemblage, with edible periwinkles and limpets being the main species represented as well as oyster, whelk, cockle and mussels (Cerón-Carrasco 2000). Bayanne appears to represent an occupation from at least the Late Bronze Age into the Later Iron Age, based on typological comparisons of both architecture and artefacts (Moore and Wilson 1999).

A note on marine molluscs in burials

One small specimen of the limpet (*Patella vulgata*) was recovered from a child's burial, dating to the

Figure showing marine mollusca species counts by context and phase. Table columns (left to right): Context, Sample, Phase, then species given by scientific name / common name: *Littorina littorea* (Periwinkle), *Littorena saxatilis* (Rough periwinkle), *Patella vulgata* (Limpet), *Nucella lapilus* (Dogwhelk), *Baccium undatum* (Whelk), *Ostrea edulis* (Oyster), *Cerastoderma edule* (Common cockle), *Venus verrucosa* (Spiny cockle), *Arctica islandica*, *Spisula solida* (Thick trough shell), *Mytilus edule* (Mussel), *Ensis sp.* (Razor shell).

Context	Sample	Phase	*L. littorea* Periwinkle	*L. saxatilis* Rough periwinkle	*P. vulgata* Limpet	*N. lapilus* Dogwhelk	*B. undatum* Whelk	*O. edulis* Oyster	*C. edule* Common cockle	*V. verrucosa* (Spiny cockle)	*A. islandica*	*S. solida* Thick trough shell	*M. edule* Mussel	*Ensis sp.* Razor shell
1		VII	1702	39	301	27	27	63	11	7	2	–	★	★
25	03	III	★	–	★	–	–	★	–	–	–	–	–	–
28	07	VI	130	45	95	–	–	5	–	–	–	–	–	–
11		VI	22	–	30	–	–	–	–	–	–	–	–	–
24	301	VI	208	–	39	1	4	6	–	3	2	–	–	–
24		VI	8	3	4	–	–	1	–	–	–	–	–	–
303/329		VI	76	–	7	–	–	4	–	–	–	–	–	–
306	302	VI	28	–	★	–	–	★	–	–	–	–	–	–
315		VI	★	–	16	–	–	–	–	–	–	–	–	–
315		VI	5	–	★	–	–	–	–	–	–	–	–	–
300	300	VI	★	–	–	–	–	1	–	–	–	–	–	–
316		VI	–	–	9	–	–	–	–	–	–	–	–	–
323		VI	120	–	45	–	–	–	–	–	–	–	–	–
332		VI	640	–	96	–	–	–	–	–	–	–	–	–
332	315	VI	780	–	192	–	–	–	–	8	6	–	–	–
333	314	III	1560	18	87	19	–	–	–	16	12	–	–	–
334	316	III	318	–	48	–	–	–	–	–	3	–	–	–
334	329	III	390	–	24	–	–	–	2	–	–	4	–	–
337		VI	196	–	58	7	–	2	–	3	–	–	–	–
337		III	182	–	45	–	–	3	–	2	–	–	–	–
318	318	VI	90	–	56	–	–	–	14	–	1	–	–	–
320	320	VI	96	23	24	–	–	–	–	3	–	–	–	–
317	317	VI	196	–	35	–	–	–	–	2	–	–	–	–
311	311	VI	320	–	1	–	–	–	–	–	1	–	–	–
SK 9 (SF 511)		III			–	–	–	–	–	–	–	–	–	–
25 (SF 46)		III	252	20	24	19	–	2	1	–	–	–	–	–
312	306	III	97	–	11	2	4	2	–	–	–	–	–	–
312		III	424	–	76	–	5	4	–	–	–	–	–	–
314		III	396	12	31	–	–	2	–	–	–	–	–	–
317		III	150	–	48	–	1	–	5	1	1	–	–	–
318	309	III	196	–	15	–	1	–	–	–	–	–	–	–
324		III	34	–	40	–	1	–	–	1	–	–	–	–
324	308	III	45	–	★★	–	–	★★	–	–	–	–	–	–
325		III	780	–	96	–	–	–	–	8	6	–	–	–
310	310	III	390	–	48	–	–	–	–	4	3	–	–	–
325	325	III	390	–	48	–	–	–	–	4	3	–	–	–
312	312	III	140	–	96	3	–	–	–	4	–	–	–	–
330		III	220	–	42	–	–	1	–	–	–	–	2	–
330/SK 12–13		III	★	–	★	–	–	–	–	–	–	–	–	–
340	327	III	120	–	43	–	–	1	–	–	–	–	–
341	326	III	★	15	★	–	–	★★	–	–	–	–	–	–
344	328	III	120	–	43	–	–	★★	6	3	6	–	–	–
345		II	780	–	96	–	–	2	–	8	6	–	–	–
309		II	83	–	8	–	–	–	–	–	–	–	–	–
310/303		II	97	–	24	–	–	–	–	–	–	–	–	–
311		II	1804	–	126	45	–	–	9	10	5	–	–	–
311/305		II	35	–	25	–	–	–	–	–	–	–	–	–
311/SK5		II	15	–	8	–	–	–	3	–	–	–	–	–
320		II	1	–	–	–	–	–	–	–	–	–	–	–
348	331	III	390	–	48	–	–	–	–	4	3	–	–	–

FIGURE 4.51

Marine mollusca species by context and phase (★: present)

	Contexts																												
	24	28	306	309	310	311	312	315	316	318	324	325	329	330	332	333	334	337	338	339	340	341	343	344	345	348	SK 3	SK 9	SK 10
Cochlicopa lubricella	*	*	**	**	*	*	*	**	*		****	*	*	**	**	***	***	***	***	**	**	*		**	**		*	*	*
Cochicopa lubrica	**		**	*	*	*	**	**	**	*	**	*	*	*	*	**	**	**	**	*	**	*	*		*	**	**		
Lauria cylindracea	*	*					*				**	*		*	*			**			**	**	*		**	*	*		
Aegopinella pura	*	*	*	*			**			*	*	*		*	**			*			**	**	*	.,		*		*	
Aegopinella nitidula	*	*	**	*				**		**			**		*			**		**	***	*	**			**			*
Oxychillus cellarius	*		**				**	**	*	*	**	*		*		*	**	**	*	*	*	*	*	*	**	*	*		*	*
Oxichillus alliarius		*																											
Arianta arbustorum	*	*	*				*	*	*	*	*			*							*			*					
Trichia hispida			*				**	***								*		*			**		*	****	**		*		
Discus rotundatus	*		****	**			****	****	*		***	**	****	****	*	***	***	****	**	***	**	**	*				*	*	
Punctum pygmaeum							*				*				*			*						*					

FIGURE 4.52

Summary of land snail species by context

10th century, found inside the infant's mouth (SK 9). As far as this author is aware, only one other such example has been found in Scotland, from the Isle of May, in Fife where a St James' shell (*Pectem maximus*) was found inside the mouth of an adult male skeleton dated 1305–1414 AD (by which time this shell was a recognised emblem of the cult of St James, related to the Santiago de Compostela pilgrimage) (James and Yeoman 2008, 180–181).

Although few, awareness of the evidence of marine shell in ritual is an interesting aspect to consider when looking at the range of possible uses of marine molluscs in antiquity.

The land snails

The summary of results of the analysis of the terrestrial snails from St Ninian's Isle is given in Figure 4.52. Identification to species was done by comparison to reference collections and to standard guides (Beedham 1972; Cameron and Redfern 1976; Kerney and Cameron 1979). Thirty-three contexts contained land snails, and twelve species belonging to six different family groups were identified in this assemblage.

Description of the land snail species identified according to family

Cochlicopidae family: the two species identified correspond to *Cochlicopa lubricella* (4.5–6.8 x 2.1–2.5mm), which is characteristic of dry places and found in limestone grassland and calcareous sand dunes, usually in mixed populations, often in dry exposed habitats, and to *Cochlicopa lubrica* (5–7.5 x 2.4–2.9mm) which is found in moderately damp places, in marshlands, grasslands and woods.

Pupillidae family: *Lauria cylindracea* is a very small snail (3–4.4 x 1.8mm), shaped like a squat turret; they are found on stone walls or under rocks.

Zonitidae family: this family occurs throughout the northern hemisphere and favours damp habitats. The species identified at St Ninian's Isle were: *Aegopinella pura* (3.5–4.2mm) and *Aegopinella nitidula* (8–10mm), which are found in moist places and, although they are found in woods, among rocks and on humanly disturbed habitats (particularly *A. nitidula*). Another species identified was *Oxychillus celarius* (9–12mm) which is found on stone walls or under rocks, and also *Oxychillus alliarius*, a small snail (5.5–7mm), with a glossy brown (sometimes greeny-white) shell with a very dark body. Its main distinguishing feature is the strong smell of garlic if disturbed. It is probably one of the most widespread snails in Shetland and inhabits woods, fields, rocks, being tolerant of poor acidic places.

Helicidae family: this family contains the largest European snails and species are found in a very wide range of habitats: within it there are groups that share features of habitat. There are six subfamilies within this group, two of which were present in this assemblage.

Subfamily: Ariantinae, species of this group have a common preference for damp habitats. *Arianta arbustorum* (10–22 x 14–18mm) is a species which inhabits walls, rocks and meadows and is nowadays also found in gardens, always in damp places. This is one of the largest snail species to occur in Shetland (it can be over 20mm).

Subfamily Hygromiinae are generally woodland snails, extending into hedges and other shady places and into open habitats where these are cool and moist. They are often found under vegetation. The species identified was *Trichia hispida* (5–6 x 5–12mm) which has a very catholic habitat; it is absent from very dry sites, but otherwise quite widespread.

Endodontidae family: a large and ancient family occuring worldwide; it is characteristic of shaded habitats. Two species of this group were identified: *Discus rotundatus,* one of the commonest species of terrestrial snails (5.5–7mm), found in moist sheltered places of all kinds, including under stones and under ground litter; and *Punctum pygmaeum* (1.2–1.5mm), found in a variety of moist and well-vegetated places.

Valloniidae family: a worldwide group is subdivided into two of which one, Valloniinae, was present at St Ninian's Isle; these are snails of open grassy habitat, with their shells often occuring in large numbers in the flood rubbish of rivers. The species identified was *Vallonia costata* (2.2–2.7mm) which is found in open calcareous places, stone walls and sand-dunes.

General discussion

The land snails from St Ninian's Isle derived mainly from Phases III and VI. These terrestrial molluscs are generally studied in archaeology to investigate the nature of the local environment in which the animals lived. It is also important to identify and record their presence because often these have not been surveyed in the areas of study. In many parts of Shetland little or no recording of these molluscs has been done and archaeologically recovered material may, in most cases, be the only means of surveying their distribution.

Terrestrial molluscs in Shetland are found mainly among dunes and on limestone. The land snails recovered at St Ninian's Isle are those found in such habitats.

Conclusion

The St Ninian's Isle edible marine molluscs were probably mainly used as food and/or as fishing bait, with their remains (i.e. the shells) being later used as components of fills to give some stability to sand. The large numbers of particularly edible periwinkles and limpets attest to this, as also the variety of edible molluscs present in this assemblage. Some lamillar shells, such as those of mussel, razor shells and oysters, disintegrate more rapidly and this may be the reason why fewer remains of such species survived in this assemblage. Shells of periwinkles and limpets are more robust and survive well in archaeological deposits.

Some species of non-edible marine molluscs may have been introduced with seaweed, whereas others may have been introduced with the edible species present in the assemblage to become components of the sandy deposits used as fills.

The terrestrial snail species present at St Ninian's Isle are taxa typical of disturbed but shaded habitats associated with stone buildings or rubble and/or sand; it is therefore assumed that these accumulated over a period of time and are likely to be modern intrusions.

4.5 THE HUMAN REMAINS

Articulated remains
Julie Roberts

This report comprises an osteological study of two assemblages of human skeletal remains from St Ninian's Isle. The same methodology for analysis was applied to both sets of remains, but the results are divided into two parts for the purpose of clarity: Part One is concerned with SK 5–13, which were excavated in the summer of 2000 and analysed in Glasgow in 2002/3. Part Two describes the remains which were analysed *in situ* during the course of excavations in 1999 and 2000 respectively (SF 60, SF 61 and SK 3).

An overall discussion will consider the importance of the remains with particular regard to changes in patterns of health and disease (that might reflect changes in the economy), mode of interment and possible relationships between the individuals.

Methodology

State of preservation

The remains were categorised as being in a poor, fair or good state of preservation. This assessment was made using three criteria: the percentage of the skeleton surviving, the extent of fragmentation of the bones, and the amount of surface erosion present.

Age at death

The methods of choice for age determination in all the immature skeletons were dental development and stages of epiphyseal fusion (Scheuer and Black 2000; Buikstra and Ubelaker 1994). In the younger individuals, aged around birth, cranial development was also used as a primary indicator of age (Scheuer and Black 2000).

Where dental and skeletal maturity were complete, age was based upon the methods outlined in *Standards for Data Collection in Human Remains* (Buikstra and Ubelaker 1994). These included assessment of the pubic symphysis, the auricular surface of the ilium, the sternal end of the right fourth rib. Degenerative changes and tooth attrition were also used as a general guide.

Sex

Secondary sexual characteristics do not start to develop until the onset of puberty and, as yet, the only reliable method of sex determination in immature individuals is by the analysis of DNA (this was attempted for the St Ninian's Isle samples, but was unsuccessful; see below). In the adults, sex was based on the sexually dimorphic features of the pelvis and cranium (Buikstra and Ubelaker 1994). Post-cranial metric data were also taken into consideration (Chamberlain 1994), although this can be variable both within and between different populations.

Health and disease

The recognition of pathological conditions in human skeletal remains is dependent on the preservation of specific skeletal elements, and the amount of surface erosion present. Certain diseases affect particular bones, and the lesions may have a characteristic distribution throughout the skeleton as a whole. Some conditions affect only the surface of the bone, causing periosteal new bone growth, in reaction to inflammation, infection or haemorrhage. If the surface of the bone has been eroded due to post-depositional disturbance, weathering, or careless excavation and post-excavation processing, evidence of pathological conditions can be lost. Even where excellent preservation exists, however, it must be remembered that many diseases, particularly acute bacterial or viral infections, do not leave a trace on the skeleton. Fortunately the remains from St Ninian's Isle were for the most part very well preserved, allowing a full palaeopathological assessment to be made. Diseases and traumatic injuries were classified according to cause with reference to a number of texts (eg Roberts and Manchester 1997; Ortner and Putschar 1981; Aufderheide and Rodríguez-Martín 1998; Stuart-Macadam 1989).

Growth and development

After birth, factors such as nutrition and disease can affect bone growth and epiphyseal fusion, whereas they have comparatively little effect on dental development. Standard growth charts have been compiled comparing chronological age and long bone length, and chronological age and dental development (Ubelaker 1989). Comparing the age based on dental development and that based on long bone length can therefore give an indication of whether a child was the correct height, small, or tall for his or her age, and therefore also of his or her nutritional status. This can be looked at in conjunction with any evidence of disease that might be present. In all but one case (SK 8) it was possible to make a comparison between dental developmental age and age based on long bone length.

In the case of adults, stature was calculated using the regression formulae devised by Trotter (1970). Shorter than normal stature can be an indication of malnourishment during childhood, although genetic factors also have to be taken into account. Childhood nutritional disorders, such as rickets and iron deficiency anaemia, can also be observed in adult skeletal remains, as can periods of arrested growth, in the form of dental enamel hypoplasia and Harris lines (although in this instance the long bones were not X-rayed).

Part 1: SK 5–SK 13 results

Preservation

Figure 4.53 summarises the condition of SK 5–13. It can be seen that the majority were in a good state of preservation, thereby enabling an accurate assessment of age at death, growth and development and skeletal pathology to be undertaken.

All the infant burials were articulated, although some were fragmented, and two, SK 8 and 12, were truncated (the latter by SK 13). The soil sample from the stomach area from SK 10 also produced over 100 infant bones and fragments with no element duplication, the long bones being from the left-hand side of the body, and this suggests a minimum of one juvenile present below and truncated by SK 10 (see Duffy below). The crania were the most frequently fragmented parts of the skeleton, due to the collapse of stone 'boxes' that had been placed around the heads. All of the children were buried supine and in semi-flexed positions. As the only adult in the group, SK 5 is described separately below.

Skeleton 5

SK 5 was a male aged 26–35 years at death. He was 165.056 ± 3.37cm (5ft 4in) tall, and of robust build. When uncovered in the ground, he was only partially articulated. It was possible to tell, however, that he lay supine, with his right hip and knee tightly flexed. The majority of his post-cranial remains were disarticulated, the exceptions being the right leg and parts of the spine. Strangely, although the vertebrae still remained in series, the spine had been divided

Skeleton No.	Percentage present	Condition
5	75	Good
6	85	Good
7	70	Good
8	20	Poor
9	90	Fair
10	70	Fair
11	85	Good
12	30	Poor
13	80	Good

FIGURE 4.53

State of preservation of burials SK 5–13

at the level of the 7th/8th thoracic vertebrae, and the upper part inverted. The 7th cervical to the 7th thoracic vertebrae were in articulation, but had been turned upside down and lay parallel to the articulated lower half of the spine, which comprised the 8th thoracic to the 5th lumbar vertebra. These were the correct way up. The 2nd to the 5th cervical vertebrae were disarticulated, and the 6th and the 1st cervical vertebrae were missing. The unusual position and partially articulated state of the remains implies that the body was moved from elsewhere and reburied when it was semi-decomposed (at the stage where some of the ligaments were still holding body parts together). Given the horrific nature of the traumatic injuries that the man had sustained (see below), a possible interpretation of events is that he was recovered from a battle site elsewhere and brought back to St Ninian's Isle to be buried.

TRAUMATIC INJURIES

SK 5 had incurred a number of severe traumatic injuries that had undoubtedly caused his death. It was possible to physically reconstruct some of the broken bones and, by studying the location and types of fractures, to reconstruct the likely sequence of his injuries, and the events immediately surrounding his death.

First in the sequence of injuries were fractures to the left fibula and tibia. The fibula had been severed in two in an oblique direction in the region of the lower third of the shaft. The tibia was not bisected, but a notch had been sliced out of it, in a location corresponding to that on the fibula. This pattern of injury is consistent with a blow from a weapon with a very sharp blade, such as a sword, slicing downwards and inwards from the fibula through to the tibia, most likely in an attempt to fell the victim (Figure 4.54).

A number of skull fractures caused by a sharp bladed weapon were present. The location of the defects, on the right occipital, parietal and temporal bones, indicated that the man was attacked from behind by a right-handed aggressor, probably once he had fallen to the ground following his leg injury. The blade thickness of the weapon was approximately 10mm, and at least two separate injuries could be distinguished. In addition, there was a skull fracture at the bregma (on the top of the head). It measured 10mm in diameter, and looked as though it might have been caused by a blunt instrument, such as the end of a pole (Figures 4.55–4.58).

Finally, an injury of the 3rd cervical vertebra was identified. The posterior half of the superior surface of the vertebral body and the right neural arch had been sliced off by a very sharp blade. There was no corresponding defect on the lower surface of the second cervical vertebrae, implying that the blade used was thin enough to have passed between the

inter-vertebral space through the disc (approximately 5mm). The angle of the defect suggested that the blade had been pulled backwards through the neck and downwards, implying that SK 5 had finally met his death by having his head lifted and throat cut from behind. The sword used to inflict the other horrific injuries would most likely have been too thick to produce a fracture of this type. A knife, perhaps similar in type to the one buried in close proximity to his remains (see Batey above), would probably have been responsible for this final act of violence.

HEALTH AND DISEASE

In addition to the injuries described above, SK 5 suffered from two disorders that were not life threatening; iron deficiency anaemia and periostitis.

There are many causes of iron deficiency anaemia, including lack of iron in the diet, metabolic disorders which prevent the absorption of iron, and

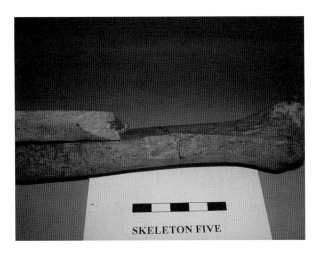

FIGURE 4.54
SK 5: fractured fibula and tibia. Photograph: J Roberts

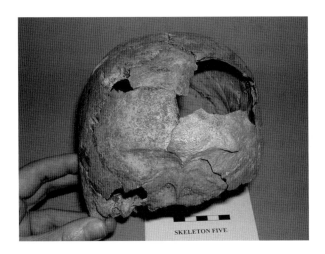

FIGURE 4.55
SK 5: fractured cranium, posterior view. Photograph: J Roberts

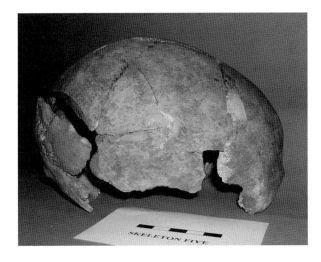

FIGURE 4.56

SK 5: fractured cranium, lateral (right side) view. Photograph: J Roberts

FIGURE 4.57

SK 5: fractured cranium, superior view. Photograph: J Roberts

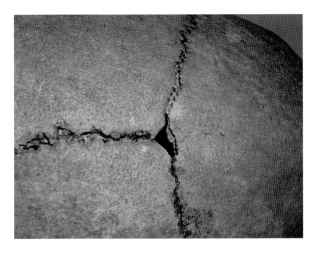

FIGURE 4.58

SK 5: fractured cranium, superior view (close-up showing bregma). Photograph: J Roberts

high pathogen load within the body. In the skeleton, iron deficiency anaemia is characterised either by lesions in the orbital vaults (*cribra orbitalia*) or pitting of the ectocranial surface of the skull and thickening and increased porosity of the diploe, the spongy layer between the inner and outer tables of the skull (*porotic hyperostosis*). SK 5 suffered from *porotic hyperostosis*, which was evident in the posterior part of the frontal bones, the anterior/medial parts of both parietals and the superior part of the occipital bone. The condition was moderate in severity and may have caused symptoms such as mild fatigue and weakness.

This iron deficiency anaemia may or may not have been related to the periostitis of the right and left tibiae and (to a lesser extent) fibulae, from which he suffered. Periostitis, inflammation of the periosteum surrounding the bone, is a frequently observed condition in archaeological skeletons, particularly in the region of the lower limbs. The reactive new bone growth, which occurs as a result of the periosteum becoming inflamed, can be caused by systemic or localised, direct infection, the latter commonly being transmitted from soft tissue injuries to the shins. Traumatic injury can also damage the periosteum itself, causing reactive new bone growth. Although in this instance, the deposits of new bone growth were quite thick covering the medial aspects of the shafts for most of their lengths, the bone was striated lamellar bone, indicating that the condition was almost healed.

The immature individuals

AGE AT DEATH

Figure 4.59 summarises the ages at death, based on dental and cranial development, of SK 6–13. Figure 4.60 presents this information graphically, and Figure 4.61 displays the information in terms of the percentage of individuals within each age category.

It can be seen from both Figures 4.60 and 4.61 that the majority of individuals were aged less than 12 months at death. Two of the infants (25%) could be classed as neonates, i.e. they died within the first 8 weeks of life. It could be said with certainty that both of the neonates had reached full term and were not premature, because even where the stage of dental development indicated birth plus *or* minus 2 months, cranial development indicated that the infants had reached an age of at least 40 weeks.

HEALTH AND DISEASE

Growth and development

Figure 4.62 summarises the differences between age indicated by dental and cranial development, and age indicated by long bone length.

It can be seen that, in five out of the seven children who had one or more intact long bones, there was a discrepancy between the age suggested by long bone length and that indicated by dental and cranial development. In all of these cases the long bone length age was younger than the dental and cranial development age, and the amount by which the two ranges differed appeared to increase with the age of the child. The two youngest individuals were the correct height for their age, implying that growth and development had been normal *in utero*. Nutrients obtained from the placenta and stored during the first few weeks of life would have initially buffered the infants against their environment, but as they got older it appears that they simply failed to thrive and grow. The pathological evidence below offers an explanation as to why this was the case.

Pathological conditions

Six of the eight children (75%) showed some kind of pathology, an unusually high percentage in an archaeological assemblage. The skeletons of infants from most pre-modern cemetery populations show little evidence of disease, and this is generally attributed to death by acute infectious disease, in otherwise relatively healthy individuals. In this instance, the diseases identified represented chronic long-term conditions.

Five of the children (SK 8–12) showed pathological changes that were characteristic of rickets (Figures 4.63–4.65). These included porosity of the cranium (SK 8, 9, 12, and to a lesser extent 10), marked fattening and porosity of the rib ends (SK 10–12), flaring of the ends, and slight deformation, of the long bones (SK 8–10), and characteristic enamel defects of the teeth (SK 9).

Rickets is a 'disease of infancy and childhood that is characterised by mineralization failure in growing cartilage and bone' (Stuart Macadam 1989, 206). There can also be poor mineralisation of the teeth, as in the case of SK 9, and, as with all of the infants aged over two months, the child is often shorter than normal for his or her age (Stuart Macadam 1989). Inadequate mineralisation can lead to deformities ranging from slight bowing of the shafts and flaring of the ends of the bones, to such severe distortion that the child is unable to walk (although the more severe changes are generally associated with older children and adolescents). Children with rickets are also prone to gastro-intestinal upsets, chest infections, and excess sweating and lethargy.

The disease is caused by insufficient vitamin D, either due to dietary deficiency, lack of sunlight, or a metabolic condition that prevents the absorption of vitamin D. It has been termed a disease of civilisation (Roberts and Manchester 1997), as it has a higher prevalence rate in crowded cities where the population are deprived of natural sunlight. It is, however, also common in populations that live at higher latitudes, for the same reason. There are two types of rickets, porotic or hypertrophic, depending

Skeleton No.	Age at death
6	0–2 months
7	4–5 years
8	12–16 months
9	16 months–2 years 8 months
10	3–6 months
11	6–9 months
12	0–2 months
13	6–12 months

FIGURE 4.59

Age at death of immature individuals SK 6–13

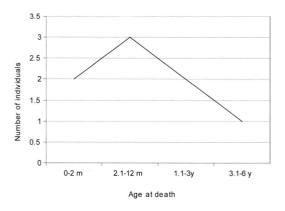

FIGURE 4.60

Number of individuals within each age category

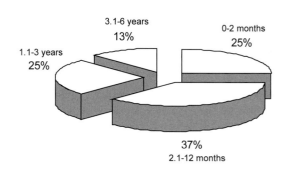

FIGURE 4.61

Percentage of individuals within each age category

SK	Dental and cranial development age	Long bone length age
6	0–2 months	0–2 months
7	4–6 years	2–3 years
8	1 year–1 year 4 months	NA
9	1 year 4 months–2 years 8 months	6–12 months
10	3–6 months	1–1.5 months
11	6–9 months	1.5–2 months
12	0–2 months	0–2 months
13	6–12 months	1–2 months

FIGURE 4.62

SK 6–13: comparison of age based on dental and cranial development, and that based on long bone length

FIGURE 4.63

SK 8: porosity of the cranium, characteristic of rickets

FIGURE 4.64

SK 9: defects of the enamel of the teeth

FIGURE 4.65

SK 10: thickening and porosity of the rib ends

on the nutritional status of the child. The changes seen in the St Ninian's Isle children were more representative of the former, which is associated with 'general undernourishment' (Stuart Macadam 1989, 207).

It has been observed that rickets 'rarely begins before four months of age because Vitamin D passes from the mother to the foetus through the placenta and is stored in the liver of the infant. The highest frequency is observed between 6 months of age and 2 years in the sunless winter months' (Ortner and Putschar 1981, 274). Ortner and Putschar also note that it occurs rarely after the age of four years. This picture fits entirely with the infants from St Ninian's Isle, with the exception of SK 12. This exception could be explained in terms of the nutritional status of the mother, i.e. if she herself was malnourished then her breast milk may have been lacking in vitamin D, which would have precluded the infant from building up an adequate store in the liver, prior to birth. This has implications for the diet of the mother, as well as that of the infants once they were weaned. It might be expected that an island community would have ready access to vitamin D rich foods in the form of fish and shellfish (and certainly a vast quantity of shells were excavated from the site), but perhaps this was not the case. In fact, isotope analysis of the bones indicated that the individuals may not have been subsisting on much of a marine-based diet at all (see below).

If the economy at the time was primarily agricultural, a decline in the climate causing poor harvests would certainly have led to endemic malnourishment and ill health. The same would also be true if the community had been reliant upon animals that could not survive the harsh conditions. It is possible that the rickets was a vitamin D resistant type, caused by X-linked hypophosphataemia. This seems unlikely though because as this type of rickets generally occurs only between the ages of 12–18 months (Blondiaux *et al* 2002). Bayesian analysis of the radiocarbon dates has indicated that SK 8–13 may have all been buried in the 10th century AD (see below). It is a distinct possibility therefore that the stunted growth and nutritional disorders observed reflected a period of decline and poverty after the Viking invasions.

The two immature individuals (SK 6 and 7) that were buried away from the main group of infants did not show any signs of rickets. SK 7 was still, however, very short in stature for his or her age, and showed evidence of a chest infection. The right 8th, 9th, 10th and 11th ribs all had periosteal new bone growth along the inner (pleural) surfaces. In some places this was quite thick, and the type of bone present indicated that the infection was of a relatively longstanding duration, but still active at the time of death. Specifically the right middle and lower lobes of the lungs appear to have been affected.

The child also suffered from Dental Enamel Hypolplasia (DEH), affecting a right maxillary first molar and a left mandibular canine. DEH is the term given to defects of the enamel of a tooth that represent a period of cessation in its growth and development. Although the causes are not fully understood, it is generally accepted that this can occur as a result of malnourishment, illnesses such as febrile infections, and physical or physiological stress. It is possible that in this case it was directly related to the chest infection.

No skeletal pathology was observed in SK 6 or 13.

Part 2: Results SF 60, SF 61 and SK 3

These remains, analysed in situ due to their potentially recent date (medieval to late 18th century) during excavations in 1999 (SF 60 and SF 61) and 2000 (SK 3), comprise the partially complete skeletons of two adults (SK 3 and SF 61) and an infant (SF 60). As they appeared to have no relationship archaeologically, they will each be discussed separately.

Skeleton 3

SK 3 was approximately 50% complete, having been truncated at the neck, and just below the hips, across the proximal shafts of the femora. The mandible and cervical vertebrae were present but disarticulated; the rest of the remains were fully articulated.

The skeleton was that of a male aged 25–30 years at death, who was 178.605 ± 4.65cm (5ft 9in) tall. Despite his tall stature and robust bones, he had a number of pathological conditions that would certainly have affected his quality of life. These included degenerative joint disease and compression fractures of the spine, a prolific chest infection that was active at the time of his death, and *spina bifida occulta* (the latter condition would have been asymptomatic).

The degenerative changes seen in the spine of SK 3 were more severe than might be expected in a man of his age. They were, however, more characteristic of trauma caused by hard manual labour, than the general 'wear and tear' type of osteoarthritis commonly seen in older individuals (Roberts and Manchester 1997). Large or medium-sized Schmorls Nodes were observed on the 4th to the 11th thoracic vertebrae (inclusive), and small ones were present on the 12th thoracic vertebra and the first three lumbar vertebrae. In five cases (T5, T6, T7, T10 and T11) these were associated with anterior compression of the vertebral bodies, indicating wedge compression fractures. These fractures are normally associated with a vertical compression force transmitted directly along the line of the vertebral bodies whilst the spine is flexed, either during a heavy fall on the feet or buttocks (Crawford-Adams 1987), or possibly the shoulders (Galloway 1999). As the damage was restricted to the anterior portion of the vertebrae, it is likely that there would have been little chance of complications involving

the spinal cord. The Schmorls Nodes represent herniations of the contents of the inter-vertebral discs onto the superior and inferior surfaces of the vertebral bodies. As with the compression fractures they can be caused by a fall when the spine is flexed, but they have also been associated with repeated flexion and lateral bending (Kennedy 1989), such as might be incurred in planting and harvesting crops.

Three left ribs and five right ribs had flecks and plaques of woven bone on the inner surfaces, indicating a chest infection that was active at the time of death. The bone growth was more prolific on the right ribs, but on the left there were also flecks on the outer surfaces of the ribs. It was not possible to determine the cause of the infection from macroscopic analysis alone, but it may have been nonspecific pleurisy or pneumonia, or even TB.

Spina bifida occulta is a congenital condition whereby the posterior neural arches of the sacrum do not fully close. The condition is asymptomatic and the affected individual is not generally aware that they are affected. It is different from the condition *Spina bifida*, where the neural canal is actually open and the spinal chord is exposed, leading to neurological deficits. In SK 3, the neural arches of the 2nd to 5th sacral vertebrae were open.

SF 60

SF 60 was a poorly preserved, disturbed infant burial. The skull was missing with the exception of two teeth, a deciduous upper central incisor and first molar. Only the left side of the torso was preserved, together with the left arm bones, and part of the left pelvis and femur, truncated at the distal end. The thoracic and lumbar vertebrae had also survived. As with the other remains in this group, no grave-cut could be found. The dentition indicated that the child was aged between birth and two months at death. No pathological conditions were observed, but it was not possible to undertake a comprehensive study as the remains were examined *in situ*.

SF 61

SF 61 was an articulated left leg (femur, patella, tibia and fibula) and intact left and right feet. The left femur had been truncated at the distal third of the shaft, and the leg was fully extended. The feet were packed closely together, as if they had once been bound or wrapped in a shroud, and no obvious grave-cut for the burial was discernable. Little can be said about the remains themselves except that they were in a good state of preservation and they belonged to an adult of unknown sex. No pathological conditions were evident.

Discussion

The skeletons analysed reflected a long tradition of burial on St Ninian's Isle and provided a valuable insight into changing modes of interment and health and disease patterns that would have reflected the changing social and economic climates.

If the group of infants is a true representation of the population living in close proximity to the island at that time, then the nutritional deficiencies described above could be an indication of a period of famine. The great number of shellfish excavated from the site would have been a potentially rich source of vitamin D, but perhaps for some reason young children did not have access to these.

SK 5 had been deposited in an unusual manner, although perhaps for different reasons. It is possible that he was a war hero, brought home to be re-buried on the island some considerable time after being killed in battle. The radiocarbon dating results suggest a Late Norse period date (1020–1240 AD at 95.4% probability). However, although the Norse had settled in Shetland by this date, there is nothing to say that SK 5 is of Norse ethnicity; he could still be of native lineage and so a desecration argument may still hold true. Whatever the reasons for the unusual arrangement of his remains, the traumatic injuries inflicted upon him provide us with irrefutable evidence of interpersonal violence during this period.

Disarticulated human remains
Paul Duffy

Specialist analysis was undertaken of an assemblage of disarticulated human remains from St Ninian's Isle recovered during the evaluation and excavation of deposits threatened by rabbit and natural erosion processes. Analysis was limited to the identification minimum number of individuals, demographic data, and skeletal pathology per context as the limited nature of the assemblages precluded further detailed analysis.

The relative frequencies of skeletal elements recovered during the excavations were also studied, in order to assess whether any spatial or temporal patterning was discernible from the disarticulated elements. Several patterns were observed in this material. Whilst the accessible material from the 1959 excavations suggests that a significant recovery bias in favour of particular skeletal elements existed during this project, it proved difficult to observe this bias in the skeletal material recovered during the 1999 and 2000 excavations. Instead, it is suggested that these patterns are more consistent with natural scavenging and decay processes.

The minimum number of individuals was determined by recording any repeated skeletal elements, or elements from individuals of clearly different biological age. The methods used to determine age at death and sex were in accordance with those outlined by Buikstra and Ubleaker (1994).

Results

The interim excavation report for the St Ninian's Isle project identified two main reasons for the presence of disarticulated remains on the island, as a result of human activity on the site and as a result of rabbit and other natural erosion processes (Barrowman 2000). The results of this analysis are therefore presented by phase and then by context. Given the chronological depth of the site and the variety of reasons for the presence of disarticulated remains, analysis of paleodemographic and paleopathological information has been limited to discussion per context. It is felt that any attempt to widen the discussion beyond this would be largely meaningless in the context of this assemblage.

The results of the skeletal analysis in terms of the interpretation of minimum number of individuals, age at death, sex, etc, are presented in the main body of the text below. These data are ordered initially by site phase, and subsequently by context. The analysis of these characteristics does not differentiate between elements recovered from a single context, but over two excavation seasons. A comprehensive skeletal catalogue is also deposited in the archive.

Phase II

— Context 309 sandy midden. A minimum of one adult male and one juvenile were identified. One male was identified. No pathology was observed.

— Context 311 sandy midden. A minimum of one adult was identified. Dental pathology in the form of heavy calculus formation was present on one adult lower left incisor.

Phase III

— Context 025=028, midden. A minimum of one adult individual was identified.

— Context 314, kerbed cairn complex over infant burials SK 8–13. A minimum of one adult was identified. Dental pathology was observed on two teeth; dental attrition on a lower left first molar, and heavy calculus formation on a second left incisor.

— Context 318, midden. A minimum of one adult was identified.

— Context 324, deposit in cist 321. A minimum of one adult was identified

— Context 325, midden. A minimum of one adult and one juvenile were identified.

— Context 330, re-deposited. Midden over SK 8–13 and below context 314. A minimum of 2 adults and 2 juveniles were identified. The age at death of one adult was estimated to be between 16–18 years, and one juvenile was estimated to be a neonate.

— Context 334, fill of cist 321. A minimum of 2 adults and 2 juveniles were identified. One male and one possible female were identified. Age at death for two individuals was calculated at between 35–45 years, and 0–6 months. The main pathological condition identified was dental disease, with subgingival calculus, evidence of severe periodontal disease, present on two teeth. Severe dental attrition was also noted on both of these teeth, as well as a third.

— Context 336, empty cist with cross slab. A minimum of one adult and one juvenile were identified.

— Context 338, fill over cross slab in cist 321, III. A minimum of one adult and one juvenile was identified.

— Context 340, sandy midden spread over east of site. A minimum of 3 adults and one juvenile were identified. One individual was male. Age at death of two of the individuals was calculated to be 24–27 years and 35–45 years. A number of pathologies were recorded. The most frequent of these was osteoarthritis, identified on a trapezoid (hand bone) and a cervical vertebra. Sub gingival calculus, evidence of severe periodontal disease, was observed on one tooth, and severe dental attrition on two teeth. Mandibular tori were also observed on an adult male mandible.

— Context 341, re-deposited sandy midden over juvenile SK 7. A minimum of 2 juveniles were identified. Age at death of two of the individuals was calculated to be 6–12 months and 12–24 months.

— Context 343, sand and midden below cross slab in 321. A minimum of one adult and one juvenile were identified.

— Context 344, sand and midden below cross slab in 321. A minimum of one adult and one juvenile were identified. Dental pathology, in the form of calculus deposits and moderate tooth attrition was identified on one lower left first premolar.

— Context 345, basal fill of wall 307. A minimum of one adult and one juvenile were identified.

Phase VI: material from 1959 excavation (Shetland Museum)

This material contained a minimum of one adult male individual, and one juvenile. Pathology was noted on the adult remains in the form of a pronounced thickening of the diploe of the frontal, parietal and occipital bones of the cranium, potentially indicative of iron deficiency anaemia. Periodontal disease was noted on the maxilla, as was external bony outgrowths known as tori. Heavy calculus and significant wear was also noted on the maxillary and mandibular teeth and moderate to heavy wear were noted on all teeth (see also Chapter 3).

Phase VI: material from 1999–2000 excavations

— Context 011, modern wall fill. A minimum of one adult individual was identified. New bone formation was noted on a rib body, suggestive of an pulmonary infection, and osteophyte formation on the proximal end of an ulna may be indicative of early arthritis.

— Context 023, re-deposited wind-blown sand. A minimum of one adult and one juvenile were identified. An estimate of age at death between 35–45 years was obtained for one individual. Pathology in the form of mandibular tori was identified in the adult individual.

— Context 024, re-deposited wind-blown sand. A minimum of 4 adults and 2 juveniles were identified. Two adults were identified as male, one possible male and one possible female. Two juveniles of between 7–11 and 1 year 4 months to 2 years 8 months were also identified. Pathology was limited to the identification of subgingival calculus on one tooth, indicative of severe periodontal disease. The majority of teeth were heavily worn, suggestive of a diet heavy in coarse food.

— Context 306, re-deposited wall tumble. A minimum of one adult and one juvenile were identified.

— Context 316, re-deposited from excavations in 1959. A minimum of one adult and 3 juveniles were identified. The majority of teeth were also heavily worn, suggestive of a diet heavy in coarse food.

— Context 329, backfill into cist from 1959 excavations. A minimum of one adult and one juvenile were identified. An age at death of 7–11 years was calculated for the juvenile individual.

— Context 332, 1959 re-deposited midden in cist. A minimum of one adult was identified.

— Context 337, modern wall fill. A minimum of one adult and one juvenile were identified.

Phase VII: topsoil and turf

— Context 01, topsoil and turf. A minimum of 4 adults and 2 juveniles were identified. One male and one female could be identified and age at death of 17–25 and 35–45 was identified for two individuals. One juvenile was further identified as between 2–4 years at death. The main pathology identified was degenerative spinal joint disease in the form of osteophyte formation on two vertebrae. The majority of teeth were also heavily worn, suggestive of a diet heavy in coarse food.

Small Finds

— Context 025 SF 37b. A minimum number of one juvenile was identified.
— Context 025 SF 50. A minimum number of one adult was identified.
— Context 025 SF 61. A minimum number of one adult was identified.
— Context 025 SF 65. A minimum number of one adult was identified.

Retents

— SK 3 Retents. A minimum of one adult was identified.

— SK 9 Retents. A minimum of one juvenile was identified.

— SK 10 Retents. A minimum of one juvenile was identified. Comparison with the burial catalogue for SK 10 suggests that these elements represent a second individual within the burial area.

Comparison of frequency of skeletal elements

A study of the skeletal elements identified from each context was designed to investigate variations in the frequency of skeletal elements in particular phases. Basic statistical analysis of the frequency of the elements was carried out, together with some re-examination of the original material. Attempts were made to undertake this analysis on both adult and juvenile material. However, the complex nature of skeletal maturation, and the fusing of the various skeletal elements at different times, rendered in-depth analysis largely meaningless.

Results and discussion

Interesting differences in the relative frequencies of adult skeletal elements were initially observed when the assemblages from the various site phases were compared. Numerically, all of the material, except that from Phase II (n=17), forms significant sample sizes on which to undertake statistical analysis (Figure 4.66). The relative frequencies of skeletal material from the earlier phases (Phase II and III) are broadly comparable in makeup, although the material from Phase II is a limited sample, with only seventeen skeletal elements from two contexts (Figure 4.67). With the exception of rib elements, these phases are also broadly comparable with the material recovered from Phase VII. Only Phase VI apparently stands out as having any major differences in the frequencies of skeletal elements recovered.

The material recovered from Phase VI is, however, inherently biased. Whilst the skeletal elements examined from Phases II, III and VII were collected exclusively during the 1999 and 2000 excavation seasons, the material from Phase VI included material excavated during O'Dell's 1959 excavation, as well as material from the 1999 and 2000 excavations. This potentially skews the results and for this reason the two different groups of material in Phase VI were described separately below.

Relative frequencies of all categories of skeletal data are found to be similar through all four phases, with a maximum difference in range of less than 10% for most of the elements. The exception to this are hand and foot bones which decrease considerably in Phase VI, as compared to the other three phases, and the frequency of rib bones, which decreases in Phases III and VII. Interestingly, however, when compared to the frequency of skeletal elements in a single adult skeleton (Figure 4.68), a different picture emerges.

Viewed in comparison to these data, it would appear that elements of the hands and feet are, in fact, consistently under-represented across all four phases, compared to the frequencies we would expect to find if all skeletal elements of the body were present. Cranial elements appear to be consistently over-represented and, similarly, ribs are over-represented in Phases III and VI. The other skeletal elements appear to be in roughly correct proportions of anatomical frequency in all phases.

Two distinct patterns therefore emerge. When the analysed assemblage is placed into the framework of the temporal site phases, and these phases compared against each other, the relative frequencies of skeletal elements are found to be broadly similar. The exception to this is the frequency of bones of the hands and feet, which drops in Phase VI, and the frequency of ribs, which decreases in Phases III and VII. In comparison with the relative frequency of skeletal elements in an average adult skeleton, it appears that hand and feet bones are consistently under-represented throughout all phases, whilst cranial elements are consistently over-represented throughout all phases. Ribs are also over-represented in Phases II and VI.

In an attempt to understand these differences, the original material from the site was re-examined. Whilst the reason for the under-representation of hands and feet was not apparent, the over-representation of the cranial elements does appear to have an explanation. These elements are particularly prone to post-mortem breakage and frequently appear in the assemblage as fragments of whole bones. The relatively large surface area of such elements, combined with post-mortem breakage, would thus appear to have led to their apparent increased frequency. The same process may explain the over-representation of ribs, although why this should occur in only two phases is unclear. The fact that the elements from Phase II form a small sample size may, however, skew the data from this phase, and the increased representation in Phase VI could therefore result from previous excavation disturbance.

A comparison between the Phase VI disarticulated material retained from O'Dell's 1959 excavation and the Phase VI material recovered from the 1999/2000 excavations suggests that the excavation methodology in 1959 produced an assemblage heavily biased in favour of long bone and cranial elements with 92% of these elements constituting the assemblage (Figure 4.69). In contrast, only 32% of the material recovered in 1999 and 2000 comprises of these elements. Furthermore, the small bones of

	Phase II	Phase III	Phase VI	Phase VII
	%	%	%	%
Other	–	4	–	7
Rib	25	14	25	12
Vertebra	13	20	13	19
H/F	43	39	17	36
Long bone	–	6	20	10
Cranial	19	17	36	16

FIGURE 4.66

Frequency of adult elements per Phase (Phase II n=17, Phase III n=173, Phase VI n=335, Phase VII n=231)

	Phase II	Phase III	Phase VI	Phase VII
	%	%	%	%
Other	–	4	4	7
Rib	25	14	14	12
Vertebra	13	20	19	19
H/F	43	39	26	36
Long bone	–	6	10	10
Cranial	19	17	22	16

FIGURE 4.67

Frequency of adult elements per Phase, excluding material excavated by O'Dell 1955–59 (Phase II n=17, Phase III n=173, Phase VI n=189, Phase VII n=231)

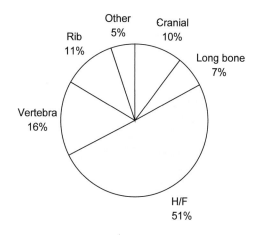

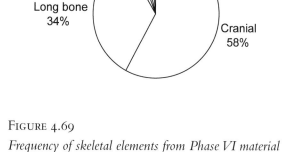

FIGURE 4.68
Frequency of skeletal elements in average adult skeleton

FIGURE 4.69
Frequency of skeletal elements from Phase VI material from Shetland Museum

the body are almost entirely absent from the 1959 sample, but were recovered in significant quantities from the 1999 and 2000 re-excavations of these layers.

What this would appear to suggest is that the disarticulated material collected during the 1959 excavation is heavily biased towards particular skeletal elements, perhaps due to active decisions as to the importance or otherwise of retaining particular parts of the skeleton, with smaller bones of the body largely absent. However, during the more recent excavations these elements are consistently under-represented in the assemblage compared to the frequency of other elements of the adult human skeleton. Although an excavation bias can, therefore, be identified during the excavations of O'Dell, this is not reflected in the material recovered during the 1999 and 2000 excavations. Instead, other factors must be considered.

The most obvious of these is the action of animal scavenging, where the extremities of the limbs are frequently targeted during the decomposition process. The bones of the hands and feet are both small and transportable, making them accessible to both large and small animals. It is possible therefore that the lack of hand and foot bones is a direct result of post-mortem taphonomic processes resulting from animal scavenging. This pattern may have been enhanced by the frequent disturbance of the excavation area by burrowing animals, which are more likely to dislodge these smaller bones that larger longbones or cranial elements, thus rendering them more accessible to scavengers. Natural processes of decay and decomposition are also likely to work more quickly on these smaller elements, and thus fewer may be found simply because more have decayed and fragmented beyond the process of archaeological recovery. O'Dell's excavations may have

further contributed to this, exposing yet more of the smaller skeletal elements to these natural processes, and so may help to explain the relative decrease in frequency of these elements in Phase VI.

In conclusion, several patterns were observed in the analysed disarticulated skeletal material from St Ninian's Isle. Whilst the study of this small assemblage from the 1959 excavations suggests that there existed a significant recovery bias in favour of particular skeletal elements during that work, the pattern suggested by the study of the skeletal material from the 1999 and 2000 excavations is more consistent with natural scavenging and decay processes apparent throughout the assemblage. The particular trends in Phase VI may represent the acceleration of these processes due to the inadvertent assistance of the excavation process.

A note on the DNA analysis of skeletal material from St Ninian's Isle
William Goodwin

DNA analysis was undertaken on a series of bone samples from St Ninian's Isle with the aim of determining the sex of infant skeletons, and whether they were genetically related. Unfortunately, to date, no endogenous DNA could be extracted and amplified from the bone samples.

Bone samples from nine skeletons were provided: SK 6–10 and 12–13, and 'Rosemary' (ABDUA 14269).

The largest section of bone provided from each skeleton was used for the purpose of DNA extraction. A DNA extraction procedure previously demonstrated to be successful when dealing with ancient DNA, was used, along with appropriate controls. After DNA extraction, amplification of mitochondrial DNA was attempted.

Results

No amplification of endogenous DNA was possible from the seven skeletons tested (all except SK 6 and 'Rosemary'). In one case some amplified product was detected; however, the amount of product was indicative of the DNA being exogenous contamination. Such contamination can be introduced by handling the bone or during the extraction procedure. It is not an uncommon hazard in this type of analysis.

There are several explanations as to why no DNA could be detected. The fact that the remains are several hundred years old means that the DNA will be highly degraded, possibly to the point of being undetectable. This possibility will be greater with this particular set of remains because they are all young children and do not therefore have the bone mass of adults that acts as a harbour for the DNA. In addition, damp conditions have been shown to be poor for its preservation. Another possible explanation for the lack of results is that the DNA extraction procedure failed to release the DNA from the mineral matrix of the bone. Compound PTB has been shown to assist the release of DNA from bone samples. If this can be obtained, it may be worth re-extracting the samples.

4.6 RADIOCARBON DATING

Radiocarbon dating of human skeletal material from the 2000 excavation
Alex Bayliss, with Rachel Barrowman, Gordon Cook and John Meadows

Dating materials

The dating programme at St Ninian's Isle focussed on the human skeletal material. Whilst several contexts from the 1999 and 2000 excavations were identified by the archaeobotanists as containing carbonised plant material with potential to be used for radiocarbon dating purposes (an unusual situation in Late Iron Age Shetland, where the burning of peat and driftwood as fuel results in very few sites with appropriate dating material present), the taphonomy of the charcoal was open to question. None of the contexts that contained carbonised material themselves reflected an episode of *in situ* burning, but rather material that had been burnt elsewhere and then dumped in, or become re-deposited into, the context in question, eg a midden, or midden re-deposited in a cist fill. The dating of the burnt material could not therefore date the feature in which it was found, providing at best a *terminus post quem* for the dumping of the midden, or interment of the burial. On a site, which from artefactual material alone is already known to be of Late Iron Age to Late Norse date, such a terminus post quem was of limited value, with no later, datable, deposits surviv-

ing on the site that could be used to 'cap' the date range (all the later deposits had already been excavated and removed from the site in the 1950s). Experience, from previous excavations, of the possible limitations on datable material from early medieval and Late Iron Age sites (Bayliss 1999; Barrowman *et al* 2007, 52–55; Ashmore 1999) serves to show that the taphonomy of the material to be dated is of crucial importance if the results obtained are to be meaningful.

Fortunately, the articulated human bone assemblage from the site had the potential to provide a more secure sequence of radiocarbon dates, particularly the assemblage excavated from the site in 2000. Two groups of bone were submitted for dating. The first group (in 2001) comprised samples from seven infants (SK 6 and SK 8-13), one juvenile (SK 7) and one adult excavated from Trench 1 in July 2000. The second group (in 2004) comprised samples from two adults ('Hubert' and 'Rosemary') and one juvenile ('Robert'), excavated in 1959, and reported in Chapter 3. In an ideal situation, when comparisons are wanted between two groups of samples whose ages do not differ by much, everything must be kept as similar as possible, i.e. all samples pre-treated together, graphitised as a batch and measured as a single batch on the AMS, preferably using the same background and modern standards when calculating the ages. In this case however this was not possible. The proviso must therefore be that the two separate sets of measurements done on skeletons from the 2000 and 1959 excavations were done several years apart using different AMS instruments. That is not to say that either group of samples is biased, merely that they could be offset slightly from one another but still within error of the correct age. It is entirely possible also for results to show the same difference between two samples measured together, but there is a higher probability of getting this difference, or greater, when the analyses are done in different laboratories at different times.

For this reason, the data are presented separately here and in Chapter 3, and only combined in the mathematical modelling below, which whilst including the relative order provided by the stratigraphy along with the radiocarbon results, must be seen only as one possible interpretative model for discussion.

Methodology

Nine radiocarbon determinations were made on human skeletons (SK 5–13) in 2001, by the Scottish Universities Environmental Research Centre, East Kilbride. Collagen samples were prepared in East Kilbride using the method outlined in Longin (1971). The collagen was combusted in sealed quartz tubes using copper oxide as the oxidant, and the CO_2 converted to graphite by the method of Slota *et al* (1987) and measured by the University of Arizona AMS Facility. Both laboratories maintain continual programmes of quality assurance procedures, in addition to participation in international inter-comparisons (Scott *et al* 1998). These tests indicate no laboratory offsets and demonstrate the validity of the precision quoted. ^{13}C analyses were carried out using a VG Isotech Sira 10 mass spectrometer. ^{15}N analyses were carried out using a Finnigan Tracer MAT mass spectrometer coupled to a Carlo Erba NA 1500 N/C/S Analyser.

Archaeological background

SK 5 was a male aged 26–35 years at death that had been inserted into a short cist (303), in an extremely flexed position. Infant burial SK 6 (aged 0–2 months) and juvenile SK 7 (aged 4–5 years) appeared to be unaccompanied burials, although two upright stones were found on one side of the skull of SK 6 suggest that it may originally have been a cist burial, and a partial headbox of small upright stones survived either side of the skull of SK 7. The remaining six infant burials (SK 8–13), were excavated from below a low kerbed stone setting (314), and marked with four small headstones, two of which were incised with crosses. They have been aged to between neonate (new born) and 2 years old and it is suggested that they were under-nourished, displaying pathological changes indicative of rickets in particular (see Roberts above).

Objectives

The objectives of the dating programme were:
— to determine whether the excavated human burials are Iron Age in date
— to determine whether the group of infant burials was contemporary with the Viking incursions into Shetland
— to determine the length of time over which the infants were interred.

Sampling strategy

All the articulated human burials from the 2000 excavations were sampled for radiocarbon dating, except for SK 3, a post-medieval burial partially disturbed by the 1959 excavations.

Interpretative approach

The Bayesian approach to modelling chronology has been adopted here (Buck *et al* 1996). This enables the stratigraphic information from the archaeological excavation to be combined with the scientific measurements, providing more precise estimates of archaeological chronology. It also moderates the influence of the inevitable statistical scatter of the radiocarbon measurements. Methodology is now available which allows us to combine these different

strands of evidence to produce realistic estimates of the dates of archaeological interest. It should be emphasised that these *posterior density estimates* are not absolute. They are interpretative *estimates*, which can and will change as further data become available and as other researchers choose to model the existing data from different perspectives.

The technique used is a form of Markov Chain Monte Carlo sampling and has been applied using the program OxCal v3.5,3 which uses a mixture of the Metropolis-Hastings algorithm and the more specific Gibbs sampler (Gilks *et al* 1996; Gelfand and Smith 1990). Details of the algorithms employed by this program are available from the on-line manual or in Bronk Ramsey (1995; 1998; 2000; 2001). The algorithms used in the model described below can be derived from the structure shown below in Figure 4.71.

Results

The results are given in Figure 4.70, and are quoted in accordance with the international standard known as the Trondheim convention (Stuiver and Kra 1986). They are conventional radiocarbon ages (Stuiver and Polach 1977).

The calibrations of these results are also given in Figure 4.70 and illustrated in Figures 4.71–4.73. All have been calculated using the datasets published by Stuiver *et al* (1998) and the computer program Ox-Cal (v3.5) (Bronk Ramsey 1995; 1998; 2001). The calibrated date ranges cited in the text are those for 95% confidence. They are quoted in the form recommended by Mook (1986), with the end points rounded outwards to 10 years. The ranges cited in plain type have been calculated according to the maximum intercept method (Stuiver and Reimer 1986); all other ranges are derived from the probability method (Stuiver and Reimer 1993). Those ranges printed in italics in the text and tables are derived from the mathematical modelling of archaeological problems.

The results of the stable isotope analyses are in the main consistent with a largely terrestrial diet, with only a minor component of marine protein (Richards and van Klinken 1997, fig 8). Two individuals have $\delta^{15}N$ and $\delta^{13}C$ values that would tend to indicate a somewhat larger marine component (*c*25–30%), however, these are both infants of 6–9 months and 6–12 months estimated ages and so these results will be complicated by a trophic shift caused by the breastfeeding effect.

Archaeological interpretation

When Professor O'Dell excavated the site in 1959, it was thought that all the short cist burials were Iron Age in date (Small 1973, 7). The results shown in Figures 4.71–4.73 demonstrate that this is not the case.

Lab no.	Sample reference	Sample description	Radiocarbon Age (BP)	δ¹³C (‰)	δ¹⁵N (‰)	Calibrated date range (95% confidence)	Posterior density estimate (95% probability)
AA-45624	SK 5	Right femur of adult (18–25 years old)	895±45	-20.3	+10.7	cal AD 1020–1260	-
AA-45625	SK 6	Right humerus and left femur of infant (0–2 months)	940±45	-21.5	+10.8	cal AD 1000–1220	-
AA-45626	SK 7	Right femur and right humerus of child (4–5 years old)	1250±45	-20.0	+12.6	cal AD 660–900	-
AA-45627	SK 8	Right femur and right tibia of infant (1– 1.5 years old)	1155±45	-20.3	+12.5	cal AD 770–990	cal AD 830–995
AA-45628	SK 9	Left femur and right humerus of infant (2–2.5 years old)	1180±45	-20.4	+14.4	cal AD 690–990	cal AD 820–990
AA-45629	SK 10	Right humerus and right tibia of infant (3–6 months old)	1045±40	-20.9	+11.1	cal AD 890–1040	cal AD 890–1030
AA-45630	SK 11	Right tibia and right femur of infant (6–9 months old)	1020±45	-18.8	+14.2	cal AD 900–1160	cal AD 890–1040
AA-45631	SK 12	Left radius and left humerus of infant (0–2 months old)	1060±45	-20.0	+12.6	cal AD 890–1030	cal AD 880–990
AA-45632	SK 13	Left tibia and left femur of infant (6–12 months old)	1150±45	-18.3	+15.3	cal AD 770–1000	cal AD 900–1000

FIGURE 4.70

Radiocarbon ages, calibrated age ranges and stable isotope values for the nine skeletons from the 2000 excavation

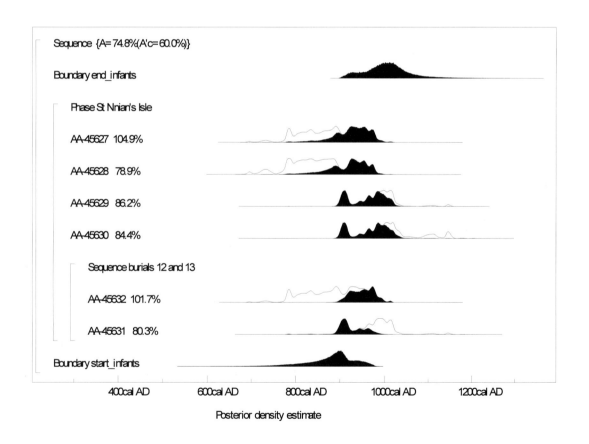

FIGURE 4.71

Probability distributions of dates from the multiple infants burial (SK 8, AA-45627–SK 13, AA-45632). Each distribution represents the relative probability that an event occurred at a particular time. For each of the radiocarbon dates two distributions have been plotted, one in outline, which is the result of simple radiocarbon calibration, and the other a solid one, which is based on the chronological model used. The large square brackets down the left hand side along with the OxCal keywords define the overall model exactly

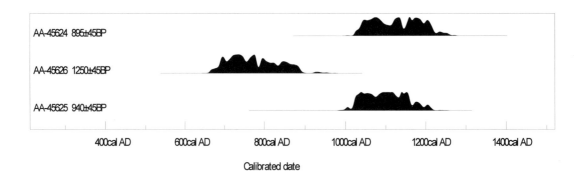

FIGURE 4.72
Probability distributions of simple calibrated dates from SK 5, SK 7 and SK 6

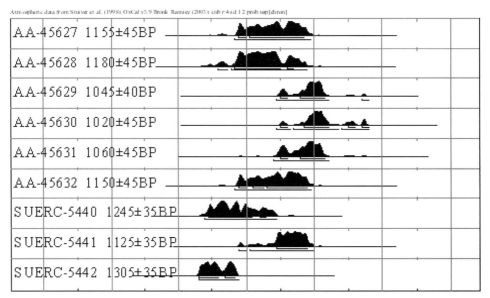

FIGURE 4.73
Probability distributions of simple calibrated dates from infant SK 8–13 (AA-45625 to AA-456532) and SK AB-DUA 14254, 14270 and 14269 (SUERC-5440 to SUERC-5442) from 1959 excavations

The six infant burials (SK 8–13) excavated from below the kerbed stone setting were all cut into the same soil (sandy midden 330) below the setting. The infants were all interred separately except SK 12 and SK 13 in the southern compartment where SK 13 clearly cut, and was therefore interred later than, SK 12.

The measurements on these children are statistically inconsistent (T'=11.7; T'(5%)=11.1; v=5; Ward and Wilson 1978). This suggests that they are not all precisely contemporary, a fact known because of the stratigraphic relationship between SK 12 and SK 13. Even if AA-45632 (SK 13) is excluded, the measurements are still significantly different (T'=10.3; T'(5%)= 9.5; v=4). This suggests that these children died over a period of time.

The model for the chronology of these six infant burials is shown in Figures 4.71 and 4.73. This demonstrates that they appear to have been interred during the 10th century AD. Insufficient measurements are available to reliably determine the length of time over which they died, although this was probably relatively short. The radiocarbon dating modelling suggests that, whilst the building of the kerbed cairn of stones above the burials may have been one event, the burials themselves may have been interred over a period of time, and this suggestion is supported by the skeletal material. Roberts and Duffy have shown that SK 8 was in a truncated and fragmentary condition, and that the interment of SK 10 had disturbed an earlier, adjacent, burial, as evidenced by the inclusion with it of disarticulated infant bones from a second individual (see Roberts and Duffy above).

The end of the 8th century, and into the 9th, was potentially a time of great upheaval in Shetland, although the first Viking impact on the native inhabitants of the Northern Isles is unknown. Recently it has been suggested that the Viking interface in Shetland was a violent one (Smith 2001, 7–8), and also that the St Ninian's Isle burials may provide evidence relevant to this debate (Barrowman 2003, 59). Examination of the probability distributions of the dates from these burials however suggests that this is unlikely to be the case as the multiple infant burials (SK 8, AA-45627–SK 13, AA-45632) are very likely to post-date AD 800 (over 95% probability), and to have been interred in the 10th century, whilst SK 5 (Figures 4.72 and 4.73), which shows signs of severe cranial trauma, died in cal AD 1020–1260 (AA-45624). Roberts independent osteological analysis however leads her to suggest above that the evidence for stunted growth and nutritional disorders amongst the infant bone assemblage from SK 8–13, reflects a period of decline and poverty after the Viking invasions, and a 10th century date is not incompatible with this suggestion.

Re-modelling of all dated samples to include those from the 1959 and 2000 excavations on St Ninian's Isle

Zoe Outram, with P Ashmore, R Barrowman and G Cook

A total of 12 radiocarbon dates have been produced for the excavations on St Ninian's Isle, Shetland. A collection of human skeletal material was recovered from a series of burials, which were used to produce the radiocarbon dates. The dates have been summarised in Figure 4.74, and span AD 650–1220, conventionally referred to as the Late Iron Age/Pictish-Norse periods. The burials are therefore significant as they date to the period Pictish–Viking interface period (Hunter 2007, 109 and 121), which is a crucial stage in Northern Isles archaeology. Unfortunately, a small plateau occurs within the radiocarbon calibration curve around 700–900 cal AD which limits the precision available within this period. The dates have been assessed in sequence in order to produce a chronology for the site. The dates have also been assessed within a Bayesian model in an attempt to refine the age ranges using the stratigraphic relationships of the sampled deposits.

The sampled material

All of the radiocarbon dates were produced on human skeletal material recovered from the excavation of a burial site. When using bone for dating, the diet of the individual must be taken into account in order to determine the contribution of marine-based plants and animals into the diet; significant marine contributions may result in an over-estimation of

the resulting date if not taken into account and would affect the choice of calibration curves used (Bayliss et al 2004; Molto et al 1997; Bronk Ramsey 2010a). The contribution of marine foods in the diet was assessed using the delta ^{13}C (δ^{13}C) ratios (Figure 4.74). A diet consisting entirely of terrestrial plants and animals would return a δ^{13}C value of approximately -20±1‰ (Richards et al 2006, 123). All of the individuals sampled from St Ninian's were within this range, with the exception of 'Hubert' (SUERC-5440), SK 13 (AA-45632) and SK 11 (AA-45630). The δ^{13}C values were just outside of the terrestrial range, being -18.8, -18.3 and -18.8 respectively. It was therefore concluded that for three of the sampled individuals the δ^{13}C values were indicative of a marine reservoir effect (MRE), but that the effect was small.

A MRE represents the measure of the offset that needs to be applied to a radiocarbon measurement, taking into account the difference between the atmospheric and oceanic carbon reservoirs that vary both temporally and spatially (Ascough et al 2009). The offset is defined by the ΔR value, which must be characterised for an area and for different periods of time. Recent work by Ascough et al (2009) has defined a ΔR value for the south mainland area of Shetland, based on samples dating to the Pictish-Norse period. This has provided a suitable ΔR value that could be applied to the samples from St Ninian's. In addition to the MRE correction, the percentage contribution of marine foodstuffs into the diet must be estimated for bones sampled from individuals with a mixed diet. However, this issue is complicated due to the potential issues regarding the trophic level effect noted in infants; further work is required to fully investigate this issue. It was therefore felt that corrections could not be confidently applied to the dataset in the light of the uncertainties still surrounding the dates.

Methodology

The archaeological information was used to arrange the dates into stratigraphic order. The dates were then statistically assessed in an attempt to reduce the size of the age ranges and increase the resolution of the resulting chronology. A Bayesian model was used, allowing the archaeological information to be combined with the chronological information through the translation of the stratigraphic order of the deposits into a statistical function (Buck et al 1991; 1994). The OxCal 4.1.4 programme was selected for the analysis as it allowed chronological models to be built easily and produces clear graphical outputs that display the models imposed on the sequence through the production of probability distributions plots of the selected dates (Bronk Ramsey 2010b). OxCal 4.1.4 also utilises the most recent calibration curve, IntCal09 (Reimer et al 2009) to calibrate the radiocarbon dates (Bronk Ramsey 2009).

Event	Sample code	Radiocarbon lab. code	Description	Uncalibrated Years BP	Calibrated 2-sigma	$\delta^{13}C$	$\delta^{15}N$
6	SK 5	AA-45624	Burial into an earlier short cist, alighned E–W	895±45	AD 1025-1220	-20.3	10.7
	SK 6	AA-45625	Infant burial, possibly once accompanied by a cist, aligned N–S	940±45	AD 1015-1210	-21.5	10.8
3	SK 8	AA-45627	Infant burial	1155±45	AD 730-990	-20.3	12.5
	SK 9	AA-45628	Infant burial	1180±45	AD 705-975	-20.4	14.4
4	SK 10	AA-45629	Infant burial	1045±40	AD 890-1120	-20.9	11.1
	SK 11	AA-45630	Infant burial	1020±45	AD 895-1155	-18.8	14.2
	SK 12	AA-45631	Infant burial	1060±45	AD 880-1120	-20.0	12.6
5	SK 13	AA-45632	Below low compartmentalised cairn, aligned E–W, cuts SK 12	1150±45	AD 770-990	-18.3	15.3
2	'Robert'	SUERC-5441	Long cist aligned E–W	1125±35	AD 780-995	-19.4	10.0
1	SK 7	AA-45626	Unaccompanied juvenile burial with a head box/cist aligned NW–SE	1250±45	AD 670-880	-20.0	12.6
	'Hubert'	SUERC-5440	Burial in early E–W long cist	1245±35	AD 680-875	-18.8	11.1
	'Rosemary'	SUERC-5442	Burial in a short cist aligned N–S. Stratigraphically and typologically earlier than 'Hubert'	1305±35	AD 655-775	-20.0	10.0

FIGURE 4.74

Summary of the dating evidence from St Ninian's Isle

All dates are presented in this report at 95% confidence (2σ) levels. The radiocarbon dates were incorporated into the model as uncalibrated dates (R-Dates), being calibrated during the statistical assessment of the sequence. The dates were arranged into a sequence, representing the stratigraphic order of the sampled deposits. A number of the dates was also placed into a 'phase', defined as an unordered group of events which have no known relationship, but which share stratigraphic relationships outside of the phase (Bronk Ramsey 2010a).

The use of the boundary function within an ordered sequence of dates is the most complicated aspect of Bayesian analysis, as the results are very sensitive to the assumptions made about the sequence (Steier and Rom 2000; Steier *et al* 2001; Bronk Ramsey 2000). A boundary was used at the beginning and end of each sequence produced with additional boundaries being used to represent breaks in the phases of activity:
— 1. A contiguous sequence: the sequence of dates before and after the break follow on from each other without a significant hiatus.
— 2. A sequential sequence: where there is a sequence of dates, a break, and another sequence of dates.

For a number of the sequences, both models were applied in order to determine the impact that they have on the dates. Following the application of the two models if a significant difference was not identified the simplest model was used for discussion in the report, which related to a contiguous sequence.

Following the application of the statistical model to a sequence, a second probability distribution was produced that demonstrated how the age ranges were affected by the inclusion of the stratigraphic information, referred to as a posterior density esti-

mate. An example has been shown in Figure 4.75. Two probability distributions are displayed for each radiocarbon date on the same plot. The light grey probability distributions represent the raw calibrated age ranges, while the dark grey probability distributions represent the posterior density estimates produced following the application of the model to the dates.

The 'agreement index' value (A-values) quantifies the degree to which the dates support the proposed model. The critical value defined for the agreement indices is set at 60%: values below this level were indicative of problems within the sequence (Bronk Ramsey 2010b); any dates highlighted as being anomalous were reassessed using the site records.

Inclusion of stratigraphic information can refine the resulting age ranges through the production of posterior density estimates, but it is important to note that these age ranges are the result of a statistical model imposed on the data and the interpretation of the stratigraphy within the field. Any new information, such as additional dating evidence or a different model being imposed on the data will produce different posterior density estimates.

The sequences of dates

The radiocarbon dates were originally assessed by Patrick Ashmore in 2005, since which time a new calibration curve has been released: IntCal09 (Reimer *et al* 2009). The dates were therefore recalibrated and the sequences reassessed in the light of the new curve. The stratigraphy recorded at the site was reassessed during the preparation of the final publication, which has resulted in two possible scenarios for the depositional sequence. The ambiguity in the sequence related to the infant burials recorded un-

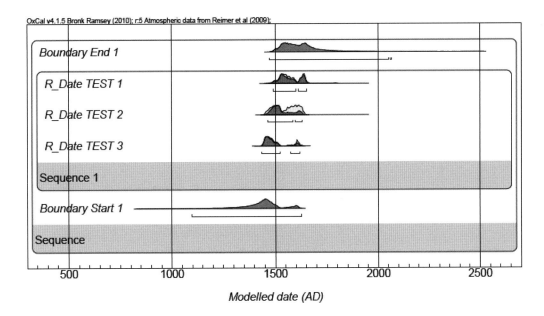

OxCal v4.1.5 Bronk Ramsey (2010); r:5 Atmospheric data from Reimer et al (2009);

Boundary End 1

R_Date TEST 1

R_Date TEST 2

R_Date TEST 3

Sequence 1

Boundary Start 1

Sequence

Modelled date (AD)

FIGURE 4.75

An example of the probability distributions produced using OxCal 4.1

der the low compartmentalised cairn (SK 8–13). It was possible to arrange some of the dates using the stratigraphic information:

— SK 8 and SK 9 (Event 3) represented the earliest burials below the low compartmentalised cairn.

— The burial referred to as SK 13 (Event 5) cut into the earlier burial SK 12 (Event 4).

It was not clear how SK 10 and SK 11 related to SK 12 and SK 13, and represented the most complicated aspect of the sequence. Two models were therefore tested:

— 1. SK 10–SK 13 were all arranged within the same 'phase', but with a small sequence reflecting the stratigraphic relationship of SK 12 and SK 13 (model 1).

— 2. A sequence that assumed that SK 10 and SK 11 were part on an earlier event than SK 12 and SK 13 (model 2).

The validity of each model will be tested and then discussed in turn in the following section.

Model 1

The first model assumed that SK 10–12 should be arranged in a 'phase' together with the addition of a small sequence that represented the stratigraphic relationship of SK 12 and SK 13. The model was investigated using a contiguous and sequential sequence; a significant difference was not noted and so the simplest model was applied, which was a contiguous sequence (Figure 4.76).

The assessment of the dates in sequence demonstrated that they respected their stratigraphic order, with the overall and individual agreement index values assigned to each date exceeding the critical value of 60%. The application of the model allowed

posterior density estimates to be produced, which have been summarised in Figure 4.77.

The assessment of the model presented in Figure 4.76 allowed the chronological information produced to be refined; the model had a significant impact on the dates from Events 2, 3, 4, and 5, refining the age ranges by between 65 to 160 years. The model could be used to suggest that the earliest burial ('Rosemary') occurred in AD 655–775, placing it at the end of the Late Iron Age/Pictish period. The burial recorded in Event 2, dated through the sample from 'Robert', was placed in AD 825–975 following the application of the model. This suggested that the earliest dated burial ('Rosemary') and the second burial event (Robert) were separated by a minimum of 50 years. If the minimum and maximum limits of the age ranges were used, however, the burials may have been separated by between 170–320 years.

Following the burial referred to as 'Robert', a series of infant burials were recorded below the low compartmentalised cairn. The earliest burials sampled in this area were SK 8 and SK 9; the burials were dated to AD 705–975, being refined to AD 875–985 following the application of the model. It is interesting to note that the raw calibrated age ranges bracket the period conventionally attributed to the Pictish-Viking phase, but the application of the model suggests that a Viking period date may be more likely when the other dating evidence is taken into account. It could also be argued that the burials recorded in Events 2 and Event 3 were separated by a minimum of 50 years, but by a maximum of 160 years. The remaining dates from below the low compartmentalised cairn returned modelled age estimates dating to AD 895–1020. A minimum of 20

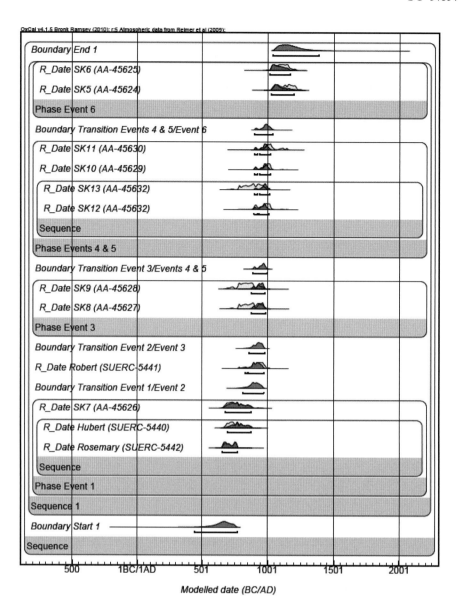

FIGURE 4.76

The probability distributions for the revised sequence of dates from St Ninian's Isle

Event	Sample code	Radiocarbon lab. code	Unmodelled age range (95% confidence)	Modelled age range (95% confidence)
6	SK 6	AA-45625	AD 1015–1210	AD 1010–1175
	SK 5	AA-45624	AD 1025–1220	AD 1020–1200
	BOUNDARY			*AD 900–1035*
5	SK 13	AA-45632	AD 770–990	AD 895–1020
4	SK 12	AA-45631	AD 880–1120	AD 895–1010
	SK 11	AA-45630	AD 895–1155	AD 895–1025
	SK 10	AA-45629	AD 890–1120	AD 895–1020
	BOUNDARY			*AD 885–1000*
3	SK 9	AA-45628	AD705–975	AD 875–985
	SK 8	AA-45627	AD 730–990	AD 875–985
	BOUNDARY			*AD 855–980*
2	'Robert'	SUERC-5441	AD 780–995	AD 825–975
	BOUNDARY			*AD 810–975*
1	SK 7	AA-45626	AD 670–880	AD 675–880
	'Hubert'	SUERC-5440	AD 680–875	AD 695–880
	'Rosemary'	SUERC-5440	AD 655–775	AD 655–775

FIGURE 4.77

Summary of the modelled age ranges estimated for the dating evidence from St Ninian's Isle (Model 1)

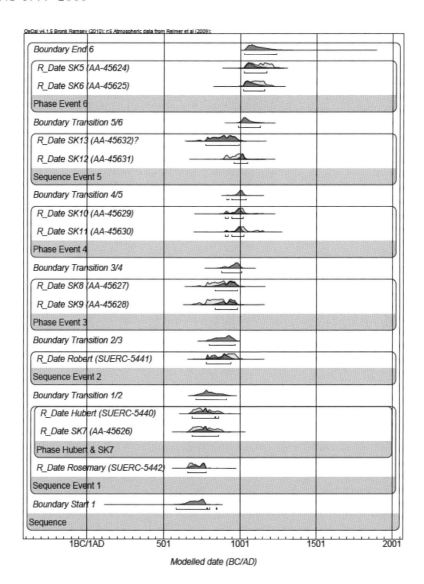

FIGURE 4.78

Posterior density estimates for the revised sequence of dates from St Ninian's Isle

years separated the earlier and later phased burials, and could be used to suggest that there was not a significant break in the activity in this area.

The final phase of activity (Event 6) was estimated to have occurred in AD 1020–1200, placing the burials firmly in the Norse-Late Norse period. It is possible to argue that Events 5 and 6 were separated by up to 100 years.

It can therefore be concluded that the proposed model used to assess the dates in this section may accurately reflect the depositional sequence. No anomalous dates were highlighted and all of the agreement index values exceeded the critical value of 60%. The application of the model suggests that the individual sampled from the earliest burial ('Rosemary') occurred towards the end of the Late Iron Age/Pictish period, and that the area was in use until the end of the 12th century AD.

Revised model 2

A second model was investigated to test the validity of the assumptions that SK 10 and SK 11 were buried earlier than SK 12 and SK 13. The model was investigated using a contiguous and sequential sequence; a significant difference was not noted and so the simplest model was applied, which was a contiguous sequence. The initial assessment of the sequence highlighted that SK 13 (AA-45632) returned an agreement of only 42.4% and therefore failed to exceed the critical value of 60%. The date produced for SK 13 appeared to be too old for its position within the proposed model; the anomalous result may indicate that the position of SK 13 within the sequence was incorrect or that residual material was sampled. However, it is also possible that the poor agreement index values related to the contribution of marine plants and animals into the diet of the individual, as SK 13 was associated with the heaviest $\delta^{13}C$ value recorded from the assemblage with a value of -18.3‰; further work is required to determine the cause of the anomalous result. SK 13 was therefore removed from the analysis of the sequence, being labelled with a question mark (?) in Figure 4.78.

The reassessment of the sequence was associated with an increase in the overall and individual agreement index values for the sequence, with all of the values exceeding the critical value of 60%. Posterior density estimates were produced for each date following the application of the model, excluding SK 13, which have been summarised in Figure 4.79.

The application of Model 2 on the dating evidence from St Ninian's allowed the size of the age ranges to be reduced; like Model 1, the application of Model 2 also had a significant impact on the dates produced from Events 2, 3, 4 and 5. The age ranges from these phases of activity were reduced by between 50–145 years.

The use of Model 2 did not alter the conclusions that could be drawn about the earliest dated burial ('Rosemary'), returning an almost identical posterior density to that produced using Model 1. A slightly older posterior density estimate however was returned for the Event 2 burial ('Robert'); a comparison of the modelled age estimates produced for 'Rosemary' and 'Robert' indicated that the two burials were either buried in quick succession, or that they were separated by up to 120–285 years if the minimum and maximum limits of the estimate age ranges were used.

It was assumed for Model 2 that three phases

of burials were sampled from underneath the low compartmentalised cairn: SK 8 and SK 9 were the earliest burials, which were followed by SK 10 and SK 11, before the burial of SK 12 and SK 13. A boundary was placed between each of these phases of use to represent the period of time that elapsed between the different periods of activity in this area. The earliest burials sampled under the low compartmentalised cairn (SK 8 and SK 9) were estimated to have occurred between AD 830–985 following the application of the model, and were very similar to the modelled age estimates produced using Model 1. The application of Model 2 supported the hypothesis stated above that SK 8 and SK 9 were probably buried in the Viking period once the additional dating evidence was taken into account. It could also be argued that the burials recorded in Events 2 and Event 3 were separated by a minimum of 55 years, but by a maximum of 210 years.

The second phase of burials below the low compartmentalised cairn (SK 10 and SK 11) were associated with estimated age ranges of AD 895–1025, suggesting that between 50–200 years elapsed between the interment of SK 10 and SK 11 and earlier phase of burials (SK 8 and SK 9). Another 60–155 years potentially elapsed before the burial of SK 12, with was associated with an estimated age range of AD 955–1050.

The application of Model 2 to the dates from Event 6 returned modelled age estimates of AD 1020–1175, which were very similar to those produced following the application of Model 1 and placed the burials firmly in the Norse-Late Norse period.

Event	Sample code	Radiocarbon lab. code	Unmodelled age range (95% confidence)	Modelled age range (95% confidence)
6	SK 5	AA-45624	AD 1025–1220	AD 1020–1175
	SK 6	AA-45625	AD 1015–1210	AD 1020–1160
	BOUNDARY			*AD 985–1130*
5	SK 13	AA-45632	AD 770–990	–
4	SK 12	AA-45631	AD 880–1120	AD 955–1050
	BOUNDARY			*AD 905–1040*
4	SK 10	AA-45629	AD 890–1120	AD 895–1025
	SK 11	AA-45630	AD 895–1155	AD 895–1025
	BOUNDARY			*AD 875–1015*
3	SK 8	AA-45627	AD 730–990	AD 835–985
	SK 9	AA-45628	AD 705–975	AD 830–985
	BOUNDARY			*AD 790–970*
2	'Robert'	SUERC-5441	AD 780–995	AD 775–940
	BOUNDARY			*AD 705–910*
1	SK 7	AA-45626	AD 670–880	AD 685–860
	'Hubert'	SUERC-5440	AD 680–875	AD 685–860
	'Rosemary'	SUERC-5440	AD 655–775	AD 655–780

FIGURE 4.79

Summary of the modelled age ranges estimated for the dating evidence from St Ninian's Isle (Model 2)

It can therefore be concluded that the application of Model 2 highlighted SK 13 as being anomalous, prompting the re-evaluation of the sampled material. The removal of this sample from the analysis was associated with an increase in the agreement index values produced for the overall sequence as well as for the individual dates. The conclusions stated following the application of Model 1 were largely supported by application of the alternate model. It is interesting to note that the burials sampled in Events 2 and below the low compartmentalised cairn were all separated by a minimum of 50–60 years, which may reflect the steady and continued use of this area as a burial ground.

Conclusions

It can be concluded that the dating evidence from St Ninian's produced a coherent chronological sequence with only one potentially anomalous sample being identified (SK 13) following the application of Model 2 to the dates; further work is required to determine the cause of the anomalous result. A small plateau within the radiocarbon calibration curve between 700 and 900 cal AD restricted the resolution available for some of the dates. The stratigraphic information was therefore used in conjunction with a Bayesian model to refine the age ranges and increase the resolution between the dated events. The raw calibrated age ranges varied in size between 200 and 250 years; the application of the models to the sequences of dates resulted in age ranges that were reduced by up to 160 years, representing a significant improvement in precision.

Two models were investigated for the dates from St Ninian's that tested two alternate hypotheses regarding the arrangement of samples SK 8–13 within the sequence. The impact of the models on the chronological information has been summarised in Figure 4.80.

The main difference noted between the two models related to the arrangement of the infant burials recorded below the low compartmentalised cairn, and the effect that the alternative hypotheses had on the dates located above and below this point in the sequence. The dates from Events 4 and 5 were subdivided into more groups for Model 2; this affected the modelled age ranges by returning a slightly younger estimate for sample SK 12 and slightly older estimates for SK 8 and SK 9. This in turn resulted in an older age estimate for the sample referred to as 'Robert'.

The application of the model to the dates has increased the resolution of the chronological evidence. It can be concluded that 'Rosemary' was buried at the end of the Late Iron Age/Pictish period. The burial attributed to Event 2 ('Robert') returned a modelled age estimate that spanned the Viking-Norse period, potentially extending back to the end of the Pictish period based on application of

'Model 2' to the dates. The burials located below the low compartmentalised cairn (Events 3–5) returned modelled age estimates that were grouped between AD 875–1020 or AD 830–1050 if Models 1 or 2 were applied respectively; these age ranges were very similar and spanned the Viking-Norse period. The final phase of burial activity sampled returned age estimates dating to the Norse period.

It can therefore be concluded that a coherent sequence of events were recorded. The assessment of the two alternative sequences of dates demonstrated that the chronological information supported both models, with the exception of sample SK 13. It is important to stress that the posterior density estimates produced related to the models that were applied to data; new information, or changes to the interpretations of the stratigraphic sequence would result in different modelled age estimates being produced. In addition, further work is required to determine the diets of the individuals sampled and the effect that this may have on the resulting radiocarbon dates.

Results of the bone stable isotope measurements
Gordon Cook, with Patrick Ashmore and Rachel Barrowman

It has been recognised for more than 20 years that radiocarbon measurements made on collagen (protein) from the bones of individuals who have subsisted on a marine-based diet will produce ^{14}C ages that are older than they actually are. This is due to the incorporation of carbon from marine resources (which has a reservoir age, marine reservoir effect, relative to the contemporaneous atmosphere) into the bone collagen of the consumers. It is possible to estimate approximately the proportion of marine carbon consumed by an individual using stable isotope analysis (δ^{13}C) and from this, the reservoir effect in individuals can be estimated, provided the 100% marine diet reservoir effect is known for that time period. The global average reservoir effect for surface waters is 400 years (i.e. carbon from a purely

		Modelled age ranges	
Event	Burials	Model 1	Model 2
6	SK 5 and SK 6	AD 1010–1200	AD 1020–1175
5	SK 13	AD 895–1020	Failed
4	SK 12	AD895–1010	AD 955–1050
	SK 10 and SK 11	AD 895–1025	AD 895–1025
3	SK 8 and SK 9	AD 875–985	AD 830–985
2	'Robert'	AD 825–975	AD 775–940
1	SK7, 'Hubert' and 'Rosemary'	AD 655–880	AD 655–860

FIGURE 4.80

A comparison of the modelled age ranges produced using Model 1 and Model 2

marine source) and this will produce an age c400 years older than a radiocarbon assay on a terrestrial sample of the same age. This will vary both temporally and spatially however. Indeed, the marine reservoir effect is now known to be suppressed in Orkney and the north coast of Scotland at c1000 AD (Ascough *et al* 2009), but no information currently exists for the Shetland Isles.

The maritime environment of Shetland, and the circumstantial evidence presented by the large numbers of shells recovered from the site, led us to suspect that a marine reservoir effect would be present in the St Ninian's Isle samples. Work by Barrett on samples from the islands of Orkney, for instance, has indicated that some individuals may have derived over 30 per cent of their dietary protein from marine sources in the ninth to eleventh centuries (Barrett *et al* 1999; 2000; 2001a), whilst prior to this time, in the Iron Age, the dietary significance of fish was limited.

The $\delta^{13}C$ measurements for burials SK 5-13 are included in Figure 4.70. The values for this assemblage are all relatively light, with the heaviest being -18.3‰ for sample AA-45632 (SK 13). This sample also has the heaviest $\delta^{15}N$ value at 15.3‰ (see below). $\delta^{13}C$ end members of −12.5‰ (100% marine diet) and −21.0‰ (100% terrestrial diet; Arneborg *et al* 1999) were used to calculate approximate percentages of marine resources in the diet of the four adults. These ranged between approximately 8 and 26%. For the infants, we used the lightest measured value of −21.5‰ as the terrestrial end member. This gave a value of 17% or less with the exception of SK 11 (24%) and SK 13 (30%). Currently, there is insufficient evidence to make a definitive statement on $\delta^{13}C$ values in relation to terrestrial versus marine diet in infants and so any calculations of their marine diet (obviously derived from the mothers) must be tentative.

The measurement of the ^{15}N isotope of nitrogen, expressed as the $\delta^{15}N$ value and measured in parts per thousand (‰), has been used in recent years to study the duration of breastfeeding in palaeopopulations (Mays *et al* 2002). $\delta^{15}N$ increases as the food chain is ascended, but a foetal or newborn infant has a $\delta^{15}N$ similar to that of its mother. Mays *et al* (2002) have demonstrated that $\delta^{15}N$ then rises during breastfeeding to give a level greater than the maternal collagen, but as the infant is weaned and the mother's milk is replaced by other foods, the $\delta^{15}N$ declines again. $\delta^{15}N$ data from the ribs of immature individuals aged from birth to 17 years from Wharram Percy, in northern England, showed mean value measurements between just below 10.0‰ and just over 13‰ for those individuals aged between birth and 18 months. From this age onwards the measurements dropped dramatically to between 10.5‰ and 5.5‰. Although the caveats of mortality bias and the small sample size must be acknowledged, the same general trend is also seen in the samples from St

Ninian's Isle (see synopsis of results in Figure 4.81).

The measurements of the $\delta^{15}N$ data for the foetal or newborn infant individuals (SK 6 and SK 12) are 10.8‰ and 12.6‰ respectively. As the infants increase in age, the values increase to between 11.1‰ and 15.3‰. Once the immature individuals reach an age where they would no longer be breastfeeding, the values decrease once again to 12.6‰ and 10.0‰. For the adult individuals, the ratios lie between 10.0‰ and 11.1‰. The exception to this general trend is seen in the data for SK 10, which is lower than might be expected. There is the possibility that this is due to malnourishment, as suggested by Roberts above in the study of the pathology of the infant burials.

Although we recognise the indications of a marine reservoir effect within this sample, in most individuals it is small. There are also so many uncertainties associated with the application of a correction (uncertainties in dietary end-points, ΔR, trophic level effect in infants, etc) that we felt it unwise to attempt. However, it would be possible for these data to be re-visited when trophic level effects in infants are better understood and a ΔR value for the Shetland Isles for this period in time is determined.

4.7 SUMMARY

Phase II

Phase II comprises the earliest excavated evidence for human activity on the site in the form of a remnant structure indicated by a double wall with a clayey core, overlaid by Late Iron Age midden deposits, in turn overlaid by an area of paving uncovered in the SW corner of the trench. Stratigraphic relationships between these features allow a sequence to be made, but a quantification of the period which elapsed between the use of each of them is difficult to ascertain. All the soils excavated from this phase contained midden material, but the provenance of any carbonised or bone material recovered from them

Individual	Age of individual	$\delta^{15}N$ (‰)
SK 6	0–2 months	10.8
SK 12	0–2 months	12.6
SK 10	3–6 months	11.1
SK 11	6–9 months	14.2
SK 13	6–12 months	15.3
SK 8	12–16 months	12.5
SK 9	16–30 months	14.4
SK 7	4–5 years	12.6
ABDUA 14270	11–14 years	10.0
ABDUA 14269	18–25 years	10.0
SK 5	26–35 years	10.7
ABDUA 14254	35–50 years	11.1

FIGURE 4.81

$\delta^{15}N$ data for all individuals submitted for dating from St Ninian's Isle, by age of individual

could not be linked to any specific features, making radio-carbon dating of limited use in locating the chronological sequence. It is possible that the paving could have been associated with the subsequent use of the site for burial, in Phase III, as it overlay the Late Iron Age midden and presumably therefore post-dates occupation associated with that midden. O'Dell's however uncovered in 1959 extensive areas of paving to the north and west of the paving found in 2000 (i.e. outwith the confines of Trench 1), and Small records that this paving was associated with Iron Age material and structures (1973, 6), and so in 2000 it was grouped in Phase II.

The finds and environmental material indicate a range of domestic activities. The 269+ sherds of coarse pottery discussed by MacSween are given a general Late Iron Age date, as is the worked stone assemblage discussed by Batey, which contains pot lids, pounders, smoothers and rubbers, and a broken quernstone, all with parallels at Iron Age sites in Shetland and Orkney. A broken black stone disc gaming piece with chamfered edges, found in this phase, is closely comparable to A21.2000.20b, a gaming piece found during O'Dell's excavations below the chapel and is common on Iron Age sites. Five worked quartz flakes, a core and a blade were found in this phase, but as Donnelly points out, worked quartz was recovered scattered throughout all phases. There are several finds of worked bone, discussed by Batey, including a whalebone spike, and chopping block, the latter with parallels on Iron Age sites such as Scalloway, and Howe, Orkney. Seven small pieces of cinder and five of slag are also identified, and may suggest domestic iron-working. Batey discusses two pieces of unworked steatite and a broken steatite hogback fishing weight found in this phase. These could be intrusive from the overlying Phase III deposits, but this is unlikely given that Phase III marks the change of use of the site to burial, and it would be unusual for such domestic finds to have been deposited with burials themselves.

The general Late Iron Age date for Phase II is refined by radiocarbon measurements from two Phase III burials above it: ABDUA 14269, the flexed female burial in a large short cist; and SK 7, a juvenile burial, possibly originally accompanied by a cist. Samples from these interments give a *terminus ante quem* of the third quarter of the 8th century, at the latest, for the deposition of the Phase II midden, which could be refined to the 7th century by modelling of the radiocarbon dates, and allowing for the build-up of midden prior to the first burial of Phase III.

Miller and Ramsay identify charred botanical remains in keeping with midden deposits: six-row barley, including five examples confidently identifiable to the hulled variety (*Hordeum vulgare* var *vulgare*), Heather sp. and cf. spruce and cf larch, as well as spot finds of apple type (Maloideae) and oak charcoal. The majority of the small animal bone assemblage from this phase is identified by Gidney as cattle and sheep, with both animal being important not just for meat, but for other products such as cheese and butter, and wool. Examples of pig are also noted from this phase and a single cat bone. The paucity of remains from companion, rather than food, animals suggests that the midden principally received household waste. Despite flotation of samples from all contexts, the fish bone assemblage is very small and Gamble and Barrett identify species that indicate shore-based fishing. Gidney points out that marine mammals do not appear to have been exploited for food, although there is evidence of whalebone working, and marine bird bones (one gannet, one gull sp. and one auk sp.). Considerable numbers of shellfish are identified from the midden by Cerón-Carrasco as mainly edible periwinkle. In addition to the sparse evidence for exploitation of marine resources from the ecofactual assemblages, marine isotope and organic residue analysis undertaken by Jones and Hedges on coarse pottery sherds from the Phase II midden (and the Phase III midden re-deposited from Phase II) are indicative of preparation/consumption of terrestrial food, identifying degraded animal fat, and no evidence of marine foodstuffs.

Phase III

The features excavated from this phase overlie Phase II and all relate to the use of the area for burial – initially in the Late Iron Age, but then extending into the Norse period. The burials, although few in number, span the transition from pre-Christian to Christian, and also variations within each. The pre-Christian period is evidenced by four short stone cists, centred on a wall or base of stones accompanied by paving, and covered by a low stone cairn. All these features were partially excavated in 1959, and the contents of the short cists removed. The largest cist is recorded as containing a female adult crouched burial, whilst three adjoining cists contained charred human bones, bones and shells, suggesting that cremation as well as burial was evidenced in this phase. This group of cists are dated by the crouched burial which has been radiocarbon dated to the mid 7th to late 8th centuries AD. To the west of this cist, a child aged 4–5 years (SK 7) was found, buried in beside the short cists and has been radiocarbon dated to the late 7th to late 9th centuries AD. Aligned NW–SE, the 'head box' of upright stones found on either side of the skull of this burial may suggest that it was Christian, although the alignment and the lack of any marker stones or cross sculpture makes this far from definite.

The second group of features however comprises the earliest definitive Christian burials on the site. These are two long cists uncovered outside the SE corner of the chapel in 1959. One cist was totally excavated, dismantled and reconstructed in 1959. A mixed assemblage of over 100 disarticulated adult, juvenile and neonate human bones identified from the upper fill, and also finds of coffin wood and weed seeds in the basal layers attest to the excavation and backfilling of the other. Both long cists were unusually shaped, being wide with the east ends of both cists narrower than the W. One of the cists had a narrow 'extension' at the east end. A socket (14) was found at the west end of cist 335, probably for a small cross slab, excavated from the site in 1959 identified by Thomas as a pre-Norse, primary cross slab (Thomas 1973, 36, Stone 11, fig 8, pl 8), and a cross-incised stone marker (SF 494), which had fallen over but was left unexcavated at the foot of the cist, has been dated by Fisher to the Early Medieval or Norse periods. An adult male ('Hubert', ABDUA 14254), that has been radiocarbon dated to the late 7th to late 9th centuries AD originated from one of these cists (321). A second skeleton from the 1959 excavation ('Robert', ABDUA 14270) has been radiocarbon dated to the late 8th to end of the 10th centuries and may originate from the other long cist although there is less evidence in the archives to confirm this. Modelling of the radiocarbon dates by Otram suggests a narrower date range and demonstrates that there is no reason from the dating evidence why 'Robert' could not pre-date the Norse burials on the site and belong to a long cist.

A third group of burials was identified to the south of the two long cists, where six infant burials (SK 8–13) were uncovered in 2000 that had not been excavated in 1959. These infants had been set into the east side of the area of the stone cairn. They were found buried with stone 'head boxes' either side of the skull, and a low linear cairn of stones and quartz pebbles, edged with upright stones and divided into small 'compartments' by smaller upright stones was built over the top. Small headstones were set at the west end of four of the small compartments, and two of these headstones were incised with unusual crosses (SF 301 and 465). Fisher describes that the two-transomed crosses, common in Byzantine tradition, are carefully designed and executed, with similar crosses being found in Argyll, Kintyre, Kerry and Iceland. The square plaiting seen on the crosses however is closely paralleled on a fragment from Papil, and Fisher identifies that it was favoured by Scandinavian patrons and so dates the St Ninian's Isle crosses to the 10th or 11th centuries. Fisher's dating is supported by the radiocarbon measurements undertaken on samples from each of the six infants. These produced dates ranging from the late 7th century at the earliest (SK 8) to the mid-12th century at the latest (SK 11), although modelling supports a 10th century date for all six infant burials, and Bayliss and Outram confirm above, that the radiocarbon dates suggest that the infants died over a period of time and were not all buried in one event, as already demonstrated by the stratigraphy. Roberts, in her study of the skeletal material, identifies age of death between new born and 32 months

and suggests that the infants suffered a poor diet, low in nutrition. The results of the bone stable isotope measurements may support this.

Artefacts were also found associated with the infant burials: a small water-worn quartz beach pebble had been placed in the mouth of infant burial SK 12 and a deliberately shaped hexagonal flat stone or smoother accompanied SK 9. Although these are not datable stylistically, Batey draws attention to the long-established association of quartz pebbles with burials, both as shroud weights and as part of cairns over Pictish burials, such as at Sandwick, Unst. Whilst only two pebbles were found directly associated with the infants, the kerbed stone cairn above the burials contained frequent quartz pebbles, as did the fills of the adult long cists 321 and 335 discussed above.

Samples taken of the soil around the infants SK 8, 9 and 11–13 contained only re-deposited soil from the sandy midden below. The soil sample from around infant SK 10 however contained over 100 infant bones and fragments with no element duplication. Duffy suggests that they belong to one individual and originate from the left-hand side of the body. The elements are also already present in SK 10 and so do not belong to that individual. It is clear that a second infant is evidenced here, and that there was already a burial in the grave or immediately adjacent to the grave, which was disturbed by the burial of SK 10. This may account for an empty area below the kerbed cairn, a 'gap' between SK 10 and SK 11; this was marked with a cross-incised headstone but contained no remains when excavated.

Sandy shell-rich midden layers containing re-deposited Phase II midden material that had become incorporated whilst the cists and burials were dug into the site, covered the immediate area around the all the cists, burials and wall base. Finds from the sandy midden, and from midden re-deposited into the cists, included worked whalebone, a bone point, lumps of cinder, nine flakes, two blades and a core of worked quartz and 71 sherds of coarse pottery, all datable to the Late Iron Age. Two bone cylindrical beads were also found that are identified by Batey as identical to the seventeen bone and antler beads found in the 1959 excavations. Coffin wood and a copper shroud pin reflect the disturbance of this layer by later medieval and later intrusive burials from above. The environmental assemblage was more diverse from this phase, containing conifer and heather family charcoal, 147 definite examples of six-rowed barley (58 of which can be identified to the hulled variety), willow, alder, oak, Scots pine type and spruce/larch charcoal and weed seeds, all of which are in keeping with the general trend of disturbance of earlier deposits caused by later burials. A slightly larger assemblage of animal bone was recovered from the midden layers around the cists than from the Phase II midden, being again predominantly cow and sheep, whilst the fish bone assemblage once again indicated shore-based fishing. Of particular note were the very large numbers of edible periwinkle (over 3,000) and limpet (with small numbers of other marine shellfish), and quartz pebbles, found in samples from the basal layers of long cist 321, short cist 304, wall base 307 and sandy midden layers 318/9, 325 and 340, specifically in the area of the cists. Whether the shellfish were originally used as a food source or not, they are clearly of ritual or decorative significance in Phase III, and defined the area of short cist burials.

The latest burials in this phase were found in and to the west side of the short cists and both have been radiocarbon dated to the 11th to 12th centuries. A neonate infant (SK 6), had been interred alongside short cist 303, possibly in a cist (only two stones remained from the 1959 excavation), or with a stone 'head box'. Immediately beside this infant burial an adult burial (SK 5) was found 'squashed' into short cist 303. It is recorded that charred human bones were excavated from this cist in 1959, and yet in doing so, the excavators did not seem to have uncovered SK 5. If the recollection of charred human bones is correct, then they either post-dated burial SK 5, or were removed when SK 5 was interred, and then re-deposited over the top. A study of the burial position and partial articulation of SK 5 has shown that it had been exhumed from elsewhere shortly after death and then inserted into the cist. This male individual had also suffered a particularly violent death, which Roberts has reconstructed by studying the location and types of fractures: The first a blow from a sharp bladed weapon slicing downwards and then a blow on the back of the head from behind. A skull fracture on the top of the head also indicates attack with a blunt instrument, such as a pole. Finally, an injury to the cervical vertebra indicates that the individual met his death by having his head lifted and throat cut from behind with a thin, sharp blade. This warrior-like death is matched by the mode of interment of this burial: the relocation of the remains to a special place, and the accompaniment of a small iron knife excavated from beside the body.

Phases IV and V

These two phases relate to the inundation of wind-blown sand (Phase IV), the building of a chapel and the interment of accompanying burials in the medieval period, and the continued use of the graveyard in the post-medieval period after the chapel had gone out of use and been dismantled (Phase V). These phases have mainly to be reconstructed from the sparse records of the 1950s excavations because most of the sand and the medieval and later burials to the south of the chapel were removed at the outset of excavations there and there remained little to re-examine in 1999/2000. Excavation of earlier phases in 1999 and 2000 did however demonstrate

that the inundation of sand commenced at the same time as the area began to be used for burial, from the late 7th to late 8th century onwards due to the presence of sand in the soils associated with the earliest (dated) burials seen in Phase III. Small's assertion that the sand provides a 'clear stratigraphical break' between the pre-Christian and Christian periods (1973, 7) can no longer be supported because the early long cists 321/336 and 335 were situated on midden at the bottom of the sandy layer, as were the infant burials under the kerbed cairn. It is clear that sand inundation began during Phase III, as sand is mixed into the cist fills, but was still a gradual and perhaps occasional event, because sand was not present to any great depth. After the Phase III burials however, a thick inundation of wind-blown sand *is* evidenced, and this is differentiated as Phase IV. It was into this sand that the four later and narrower medieval long cists (03–06) were cut in Phase V, although wind-blown sand continued to periodically inundate the site through the medieval and post-medieval periods.

The contents of all four medieval long cists were excavated in 1959. Phase V cist 06 was fully dismantled, and the earlier long cists below it re-examined. As has been discussed in Phase III above, burials 'Hubert' and 'Robert' excavated from the earlier phase long cists in 1959 have been radiocarbon dated to the end of the 10th century AD at the latest, whereas the later narrower long cists (03–06), excavated from above the sand, are provided with a *terminus post quem* for their interment, by the latest burials of Phase III below the sand, of the mid-11th century at the absolute earliest.

Three further post-medieval burials were uncovered in 1999 and 2000. SK 3 was partially excavated from the east edge of the trench and had been damaged by rabbit burrowing and the 1959 excavations. SK 60, an almost complete neonate infant burial, and SK 61, part of an adult burial, were analysed in situ in Trial Trench 1. SK 60 was possibly an unbaptized infant as it had been interred close to the wall of the ruined chapel.

Phases VI and VII

Phase VI represents the backfill from the excavations undertaken by O'Dell's team south of the chapel in 1958 and 1959, and the consolidated and to some extent, reconstruction of features at the end of the 1959 season. It is these consolidated remains that were planned and published in the 1973 volume (Figure 1.2). The mixed finds and environmental assemblage from this phase all derive from lower phases on the site and include a small headstone with an unusual incised cross (SF 433) from the backfill. Fisher identifies the graffito-style oval shape of the ringed cross as having similarities with an example from the Faroes that can be dated to the 10th century, and suggests that the St Ninian's Isle example is a small headstone comparable to those found marking the infant burials below the kerbed cairn of Phase III, although the design of the cross is different. Batey discusses a possible knife tang and a piece of an iron key (SF 551) which joins with another piece found in the topsoil Phase VII, the latter identified as being of a type common in the 8th to 11th centuries. She also discusses three pieces of antler time, carefully worked into a bead of the same type as the bone and antler necklace found in 1959 (PLATE 14), and a bead found in Phase III (SF 460 and 512). The majority of the botanical remains recovered from Phase VI comprised modern material, and rabbit bones were ubiquitous. A gaming piece, pieces of pumice and iron nails and roves were also recovered from the topsoil, Phase VII. All these finds are in keeping with the disturbance of the site by the excavations in 1959, and the subsequent re-deposition of topsoil and excavation spoil over the site. Coffin wood fragments, disarticulated human bone, and modern material all attest to the disturbance seen in this phase.

Notes

[1] The term 'bogus' was used for this category in the original archive report.

[2] See also the site of the International Bryozoology Association at www.naturalhistory.org.uk/hosted_sites/iba/assoc.html.

[3] http://units.ox.ac.uk/departments/rlaha.

DISCUSSION

5.1 OVERALL SYNTHESIS

This volume has presented the results of a small research project undertaken between 1999 and 2004 with the aim of revisiting the archaeology at St Ninian's Isle through a study of the archive material from the 1950s excavations, and renewed survey and excavation work on the Isle over two summer seasons (1999 and 2000). It is enriched by the addition of Forsyth's analysis of the ogham inscription in Chapter 2, and the various specialists' reports on the artefactual, environmental and dating material from the site. Given the complicated nature of the remains excavated on the Isle, and the fragmented way that the site has been excavated and published, it was felt that a wider discussion was needed to bring out the most salient points for future research. The results have thrown up several issues relating to the archaeology on St Ninian's Isle, which can now be discussed against a more substantial background of evidence. It is hoped that this discussion will bring to the fore the more interesting preliminary conclusions that may otherwise remain buried within the density of the excavation and archive reports, so that they may be used by others to further debate on the many aspects of material culture and belief relevant to the interpretation of the archaeology at St Ninian's Isle, and the wider implications for Shetland in the Late Iron Age and Norse periods.

Figure 5.1 is a combined illustration of the plan published by the late Alan Small in the 1973 volume showing the area to the south of the chapel as dug in 1959, Charles Thomas' plan in the same volume that he drew as part of his own investigations into the find spots for the stone sculpture from the site in 1967, O'Dell's 1959 plan, as published in 1960 and Helen Nisbet's 1959 excavation sketch.[1] Superimposed onto to this are the features that were uncovered and examined when the area south of the chapel was re-opened in 2000 (Trench 1). By combining the results of the 1950s excavations, the recent archive study, and the renewed 1999–2000 excavations, it is possible to propose an overall succession of phases of activity at the site. Thomas proposed a similar series of events based on his own research into the 1950s excavations (1973, 13), and when the two sequences are compared they are shown to be largely compatible (Figure 5.2). This is re-assuring as it demonstrates that, despite the short-comings of the 1950s excavations, the basic order of events in the 1973 volume (based on O'Dell's findings) still stands. There are, however, some important small differences between the two sequences as extra information has come to light from the re-assessment; in particular the position of the thick wind-blown sand inundation within the sequence, and the evidence for the use of the burial ground in the Norse period, prior to that sand inundation.

Thomas identified (1973, 13) six phases of activity on the site: 1, Iron Age occupation probably commencing in the first few centuries BC and lasting until the 3rd or 4th AD; 2, a pre-Christian burial ground of short-cist inhumations used over the next two or three centuries; 3, the continuation of the burial-ground, but as a Christian one, with oriented extended inhumations in long cists and an accompanying stone chapel, dated to the late 7th or 8th century; 4, the building in the 12th century of a slightly larger Norse chapel over the first, after the burial of the hoard and a hiatus caused by the Norse raids c800, with a resulting, 'perhaps a considerable', interval; 5, the enlarging of this chapel at the end of the 12th or into the early 13th century; and finally, 6, the decay of this building after the Reformation until shortly after 1744.

The recent re-assessment of the archives and the renewed excavations on the site have also identified six phases of activity at the site (Phases I-VI), although they are differently grouped (Figure 3.34). Phase I encompasses the schist bedrock and unexcavated deposits, and Phase II, Iron Age domestic occupation and middens. Unlike Thomas' phasing, however, both non-Christian and Christian burials are then incorporated into a single phase, Phase III, which includes short cists and cremations, a stone cairn and paving, as well as extended Christian inhumations in long cist burials, infant graves, infants burials below a low cairn and crosses, the first church building on the site and the corner-post shrine(s), the hoard and an unusual Norse burial. This phase is sealed by Phase IV, sand inundation, above which, in Phase V, the new medieval chapel was built, later extended, and accompanied by narrow extended long cists, before being demolished in 1744, and then uncovered 200 years later by O'Dell's excavations (Phase VI).

Further information on the dating and sequence of some of the features has been possible from the

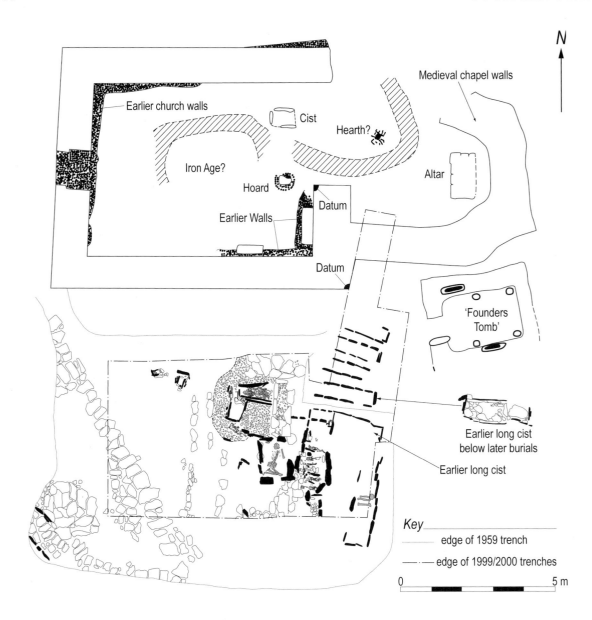

FIGURE 5.1

Illustration combining plans published by Small (1973, fig 5), Thomas (1973, fig 8) and O'Dell (1960, fig 1), a sketch made by Thomas and now in his archive, and Helen Nisbet's 1959 excavation sketch

recent re-assessment. This includes the dating of the Iron Age occupation (Phase II), which is now pushed later from Thomas' suggested date of the 3rd or 4th centuries AD, to the Late Iron Age by Mac-Sween's identification of the coarse pottery from the Phase II middens has having more in common with other Late Iron Age assemblages in Shetland than with earlier Iron Age 'broch-related' assemblages, and the radiocarbon date of the late 7th to late 8th centuries for the earliest burial identified from Phase III above. Batey identifies the majority of the finds from this phase from both excavations as belonging to the Iron Age, with excavated parallels being found from most of the bone and stone artefacts, such as gaming pieces, whalebone objects, whorls, coarse tools and beads, in the Iron Age/Late

Iron Age levels at sites such as Scalloway, Jarlshof and Clickhimmin in Shetland, and Howe in Orkney. The exception to this are a small group of steatite objects, in particular a fishing weight found in Phase II in the 2000 excavations, and a finely worked small steatite food vessel found during O'Dell's excavations, which although out of context with no record of where on the site it was found, suggests activity on the site in the Norse period, other than burial.

The Late Iron Age middens, identified as the final event of the phase by both excavation campaigns, covered the footings of earlier buildings, although it is not possible to tell from the available evidence whether the disuse of these buildings represents a total dismantling and abandonment of settlement on St Ninian's Isle in the Late Iron Age, or merely a settlement shift to a nearby location (from which the middens, presumably, originated). All evidence is in agreement however that after Phase II and the disuse and covering of the buildings, the nature of this small area of the Isle changed completely from the domestic to the spiritual. There is an absence of any indications of domestic occupation or structures in any of the levels above Phase II, apart from the re-deposition of Phase II midden material into later features. From Phase III, all the features excavated on the site relate to burial and worship. St Ninian's Isle fits a pattern in this respect; the occurrence of early ecclesiastical sites over Iron Age settlements in the Northern Isles is a recognised phenomenon (Lamb 1995; Lowe 1987). At St Ninian's Isle, however, as at Papa Stronsay, Orkney (Lowe 2002; Lowe *et al* 2000) there is evidence in the form of short cist burials, cremations and paved areas, and a stone

cairn, that the site was used for burial and ceremony before Christianity reached Shetland.

Unlike Thomas' suggested groupings, this transition from pagan to Christian is amalgamated into the same phase (Phase III) by the recent work, as no clear stratigraphical break between the two was evidenced although there were descriptions in the archives from the previous work of a thin layer of peat and sandy soil between the short cists and the base of the early church above them. The burials from Phase III are a diverse group (Figure 5.3), and the only overtly non-Christian burial has been radiocarbon dated to 660–780 cal AD, a comparable range with the earliest dated Christian burials on the site (SK 7 660–900 cal AD, and ABDUA 14254 'Hubert' 680–890 cal AD), suggesting that it is not out of the question that the burials, if not contemporary, closely followed one another. In addition to

1999-2000 excavations (Chapters 3-4, above)		1955-59 excavations (Thomas 1973, 11-13)
Phase I:	Bedrock and unexcavated deposits	Bedrock covered by thin layer of peat below church
Phase II:	Iron Age occupation Wall footings, paving and midden LIA up to 7th–8thC AD	1.	Iron Age occupation Stone walls, rubble collapse, paved areas, occupation debris From first few centuries BC to 3rd/4thC AD
Phase III:	Pre-Christian – Christian spiritual site Short cists, cremations, paving, wall base and rubble mound Large crouched burial: ABDUA 14269: 660–780 cal AD Long cists: ABDUA 14254: 680–890 cal AD, ABDUA 14270: 780–1000 cal AD Infant inhumation SK7: 670–890 cal AD Accompanying small church and shrine Hoard buried some time from the 8th century onwards Christian infant burials below low kerbed cairn SK8 AA 45627: 770–990 AD SK9 AA 45628: 720–980 AD SK10 AA 45629: 890–1160 AD SK11 AA 45630: 890–1160 AD SK12 AA 45631: 880–1040 AD SK13 AA 45632: 770–990 AD Can all be refined to some time in the 10th century (see Chapter 4.6) Ogham inscription Warrior burial in cist SK 5: 1020–1240 cal AD Infant burial SK 6: 1010–1220 cal AD	2. 3.	Burial ground, initially Pagan Short- or medium-length slab cists with crouched inhumations, pottery and human bone fragments Large crouched burial over wall 3rd/4th– 6th/7th centuries Christian burial ground; oriented extended inhumations in long cists Late 7th and 8th centuries Accompanying stone chapel and shrine c800AD Hoard buried and Viking hiatus
Phase IV:	Sand inundation	4.	A 'considerable interval' resulting from the Viking raids
Phase V:	New chapel built end of 11th or in 12th century Accompanied by narrow extended long cists Chapel enlarged and chancel added Demolished 1744 Burial ground continues in use until mid-19th century	5.	New chapel built. No earlier than 12th century. Chapel enlarged, chancel added. End of 12th/early 13th century Burial ground continues in use until mid-19th century

FIGURE 5.2

A comparison of the phases of activity evidenced from the 1950s and 1999/2000 excavations

Burial	Age at death	Sample code	Calibrated date range (95% confidence)	Headbox	Long cist	Short cist	Cross-incised stone	Alignment	Quartz pebbles
SK5	26–35 years	AA 45624	1020–1240 AD					E–W	●
SK6	0–2 months	AA 45625	1010–1220 AD	●	?			N–S	
SK7	4–5 years	AA 45626	670–890 AD	●	?			NW–SE	
SK8	12–16 months	AA 45627	770–990 AD	●			●	E–W	●
SK9	16–32 months	AA 45628	720–980 AD	●			●	E–W	●
SK10	3–6 months	AA 45629	890–1160 AD	●			●	E–W	●
SK11	6–9 months	AA 45630	890–1160 AD	●			●	E–W	●
SK12	0–2 months	AA 45631	880–1040 AD	●			●	E–W	●
SK13	6–12 months	AA 45632	770–990 AD	●			●	E–W	●
ABDUA 14254	>40 years	SUERC 5440	680–890 AD		●		●	E–W	●
ABDUA 14269	18–25 years	SUERC 5442	660–780 AD			●		N–S	●
ABDUA 14270	11–14 years	SUERC 5441	780–1000 AD		●			E–W	

FIGURE 5.3

The burials from Phase III

this, eight short cists are mentioned in the archives as having been excavated from below the chapel in the 1950s, and at least three of these are recorded as having contained cremated human bone, and human bone fragments and two of which also contained urns.

The advent of Christianity during Phase III is demonstrated by a change in burial practice to extended long cists marked with cross-incised stones, and the building of a small stone church in the 8th century. The renowned St Ninian's Isle hoard was apparently dug into the floor of this primary church building, although no trace of a floor was found by the excavators in 1957–58 (O'Dell 1960, 5), and it also probably housed the one, or possibly two, corner post shrines, the components of which were excavated from a secondary position on the site in 1957 (O'Dell 1957; Thomas 1973, 12; 1998).

Through the succeeding four centuries, the area continued to be used for burial, with several different forms of burial rite evidenced. The burial assemblage has been put into a table (Figure 5.3) so as to make the discussion of what is a complicated series of features and dates, easier to illustrate. The majority of the burials are of infants and children, and there is no dominant burial rite: unprotected dug graves (O'Brien and Roberts 1996, 163), long cists, and a cairn over dug graves are all evidenced, and alignments are not always E–W. Headstones, some with crosses incised, are incorporated into some, but not all, burials, as are stone head boxes, or 'ear muffs' (O'Brien and Roberts 1996, 163, 164). An unusual adult burial re-buried in an older short cist ends the phase. Despite the very small assemblage, the diversity of burials during Phase III points to a continuous loyalty to place, despite significant changes in belief and the upheaval resulting from the Norse incursions. The St Ninian's Isle ogham stone also belongs to this phase, although Goudie recovered it from the thick wind-blown sand covering the site and its original location is unknown.

It is difficult from the archive evidence alone to either support or refute the suggestion that there was a 'hiatus' on the site at the time of the Viking invasions around AD 800 (Thomas 1973, 13). A sketch in the archive of a section of the exterior face of the medieval chapel wall and below it annotates 'earth infill' over the earlier church walls, but there is not enough further information to be able to characterise it, and it could as easily be either part of the medieval chapel wall foundations, the earlier church walls, or a layer of abandonment. In the excavation pits inside the chapel, excavated in 1957-9, no evidence was found of stonework between the early church and the medieval chapel walls, which sat directly over them. Certainly the range of radiocarbon measurements from the six infant burials below the low cairn (SK 8–13) and one of the long cist burials ('Robert', ABDUA 14270) confirm that the site continued to be used for burial through the 9th and 10th centuries, and at present there is nothing to suggest that the church was not still in use then too. The final radiocarbon-dated event of Phase III is the insertion of one particularly unusual burial of an adult male who died a violent death some time between the early 11th and mid-12th centuries, was exhumed from elsewhere and then re-buried with a small iron knife, in one of the earlier short cists from this phase. An infant burial (SK 6) adjacent to this cist was found to date to the same period, although it is harder to argue from these two burials alone that the first church building was still in use in the 11th–12th centuries.

Certainly by the end of the 11th century sand began to appear on the site more frequently. Sand is also seen in Phase III, initially only in small quantities, and possibly imported onto the site with shells. The area around the Phase III burials was covered in a layer of sand mixed with clay and midden that had been dug up from the Phase II midden below and become incorporated with the soil around the cists and burials when they were constructed. Not surprisingly, this sandy midden layer contained the same range of material as the Phase II middens, but with a much larger marine shellfish component. Over 3,000, mainly edible periwinkle, shells were found, mixed with quartz pebbles, in and around the short cists. It is not known whether the shellfish were originally used as a food source or not, but they were clearly of significance in the arrangement of the cists during Phase III, and Cerón-Carrasco suggests that they may have been used to stabilise the sand in cist fills.

The early church building itself was built onto sand and sandy soils also appear in the fills of the long cists on the site in Phase III, which themselves were situated at the base of a thick sand layer. It is possible that the increased presence of wind-blown sand on the site is what caused it to be abandoned as a settlement in Phase II. Even a gradual accumulation, or occasional sand storm, would have made occupation on the site difficult, and certainly by the end of Phase III, the sand was blowing into the site to form thick layers. A pit dug in 1958 to the SE of the chapel, at the sloping sandy cliff edge, found long cist burials dug into a clay midden layer, overlying sand, which is recorded in this pit at a greater depth than elsewhere on the site, and this may reflect that the first wind blows of sand would have accumulated at the east edge of the settlement, up from the sandy shore to the east. It may have been the first sand inundation here that caused the settlement to be abandoned (presumably re-located) and then used to dump midden. It is known that the climate was increasingly stormy at this time, when the sea level was particularly high after an increasingly warm regime. The resulting formation of new sand dunes was particularly active towards AD 700, and again between 800 and 900 (Lamb 1981, 61). On St Ninian's Isle it was therefore at the time of the abandonment of settlement and change of use of the site to burial, that the beach and tombolo began to form, ultimately connecting St Ninian's Isle to mainland Shetland.

The extension of a thick layer of wind-blown sand (Phase IV) across the whole site marks the end of Phase III, and the lack of turf build-up evidenced in the bottom part of this layer suggests that it represents a massive and catastrophic inundation. Small (1973, 7) describes this sand as being a clear stratigraphic break between the pre-Christian and Christian burials on the site, although Thomas draws attention instead to the 'apparently continuous use of the cemetery from pre-Christian into Christian times' (Thomas 1973, 13). The recent reappraisal has shown that although sand begins to be evidenced at the beginning of Phase III, the massive and catastrophic sand inundation post-dates the early Christian burials on the site. Above this thick sand layer a new unicameral chapel was built, on the same alignment as the earlier small church and accompanied by narrow, extended long cists concentrated to the south and east of the building. This

new chapel (Phase V) and the sand inundation before it (Phase IV) are both given a *terminus post quem* by the latest burial of Phase III of at least the mid-11th century, possibly as late as the latter half of the 12th, and this corresponds also to Thomas' suggestion of late 11th/12th century date for the medieval chapel. Three broken steatite cross-incised slabs, and a hogback grave cover, found above the sand, may be contemporary with this primary phase of the medieval chapel, and the narrow long cists excavated from above the sand at the SE corner of the building. After a short time an apsidal east end, possibly vaulted, and housing a free-standing dry stone altar was added to the chapel and there was undoubtedly an extensive associated graveyard. It is not known when the chapel was abandoned, although we know it was finally demolished in 1744, and the stone used to build a retaining wall on the east side of the Isle. The ruined church continued to be considered sacred even after its destruction, as demonstrated by votive finds of Limoges enamel fragments and a coin pushed into the ruined altar. Periodic sand inundation and erosion continued at this time, especially in the period of particular storminess in north Scotland in the late eighteenth century, and the ruined chapel became covered in sand. The last burial took place on the Isle c1840, and the site of the chapel was lost until O'Dell's excavations began in 1955, just over a hundred years later (Phase VI).

5.2 PHASE II: EVIDENCE OF IRON AGE SETTLEMENT

The structures and middens

The earliest features identified above the bedrock (Phase I) were the remains of Iron Age structures built onto the clay subsoil below and to the south of the chapel. Below the chapel there was evidence that they were set onto a thin layer of peat over the bedrock, and Small describes 'an extensive complex of fragments of paving and walls' (Small 1973, 5) and the terms 'platform' and 'pavement' are found in the archives, as well as references to hearth material, pottery, a stone whorl or bead, and whale and fish bone, although the stratigraphy was so confused here that it is possible that these artefacts derived from a thick midden layer that accumulated above the disused structures. Small (1973, 5) describes the remains to the south of the chapel as the floors of two huts with a pathway between them and a pathway above them to the west, although again it is hard to ascertain from the sparse descriptions and sketches, and from the ephemeral remains of a wall re-examined in 2000 to the south of the chapel, the original form of the buildings. Small describes that there were 'several periods of rebuilding in the pre-Christian phases'.

The archive descriptions of the buildings below the chapel suggest they were small and circular, possibly comprising conjoining cells, and reminiscent of huts rather than substantial round houses. Similarly the structural remains excavated on the west side of the area south of the chapel comprised hut floors, and paved paths and areas. Small, cellular dry stone buildings and paving have been excavated at nearby Scalloway (Sharples 1998, 62–73) and particularly Old Scatness broch (Dockrill et al 2002, 205–207; 2003, 118–119), where the imminent publication of the Late Iron Age (Pictish) cellular buildings and associated artefactual and environmental material (J Bond pers comm) is eagerly awaited. Sharples when discussing the Scalloway cellular buildings (1998, 205) draws attention to comparable figure-of-eight houses at Birsay in Orkney (Hunter 1986; Morris 1989), for which an 8th-century date is suggested, and the pathways excavated at Scalloway are particularly reminiscent of those excavated to the south of the chapel at St Ninian's Isle as shown on Small's final plan (Figure 5.1; cf. figs 59–61 in Sharples 1998, 68–69), as are those found at Kebister on the east coast of mainland Shetland (Owen and Lowe 1999, 122–126, Structure 5, pl 15) and dated to the Late Iron Age.

The structural remains were covered by differing layers of clayey midden dark yellowish brown in the area south of the chapel, and black below and to the east of the chapel, where it was excavated in 1958–59. The latter layer is described as being a foot thick, and may have extended to the west, where it is described as a clay humus layer. These layers accumulated over the structures once they had gone out of use, and they pre-date all the burials on the site. It is not possible to say what structures or occupation these middens are associated with. They presumably relate to occupation elsewhere on the site, probably nearby, but it is also possible that within this general Iron Age Phase II, several phases of occupation are represented, with settlement shift around different parts of the site. Unfortunately the ad hoc and keyhole nature of the 1950s excavation, the sparse archive, the undoubted re-use of stone on the site in antiquity, and the centuries of use for burial, have all conspired to make it impossible to unravel the various glimpses of early structures, or to shed any further light on this era of settlement on the Isle except to say that there evidently was settlement on the Isle in the Late Iron Age. Nearby settlement is also suggested by eroding Iron Age midden deposits that have been recorded from across the bay at Ireland (Shetland Museum 1997b).

The artefactual assemblages from the middens: character and dating

The artefactual assemblage from the Phase II middens does provide us with more of a picture of the Late Iron Age settlement on the Isle, and reflects a range of domestic activities. Those finds that are diagnostic are all Late Iron Age in character, possibly bar one steatite weight (discussed by Batey in

Chapter 4, and below) and two examples amongst the material from the 1959 excavations of earlier Iron Age forms of coarse ceramics and one heavily steatitic sherd which may date to the later Bronze Age/Early Iron Age (MacSween, Chapter 3). Batey reports on the non-pottery finds from the 1950s excavations, most of which are also from this phase and are identifiably of Late Iron Age date, including a stone weight, a stone bead or whorl, a pebble gaming piece, pumice, an iron bolt, the shaft of a broken bone pin and a glass bead (Chapter 3). The finds from the recent excavations show a similar date and range of domestic activities. The artefactual assemblage (Chapter 4) includes over 80 sherds of coarse pottery, stone tools, a broken quern stone, stone pot lid and a broken stone gaming piece that is similar to gaming pieces found at other Iron Age sites, such as Scalloway in Shetland, and the Howe in Orkney. A whalebone spike or stake and a chopping block, a bone point, two lumps of un-worked steatite, small lumps of possible smithing slag and flaked quartz complete the assemblage.

The recovery of flaked quartz from the midden layers, including some showing signs of utilization and retouch, and also a blade, adds an extra dimension to the study of the economy of the Late Iron Age settlement on the site. Donnelly draws attention to the fact that quartz assemblages on sites such as St Ninian's Isle are often seen as residual, without necessarily any evidence for such, and that in Shetland, the lack of good flint and resulting reliance on quartz has resulted in undiagnostic assemblages. Only the recent excavations at St Ninian's Isle recovered any quartz artefacts, and Donnelly suggests that the previous excavators may have failed to recognise many lithics, in common with many of the later prehistoric sites on Shetland (and Orkney) that were investigated in the early parts of last century, when the excavators did not appear to have been aware of the wide-scale use of quartz in later levels. He concludes that the quartz lithics from St Ninian's Isle probably do relate to quartz use in the Iron Age, although the possibility that the material relates to a much earlier site dating to the end of the Neolithic or the Bronze Age should also be considered.

The general Late Iron Age date for the middens, as indicated by the artefactual assemblage contained within it, can be refined by the radiocarbon dating of the earliest burial in Phase III above to the late 7th to late 8th centuries AD, and by the stylistic dating of the shrine posts and early cross-incised stones found in the 1950s from features above the midden layers. Whilst the shrine posts were found in a secondary position, one cross-incised stone in particular (Stone 11; Thomas 1973, 36) was found associated with the earliest phase of long cists on the site, and is dated by Thomas to the early half of the 8th century. Allowing for accumulation therefore, the middens were probably deposited no later than the end of the 7th century AD.

The only analogous object from the Phase II artefactual material may be the broken steatite fishing weight, which Batey has suggested has similarities to a type known as a hogback fishing weight, (a type described by Clarke and Sharman as a 'distinctive Norse object'; 1998, 149, fig 95, no. 4), which would conventionally be dated later than Phase II. Whilst it is possible that the weight may be intrusive, given the disturbance on the site from later burials, it is unlikely that the weight derives from later phases on the site, as these correspond to a change in use to burial and worship, with no evidence for settlement or occupation and a broken fishing weight would be an unusual grave good to be included with the burials of Phase III. A finely made, small steatite food vessel found during O'Dell's excavations is identified by Batey (Chapter 3) as potentially Norse. Unfortunately this find could not be tied to a particular excavated feature or even year of excavation on the site. Its very presence however may suggest that there was activity other than burial at the site in the Norse period, unless it is associated with a funerary or ritual/religious function.

Certainly the use of steatite is not in itself an indication of Norse ethnicity; whilst a boom in the Shetland steatite industry occurred in the Norse period (Buttler 1989), the natural steatite resources on the islands were exploited throughout prehistory and into the Iron Age (Sharman 1998d, 138), and Iron Age steatite vessels have been found in Shetland at sites such as Scalloway (see below) and Kebister (Sharman 1999, 169–170). Whilst the historical record defines the onset of Norse raiding (as opposed to settlement) of Scotland from across the North Sea as being at the end of the 8th/beginning of the 9th century, an earlier date in the middle of the 8th century has been suggested for contact by Morris (1998, 73, 74, 83–85), who questions the 'purely inferential' arguments that Viking settlement in the Northern Isles began at the end of the 8th century as a convenient base from which to raid the Western Isles and mainland Scotland, although Graham-Campbell (and Buteaux) argue against such 'informal settlement' (2003b and references therein; discussed also in Hunter 2007, 121–146). The recent discovery of an early Viking settlement at Norwick, Unst, includes an accompanying culturally early Viking period assemblage of steatite and pottery. Radiocarbon dating from the site leads Ballin Smith to conclude that 'The settlement is clearly early, with the dates indicating occupation well before the late 8th century, and possibly as much as a century before' (2007, 294). Evidence of early Viking occupation has also been uncovered at Old Scatness (Batey, cited in Ballin Smith 2007, 294; Bond *et al* forthcoming).

In contrast, at Upper Scalloway, there is an 'absence of evidence for contact with Scandinavia' (Sharples 1998, 211), and Iron Age steatite vessels have been found with clear evidence of pre-Norse tooling techniques (Sharman 1998a). Three elaborate steatite objects were found: a mould for the manufacture of bar ingots (Campbell with Sharman 1998, 161–162), a lamp (Sharman 1998b, 149), and a carved and elaborately decorated weight (Clarke and Sharman 1998), recovered from early Phase III, House One, and dated to AD 500–650 by other elements of the artefactual assemblage and radiocarbon dating (Sharples 1998, 83–88). Sharples draws our attention to the fact that the steatite bar mould would have been dated to the Viking period if it had been found out of context, and that normally the form (rather than the tooling) of the steatite vessels (Sharman 1998d, 138–139) would have led them to be dated to the Viking period also. This could also be said of the steatite, possibly 'hogback' fishing weight, and fine miniature vessel, from St Ninian's Isle.

The environmental assemblage: nature and economy

In common with the artefactual assemblage, the ecofactual material from the recent excavations of the Phase II middens suggests that they received principally domestic waste (Chapter 4). Although the assemblage is small, Miller and Ramsay identify evidence amongst the archaeobotanical material that barley was cultivated in the vicinity. Chance gifts from the sea, such as driftwood or whale carcasses, were also utilised, but there seems to have been little exploitation of the wider marine environment. The use of driftwood is suggested by the presence of conifer charcoal, and a small glimpse into the environment at the time is given by examples of Heather sp., apple type and oak charcoal. The contents of the small faunal assemblage from the recent excavations reported by Gidney suggest that the midden received household waste, and the tiny fish bone assemblage and larger edible periwinkle and other marine shellfish assemblage both indicate only shore-based fishing and gathering. Gidney identifies only a small number of marine bird bones and there is no evidence that marine mammals were used for food, with whale bone recovered as artefacts rather than as food waste from the middens.

The marine isotope analysis by Hedges of samples from coarse pot sherds from this phase also produced results that were well within what is expected from terrestrial sources, and organic residue analysis by Jones of the pottery sherds showed a clear result indicative of degraded animal fat. A predominantly terrestrial-based diet is also indicated by the marine isotope analysis of the skeletal remains from Phase III. With the caveat that this is only a small assemblage, the analyses are backed up by observations made on site concerning the lack of fish bone recovered, despite the environmental flotation undertaken of soil samples, and the dominance of shore-collected shellfish. It is possible that more fishing did take place but that the bone was dumped elsewhere, and also that the indications from analysis of a small sample of pot sherds is unrepresentative of general diet. The paucity of fish bone however is surprising in the Phase II midden. In the 1958 excavations, O'Dell and his team found thick black midden dumps down the cliff at the seaward edge of the site, but here there is also no mention of fish bone in the, admittedly sketchy, archive notes. The presence of a few small fish bones in the archive collection from 1959 suggests that the excavation team knew fish bone when they saw it, and one would expect that the fish bone would be mentioned (as animal and human bone is) if it had been present in any great number.

These observations of a largely terrestrial and shore-based economy at St Ninian's Isle in the Late Iron Age fit with a growing body of evidence for a land-based economy in the Late Iron Age, or 'Pictish' period (Barrett *et al* 2001a; 2001b), although the skeletal material from St Ninian's Isle that has been radiocarbon dated to the later Norse period also displays evidence of a largely terrestrial diet (see below).

5.3 PHASE III: CENTURIES OF CHANGE: BURIAL AND WORSHIP, PAGAN AND CHRISTIAN, NATIVE AND NORSE

Short cists, cremations and a rubble mound: were there pagan Picts at St Ninian's Isle?

Eight cists containing cremations or burials and cut into the midden layer above the Iron Age structures, are mentioned in the archives from the excavations below the chapel, of which five are identified as probably pre-Christian, and two as containing cremation urns and burnt bone, although this cannot be verified as the urns have subsequently been lost. The cists were set into a thick black clayey midden layer up to a foot thick, which covered the disused buildings below the chapel, and included cist A, set at a similar depth below the chapel as the short cists excavated in 1959 to the south. This group of four short cists was excavated from above the Phase II middens south of the chapel, and were re-examined in 2000. The largest of them (305) contained a flexed female burial lying prone and aligned N–S, and dated to between the mid 7th and end of the 8th century, the remaining three cists were all emptied in 1959 and are described as containing charred human bones, shells and human bones, although these have since been lost.

The cists were centred on a small wall or base of stonework and covered by a stone cairn, which had been dug into when later (Christian) burials were inserted into the sides. The stonework of the wall base in the centre was clearly defined, and discrete, with short cists abutting it to the south and west and paving and shells mixed with earlier midden found spread around it to the north and west. Its dimen-

sions were the same as those of the early long cists on the site, i.e. the size required for an adult human body to lie extended, and it could be postulated that it fulfilled some kind of funerary function associated with the short cist burials given its central position amongst them, perhaps it served as a base for an upright stone, or marker, although no evidence of a socket or other supporting stonework was found within it. Ultimately, due to the partial excavation and removal of features from around the base in 1959, and the scarcity of information concerning the original contents of the short cists, this can only remain conjecture. It is certainly possible however that this feature was associated with funerary ritual, either as a marker or as some sort of mortuary platform.

In the area around the south and west sides of the cists, where the rubble mound had been excavated in 1959, a layer of mixed midden was identified in a semi-circular area at the interface with the Phase II middens below. It contained many finds that are datable to the Late Iron Age and had become re-deposited from the midden as a result of the construction of the rubble mound and cists above, including artefacts such as a bone point and worked whalebone, including a possible mallet and carbonised inclusions from the midden below, such as burnt cereal grains and Scots pine charcoal. Two bone cylindrical beads closely comparable to the seventeen bone and antler beads found below the rubble cairn in 1959 were also found in this midden. They are similar to examples from other Iron Age sites in Shetland, and Batey suggests that the examples from St Ninian's Isle may well have served as a necklace, as Small suggested, and it is not unlikely that they were originally associated with a burial.

The radiocarbon date from burial ABDUA 14269 in the large short cist (305) identifies it to the period when the Picts, descendants of the Late Iron Age tribes of Scotland, are recognizable as an archaeological and historical entity, and had begun to be converted to Christianity (Foster 1996, 13, 79) and St Ninian's Isle is one of several sites known from the southern half of mainland Shetland with clear evidence for Pictish influence, if not presence. In addition to Papil, West Burra (Thomas 1973) and Jarlshof (Hamilton 1956), recent excavations at the nearby multi-period site at Old Scatness broch in particular have found evidence not only for Late Iron Age cellular buildings, but also incontrovertible evidence of Pictish culture in the form of Pictish symbol stones (eg Dockrill *et al* 2006). Culturally Pictish artefacts have also been recovered from Upper Scalloway (Sharples 1998). A Pictish stone has also been found as a stray find at Breck of Hillwell nearby (Shetland Museum 1997a) and Forsyth draws attention to the Shetlandic corpus of ogham inscriptions, including Cunningsburgh, in the south of mainland Shetland, amongst others (see Chapter 2). Friell and Watson (1984) were in no doubt that

Shetland was part of what is recognised as Pictish culture and this has led Turner, for instance, to state that 'by the 6th century Shetland was very much part of the mainstream of Pictish politics and life' (Turner 1998, 85). Woolf, in his *From Pictland to Alba* (2007) is not quite so enthusiastic, writing of the Atlantic littoral, from Ardnamurchan to Shetland, with the exception of Orkney 'Although there are examples of Pictish art from all these regions they are few and far between and might reflect sporadic links rather than full engagement with the Verturian hegemony' (2007, 13). Forsyth, in her discussion in Chapter 2 of the ogham stone from the site, writes however that 'The archaeological and palaeographical diversity of the Shetland oghams shows that they were not the product of an isolated burst of ogham carving activity ... Instead the impression is of an on-going participation in the Scottish ogham tradition over a potentially extended period'.

The short cist grave 305, with its flexed and prone burial (ABDUA 14269), does not however fit easily as there is nothing particularly Christian, or Pictish, about it. If it is compared to the other burials from the site, it differs in most points, other than the presence of quartz pebbles (Figure 5.3). It is not accompanied by any Christian sculpture, but also does not generally fit the most commonly evidenced mode of burial in the Late Iron Age: the Pictish circular or square burial cairn, usually with a stone kerb, and overlying a long cist covered by a layer of sterile sand, now recognized as the distinctive Pictish burial form in the north of Scotland (Ritchie 1974, 31–32; Ashmore 1980; McNeill and MacQueen 1996, 49; Close-Brooks 1984), with an example from Shetland (Sandwick in Unst; Bigelow 1984) as well as Orkney, Caithness, Sutherland and the Western Isles (Morris 1991, 74; 1989, 109–127; Graham-Campbell and Batey 1998, 11; Ashmore 1980; 2003; Brennand *et al* 1998a; 1998b; Downes and Badcock 1998a; 1998b; Mulville *et al* 2003). The burials in long cists below cairns at the Brough Road, Birsay, are radiocarbon dated to between the 1st and 6th centuries AD (Morris 1991, 74), and that from Cille Pheadair, Uist to 620–780 cal AD (Brennand *et al* 1998a; 1998b, 38–46; Mulville *et al* 2003, 24–27). The St Ninian's Isle burial is of a similar date to these burials (especially Cille Pheadair), and comparisons could also be made between the evidence for post-mortem re-positioning of the Cille Pheadair example ('Kilphedir Kate') and ABDUA 14269 ('Rosemary'), which was also supported on her left side by stones, and whose left arm was missing (but with the left shoulder and the left hand bones and fingers intact), and the presence of the stone cairn around the cists on St Ninian's Isle. Here the comparison ends however. Roberts' study of 'Rosemary' (Chapter 3) demonstrates that she was flexed and prone, rather than supine, and there was no evidence of dismemberment, and she was buried in a short, not long, cist. What is clear is that the St Ninian's Isle

example is altogether an unusual burial, for which it is difficult to find parallels.

'Rosemary' is the only probable non-Christian burial (rather than cremation) for which there is surviving evidence from the site, although short cists containing quartz pebbles and bones were excavated below the church in 1958–59. Features such as the orientation of the grave cannot necessarily be taken as a reliable guide to the belief system respected by the individual buried. E–W alignment, for instance, is as likely to be solar-related as Christian, and is seen in both Anglo-Saxon and Pictish burials from this period (discussed by Ritchie 2003, 4). Similarly the radiocarbon date for 'Rosemary' cannot determine whether this is a pagan or Christian burial. The radiocarbon date range for the first evidently Christian burials excavated to the south of the church for instance, a NW–SE aligned child grave (SK 7) with a 'head box', which may have been buried in a cist, and an early long cist burial (ABDUA 14254, 'Hubert'), aligned E–W with a cross-marked head stone (Figure 5.3), both have a similar date range as 'Rosemary'. Unfortunately, other than the square cairn at Sandwick mentioned above, which we have already seen is not comparable to the St Ninian's Isle burial, there is a paucity of Iron Age burial evidence from Shetland with which to compare 'Rosemary' (ABDUA 14269), at inverse proportion to the number of excavations undertaken on Iron Age settlement sites. Comparable pre-Christian, Late Iron Age burials may be identified at St Nicholas' chapel, Papa Stronsay, where two pre-Christian, slightly-flexed, inhumations, lying on their right sides, were found in an inhumation grave to the south of and below the 11th-century chapel (Lowe 2002, 91), but there were no cists associated with these burials.

One feature that links all the short cists from Phase III, and possibly the cremations also, is the presence of quartz pebbles. These are noted in the archives as being found in the short cists below the chapel and they were also found incorporated into the later, Christian, burials on the site. The use of quartzite for special, perhaps even magical, purposes has a long history, with origins that pre-date the Late Iron Age, and continue into the Christian period. Ritchie (1998, 178) draws attention to Culcharron in Argyll where quartzite pebbles were sprinkled thickly around the base of the kerb-stones of a cairn dating to the second millennium BC, and to Whithorn, where burials were accompanied by significant numbers of pebbles. Many other examples exist. Several thousand pebbles were excavated at Whithorn (Hill 1997), and a short distance along the coast at Barhobble, Mochrum, white quartzite pebbles were found in medieval burials (Cormack 1995), whilst those found over medieval burials on the Isle of May have prompted one writer to suggest that they may be equated to a miracle involving a white stone in Adomnan's *Vita Columba* (Kermack 1996). Adomnan's story is also cited by

Ritchie, when discussing painted white quartzite pebbles found in contemporary archaeological contexts (Ritchie 2003, 4).

The remaining evidence for pre-Christian burial practice at the commencement of Phase III is found in the three short cists adjacent to cist 305, excavated in 1959 and said to contain cremated or charred, probably human bone fragments (according to archive notes). It is unfortunate that none of the cremation remains can be located, so this cannot be confirmed. It is not possible, for instance, to determine whether the cremations are earlier than ABD-UA 14269 or contemporary with it. It is also impossible from the archive descriptions alone to discern whether the cremations excavated from below the chapel are contemporary with the short cists to the south of the chapel. It is tempting on burial mode alone to assume, as O'Dell did, that the cremations pre-date the burials. Assumptions however are often shown to be misguided on this site.

Ritchie's recent discussion of paganism among the Picts in Orkney gives us a glimpse into the potential archaeological manifestations of Pictish pagan belief systems (2003). She cites St Nicholas' Chapel in Papa Stronsay, Orkney, a site comparable to St Ninian's Isle, where an enclosed Late Iron Age settlement has been excavated from below the 11th-century chapel (Buteux et al 1998; 1999; Lowe 2002; Lowe et al 2000). The most significant building excavated was a small, oval, corbelled building, with a rectangular stone setting in the centre, and an upright stone at one end (Lowe 2002, 91). This building lay under the later chapel and was also the focal point of a stone-lined pathway, which approached if from the south, continued under the west gable of the later chapel, and then extended south and west towards the sea. A small fragment of green porphyry was recovered from infill into this building. A second, larger building was identified next to it to the east (Lowe 2002, 92). Ritchie suggests that if the porphyry belongs to the construction of St Nicholas' Chapel, 'the circular building is freed of all Christian connotations and could become the pagan shrine that attracted Christian activities in the first place' (Ritchie 2003, 5). The two pre-Christian slightly-flexed inhumations found to the south of the chapel may also support her suggestion (Lowe 2002, 91).

The stone pathways found at St Nicholas' chapel are reminiscent of the pathways described by Small from both below and to the south of the chapel on St Ninian's Isle. Here, above the Iron Age structures and midden/occupation layers, Small described a later, kerbed and flagged, pathway some 1.3m wide, in the SW corner of the excavation area, where up to 3m length was uncovered. Unfortunately the majority of this part of the 1959 trench lay outwith the confines of the 2000 trench, and so only a small corner of the Iron Age structures there were re-examined in 2000. This re-examination however

has shown that there were clearly at least two phases of structure here, and that the paved pathways that overlay the midden in this area could potentially be placed into Phase III, and therefore be connected with the use of the site for burial. A small area of paving was also uncovered at the edge of the short cists south of the chapel, which were themselves centred on a wall or stonework base of unknown function, suggested above as either a platform or marker, protruding through the rubble mound which covered the cists. Like St Nicholas', Papa Stronsay, St Ninian's Isle was singled out as a special place to lay the dead to rest before the advent of Christianity, and remained significant to the population using it, through change in use and religious belief.

Long cists, 'head-boxes' and cross-incised stones: the arrival of Christianity and the continuity of place

The arrival of Christianity on the Isle is signalled in the burial record by three features: the marking of burials with cross-incised stones, the interment of burials in long cists, and the use of 'head boxes'.

The long cists excavated on the site were separated into two distinct groups, an earlier, Phase III, group situated below the sand, and a later medieval Phase V group situated above it. Two long cists from the earlier group were excavated 2000 (cists 321 and 335) and the presence of over 100 disarticulated mixed adult, juvenile and infant bones in the re-deposited fill of cist (321), and of weed seeds and coffin wood in the basal fills of both cists, demonstrated that they had been dug into and then backfilled in 1959. A small cist 'extension' (336), or thinning of cist 321 at the east end, was covered by a cross-incised slab, possibly a fallen stone, which can be dated stylistically to the early medieval or Norse periods. The study of archive slides and notes revealed that an extended male burial 'Hubert' (ABDUA 14254) dated to the end of the 7th to the end of the 9th centuries was probably excavated from cist (321). Adjacent to this cist, a second long cist (335) was totally excavated and partially dismantled during the 1959 excavations, and a cross-incised stone was found set upright at its west end (Thomas 1973, 30, 36, Stone 11, who identifies it as a primary cross slab dating to the pre-Norse period of early Christianity on Shetland). It is tempting to ascribe a second, juvenile excavated from the long cists on the site in 1959, skeleton ABDUA 14270 'Robert', to this cist, but there is no evidence in the archives unfortunately to link the two. 'Robert' is described in an archive letter as originating from a wooden coffin (which showed as a stain in the sand) within a long cist but he has been radiocarbon dated to the late 8th to end of the 10th centuries, which would place this burial below the sand, rather than in the later Phase V medieval long cists above it.

Batey's study (Chapter 3) of the two groups of magnificent glass beads found during the 1950s excavations concludes that they most likely belong to Phase III, with Group One recorded as having been found in the long cists SE of the chapel, and Batey identifies that they have close similarities with beads from other long cist cemeteries in Scotland, and could conceivably be from the same chronological context as the Pictish hoard. The Group Two beads, of a different character to those in the other group, may have come from a second grave, but there is no evidence that this was the case, and archive information instead suggests that they may have originated from the Iron Age levels below the medieval chapel excavated in 1959, with similar, but smaller, beads being noted from Iron Age contexts at Clickhimin Broch, Shetland (Batey citing Hamilton 1968, 90). It is still possible however that they may have originated from an early long cist, as there are descriptions in the archives of further cists, possibly long cists, uncovered below the medieval chancel at what would have been the SE corner of the early church building below.

Further early long cists were excavated from the Isle in 1958 and 1959, but there is regrettably little further information to be found concerning their form, stratigraphical position or contents. What was possibly a long cist with a lintel cover was excavated from below the east end of the medieval nave in 1958, pre-dating the nave and therefore possibly situated in the interior east end of the earlier church below it. Two cists, probably long cists, that extended under the timber shoring of the trench at the interior edge of and below the medieval south chancel wall, probably belonged to the same group as (321) and (335) discussed above. In addition to this, long cists are noted cut into a black midden layer to the east of the church in a pit dug down the slope to the SE of the medieval chapel in 1958, but there is unfortunately no further information in the archive as to the number of cists, their form or contents. These long cists at the bottom of the sand outside the SE corner of the putative earlier church, plus the possible long cist with the lintel situated inside the early church at its east end, represent the first phase of a long cist cemetery on the site, probably associated with the primary church building.

Large long cist cemeteries are generally recognised in the area of SE Scotland (Foster 1996, 79; Alcock 1992; Henshall 1956), but long cists have also been identified singly, or in small groups, in northern and western Scotland (eg Ponting 1989; Hedges 1978), where there is growing evidence for long cist cemeteries (Proudfoot 1996, illus 27, 445, cited in Neighbour et al 2000, 575; forthcoming; Ashmore 2003, 39–40) dated to between the 5th and 9th centuries (see Close-Brooks 1984). Radiocarbon estimates from Hallow's Hill, in Fife (Proudfoot 1996), suggest a date centred on the 6th century AD, and it has been suggested that long cist cemeteries be-

gan before the advent of Christianity (Alcock 1992, 127). The examples from St Ninian's Isle sit at the later end of the range, and in common with the Orkney examples (Ashmore 2003, 41), date to the second half of the first millennium. It is impossible from the available evidence to determine whether the long cist cemetery at St Ninian's Isle pre-dates the primary church on the site or not.

Westness, Rousay, Orkney, is the largest comparative native and Norse cemetery to be excavated in the Northern Isles. It contained a wide range of burial types of men, women and children, including Christian long cist inhumations and head-box burials, some displaying evidence for insufficient nutrition, and also a pregnant adult female in a cist grave with two children in cut graves alongside, overlaid by pagan Norse boat-shaped graves, boat burials and stone-lined pits (S H H Kaland pers comm; Kaland 1993; see also Barrett et al 2000; Ashmore 2003, 46–49). The ethnicity of the individuals buried in the long cist on St Ninian's Isle is unknown, although Thomas considers the upstanding cross-incised stone from the head of cist 335 to be pre-Norse, whilst Fisher identifies parallels in both the early medieval and Norse periods for the simple form of Latin cross-incised grave marker found flat at the east end of cist 321.

Forsyth suggests in Chapter 2 that a plausible explanation for the ogham-inscribed slab from St Ninian's Isle is that it was once part of a cist-grave, perhaps a side panel. The fact that the slab was already fractured when Goudie found it suggests that either it was a secondary use in the cist-grave, or it may have formerly stood upright and been toppled over, so causing the break. The slab may have been trimmed for re-use, but there is no evidence of tool marks, and it seems more likely that the stone has broken along a natural jointing plane. The St Ninian's Isle ogham is one of eight ogham-inscribed stones from Shetland, seven of which were found on or near churchyards.

Thomas argued that Christianity arrived in Shetland 'arguably in the early 7th century, more probably in the mid 7th, most improbably before AD 600' (Thomas 1973, 27). The growth in the number of excavations of early medieval and Norse ecclesiastical sites in recent years has meant that there is increasing archaeological evidence for, and discussion of, the spread of Christianity (eg Carver 2003). The principal evidence for conversion to Christianity in Shetland however is sculpture, the prime examples of which are still to be found in the fertile southern half of mainland Shetland and the adjacent smaller isles, including St Ninian's Isle. As discussed above in Chapter 3, Thomas dates the composite shrine posts at St Ninian's Isle to the 8th century (1973, 23; 1998, 94–95), although Stevenson has suggested a later date in the 9th century (Stevenson 1981, 287–288; see also Lamb 1995). There are also the 'primary' cross-incised stones from St Ninian's Isle, divided into grave markers (pebbles or stone fragments marked with a cross and laid over the head of the deceased) and cross-slabs (cross-incised slabs or little pillars which are thought to have stood upright at one end of the grave), which Thomas dates to the pre-Norse period (1973, 28–29): Stone 11 from the head end of cist 335, re-examined in 2000; Stone 10 found face downwards in the nave in 1959; and Stone 15 found over the treasure. Thomas also suggested that the 'S-dragons' on one of the shrines might demonstrate the survival, through the transition from paganism to Christianity, of an old 'guardian' symbol, suggesting a degree of continuity between the two beliefs (1973, 24–25), although this was rejected by Stevenson (1981, 287–288).

St Ninian's Isle was clearly in an area not only rich in Pictish culture, as seen at nearby Scatness, Jarlshof and Scatness, but also Christian belief. Thomas highlighted the links between Papil, West Burra and St Ninian's Isle along the coast in the 1973 volume. The impressive collection of early Christian sculpture from Papil, includes shrine posts, the famous shrine panel, or 'Burra stone', which depicts clerics with crosiers and book satchels, travelling towards a cross (Thomas 1973, 42 and refs therein; Fisher 2002, 53–54, fig 3.8; Lamb 1995, 9–12, 20–22), the 'Papil stone', a cross-slab depicting clerics around a cross, and bird-headed men (Fisher 2002, 53–54, fig 3.9), and a broken cross-incised slab (Thomas 1973, 29, pl xv; Fisher 2002, 53–54, fig 3.10). This collection indicates a major site from the 8th century onwards (discussed with the St Ninian's Isle corpus by Thomas 1973; 1971, 156–157; and Fisher 2002, 53–54), with the Papil shrine panel being alternatively dated 'well into the 9th century' by Stevenson (1981, 288–289), and the broken cross-incised slab into the 10th century by Fisher (2002, 54).

A concentration of early Christian sculpture is also found on the east side of south mainland, at Bressay. The 'Bressay stone', a cross-slab sculptured in relief, with ogham inscriptions on the two narrow sides, is said to have been inspired by the Papil Stone (Stevenson 1981, 284–285; Lamb 1995, 21). Cross-incised slabs (Thomas 1971, 118–119) and a corner-post shrine post (and a rune stone) have also been recovered from the old graveyard at Gungstie, Noss, across the sound of Ness from Bressay. This site has a nearby 'Papar' name, Papil Geo, and has been the subject of a small rescue excavation by Val Turner (1994; 1998, 113; forthcoming; discussed by Fisher in 2002, 54–55). Finally, at Mail, Cunningsburgh,, grave-markers, including three ogham stones, three rune stones, and another Pictish stone have also been recovered, and there are local references to further carved stones, now lost, uncovered during grave-digging (Thomas 1973, 9; Turner 1998, 96; Brian Smith pers comm; see Forsyth in Chapter 2).

Even this brief survey of sites illustrates that St Ninian's Isle was part of a rich and vibrant early Christian landscape in the southern half of mainland Shetland in the 8th to 10th centuries, and was perhaps chosen as an early church site because it was already considered a special place by the local population. This is suggested by the chosen position of the earliest dated, manifestly Christian, burials, the long cists set into the sandy ground less than a metre away to the east of the pagan short cists and rubble mound, and aligned with the mysterious base of stonework upon which the short cists were also centred. The long cists were buried at the same level as the short cists, and into the same thin layer of sand. From the lack of soil deposits it is clear that the pagan short cists and mound were upstanding and visible when the first Christian burials were inserted (there was no soil build up between the two). This location was deliberately chosen and continued to have special significance to the Christian converts, an occurrence that has been noted at other sites (Ashmore 1980).

Eight of the twelve burials located in the area south of the chapel in Phase III, either excavated in 2000, or for which there is enough archive material available, are of infants or children, and all include head boxes with the burials. Head-box burials have a widespread distribution in Scotland and the Isle of Man, in male and female, child and adult burials, and are evidenced in early historic and medieval contexts, from Barhobble, Mochram, in Dumfries and Galloway (Cormack 1995), to Newhill Point, Balblair, Ross and Cromarty (Reed 1995), Skaill House, Sandwick in Orkney (James 1999) and Peel Castle, Isle of Man (Freke 2002), to name just a few examples. They are a Christian phenomenon, with a widespread date distribution from the earliest Christian to the later medieval periods. One of the earliest dated examples from Kirkhill, St Andrews (Reed 1995, 789) is radiocarbon dated to AD 661–778 at one sigma level of confidence, comparable in date to SK 7 from St Ninian's Isle, the earliest dated child burial. The remaining head-box burials at St Ninian's Isle, the 10th-century infant burials and a single infant grave (SK 6), possibly once accompanied by a cist and dated to the early 11th to early 13th centuries, are comparable to examples from Skaill, Orkney, dated to the 11th or 12th century (James 1999, 769), and Barhobble, Dumfries and Galloway, dated to the 11th-13th centuries (Cormack 1995, 43–44, 93).

The presence of infant burials in a cemetery has in itself been linked to the introduction of Christianity, particularly on Roman-period sites, with infant burials often being allocated their own particular space within larger cemeteries (Scott 1999, 114, 123). Separate burial grounds for neonate (i.e. un-baptised) infants are found in Ireland from the medieval period onwards, where Finlay draws attention to examples of child cemeteries being singled out for the burial of adults that deviated from the norm, such as unrepentant murderers and their victims, those of differing religious beliefs, or victims of famine (Finlay 2000, 408–410). However, whilst on first appearance there does seem to be a disproportionately large number of infant compared with adult individuals excavated from St Ninian's Isle and evidenced in the disarticulated bone assemblages found scattered in grave fills and other re-deposited soils, this is as likely to be result of excavation and preservation bias, considering the nature of the work at the site in the 1950s, and the continued use of the site for burial from the medieval period to the 19th century.

The first church building on the site

There is a lack of direct stratigraphical information available in the archives concerning the early church building other than the *terminus ante quem* provided by the building of the later medieval chapel foundations above some time in the 12th to 13th centuries. There are however scraps of evidence that can be pieced together to give an overall indication of the likely dimensions and appearance of its lower wall courses. By 1959, the south and west sides, possibly half of the east side, and a small portion of the north side, of an earlier building below the chapel had been uncovered (Figure 5.1). This earlier building measured some 6.5 x 5 m and lay directly below the medieval chapel on roughly the same alignment and internal measurements as the nave. The walls overlay a thin layer of sand above the earlier short cists and midden, and were built from dry-stone rectangular blocks, plastered on the inner face. Only the basal three courses survived, the stone presumably having been re-used to build the later medieval chapel.

There is no direct evidence for the nature of this earlier building, and no definitive evidence that it was an earlier church, but this is the most probable interpretation given the circumstantial evidence, namely its situation directly below the medieval chapel and on the same alignment, and its location adjacent to the group of early long cists below the wind-blown sand. The shrine posts and collection of stone sculpture that have been recovered from the site also support the existence of a contemporaneous church. This includes a cross-marked stone described found marking one of the long cists (Stone 11; Thomas 1973, 36, fig 8, pl VIII) and a broken cross-incised sandstone slab (Stone 10; Thomas 1973, 36, fig 8, pl VIII) found face downwards in the SW part of the nave of the medieval chapel in 1959, but which Thomas dates to the 8th century or a little earlier (Thomas 1973, 28). A small fragment of porphyry (Stone 21; Thomas 1973, 38) was also found in excavations in the nave, but may be a later introduction to the site. Levels taken on the top of the footings of the earlier chapel walling in 1999 compare with levels taken on the top of the side slabs of the earlier long cists below the sand at the SE corner of the church, and support the suggestion that the early church building and the early long

cists were set into a contemporary ground surface. If the first church building accompanied the first long cists on the site, then it can be dated to between the late 7th and the late 9th centuries from the radiocarbon dating of the cists, a date which is in keeping with the excavator's own conclusion that both belonged to the 'pre-Norse' period (O'Dell and Cain 1960, 5).

It is clear from the archives that at the beginning of the excavations O'Dell was greatly influenced by Douglas Simpson and his idea that the first church on the site had been founded by St Ninian or his followers. O'Dell was keen to find evidence of white plaster on the inside and outside of the chapel walls, because such would be a sign that the building was linked to St Ninian, from Bede's brief reference to Ninian building a stone church, known as 'Candida Casa' (the White or Shining House) at Whithorn in his mission to the Britons. As the excavations progressed, however, O'Dell accepted that the Ninianic dedication was a medieval one, although this does not negate an early date for the primary church building or O'Dell's identification of plaster, or mortar, on the earlier church walls, which has been evidenced on other early church buildings, such as at Iona (O'Sullivan 1994, 354–356).

It has been suggested that there was an earlier timber church at St Ninian's Isle (Morris 1990, 9–10; 1996b, 189). An initial phase of timber church building has been proposed at early church sites, such as Deerness, Orkney (Morris with Emery 1986a, 315–320; 1986b), which is thought to have been clad externally with dry-stone walling, and Kebister, Shetland (Owen and Lowe 1999, 84–87, 290–292) in the North, or Barhobble, Dumfries and Galloway (Cormack 1995, 23–24) and Ardwall Isle in the South (Thomas 1967). There is no evidence in the archive for such, however, which is perhaps not surprising given the availability of stone from the earlier, abandoned, Iron Age structures on the site.

There are few excavated parallels from Scotland for the early church building at St Ninian's Isle. Cant lists several earlier chapels in Shetland (Cant 1975, 21–23), whilst Lamb (1995) and Lowe's (1987) work on the phenomena of early ecclesiastical sites either on the edges of, or directly over, earlier Iron Age settlements (see summary in Lowe 1998, 204), identified several potential parallels in Shetland, such as St Mary's Church at Culbinsbrough on Bressay, and possibly Kirkaby on Unst (Macdonald and Laing 1969, 127–128), as does recent survey work on Unst, Fetlar and Yell (Morris 2001). None of these however have been excavated and St Ninian's Isle remains a unique excavated Shetlandic example. Further south in Orkney, St Boniface, Papa Westray, was singled out by Lamb as being of particular promise (1995, 19–20), and has since been excavated with exciting results (Lowe 1998). In general, however, the distribution of known early stone churches in Scotland is sparse to say the least. This is probably because later sites were built directly on top of older ones, so obliterating the earlier evidence. For instance, Alcock in his comprehensive study of North Britain AD 550–850 (Alcock 2003) is able to list a small number of early church buildings for which there is material evidence, but north of the Forth-Clyde, acknowledges that 'material evidence of churches is extremely hard to find' (Alcock 2003, 285), and indeed excludes both the Northern and Western Isles from consideration due to the lack of evidence. Of those identified in mainland North Britain, only Heysham, on a headland on the NW coast of England (Potter and Andrews 1994) and Ardwall Isle, in the Solway Firth (Thomas 1967) are comparable to the early church building on St Ninian's Isle. Although survey and documentary research can identify possible early church buildings, excavation is ultimately the only means of confirming an early date, and this is usually a last resort on early church sites, the majority of which are below later churches and/or burial grounds, which are often still in use. As a result, churches pre-dating the Reformation in Scotland are sometimes lumped together in local tradition as 'early' chapels and, in the absence of documentary evidence, it can be difficult to unravel their true date. Recent survey by the author of sites in Lewis, in the Western Isles, that have been described as 'early chapels' in local tradition for instance, has shown that they are varied in size, form and date, some being in use from possibly the earliest Christian centuries, others not built until the late medieval period and used up to the 17th century (Barrowman 2005; 2008).

The sparse archive and the lack of any recorded floor layer make the dating of the early church building on St Ninian's Isle problematic. A *terminus post quem* of the late 7th century at the earliest is provided by the pre-Christian, short cist burial dated from the site. Also, if the first long cists on the site accompanied the first church on the site, which seems likely, then the earliest radiocarbon date for the early long cists on the site, gives a range of the late 7th to the late 9th centuries. Taken together this small sample of dates, and the associated shrine sculpture and cross stones, suggest that the church was already in existence in the 8th century, and was not built in the later, Norse, period (Morris 1990, 9–10; 1996b, 189), although there may be evidence that it continued in use into that period. Having said this, there is no evidence in the archives that an intermediate structural phase was excavated between the early church building and the layer of sand and medieval chapel above it, so whilst the early church may have been built any time in 8th century, it could well have continued in use into the Norse period, and indeed this may be suggested by the interment of burials in the 10th century on the site (see below).

There are layers of earth and sand 'infill' shown between the 'Celtic horizon' i.e. the early church,

and the medieval one, recorded on a rough sketch section in the archives (Figure 3.14), and it could be that this represents collapse of the earlier church building before the building of the later chapel above it, or perhaps the rubble foundations for the medieval chapel, but with no other information in the archives to clarify this partial section it is hard to say. Also, slides of the section below the wall *inside* the chapel show that the chapel walls were built straight onto the early church wall footings, so do not match up. Consequently it is hard to draw any definite conclusions as to how much time elapsed between the ruination of the first building and the construction of the second. Thomas' original assumption that 'the chapel on St Ninian's Isle was unquestionably rebuilt, but apparently not before the late eleventh or 12th century AD; and no structure phase can be seen between this horizon and the 8th century', is still supported by the recent re-assessment, although there is not enough evidence surviving in the archives to establish how long the earlier church building was in use and whether it had already been abandoned when the massive sand inundation of Phase IV occurred in the late 11th-12th centuries.

It has been suggested by Thomas that the exceptional carved shrine posts found in 1957 just south of the east end of the chapel in a 'curious little unroofed structure' which became known as the 'Founder's Grave', or 'Founder's Tomb' originated in the early church building, and date to the 8th century. The Founder's Tomb, despite its name, was a secondary feature, which Thomas argues was 'no more than a muddled, and probably very late, repositioning of corner-posts from two distinct shrines' (Thomas 1973, 20). He describes the mixing of the shrine posts two, possibly three, shrines as a secondary attempt to re-erect a shrine in the Middle Ages (1971, 157; 1983, 285; 1998, 96) and suggests that they would have originally stood in a church, probably at the east end, as the decoration would need to be looked at from the side, and possibly against the wall as the shrines would have needed support (see Thomas 1983, fig 122 in particular). This is supported by Helen Nisbet's recollections that the bones of the partially articulated and extremely flexed burial found in the Founder's Tomb, were in poor condition and appeared to have originated from a wetter environment than the free-draining sand. Thomas reconstructs the shrine within the early church building, and suggests that the hoard may even have been deposited within one of the shrines, given its find spot within *c*1m of the east end of the church (1983, 291), and it is possible that the translated human remains found in the Founder's Tomb also originated from the shrine in the damper clay environment of the deposits in the early church. In total nine shrine stones were found, identified by Thomas (1973, 20–26, 33–35, pls III–VII) as belonging to one double shrine 'A' (Stones 1–7, and

20; including 3 corner-posts, 2 median posts and 2 panel and lid fragments; Thomas 1973, fig 10), and a second, also possibly double, shrine 'B' (Stones 8–9; Thomas 1973, fig 11), although he has subsequently suggested that this latter shrine could comprise two separate shrines (Thomas 1983, 285; 1998, 96). Although Stevenson has argued for a date later in the 9th century (Stevenson 1981, 287–288), Thomas has since re-iterated his late 8th-century dates for composite shrines from Shetland, with 'a limited but undatable diffusion to Iona; and more such shrines during the 9th century' (Thomas 1998, 5).

A possible 'garth' or enclosure wall was excavated in 1957 to the north of, and parallel to, the north medieval nave wall; this was traced for almost 30ft (9.14m), at which point it was found to turn south and extended under the nave wall. This wall could possibly have been associated with the earlier church building, but was built onto sand, and references to it in the archive are sketchy and suggest that it may perhaps have been later, although with the lack of evidence this hard to confirm or deny. A separate bank further to the NE of the chapel was identified by the survey and trial trench excavations in 1999 as a bank of spoil from O'Dell's excavations (Harry 2000, 40–41) and not an enclosure wall.

The low cairn and infant graves and a warrior burial: Norse and native influences

To the south of the early church and long cists, and below the wind-blown sand, a small, low cairn of stones and quartz pebbles was excavated, partially defined on the south, east and north sides by a kerb of upright stones. It was set into the east side of the rubble cairn which covered the short cists, and within the outer kerb was divided using small upright stones, into six small compartments. Some of the outer kerb and compartments had been damaged by later burials on the site, but the form of the cairn was still clear. Four of the six compartments had small upright headstones marking the west end, and two of these headstones had double transom crosses incised on them. Below the cairn six infants were found, cut into the midden below, and covered by a thin layer of sand and re-deposited midden. The burial position of each infant corresponded to the areas defined above by the compartments, except that one compartment was found empty, and another held two burials, one truncating the other. There was also evidence in the fill of one of the burials (SK 10) that an earlier neonate infant had been present, which had then been displaced by the burial of the second. Each infant also had a small upright stone either side of the skull (a 'head box'). Comparisons with other known burial forms include Pictish kerbed cairns found in the north of Scotland (Ashmore 1980), but possibly also Viking (pagan) oval mounds, possibly constructed with small stones or outlined with a kerb of stones set on end, visible as stone set-

tings at sites such as Westness (S H H Kaland pers comm), Lunna, Lunnasting and Belmont, Unst in Shetland (Turner 1998, 111; see also McNeill and MacQueen 1996, 71; Graham-Campbell and Batey 1998, 56–65).

Radiocarbon measurements on the infants give a date range of the late 8th to mid 12th centuries (Figure 5.3), although by using the stratigraphical relationship evidenced by the truncated burials, this can be refined down through modelling to a 10th century date for the death of all of the infants. The modelling also confirms that the infants were buried sequentially over time, perhaps over 3 or 4 generations. Fisher (Chapter 3) dates the cross-incised headstones stylistically most likely to the Norse period (the late 10th or early 11th centuries), and draws comparisons in the square plaiting design to sculptured stones from nearby Papil. Stevenson has already identified, from amongst the sculptured stones of Shetland (including St Ninian's Isle and Papil) 'acceptable evidence of the continuation of Christian sculpture … in the period 800–1050' (Stevenson 1981, 291). Whilst the infant burials date to the Norse period, they were not necessarily themselves of Norse ethnicity, and indeed, the cairn below which they were buried, and their position adjacent to existing, earlier, short and long cists, suggests a continuity of native traditions and loyalty to place.

There is considerable evidence from the stone sculpture, and now from the burials on the site, for the continuation of native Christian influence in the Norse period at St Ninian's Isle. Forsyth (Chapter 2) is of the opinion that the text of the St Ninian's Isle ogham stone, if correctly interpreted, is 'scarcely later than the 7th century', but also that 'This is remarkably early and does not sit well with the general aspect of the script' and that it is quite possible that many of the Shetlandic examples date to the Norse period. Within the arena of the ongoing arguments surrounding the Norse impact on the native population of the Northern Isles (eg Crawford 1981; Buteux 1997, 262–263; Backlund 2001; Smith 2001; 2003; Barrett 2003a; 2004; Hunter 2007), there have been suggestions that the Norse, when they settled in Shetland, quickly adopted Christian practices and continued to use sites that already had local sacred importance, even perhaps with Christian and pagan communities co-existing (eg Barrett 2003b, 220–221). It is entirely possible therefore that the early church building at St Ninian's Isle, although probably built some time in the 8th century when the earliest long cists were interred on the site, may have continued in use in the 9th or 10th centuries.

The latest two burials excavated from below the sand in Phase III were an infant grave (SK 6) and an unusual adult burial (SK 5) interred in a short cist. The infant grave, aligned N–S, had probably originally been accompanied by a cist, on the west side of the short cists, although only two of the cist stones remained when the burial was excavated in 2000. It was thought initially that this burial, and an earlier dated juvenile burial SK 7 to the south of it, were cut directly into the Iron Age midden layers on the site, with no accompanying cist (Barrowman 2003, 58), although each burial was accompanied by a 'head-box'. Further study in post-excavation identified however that upright stones adjacent to these burials, uncovered both in 1959 and 2000, were probably the remains of cist stones. Infant (SK 6) has been radiocarbon dated to the first quarter of the 11th to the mid-12th century. The remains of the 'head box' could be used to suggest that it is a Christian burial, despite its N–S alignment, but cannot be confirmed. There is nothing specifically Christian about the adult burial (SK 5), situated immediately beside this infant grave. The remains of the partially articulated adult male had been arranged in an extremely flexed position, so as to be packed into short cist 303, from which the 1959 excavators had already removed charred human bone (if this was correctly recalled and identified as such; the bone has since been lost). Radiocarbon dating of burial SK 5 has produced a date of the first quarter of the 11th to early 13th century at the latest, and study of the remains shows that the body had been exhumed from elsewhere and then inserted into the cist in a partially decomposed state. Roberts' analysis of the pathology (Chapter 4) has demonstrated that the individual had died a violent death, suffering a sequence of injuries, culminating in his having his head lifted and his throat cut from behind. This warrior-like death led Roberts to suggest that a possible interpretation of events is that this individual was recovered from a battle site elsewhere, and brought back to St Ninian's Isle to be buried, where his remains were placed into a cist south of the church.

This burial stands out as being special, and the re-burial of the remains in a small stone cist is oddly reminiscent of Thomas' description of the translation of saints, relics, when the skeleton would be exhumed, possibly partially articulated, and then re-deposited in a stone shrine, which would only need to be long enough to house the longest bones (Thomas 1973, 17). What is missing from this scenario, however, is any indication, other than possibly the E–W alignment of the cist, that SK 5 is a Christian burial. The inclusion of a small iron knife with the burial could be taken as a grave good, but could also have been included with clothing (O'Brien and Roberts 1996, 165), and indeed, the clothing on the body, or the binding of it, would have facilitated the re-deposition of the remains in a semi-decomposed state (as indicated by the partical articulation). There are two other burials from the previous excavations that are described as being re-deposited extremely flexed 'with the thigh bones touching the skull' – a skeleton found in the pit dug in the Founder's Tomb in 1957 but subsequently lost, and a burial code-named 'Elizabeth', excavated from the site two years later and located during the archive study. Frustratingly, these tantalising glimpses of two further examples of extremely flexed, and possibly translated burials, have to remain as such as there is no more information to be found in the archives concerning them. The final laying to rest of the warrior on the Isle does suggest that it was still regarded as a special place in the later, Norse, centuries however.

The economy and diet of the Phase III burials

The evidence from the Phase II midden layers on the site suggests that the inhabitants on St Ninian's Isle prior to the 8th century operated a largely terrestrial, shore-based economy, and this fits well with a general picture that has been emerging over the last 20 years of limited deep-water fishing in the Iron Age (Barrett *et al* 1999 and refs therein; Barrett *et al* 2001a; 2001b). Once the site began to be used for burial instead of settlement, no further midden deposits are found, other than small pockets re-deposited in and around the burials, and in order to study the economy of the community that these burials represent, it was necessary to study the individuals themselves. At many sites in the Northern Isles a change in fishing strategies has been identified at the Late Iron Age/Viking period transition, with typically an intensification of fishing (see Barrett 2003a, 88–90; 2003b). The δ^{13}C isotope analysis of the skeletal material from St Ninian's Isle suggests however a largely terrestrial-based diet for all of the burials from the Isle that have been radiocarbon dated, from both the Late Iron Age and later periods, with the estimate of 8–26% marine component suggested for the four adult burials, and values of less than 30% for all the infant burials (Figures 3.33 and 4.70). Although it must be stressed that these are only estimates, it can be said that the measurements are certainly not strongly indicative of a marine diet (for an example of a strongly indicative result, see Richards and Mellars 1998; also Barrett *et al* 2000).

Within this portrayal of a largely terrestrial-based diet must be placed the six 10th-century infant burials (SK 8–13), buried together over a period of time under a low kerbed cairn. Study of the articulated remains has shown that the infants displayed signs of rickets (lack of Vitamin D) and malnourishment, implying that their mothers (all the infants were young enough that they were still breastfeeding) were also low in nutrients and this seems strange when the population lived in a coastal environment, a source of marine food high in Vitamin D.

Ultimately any further interpretation is only speculation, with such a small sample size and only estimates possible from the isotope measurements. The most obvious speculation however must be that these results reflect period of hardship resulting in starvation and malnourishment. Increasingly stormy conditions are suggested by the evidence of gradual sand inundation in this phase (Phase III, Late Iron Age onwards), and this may have had an effect on the crops and resources available to the local population, but it is also possible that an element of economic or social control of resources is in evidence here.

The St Ninian's Isle hoard

O'Dell wrote that 'No definitive traces of floor could be seen but at the horizon of this, as given by the lower edge of plastering on the wall, the hoard was found…' (O'Dell and Cain 1960, 5). Information in the archives confirms that the hoard was indeed found between the Iron Age levels and the medieval chapel foundations, i.e. at the level of the early church building, but its position is recorded only in relation to the base of the wall of this building. An archive slide (PLATE 9) shows the hoard set into the black clay midden layer below the church, with sand above it at the sides of the pit, confirming that the hoard was buried in Phase III, above the Iron Age structures and midden (Phase II), but below the sand (Phase IV). This does not therefore confirm that the hoard was deposited *into the floor* (or indeed, under the floor) whilst the earlier church building was in use, just that it was buried in the church during Phase III whilst the building was still open and accessible, and can have been deposited no earlier than the 8th century when the church was built.

Wilson recognised that the impact of the Vikings on the site was crucial in an almost circular argument whereby the date of the Viking attacks on Shetland was used to provide an end-date for the deposition of the treasure. On stylistic grounds he put the uninscribed sword chape (no. 16) and the pommel (no. 11) as the latest objects in the hoard, dated to within 25 years one way or the other of AD 800 (Wilson 1973, 147), but the date for the deposition of the hoard relies on the hypothesis that it was laid down in the face of Viking attacks. He concludes however that 'In the face of all these intangibles and on the basis of the available comparative material the situation must be left in this most unsatisfactory state' (Wilson 1973, 148). There is actually very little evidence of a 'hiatus' on the site around AD 800. In fact it could be said that there is evidence for continuity in burial practice. The arrangement of the short cists, long cists, infant burials and later, unusual (re-) burial within the same small area, with the remains dating to several points within a range of up to 500 years, suggests that St Ninian's Isle continued to be considered a special place by the population(s) who buried their dead and worshipped there. Despite the possible evidence for disruption and decline seen

in the pathology of the 10th century infant burials, continuity is suggested by the positioning of the long cists and infant burials, respecting the wall base and large pre-Christian cist burial interred in the late 7th to 8th centuries.

One could go further and say that given that the earliest dated identifiably Christian burial may be dated as late as the end of the 9th century, that the shrine posts have been dated by Stevenson to 'well into the 9th century' (1981), and that there is no end date for the use of the early church until the thick inundation of sand in the 11th or 12th centuries, then it is entirely possible archaeologically that the hoard was deposited in the 9th century, or even later, whilst the church was still open. There *is* evidence of decline and poverty from the site, but as we have seen above, it is evidenced a century later in the 10th century infant burials, and it can be speculated that this decline was due to cultural or economic upheaval at the time. Although the infants died during the late Viking Age, they need not have been of Norse ethnicity. Perhaps a native population continued to worship and bury on St Ninian's Isle into the Viking period, and it is not so much the threat of a Viking raid in AD 800 that is relevant in determining the end date for the dating and deposition of the hoard, but a declining and struggling population of the succeeding centuries. Indeed it was Thomas who initially suggested that 'it is wholly feasible, that this chapel and cemetery were in sporadic use through the ninth, tenth and eleventh centuries, if only by a few surviving Christian islanders or Picts under the domination of pagan Norse landholders' (Thomas 1973, 13).

As important as, and probably inextricably linked with, the date of the deposition of the hoard is the discussion of the nature of the objects in it. The original discussion immediately polarised in the main into two opposing arguments, secular or Christian, with the Christian suggestion coming first in the *Antiquity* article (Bruce-Mitford 1959, 259), to be developed by Monsignor McRoberts (1962; 1965). Bruce-Mitford however was not of the opinion that the hoard was ecclesiastical, saying 'the hoard is not church plate in any normal sense. For one thing, where are the chalice and paten?', and he goes on to suggest that the hoard represents either the personal wealth of various members of a small community that served the church, or more likely, the moveable wealth of the church in the form of gifts received (Bruce-Mitford 1959, 266–267). McRoberts' argument for the hoard being church plate, comprising 'six bowl-shaped silver chalices, a liturgical hand-basin, a hanging bowl or votive chalice, the abbot's brooch, eleven smaller brooches which were accessories of the deacon's vestments, two ornamental girdle-ends, a communion spoon, a knife for the Fractio panis and a silver pommel and three other silver fittings from a Eucharistic flabellum' provided a coherent explanation of the whole hoard, with all its peculiarities (McRoberts 1962, 313). Wilson subsequently countered this in his analysis of each separate piece (Wilson 1970, 2; 1973, 104–105, 110–111, 114–115; 117–122; 145), together with the general considerations that the hoard could not be ecclesiastical because there is no chalice, and that it differs completely from other hoards of an ecclesiastical nature found in the British Isles. He also argues that there is no single piece in the hoard that has a specifically Christian function, and that: 'It would … be an extremely odd community that would not include precious vessels of a specifically and uncontrovertibly ecclesiastical nature in its treasure' (Wilson 1973, 145).

Wilson concludes that 'If this hoard did originally belong to a church it must be seen as the secular portion of a rich treasury' (Wilson 1973, 145–146), with the differing states of wear on the objects indicating the accumulation of a family's silver, stating that 'It would seem reasonable to suppose that the hoard from St Ninian's Isle represents the treasure of a family brought for sanctuary to the church in the time of threatened attack and never reclaimed by its owners for obvious reasons' (Wilson 1973, 146). Recent interpretations have subsequently favoured the idea that the hoard was accumulated wealth, but possibly of several families, and that it was deposited in the church for safe-keeping, rather like an early medieval bank (first hinted at by Wilson 1973, 104–105; see also Graham-Campbell 2003a, 22–23, who favours Hughes 1980, supposing it to be a secular silver, but presented to the church; see also Henderson 1967).

The possibility that there are both secular and Christian objects in the hoard is hinted at by Wilson in relation to the brooches and other hoards containing brooches, such as the Trewhiddle hoard from Cornwall (Wilson 1973, 104–105). He confirms that the hoard objects were accumulated over a long time, the earliest piece, the hanging bowl, dated no later than AD 700, the un-inscribed sword chape and the sword pommel to the end of the 8th/beginning of the 9th centuries, and from a wide geographical distribution, with the collection, whilst Pictish, having stylistic links to Ireland, Northumbria and southern England (Wilson 1973, 144–146, 147), and Webster has more recently suggested Anglo-Saxon manufacture (cited in Graham-Campbell 2003a, 31–32; but see also Graham-Campbell forthcoming; Forsyth in Chapter 2 above; Forsyth forthcoming b). This widespread chronological and geographical spread can be explained by Wilson's suggestion (crediting Hughes) that 'in a society without a monetary economy, where exchange of precious objects would form a means of trade, there would seem to be no reason why churches should not keep a hoard of precious objects for economic purposes' (Wilson 1973, 104). This interpretation could be taken one step further to suggest that the hoard represents the wealth of several individuals or families, who gathered together at the point of deposition, to keep the hoard safe.

Such interpretation allows for the possibility that, although the hoard cannot be exclusively ecclesiastical, it may contain a combination of secular and ecclesiastical objects. Wilson's identification of the seven shallow bowls as tableware (Wilson 1973, 106–107) does not in itself rule out an ecclesiastical function, and he also describes how 'the idea of the spoon as a Christian object dies hard'. He attempts to kill it quite convincingly, however, stating that together with the claw-like object, 'there is no particle of evidence to suggest that it was ever used in the mass' (Wilson 1973, 118). The inscription on the sword chape (Forsyth in Chapter 2, above) is dismissed by Wilson as a 'pious platitude' because secular objects bearing Christian symbols are quite common in this period (Wilson 1973, 122). One must be careful however not to underestimate the words 'in the name of God the highest'. A community or individual with faith would believe that an object inscribed with these words would confer powerful protection, regardless of whether or not the object itself (in this case a sword chape) had a liturgical or other ecclesiastical use.

Ritchie has suggested that the treasure may have been the accumulated wealth of a Viking marauder (2003, 8–9; quoting Cummins 2001, 91–93; previously discounted by Wilson, 1973, 146). The accumulation of objects over time, their widespread geographical origins, the mixture of secular and ecclesiastical, could all support Ritchie's vision of 'the fruits of a Viking raid on eastern Scotland' (2003, 9). Indeed the opening up of the end date for the deposition of the hoard to the 9th, or even 10th, centuries, introduces the possibility that the depositor of the hoard was of Norse ethnicity. Hughes suggests that the early church on St Ninian's Isle was abandoned and possibly sacked at this time, with the shrine smashed and dispersed (Hughes 1980, 12), and this is possible from the archaeological evidence as the shrine posts were found in a dismantled and secondary position in the wind-blown sand adjacent to the medieval chapel. It is more likely however that the shrine posts were re-located when the medieval chapel was built above the earlier church and presumably re-used the stone from it.

The unusual addition of the porpoise jawbone in the hoard has also been pondered over since its discovery. Graham-Campbell follows the various discussions concerning the porpoise bone and concludes by agreeing with Wilson's own conclusion that 'The deeper meaning of this bone is an enigma' (Wilson 1973, 123–124; Graham-Campbell 2003a, 23–25). It is very unlikely that the porpoise bone 'may have been thought to have been a human bone which had been part of an early Pictish saint or teacher' (O'Dell 1960, 7) by the depositors of the hoard. The individuals associated with St Ninian's Isle were presumably familiar with porpoise bones, being situated on a coastal site where washed-up dead porpoise, whale and dolphin carcasses would have been a relatively frequent occurrence, and indeed important resource.

This leaves two possibilities: either the porpoise bone was not actually buried with the hoard and was mistakenly included with it by the 1958 excavators, or it was deliberately deposited with the treasure. Although the first suggestion is a possibility, in the archive discussed however there are records of pot sherds found next to the treasure which were recorded separately and not included with it, so surely if the porpoise bone was separate to the hoard, it would also have been recorded separately. Of greater significance is the green staining on the bone itself, noted when the hoard was first 'unpacked' by O'Dell, who described how 'entangled on the east side and below the bowls were the other items including the porpoise bone. Earth had penetrated but slightly between the objects and there were many voids' (D1/359/1/11/24 in the Shetland Archives). This does not allow for accidental digging into the black clayey midden below, and it can reasonably be said to dismiss the option that the porpoise bone was mistakenly included in the hoard. This leaves us with the conclusion that the bone was deliberately deposited with the silver and that the depositors of the hoard knew that it was a porpoise bone and deliberately chose to include it as such. It does not unfortunately tell us whether the depositor(s) and owner(s) of the hoard were one and the same person(s).

The suggestion that the hoard itself represents the 'moveable wealth' of the church, or community, could be expanded to suggest that the owner(s) of the hoard may have been 'moveable', perhaps itinerant churchmen, or from a nearby Christian community. The unusual collection of pieces in the hoard may reflect at one and the same time portable ecclesiastical objects used perhaps for the sacraments of baptism or communion in the early Church for instance, and also the precious items acquired through, and for, economic purposes. Perhaps the varied objects reflect the accumulated wealth of travelling early converts, in the form of donations made to the church community in south mainland Shetland, and also some of the liturgical equipment needed to celebrate the sacraments at the fledgling early Christian communities they visited. The porpoise jawbone would have had deeper symbolic meaning if the owners of the treasure were fellow sea voyagers - a companion to those travelling across the seas between the islands of Shetland. Or perhaps, as Thomas suggests in relation to the unique sculptured shrine-panel from nearby Papil, dated to the 9th century (Stevenson 1981, 288–289), the symbolism of the porpoise bone refers to a traditional story of the introduction of Christianity to Shetland, when early clerics (i.e. the papar themselves) travelled across the sea to carry out their missionary and pastoral duties (Thomas 1971, 156; Lamb 1995, 21).[2]

The treasure was found (and had been transported?) in a larch wood box (see Graham-Campbell 2003a, 25–27 for discussion of the identification of the larch wood). Spruce/larch (*Picea/Larix*) charcoal was also, with the heather family (*Ericaceae*) charcoal, the most frequently encountered type of charcoal evidenced from the 1999/2000 excavations at St Ninian's Isle, and this indicates the value put upon this important resource. Although, due to the flaked and small size of the charcoal recovered from the flotation samples, it was impossible for Miller and Ramsay (above) to be confident in separating these two very similar genera, two small finds of larger pieces of charcoal from the Phase II middens could be identified to *cf* Larch (*cf Larix*) and *cf* Spruce (*cf Picea*). In addition to this, the three large pieces of charcoal in the 1950s excavation assemblage comprised a single, large fragment of fir (*Abies*) charcoal, and two smaller and pieces identifiable only to fir/spruce/larch (*Abies/Picea/Larix*). Neither spruce nor larch is native to Scotland, and it is most likely that they came to the site as North American driftwood, as they did to other sites in Shetland, such as Papa Stour (Miller and Ramsay in Chapter 4), although spruce timber could also have been harvested or traded from southern Scandinavia. It is interesting that such driftwood, commonly found on sites in the treeless Northern and Western Isles (Dickson 1992) was used for the treasure box when it is generally accepted that the treasure itself does not originate from Shetland. Perhaps the treasure was brought to Shetland in a different container, and put into the larch wood box when it got to the Isles. There is no mention in the archives of the box having had any nails or other metal fittings, perhaps suggesting that the box was chosen at the time of deposition, rather than being a ceremonial 'presentation casket', or similar (Graham-Campbell 2003a, 25–26) that had travelled with the treasure.

What is perhaps more intriguing is the fact that the hoard was covered by a cross-incised stone, which Graham-Campbell has recently confirmed was placed with the cross face upwards, not downwards as previously reported by Thomas (1973, 37). This could be taken as evidence to support its deposition by a Christian. The fact that the stone was broken, with only part of the cross apparent, might question however whether the slab was deliberately chosen because it was a cross-slab, or whether it was simply a handy flat slab found nearby. It may be that there was no time for the depositor to scratch his/her own small cross onto a slab, and so the broken cross slab was chosen instead, but what is perhaps most telling is that this broken cross slab was lying around at all on a site that supposedly was in the nascent phase of Christian use, where the re-use of older slabs was not yet the norm. The fact that this stone was already broken and discarded in the first place in such a way as to be available as a handy cover for the treasure suggests that the hoard was buried when the church and Christian burial ground had been in use for some considerable time.

5.4 PHASES IV AND V: SAND INUNDATION, THE MEDIEVAL CHAPEL, FOUNDER'S TOMB AND BURIALS

The majority of the evidence for this phase of the site's history was excavated during the 1955–59 excavations, when over 6m of sand, and thousands of medieval and later interments, were removed. The major catastrophic sand inundation event occurs in Phase IV, when a thick layer of clean sand of at least a metre in depth completely covered the early church and burials of Phase III. Almost all of this sand was removed during the previous excavations, and so it has not been possible to analyse the sand build-up in any detail. However, a small proportion of it was left *in situ* after the 1959 excavation, in the NE corner of the excavation area south of the church, and slides taken at the time give an idea of the depth and extent of the sand.

Both the 1959 and 2000 excavation campaigns investigated four long cists that had been set into the top of the thick layer of sand outside the SE corner of the chapel. The previous excavators had referred to them as the earliest Christian interments, but this is not the case. They represent a later phase of long cists (Phase V, contemporary with the building and use of the medieval chapel) and differed from those excavated from Phase III *below* the thick layer of sand, in that they were of a consistent width along their entire length, and were narrower than the earlier cists. Wind-blown sand continued to accumulate after Phase IV and also in Phase V, although the removal of all the archaeological evidence for Phase V, other than four long cists and the standing remains of the medieval chapel, has precluded any study of this in the recent work. Shifting blown sand is a common and well-known occurrence in Shetland (and indeed Orkney and the Western Isles), and accounts for the survival of many well-preserved, remarkable archaeological sites.

A *terminus post quem* for the building of the medieval chapel on St Ninian's Isle is provided by the latest burials from Phase III (SK 5 and SK 6), which date to between the 11th and the end of the 12th centuries. Allowing for the sand inundation of Phase IV, the chapel could have been built any time from the mid-11th century onwards, at the earliest. The chapel was originally a unicameral building, probably with a sandy, or earthern, floor and a thatched roof, and a central doorway in the west wall. As Thomas suggests (1973, 12), a rounded chancel or 'apsidal east end' was then added, the east wall broken down and perhaps a chancel arch or small doorway made to gain access from the nave to the new chancel. It is possibly at this time, when the main altar was put into the rounded chancel, that a side altar was added in the SE interior corner of the nave, possibly with a second altar in mirror position in the NE corner. The chancel, which is also described in the archive as an 'apse' due to its rounded internal wall, may have been vaulted, and with its free standing dry-stone altar, was built onto wind-blown sand and may have required buttressing, or a thickening of the east end as support, whereas the nave was built onto what appears to be a foundation of rubble and sandy soil above the remains of the earlier church below. There is no evidence of an intermediate building between the early church and the medieval chapel. The walls were mortared, possibly at a later date. No evidence was found for any other internal stone furniture, other than the side altar.

There is no stratigraphic information from above these burials that could be used to narrow down the date range for the building of the medieval chapel, as this was all excavated in 1959. Four carved steatite grave markers (Thomas 1973; Stones 12–14, and 16), three of which had crosses carved on to them, and the fourth shaped into a cross, and a hogback grave cover (Stone 17), are dated by Thomas in his catalogue as 10th to 12th centuries, and 'Christian Norse' (Thomas 1973, 30). They could conceivably belong to the earlier Phase III which has evidence for 10th to late-11th century burials. The grave markers however were found in 1956 in the upper sandy levels of the site and probably therefore post-date the wind-blown sand of Phase IV. The hogback stone from the Isle was placed by Lang (1974, 231) in the 11th century, although St Boniface, Papa Westray, Orkney, is comparable to St Ninian's Isle, and has a 12th-century church and a hogback stone, which Lang dates to the 12th century (1974, 230). Cross-incised stones and a shrine panel fragment were also recovered from St Boniface (Lowe 1998), and Lowe is of the opinion that 'there is a greater likelihood, than not, of continuity between the earlier and later phases of ecclesiastical use of the site' (1998, 206). This has been arrived at through 'tight radiocarbon chronology' for the dating of plaggen soil, a buried ground surface and an overlying ash mound. He also argues that 'Continuity can also be inferred on the basis of the spatial relationship between the earlier and later cemeteries' (Lowe 1998, 206). At St Ninian's Isle there is not such 'tight radiocarbon chronology', with the only dating evidence available to date the Phase IV event of sand inundation, and the subsequent Phase V building of the medieval chapel, is that of the latest radiocarbon dates from Phase III of the latter half of the 11th century, to as late as the 13th century. It is very likely that the 'Christian Norse' sculpture catalogued by Thomas, particularly the hogback stone, may have originated from burials associated with the earlier unicameral phase of the medieval chapel. A small assemblage of finds recorded from the earlier excavations can be linked to the later phase of the chapel after the addition of the apsidal east end (a cresset lamp and a cross slab found face down in the nave during the 1957 excavations both probably date to the 12th–13th centuries), after the addition of the chancel, and fragments of a Limoges enamel cross found pushed into the stones of the altar may date to the 13th century or later, although the fragments are very worn and were most probably a later votive offering (see below). A lump of porphyry found in rubble in the chapel in 1956 is one of ten samples listed in the Kebister volume (Owen 1999), and a fragment found at St Nicholas chapel, Papa Stronsay (Lowe 2002, 92–94), adds a further example. This latter fragment is from a pre-11th century context, but the St Ninian's Isle example could as easily be a later.

The 12th century was a time of great vigour in the Church in the Northern Isles, when the Norse colonies of Orkney and Shetland were still both under the archipiscopal see of Trondheim, with a local bishop's seat at Birsay (Crawford 1987; Cant 1973; Øien 2005). There was also a growing economy in the Northern Isles in the Late Norse period, from the 12th-13th centuries and onwards (eg Clarke and Heald 2002 with refs). The Ninianic dedication undoubtedly belongs to the chapel built on the Isle at this time, when the Ninianic cult arrived in the North, although in the case of St Ninian's Isle, the dedication is made to a genuinely pre-Norse, Christian site (Thomson 2007, 522–523).

Cant describes the chapel as relatively ambitious in design, but not a head church in the parochial system developed in Shetland from the 12th century onwards (Cant 1975, 9–10). In general size and form the later chapel is reminiscent of many contemporary small rural chapels identified in Shetland, Orkney and the Western Isles (eg Cant 1975, 9–13, fig 2; Flemming and Woolf 1992; Morris 1990; 2001; Morris and Brady 1999; Brady 2000; Brady and Johnson 1998; 2000; Brady and Morris 2000; Lowe et al 2000; Barrowman 2005; 2008). The dimensions of the St Ninian's Isle chapel (nave 7 x 5.1m, chancel 4.5 x 3.8m) are comparable to other bi-cameral chapels in north and west Scotland (eg see Flemming and Woolf 1992; 341–343, 349, Appendix), such as Teampall Pheadair, Siadar and Teampall Eoin in Bragar, Lewis (Barrowman 2008) and St Nicholas on Papa Stronsay, Orkney. The latter example is directly comparable to that on St Ninian's Isle, being originally a unicameral structure 5.32 x 3.93m, with a small (albeit square-ended) chancel 2.7 x 2.5m internally, added later. In its final form it had three altars: two in the corners of the nave, one at the east end of the chancel; Lowe 2002, 87; Lowe et al 2000. Similarly, the chapel also had a sandy mortar floor, and an altar slab was found broken with three of the four fragments set into the floor (the fourth was unstratified) (Lowe 2002, 88–90). The slab is provisionally dated to the 11th or 12th centuries and is probably associated with the final refurbishment of the building into the form it is seen in now.

The Founder's Tomb containing the shrine posts at St Ninian's Isle is contemporary with, or was added to, the medieval chapel. The re-positioning of the shrine posts from their original location (within the earlier church?) into this unroofed structure may

have become necessary when the later chapel was first built. For comparisons for this structure from the later Middle Ages onwards, it is possible to look to the tombs built on the north side of the presbytery in later medieval churches (see Fawcett 1996), and also perhaps in the later, post-Reformation practice of erecting a separate burial place or aisle, attached to a church, to enabling the wealthy to be buried as near as possible to the church (Dunbar 1996). A burial excavated in the Founder's Tomb in 1957 was described as 're-located' and was clearly in an extremely flexed, partially disarticulated position, 'with the thigh bones touching the skull'. It is not possible to tell from the photographs or brief description whether this jumble of bones originated from below the bottom of the later medieval structure, or from within it. It is possible that they were the translated remains from the original corner post shrine.

Few cemeteries dating to the medieval period have been excavated in the Northern and Western Isles, and this is usually because they are below a later burial ground, which is often still in use. The discovery of a medieval cemetery in Shetland at nearby Scalloway is unusual, but as Sharples points out, this is due to the restrictions on excavation rather than anything else. Medieval cemeteries over or around abandoned churches are well-evidenced in the isles; what is unusual about Scalloway is that the burial ground was abandoned and forgotten (Sharples 1998, 197). Overall the 14th-16th centuries and the 'Scottification' of Shetland society are still poorly understood (Bigelow 1992, 13–15).

Little remains of the medieval post-medieval period on the site. The Isle was inhabited until the last quarter of the eighteenth century, and a small trial trench excavated in 1999 revealed evidence of cultivation in the recent past (Harry 2000, 42–43) 80m north of the chapel, on the east side of the Isle. Almost all of the late medieval and post-medieval burials on the site were removed in the 1950s excavations, but three burials were found in 1999 and 2000 that date to this period: two only partially intact, and one neonate infant buried up against the chancel wall. Excavations in Trench 2 in 2000 found evidence for post-medieval burials (Barrowman 2000), and the archive study has identified skeletal material held in the Natural History Museum in London that derives from the 1950s spoil heaps, and is no doubt of medieval/post-medieval date. There is also a small assemblage of late medieval (13th–14th century) and post-medieval (16th–17th century) pottery sherds amongst the Shetland Museum collection, discussed by Will (Chapter 3), that may derive from settlement close to the medieval chapel. These sherds date to a period when Shetland had strong trading links with mainland Europe, being on an important shipping route from Scandinavia to Britain and Western Europe, particularly Holland. A late 17th-century coin and worn Limoges enamel cross fragments found pushed into the fabric of the altar may be votive offerings by visitors to the Isle at that time (see Stevenson 1986 who discusses votive coin deposition at Deerness, and elsewhere in Orkney and Shetland), although the chapel was demolished by the mid-18th century. It is also possible that the enamel fragments originated from a burial, as eg at Teampall Bhuirigh, Benbecula in the Western Isles (Caldwell 1978). Also, the burial close to the chapel wall of the neonate infant, which was possibly un-baptized and therefore not able to be buried in a functioning graveyard, suggests that the chapel was still viewed as a spiritual and holy place after the Reformation (as also at Deerness). The chapel was finally demolished by John Bruce Stewart in 1744, when the stone was re-used to build a revetment wall at the east side of the Isle.

5.5 PHASE VI: O'DELL'S EXCAVATIONS

At the end of the final season of O'Dell's excavations in 1959, the site was backfilled and consolidated, with the main features reconstructed, and recorded on a final plan. A retaining wall was built around the foot of the steep sandy banks around the 6m deep trench that had been dug into the sandy hill side south of the chapel, and the trench inside the chapel was backfilled and the position of the treasure marked. A mixture of finds was recovered from the 1950s backfill and topsoil in these features. Batey (Chapter 4) discusses a possible pot lid and hones, pumice and a complete gaming piece with grozed edges, all of which belong to the Iron Age levels and were found re-deposited and out of context. Metalwork finds include two conjoining pieces of an iron key, identified by Batey as being common in the 8th–11th centuries but found in backfill and topsoil. A broken fragment of a knife blade, with part of the tang remaining, was also found, and may originally have been from another grave context disturbed by O'Dell's excavations, like the example found with SK 5 in Phase III, because it was found in the back-fill from the earlier work, although Batey concludes that a settlement context would perhaps be more usual. The remaining metalwork assemblage for this comprises eleven iron nails and roves, identified as being of different forms, which Batey suggests mostly derive from the re-use of old timbers. A 1957 halfpenny that may have been dropped by the excavators completes the metalwork assemblage. A broken antler bead, comparable to that found in phase III and the previous excavations was found in backfill over the rubble mound and two worked pieces of bone, possibly used as handles or awls, both originally derive from the Iron Age levels of Phase II. The remaining assemblage comprises a scattering of coarse pottery sherds throughout the contexts, amounting to 23 vessels in total. Again these would have derived originally from the earlier midden contexts on the site.

The majority of the animal bone found from the site was found in these late phases, re-deposited in the topsoil and backfill from earlier contexts. Rabbit bones were ubiquitous. Fish bone was also present in these upper phases, although in lesser numbers than earlier phases, and marine shells were scattered throughout the backfill and topsoil layers. Duffy's analysis of the disarticulated bone assemblage from both the 1950s and 1999/2000 excavation campaigns studies the reasons for the drop in representation of hand and foot bones in Phase VI, concluding that that there existed a significant recovery bias in favour of particular skeletal elements during the 1950s work. He identifies a total minimum of 16 adult and 12 juvenile individuals represented by the disarticulated bone from these upper phases, although they are but a small remnant of the thousands of medieval and later interments that were removed, together with sand and rubble, from the area south of the chapel.

5.6 CONCLUSION

O'Dell's excavations on St Ninian's Isle uncovered one of the most fascinating and important Late Iron Age and Norse/medieval sites in Scotland, and close study, re-examination and new analyses of the fragmentary archive notes, published accounts and excavated material form the 1950s excavations can still tell us much about this important site. Alan Small's notes and slides, together with Helen Nisbet's site diary, photographs and slides are the primary excavation record for the 1950s excavations.

There is no doubt that the site was first an Iron Age settlement, probably of cellular buildings and paving, and all indications from the excavations are that it was an extensive settlement, rebuilt and reused over several phases of occupation. This settlement remains largely intact, lying on the clay subsoil below the extensive layers of wind-blown sand on the east side of the Isle. The artefactual assemblage from the middens overlying the abandoned settlement date to the Late Iron Age (but no later than the 7th century AD), although there are tiny glimpses of Early Iron Age/Late Bronze Age occupation in the form of single sherds in the ceramic assemblage from the 1950s excavations which could suggest older occupation in the local vicinity.

After the settlement had been abandoned the site was used for burial and ritual, both pre-Christian and Christian, and no further evidence for structures or domestic occupation was found. Short cist cremations were excavated, set into a thick midden layer over the Iron Age structures below the chapel on the site, and a group of short cists were found arranged around a stonework base, and bounded on one side by paving in the trench on the south side of the chapel. An adult female burial had been placed in a prone and twisted position in the largest of the short cists in the late 7th to 8th centuries, and the whole group was covered in a low stone cairn, at the edges of which were found bone and antler beads. At the side and above the mound two long cists were excavated, one containing an extended inhumation that has been dated to the late 7th to late 9th centuries. These cists represent the earliest evidence for Christian burial, although the stone sculpture from the previous excavations may suggest an earlier date in the 7th century for the introduction of Christianity to the site.

The arrangement of the cists, burials and associated burial features on the site suggest gradual change and assimilation, where the loyalty to place and respect for what had gone before was strong. It is undoubtedly the already-existing specialness of place that led this area on St Ninian's Isle to be chosen for the building of a small church in the 8th century. This superimposition of the new Faith onto the old is a common pattern on Late Iron Age sites in the Northern Isles and the outstanding collection of shrine posts and other stone sculpture, demonstrate that this was no ordinary place, and of particular significance during the early years of Christianity on Shetland. This is undoubtedly why the church on St Ninian's Isle was chosen as the site for the hiding of the magnificent hoard: a special place that conferred special protection.

Continuity of place is evidenced in the small assemblage of Norse burials, which were interred into the edges of the same stone cairn that originally covered the short cists buried two centuries earlier. A study of the archive evidence has shown that the church may still have been in use at this time in the 9th or 10th centuries, and that the hoard need not necessarily have been deposited in the early church in AD 800 in the face of Viking attack. The ogham stone has also been re-assessed and thought as likely to be 10th century as 7th century, and could fit with the growing corpus of 10th century sculpture from Shetland. The indications of malnutrition amongst the group of infant burials interred below a complex of upright stones filled with pebbles and marked with small headstones carved with crosses and dated to the 10th century may be taken as evidence of hardship and straightened times amongst the population buried on the Isle at this time. Despite the 10th-century date and the stylistically Norse crosses, the choice of resting place for these infants, alongside older burials and into the side of an existing mound, strongly suggests a native rather than an incoming population was buried here. The latest dated burials from this phase date to the 11th/12th centuries. An infant in a cist and an adult male burial excavated from a short cist, who, when analysed, was found to have suffered a violent death

and been moved post-mortem, again suggesting that the Isle was considered a special place.

Following thick and catastrophic inundations of wind-blown sand in the 11th or 12th centuries, a new chapel was built over the old, at first just a small nave, with accompanying long cists buried at the south and east sides. Subsequently an internally rounded chancel was added with a free-standing dry-stone altar. This chapel was abandoned in the 18th century, but the graveyard at the site continued to be used through the post-medieval period and into the 19th century.

The physical situation of St Ninian's Isle, at once removed from the mainland yet easily accessible and visible, gives it a feeling of being a special place apart, and Professor Andrew O'Dell, a talented historical geographer with an enthusiasm for Shetland and the Isles, no doubt felt this himself when he first stepped foot on it. It is hoped that the recent work and research presented in this volume has built upon his enthusiasm in bringing out into the wider domain the remarkable archaeological site he uncovered there.

Notes

[1] I am grateful to Prof James Graham-Campbell, who reminded me to include the portion of the west wall of the earlier chapel that appears on O'Dell's 1959 plan (published in O'Dell and Cain, 1960, fig 1), and that the west wall, whilst not on Thomas' published plan in the 1973 volume, is recorded on his original sketch-plan made after interviewing O'Dell, and meeting with Alan Small whilst researching the carved stones from the site.

[2] Many primary Shetland Christian sites were given a 'Papa' place-name by the Norse, from *papar*, meaning priests, eg Papil Geo, Noss, and Papil, West Burra (although see MacDonald 2002; Gammeltoft 2004) and Lamb concludes that the *papar* names in the Northern Isles indicate 'rich, revenue-yielding agricultural estates which were the basis of all wealth and social position in early medieval society' (Lamb 1995, 17). Recent work by the 'Papar project' (http://www.rcahms.gov.uk/papar/) directed by Crawford, Ballin Smith and Simpson, has concentrated on looking at the depth of soils associated with *papar* sites in Orkney, Caithness, Shetland and the Western Isles to investigate this hypothesis (see Simpson with Guttmann 2002; Ballin Smith pers comm; Ballin Smith *et al* 2004; Crawford 2005), and excavations by colleagues on Brei Holm, Papa Stour, a cliff stack site traditionally described as an eremitic monastic settlement (Lamb 1973, 89; Brady 2002; Brady and Batey 2009) has produced crucial radiocarbon dating evidence from residues from coarse pottery, typologically dated to the Late Iron Age to Norse periods, although 'nothing recovered in this limited excavation can establish any link between this site and an ecclesiastical use …' (Brady 2002, 81). In relation to *papar* names in Orkney, Thomson writes 'the papar are likely to have been clergy living in places where they were associated with secular communities rather than hermits seeking isolation' (Thomson 2007, 515).

APPENDIX 1

Finds in the Shetland Museum from
O'Dell's excavations in 1958–59

Box: A21.2000. St Ninian's Isle Items 797 and 798

★ = illustrated, EIA = Early Iron Age, LIA = Later Iron Age

Number	Material	Description	No. of pieces	Label	Year	Item no.
A21.2000.1a	Pottery	LIA (22 body and one base sherds)	23	*Ian and Alan K15 h (peat ash) bde associated with structure*		798
A21.2000.1b★	Stone	Stone with perforation	1	*12" below. Iron Age level (pavement) 29/7/59 Pot and sandstone with hole!*	1959	798
A21.2000.2a	Pottery	LIA (3 rim and 5 body sherds)	8	*9.8.59 Y.3.a/b Outside lower of two box kerbstone edges in peat ash. 69" below kerbstone. Bone found 11/2 ft to ESE. Also a drawing*	1959	798
A21.2000.2b★	Animal bone	Worked sheep/goat tibia, possibly turned	1	*Ditto*	1959	798
A21.2000.3	Animal bone	Burnt indet unworked bone	1	*2X*		798
A21.2000.4★	Pottery	LIA (1 rim and 3 body conjoining sherds)	4	*S*		798
A21.2000.5	Pottery	LIA conjoining body sherds	26	*Ek*		798
A21.2000.6a	Pottery	LIA base and body sherds	2	*Y.3.h 54" below medieval fdation to S of large kerbstone*		798
A21.2000.6b	Pumice	Water-rounded pumice	1	*Ditto*		798
A21.2000.7★	Pumice	Worked pumice	1			798
A21.2000.8a	Animal bone	Sheep/goat, cow and indet frags	10	*K11g*		798
A21.2000.8b	Pumice	Worked pumice	1	*Ditto*		798
A21.2000.9a	Pottery	LIA 5 rim and 28 body conjoining sherds	32	*None*		798
A21.2000.9b	Pumice	Worked pumice	1	*Ditto*		798
A21.2000.10a	Pottery	Body sherds	13	*Bf*		797
A21.2000.10b	Human bone	Infant left femur	1	*Ditto*		797
A21.2000.10c	Animal bone	Cow and indet animal bone and teeth	6	*Ditto*		797
A21.2000.11	Pumice	Water-rounded pumice	1	*Pumice centre of nave*		798
A21.2000.12a	Animal bone	Cow bone frags and teeth	4	*Ba*		797
A21.2000.12b	Human bone	Highly eroded human manible frags	3	*Ditto*		797
A21.2000.13a	Industrial waste	Slag	1	*Below X1*		798
A21.2000.13b	Animal bone	Cow and indet animal bone frags and teeth	14	*Ditto*		798
A21.2000.15a★	Pottery	LIA base, 3 body sherds and 2 frags	6	*Be*		798
A21.2000.15b	Animal bone	Cow and indet animal bone frags and teeth	10	*Ditto*		798
A21.2000.16a	Pottery	LIA 1 rim, 6 body sherds and 3 frags	10	*June Jean Greig X4a 59" below Med foundations level*		797
A21.2000.16b	Human bone	Right fifth metacarpal, unfused end	1	*Ditto*		797
A21.2000.17a	Pottery	LIA 2 body sherds and 2 frags	4	*Douglas US 28/7/59 5Ug 5 Ub 54" below Med*	1959	797
A21.2000.17b★	Schist	Worked schist object with two partial holes along edge	1	*Ditto*		797
A21.2000.18a	Pottery	LIA body sherds	1	*U3i - GO or CO" Douglas*		798
A21.2000.18b	Pumice	Worked pumice	1	*Ditto*		798
A21.2000.19a	Pottery	LIA body sherd	1	*U.6.e pot ca 5ft below fdation. Pumice directly below pot*		798
A21.2000.19b	Pumice	Water-rounded pumice	1	*Ditto*		798
A21.2000.20a	Pottery	LIA body sherds	5	*Af*		798

Number	Material	Description	No. of pieces	Label	Year	Item no.
A21.2000.20b★	Stone	Gaming pieces	2	Ditto		798
A21.2000.21a	Pottery	LIA body sherds	2	Sun 9th Aug Y1 - in 65"	1959	798
A21.2000.21b	Glass	Yellow glass bead	1	Ditto	1959	798
A21.2000.22a	Pottery	LIA 5 body sherds and 1 base	6	El		798
A21.2000.22b	Stone	Gaming piece?	1	Ditto		798
A21.2000.22c	Quartz	Unworked quartz frag	1	Ditto		798
A21.2000.23a	Pottery	LIA body sherds	5	Bk		798
A21.2000.23b	Pumice	Worked pumice	1	Ditto		798
A21.2000.24	Pottery	LIA body sherd	1	Z		798
A21.2000.25	Pottery	LIA body sherd	1	Ed		798
A21.2000.26	Flint	Unworked flint waste chips	2	Margaret 8.7.59 In SE of nave above whalebone complex	1959	798
A21.2000.27	Pottery	LIA body sherd	1	Ea		798
A21.2000.28	Pottery	LIA 3 body and 2 rim sherds	5	E		798
A21.2000.29	Pottery	LIA body sherds	2	D. South 2		798
A21.2000.30★	Pottery	LIA base and 32 body conjoining sherds	33	Site F below D North Ian's pot		798
A21.2000.31★	Pottery	LIA body sherds (one sherd illus)	3	L.12.h. ca.1ft. Below occupation level		798
A21.2000.32	Pottery	LIA body sherds	2	Ee		798
A21.2000.33	Pottery	LIA 2 body and 1 frag conjoining	3	Eq		798
A21.2000.34★	Pottery	LIA 18 body and 2 conjoining rim sherds	20	H and H Paper with map taken out of bag and attached to specimen list		798
A21.2000.35	Pottery	LIA 6 body and 1 base sherd	7	K12 a and d Near top of occupation surface		798
A21.2000.36	Pottery	LIA body sherds	3	A		798
A21.2000.37	Pottery	LIA base sherds	3	CB		798
A21.2000.38	Pottery	LIA body sherd	1	8		798
A21.2000.39	Pottery	LIA body sherds	3	Ad		798
A21.2000.40	Pottery	LIA 3 body sherds and 2 base	5	None		798
A21.2000.41	Pottery	LIA 3 body sherds and 1 base	4	Alan's Pit Below X1		798
A21.2000.42	Pottery	LIA 2 body sherds and 1 rim	3	Stewart X4f 7/9/59 SE Corner of square box 75" below	1959	798
A21.2000.43a	Pottery	LIA body sherds	1	P and Q		798
A21.2000.43b	Animal bone	Sheep/goat, cow and indet animal bone frags and teeth	14	Ditto		798
A21.2000.44	Pottery	LIA body sherds, 3 conjoining	5	Ak		798
A21.2000.45	Pottery	LIA body sherds	1	Top of Prof's body		798
A21.2000.46	Pottery	LIA body sherds	2	Em		798
A21.2000.47	Pottery	LIA 2 body sherds and 1 base	3	John and Evie's Pit		798
A21.2000.48	Pottery	LIA base sherd	1	Aa		798
A21.2000.49a	Pottery	LIA rim sherd	1	White stone - S trench		798
A21.2000.49b	Animal bone	Cow tooth	1	Ditto		798
A21.2000.50	Pottery	LIA body sherds	3	X3		798
A21.2000.51a	Iron	Very corroded frags of Fe bolt	1	En		798
A21.2000.51b	Pottery	LIA body sherds	1	Ditto		798
A21.2000.52	Pottery	LIA body sherds	1	Cc		798
A21.2000.53	Pottery	LIA body sherds	1	Y5e 71" and 72" 4/8/59 Douglas	1959	798
A21.2000.54	Pottery	LIA body sherds	1	Eh		798
A21.2000.55	Pottery	LIA body sherds	2	6 x fg 80" below Just above pavement - set on "glay"?hut circle, Alan 7/8/59	1959	798
A21.2000.56	Animal bone	Cow bone in poor condition	1	G.13.d 6" Below occupation surface		798
A21.2000.57	Pottery	LIA body sherds	2	Bd		798
A21.2000.57a	Pottery	LIA body sherd	1	None		798
A21.2000.58	Pottery	LIA 5 body sherds and 1 base sherd	6	Ag		798
A21.2000.59	Pottery	LIA body sherd	1	P		798
A21.2000.60	Industrial waste	Slag, conjoining	6	None		798
A21.2000.61	Peat	Four peat frags	4	Ef		798
A21.2000.62	Pottery	LIA body sherd	1	Bl		798
A21.2000.63	Pottery	LIA base and 2 conjoining body sherds	3	?E about 1 ft above Ian's pot		798
A21.2000.64	Pottery	LIA 4 body and 1 rim sherd	5	Ab		798
A21.2000.65	Pottery	LIA body sherd	1	10x		798
A21.2000.66	Pottery	LIA body sherd	1	Bn		798
A21.2000.67	Pottery	LIA 5 body sherds, 3 conjoining and 1 frag	6	Bc		798
A21.2000.68	Pottery	LIA body sherds	2	"Ac"		798

Number	Material	Description	No. of pieces	Label	Year	Item no.
A21.2000.69a	Charcoal	Abies (Fir) charcoal	1	*Ca*		798
A21.2000.69b	Pottery	LIA body sherd	1	*Ditto*		798
A21.2000.70a	Peat	5 lumps of peat	5	*Bb*		798
A21.2000.70b	Pottery	LIA body sherds	2	*Ditto*		798
A21.2000.71	Pottery	LIA 7 body sherds and 3 rim	10	*Ae*		798
A21.2000.72	Pottery	LIA body sherd	1	*Bd*		798
A21.2000.73★	Pottery	LIA 2 rim sherds conjoining and 1 body poss also conjoining and 3 separate conjoining sherds of body	6	*J.a.n 6" below occupation surface*		798
A21.2000.74a	Peat	Two frags of peat, conjoining	2	*Sheila 8.7.59 W third of hollow*	1959	798
A21.2000.74b	Pottery	LIA body sherds: 2, 2 conjoining and 2 conjoining	6	*Ditto*		798
A21.2000.74c	Fish bone	One gunard dentary and 2 unident fish bone	3	*Ditto*		798
A21.2000.75	Pottery	LIA 7 body, 1 base and 1 rim	9	*nave*		798
A21.2000.76	Pottery	LIA 2 body sherds and 1 base	3	*Below X1*		798
A21.2000.77a	Pottery	LIA body sherds	2	*I12 ef 6" I.12.e.qf. In top 6in*		798
A21.2000.77b	Iron	Worn Fe frags of rivet/nail head?	1	*Ditto*		798
A21.2000.78	Pottery	LIA 3 rim, 3 bases and 6 body sherds	12	*OG or O6 Douglas Depth behind wall, 6ft to thin slab flooring*		797
A21.2000.79	Pottery	LIA 2 base, 8 body sherds and 1 frag	11	*Wed 5th Aug J14 n 12" below level of broad diagonal wall*	1959	797
A21.2000.80	Pottery	LIA body sherds	2	*G.19.I alongside cist wall above skull - ?part of midden waste*		797
A21.2000.81	Pottery	LIA body sherds	3	*Alan 29/7/59 2Uf 48" below*	1959	797
A21.2000.82	Pottery	LIA body sherds	3	*Thurs Aug 6th Nave X7n 66" below Medieval foundations*	1959	797
A21.2000.83	Pottery	LIA body sherds	2	*D south 4*		797
A21.2000.84	Pottery	LIA body sherd	1	*V.3.d. 60" below medieval fdation*		797
A21.2000.85	Pottery	LIA body sherds	5	*Irene 25/7/59 X4 a/d 64" below Med Horiz*	1959	797
A21.2000.86	Pottery	LIA frag and sherd conjoining	2	*58" V3i Douglas*		797
A21.2000.87a	Pottery	LIA body sherds	2	*Y4e 62"*		797
A21.2000.87b	Charcoal	Picea/Abies/Larix (Spruce/Fir/Larch) charcoal frags	20	*Ditto*		797
A21.2000.88	Pottery	LIA body sherds	2	*Wz.f./I 58" Douglas*		797
A21.2000.89	Pottery	LIA body sherds	6	*Ian and Alan 30/7/59 I 14 g 5 pot 27" below Med fdn*	1959	797
A21.2000.90a	Fish bone	Two gunard bones and 31 unident fish bone frags	33	*H.18.I immediately below top stones*		797
A21.2000.90b	Industrial waste	2 conjoining slag pieces	2	*Ditto*		797
A21.2000.90c	Shell	Littorina littorea (edible periwinkle) shells	4	*Ditto*		797
A21.2000.91a	Tile	Tile sherd	1	*None*		797
A21.2000.91b	Pottery	Medieval SMR hollow handle	1	*Ditto*		797
A21.2000.91c	Industrial waste	VFA	1	*Ditto*		797
A21.2000.91d	Pottery	Glazed medieval LHDW body conjoining sherds	2	*Ditto*		797
A21.2000.91e	Pottery	N European medieval hollow rod handle, 16th/17th century	?	*Ditto*		797
A21.2000.92a	Animal bone	Sheep/goat bone, conjoining	2	*W third of hollow*		797
A21.2000.92b	Pottery	LIA rim sherd	1	*Ditto*		797
A21.2000.93	Pottery	LIA base sherd	1	*X36 50" below Med hrizon Base Irene*		797
A21.2000.94	Pottery	LIA 2 body sherds and 1 base	3	*6/8/59 4Yd/e 68" Douglas*	1959	797
A21.2000.95	Pottery	LIA body sherds	1	*F13 h top layer top of occupation layer*		797
A21.2000.96	Pottery	LIA body sherds	2	*irene 29/7/59 X4 g/h 64" below med horizon*	1959	797
A21.2000.97	Pottery	LIA body sherds	3	Three labels: (1) *A plan of excavation pits.* (2) *Plan of location of pits within church.* (3) *John and Eric 30.6.59*	1959	797
A21.2000.98	Pottery	LIA 7 body and 1 rim sherd	8	*H14e 18-27" below occ layer. Ian 3/8/59*	1959	797
A21.2000.99	Pottery	LIA 10 body and 1 base	11	*Ian and Alan J15 h/I 10" below Iron Age level (associated with structure P.1 29/7/59*	1959	797
A21.2000.100a	Burnt bone	2 conjoining frags of indet burnt bone	2	*Close together at the edge of "cairn" about 11/2 to 2 ft below occupation surface. L.16. hdi. M.17.a*		798
A21.2000.100b	Pottery	LIA 2 body, 1 basal sherds and 1 frag	4	*Ditto*		798

Number	Material	Description	No. of pieces	Label	Year	Item no.
A21.2000.101a	Pottery	LIA 2 body sherds, 1 rim and 1 base	4	*Thur 6 Aug Nave X6 /\ 70" below medieval foundations*	1959	798
A21.2000.101b	Charcoal	4 pieces of Picea/Abies/Larix (Spruce/Fir/Larch) charcoal	4	Ditto	1959	798
A21.2000.102	Pottery	LIA body sherd	1	*3Vd. 55" Douglas*		798
A21.2000.103a	Pottery	LIA 2 body sherds, 1 base sherd	3	*DS2 ?Iron nails worked down from burial ?microlith*		798
A21.2000.103b	Iron	Corroded Fe coffin fittings? 2 nail shanks and one poss nail head	3	Ditto		798
A21.2000.103c	Flint	Waste chip, probably natural	1	Ditto		798
A21.2000.104★	Pottery	LIA 2 rims and 10 body sherds; one sherd illus	12	None		798
A21.2000.105	Pottery	LIA 2 body sherds	2	*9z or zb*		798
A21.2000.106a	Pottery	LIA 1 base and 1 body	2	*X4 - North end*		798
A21.2000.106b	Peat	Frag of peat	1	Ditto		798
A21.2000.107	Pottery	LIA 1 base and 5 body	6	*Ae*		798
A21.2000.108	Pottery	LIA 29 body sherds, very thin, burnished	29	*Irene 28/7/59 X4 g 64" Below med. Found*	1959	798
A21.2000.109	Pottery	LIA 5 body sherds, 3 of which conjoin	5	*F (Below D north)*		798
A21.2000.110	Pottery	LIA 2 body sherds	2	*K.10,i*		798
A21.2000.111	Pottery	LIA 1 base and 1 frag	2	*Eb*		798
A21.2000.112	Pottery	LIA abraded body sherd	1	*Prof's wall*		798
A21.2000.113	Pottery	LIA body sherd	1	*I*		798
A21.2000.114	Pottery	LIA body sherd	1	*Bm*		798
A21.2000.115	Pottery	LIA frag	1	*6*		798
A21.2000.116	Pottery	Large fragment of 16th/17th century N European earthernware pipkin rim sherd with handle scar	1	*Outside W wall to S of main door c. 1 ft above founds*		797
A21.2000.117	Pottery	LIA 2 body sherds	2	*Douglas 4 Ue 28/7/59 51" below Med hor*	1959	797
A21.2000.118	Pottery	LIA 5 body sherds	5	*DSz or 2 - western facies*		797
A21.2000.119	Pottery	LIA 4 body sherds	4	*Douglas 3/8/59 2 Wd 50" below medieval horizon*	1959	797
A21.2000.120a	Pottery	LIA 5 body sherds and 1 rim	6	*Helen W third of hollow*		797
A21.2000.120b	Animal/human bone	Cow tooth, indet bone and 2 human teeth	4	Ditto		797
A21.2000.121	Pottery	LIA body sherds	2	*Y.4.h 59" below medieval foundation*		797
A21.2000.122a	Whale bone	Whale bone frags	2	*U6a Douglas same pot as U.6*		797
A21.2000.122b	Pottery	LIA 1 rim, 8 body sherds and 2 frags	11	Ditto		797
A21.2000.123a	Pottery	LIA 18 body, 1 base and 1 rim	20	*71" below Medieval foundations level x5g*		797
A21.2000.123b	Stone	Gaming piece	1	Ditto		797
A21.2000.124	Pottery	LIA base sherd	1	*C1*		797
A21.2000.125a	Pottery	LIA 15 body sherds, 1 base and 11 frags	27	None		797
A21.2000.125b	Pottery	16th/17th century pipkin (N European earthenware) foot sherd	1	Ditto		797
A21.2000.126	Pottery	LIA body sherds	2	None		797
A21.2000.127a	Pottery	LIA body sherds	5	*D south Edge of Jimmy's hole - top layer*		797
A21.2000.127b	Copper alloy	Copper-alloy frags, very decayed	3	Ditto		797
A21.2000.128a	Pottery	LIA body sherds	4	*Rosemary and Chris 9 - 18" below occupation layer H 15 3/8/59 4 pot 1 bone*	1959	797
A21.2000.128b	Bird bone	Bird sp. furcula	1	Ditto		797
A21.2000.129	Pottery	LIA body sherd	1	*U.3.f 59" below medieval foundation*		797
A21.2000.130	Pottery	LIA 3 body sherds and 2 base	5	*Wed 5th Aug H14 12" below level of broad diagonal wall*	1959	797
A21.2000.131	Animal bone	Pig and carnivore teeth	2	*F13*		797
A21.2000.132	Pottery	LIA body sherds	2	*Y4c 58" below Med horizon 2/8/59 Prof*	1959	797
A21.2000.133	Pottery	LIA body and base sherds	2	*Irene 29/7/59 X3f 64" below med hor*	1959	797
A21.2000.134	Pottery	LIA body sherd	1	*Ian 3/8/59 H15 9-18" below occupation layer*	1959	797
A21.2000.135a	Pottery	LIA 4 body sherds, 1 base and 1 fragment	6	*Chancel pit*		797
A21.2000.135b	Iron	Triangular sheet of Fe fragment of indet form	1	Ditto		797
A21.2000.136	Pottery	LIA body sherds	2	*Margaret Fraser 8.7.59 SE corner of nave*	1959	797
A21.2000.137	Pottery	LIA body sherds	2	*Alan 7.8.59 X6 77" above pavement on 'gley'*	1959	797

Number	Material	Description	No. of pieces	Label	Year	Item no.
A21.2000.138a	Animal bone	Cow incisor	1	G.17-18 Alan's midden pit		797
A21.2000.138b	Pottery	LIA body sherds	5	Ditto		797
A21.2000.139	Pottery	LIA body sherds	5	U4 c 61" Douglas		797
A21.2000.140	Pottery	LIA base sherd	1	K.16 (SW quadrant) In top 9ins of occupation layer		797
A21.2000.141	Pottery	LIA 3 body sherds and 1 rim	4	X4 In Stewarts Bay 71		797
A21.2000.142	Pottery	LIA 4 body sherd frags	4	F.13.f.top of occupation layer		797
A21.2000.143	Pottery	LIA body sherd	1	6/8/59 7Xe 72" Stewart	1959	797
A21.2000.144	Pottery	LIA smashed pot, partially complete (53 body and 10 rim sherds)	63	None		797
A21.2000.145★	Pottery	LIA 2 base, 1 rim and 2 body sherds; 1 sherd illus	5	Ah		797
A21.2000.146	Pottery	LIA 14 body sherds, 4 base, 3 rim and 1 frag	22	Ej		797
A21.2000.147	Pottery	LIA 35 body sherds	35	None		797
A21.2000.148	Pottery	LIA body sherds	2	None		797
A21.2000.149	Pottery	LIA body sherds and frags	8	cist		797
A21.2000.150	Pottery	LIA body sherd	1	about 6" above CIST 5		797
A21.2000.151a	Pottery	LIA body sherd	1	Founder's Tomb pit		797
A21.2000.151b	Animal bone	Indet animal bone and seal? tooth	2	Ditto		797
A21.2000.151c	Quartz	Natural quartz chunks	2	Ditto		797
A21.2000.152	Pottery	LIA base sherd	1	Wed 5th Aug H - 15 n 6" below level of broad diagonal wall	1959	797
A21.2000.153a	Pottery	LIA 18 body sherds, 3 rim and 5 frags	26	Cist S		797
A21.2000.153b	Pumice	Water-rounded pumice	1	Ditto		797
A21.2000.154a	Pottery	LIA 18 body sherds and 4 frags	22	Bi		797
A21.2000.154b	Animal bone	Cow and indet animal bone frags	6	Ditto		797
A21.2000.155	Pottery	LIA 9 body and 2 rim sherds	11	D North (1)" with a sketch		797
A21.2000.156	Pottery	LIA body and base sherds	2	D North 2 (about 4" below D.N.1.)		797
A21.2000.157	Pottery	LIA body sherd	1	Tues 4th Aug I.14. - 6" below level of broad diagonal wall	1959	797
A21.2000.158	Pottery	LIA rim sherd	1	W2 63" g/h Douglas		797
A21.2000.159	Pottery	LIA body sherd	1	Y5b 58" 4/8/59 Douglas	1959	797
A21.2000.160	Pottery	LIA body sherd	1	Y3c 7/8/59 59"	1959	797
A21.2000.161	Pottery	LIA body sherd	1	X3e 2" above floor approx. Douglas 6/8/59	1959	797
A21.2000.162	Pottery	LIA body sherd	1	Y5a 67" 4/8/59 Douglas	1959	797
A21.2000.163	Pottery	LIA body conjoining sherd	2	Y3h 55" 7/8/59 Douglas	1959	797
A21.2000.164a	Pottery	LIA body sherds	3	59 X1b 64" X1C		797
A21.2000.164b	Animal bone	Indet fragment, possibly whalebone	1	Ditto		797
A21.2000.165a	Pottery	LIA base sherd	1	Y3h 53" 7/8/59 Douglas	1959	797
A21.2000.165b	Animal bone	Indet fragment	1	Ditto		797
A21.2000.166	Pottery	LIA body sherd	1	13B		797
A21.2000.167	Pottery	LIA 7 body sherds and 1 rim	8	Hh		797
A21.2000.168	Pottery	LIA 7 body sherds and 5 frags	12	None		797
A21.2000.169	Pottery	LIA body sherd	1	Cist S		797
A21.2000.170	Pottery	LIA body sherd	1	Wed 5th Aug I 14 n 16" below level of broad diagonal wall	1959	797
A21.2000.171	Pottery	LIA body sherds	3	Ap NW angle of stone platform - layer just above 'cist' - above Ah		797
A21.2000.172	Pottery	LIA 2 body sherds, 3 rims and 1 base	6	Bj		797
A21.2000.173	Pottery	LIA body sherd	1	None		797
A21.2000.174	Pottery	LIA body sherd	1	12A		797

APPENDIX 2

Features excavated in 1958 and 1959

Features excavated in 1958 and 1959 with the corresponding finds labels and find from the Shetland Museum (Small) Collection

Finds label	Sketch (Yes/No)	Location (from O'Dell's notebook/ Nisbet archive/ finds label)	Finds no. in Shetland museum	Material	Date found
'Cist'			A21.2000.149	Pottery	-
8	N		A21.2000.38	Pottery	-
10X	N		A21.2000.65	Pottery	-
12A	N		A21.2000.174	Pottery	-
13B	N		A21.2000.166	Pottery	-
6	N		A21.2000.115	Pottery	-
A	Y	Cist in nave, north of side altar	A21.2000.36	Pottery	-
Aa	N	Nave Stewart. E end of timbering in nave; one piece very coarse pot blackened	A21.2000.48	Pottery	-
Ab	N	Nave Helen. E end of clay bonded wall in nave pieces pot and charcoal	A21.2000.64	Pottery	-
Ac	N	Nave 4' N of S wall. 7'W of front wall side altar. Bits of pot and lump of charcoal	A21.2000.68		
	Pottery	-			
Ad	N	Nave, 4" below Ac and 2ft to NW of it	A21.2000.39	Pottery	-
Ae	N	Nave, 3rd layer down and 5 ft NW of NW corner of side altar	A21.2000.71, A21.2000.107	Pottery	-
Af	N	Nave, 4th layer 2" under Ae	A21.2000.20	Pottery and two gaming pieces	-
Ag	N	Nave, 4th layer 4" under Af and 18" to NW of Ae	A21.2000.58	Pottery	-
Ah pot	N, but small diagram showing Ah next to Ian's pot	W side of nave, Fiona. Coarse pot in base of angle between 4th step and south side of pit as 1st enlargement. Adjoining 4 pieces finer pot.	A21.2000.145	Pottery	
Aj	N	E end of nave, Helen. Foot of clay bonded wall to E of Ab. 5 small pieces of pot and piece of charcoal	-	-	-
Ak	N	Nave, Helen. Top of Prof's Wall N end	A21.2000.44	Pottery	-
Al	N	Nave, at foot of clay bonded wall 3" above subsoil ?pot yellow	-	-	-
Am	N	Nave, 4th layer 5" to W of Ag ?part of same pot as Ag	-	-	-
An	N	Nave, same level as Af but 5" to W	-	-	-
Ap	N	Nave, Fiona. Coarse pot above Ah. NW angle of stone platform layer just above cist – above Ah	A21.2000.171	Pottery	-
Aq	N	Nave, pot pieces from under hoard	-	-	-
Ar	N	'Mixture' from top layer above stone platform	-	-	-
?Cist B	Y	Possibly in NW corner of nave	-	-	-
Ba	N	Fiona. Teeth from platform (top layer) above stones complex, to W end	A21.2000.12	Animal and human bone	-
Bb	Y	Nave, Bone and 2 pieces pot (midway) below top of wall	A21.2000.70	Peat lumps and pottery	-
Bc	N	Nave, Helen. In crevices between stones. Larger piece preserved under schist.	A21.2000.67	Pottery	-
Bd	N	Nave, Helen. 3 pieces pot near surface ?same as Aa Another piece found later adjoining Bd	A21.2000.57, A21.2000.72	Pottery	-
Be	Y	Fiona. W end of stone zone, in yellow clay in 'cist'	A21.2000.15	Pottery and animal bone	-
Bf	Y	Nave, Muriel and Fiona	A21.2000.10	Pottery, human and animal bone	-
Bg	Y	Douglas. Tooth and pot piece	-	-	-
Bh	N	Nave, Fiona. 2nd layer immediately above stone layer under 1957 steps ?burnt bone, teeth and 1 piece pot	-	-	-

Finds label	Sketch (Yes/No)	Location (from O'Dell's notebook/ Nisbet archive/ finds label)	Finds no. in Shetland museum	Material	Date found
Bi	N	Fiona. 2nd layer, immediately above stones. Many pieces pot scattered piece of bone and ?bark close to teeth	A21.2000.154	Pottery and animal bone	–
Bj	N	Pot pieces S of Bc in crevices between stones	A21.2000.172	Pottery	–
Bk	N	Nave, Pot pieces found below Bd at level immediately above ?stone pavement	A21.2000.23	Pottery and pumice	–
Bl	N	Nave, Jimmy and Helen. Found about 4'6" above 'stone pavement' between crevices of smallish fallen pieces. Coarse.	A21.2000.62	Pottery	–
Bm	N	Nave, 3" below Bl and close to 'stone pavement'	A21.2000.114	Pottery	–
Bn	N	'Upper' level; gritty piece of pot	A21.2000.66	Pottery	–
Bo	N	Stone ring. Close to Bn. Immediately above stone pavement under protecting stone	–	–	–
Brown beads	N	Inside nave 6'W of side altar and 4' N of south wall	–	–	–
Cist C	Y	Centre of nave to south of clay-bonded wall and Cist S	A19.1998.7 A21.2000.124 (labelled C1)	Pottery	1959
Ca	N	Douglas. To W of large block. Top layer; 1 piece pot	A21.2000.69	Charcoal and pottery	–
Cb	N	2nd layer pot (2 pieces) and ?burnt bone	A21.2000.37	Pottery	–
Cc	N	Small fragment pot? 4th layer under a stone	A21.2000.52	Pottery	–
Chancel pit			A21.2000.135	Pottery and iron	–
E			A21.2000.28	Pottery	–
E12	N	b1 written on sherd, 25 written on stone bead	A19.1998.8	Pottery	–
Ea	Y	Nave, SE angle of timbering. Pot near base of 1958 wall	A21.2000.27	Pottery	–
Eb	Y	Nave, SE angle of timbering. Pot 6" higher than Eq	A21.2000.111	Pottery	–
Ec	Y	Nave, 2 pieces of pot in clay at base of stone	–	–	–
Ed	Y	Nave, Pot fragment on clay layer at level base of ?fallen stone	A21.2000.25	Pottery	–
Ee	N	Nave, 2 pieces pot 9" below previous layer Eb	A21.2000.32	Pottery	–
Ef	N	Nave, Piece charcoal near Ec	A21.2000.61	Peat frags	–
Eg	N	Nave, Pot rim upper layer	–	–	–
Eh	N	Nave, Pot fragment	A21.2000.54	Pottery	–
Ej	Y	Nave, Q10. Numerous fragments of pot and charcoal fragment under fallen stones to N end of Prof's wall appeared to have been smashed by fallen stone. Number of small chuckie stones.	A21.2000.146	Pottery	–
Ek	Y	Nave, ACO. Large reddish pot, thick and firm curve to rim. Found as Ej under pile of boulders continuing approx line of Prof's wall. At least 3 large white quartz boulders in pile of stones above pot. Stones continue under timbering on north side. Pot had sand (blown) underneath. Pieces of charcoal about pot and in stones above to E decayed bone. (SN)	A21.2000.5	Pottery	–
El	Y	Nave, Douglas. 2nd layer yellow ashes under, all slab with bones.	A21.2000.22	Gaming piece, natural quartz, pottery	–
Em	Y	Nave, Douglas under wall to E of lozenge. Pieces under Prof's wall thinner pot and ?edge 2 pieces under wall to W thicker pot	A21.2000.46	Pottery	–
En	Y	Nave, Below 2nd slab ?iron and pot	A21.2000.51	Iron and pottery	–
Eo	Y	Nave, Pot found below 42" on plan	–	–	–
Ep	N	Nave, Pot 1ft to S of Ej and c 4ins higher in stones	–	–	–
Eq	N	Nave, 3 pot fragments about 1 ft to W of Ep	A21.2000.33	Pottery	–
Er	Y	Nave, Knocking stone, 2nd layer slightly above platform	–	–	–
F	N	Nave, Below D North Ian's pot	A21.2000.30	Pottery	–
F13	N		A21.2000.131	Animal bone	–
F.13.f	N	Top of occupation layer, S of chapel	A21.2000.142	Pottery	–
F.13.h	N	Top layer of occupation layer, S of chapel	A21.2000.95, A21.2000.109	Pottery	–
Frags of whalebone	N	Nave, ?brush 5'6"W of front of side altar and 6ft north of S wall and 4' below nave floor	Associated with A19.1998.6?	Fishbone	–
G.13.d	N	6" below occupation surface, S of chapel,	A21.2000.56	Animal bone	–
G14	N	Flint	A19.1998.4	Flint	–
G.14.a	N	Elizabeth from Spygie 3" below Iron Age. Bone needle.	A19.1998.3	Bone pin point	29/7/59
G17-18		Alan's midden pit	A21.2000.138	Animal bone and pottery	–

Finds label	Sketch (Yes/No)	Location (from O'Dell's notebook/ Nisbet archive/ finds label)	Finds no. in Shetland museum	Material	Date found
G.19.I	N	Alongside cist wall above skull, ?part of midden waste	A21.2000.80	Pottery	–
H	Y	Nave, uprights at right angles to each other shown on Nisbet's plan as (5) and on sketch in SN. To the south of and adjacent to Cist A. Junction of nave and chancel			
Pot fragment above wall (SN)	A21.2000.34	Pottery		–	
H14	N	12" below level of broad diagonal wall, S of chapel	A21.2000.130	Pottery	5/8/59
H14e	N	18-27" below occupation layer Ian, S of chapel	A21.2000.98	Pottery	3/8/59
H15	N	Rosemary and Chris 9; 18" below occupation layer H15, S of chapel	A21.2000.128	Pottery and bird bone	3/8/59
H15	N	Ian 9-18" below occupation layer, S of chapel	A21.2000.134	Pottery	3/8/59
H15n	N	6" below level of broad diagonal wall, S of chapel	A21.2000.152	Pottery	5/8/59
H.18.I	N	Immediately below top stones	A21.2000.90	Fishbone, slag and shell	–
Hh	N	Nave, at western foot of Prof's wall behind <> boundary stone (ie lozenge stone) associated with large quartz block ?part of a pot running towards <> stone. Labelled 'John and Evie's pit'.	A21.2000.47	Pottery	–
I	N	Grid ref from area south of church (on slide in Shetland Museum)	A21.2000.113	Pottery	–
I12.ef	N	I12 ef 6" and I.12.e.qf In top 6 ins, S of chapel	A21.2000.77	Pottery and iron	–
I14	N	6" below level of broad diagonal wall, S of chapel	A21.2000.157	Pottery	4/8/59
I14g5	N	Ian and Alan Pot 27" below Med fdn, S of chapel	A21.2000.89	Pottery	30/7/59
I14n	N	16" below level of broad diagonal wall, S of chapel	A21.2000.170	Pottery	5/8/59
I.17.g	N	'Beads' at edge of cairn, under lip of stone, S of chapel	No find – envelope empty	?Bone and antler beads	1959
J14n	N	12" below level of broad diagonal wall, S of chapel	A21.2000.79	Pottery	5/8/59
J15 h/l	N	See P1 below	A21.2000.99	Pottery	1959
J.20?	N	Fe object. Chris? Irene found in shovel. Iron object found in debris from E edge of 'cairn' at southern section of it, S of chapel	A19.1998.1	Iron object	24/7/59
J.a.n	N	6" below occupation surface, S of chapel	A21.2000.73	Pottery	–
K.10.i	N	South of chapel	A21.2000.110	Pottery	–
K.11.g	N	South of chapel	A21.2000.8	Animal bone, stone bead and pumice	–
K.12.a and d	N	Near top of occupation surface, S of chapel	A21.2000.35	Pottery	–
K.15.h	N	Ian and Alan (peat ash) bde associated with structure. 12" below Iron Age level (pavement) pot and sandstone with hole!, S of chapel	A21.2000.1	Pottery and perforated stone	29/7/59
L.12.h	N	ca. 1ft Below occupation level, S of chapel	A21.2000.31	Pottery	–
L.16. hdi/M.17.a	N	Close together at the edge of 'cairn' about 1½ to 2 ft below occupation surface, S of chapel	A21.2000.100	Burnt bone and pottery	–
OG or O6	N	Nave, Douglas depth behind wall, 6ft to thin slab flooring	A21.2000.78	Pottery	–
Structure P1	N	J15 Structure P1 below the IA level. S of the chapel	A21.2000.99	Pottery	1959
Cist P	Y	South side of chancel	–	–	–
Cist Q	Y	South side of chance	–	–	–
Ss	N	Nave, higher level than Cist S and to W. towards 4th step 3 bits pot and teeth	–	–	–
T	Y	Nave, adjacent west of D South and Jimmy's Hole	'Fiona's pot'		
NB. Does this = Ah pot?	–	–			
2Uf	N	Nave, Alan 48" below	A21.2000.81	Pottery	29/7/59
U3f	N	Nave, 59" below Medieval foundation	A21.2000.129	Pottery	–
U3i	N	Nave, GO or CO Douglas	A21.2000.18	Pottery and pumice	–
U4c	N	Nave, 61" Douglas	A21.2000.139	Pottery	–
4 Ue	N	Nave, 51" below Medieval horizon	A21.2000.117	Pottery	28/7/59
5Ug 5Ub	N	Nave, Douglas US 54" below Med	A21.2000.17	Pottery and schist object	28/7/59
U6a	N	Nave, Douglas same pot as U6	A21.2000.122	Whale bone and pottery	–
U.6.e	N	Nave, pot ca 5ft below fdation. Pumice directly below pot	A21.2000.19	Pottery and pumice	–
V3i	N	Nave, 58" Douglas	A21.2000.86	Pottery	–
V.3.d	N	Nave, 60" below Medieval fdation	–	–	–
3Vd	N	Nave, 55" Douglas	A21.2000.102	Pottery	–

Finds label	Sketch (Yes/No)	Location (from O'Dell's notebook/ Nisbet archive/ finds label)	Finds no. in Shetland museum	Material	Date found
W2	N	Nave, 63" g/h Douglas	A21.2000.158	Pottery	–
2 Wd	N	Nave, 50" below Medieval horizon Douglas	A21.2000.119	Pottery	3/8/59
West third of hollow	N	Sheila	A21.2000.92 A21.2000.74	Peat, pottery, fish bone, animal bone	8/7/59
Wz.f/l	N	Nave, 58" Douglas	A21.2000.88	Pottery	–
X1	Y – on another sketch	Nave			
Also a table of a section below X1, with levels	A21.2000.13: Below X1, A21.2000.76: 'below X1', A21.2000.41: 'Alan's pit Below X1'	Slag, animal bone and pottery	–		
X1b/c	N	Nave, 59" X1b 64" X1c	A21.2000.164	Pottery and animal bone	–
2X	N		A21.2000.3	Animal bone	–
X3	N		A21.2000.50	Pottery	–
X3e	N	Nave, 2" above floor approx Douglas	A21.2000.161	Pottery	6/8/59
X3f	N	Nave, 64" below Medieval horizon Irene	A21.2000.133	Pottery	29/7/59
X4	N	In Stewart's Bay 71	A21.2000.141	Pottery	–
X4a	N	Nave, June Jean Greig 59" below Med foundations level	A21.2000.16	Pottery and human bone	–
X4a/d	N	Nave, Irene 64" below Med Horiz	A21.2000.85	Pottery	25/7/59
X4f	N	Nave, Stewart SE Corner of square box 75" below	A21.2000.42	Pottery	7/9/59
X4g/h	N	Nave, Irene 64" below Medieval horizon	A21.2000.96	Pottery	29/7/59
X4		North end	A21.2000.106	Pottery and peat	–
X4g	N	Nave, Irene 64" Below med. Found.	A21.2000.108	Pottery	28/7/59
X5g	N	Nave, 71" below Medieval foundations level	A21.2000.123	Pottery and gaming piece	–
X6	N	Nave, Alan 77" above pavement on 'gley'	A21.2000.137	Pottery	7/8/59
X6	N	Nave 70" below medieval foundations	A21.2000.101	Pottery and charcoal	6/8/59
6Xfg	N	Nave, 80" below Just above pavement – set on 'glay' ?hut circle, Alan	A21.2000.55	Pottery	7/8/59
7Xe	N	Nave, 72" Stewart	A21.2000.143	Pottery	–
X7n	N	Nave 66" below Medieval foundations	A21.2000.82	Pottery	6/8/59
X36	N	Nave, 50" below Med horizon base Irene	A21.2000.93	Pottery	–
Y1	N	Nave, In 65"	A21.2000.21	Pottery and glass bead	9/8/59
Y.3.a/b	N	Nave, Outside lower of two box kerbstone edges in peat ash. 69" below kerbstone. Bone found 1½ ft to ESE	A21.2000.2	Pottery and animal bone	9/8/59
Y3c	N	Nave, 59" Douglas	A21.2000.160	Pottery	7/8/59
Y3h	N	Nave, 55" Douglas	A21.2000.163	Pottery	7/8/59
Y3h	N	Nave, 53" Douglas			
54" below Medieval fdation to S of large kerbstone	A21.2000.165				
A21.2000.6	Pottery, animal bone and pumice	7/8/59			
Y4c	N	Nave, 58" below Medieval horizon Prof	A21.2000.132	Pottery	2/8/59
4Yd/e	N	Nave, 68" Douglas	A21.2000.94	Pottery	6/8/59
Y4e	N	Nave, 62"	A21.2000.87	Pottery and charcoal	–
Y4h	N	Nave, 59" below Medieval foundation	–	–	–
Y5a	N	Nave, 67" Douglas	A21.2000.162	Pottery	4/8/59
Y5b	N	Nave, 58" Douglas	A21.2000.159	Pottery	4/8/59
Y5e	N	Nave, 71" and 72" Douglas	A21.2000.53	Pottery	4/8/59
9z or Zb	N		A21.2000.105	Pottery	–
S of S wall 2' below wall top	N	Stone labelled in pencil 'S of S wall E end (or cut) 2 (feet) below wall top. Prob south of chapel'	A19.1998.2	Stone weight	–
Stone platform	N		A19.1998.5, A19.1998.6	Fish bone	–
Top of Prof's body	N		A21.2000.45	Pottery	–

APPENDIX 3

Coarse pottery held in the Shetland Museum

Coarse pottery held in the Shetland Museum (Small) collection (A19.1998 and A21.2000).
Fabric 1: sandy clay;
Fabric 2: fine sandy clay;
Fabric 3: fine clay;
Fabric 4: steatitic clay;
Fabric 5: sandy steatitic clay.
Int: interior; ext: exterior. Surface finish: S (smoothed), B (burnished).

SF no.	No. of sherds	Weight (g)	Width (mm)	Description	Decora-tion (y/n)	Surface finish	Fabric	Sooting	Comment
A19.1998.7	1	12	8	1 rim	n		1+10%	Both	Rolled
A19.1998.8a	1	9	8	1 rim	n	S	1	Int	Slightly everted rim
A19.1998.11	1	22	8	1 body	y	S	1	Both	Flat rim, applied fingertip impressed band just below lip
A19.1998.12	1	26	7	1 body	y	S	4+10% st	Ext sooted, int residue	Shouldered, incised chevron above shoulder
A19.1998.13	1	118	23	1 body	n		st clay+40% st		N-shaped junction
A19.1998.14	1	19	8	1 base	n	S	3+10% st	Both	Angled base
A19.1998.15	1	29	9	1 body	n	polished	4+10% st	Both	Polished ext and int (black)
A19.1998.16.1	1	7	9	1 rim	n		4+20% st	Both	Probably necked
A19.1998.16.2	1	3	6	1 rim	n		2	Int	Rolled rim
A19.1998.16.3	1	9	7	1 rim	n		4+10% st	Ext	Well-defined neck, lip missing
A19.1998.16.4	1	5	6	1 rim	y		4+10% st		Inverted rim, deep groove 8mm below
A19.1998.16.5	1	4	8	1 rim	y		3+10% st	Both	Rolled rim, groove under
A21.2000.1a.1	8	59	7	8 body	n		1+10%	Both	
A21.2000.1a.2	1	21	14	1 body	n		1+10%	Ext	
A21.2000.1a.3	1	14	8	1 base	n	S	1+20%	Int	From angle of base
A21.2000.1a.4	2	9	7	2 body	n		1+shell	Both	
A21.2000.1a.5	6	29	6	1 base, 5 body		B	1	Both	Small sherd from angle of base
A21.2000.1a.6	2	8	7	2 body	n		1	Int residue	
A21.2000.1a.7	1	8	7	1 body	n	S	1		
A21.2000.1a.8	1	7	7	1 body	n	S	1	Int	
A21.2000.1a.9	1	3	6	1 body	n	S	1	Int	
A21.2000.2a	8	84	10	3 rims, 5 body	n	S	1	Both	Slightly everted rim
A21.2000.4	4	104	8	1 rim, 3 body	n	S	1+10%	Both	Plain rim, slightly inverted (dia 140mm)
A21.2000.5	26	424	9	26 body	n		1+10%	Both	
A21.2000.6a.1	1	32	15	1 base	n		1+10%	Int	
A21.2000.6a.2	1	13	9	1 body	n	S	1+10%	Ext	
A21.2000.9a	32	322	6	5 rim, 28 body	y		1+10%	Both	Applied pinched neckband just below lip
A21.2000.10a.1	4	57	8	4 body	n		1	Ext	
A21.2000.10a.2	1	4	10	1 body	n		1		
A21.2000.10a.3	3	9	6	3 body	n		1	Ext	
A21.2000.10a.4	1	4	8	1 body	n	B	2	Int	
A21.2000.10a.5	1	18	9	1 body	n		2+10%	Both	
A21.2000.10a.6	2	20	8	1 body, 1 frag	n		2+10%	Int	
A21.2000.10a.7	1	33	11	1 body	n	B	1+10%	Both	

SF no.	No. of sherds	Weight (g)	Width (mm)	Description	Decora-tion (y/n)	Surface finish	Fabric	Sooting	Comment
A21.2000.15a	6	36	9	1 base, 3 body, 2 frags	n	B	2+10%		Dished base
A21.2000.16a.1	9	20	3 to 7	1 rim, 5 body, 3 frags	n	B	1+10%	Ext	Everted; very fine lip, frag-mented
A21.2000.16a.2	1	17	7	1 body	n	S	1+10%	Ext	
A21.2000.17a.1	1	36	9	1 body	n	S	1+10%	Both	
A21.2000.17a.2	1	9	10	1 body	n		1+10%	Int	
A21.2000.17a.3	2	7	0	2 frags	n	S	1+10%	Int	
A21.2000.18a	1	9	6	1 body	n	S	1		
a21.2000.19a	1	11	7	1 body	n	S	1	Ext	
A21.2000.20a.1	1	8	10	1 body	n	S	2+10%	Both	
A21.2000.20a.2	2	6	6	2 body	n	S	2	Ext	
A21.2000.20a.3	2	4	6	2 body	n		4+50% steatite	Int	
A21.2000.21a	2	43	10	2 body	n		1+10%		Join
A21.2000.22b.1	2	8	4	2 body	n	B	2	Ext	
A21.2000.22b.2	1	3	3	1 body	n	B	3		
a21.2000.22b.3	1	2	6	1 body	n		1	Int residue	
A21.2000.22b.4	1	4	6	1 body	n		1	Ext	
A21.2000.22b.5	1	2	5	1 base	n	S	1	Ext	From angle of base
A21.2000.23a.1	1	16	8	1 body	n		1+10%	Ext	
A21.2000.23a.1	4	11	5	4 body	n		2	Both	
A21.2000.24	1	2	6	1 body	n	B	1	Ext	
A21.2000.25	1	9	5	1 body	n	S	1+10%	Ext sooted, int residue	
A21.2000.27	1	7	8	1 body	n		3+10%		
a21.2000.28.1	2	38	10	1 rim, 1 body	n	S	4+20% steatite	Both	Int bevel
A21.2000.28.2	1	9	10	1 body	n		1+10%	Int	
A21.2000.28.3	2	9	7	1 body, 1 rim	n		2	Both	Everted rim, abraded
A21.2000.29	2	36	8	2 body	n	B	2+10%	Both	
A21.2000.30	33	433	7	1 base, 32 body	n		1+10%	Ext sooted, int residue	Flat base (reconstructed), angled sides (dia 120mm)
A21.2000.31.1	1	27	6	1 body	y	B	1	Ext	Parallel grooves below neck
A21.2000.31.2	1	10	5	1 body	n	B	3		
a21.2000.31.3	1	6	9	1 body	n	S	1+10%	Int	
A21.2000.32	2	16	10	2 body	n	S	1+20%	Int	One from angle of base
A21.2000.33	3	5	6	2 body, 1 frag	n		2	Ext	
A21.2000.34.1	17	210	8	17 body	n		1+10%	Both	
A21.2000.34.2	2	24	9	2 rims	n	B	1	Both	Rolled rim (sherds join)
A21.2000.34.3	1	4	9	1 body	n	S	5	Ext	
A21.2000.35.1	6	25	7	1 base, 5 body	n	S	2+10%	Both	
A21.2000.35.2	1	1	3	1 body	n	Polished	3		From neck of a very finely made vessel
A21.2000.36.1	1	15	7	1 body	n	B	1	Int residue	
A21.2000.36.2	2	5	7	2 body	n	B	1	Ext	Possibly applied decoration (sherds join)
A21.2000.37.1	2	10	10	2 base	n		1+30%	Ext sooted, int residue	From angle of base
A21.2000.37.2	1	8	10	1 base	n		1	Int	From flat part of base
A21.2000.38.1	1	1	0	1 frag	n		2		
a21.2000.39	3	29	7	3 body	n	S	5	Ext	
A21.2000.40	5	51	6	2 base, 3 body	n	S	1+20% steatite	Ext	From flat part of base
A21.2000.41.1	1	17	11	1 body	n	S	1	Int residue	
A21.2000.41.2	2	10	7	2 body	n	S	1+10%	Int residue	
A21.2000.41.3	1	30	12	1 base	n	S	1+10%	Both	From flat part of base
A21.2000.42.1	1	2	9	1 rim	y		1	Ext	Plain rim, groove 8mm under
A21.2000.42.2	1	5	6	1 body	n	B	1	Int	
A21.2000.42.3	1	4	5	1 body	n	B	1	Ext	
A21.200.43a	1	8	8	1 body	n	B	1	Ext	
A21.2000.44.1	1	26	10	1 body	n	S	2+10%		
A21.2000.44.2	1	21	9	1 body	n	B	2+30%	Ext	
A21.2000.44.3	3	23	10	3 body	n		3+org+10% steatite	Both	Pitted

SF no.	No. of sherds	Weight (g)	Width (mm)	Description	Decora-tion (y/n)	Surface finish	Fabric	Sooting	Comment
A21.2000.45	1	4	8	1 body	n		2		
a21.2000.46.1	1	51	6	1 body	n	B	1+10%	Both	
A21.2000.46.2	1	5	8	1 body	n		1	Both	
A21.2000.47.1	1	6	7	1 base	n		1	Both	
A21.2000.47.2	1	8	10	1 body	n		1+10%	Int	
A21.2000.47.3	1	6	9	1 body	n		1+10%	Ext	
A21.2000.48	1	44	14	1 base	n		5+10% st	Int	Flat part of base
A21.2000.49a	1	8	9	1 rim	n		5		Abraded
A21.2000.50	3	32	9	3 body	n	B	2+10%	Int residue	
A21.2000.51b	1	5	8	1 body	n		3		
a21.2000.52	1	3	10	1 body	n		2		
a21.2000.53	1	7	6	1 body	n	B	1	Ext	
A21.2000.54	1	3	7	1 body	n	B	1	Ext	
A21.2000.55	2	28	7	2 body	n	S	1	Both	
A21.2000.57	2	24	10	2 body	n	B	1+10%	Ext sooted, int residue	
A21.2000.57a	1	4	9	1 body	n	S	st sandy clay	Ext	
A21.2000.58	6	105	15	1 base, 5 body	n	S	1+10%	Int residue	Flat base, angled sides
A21.2000.59	1	4	9	1 body	n	B	1	Ext	
A21.2000.62	1	48	12	1 body	n	S	1+10%	Ext sooted, int residue	
A21.2000.63.1	1	10	9	1 base	n		2	Int	From angle of base
A21.2000.63.2	2	13	6	2 body	n	S	1	Ext	
A21.2000.64.1	1	6	7	1 rim	n	B	2		Plain rim
A21.2000.64.2	2	8	9	2 body	n		1	Ext	
A21.2000.64.3	2	12	7	2 body	n	B	2	Both	
A21.2000.65	1	6	8	1 body	n		1	Ext	
A21.2000.66	1	9	9	1 body	n		coarse sand		?Industrial ceramic
A21.2000.67.1	2	37	9	2 body	n	B	1+10%	Both	
A21.2000.67.2	1	11	9	1 body	n	B	1+10%	Ext	
A21.2000.67.3	1	12	9	1 body	n	S	2+10%		
a21.2000.67.4	2	5	8	1 body, 1 frag	y		1+10%	Both	Fragment is from a finger-impressed neckband (joins body)
A21.2000.68.1	1	16	6	1 body	n	S	1	Ext	
A21.2000.68.2	1	12	11	1 body	n	S	2+20%		N-shaped coil junction
A21.2000.69b	1	5	7	1 body	n	S	1	Ext	
A21.2000.70b	2	8	10	2 body	n	S	1	Both	
A21.2000.71	10	53	8	3 rim, 7 body	n	S	3		?Flat lip, short neck
A21.2000.72	1	7	8	1 body	n	S	5		
a21.2000.73.1	3	11	8	2 rims, 1 body	n	S	1	Both	Beaded rim
A21.2000.73.2	3	26	10	3 body	n	S	1+10%	Int	
A21.2000.74b.1	2	26	8	2 body	n	S	1	Int	
A21.2000.74b.2	2	22	7	2 body	n		2+40%	Ext & int residue	
A21.2000.74b.3	2	5	6	2 body	n	B	2+10%	Both	
A21.2000.75.1	3	56	10	1 base, 2 body	n	S	1	Ext	Flat base, angled sides
A21.2000.75.2	1	18	10	1 body	n	S	1+10%	Int	
A21.2000.75.3	1	8	10	1 body	n	S	1+10%	Both	
A21.2000.75.4	1	6	8	1 body	n	S	2+10%	Ext	
A21.2000.75.5	1	8	11	1 body	n	S	1	Ext	
A21.2000.75.6	1	5	7	1 body	n	S	2	Ext	
A21.2000.75.7	1	4	5	1 rim	n	S	1		Everted rim, small sherd
A21.2000.76.1	1	16	11	1 body	n	S	1	Int residue	Broken along coil junction
A21.2000.76.2	1	15	10	1 base	n	S	1+10%		?Light-coloured coating in int; flat base, angled walls
A21.2000.76.3	1	6	9	1 body	n	S	1		
A21.2000.77a.1	1	8	10	1 body	n	S	1	Int	
A21.2000.77a.2	1	3	7	1 body	n	S	5	Both	
A21.2000.78	12	99	9	3 rim, 3 base, 6 body	n	S	1	Ext	Fragmented everted rim & neck sherds, flat base, angled walls

SF no.	No. of sherds	Weight (g)	Width (mm)	Description	Decoration (y/n)	Surface finish	Fabric	Sooting	Comment
A21.2000.79.1	1	23	13	1 base	n	S	1+30%	Ext	
A21.2000.79.2	5	42	10	1 base, 3 body, 1 frag	n	S	1+10%		Flat base, angled sides
A21.2000.79.3	4	38	7	4 body	n	S	1+10%	Both	
A21.2000.79.4	1	4	6	1 body	n		1+10%		
a21.2000.80.1	1	9	7	1 body	n	S	1	Both	
A21.2000.80.2	1	4	8	1 body	n		3		
a21.2000.81	3	27	10	3 body	n	S	2+10%	Ext	Int missing on one sherd
A21.2000.82	3	65	10	3 body	n	S	1+10%	Ext	
A21.2000.83	2	12	8	2 body	n	S	1+10%	Both	
A21.2000.84	1	23	10	1 body	n	S	1+10%	Both	
A21.2000.85.1	4	97	10	4 body	n		1+30%	Int	
A21.2000.85.2	1	6	6	1 body	n	S	2+10%	Int	
A21.2000.86	2	10	8	1 body, 1 frag	n	S	1+10%	Both	
A21.2000.87a.1	1	21	9	1 body	n		sandy clay+10%	Ext residue, int sooted	
A21.2000.87a.2	1	4	6	1 body	n	S	2+10%	Int residue	
A21.2000.88	2	5	9	2 body	n		1	Ext	
A21.2000.89	6	55	8	6 body	n	S	2+10%	Ext sooted, int residue	
A21.2000.92b	1	7	8	1 rim	n	S	1+10%	Ext	Plain rim
A21.2000.93	1	9	9	1 basal sherd	n	B	2+10%	Ext	
A21.2000.94.1	2	40	7	2 body	n	S	2+10%	Ext sooted, int residue	
A21.2000.94.2	1	10	11	1 base	n	S	1+10%	Both	From angle of base
A21.2000.95	1	14	11	1 body	n	S	1	Int	
A21.2000.96.1	1	10	7	1 body	n	S	1+10%	Both lightly sooted	
A21.2000.96.2	1	11	6	1 body	n	S	1+10%	Ext sooted, int residue	
A21.2000.97	3	15	8	3 body	n		4+organics+10%	Int	One sherd from angle of base
A21.2000.98.1	7	57	8	1 rim, 6 body	n	B	1	Ext	Plain rim, angle not determined
A21.2000.98.2	1	7	6	1 body	n		1	Residue both sides	
A21.2000.99.1	10	28	4	1 base, 9 body	n		3+10%	Both	Flat base, angled sides
A21.2000.99.2	1	9	9	1 body	n		5	Ext	
A21.2000.100b.1	1	10	8	1 base	n		2	Int	From flat part of base
A21.2000.100b.2	2	6	8	1 body, 1 frag	n	S	2	Both	
A21.2000.100b.3	1	5	7	1 body	n	Wiped	1	Int	
A21.2000.101a.1	2	52	11	1 base, 1 body	n	S	1+10%	Ext sooted, int residue	From flat part of base
A21.2000.101a.2	1	11	7	1 rim	n	S	1	Both	From neck of vessel
A21.2000.101a.3	1	4	3	1 body	n		1	Ext sooted, int residue	
A21.2000.102	1	8	7	1 body	n	S	1	Ext sooted, int residue	
A21.2000.103a.1	3	44	11	1 base, 2 body	n		2+10%	Both	From angle of base
A21.2000.104.1	1	5	9	1 body	n	S	2+10%	Ext	
A21.2000.104.2	1	6	9	1 body	n	S	1		
a21.2000.104.3	2	16	7	2 body	n	Wiped	1	Both	
A21.2000.104.4	2	23	7	2 body	n	S	1+10%	Int residue	
A21.2000.104.5	2	21	8	2 body	n	S	2	Int	
A21.2000.104a.1	1	12	5	1 rim	n	B	2	Ext	Everted
A21.2000.104a.2	1	10	7	1 rim	n		1	Both	Inverted
A21.2000.104a.3	1	6	7	1 body	n		1		
a21.2000.104a.4	1	7	10	1 body	n		1+10%	Int	
A21.2000.105.1	1	5	8	1 body	n	Wiped	1		
a21.2000.105.2	1	2	7	1 body	n		3	Ext	
A21.2000.106a	2	19	10	1 base, 1 body	n		1+10%		From angle of base
A21.2000.107.1	1	8	7	1 body	n	B	1		
a21.2000.107.2	1	12	11	1 base	n		2+10%	Ext	From flat part of base

SF no.	No. of sherds	Weight (g)	Width (mm)	Description	Decora- tion (y/n)	Surface finish	Fabric	Sooting	Comment
A21.2000.107.3	1	2	8	1 body	n	B	3	Both	From neck of vessel
A21.2000.107.4	3	13	0	3 body	n		1	Int	
A21.2000.108	29	38	5	20 body, 9 frag	n	B	1	Both	
A21.2000.109	5	75	7	5 body	n	S	1+10%	Ext sooted, int residue	Broken along coil junction
A21.2000.110.1	1	12	9	1 body	n	S	1	Int	
A21.2000.110.2	1	7	6	1 body	n	S	1	Both	
A21.2000.111	2	6	11	1 base, 1 frag	n	B	3+10%	Ext	From flat part of base
A21.2000.112	1	7	11	1 body	n		2	Int	Abraded
A21.2000.113	1	3	7	1 body	n		2		Abraded
A21.2000.114	1	7	7	1 body	n	B	2	Both	
A21.2000.115	1	1	0	1 frag	n		2		
a21.2000.117.1	1	4	8	1 body	n	B	1	Ext	
A21.2000.117.2	1	4	5	1 body	n	B	1	Both	
A21.2000.118a.1	3	68	9	3 body	n	B	2+10%	Both	N-shaped junctions
A21.2000.118a.2	1	10	10	1 body	n	S	1		
a21.2000.118a.3	1	2	9	1 body	n	B	1		
a21.2000.119	4	10	9	4 body	n		2+10%	Ext	Abraded
A21.2000.120a.1	1	11	8	1 body	n	S	5+organics	Both	
A21.2000.120a.2	1	7	8	1 body	n		1	Ext residue	
A21.2000.120a.3	1	2	0	1 body	n		1+10%		Ext abraded
A21.2000.120a.4	1	2	5	1 rim	n	S	2		Small rim, plain lip
A21.2000.120a.5	1	2	0	1 body	n		2+10%	Int	Ext abraded
A21.2000.120a.6	1	2	0	1 body	n	S	2+10%		Int abraded
A21.2000.121a	1	3	7	1 body	n		2+10%	Ext	
A21.2000.121b	1	6	7	1 body	n		1+10%	Ext	
A21.2000.122b	11	58	10	1 rim, 8 body, 2 frag	n	S	1+10%	Ext	Flat lip, probably everted
A21.2000.123a.1	18	288	12	1 rim, 1 base, 16 body	n	S	1+10%	Both	Angled base (dia 200mm), small everted rim fragment
A21.2000.123a.2	2	33	11	2 body	n	S	2+10%		
a21.2000.124	1	10	8	1 base	y	S	1	Both	Flat base, slightly angled sides, incised
A21.2000.125a.1	1	25	10	1 body	n	S	1+10%	Ext	
A21.2000.125a.2	3	11	10	1 base, 2 frags	n		1+10%		Flat part of base
A21.2000.125a.3	2	10	10	2 body	n	S	1	Int	
A21.2000.125a.4	5	17	8	5 body	n	B	1	Both	
A21.2000.125a.5	2	12	9	1 body, 1 frag	y	S	1+10%	Int	Possible incised lines
A21.2000.125a.6	2	11	8	1 body, 1 frag	y	S	1+10%	Both	Possible frag from applied finger-impressed band
A21.2000.125a.7	10	30	8	3 body, 7 frags	n	S	2+10%	Both	
A21.2000.125a.8	2	8	8	2 body	n		3+20%+org	Both	
A21.2000.126.1	1	46	9	1 body	n	S	1+10%	Both	
A21.2000.126.2	1	6	7	1 body	n	S	1+10%	Ext	
A21.2000.127a.1	1	13	11	1 body	n	S	1+10%		
a21.2000.127a.2	1	7	7	1 body	n	B	2+10% steatite		From neck of vessel
A21.2000.127a.3	1	7	11	1 body	n		2+20% steatite	Ext	
A21.2000.127a.4	1	4	10	1 body	n		3		
a21.2000.127a.5	1	4	9	1 body	n	S	1	Int	
A21.2000.128a.1	1	13	6	1 body	n	S	1+10%	Ext sooted, int residue	
A21.2000.128a.2	1	6	6	1 body	n	S	4+10% steatite	Int	
A21.2000.128a.3	1	4	7	1 body	n	S	1+10%		
a21.2000.128a.4	1	1	6	1 body	n	B	1	Ext	
A21.2000.129	1	6	9	1 body	n		4+10%	Ext	
A21.2000.130.1	2	17	6	2 body	n	S	1	Ext sooted, int residue	
A21.2000.130.2	1	3	7	1 body	n	S	1	Both	
A21.2000.130.3	1	4	0	1 base	n		1		Flat part of base, int abraded
A21.2000.130.4	1	16	9	1 base	n		1		Flat part of base
A21.2000.132.1	1	17	9	1 body	n	S	1+10%	Both	
A21.2000.132.2	1	4	4	1 body	n	B	2	Ext	
A21.2000.133.1	1	13	9	1 base	n		1+10%	Both	Flat part of base

SF no.	No. of sherds	Weight (g)	Width (mm)	Description	Decora- tion (y/n)	Surface finish	Fabric	Sooting	Comment
A21.2000.133.2	1	4	9	1 body	n	B	2+10%	Ext	
A21.2000.134	1	2	6	1 body	n	B	1	Ext	
A21.2000.135a.1	4	8	9 to 12	3 body, 1 frag	n		1	Int	
A21.2000.135a.2	1	2	8	1 body	n		2+10% steatite	Int	
A21.2000.135a.3	1	2	0	1 basal frag	n	B	2+10%	Ext	Ext fragment of base
A21.2000.136	2	15	9	2 body	n	S	1+10%	Int res	One sherd has surface missing
A21.2000.137	2	33	10	2 body	n	S	1+10%	Ext sooted, int residue	
A21.2000.138.1	3	11	5	1 body, 2 frags	n	S	1	Both	
A21.2000.138.2	2	9	9	2 body	n		5+10%	Int	
A21.2000.139.1	2	6	9	2 body	n	S	1+10%	Ext	
A21.2000.139.2	3	6	7	3 body	n		2+10%	Int	
A21.2000.140	1	37	9	1 base	n	S	2+10%	Int	Flat base, angled sides
A21.2000.141.1	2	20	7	2 body	n	S	1+30%	Both	
A21.2000.141.2	1	8	8	1 body	n		2+10%		
a21.2000.141.3	1	14	7	1 rim	n		1+10%	Both	Plain rim, bowl
A21.2000.142	4	8	6	4 body	n		2+10%	Int	
A21.2000.143	1	4	4	1 body	n	S	1	Both	
A21.2000.144.1	15	81	3	6 rim, 9 body	n	B	2+10%	Both	Inverted rim, very fine
A21.2000.144.2	19	137	7	19 body	n	Wiped	1+10%	Both	
A21.2000.144.3	1	28	10	1 body	n		1+10%	Both	
A21.2000.144.4	4	9	8	4 body	n	Wiped	1+10%	Int	
A21.2000.144.5	24	682	8	4 rim, 20 body	n	B	1+10%	Ext sooted, int residue	Flat rim (240mm)
A21.2000.145.1	1	105	10	1 base	n	S	1	Ext sooted, int residue	Flat base (160mm)
A21.2000.145.2	1	14	7	1 base	n		1+10%	Int residue	Flat part of base
A21.2000.145.3	1	3	10	1 body	n		2+10%		Abraded
A21.2000.145.4	1	7	7	1 body	n	B	1	Ext sooted	
A21.2000.145.5	1	8	7	1 rim	y		2+10%	Both	Plain lip, shallow groove 9mm below
A21.2000.146.1	13	179	9	3 rim, 2 base, 7 body, 1 frag	n		2+10%	Both	Everted rim, flat base
A21.2000.146.2	3	11	9	3 body	n		2+10%	Ext sooted	
A21.2000.146.3	1	4	10	1 base	n		1+10%	Both	Flat part of base
A21.2000.146.4	4	13	6	1 base, 3 body	n		1	Both	Barrel-shaped
A21.2000.146.5	1	33	8	1 body	n		2	Both	
A21.2000.147	35	327	8	35 body	n	S	2	Int	
A21.2000.148.1	1	52	9	1 body	n	B	1+10%	Int	B surface abraded
A21.2000.148.2	1	33	9	1 body	n	S	1+10%	Both	
A21.2000.149.1	1	5	6	1 body	n		2+10%	Ext	
A21.2000.149.2	2	6	8	2 body	n	B	1	Ext	
A21.2000.149.3	1	15	9	1 base	n		1+10%	Ext	Flat part of base
A21.2000.149.4	4	15	10	2 body, 2 frags	n	S	2+10%		
a21.2000.150	1	3	8	1 body	n		1		
a21.2000.151a	1	6	7	1 body	n	B	3+10%		
a21.2000.152	1	9	9	1 base	n	S	1+10%		Angle of base
A21.2000.153a.1	15	68	7	3 rim, 13 body, 1 frag	n		1	Ext sooted, int residue	Plain rim
A21.2000.153a.2	2	11	10	2 body	n		1	Both	
A21.2000.153a.3	6	10	5	3 body, 4 frags	n		1	Both	
A21.2000.154a.1	19	110	8	15 body, 4 frags	n		1	Ext	
A21.2000.154a.2	2	34	6	1 body	n	S	1	Int residue	
A21.2000.154a.3	1	26	9	1 body	n	S	1	Int residue	
A21.2000.154a.4	1	10	7	1 body	n	S	1	Ext	
A21.2000.155.1	1	12	8	1 body	n		4+10% st	Both	
A21.2000.155.2	1	23	11	1 body	n	S	2+30%		
A21.2000.155.3	1	8	9	1 rim	n	S	2+10% steatite		
A21.2000.155.4	1	3	7	1 body	n		1		

SF no.	No. of sherds	Weight (g)	Width (mm)	Description	Decora-tion (y/n)	Surface finish	Fabric	Sooting	Comment
A21.2000.155.5	1	4	8	1 body	n		1		
A21.2000.155.6	2	6	6	1 body, 1 rim	n	S	1	Both	Possible everted rim
A21.2000.155.7	1	6	12	1 body	n	S	1		
A21.2000.155.8	3	13	9	3 body	n	S	5	Both	
A21.2000.156.1	1	18	9	1 base	n		1+10%	Int	Flat part of base
A21.2000.156.2	1	2	6	1 body	n	S	1	Int	
A21.2000.157	1	5	8	1 body	n		1		
A21.2000.158	1	13	9	1 rim	n		1	Ext	Plain rim
A21.2000.159	1	12	10	1 body	n		1		
A21.2000.160	1	10	11	1 body	n	S	1+10%	Int residue	
A21.2000.161	1	6	0	1 body	n	B	2		Int missing
A21.2000.162	1	25	9	1 body	n	S	1+10%	Both	
A21.2000.163	2	5	6	2 body	n	S	1	Int residue	
A21.2000.164a.1	1	12	10	1 body	n	S	2+10%		
A21.2000.164a.2	2	35	10	2 body	n		1B	Both	
A21.2000.165a	1	55	18	1 base	n		1	Both	Flat part of base
A21.2000.166	1	3	7	1 body	n	S	2	Ext	
A21.2000.167.1	4	90	10	4 body	n	S	1	Int	
A21.2000.167.2	2	12	9	2 body	n	S	2+10%		
A21.2000.167.3	1	6	10	1 body	n	S	1	Int	
A21.2000.167.4	1	4	7	1 rim	y	S	1	Both	Small rim, plain lip, groove under
A21.2000.168	12	100	9	7 body, 5 frags	n	S	1	Ext	
A21.2000.169	1	17	8	1 body	n		1+10%	Ext sooted, int residue	N-shaped coil junction
A21.2000.170	1	20	12	1 body	n		2+10%	Both	V-shaped coil junction
A21.2000.171	3	131	8	3 body	n		1	Ext	Int surface scraped
A21.2000.172.1	2	69	11	2 body	n	S	1	Both	
A21.2000.172.2	1	30	8	1 rim	n	S	2+10%	Ext	Plain rim
A21.2000.172.3	1	10	8	1 rim	n	S	1	Both	Beaded rim
A21.2000.172.4	1	4	6	1 rim	n	S	1	Both	Plain rim (small sherd)
A21.2000.172.5	1	13	9	1 base	n		1	Int	Flat part of base
A21.2000.173	1	4	8	1 body	n	B	1	Ext	
A21.2000.174	1	1	7	1 body	n	B	2	Int	From neck of vessel

APPENDIX 4

St Ninian's Isle, Shetland 1999–2000.

Context descriptions

Number	Description	Year excavated	Trench	Phase
01	Turf and topsoil	1999	T1/TT1	VII
02	South wall of east end of chancel/apse	1999	TT1	V
03a	Northernmost long cist aligned E–W in NE corner of trench	1959	T1/TT1	V
03b	Re-filled long cist partially reconstructed after 1959 excavation	1999/2000	T1/TT1	VI
04a	Long cist aligned E–W in NE corner of trench	1959	T1/TT1	V
04b	Re-filled long cist partially reconstructed after 1959 excavation	1999/2000	T1/TT1	VI
05a	Long cist aligned E–W in NE corner of trench	1959	T1/TT1	V
05b	Re-filled long cist partially reconstructed after 1959 excavation	1999/2000	T1/TT1	VI
06a	Long cist aligned E–W in NE corner of trench	1959/2000	T1/TT1	V
06b	Re-filled long cist partially reconstructed after 1959 excavation	1999/2000	T1/TT1	VI
07	Stone collapse; part of 1959 backfill	1959/1999	TT1	VI
08	Stone collapse; part of 1959 backfill	1959/1999	TT1	VI
09	Topsoil/backfill	1959/1999	TT1	VI
10	Revetment wall	1959/1999	TT1	VI
11	Wall fill	1959/1999	TT1	VI
12	Revetment wall = 328	1959/1999	TT1	VI
13	Group of quartz pebbles backfill	1959/1999	TT1	VI
14	Post setting?	1959/1999	TT1	III
15	Wall = 307	1959/1999	TT1	VI
16	Topsoil/backfill from 1950s	1959/1999	TT1	VI
17	Topsoil/backfill from 1950s	1959/1999	TT1	VI
18	Wind-blown sand = 024	1959/1999	TT1	VI
19	Wind-blown sand = 024	1959/1999	TT1	VI
20	Wind-blown sand = 024	1959/1999	TT1	VI
21	Wind-blown sand = 024	1959/1999	TT1	VI
22	Wind-blown sand = 024	1959/1999	TT1	VI
23	Wind-blown sand = 024	1959/1999	TT1	VI
24a	Wind-blown sand	1959	T1/TT1	IV
24b	Re-deposited wind-blown sand around reconstructed long cists	1999/2000	T1/TT1	VI
25	Midden deposit = 317 = 308 = 312	1999	TT1	III
26	Unexcavated; patches of sand within 025	1999	TT1	III
27	Unexcavated; patches of sand within 025	1999	TT1	III
28	Midden and shells, same as 025	1999	TT1	III
300	Area of paving truncated by trench edge	1959/2000	T1	II
301	Alignment of stones, probably wall	2000	T1	II
302a	Short cist	1959	T1	III
302b	Short cist aligned N–S, partially reconstructed after 1950s	2000	T1	VI
303a	Short cist	1959	T1	III
303b	Short cist, aligned N–S, partially reconstructed after 1950s	2000	T1	VI
304a	Short cist	1959	T1	III
304b	Short cist, aligned N–S, partially reconstructed after 1950s	2000	T1	VI
305a	Short cist	1959	T1	III
305b	Short cist, aligned N–S, partially reconstructed after 1950s	2000	T1	VI
306a	Rubble mound, tumbled stones	1959/2000	T1	III
306b	Tumble of stones partially excavated in 1950s	1959/2000	T1	VI
307a	Stone wall or base aligned N–S	2000	T1	III
307b	Upper courses of stone wall, reconstructed after 1950s excavations	1959/2000	T1	VI
308	Sandy soil, containing stone, pebbles, bone and shell. Unexcavated. Probably = 312, 317 and 025	2000	T1	III
309	Thick layer of clayey midden, same as 311, over 301	2000	T1	II
310	Area of cobbles and gravel below and covering same area as paving 300 above	2000	T1	II
311	Midden material spread over area to the west of cists 302 etc, same as 309	2000	T1	II

Number	Description	Year excavated	Trench	Phase
312	Layer of sandy shell midden, same as 25 from 1999 and 317 = 308	2000	T1	III
313	Area of paving stones to the north of 307, partially excavated and replaced after 1950s excavations	1959/2000	T1	VI
314	Compartmentalised low kerbed cairn complex over infant burials (SK 8–13)	2000	T1	III
315	Loose dark brown sand and shell, probably re-deposited midden, between stones of 306	1959/2000	T1	VI
316	Sand infill into hollow cut to find bedrock in 1959	1959/2000	T1	VI
317	Same as 25 and 312 = 308, sandy midden deposit	2000	T1	III
318	Sandy shell midden with bone and charcoal	2000	T1	III
319	Same as 318	2000	T1	III
320	Fill between outer lines of stones of possible wall 301	2000	T1	II
321	Long cist aligned E–W with 3 sides present, below sand 24 and later cist 06, partially excavated in 1959 (see also 336)	2000	T1	III
322	Same as 347. Loose sand within cist 305. Backfill from O'Dell's excavations	1959/2000	T1	VI
323a	Rubble to east of cist 305 forming east edge of cist	1959	T1	III
323b	Rubble wall collapsed and added to during 1950s excavations	1959/2000	T1	VI
324a/b	Concentration of quartz pebbles with occasional schist and sandstone, within sand matrix, on top of/within cist 321	2000	T1	III/V/VI
325	Layer of sandy shell midden, overlying 309 in west of trench	2000	T1	III
326a/b	Layer of angular schist and sandstone flags, paving within or at the bottom of, cist 321	2000	T1	III/V/VI
327	Paving of flat angular stones, sandstone and schist, to north of wall 307. Unexcavated	2000	T1	III
328	Mortared E–W 1950s wall below wall 010 1999, same as 012 1999	1959/2000	T1	VI
329	Sandy backfill within cist 303	1959/2000	T1	VI
330	Sandy shell, stones and gravel midden. Probably 325 re-deposited	2000	T1	III
331	Discrete dump of pottery sherds and reddish-brown or grey clay specific to dump, possibly ash	2000	T1	II
332	Mixed sandy midden material with shell and mixed human and animal bone (occasional), probably backfill, within 302	1959/2000	T1	VI
333	Shell and quartz pebbles in silty sand. Backfill, or at least disturbed during 1950s excavations. Within cist 304	1959/2000	T1	VI
334a/b	Fill of cist 321 below paving 326, sand and pebbles with shells	2000	T1	?III/V/VI
335	Rectangular cist, aligned E–W 3 sides remaining and south side replaced by modern wall 328. Filled by re-deposited sand 24, cuts sand and stones 340. Excavated in 1950s but left cist stones in situ	1959/2000	T1	VI
336	East end of cist 321, S and E stones only in situ, contains fallen cross-incised slab RF494	2000	T1	III
337	Sand and pebbles associated with laying of wall 328	2000	T1	VI
338	Sand and quartz pebbles over cross-slab RF 494	2000	T1	III
339	Fill between stones of wall 307. Probably re-deposited when upper courses of 307 added to after O'Dell's excavations	1959/2000	T1	VI
340	Same as 308, sand and stones in SW corner of trench. Largely unexcavated	2000	T1	III
341	Re-deposited and disturbed sandy midden over juvenile burial SK 7	2000	T1	III
342	Possible cut for juvenile crouched burial SK 7, aligned NW–SE	2000	T1	III
343	Sand and stones below cross-slab RF 494	2000	T1	III
344	Quartz (75%) and other pebbles below RF 494, above layer 343. Also frequent shells, occasional human bone fragments and pebbles with whitish deposit	2000	T1	III
345	Basal fill of wall 307. Undisturbed, and below cist 305. Same as 307	2000	T1	III
346	Irregular cut within 336, filled by pebbles 344	2000	T1	III
347	1950s backfill of sand into cist 305. Over clay 348. Same as 322	1959/2000	T1	VI
348	Clay inside cist 305. Surface of O'Dell's excavations, compact from trample		T1	III
349	Rounded, amorphous cut down to bedrock, made in 1959, to find bedrock. Cuts 309, and thick layer of clay below it (both unexcavated)	1959/2000	T1	VI
350	Schist bedrock	1959/2000	T1	I
351	Stone setting of flat, angular stones set upright in square shape. Partially excavated, east of a further setting 352, below 309 and 311	2000	T1	II
352	Square stone setting of upright angular stones, similar to 351 and to the west. Partially excavated	2000	T1	II

APPENDIX 5

Finds from the 1999–2000 excavations
by phase, context and small find number

★ = illustrated

Find no.	Context	Trench	Material	Description	No. of pieces	Phase
376	300	T1	Stone	Saddle quern	1	II
377	300	T1	Stone	Probably natural	1	II
378	300	T1	Stone	Probably natural	1	II
517	309	T1	Pottery	Body and rim sherds, fabric 1 (from BS 307). Lipid analysis	13	II
537	309	T1	Pottery	Body sherd, fabric 1	1	II
539	309	T1	Animal bone	Fragment of whittled long bone shaft	1	II
578	309	T1	Wood	Indeterminate mineralised wood	1	II
603	309	T1	Pottery	Body sherd, fabric 4, possibly base (from BS 307)	1	II
304b	309	T1	Wood	Indet mineralised wood	1	II
305b	309	T1	Charcoal	Apple type frags up to 2cm	4	II
604	310	T1	Pottery	Body and rim sherds, fabric 2 (from BS 303)	2	II
516	311	T1	Pottery	Body sherd, fabric 2 (from BS 305)	1	II
563	311	T1	Slag	Indeterminate lump of ferrous slag. 18 x 11 x 10mm (from BS 305)	1	II
464	331	T1	Animal bone	Not worked; cattle rib shaft section in very poor condition	1	II
520	331	T1	Pottery	Body sherds, fabric 1 (from BS 313)	6	II
390★	331	T1	Pottery	Rim, base and body sherds, fabric 1. Lipid analysis on 8 sherds	160 + frags	II
300	301	T1	Stone	Possible broken ard or mattock head	1	II
302	309	T1	Pottery	Body sherd, fabric 2	1	II
310	309	T1	Slag	Lump	1	II
314	309	T1	Pottery	Body sherd, fabric 1	1	II
318	309	T1	Pottery	Body sherd, fabric 2	1	II
320	309	T1	Pottery	Body sherd, fabric 1	1	II
322	309	T1	Pottery	Body sherd, fabric 4	1	II
323	309	T1	Pottery	Body sherd, fabric 4	1	II
324	309	T1	Pottery	Body sherd, fabric 2	1	II
325	309	T1	Pottery	Body sherd, fabric 1. Lipid analysis.	1	II
326	309	T1	Stone	Unworked	1	II
327	309	T1	Pottery	Body sherd, fabric 3	1	II
328	309	T1	Pottery	Body sherd, fabric 1	1	II
329	309	T1	Pottery	Body sherd, fabric 1. Lipid analysis.	1	II
332	309	T1	Burnt bone	Indeterminate partly calcined	1	II
333	309	T1	Quartz	Flake (cat. 2)	1	II
334	309	T1	Pottery	Body sherd, fabric 2	1	II
335	309	T1	Burnt bone	Indeterminate, charred	1	II
336	309	T1	Pottery	Body sherd, fabric 1	1	II
337	309	T1	Pottery	Body sherd, fabric 2	1	II
338	309	T1	Burnt bone	Indeterminate, charred (?pig mandible frag)	1	II
339	309	T1	Pottery	Body sherd, fabric 2	1	II
340	309	T1	Pottery	Body sherd, fabric 1	1	II
341	309	T1	Burnt bone	Indeterminate, charred	1	II
342	309	T1	Pottery	Body sherds, fabric 1	2	II
343	309	T1	Burnt bone	Charred cattle ischium; cojoins with SF 367	1	II
344	309	T1	Pottery	Body sherd, fabric 2	1	II
345	309	T1	Burnt bone	Indeterminate, charred	1	II
346	309	T1	Quartz	Flake (cat. 3)	1	II
347	309	T1	Pottery	Body sherd, fabric 1	1	II
349	309	T1	Human bone	Indeterminate fragment	1	II
350	309	T1	Stone	Possible hammerstone	1	II
351	309	T1	Stone	Unworked	1	II

Find no.	Context	Trench	Material	Description	No. of pieces	Phase
354	309	T1	Charcoal	cf larch	1	II
355	309	T1	Pottery	Body sherds, fabric 2	3	II
356	309	T1	Stone	Natural unworked stone	1	II
357	309	T1	Pottery	Body sherd, fabric 1	1	II
358	309	T1	Pottery	Body sherd, fabric 4. Marine residue analysis	1	II
359	309	T1	Pottery	Body sherd, fabric 1	1	II
360	309	T1	Stone	Pebble	1	II
361	309	T1	Slag	Lump	1	II
363	309	T1	Pottery	Body sherds, fabrics 2 and 3	2	II
364	309	T1	Quartz	Core (cat. 6)	1	II
365	309	T1	Slag	Lump	1	II
366	309	T1	Pottery	Body sherd, fabric 1	1	II
367	309	T1	Burnt bone	Charred frag cattle ischium; cojoins with SF 343	1	II
368	309	T1	Pottery	Body sherd, fabric 1	1	II
369	309	T1	Human bone	Fragments of infant skull from SK 6; reunited with SK 6 and included in skeletal report	c20	II
373	309	T1	Pottery	Body sherd, fabric 1	1	II
380	309	T1	Charcoal	Spruce/larch	1	II
381	309	T1	Pottery	Body sherd, fabric 4	1	II
382	309	T1	Pottery	Body sherd, fabric 2	1	II
387	309	T1	Pottery	Body sherd, fabric 2. Lipid analysis.	1	II
391	309	T1	Animal bone	Cattle and sheep/goat	9 + many indet	II
393	309	T1	Pottery	Body sherd, fabric 2	1	II
395	309	T1	Quartz	Possible flake (cat. 7)	1	II
406	309	T1	Pottery	Body sherd, fabric 2	1	II
408	309	T1	Pottery	Body sherd, fabric 1	1	II
410	309	T1	Pottery	Body sherd, fabric 1	1	II
411	309	T1	Burnt soil/cinder	Lump	1	II
412	309	T1	Pottery	Fragment, too small for identification	1	II
413	309	T1	Slag	Lump	1	II
414	309	T1	Pottery	Body sherd, fabric 2	1	II
415	309	T1	Animal bone	Indeterminate, calcined	1	II
416	309	T1	Burnt soil/cinder	Lump	1	II
417	309	T1	Pottery	Body sherd, fabric 1	1	II
418	309	T1	Pottery	Body sherd, fabric 2	1	II
419	309	T1	Pottery	Body sherd, fabric 1	1	II
420	309	T1	Quartz	Probable blade (cat. 11)	1	II
436	309	T1	Pottery	Body sherds, fabric 2	2	II
437	309	T1	Pottery	Body sherds, fabric 2. Marine residue analysis	4	II
438	309	T1	Pottery	Body sherds, fabric 2. Marine residue analysis	3	II
439	309	T1	Pottery	Body sherds, fabric 2. Marine residue analysis	3	II
440	309	T1	Pottery	Body sherd, fabric 3	1	II
441	309	T1	Pottery	Body sherd, fabric 1	1	II
448	309	T1	Pottery	Body sherds, fabric 1. Marine residue analysis	2	II
449	309	T1	Pottery	Body sherd, fabric 1	1	II
450	309	T1	Pottery	Body sherd, fabric 1	1	II
457	309	T1	Burnt soil/cinder	Lump	1	II
458	309	T1	Charcoal	Spruce/larch	1	II
468	309	T1	Pottery	Body sherd, fabric 3	1	II
469	309	T1	Animal bone	Cattle fragment	1	II
475	309	T1	Pottery	Body sherd, fabric 1	1	II
508	309	T1	Pottery	Body sherd, fabric 4	1	II
303*	309	T1	Pottery	Body sherd, fabric 1	1	II
304a	309	T1	Bone	Cattle, broken shaft frag of metatarsal	1	II
305a	309	T1	Calcined bone	Indeterminate bone	1	II
330a	309	T1	Burnt soil/cinder	One piece	1	II
330b	309	T1	Pottery	Body sherd, fabric 2	1	II
348*	309	T1	Whalebone	Whalebone long point broken into three pieces	1	II
362a	309	T1	Quartz	Probable flake (cat. 4)	1	II
362b	309	T1	Quartz	Possible waste (cat. 5)	1	II

Find no.	Context	Trench	Material	Description	No. of pieces	Phase
370★	309	T1	Stone	Irregularly trimmed slate disc with probably natural markings	1	II
392★	309	T1	Stone	Half a circular chamfered black stone disc; gaming piece?	1	II
409★	309	T1	Pottery	Rim sherd, fabric 2	1	II
514★	309	T1	Animal bone	Whalebone lump, chipped and shaped block	1	II
306	311	T1	Charcoal	Cf spruce	1	II
307	311	T1	Burnt bone	Charred, sheep/goat frag	1	II
308	311	T1	Pottery	Body sherd, fabric 1	1	II
309	311	T1	Pottery	Body sherd, fabric 1	1	II
311	311	T1	Pottery	Body sherd, fabric 2	1	II
313	311	T1	Pottery	Body sherd, fabric 2	1	II
315	311	T1	Pottery	Body sherd, fabric 1	1	II
316	311	T1	Quartz	Flake (cat. 1)	1	II
317	311	T1	Pottery	Body sherd, fabric 2	1	II
331	311	T1	Burnt bone	Indeterminate, charred	1	II
352	311	T1	Pottery	Body sherd, fabric 1	1	II
371	311	T1	Pottery	Body sherd, abraded	2	II
374	311	T1	Stone	Steatite chunk unworked	1	II
375	311	T1	Pottery	Body sherds, fabric 1	2	II
379	311	T1	Cinder	Cinder	1	II
383	311	T1	Pottery	Body sherds, fabric 1	2	II
384	311	T1	Pottery	Body sherd, fabric 2	1	II
385	311	T1	Pottery	Body sherd, fabric 3	1	II
386	311	T1	Pottery	Body sherd, fabric 2	1	II
388	311	T1	Pottery	Body sherd, fabric 2	1	II
389	311	T1	Burnt soil/ cinder	Lump	1	II
394	311	T1	Pottery	Body sherd, fabric 2	4	II
396	311	T1	Pottery	Body sherd, fabric 1	1	II
397	311	T1	Pottery	Body sherd, fabric 3	2	II
398	311	T1	Charcoal and burnt soil/ cinder	One lump of oak, three lumps of cinder	1	II
405	311	T1	Pottery	Body sherd, fabric 2	1	II
407	311	T1	Stone	Unworked steatite lump	1	II
372★	311	T1	Stone	Steatite weight fragment	1	II
459	320	T1	Burnt soil/ cinder	Lump	1	II
44	25	TT1	Human bone	Undiagnostic tiny fragment	1	III
46	25	TT1	Shell	Two oyster, one cockle	3	III
47	25	TT1	Pottery	Body sherd, fabric 4	1	III
50	25	TT1	Human bone	Adult thoracic vertebra	1	III
53	25	TT1	Animal bone	Indeterminate fragment	1	III
54	25	TT1	Slag			III
55	25	TT1	Animal bone	Sheep/goat scapula, sheep long bone shaft frag, gull sp femur, and indet	4	III
56	25	TT1	Slag			III
64	25	TT1	Pottery	Body sherd, fabric 1	1	III
65	25	TT1	Human bone	Adult thoracic vertebra		III
67	25	TT1	Pottery	Body sherds, fabrics 2 and 3	3	III
51a	25	TT1	Animal bone	Not located	Not located	III
51b	25	TT1	Pottery	Body sherd, fabric 4	1	III
57a	25	TT1	Animal bone	Dog canine	1	III
57b	25	TT1	Human bone	Juvenile left scapula	1	III
63	27	TT1	Pottery	Body sherd, fabric 1. Lipid analysis.	1	III
402	312	T1	Quartz	Flake (cat. 8)	1	III
403	312	T1	Quartz	Core (cat. 9)	1	III
404	312	T1	Quartz	Blade (cat. 10)	1	III
312	314	T1	Pottery	Body sherd, fabric 2	1	III
301★	314	T1	Stone	Cross-incised stone	1	III
465★	314	T1	Stone	Inscribed with cross, schist	1	III
421	318	T1	Stone	Natural unworked stone	1	III
422	318	T1	Pottery	Body sherd, fabric 1	1	III
423	318	T1	Pottery	Body sherd, fabric 2	1	III
424	318	T1	Animal bone	Indeterminate, charred	1	III
425	318	T1	Pottery	Body sherd, fabric 2	1	III

Find no.	Context	Trench	Material	Description	No. of pieces	Phase
426	318	T1	Pottery	Body sherds, fabric 1	3	III
427	318	T1	Pottery	Body sherd, fabric 2	1	III
431	318	T1	Pottery	Body sherd, fabric 1	1	III
434	318	T1	Animal bone	Indeterminate, charred	1	III
435	318	T1	Pottery	Body sherd, fabric 1	1	III
443	318	T1	Animal bone	Indeterminate, charred	1	III
445	318	T1	Pottery	Body sherd, fabric 1	1	III
451	318	T1	Pottery	Body sherd, fabric 1. Marine residue analysis	1	III
452	318	T1	Pottery	Body sherds, fabric 1. Marine residue analysis	2	III
453	318	T1	Quartz	Possible flake (cat. 18)	1	III
455	318	T1	Pottery	Body sherd, fabric 1. Marine residue analysis	1	III
456	318	T1	Pottery	Body sherd, fabric 1	1	III
461	318	T1	Pottery	Body sherds, fabric 1	2	III
462	318	T1	Pottery	Body sherds, fabric 2	2	III
518	318	T1	Pottery	Body sherd, fabric 1 (from BS 309)	1	III
460★	318	T1	Animal bone	Worked bead, cattle metatarsal shaft section	1	III
512★	318	T1	Animal bone	Worked; cattle metatarsal shaft section	1	III
400	325	T1	Slag	Lump	1	III
401	325	T1	Stone	Natural	1	III
503	325	T1	Charcoal	Scots pine type	1	III
556	325	T1	Fe	Indeterminate fragment of corroded metal, flat. 35 x 25 x 4mm (from BS 310)	1	III
399★	325	T1	Animal bone	Bone peg whittled from long bone shaft	1	III
432★	325	T1	Bone	Worked whale bone, shaped piece with neatly drilled central hole	1	III
467	330	T1	Pottery	Body sherd, fabric 2	1	III
471	330	T1	Stone	Headstone	1	III
472	330	T1	Stone	Headstone	1	III
498	330	T1	Pottery	Body sherd, fabric 1	1	III
499	330	T1	Pottery	Body sherd, fabric 2	1	III
500	330	T1	Pottery	Body sherd, fabric 2	1	III
501	330	T1	Pottery	Body sherd, fabric 2	1	III
504	330	T1	Pottery	Body sherd, fabric 4. Lipid analysis	1	III
505	330	T1	Pottery	Body sherd, fabric 2	1	III
519	330	T1	Pottery	Body sherds, fabric 1 (from BS 312)	2	III
507a	330	T1	Quartz	Probable flake (cat. 23)	1	III
507b	330	T1	Quartz	Flake (cat. 24)	1	III
494★	336	T1	Stone	Cross inscribed, schist	1	III
483	338	T1	Pebble with residue	White residue encrusted on pebble	1	III
522	338	T1	Pottery	Body sherds, fabric 2 (from BS 320)	2	III
488★	338	T1	Animal bone	Shaped lump of whalebone vertebra centrum	1	III
491	340	T1	Fe	Highly corroded object flat-sectioned piece	1	III
495	340	T1	Pottery	Body sherd, fabric 2	1	III
496	340	T1	Pottery	Body sherd, fabric 1	1	III
523	340	T1	Pottery	Body sherds, fabric 1 (from BS 325)	4	III
555	340	T1	Fe	Nail shank, very badly corroded (from BS 325)	1	III
606	340	T1	Pottery	Body and rim sherd, fabric 1 (from BS 325)	1	III
525	341	T1	Pottery	Body sherd, fabric 1 (from BS 327)	1	III
560	341	T1	Cu alloy	Top part of wire-wound pin ? shroud pin. 15 x 2 x 2mm (from BS 327)	1	III
529	343	T1	Pottery	Body and ?rim sherds, fabrics 1 and 2 (from BS 332). Lipid analysis	10	III
530	343	T1	Pottery/daub?	?Daub frags. (from BS 343)	frags	III
586	343	T1	Quartz	Flake (from BS 332) (cat. 34)	1	III
524	344	T1	Pottery	Body sherd and frag, fabric 2 (from BS 326)	1 + frag	III
587	344	T1	Quartz	Flake (from BS 326) (cat. 31)	1	III
588	344	T1	Quartz	Flake (from BS 326) (cat. 32)	1	III
575	345	T1	Stone	Pebble with one short edge slightly smoothed. ?rubber. 120 x 70 x 30mm (from BS 328)	1	III
528	348	T1	Pottery	Body sherds, fabric 2 (from BS 331)	5	III
510★	330/SK 9	T1	Stone	Deliberately shaped possibly through use as a smoother	1	III
509	SK 12	T1	Quartz	Natural unworked quartz (cat. 25); missing	1	III
511	SK 9	T1	Shell	Limpet in mouth of SK 9	1	III
497	SK5	T1	Fe	Knife blade with SK 5; blade and most of tang with traces of wooden haft remaining in corrosion	1	III

Find no.	Context	Trench	Material	Description	No. of pieces	Phase
466	334	T1	Pebble with residue	White residue encrusted on pebble	1	III/VI
473	334	T1	Pottery	Body sherd, fabric 3	1	III/VI
478	334	T1	Quartz	Possible waste (cat. 22)	1	III/VI
502	334	T1	Burnt soil/cinder	Lump	1	III/VI
506	334	T1	Stone	Unworked	1	III/VI
521	334	T1	Pottery	Body sherd, fabric 2 (from BS 316)	1	III/VI
526	334	T1	Pottery	Body sherds, fabric 1 (from BS 329)	4	III/VI
577	334	T1	Mortar	Fragment (2cm long)	1	III/VI
589	334	T1	Quartz	Blade (from BS 316) (cat. 26)	1	III/VI
590	334	T1	Quartz	Flake (from BS 316) (cat. 27)	1	III/VI
591	334	T1	Quartz	Flake (from BS 316) (cat. 28)	1	III/VI
592	334	T1	Quartz	Waste (from BS 316) (cat. 29)	1	III/VI
593	334	T1	Quartz	Waste (from BS 316) (cat. 30)	1	III/VI
561	1	T1	Slag	Indeterminate lump of ferrous slag. 16 x 13 x 12mm (from bag 3)	1	VI
562	1	T1	Slag	Indeterminate lump of ferrous slag. 22 x 20 x 13mm (from bag 4)	1	VI
538	315	T1	Bone	Worked animal bone (from BS 302)	1	VI
319	316	T1	Pottery	Body sherd, fabric 2	1	VI
513	316	T1	Pottery	Body sherd, fabric 1	1	VI
527	316	T1	Pottery	Body sherds, fabrics 1 and 2 (from BS 330)	3	VI
550	316	T1	Fe	Nail with round head and broken shank. 36 x 11 x 7mm	1	VI
463	329	T1	Quartz	Natural unworked quartz (cat. 20); discarded	1	VI
481	333	T1	Pottery	Body sherd, fabric 1	1	VI
482	333	T1	Pottery	Body sherd, fabric 1	1	VI
484	333	T1	Pottery	Body sherd, fabric 1	1	VI
485	333	T1	Pottery	Body sherd, fabric 1	1	VI
486	333	T1	Stone	Natural unworked stone	1	VI
487	333	T1	Animal bone	Indeterminate, charred	1	VI
489	333	T1	Pottery	Body sherd, fabric 2	1	VI
490	333	T1	Pottery	Body sherd, fabric 3	1	VI
492	333	T1	Animal bone	Indeterminate, charred	1	VI
493	333	T1	Animal bone	Indeterminate, charred	1	VI
565	333	T1	Plastic	Short length of green plastic wire sheathing (from BS 314)	1	VI
566	333	T1	Stone	Small pebble with two grooves on one face, possibly manmade (from BS 314)	1	VI
576	333	T1	Mortar	Fragments (largest 2cm long)	2	VI
476	337	T1	Charcoal	Spruce/larch	1	VI
477	337	T1	Quartz	Possible core (cat. 21)	1	VI
479	337	T1	Pebble with residue	White residue encrusted on pebble; analysed by XRD and SEM	1	VI
480	337	T1	Stone	Unworked	1	VI
605	337	T1	Pottery	Body sherd, fabric 1 (from BS 318)	1	VI
474	339	T1	Pottery	Body sherd, fabric 4	1	VI
594	339	T1	Quartz	Flake (from BS 317) (cat. 43)	1	VI
595	339	T1	Quartz	Waste (from BS 317) (cat. 44)	1	VI
596	339	T1	Quartz	Waste (from BS 317) (cat. 45)	1	VI
557	306b	T1	Fe	Nail with narrow flat head and bent shank at lower end. 30 x 5 x 5mm (from BS 302)	1	VI
559	306b	T1	Fe	Flat piece, expanded at one end, possible knife tang or part fo a tool? 50 x 17 x 2mm (from BS 302)	1	VI
564	306b	T1	Slag	Indeterminate lump of ferrous rich slag. 35 x 25 x 5mm (from BS 302)	1	VI
579	306b	T1	Quartz	Blade (from BS 302) (cat. 36)	1	VI
580	306b	T1	Quartz	Flake (from BS 302) (cat. 37)	1	VI
581	306b	T1	Quartz	Flake (from BS 302) (cat. 38)	1	VI
582	306b	T1	Quartz	Flake (from BS 302) (cat. 39)	1	VI
583	306b	T1	Quartz	Flake (from BS 302) (cat. 40)	1	VI
584	306b	T1	Quartz	Waste (from BS 302) (cat. 41)	1	VI
585	306b	T1	Quartz	Waste (from BS 302) (cat. 42)	1	VI
515a★	306b	T1	Antler	Bead; hollowed out tine	1	VI
515b	306b	T1	Pottery	Body sherds, fabric 2 (from BS 302)	2	VI
540★	306b	T1	Bone	Cattle metatarsal with hole made in proximal end		VI
541★	306b	T1	Bone	Sheep/goat metacarpal, proximal end worked and polished, opposite end broken		VI

Find no.	Context	Trench	Material	Description	No. of pieces	Phase
558★	306b	T1	Fe	Loop with one end broken and twisted shank. ?Key. 43 x 10 x 5mm (from BS 302) (conjoins with SF 551)	1	VI
60	24	TT1	Human bone	Infant burial, in situ	–	VI
61	24	TT1	Human bone	Adult burial, in situ	–	VI
353	24	T1	Pottery	Body sherd, fabric 1	1	VI
428	24	T1	Quartz	Flake (cat. 12) + 1 natural unworked (cat. 13); discarded	1	VI
430	24	T1	Pebble with residue	Pinkish white residue encrusted on pebble	1	VI
442	24	T1	Wood	Indeterminate mineralised wood - cf coniferales (coniferous)	1	VI
444	24	T1	Mortar	Lump of shell mortar	1	VI
446	24	T1	Mortar	Lumps of shell mortar	2	VI
447	24	T1	Quartz	Natural unworked quartz (cat. 17); discarded	1	VI
454	24	T1	Quartz	Flake tool (cat. 19)	1	VI
470	24	T1	Stone	Unworked	1	VI
429a	24	T1	Quartz	Probable flake (cat.15) +5 bogus (cat. 14); discarded	1	VI
429b	24	T1	Quartz	Flake (cat. 16)	1	VI
433★	24	T1	Stone	Inscribed with cross, schist	1	VI
531	1	T1	Pottery	Body sherds, fabric 2 (from general finds; no date)	6	VII
532	1	T1	Pottery	Body sherd, fabric 2 (from general finds 03/07/00)	1	VII
533	1	T1	Pottery	Body sherds, fabric 2 (from general finds 04/07/00)	8	VII
534	1	T1	Pottery	Body sherd, fabric 1 (from general finds 09/07/00)	1	VII
535	1	T1	Pottery	Body sherds, fabric 1 (from general finds 11/07/00)	3	VII
536	1	T1	Pottery	Body sherd, fabric 2 (from general finds 12/07/00)	1	VII
542	1	T1	Fe	Flat topped iron nail with small head. 51 x 6 x 5mm (from bag 1)	1	VII
543	1	T1	Fe	Rove, with part of shank. 34 x 24 x 19mm max (from bag 1)	1	VII
544	1	T1	Fe	Rove, broken and incomplete. 19 x 17 x 8mm (from bag 2)	1	VII
545	1	T1	Fe	Rove, broken and incomplete. 21 x 14 x 11mm (from bag 2)	1	VII
546	1	T1	Fe	Large round headed nail with short shank. 25 x 23 x 22mm (from bag 2)	1	VII
547	1	T1	Fe	Small nail, highly corroded. 18 x 7 x 4mm (from bag 2)	1	VII
548	1	T1	Fe	Long nail, broken shank, head expanded and corroded. 48 x 17 x 12mm (from bag 2)	1	VII
549	1	T1	Fe	Small iron fragment with traces of wood in corrosion. 16 x 14 x 5mm (from bag 2)	1	VII
552	1	TT1	Fe	Broken nail shank, square section. Overall c38 x 10 x 5mm (from bag 5)	1	VII
553	1	TT1	Fe	Quantity of shattered iron fragments, originally a nail. No dimensions (from bag 6)	many	VII
554	1	T1	Fe	Halfpenny of 1957. Light corrosion. Dia 25mm	1	VII
569	1	T1	Stone	Waterworn pebble with one face very smoothed, possible hone?. 83 x 26 x 15mm (from bag 9)	1	VII
570	1	T1	Stone	Crudely chipped schist disc. ?Pot lid. 98 x 118 x 17mm (from bag 10)	1	VII
571	1	T1	Stone	Quatzite pebble with rose patch. ?Selected. 67 x 60 x 32mm (from bag 10)	1	VII
572	1	T1	Stone	Eliptical pebble, possibly utilised at each end. 1000 x 62 x 18mm (from bag 10)	1	VII
574	1	T1	Stone	Long pebble with two long faces smoothed. ?Doubtful hone. 95 x 25 x 20mm (from bag 11)	1	VII
597	1	T1	Quartz	Flake (from general finds 4/7/00) (cat. 46)	1	VII
598	1	T1	Quartz	Flake (from general finds 10/7/00) (cat. 47)	1	VII
599	1	TT1	Quartz	Flake (from general finds 25/8/99) (cat. 48)	1	VII
600	1	TT1	Quartz	Core (from general finds 25/8/99) (cat. 49)	1	VII
601	1	TT1	Quartz	Flake (from general finds 25/8/99) (cat. 50)	1	VII
602	1	T1	Quartz	Flake (from SK 10) (cat. 33)	1	VII
551★	1	T1	Fe	Elongated iron piece with rounded shafting at one end, incomplete circumference. ? Projectile point or key, bent and incomplete. 42 x 10 x 8mm (from bag 4)(conjoins with SF 558)	1	VII
567★	1	T1	Stone	Two water-worn pieces of pumice, one has smoothed face (a). a) 35 x 25 x 11mm; b) 32 x 25 x 2mm (from bag 7)	2	VII
568★	1	T1	Stone	Broken shaped quartz fragment, possible traces of perforation at one edge. 25 x 18 x 9mm (from bag 8 w/I N–S wall))	1	VII
573★	1	T1	Stone	Complete disc with ground edges. Flat. Gaming piece 26 x 24 x 6mm (from bag 11)	1	VII

APPENDIX 6

Catalogue of quartz

from the 1999–2000 excavations

Cat.	SF	Q-Cat	P/S/T	Type*	Sub-type	L	W	Bth	Bulb	P-W	P-D	Platform*	Terminal*	Direction*	Pattern	Pat	Cort	Burnt	Retouch	Macro/Evidence	Context
Trench 1 contexts																					
1	316	Def	S	F	regular	31	10	8	F	3	2	S	F	O	4, 2s 2r	na	na	x	R/Md/Sr D/Cnt/R/m	heavy damage dorsal distal	311
2	333	Def	S	F	regular	21	23	8	D	17.5	7.5	F	F	B	5, 3s 2 90	na	na	x	x	utilised? V/L/m	309
3	346	Def	I	F	regular	23	13	5	P	12	1.5	L	F	O	6, 3s 3r	na	na	x	x	x	309
4	362.1	Prob	I	F	irregular	23	15	5	F	3	1.5	S	H	B	3, 1s 2 90	na	na	x	x	damage dorsal left mid-lower	309/311
5	362.2	Poss	S	W	chunk	21	13	8	na	na	na	na	na	na	na	na	na	x	x	heavy damage to both lateral margins	309/311
6	364	Def	I	C	bipolar	25	12	8	na	many	many	M	na	M	11, varios d	na	na	x	x	x	309/311
7	395	Poss	P	F	irregular	10x	8x	3x	?	?	?	?	?	F	na	0	na	na	x	x	distal fragment	309
8	402	Def	I	F	regular	21	17	4	D	5	1	V	F	M	6, 1s 4r 1 270	na	na	x	? Ir/Md/Sc D/L/m-l	damage, utilised? D/L/m-l	312
9	403	Def	S	C	bipolar	30	22	11	na	many	many	M	na	BO	10, various d	na	na	x	x	x	312
10	404	Def	I	B	bladelet	18	7	3	D	1	1.5	S	F	U	4s	na	na	x	x	x	312
11	420	Prob	I	B	blade	23	9	3	F	7	2.5	V	F	O	3, 1s 1r 1?	na	na	x	x	x	309
12	428.1	Def	I	F	regular	17	24	8	F	6	1.5	L	F	B	4, 3s 1 90	na	na	x	R/Fn-Md/Pl/S-abt D/L/u-l	x	24
13	428.2	Nat	x	x	x	x	x	x	x	x	x	x	x	x	x	x	x	x	x	x	24
14	429.1	Nat	x	x	x	x	x	x	x	x	x	x	x	x	x	x	x	x	x	x	24
15	429.2	Prob	P	F	decortical	17	28	8	P	25	7	F	F	na	o	na	na	x	x	x	24
16	429.3	Def	S	F	irregular / core-prep	24	15	13	F	9.5	2.5	F	P	O	6, 2s 2r 2r	na	na	x	x	x	24
17	447	Nat	x	x	x	x	x	x	x	x	x	x	x	x	x	x	x	x	x	x	24
18	453	Poss	P	F	decortical	39	41	7	F	36	5.5	F	K	na	o	na	na	x	x	x	318
19	454	Def	I	FT	side scraper	35x	11x	10x	?	?	?	?	?	U	2s	na	na	x	R/Hv/Sc/S-Abt D/L/u-l	snap lateral right	24
20	463	Nat	x	x	x	x	x	x	x	x	x	x	x	x	x	x	x	x	x	x	329
21	477	Poss	S	C	Uni/SPC/conical/fl	31	27	10	na	24	9.5	F	na	U	4s	na	na	x	x	x	337
22	478	Poss	S	W	shatter over 10mm	13	8	4	na	na	na	na	na	na	na	na	na	x	x	x	334
23	507.1	Prob	P	F	decortical	20	27	12	P	23	12	F	S	na	o	na	na	x	x	x	330
24	507.2	Def	S	F	irregular	16	14	5	P	13	5.5	F	P	U	2, 1s 1?	na	na	x	x	x	330
25	509	Nat	x	x	x	x	x	x	x	x	x	x	x	x	x	x	x	x	x	x	SK12
Trench 1 samples																					**Sample**
26	[316.1]	Def	I	B	chip	11	4	2	D	2	1.5	V	F	U	2s	na	na	x	x	x	334, [316]
27	[316.2]	Prob	S	F	irregular	9	8	3	P	4	2	F	F	U	3s	na	na	x	x	x	334, [316]
28	[316.3]	Prob	P	F	decortical	10	8	3	P	3	1.5	C	F	na	0	na	na	x	x	x	334, [316]
29	[316.4]	Poss	S	W	shatter less than 10mm	x	x	x	na	na	na	na	na	na	na	na	na	x	x	x	334, [316]
30	[316.5]	Poss	S	W	shatter less than 10mm	x	x	x	na	na	na	na	na	na	na	na	na	x	x	x	334, [316]
31	[326.1]	Prob	P	F	decortical	23	15	6	F	4.5	1.5	F	F	na	0	na	na	x	x	x	344, [326]
32	[326.2]	Poss	P	F	decortical	24	15	4	P	3	1	C	F	na	0	na	na	x	x	x	344, [326]
33	SK 10	Def	P	F	decortical	20	13	4	F	9.5	2.5	F	P	na	0	na	na	x	x	x	SK 10
34	[332.1]	Prob	I	F	irregular	12	10	2	F	8	2	F	P	U	3s	na	na	x	x	x	343, [332]
35	[305.1]	Nat	x	x	x	x	x	x	x	x	x	x	x	x	x	x	x	x	x	x	311, [305]
36	[302.1]	Def	I	B	blade	21	9	3	F	8	2.25	F	F	U	4s	na	na	x	x	x	306, [302]
37	[302.2]	Def	S	F	irregular / core-prep	17	11	3	P	4	2	V	F	B	2, 1s 1 270	na	na	x	x	x	306, [302]
38	[302.3]	Prob	I	F	regular	21	8	5	F	1.5	1	F	F	B	4, 3s 1 90	na	na	x	x	x	306, [302]
39	[302.4]	Prob	S	F	irregular	12	7	3	D	4.5	1	F	F	B	3, 1s 2 90	na	na	x	x	x	306, [302]
40	[302.5]	Def	I	F	irregular	11	8	2	F	5	0.5	L	F	U	3s	na	na	x	x	x	306, [302]

Cat.	SF	Q-Cat	P/S/T	Type*	Sub-type	L	W	Bth	Bulb	P-W	P-D	Platform*	Terminal*	Direction*	Pattern	Pat	Cort	Burnt	Retouch	Macro/Evidence	Context
41	[302.6]	Poss	S	W	shatter over 10mm	11	6	3	na	na	na	na	na	na	na	na	na	x	x	x	306, [302]
42	[302.7]	Prob	I	W	shatter less than 10mm	x	x	x	na	na	na	na	na	na	na	na	na	x	x	x	306, [302]
43	[317.1]	Def	I	F	regular	14	12	3	P	10	3	F	F	B	4 90	na	na	x	x	x	339, [317]
44	[317.2]	Prob	I	W	shatter over 10mm	11	6	3	na	na	na	na	na	na	na	na	na	x	x	x	339, [317]
45	[317.3]	Prob	I	W	shatter less than 10mm	x	x	x	na	na	na	na	na	na	na	na	na	x	x	x	339, [317]
Trial Trench 1 contexts																					
46	335?	Def	S	F	regular	32	18	10	P	13.5	9.5	F	F	O	2r	na	na	x	x	x	1
47	336?	Def	S	F	irregular	13	8	3	P	3	1.5	V	F	B	2, 1s 1 90	na	na	x	x	x	1
48	337.1?	Def	S	F	regular / cor prep	21	18	9	P	13	5	Co	P	U	3s	na	na	x	x	x	1
49	337.2?	Prob	S	C	Bif-Opp-PC-semi-conical-fl	23	20	17	na	14.5/14.5	18/8.5	F/F	na	O	4, 3s 1r	na	na	x	x	x	1
50	337.3?	Prob	S	F	regular / cor prep	14	16	10	P	14	9.5	F	P	U	4s	na	na	x	x	x	1

*

Type:
B: blade
C: core
F: flake
FT: flake tool
W: waste
x: n/a

Platform:
C: cortical
Co: concave
F: flat
L: linear
M: many
S: shattered
V: vestigial

Terminal:
F: fine
H: hinge
K: kam step
P: plungeing
S: step

Direction:
B: bi-directional
BO: bipolar opposed
M: multi-directional
O: opposed
U: uniplane

APPENDIX 7

Catalogue of coarse pottery

from the 1999–2000 excavations

★ : Maximum measurements for smallest sherd present in range   ★★ : Sherd submitted for analysis
Surface finish: S (smoothed), B (burnished)

SF	Context	Trench	Year	Sherds	Weight (g)	Width (mm)★	Longest axis (mm)★	Decoration (y/n)	Surface finish	Fabric	Sooting	Comment	Phase
302	309	1	2000	1	18.7	8.0	55.0	n	S	2 + 10%	n	spatula marks in interior	II
303	309	1	2000	1	5	9.0	24.5	?y	B	1	n	possible faint linear and herringbone décor	II
308	309	1	2000	1	2.6	5.0	25.0	n	B	1	int		II
309	309	1	2000	1	1.9	6.5	22.5	?y	n	1	ext	faint linear; residue on exterior	II
314	309	1	2000	1	6.1	8.0	31.5	n	n	1+ 20% inc	n	?interior abraded	II
320	309	1	2000	1	4.0	7.0	25.5	n	n	1+ 10% inc	both		II
322	309	1	2000	1	10.3	8.5	39.0	n	S	4+ 10% inc	ext	interior part abraded	II
323	309	1	2000	1	8.3	8.0	40.5	n	n	4+ 20% inc	both		II
324	309	1	2000	1	2.7	6.5	25.0	n	S	2+10% inc	both		II
325	309	1	2000	2	10.9	7.0 (6.5)	38.5 (33.0)	n	S	1+10% inc	both	conjoining; dimensions 7.0 x 42.5; int res	II
327	309	1	2000	1	1.9	4.0	26.5	n	B	3	n	both surfaces burnished black	II
328	309	1	2000	1	2.9	9.0	24.5	n	int B	1+ 10% inc	n		II
329	309	1	2000	1	9.2	8.0	42.0	n	S	1+ 10% inc	both	residue on interior	II
334	309	1	2000	1	6.5	8.0	36.0	n	n	2	int		II
336	309	1	2000	1	3.7	7.0	29.5	n	B	1	n		II
337	309	1	2000	1	11.4	10.5	35.0	n	B	2	both		II
342	309	1	2000	2	12.1	8.0 (5.5)	45.5 (36.0)	?y	comb/burn	1	ext	interior combed	II
344	309	1	2000	1	1.2	4.0	19.5	n	n	2	ext	thin walled	II
347	309	1	2000	1	5.8	6.5	31.0	n	B	1	int		II
355	309	1	2000	3	1.1	4.0 (4.0)	14.5 (11.0)	n	B	2	n	thin walled	II
356	309	1	2000									stone	II
357	309	1	2000	1	2.6		22.5	n	n	1	ext	?part of a round cordon	II
358★★	309	1	2000										II
359	309	1	2000	1	3.1	10.5	23.0	n	n	1+ 10% inc	n	prob flat part of base	II
363	309	1	2000	2	2.1	3.5 (6.0)	22.5 (11.5)	n	n	2 and 3+10% inc	ext	2 different pots; thin-walled	II
368	309	1	2000	1	9.7	8.0	30.5	n	n	1+ 10% inc	int		II
373	309	1	2000	1	7.1		27.5	n	B	1	ext	1 body, 1 flat part of base (prob same vessel)	II
381	309	1	2000	1	8.0	10.5	31.5	n	n	4+ 30% steatite	n	abraded	II
382	309	1	2000	1	5.5	5.0	38.0	n	burnished	2+ 10%	both		II

SF	Context	Trench	Year	Sherds	Weight (g)	Width (mm)*	Longest axis (mm)*	Decoration (y/n)	Surface finish	Fabric	Sooting	Comment	Phase
387	309	1	2000	1	6.8	6.0	40.0	n	n	2	both		II
393	309	1	2000	1	17.0	8.5	40.0	n	n	2+ 10%	ext		II
406	309	1	2000	1	4.5	6.5	27.5	n	n	2	both		II
408	309	1	2000	1	7.6	7.5	43.5	n	n	1+ 10% inc	both	residue on interior	II
409	309	1	2000	1	6.2	7.0	30.0	n	n	2	ext	rim beaded to interior	II
410	309	1	2000	1	4.2	9.5	23.5	n	n	1	ext	from angle of base	II
414	309	1	2000	1	5.5	8.0	32.0	n	n	2	both		II
417	309	1	2000	1	4.5		35.0	n	n	1	ext	?abraded	II
418	309	1	2000	1	3.9	6.0	30.0	n	n	2	both		II
419	309	1	2000	1	10.1	8.0	37.5	n	n	1+ 10%	int		II
436	309	1	2000	2	5.3	5.5 (6.0)	32.5 (26.0)	n	n	2	n		II
437**	309	1	2000										II
438**	309	1	2000										II
439**	309	1	2000										II
440	309	1	2000	1	0.5	4.0	14.0	n	n	3	n		II
441	309	1	2000	1	5.0	6.0	28.0	n	n	1+ 10% inc	both		II
448**	309	1	2000										II
449	309	1	2000	1	3.0	5.5	25.0	n	n	1	both		II
450	309	1	2000	1	6.5	7.5	27.5	n	n	1+ 10% inc	both		II
468	309	1	2000	1	10.3	10.5	34.0	n	S	3+ 10% inc	n		II
474	309	1	2000	1	2.4	6.0	22.0	n	n	4+ 10% inc	both		II
475	309	1	2000	1	1.0	5.5	13.0	n	n	1	int		II
508	309	1	2000	1	1.9	6.0	20.0	n	n	4+ 20%	ext		II
517	309	1	2000	13	24.1	6.0 (-)	34.0 (7.0)	n	n	1 and 1+ 10% inc	ext	smallest sherd, abraded frag (BS 307); all different vessels (one rim)	II
311	311	1	2000	1	2	5.5	20.5	n	n	2	int		II
313	311	1	2000	1	1.4	6.0	17.0	n	n	2	ext		II
315	311	1	2000	1	3.5	9.0	20.5	n	n	1	n		II
317	311	1	2000	1	1.4	4.0	20.5	n	n	2	both	same vessel as 318	II
318	311	1	2000	1	2.2	3.0	28.0	n	n	2	both	very thin-walled	II
339	311	1	2000	1	3.4	6.0	32.0	n	n	2	both		II
340	311	1	2000	1	1.7	5.5	20.0	n	B	1	ext		II
352	311	1	2000	1	3	10.5	26.0	n	n	1	n	exterior abraded	II
366	311	1	2000	1	5.4	9.5	25.5	n	n	1+ 10% inc	ext		II
371	311	1	2000	2	14.5	8.5 (-)	34.5 (24.0)	n				?abraded	II
375	311	1	2000	2	7.5	5.0 (5.5)	40.5 (20.5)	n	n	1	ext		II
383	311	1	2000	2	2.0	5.5 (5.5)	16.0 (11.0)	n	n	1	both	prob different vessels	II
384	311	1	2000	1	1.8	6.0	20.0	n	n	2	int		II
385	311	1	2000	1	4.3	9.5	26.0	n	n	3+ 10%	ext		II
386	311	1	2000	1	1.6	4.0	21.5	n	B	2	int		II
388	311	1	2000	1	2.8	8.5	23.5	y	combed	2+ 10% inc	n	combing on both faces	II
394	311	1	2000	4	4.0	7.5 (4.0)	19.5 (13.0)	n	n	2	both	thin walled	II
396	311	1	2000	1	2.7	6.5	26.0	n	B	1	ext		II
397	311	1	2000	2	3.3	7.0	25.5	n	n	3	int		II
405	311	1	2000	1	6.5	7.5	32.5	n	n	2+ 10%	both		II
516	311	1	2000	1	1.7	4.0	23.5	n	n	2	ext	(from BS 305); coil junction; thin-walled	II
390	331	1	2000	160 & frags	889.0	8.0 (6.0)	83.0 (12.5)	n	B	1	both	flat rim; flat base, angled walls	II
481	331	1	2000	1	11.1	7.5	43.5	n	n	1+ 10% inc	both		II
520	331	1	2000	6	17.8	8.0 (8.0)	27.0 (11.5)	n	n	1+ 10% inc	int	(from BS 313) all same vessel	II

SF	Context	Trench	Year	Sherds	Weight (g)	Width (mm)*	Longest axis (mm)*	Decoration (y/n)	Surface finish	Fabric	Sooting	Comment	Phase
47	25	TT1	1999	1	14.3	8.5	44.5	n	S	4 + 20% inc	both		III
51	25	TT1	1999	1	3.9	5.5	29	n	B	4 + 10% inc	n		III
64	25	TT1	1999	1	5.2	11	25	n	n	1 + 10% inc	both	from just above base; residue on interior	III
67	25	TT1	1999	3	8	7	21	n	n	2 and 3	some	all different vessels	III
63	27	TT1	1999	1	8.9	7	39	n	n	1	ext	burnt residues present on ex-terior	III
312	314	1	2000	1	7.4	7.0	37.0	n	n	2	n		III
421	318	1	2000									stone	III
422	318	1	2000	1	1.6		16.0	n	n	1	n	?abraded	III
423	318	1	2000	1	7.7	7.0	36.0	n	B	2	n	both surfaces burnished	III
425	318	1	2000	1	3.6	8.5	23.0	n	B	2	ext		III
426	318	1	2000	3	8.5	5.5 (4.0)	37.5 (26.0)	n	n	1	both		III
427	318	1	2000	1	2.9	7.0	24.0	n	n	2	n		III
431	318	1	2000	1	5.5	6.5	30.0	n	B	1	ext		III
435	318	1	2000	1	6.4	6.5	36.0	n	B	1	ext	same vessel as 431	III
445	318	1	2000	1	1.8	5.5	22.5	n	S	1	ext		III
451**	318	1	2000										III
452**	318	1	2000										III
455**	318	1	2000										III
456	318	1	2000	1	2.9	6.0	25.0	n	n	1	n		III
461**	318	1	2000										III
462	318	1	2000	2	5.6	7.0 (7.0)	27.5 (16.0)	n	S	2	n	conjoining; dimensions 7.0 x 37.0	III
513	318	1	2000	1	3.5	6.5	27.0	n	n	1	n		III
518	318	1	2000	1	1.1	6.0	16.5	n	n	1	int	(from BS 309)	III
467	330	1	2000	1	5.4	5.5	31.0	n	B	2	int		III
498	330	1	2000	1	10.2	7.0	46.0	n	S	1	ext		III
499	330	1	2000	1	1.8	6.0	19.0	n	B	2	int		III
500	330	1	2000	1	5.4	6.5	30.5	n	S	2	n		III
501	330	1	2000	1	1.9	6.0	19.0	n	n	2	int	residue on in-terior	III
504	330	1	2000	1	5.5	9.0	30.5	n	n	4+ 10% inc	int	residue on in-terior	III
505	330	1	2000	1	2.4	7.5	22.0	n	n	2	n		III
519	330	1	2000	2	11.4	7.5 (7.5)	33.5 (23.5)	n	n	1	both	(from BS 312) dif-ferent vessels	III
473	334	1	2000	1	5.4	6.5	33.5	n	S	3	n		III
521	334	1	2000	1	5.3	6.0	30.0	n	S	2+ 10% inc	both	(from BS 316)	III
526	334	1	2000	4	19.3	8.0 (4.5)	45.0 (18.5)	n	n	1	n	(from BS 329) dif-ferent vessels; one plain rim	III
522	338	1	2000	2	1.2	7.5 (-)	15.0 (12.5)	n	n	2	both	(from BS 320)	III
495	340	1	2000	1	4.6	6.0	27.5	n	n	2	int		III
496	340	1	2000	1	3.5	7.5	23.5	n	S	1	int		III
523	340	1	2000	4	6.8	9.0 (7.0)	26.0 (12.5)	n	n	1	n	(from BS 325) 2 dif vessels; includes flat part of base	III
525	341	1	2000	1	1.4	5.5	17.0	n	B	1+ 10%	ext	(from BS 327)	III
529	343	1	2000	10	48.6	6.5 (-)	42.5 (13.5)	n	B S	different	both	(from BS 332) dif vessels - fabrics 1, 2, 1+10% inc, 2+ 10% inc	III
530	343	1	2000	frags.	26.6	7.2 (3.1)	26.9 (7.3)	n				(from BS 343) ?burnt clay from around a hearth	III
524	344	1	2000	1 & frag.	4.1	7.5	27.5	n	S	2+ 10%	int	(from BS 326)	III
528	348	1	2000	5	9.2	13.5 (7.5)	24.0 (9.5)	n	S	2	n	(from BS 331) dif-ferent vessels	III

SF	Context	Trench	Year	Sherds	Weight (g)	Width (mm)*	Longest axis (mm)*	Decoration (y/n)	Surface finish	Fabric	Sooting	Comment	Phase
531	1	1	2000	6	20	10 (5)	35	n	S	2	both	3 vessels (1x1; 1x1; 4x1)	VI
532	1	1	2000	1	2.7	7	2	n	n	2	n		VI
533	1	1	2000	8	60.4	8 (6)	46	n	B	2	both	3 vessels (1x1; 1x1; 5x1)	VI
534	1	1	2000	1	7.5	6	35	n	S	1+ 10% inc	ext		VI
535	1	1	2000	3	13.5	8 (5)	43	n	n	1	int		VI
536	1	1	2000	1	7.1	8	35	n	n	2	n		VI
537	1	1	2000	1	6.6	8	31	n	n	1	ext	probably 3 different vessels; includes flat rim	VI
Gen find	1	TT1	1999	1	5.9	6	37.5	n	B	1	int		VI
353	24	1	2000	1	6.2	1.9	29.5	n	S	1+ 10% inc	n		VI
Gen find	24	TT1	1999	1	5.3	7	29	n	B	1 + 10% inc	n	inclusions possibly steatite/mica	VI
319	316	1	2000	1	6.5	7.5	34.0	n	S	2	n		VI
527	316	1	2000	3	8.4	8.0 (6.0)	26.0 (18.0)	y	n	1, 2 and 1+10%inc	both	(from BS 330) different vessels	VI
482	333	1	2000	1	7.5	9.5	33.5	n	n	1+ 10% inc	n		VI
484	333	1	2000	1	2.5	9.0	21.0	n	n	1	both		VI
485	333	1	2000	1	3.4	6.0	29.0	n	n	1	ext		VI
486	333	1	2000									stone	VI
489	333	1	2000	1	1.6	7.5	18.0	n	n	2	n		VI
490	333	1	2000	1	4.9	7.0	32.0	n	B	3	n		VI
515	306b	1	2000	2	13.5	6.5 (6.5)	42.0 (32.0)	n	S	2+ 10% inc	n	different vessels – sherd from BS 302 has perforation	VI

APPENDIX 8

The TIC chromatogram of SF 329, context 309

Peaks 4, 6 and 7 correspond to the C16, C18:1 and C18:0 fatty acids respectively

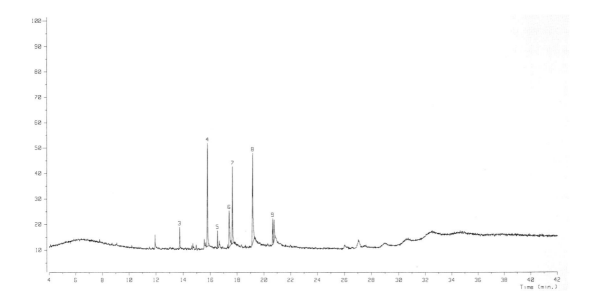

APPENDIX 9
Element and quantification codes used
in fish bone identification

Element	Element code	Quantification code
Articular	a	1
Basioccipital	bo	1
Ceratohyal	ch	1
Cleithrum	cl	1
Dentary	d	1
Hyomandibular	hy	1
Infrapharyngeal	iph	1
Maxilla	mx	1
Opercular	o	1
Palatine	pa	1
Parasphenoid	par	1
Preopercular	po	1
Post-temporal	pt	1
Premaxilla	px	1
Supercleithrum	scl	1
Scapula	scp	1
Quadrate	qd	1
Vomer	vo	1
Abdominal vertebra	av	2
Abdominal vertebra group 1	av1	2
Abdominal vertebra group 2	av2	2
Abdominal vertebra group 3	av3	2
Caudal vertebra	cv	2
Caudal vertebra group 1	cv1	2
Caudal vertebra group 2	cv2	2
Penultimate vertebra	puv	2
Ultimate vertebra	uv	2
Vertebra	v	2

BIBLIOGRAPHY

ABBREVIATIONS

ADS	Archaeology Data Service
DES	*Discovery and Excavation in Scotland*
DGSA	*Dumfries and Galloway Standard Advertiser*
Dia	Diameter
EIA	Early Iron Age
GAGM	Glasgow Art Gallery and Museums
GUAD	Glasgow University Archaeology Department
GUARD	Glasgow University Archaeological Research Division
LHDW	Low Countries Highly Decorated Ware
LIA	Late Iron Age
NHM	Natural History Museum
NMRS	National Monuments Record of Scotland
SF	Small find
SMR	Sites and Monuments Record
SN	Site notebook (D1/359/6) held in the Shetland Archives
PDR	*Preliminary Report of excavations at St Ninian's Isle, 1955–8,* written by O'Dell in 1958 (D.1/359/7, D1/359/8/2 and D1/359/1/11/24), in Shetland Archives
RCAHMS	Royal Commission on the Ancient and Historical Monuments of Scotland
Th	Thickness
VFA	Vitrified fuel ash

REFERENCES

Addyman, P V and Priestley, J, 1977 'Baille Hill, York: A report on the Institute's Excavations', *Archaeological Journal* 134, 115–156

Ahronson, K, 2002 'Testing the evidence for northern North Atlantic *papar*: a cave site in southern Iceland', in B E Crawford (ed), *The Papar in the North Atlantic: environment and history*, St John's House Papers 10, St Andrews, 107–120

Alcock, E, 1992 'Burials and cemeteries in Scotland', in N Edwards and A Lane (eds), *The early church in Wales and the West. Recent work in early Christian archaeology, history and place-names,* Oxbow Monograph 16, Oxford, 125–129

Alcock, L, 2003 *Kings, warriors, craftsmen and priests in northern Britain AD 550–850*, Society of Antiquaries Monograph Series 24, Edinburgh

Allen, J R and Anderson, J, 1903 *The early Christian monuments of Scotland* (reprinted with introduction by Henderson, 1994), Pinkfoot Press, Balgavies

Anderson, J, 1904 'Notices of a sculptured stone with ogam inscription from Latheron, presented to the National Museum by Sir Francis Tress Barry, Bart. M.P. Hon. F.S.A.Scot., Keiss Castle, Caithness; and of two Sculptured stones recently discovered by Rev. D. Macrae, B.D. at Edderton, Ross-shire', *Proceedings of the Society of Antiquaries of Scotland* 38, 534–541

Anon. 1878 'Donations to and purchases for the museum [St Ninian's Isle]', *Proceedings of the Society of Antiquaries of Scotland* 12, 11

Arneborg, J, Heinemeier, J, Lynnerup, N, Nielsen, H L, Rud, N, and Sveinbjörnsdóttir, Á E, 1999 'Change of diet of the Greenland Vikings determined from stable carbon isotope analysis and ^{14}C dating of their bones', *Radiocarbon* 41(2), 157–168

Ascough, P L, Cook, G T and Dugmore, A J, 2009 'North Atlantic marine 14C reservoir effects: implications for late-Holocene chronological studies', *Quaternary Geochronology* 4, 171–180

Ashmore, P, 1980 'Low Cairns, long cists and symbol stones', *Proceedings of the Society of Antiquaries of Scotland* 110, 346–355

Ashmore, P, 1999 'Radiocarbon dating: avoiding errors by avoiding mixed samples', *Antiquity* 73, 124–130

Ashmore, P, 2003 'Orkney burials in the first millennium AD', in J Downes and A Ritchie (eds), *Sea change: Orkney and Northern Europe in the later Iron Age AD 300–800*, Pinkfoot Press, Balgavies, 35–50

Atkinson, J A, Donnelly, M, MacGregor, G and Lelong, O, 2000 *The Ben Lawers Historic Landscape Project: the pilot seasons 1996–1999*, Glasgow University, Glasgow

Aufderheide, A C and Rodríguez-Martín, C, 1998 *The Cambridge Encyclopaedia of Human Palaeopathology*, Cambridge University Press, Cambridge

Backlund, J, 2001 'War or peace? The relations between the Picts and the Norse in Orkney', *Northern Studies* 36, 33–48

Baldwin Brown, G, 1915 'Notes on a necklace of glass beads found in a cist in Dalmeny Park, South Queensferry', *Proceedings of the Society of Antiquaries of Scotland* 49, 332–338

Ballantyne, J and Smith, B (eds), 1994 *Shetland documents 1518–1611*, Shetland Islands Council and Shetland Times Ltd, Lerwick

Ballin Smith, B, 2007 'Norwick: Shetland's first Viking settlement?', in B Ballin, S Smith and G Williams (eds), *West over the sea. Studies in Scandinavian sea-borne expansion and settlement before 1300: a festschrift in honour of Dr Barbara E Crawford*, Brill, Leiden, 287–298

Ballin Smith, B with Collins, G, 1994 '8.3 Stone artefacts', in B Ballin Smith (ed), *Howe: four millennia of Orkney prehistory*, Society of Antiquaries of Scotland Monograph Series 9, Edinburgh, 185–212

Ballin Smith, B with Constantine, J, 1994 '8.2 Bone artefacts', in B Ballin Smith (ed), *Howe: four millennia of Orkney prehistory*, Society of Antiquaries of Scotland Monograph Series 9, Edinburgh, 168–185

Barrett, J H, 1995 *'Few know an earl in fishing-clothes'. Fish middens and the economy of the Viking Age and Late Norse earldoms of Orkney and Caithness, northern Scotland*, PhD, University of Glasgow

Barrett, J H, 1997 'Fish trade in Norse Orkney and Caithness: a zooarchaeological approach', *Antiquity* 71, 616–638

Barrett, J H, 2003a 'Culture contact in Viking Age Scotland', in J Barrett (ed), *Contact, continuity and collapse: the Norse colonization of the North Atlantic*, Turnhout, Belgium, 73–111

Barrett, J H, 2003b 'Christian and pagan practice during the conversion of Viking age Orkney and Shetland', in M Carver (ed), *The cross goes North: processes of conversion in Northern Europe, AD 300–1300*, University of York, York Medieval Press, York, 207–226

Barrett, J H, 2004 'Beyond war or peace: the study of culture contact in Viking-age Scotland', in J Hines, A Lane, and M Redknap (eds), *Land, sea and home: proceedings of a conference on Viking-period settlement*, Society for Medieval Archaeology Monograph 20, Maney, Leeds, 207–218

Barrett, J H, Nicholson, R A and Cerón-Carrasco, R, 1999 'Archaeo-ichthyological evidence for long-term socioeconomic trends in northern Scotland: 3500 BC to AD 1500', *Journal of Archaeological Science* 26, 353–388

Barrett, J H, and Oltmann, J, 1998 *A report on mammal, bird and fish bone from excavations at Sandwick North, Unst, Shetland, 1995*, Department of Anthropology, University of Toronto

Barrett, J H, Beukens, R P and Brothwell, D R, 2000 'Radiocarbon dating and marine reservoir correction of Viking Age Christian burials from Orkney', *Antiquity* 74, 537–543

Barrett, J H, Beukens, R P and Nicholson, R A, 2001 'Diet and ethnicity during the Viking colonisation of northern Scotland: evidence from fish bones and stable carbon isotopes, *Antiquity* 75, 145–154

Barrett, J, Beukens, R, Simpson, I, Ashmore, P, Poaps, S and Huntley, J, 2001 'What was the Viking Age and when did it happen? A view from Orkney', *Norwegian Archaeological Review* 33(1), 1–39

Barrowman, R, 2000 *St Ninian's Isle, Shetland. Excavations in July 2000*, Archaeology Department Report, Glasgow University

Barrowman, R, 2003 'A decent burial? Excavations at St Ninian's Isle in July 2000', in J Downes and A Ritchie (eds), *Sea change: Orkney and Northern Europe in the later Iron Age AD 300–800*, Pinkfoot Press, Balgavies, 51–61

Barrowman, R C, 2005 'Lewis Coastal Chapel Sites Survey', *Discovery and Excavation in Scotland* New Series 6, 143–144

Barrowman, R C, 2008 *Lewis Coastal Chapel-Sites Survey 2007–8. Project 2593*, Glasgow University, Glasgow

Barrowman, R forthcoming, 'Putting things in context: revisiting the St Ninian's Isle excavations', in B Smith (ed), *The St Ninian's Isle treasure. Fifty years on*, Lerwick

Barrowman, R C, Batey, C E and Morris, C D, 2007 *Excavations at Tintagel, Cornwall 1990–1999*, Society of Antiquaries of London, London

Batey, C E, 1987 *Freswick Links, Caithness. A re-appraisal of the Late Norse site in its context*, British Archaeological Reports, British Series 179, Oxford

Batey, C E, 1989 'Excavations beside the Brough Road, Birsay: The artefact assemblage', in C D Morris, *The Birsay Bay Project Volume 1. Brough Road excavations 1976–1982*, Department of Archaeology, University of Durham, Monograph Series 1, Durham, 191–229

Batey, C E, with contributions from J Henderson and the late A Small, 2008 'The glass beads from St Ninian's Isle, Shetland', in C Karkov and H Damico (eds), *Aedificia nova: studies in honor of Rosemary Cramp*, Medieval Institute Press, 254–267

Batey, C E, with Freeman, C, 1986 'Lavacroon, Orphir, Orkney', *Proceedings of the Society of Antiquaries of Scotland* 116, 285–300, fiche 5: A3–D9

Batey, C E and Newton, A, 2009 'The Pumice', in K Brady and C Batey, 'Excavations and survey on Brei Holm and Maiden Stack, Papa Stour, Shetland', *Scottish Archaeological Journal* 30 (Oct 2008), 49 (1–64)

Batey, C E, Jesch, J and Morris, C D (eds), 1993 *The Viking Age in Caithness, Orkney and the North Atlantic. Select papers from the Proceedings of the Eleventh Viking Congress, Thurso and Kirkwall*, Edinburgh University Press, Edinburgh

Bayliss, A, 1999 'On the taphonomy of charcoal samples for radiocarbon dating', in J Evin, C Oberlin, J P Daugas and J F Salles (eds), *Actes du 3ème congrès international 'Archaéologie et 14C', Lyon, 6-10 Avril 1998, Revue d'Archéométrie Suppl 1999 et Soc Préhist Fr Mémoire* 26, 51–56

Bayliss, A, Shepherd Popescu, E, Beavan-Athfield, N, Bronk Ramsey, C, Cook, G T, and Locker, A, 2004 'The potential significance of dietary offsets for the interpretation of radiocarbon dates: an archaeologically significant example from medieval Norwich', *Journal of Archaeological Science* 31, 563–575

Beedham, G E, 1972 *Identification of the British mollusca*, Pitman Press, Bath

Beijerinck, W, 1947 *Zadenatlas der Nederlandsche Flora*, Veenman & Zonen, Wageningen

Bertrand, E, 1995 *Emaux Limousins du Moyen Âge*, Brimo de Laroussilhe, Paris

Best, M R (ed), 1986 *Gervase Markham: the English housewife*, McGill-Queen's University Press, Canada

Bigelow, G, 1984 'Two kerbed cairns from Sandwick, Unst, Shetland', in J G P Friell and W G Watson (eds), *Pictish studies. Settlement, burial and art in Dark Age Northern Britain*, British Archaeological Reports, British Series 125, Oxford, 115–129

Bigelow, G, 1992 'Issues and prospects in Shetland Norse Archaeology', in C D Morris and D J Rackham (eds), *Norse and later settlement and subsistence in the North Atlantic*, Department of Archaeology, University of Glasgow, Occasional Paper Series, 19–32

Birkeli, F, 1973 *Norske Steinkors i tidlig Middelalder*, Oslo

Black, G F, 1891 'Report on the archaeological examination of the Culbin Sands, Elginshire, obtained under the Victoria Jubilee Gift of His Excellency Dr R H Gunning', *Proceedings of the Society of Antiquaries of Scotland* 25 (1890–91), 484–511

Blondiaux, G, Secousse, F, Cotton, A, Danze, P and Flipo, R, 2002 'Rickets and child abuse: the case of a two year old girl from the fourth century in Lisieux (Normandy)', *International Journal of Osteoarchaeology* 12, 209–215

Bond, J M, Dockrill, S J, Batt, C M, Nicholson, R A, Batey, C E, Turner, V, Forster, A L and Outram, Z, forthcoming *First contact? New evidence for the visibility of Viking settlement in the Northern Isles*

Borland, J, 2005 'Understanding what we see, or seeing what we understand: graphic recording, past and present, of the early medieval sculpture of St Vigeans', in S Foster and M Cross (eds), *Able minds and practised hands: Scotland's early medieval sculpture in the 21st century*, Society for Medieval Archaeology Monograph 23, London, 201–214

Brady, K, 2000 *Yell chapel-sites survey, 1999–2000*, Glasgow University Archaeological Research Division unpublished report, Glasgow

Brady, K, 2002 'Brei Holm, Papa Stour: in the footsteps of the papar?', in B E Crawford (ed), *The Papar in the North Atlantic: environment and history*, St John's House Papers 10, St Andrews, 69–82

Brady, K and Batey, C, E, 2009 'Excavations and survey on Brei Holm and Maiden Stack, Papa Stour, Shetland', *Scottish Archaeological Journal* 30 (Oct 2008), 1–64

Brady, K and Johnson, P G, 1998 *Unst chapel survey 1998: Phase I: Report 1*, Glasgow University Archaeological Research Division unpublished report, Glasgow

Brady, K and Johnson, P G, 2000 *Unst chapel-sites survey 1999: Phase I: Report 2*, Glasgow University Archaeological Research Division unpublished report, Glasgow

Brady, K and Morris, C D, 2000 *Fetlar chapel sites survey*, Glasgow University Archaeological Research Division unpublished report, Glasgow

Branch, G M, 1985 'Limpets: their role in littoral and sublittoral community dynamics', in P G Moore and R Seed (eds), *The ecology of rocky coasts*, Hodder & Stoughton, London

Brand, Rev J, 1701 *Brief description of Orkney, Zetland, Pightland-Firth, and Caithness, etc*, Edinburgh

Brash, R R, 1879 *The ogam inscribed monuments of the Gaedhil in the British Islands* (ed G M Atkinson), London

Brennand, M, Parker-Pearson, M and Smith, H, 1998a 'Cille Pheadair (Kilpheder): 'Pictish' square cairn and disturbed skeleton', *Discovery and Excavation in Scotland*, 103

Brennand, M, Parker-Pearson, M and Smith, H, 1998b *The Norse settlement and Pictish cairn at Kilpheder, South Uist. Excavations in 1998*, University of Sheffield Department of Prehistory and Archaeology, unpublished report, Sheffield

Bronk Ramsey, C, 1995 'Radiocarbon calibration and analysis of stratigraphy', *Radiocarbon* 36, 425–430

Bronk Ramsey, C, 1998 'Probability and dating', *Radiocarbon* 40, 461–474

Bronk Ramsey, C, 2000 'Comment on "The use of Bayesian statistics for ^{14}C dates of chronologically ordered samples": a critical review', *Radiocarbon* 42(2), 199–202

Bronk Ramsey, C, 2001 'Development of the radiocarbon calibration program OxCal', *Radiocarbon* 43, 355–363

Bronk Ramsey, C, 2009 'Bayesian analysis of radiocarbon dates', *Radiocarbon 51*(1), 337–360

Bronk Ramsey, C, 2010a *OxCal 4.1.4 programme*, available from http://c14.arch.ox.ac.uk/embed.php?File=oxcal.html, last accessed 28/5/2010

Bronk Ramsey, C, 2010b *OxCal 4.1 Manual*, available from http://c14.arch.ox.ac.uk/oxcalhelp/hlp_contents.html, last accessed 28/5/2010

Brooke-Freeman, E, 2005 'Shetland place-names project', in P Gammeltoft, C Hough and D Waugh (eds), *Cultural contacts in the North Atlantic Region: the evidence of names*, Shetland Times Ltd, Lerwick, 42–57

Brooks, S T and Suchey, J M, 1990 'Skeletal age determination based on the Os Pubis: a comparison of the Ascadi-Nemeskeri and Suchey-Brooks methods', *Human Evolution* 5, 227–238

Brown, M P, 1989 'Catalogue number 102', in S Youngs (ed), *'The work of angels': masterpieces of Celtic metalwork, 6th-9th centuries AD*, British Museum, London, 110

Brown, G and Roberts, J A, 2000 'Excavations in the medieval cemetery at the city churches, Dundee', *Tayside and Fife Archaeological Journal* 6, 70–86

Brown, T J, 1993 'St Ninian's Isle silver hoard: the inscriptions', in J Bately, M Brown and J Roberts (eds), *A palaeographer's view: the selected writings of Julian Brown*, Harvey Miller Publishers, London, 245–251 [originally published as part of a joint paper with A C O'Dell, R B K Stevenson, H J Penderleith and R L S Bruce-Mitford, in *Antiquity* 33 (1959), 250–255]

Bruce-Mitford, R L S, 1959 'Comments on the bowls and miscellaneous silver and general conclusions', in A C O'Dell, R B K Stevenson, T N Brown, H J Plenderleith and R L S Bruce-Mitford, 'The St Ninian's Isle Silver Hoard', *Antiquity* 33, 1959, 241–243 (241–268)

Bruce-Mitford, R L S, 1960 'The treasure of St Ninian's', *Scientific American* 203:5, 154–166

Buck, C E, Cavanagh, W G, and Litton, C D, 1996 *Bayesian approach to interpreting archaeological data*, Wiley, Chichester

Buck, C E, Christen, J, A, Kenworthy, J B, and Litton, C D, 1994 'Estimating the duration of archaeological activity using ^{14}C determinations', *Oxford Journal of Archaeology* 3(2), 229–240

Buck, C E, Kenworthy, J B, Litton, C D and Smith, A F M, 1991 'Combining archaeological and radiocarbon information: a Bayesian approach to calibration', *Antiquity* 65, 808–821

Buikstra, J E and Ubelaker, D H (eds), 1994 *Standards for data collection from human skeletal remains*, Arkansas Archaeological Survey Research Series 44

Buteux, S, 1997 *Settlements at Skaill, Deerness, Orkney. Excavations by Peter Gelling of the prehistoric, Pictish, Viking and later periods, 1863–1981*, British Archaeological Reports, British Series 260, Oxford

Buteux, S, Hunter, J and Lowe, C, 1998 'St Nicholas Chapel, Papa Stronsay', in *Discovery and Excavation in Scotland* 1998, 72

Buteux, S, Hunter, J and Lowe, C, 1999 'St Nicholas Chapel,

Papa Stronsay', in *Discovery and Excavation in Scotland* 1999, 68–69

Buttler, S, 1989 'Steatite in Norse Shetland', *Hikuin* 15, 193–206

Buttler, S, 1991 'Steatite in the Norse North Atlantic', *Acta Archaeologica* 61, 228–232

Calder, G, 1917 (ed) *Auraicept na n-Éces*, John Grant, Edinburgh

Calder, W M and Jackson, K H, 1957 'An inscription from Altyre', *Proceedings of the Society of Antiquaries of Scotland* 90, 246–250

Caldwell, D H, 1978 'An enamelled plaque from Borve, Benbecula', *Proceedings of the Society of Antiquaries of Scotland* 109, 378–380

Cameron, R A D and Redfern, M, 1976 *British land snails*, Sypnoses of the British Fauna (New Series) 6, The Linnean Society of London, Academic Press

Campbell, A C, 1989 *Seashores and shallow seas of Britain and Europe*, Hamlyn, London

Campbell, E, 1998a 'Miscellaneous iron tools', in N Sharples, *Scalloway. A broch, Late Iron Age settlement and medieval cemetery in Shetland*, Cardiff Studies in Archaeology, Oxbow Monograph 82, Oxford, 159–160

Campbell, E, 1998b 'Metal fittings', in N Sharples, *Scalloway. A broch, Late Iron Age settlement and medieval cemetery in Shetland*, Cardiff Studies in Archaeology, Oxbow Monograph 82, Oxford, 165–166

Campbell, E and Smith, A N, 1998 'Points', in N Sharples, *Scalloway. A broch, Late Iron Age settlement and medieval cemetery in Shetland*, Cardiff Studies in Archaeology, Oxbow Monograph 82, Oxford, 150

Campbell, E with Sharman, P, 1998 'Metalworking debris', in N Sharples, *Scalloway. A broch, Late Iron Age settlement and medieval cemetery in Shetland*, Cardiff Studies in Archaeology, Oxbow Monograph 82, Oxford, 161–164

Cant, R G, 1973 'The church in Orkney and Shetland and its relations with Norway and Scotland in the middle ages', *Northern Studies* 1, 1–18

Cant, R G, 1975 *The medieval churches and chapels of Shetland*, Shetland Archaeological and Historical Society, Lerwick

Carter, S P, McCullagh, R P J and MacSween, A, 1995 'The Iron Age in Shetland: excavations at five sites threatened by coastal erosion', *Proceedings of the Society of Antiquaries of Scotland* 125, 429–482, fiche 2: C7–C14

Carver, M, (ed) 2003 *The cross goes North: processes of conversion in Northern Europe, AD 300–1300*, University of York, York Medieval Press, York

Cerón-Carrasco, R, 1993 *Upper Scalloway, Shetland: the fish bone remains*, AOC (Scotland) Ltd unpublished report

Cerón-Carrasco, R, 1998 'Fish', in N Sharples, *Scalloway. A broch, Late Iron Age settlement and medieval cemetery in Shetland*, Cardiff Studies in Archaeology, Oxbow Monograph 82, 112–116

Cerón-Carrasco, R, 2000 '*The marine mollusc remains from Bayane, Yell, Shetland, with a note on the land snails*', unpublished report

Challinor, C, Brown, L D and Heron, C, 1998 'Molecular information from ceramics: a case study from the Northern Isles', in R A Nicholson and S J Dockrill, *Old Scatness Broch, Shetland: retrospect and prospect*, Bradford Archaeological Sciences Research 5, Bradford, 139–149

Chamberlain, A, 1994 *Human remains*, British University Press, London

Christie, H and Svarstad, C, 1963 *Kinsarvik Kirke*, Fortidsminner 46, Oslo

CIIC = Macalister, R A S, 1945 *Corpus Inscriptionem Insularum Celticarum*, vol. 1, Stationery Office, Dublin

Clarke, A, 1998a 'Miscellaneous stone tools', in N Sharples, *Scalloway. A broch, Late Iron Age settlement and medieval cemetery in Shetland*, Cardiff Studies in Archaeology, Oxbow Monograph 82, Oxford, 140–147

Clarke, A, 1998b 'Small rounded pebbles', in N Sharples,

Scalloway. A broch, Late Iron Age settlement and medieval cemetery in Shetland, Cardiff Studies in Archaeology, Oxbow Monograph 82, Oxford, 178–180

Clarke, A, 1999 'The flaked quartz', in O Owen and C Lowe, *Kebister: the four-thousand-year-old story of one Shetland township*, Society of Antiquaries of Scotland Monograph Series 14, Edinburgh, 164–166

Clarke, A and Sharman, P, 1998 'Weights', in N Sharples, *Scalloway. A broch, Late Iron Age settlement and medieval cemetery in Shetland*, Cardiff Studies in Archaeology, Oxbow Monograph 82, Oxford, 147–149

Clarke, D V, 1990 'The National Museums' stained-glass window', *Proceedings of the Society of Antiquaries of Scotland* 120, 201–224

Clarke, D and Heald, A, 2002 'Beyond typology: combs, economics, symbolism and regional identity in Late Norse Scotland', *Norwegian Archaeological Review* 35(2), 81–93

Close-Brooks, J, 1984 'Pictish and other burials', in J G P Friell and W G Watson (eds), *Pictish studies. Settlement, burial and art in Dark Age Northern Britain,* British Archaeological Reports, British Series 125, Oxford, 87–114

Close-Brooks, J, 1989 *Pictish Stones in Dunrobin Castle Museum,* (The Sutherland Trust), Pilgrim Press, Derby

Close-Brooks, J and Stevenson, R B K, 1982 *Dark Age sculpture,* Her Majesty's Stationery Office, Edinburgh

Cohen, A and Serjeantson, D, 1986 *A manual for the identification of bird bones from archaeological sites,* A Cohen, London

Collingwood, R G and Wright, R P, 1965 *The Roman Inscriptions of Britain* (RIB), vol. 1, Oxford University Press, Oxford

Cormack, W F, 1995 'Barhobble, Mochrum: excavation of a forgotten church site in Galloway', in F Williams and W F Cormack (eds), *Transactions of the Dumfriesshire and Galloway Natural History and Antiquarian Society: Barhobble Volume,* Third Series 70, 5–106

Coull, J, 2003 'The shaping of Shetland: an archipelago's landscape history', *Landscape* 2, 67–89

Cowie, T, Bruce, M and Kerr, N, 1993 'The discovery of a child burial of probable Viking-Age date on Kneep Headland, Uig, Lewis, 1991: interim report', C E Batey, J Jesch and C D Morris (eds), *The Viking Age in Caithness, Orkney and the North Atlantic. Select papers from the Proceedings of the Eleventh Viking Congress, Thurso and Kirkwall,* Edinburgh University Press, Edinburgh, 165–172

Crawford, B E, 1987 *Scandinavian Scotland,* Leicester University Press, Leicester

Crawford, B E, 2005 'The Papar: Viking reality or 12th-century myth?', in P Gammeltoft, C Hough and D Waugh (eds), *Cultural contacts in the North Atlantic region: the evidence of names,* NORNA, Scottish Place-Name Society and Society for Name Studies in Britain and Ireland, Lerwick, 83–99

Crawford, B E and Ballin Smith, B, 1999 *The Biggings, Papa Stour, Shetland: the history and excavation of a royal Norwegian farm,* Society of Antiquaries of Scotland and Det Norske Videnskaps-Akademi, Edinburgh

Crawford, I A, 1981 'War or peace: Viking colonisation in the Northern and Western Isles of Scotland reviewed', in H Bekker-Nielson, P Foote, and O Olsen (eds), *Proceedings of the Eighth Viking Congress, Aarhus 1977,* Odense, 259–269

Crawford-Adams, J, 1987 *Outline of fractures,* Churchill Livingstone, Edinburgh (9th edition)

Crone, A, 2000 *The history of a Scottish lowland crannog: excavations at Buiston, Ayrshire 1989-90,* Scottish Trust for Archaeological Research (STAR) Monograph, Edinburgh

Cummins, W A, 2001 *The last language of the Picts,* The Pinkfoot Press, Balgavies

Dalland, M and MacSween, A, 1999 'The coarse pottery', in O Owen and C Lowe, *Kebister: the four-thousand-year-old story of one Shetland township*, Society of Antiquaries of Scotland Monograph Series 14, Edinburgh, 178–200

Dargie, T C D, 1998 *Sand dune vegetation survey of Scotland. Shetland,* Scottish Natural Heritage, Edinburgh

Davies, W [*et al*], 2000 *The inscriptions of early medieval Brittany*, Celtic Studies Publications 5, Aberystwyth

Dickson, J H, 1992 'North American driftwood, especially *Picea* (spruce) from archaeological sites in the Hebrides and Northern Isles of Scotland', *Review of Palaeobotany and Palynology* 73, 49–56

Dickson, C A and Dickson, J H, 2000 *Plants and people in ancient Scotland,* Tempus, Stroud

DIL: *Dictionary of the Irish Language, based mainly on Old and Middle Irish materials*, edited by E G Quin *et al,* Royal Irish Academy, Dublin, 1913–76, (compact edition, 1983)

Dockrill, S J, 2003 'Broch, wheelhouse, and cell: redefining the Iron Age in Shetland', in J Downes and A Ritchie (eds), *Sea change: Orkney and Northern Europe in the later Iron Age AD 300–800,* Pinkfoot Press, Balgavies, 82–94

Dockrill, S J, Bond, J M and Turner, V E, 2001 *Old Scatness Broch and Jarlshof Environs Project: field season 2000: interim report No. 6,* Bradford Archaeological Sciences Research 10, Bradford

Dockrill, S J, Turner, V E and Bond, J M, 2000 'Old Scatness/Jarlshof Environs Project', *Discovery and Excavation in Scotland,* New Series 1, 79–80

Dockrill, S J, Turner, V E and Bond, J M, 2002 'Old Scatness/Jarlshof Environs Project', *Discovery and Excavation in Scotland,* New Series 3, 105–107

Dockrill, S J, Turner, V E and Bond, J M, 2003 'Old Scatness/Jarlshof Environs Project', *Discovery and Excavation in Scotland,* New Series 4, 118–119

Dockrill, S J, Turner, V E and Bond, J M, 2004 'Old Scatness/Jarlshof Environs Project', *Discovery and Excavation in Scotland,* New Series 5, 117–118

Dockrill, S J, Bond, J M, Turner, V E, Cussans, J E, Bashford, D and Brown, L D, 2006 'Old Scatness/Jarlshof Environs Project', *Discovery and Excavation in Scotland,* New Series 6, 126–127

Donaldson, G, 1954 *The Court-book of Orkney and Shetland 1602–4,* Scottish Record Society, Edinburgh

Donations 1878 'Donations to and purchases for the Museum and Library, with exhibits', *Proceedings of the Society of Antiquaries of Scotland* 12, 615, 628–630

Donations 1928 'Donations to the Museum 4, 12 March 1928, Rev James M Pattullo', *Proceedings of the Society of Antiquaries of Scotland* 42, 165

Downes, J and Badcock, A, 1998a 'An Corran, Boreray', *Discovery and Excavation in Scotland* 1998, 100

Downes, J and Badcock, A, 1998b 'Berneray causeway', *Discovery and Excavation in Scotland* 1998, 101

Dulley, A J F, 1967 'Excavations at Pevensey, Sussex 1962–66', *Medieval Archaeology* 11, 209–232

Dunbar, J G, 1996 'The emergence of the reformed church in Scotland *c*1560–*c*1700', in J Blair and C Pyrah (eds), *Church archaeology: research directions for the future,* Council for British Archaeology Research Report 104, London, 127–143

Earwood, C, 1993 *Domestic wooden artefacts in Britain and Ireland from Neolithic to Viking times,* University of Exeter Press, Exeter

Evans, D E, 1967 *Gaulish personal-names: a study of some continental formations,* Clarendon Press, Oxford

Evershed, R P, Dudd, S N, Copley, M S, Berstan, R, Stott, A W, Mottram, H, Buckley, S A and Crossman, Z, 2002 'Chemistry of archaeological animal fats', *Accounts of Chemical Research* 35, 660–668

Fawcett, R, 1996 'The archaeology of the Scottish church in the later Middle Ages', in J Blair and C Pyrah (eds), *Church archaeology: research directions for the future,* Council for British Archaeology Research Report 104, London, 85–103

Fawcett, R, forthcoming 'Chapter 6. An architectural analysis of the church and related buildings on the Brough of Birsay', in C

D Morris with C E Batey, et al, *The Birsay Bay Project Volume 3: The Brough of Birsay, Orkney, investigations 1957–2007*, Society of Antiquaries of Scotland

Fenton, A, 1978 *The Northern Isles: Orkney and Shetland*, John Donald, Edinburgh

Fenton, A, 1984 'Notes on shellfish as food and bait in Scotland', in B Gunda (ed), *The fishing culture of the world. Studies in ethnology, cultural ecology and folklore*, vol. 1, Akadémiai Kiadó, Budapest, 121–141

Fenton, A, 1986 'Seaweed manure', in A Fenton (ed), *The shape of the past 2*, John Donald, Edinburgh, 48–82

Ferguson, S, 1887 *Ogham inscriptions in Ireland, Wales and Scotland*, Douglas, Edinburgh

Finlay, N, 2000 'Outside of life: traditions of infant burial in Ireland from Cillin to Cist', *World Archaeology* 31, No. 3 (Feb 2000), 407–422

Finlayson, W, 2000 'Chipped stone assemblage', in R Lamb and J Downes, *Prehistoric Houses at Sumburgh in Shetland*, Oxbow Books, Oxford, 104–109

Fisher, I, 2001 *Early medieval sculpture in the West Highlands and Islands*, Royal Commission on the Ancient and Historical Monuments of Scotland and Society of Antiquaries of Scotland, Monograph Series 1, Edinburgh

Fisher, I, 2002 'Crosses in the Ocean: some *papar* sites and their sculpture', in B E Crawford (ed), *The Papar in the North Atlantic: environment and history*, St John's House Papers 10, St Andrews, 39–57

Fisher, I, 2005 'Cross-currents in North Atlantic Sculpture', in A Mortensen and S V Arge, *Viking and Norse in the North Atlantic: select papers from the proceedings of the Fourteenth Viking Congress, Tórshavn, 19–30 July 2001*, Tórshavn, 160–166

Fisher, I, 2010 'Norwegian crosses in Shetland and the Hebrides?', in J Sheehan and D Ó Corráin (eds), *The Viking age: Ireland and the West: papers from the proceedings of the fifteenth Viking Congress, Cork, 18–27 August 2005*, Four Courts Press, Dublin

Fisher, I and Scott, I G, 2007 'Early medieval sculpture from the Faroes: an illustrated catalogue', in B Ballin, S Smith and G Williams (eds), *West over the sea. Studies in Scandinavian sea-borne expansion and settlement before 1300: a festschrift in honour of Dr Barbara E Crawford*, Brill, Leiden, 363–378

Fitzhugh, W W and Ward, E I (eds), 2000 *Vikings: the North Atlantic Saga*, Smithsonian Institution Press in association with the National Museum of Natural History, Washington, London

Fleming, A and Woolf, A, 1992 'Cille Donnain: a late Norse church in South Uist', *Proceedings of the Society of Antiquaries of Scotland* 122, 329–350

Flinn, D, 1997 'The role of wave diffraction in the formation of St Ninian's Isle ayre (tombolo) in Shetland, Scotland', *Journal of Coastal Research* 13:1, 202–208

Fojut, N, 1993 *A guide to prehistoric and Viking Shetland*, Shetland Times Ltd, Lerwick

Forsyth, K, 1995 'The inscriptions on the Dupplin Cross', in C Bourke (ed), *From the Isles of the North: medieval art in Ireland and Britain (Proceedings of the Third International Conference on Insular Art)*, HMSO, Belfast, 237–244

Forsyth, K, 1996a *The Ogham Inscriptions of Scotland: An Edited Corpus*, PhD Dissertation, Harvard University (Ann Arbor: UMI)

Forsyth, K, 1996b 'The ogham-inscribed spindle whorl from Buckquoy: evidence for the Irish language in pre-Viking Orkney?', *Proceedings of the Society of Antiquaries of Scotland* 125, 677–696

Forsyth, K, 1998 'Literacy in Pictland', in H Pryce (ed), *Literacy in medieval Celtic societies*, Cambridge University Press, Cambridge, 39–61

Forsyth, K, 2001 'Appendix 1: The ogham inscription at Dunadd', in A Lane, *Excavations at Dunadd, Argyll*, Oxbow Books, Oxford, 264–272

Forsyth, K, 2007 'An ogham-inscribed plaque from Bornais, South Uist', in B Ballin-Smith, S Taylor and G Williams (eds), *West over the sea. Studies in Scandinavian sea-borne expansion and settlement before 1300: a festschrift in honour of Dr Barbara E Crawford*, Brill, Leiden, 460–477

Forsyth, K, forthcoming a, 'An ogham-inscribed slab from Broch of Burrian, found in 1870', in P Sharman, 'Investigations at the Broch of Burrian, North Ronaldsay, Orkney'

Forsyth, K, forthcoming b, 'Language and literacy in pre-Viking Shetland: the evidence from St Ninian's Isle', in B Smith (ed), *The St Ninian's Isle treasure. Fifty years on*, Lerwick

Foster, S M, 1990 'Pins, combs and the chronology of later Atlantic Iron Age Settlement', in I Armit (ed), *Beyond the brochs: Changing perspectives on the Atlantic Scottish Iron Age*, Edinburgh University Press, Edinburgh, 143–174

Foster, S M, 1996 *Picts, Gaels and Scots*, Batsford, London

Friell, J G P and Watson, W G (eds), 1984 *Pictish studies. Settlement, burial and art in Dark Age Northern Britain*, British Archaeological Reports, British Series 125, Oxford

Freke, D, 2002 *Excavations on St Patrick's Isle, Peel, Isle of Man, 1982–88: prehistoric, Viking, medieval and later*, Liverpool Monographs in Archaeology and Oriental Studies 2 (200), Liverpool University Press, Liverpool

Galloway, A (ed), 1999 *Broken bones, anthropological analysis of blunt force trauma*, Charles C Thomas, Springfield, Illinois

Gammeltoft, P, 2004 'Among Dímons and Papeys: what kind of contact do the names really point to?', *Northern Studies* 38, 31–50

Geddes, J and Carter, A, 1977 'Objects of non-ferrous metal, amber and paste', in H Clarke and A Carter, *Excavations in King's Lynn, 1963–70*, Society for Medieval Archaeology Monograph 7, 287–291

Gelfand, A E, and Smith, A F M, 1990 'Sampling approaches to calculating marginal densities', *Journal of the American Statistical Association* 85, 398–409

Gilks, W R, Richardson, S and Spiegelhalther, D J, 1996 *Markov Chain Monte Carlo in practice*, Chapman and Hall, London

Goodall, I H and Carter, A 1977 'Iron objects', in H Clarke and A Carter, *Excavations in King's Lynn 1963-1970*, Society for Medieval Archaeology Monograph 7, 291–298

Goudie, G, 1879 'On two monumental stones with ogham inscriptions recently discovered in Shetland', *Proceedings of the Society of Antiquaries of Scotland* 12, 20–32

Goudie, G, 1904 *The Celtic and Scandinavian antiquities of Shetland*, William Blackwood, Edinburgh

Goudie, G, 1912 'The ecclesiastical antiquities of the southern parishes of Shetland', *Transactions of the Scottish Ecclesiological Society* iii, part 3, 36–50

Graham-Campbell, J, 1975 'Bossed penannular brooches: a review of recent research', *Medieval Archaeology* 19, 33–47

Graham-Campbell, J, 1985 'A lost Pictish treasure (and two Viking-age gold arm-rings) from the Broch of Burgar, Orkney', *Proceedings of the Society of Antiquaries of Scotland* 115, 241–261

Graham-Campbell, J, 1995 *The Viking-age gold and silver of Scotland (AD 850–110)*, National Museums of Scotland, Edinburgh

Graham-Campbell, J, 2003a *Pictish silver: status and symbol*, H M Chadwick Memorial Lectures 4, Cambridge

Graham-Campbell, J, 2003b 'The Vikings in Orkney', in D J Waugh (ed), *The faces of Orkney: stones, skalds and saints*, Scottish Society for Northern Studies, Edinburgh, 128–137

Graham-Campbell, J, forthcoming 'The St Ninian's Isle treasure: contents and context', in B Smith (ed), *The St Ninian's Isle Treasure. Fifty years on*, Lerwick

Graham-Campbell, J and Batey, C E, 1998 *Vikings in Scotland: an archaeological survey*, Edinburgh University Press, Edinburgh

Grant, F J, 1893 *The county families of the Zetland Islands*, Lerwick

Hall, A J, 2000 'Geoarchaeological report and observations', in

R Barrowman, *St Ninian's Isle, Shetland. Excavations in July 2000*, Archaeology Department Report, Glasgow University, 39–45

Hall, D and Lindsay, W J, 1983 'Excavations at Scalloway Castle, 1979', *Proceedings of the Society of Antiquaries of Scotland* 113, 565–577

Hallén, Y, 1994 'The use of bone and antler at Foshigarry and Bac Mhic Connain, two Iron Age sites on North Uist, Western Isles', *Proceedings of the Society of Antiquaries of Scotland* 124, 189–231

Hamilton, J R C, 1956 *Excavations at Jarlshof, Shetland*, Ministry of Works Archaeological Reports 1, Edinburgh

Hamilton, J R C, 1968 *Excavations at Clickhimin, Shetland*, Department of the Environment Archaeological Reports 6, Edinburgh

Harland, J F, Barrett, J H, Carrott, J, Dobney, K and Jaques, D, 2003 'The York System: an integrated zooarchaeological database for research and teaching', *Internet Archaeology* 13: http://intarch.ac.uk/journal/issue13/harland_index.html.

Harry, R, 2000 *St Ninian's Isle survey and excavation 1999*, Glasgow University Archaeological Research Division unpublished report 689, Glasgow University

Harry, R and Morris, C D, 1997 'Excavations on the Lower Terrace, Site C, Tintagel Island 1990–1994', *Antiquaries Journal* 77, 1–144

Harvey, A, 1987 'The ogam inscriptions and their geminate consonant symbols', *Ériu* 38, 45–71

HE: (Bede's *Historia Ecclesiastica*) Colgrave, B and Mynors, R A B (eds and transl), 1969 *Bede's Ecclesiastical History of the English History*, Clarendon Press, Oxford

Hedges, J W, 1978 'A long cist at Sandside, Graemsay, Orkney', *Proceedings of the Society of Antiquaries of Scotland* 109, 374–378

Hedges, J W, 1987 *Bu, Gurness and the Brochs of Orkney*, 3 vols, British Archaeological Reports, British Series, Oxford, 163–165

Hencken, H, 1950 'Lagore Crannog: an Irish royal residence of the 7th to 10th centuries AD', *Proceedings of the Royal Irish Academy,* 53c, 1–247

Henderson, G and Henderson, I, 2004 *The art of the Picts. Sculpture and metalwork in early medieval Scotland*, Thames and Hudson, London

Henderson, I, 1967 *The Picts, Ancient peoples and places 54*, Thames & Hudson, London

Henshall, A, 1956 'The long cist cemetery at Lasswade, Midlothian', *Proceedings of the Society of Antiquaries of Scotland* 89, 252–283

Hibbert, S, 1822 *A description of the Shetland Islands, comprising an account of their geology, scenery, antiquities and superstitions*, A Constable and Co., Edinburgh

Hill, P, 1997 *Whithorn and St Ninian. The excavation of a Monastic Town, 1984–91*, Sutton Publishing for the Whithorn Trust, Stroud

Hughes, K, 1980 *Celtic Britain in the Early Middle Ages: studies in Welsh and Scottish sources*, editor D Dumbille, Boydell, Woodbridge

Hunter, J R, 1986 *Rescue excavations on the brough of Birsay 1974–82*, Society of Antiquaries of Scotland Monograph Series 4, Edinburgh

Hunter, J R, 1985 [notice of discovery of Pool ogham-inscribed stone], *Discovery and Excavation in Scotland*, 66

Hunter, J, 2007 'The interface and Scandinavian settlement', in J Hunter, J M Bond and A N Smith (eds), *Investigations in Sanday, Orkney. Vol. 1: excavations at Pool, Sanday. A multi-period settlement from Neolithic to late Norse times*, The Orcadian Ltd/ Historic Scotland, Orkney, 121–146

Hylleberg, J and Christensen, J T, 1977 'Phenotypic variation and fitness of periwinkles (Gastropoda: Littorinidae) in relation to exposure', *Journal of Molluscan Studies* 43, 192–199

Jackson, K H, 1955 'The Pictish language', in *The problem of the Picts*, ed. F T Wainwright, Nelson, Edinburgh (repr. 1980, Melven Press, Perth), 129–160

Jackson, K H, 1960 'The St Ninian's Isle inscription: a re-appraisal', *Antiquity* 34, 38–42

Jackson, K H, 1973a 'The Inscriptions', in A Small, C Thomas and D M Wilson, *St Ninian's Isle and its treasure*, 2 vols, Aberdeen University Studies 152, Oxford University Press, Oxford, 167–173

Jackson, K H, 1973b 'An ogam inscription near Blackwaterfoot', *Antiquity* 47, 53–54

Jackson, K H, 1977 'The ogam inscription on the spindle whorl from Buckquoy, Orkney', in A Ritchie, 'Excavation of Pictish and Viking-age farmsteads at Buckquoy, Orkney', *Proceedings of the Society of Antiquaries Scotland 108*, 221–222

Jacobsen, L and Moltke, E, 1941 'Danmarks', *Runeindskrifter*, 1 text; 2 atlas (plates), Copenhagen

Jakobsen, J, 1993 *The place-names of Shetland*, The Orcadian Ltd, Kirkwall

James, H, F, 1999 'Excavations of a medieval cemetery at Skaill House, and a cist in the Bay of Skaill, Sandwick, Orkney', *Proceedings of the Society of Antiquaries of Scotland* 129, 753–777

James, H F and Yeoman, P, 2008 *Excavations at St Etherman's Monastery, Isle of May, Fife, 1992–7*, Tayside and Fife Archaeological Committee Monograph 6, Edinburgh

Johnson, P G, 2000 'Geophysical survey', in R Harry, *St Ninian's Isle survey and excavation 1999*, Glasgow University Archaeological Research Division unpublished report 689, Glasgow University, 25–36

Kaland, S H H, 1993 'The settlement of Westness, Rousay', in C E Batey, J Jesch and C D Morris (eds), *The Viking Age in Caithness, Orkney and the North Atlantic. Select papers from the Proceedings of the Eleventh Viking Congress, Thurso and Kirkwall,* Edinburgh University Press, Edinburgh, 308–317

Kay, G, 1908 'A description of Dunrossness by G Kay, minister thereof', Description of ye Countrey of Zetland (ed. G Bruce), Edinburgh

Kennedy, K A R, 1989 'Skeletal markers of occupational stress', in M Yaşar İşcan and K A R Kennedy (eds), *Reconstruction of life from the skeleton*, Liss, New York, 129–160

Kermack, S, 1996 'Passports to paradise', in the *Pictish Arts Society Journal* 10 (Winter 1996), Pictish Arts Society, Edinburgh, 23–25

Kermode, P M C, 1907 *Manx Crosses*, London (Pinkfoot Press reprint with introduction by D M Wilson, Balgavies 1994)

Kermode, P M C, 1930 'Notes on early cross-slabs from the Faeroe Islands', *Proceedings of the Society of Antiquaries of Scotland* 65, 373–378

Kerney, M P and Cameron, R A D, 1979 *Land snails of Britain and North-West Europe*, Harper Collins Publishers, London

Kitching, J A, 1985 'The ecological significance and control of shell variability in dod-whelks from temperate rocky shores', in P G Moore and R Seed (eds), *The ecology of rocky coasts*, Hodder and Stoughton, London

Koch, J T, 1983 'The loss of final syllables and loss of declension in Brittonic', *Bulletin of the Board of Celtic Studies* 30, 201–233

Lager, L, 2002 *Den synliga tron: runstenskors som en spegling av kristandet i Sverige*, Uppsala

Laing, L R, 1975 *The archaeology of late Celtic Britain and Ireland c. 400 –1200 AD*, Methuen, London

Lamb, R G, 1976 'The Burri Stacks of Culswick, Shetland, and other paired stack settlements', *Proceedings of the Society of Antiquaries of Scotland* 107, 144–154

Lamb, H, 1981 'Climate from 1000 BC to 1000 AD', in M Jones and G Dimbleby (eds), *The Environment of Man: The Iron Age to the Anglo-Saxon Period*, British Archaeological Reports, British Series 87, Oxford, 53–65

Lamb, R G, 1973 'Coastal settlements of the North', in *Scottish Archaeological Forum* 5, 76–98

Lamb, R G, 1995 'Papil, Picts and Papar', in *Northern Isles Connections. Essays from Orkney & Shetland presented to Per Sveaas Andersen*, The Orkney Press, Kirkwall, 9–27

Lamb, R and Downes, J, 2000 *Prehistoric Houses at Sumburgh in Shetland*, Oxbow Books, Oxford

Lang, J T, 1974 'Hogback monuments in Scotland', *Proceedings of the Society of Antiquaries of Scotland* 105, 206–235

Lindeman, F O, 2006 'Celtic *namant-', *Zeitschrift für Celtische Philologie* 55, 18–23

Longin, R, 1971 'New method of collagen extraction for radiocarbon dating', *Nature* 230, 241–242

Low, Rev G, 1879 *Tour through the islands of Orkney and Shetland*, Kirkwall

Lowe, C E, 1987 *Early ecclesiastical sites in the Northern Isles and Isle of Man: an archaeological field survey*, 2 vols, unpublished PhD thesis, Department of Archaeology, Durham University

Lowe, C E, 1998 *Coastal erosion and the archaeological assessment of an eroding shoreline at St Boniface Church, Papa Westray, Orkney*, Sutton, Stroud

Lowe, C E, 2002 'The *papar* and Papa Stronsay: 8th century reality or 12th century myth?', in B E Crawford (ed), *The Papar in the North Atlantic: environment and history*, St John's House Papers 10, St Andrews, 83–95

Lowe, C E, Buteux, S and Hunter, J, 2000 'St Nicholas Chapel, Papa Stronsay', *Discovery and Excavation in Scotland*, New Series 1, 67–68

Macalister, R A S, 1940 'The inscriptions and language of the Picts', in J Ryan (ed), *Feíl-Sgríbhinn Eóin mhic Néill, Essays and Studies Presented to Professor Eoin MacNeill*, Dublin, 184–226

Macalister, R A S, 1945 *Corpus Inscriptionem Insularum Celticarum*, vol. 1, Stationery Office, Dublin (= CIIC)

MacDonald, A, 2002 'The Papar and some problems: a brief review', in B E Crawford (ed), *The Papar in the North Atlantic: environment and history*, St John's House Papers 10, St Andrews, 13–29

MacDonald, A D S and Laing, L R, 1969 'Early ecclesiastical sites in Scotland: a field survey, Part 1', *Proceedings of the Society of Antiquaries of Scotland* 100, 123–134

MacGregor, A, 1976 'The broch of Burrian, North Ronaldsay, Orkney', *Proceedings of the Society of Antiquaries of Scotland* 105, 63–118

McKinney, F K and Jackson, J B C, 1989 *Bryozoan evolution*, Unwin Hyman, London

McManus, D, 1986 'Ogam: archaizing, orthography and the authenticity of the manuscript key to the alphabet', *Ériu* 37, 1–31

McManus, D, 1988 'Irish letter-names and their kennings', *Ériu* 39, 127–168

McManus, D, 1991 *A guide to ogam*, Maynooth Monographs 4, An Sagart, Maynooth

McNeill, P G B and MacQueen, H L (eds), 1996 *An atlas of Scottish history to 1707*, Scottish Medievalists, Department of Geography, University of Edinburgh, Edinburgh

McRoberts, D, 1962 'The ecclesiastical significance of the St Ninian's Isle treasure', *Proceedings of the Society of Antiquaries of Scotland* 94, 301–313

McRoberts, D, 1965 'The ecclesiastical significance of the St Ninian's Isle treasure', in A Small (ed), *The Fourth Viking Congress York, August 1961*, published for the University of Aberdeen by Oliver and Boyd, 224–246

MacSween, A, 1998a 'Ceramics', in N Sharples, *Scalloway. A broch, Late Iron Age settlement and medieval cemetery in Shetland*, Cardiff Studies in Archaeology, Oxbow Monograph 82, Oxford, 12, 91, 96–99, 121–123, 132–136

MacSween, A, 1998b 'Preliminary comments on the Old Scatness pottery', in R A Nicholson and S J Dockrill, *Old Scatness broch, Shetland: retrospect and prospect*, Bradford Archaeological Sciences Research 5, Bradford, 85–87

MacSween, A, 2002 'Dun Beag and the role of pottery in interpretations of the Hebridean Iron Age', in B Ballin Smith and I Banks (eds), *In the shadow of the brochs: the Iron Age in Scotland*, Tempus, Stroud, 145–152

Mather, A D and Smith, J S, 1974 *Beaches of Shetland*, Department of Geography, University of Aberdeen, Aberdeen

Mays, S A, Richards, M P and Fuller, B T, 2002 'Bone stable isotope evidence for infant feeding in mediaeval England', in *Antiquity* 76, 654–656

Metropolitan Museum of Art, 1996 *Enamels of Limoges 1100–1350*, Metropolitan Museum of Art, New York

Moar, P, 1952 'Two Shetland finds', *Proceedings of the Society of Antiquaries of Scotland* 86, 206

Molto, J E, Stewart, J D, and Reimer, P, 1997 'Problems in radiocarbon dating human remains from arid coastal areas: an example from the cape region of Baja California', *American Antiquity* 62(3), 489–507

Mook, W G, 1986 Business meeting: Recommendations/Resolutions adopted by the Twelfth International Radiocarbon Conference, *Radiocarbon* 28, 799

Moore, H and Wilson, G, 1999 *The Bayanne Project. Interim report 1995–1997*, Shetland Amenity Trust and Historic Scotland

Morris, C D, 1989 *The Birsay Bay Project Volume 1. Brough Road excavations 1976–1982*, Department of Archaeology, University of Durham, Monograph Series 1, Durham

Morris, C D, 1990 *Church and monastery in the far North: an archaeological evaluation*, Jarrow Lecture, 1989 (Jarrow: Rector and Parish of St Paul's, 1990)

Morris, C D, 1991 'Native and Norse in Orkney and Shetland', in C Karkov, and R Farrell (eds) *Studies in insular art and archaeology*, American Early Medieval Studies 1, 61–80

Morris, C D, 1996a 'The Norse impact in the northern Isles of Scotland', in J F Kroger and H Naley (eds), *Nordsjøen: Handel, religion og politikk: Karmøyseminaret 1994 og 1995*, Dreyer Bok, Stavanger, 69–83

Morris, C D, 1996b 'Church and monastery in Orkney and Shetland. An archaeological perspective', in J F Kroger and H Naley (eds), *Nordsjøen: Handel, religion og politikk: Karmøyseminaret 1994 og 1995*, Dreyer Bok, Stavanger, 185–206

Morris, C D, 1996c 'From Birsay to Tintagel: a personal view', in B E Crawford (ed), *Scotland in Dark Age Britain*, St John's House Papers 6, Aberdeen, 53–55

Morris, C D, 1998 'Raiders, traders and settlers: the early Viking age in Scotland', in H B Clarke, M Ní Mhaonaigh and R Ó Floinn, *Ireland and Scandinavia in the Early Viking Age*, Dublin, 73–103

Morris, C D, 2001 'Norse Settlement in Shetland: the Shetland chapel-sites project', in G Fellows-Jensen (ed), *Denmark and Scotland: the cultural and environmental resources of small nations, Joint symposium of the Royal Society of Edinburgh and the Royal Danish Academy of Sciences and Letters held in Copenhagen 15th–18th September 1999*, København, 58–78

Morris, C D, 2003 'Christian Vikings in the North Atlantic Region', in S Lewis-Simpson (ed), *Vinland revisited: the Norse world at the turn of the first millennium: Selected papers from the Viking Millennium International Symposium, 15–24 September 2000, Newfoundland and Labrador*, Historical Sites Association of Newfoundland and Labrador Inc, St John's, Newfoundland, 305–318

Morris, C D, 2004 'From Birsay to Brattahlid. Recent perspectives on Norse Christianity in Orkney, Shetland and the North Atlantic region', in J Adams and K Holman (eds), *Scandinavia and Europe 800–1350: Contact, continuity and coexistence*, Brepols, Turnhout, 177–196

Morris, C D and Barrowman, R C, 2008 'The Shetland Chapel-Sites Project: further investigations and resume', in C Paulsen and H D Michelsen (eds), *Símunarbók. Heiðursrit til Símun V Arge á 60 ára degnum 5 september 2008*, Froðskapur-Faroe University Press, Tórshavn, 166–192

Morris, C D and Brady, K J, with a contribution from Johnson, P G, 1999 'The Shetland Chapel-Sites Project 1997–98', *Church Archaeology* 3, 25–33

Morris, C D with Emery, N, 1986a 'The chapel and enclosure on the Brough of Deerness, Orkney, survey and excavations 1975–7', *Proceedings of the Society of Antiquaries Scotland* 116, 301–374

Morris, C D with Emery, N, 1986b 'The setting for the Brough of Deerness, Orkney', *Northern Studies* 23 (1986), 301–374, microfiche 2–4

Muir, T S, 1861 *Shetland: an ecclesiological sketch*, T&T Clark, Edinburgh

Mulville, J, Parker Pearson, M, Sharples, N, Smith, H and Chamberlain, A, 2003 'Quarters, arcs and squares: human and animal remains in the Hebridean Late Iron Age', in J Downes and A Ritchie (eds), *Sea change: Orkney and Northern Europe in the later Iron Age AD 300–800*, Pinkfoot Press, Balgavies, 21–34

Murray, J C, (ed) 1982 *Excavations in the medieval burgh of Aberdeen 1973–81*, Society of Antiquaries of Scotland Monograph Series 2, Edinburgh

Mykura, W, 1976 *Orkney and Shetland*, British Regional Geology Series, HMSO, Edinburgh

Name Book, *Original Name Books of the Ordnance Survey*, Book 10

Nash-Williams, V E, 1950 *The early Christian monuments of Wales*, University of Wales Press, Cardiff

NMAS Cat 1892 *Catalogue of the National Museum of Antiquities of Scotland*, printed for the Society of Antiquaries of Scotland, Edinburgh

Nature Conservancy Council, 1976 *Shetland: localities of geological and geomorphological importance*, Lerwick

Neighbour, T, Knott, C, Bruce, M, F and Neill, W K, 2000 'Excavation of two burials at Galson, Isle of Lewis, 1993 and 1996', *Proceedings of the Society of Antiquaries Scotland* 130, 559–584

Neighbour, T, Church, M and Heald, A, with contributions by Cerón-Carrasco, R, Johnson, M, Tams, A and Thomas, J, forthcoming *The eroding settlement and cemetery at Galson, Isle of Lewis*

Nicholson, R A, 1998 'Fishing for facts: a preliminary view of the fish remains from Old Scatness Broch', in R A Nicholson and S J Dockrill (eds), *Old Scatness Broch, Shetland: retrospect and prospect*, Bradford Archaeological Sciences Research 5, Bradford, 97–110

Nicholson, R A and Dockrill, S J, (eds) 1998 *Old Scatness Broch, Shetland: retrospect and prospect*, Bradford Archaeological Sciences Research 5, Bradford

Nisbet, H C, 1958 'Chapel and village, North Rona', *Discovery and Excavation in Scotland*, 1958, 33

Nisbet, H C and Gailey, R A, 1962 'A survey of the antiquities of North Rona', *Archaeological Journal* 117, 88–115

O'Brien, M A, 1976 (reprint) *Corpus Genealogiarum Hiberniae*

O'Brien, E and Roberts, C, 1996 'Archaeological study of church cemeteries: past, present and future', in J Blair and C Pyrah (eds), *Church archaeology: research directions for the future*, Council for British Archaeology Research Report 104, London, 159–181

O'Brien, M A, 1962 *Corpus Genealogiarum Hiberniae*, vol. 1, Dublin Institute for Advanced Studies, Dublin

O'Dell, A C, 1939 *The historical geography of the Shetland Islands*, Manson, Lerwick

O'Dell, A C, 1957 'St Ninian's Isle', *Discovery and Excavation in Scotland*, 35

O'Dell, A C, 1958 'St Ninian's Isle', *Discovery and Excavation in Scotland*, 34–35

O'Dell, A, 1959a 'Excavations at St Ninian's Isle', *The Scottish Geographical Magazine* 75, 41–43

O'Dell, A, 1959b 'Introduction', in A C O'Dell, R B K Stevenson, T N Brown, H J Plenderleith and R L S Bruce-Mitford, 'The St Ninian's Isle Silver Hoard', *Antiquity* 33, 1959, 241–243 (241–268)

O'Dell, A C, 1959c 'St Ninian's Isle', *Discovery and Excavation in Scotland*, 34–35

O'Dell, A C, 1960 'St Ninian's Isle excavations', in A C O'Dell and A Cain, *St Ninian's Isle Treasure*, Edinburgh, 4–5

O'Dell, A C and Cain, A, 1960 *St Ninian's Isle Treasure*, Oliver and Boyd for the University of Aberdeen, Edinburgh

O'Dell, A C, 1962 *The Highlands and Islands of Scotland*, T Nelson, London

O'Donovan, J, 1868 *Cormac's Glossary*, translated and annotated by John O'Donovan, edited by Whitley Stokes, Calcutta

Øien, T, 2005 'The Northern Isles – between two nations', *Northern Studies* 39, 80–104

Okasha, E, 1985 'The non-ogam inscriptions of Pictland', *Cambridge Medieval Studies* 9, 43–69

Okasha, E, 1992 'The inscriptions: transliteration, translation and epigraphy', in D Tweddle (ed), *The Anglian helmet from Coppergate*, The Archaeology of York 17/8, London, 1012–15

O'Meadhra, U, 1979 *Early Christian, Viking and Romanesque Art: motif-pieces from Ireland*, Theses and papers in North-European Archaeology 7, Stockholm

O'Sullivan, J, 1994 'Excavation of an early church and a women's cemetery at St Ronan's medieval parish church, Iona', *Proceedings of the Society of Antiquaries Scotland* 124, 327–365, fiche 3: A5–D11

O'Sullivan, A and Sheehan, J, 1996 *The Iveragh Peninsula: an archaeological survey of South Kerry*, Cork University Press, Cork

Ortner, D J and Putschar, W G J, 1981 *Identification of palaeopathological conditions in human skeletal remains*, Smithsonian Institution Press, Washington

Ottaway, P, 1992 *Anglo-Scandinavian ironwork from Coppergate*, The Archaeology of York The Small Finds 17/6, York

Owen, O, 1999 'The exotic porphyry', in O Owen and C Lowe, *Kebister: the four-thousand-year-old story of one Shetland township*, Society of Antiquaries of Scotland Monograph Series 14, Edinburgh, 223–225

Owen, O and Lowe, C, 1999 *Kebister: the four-thousand-year-old story of one Shetland township*, Society of Antiquaries of Scotland Monograph Series 14, Edinburgh

Padel, O P, 1972a *Inscriptions of Pictland*, Unpublished M Litt Thesis, University of Edinburgh

Padel, O P, 1972b 'A note on the ogham inscriptions on the stones at Newton and Logie House', *Archaeology Journal* 129, 196–198

Peterkin, A, 1839 *The booke of the universal kirk of Scotland*, The Edinburgh Printing and Publishing Co. and William Blackwood and Sons, Edinburgh

Pollard, A J, 1994 *A study of marine exploitation in prehistoric Scotland, with special reference to marine shells and their archaeological contexts*, unpublished PhD thesis, Glasgow University

Ponting, M R, 1989 'Two Iron-Age cists from Galson, Isle of Lewis', *Proceedings of the Society of Antiquaries Scotland* 119, 91–100, fiche 3: F1–G14

Potter, T W and Andrews, R D, 1994 'Excavation and survey at St Patrick's chapel and St Peter's church, Heysham, Lancashire, 1977–78', *Antiquaries Journal* 74, 55–134

Proudfoot, E, 1996 'Excavations at the long cist cemetery on the Hallow Hill, St Andrew's, Fife 1975–7', *Proceedings of the Society of Antiquaries Scotland* 126, 387–454

Proudfoot, E and Aliaga-Kelly, C, 1996 'Towards an interpretation of anomalous finds and place-names of Anglo-Saxon origin in Scotland', *Anglo-Saxon Studies in Archaeology and History* 9, 1–13

Rackham, D J, 1987 'Assessing the relative frequencies of species by the application of a stochastic model to a computerised database of fossil or archaeological skeletal material', in L van Wijngaarden-Bakker (ed), *Data Management of Archaeological Skeletal Material*, PACT

Rackham, D J, with others, 1996 'Beachview, Birsay: The Biological Assemblage', in C D Morris, *The Birsay Bay Project*

Volume 2. Sites in Birsay Village and on the Brough of Birsay, Orkney, Department of Archaeology, University of Durham, Monograph Series 2, Durham, 161-191

Radford, C A R, 1959 The Early Christian and Norse Settlements at Birsay, Orkney, Department of the Environment Official Guide, Edinburgh

Radford, C A R, 1962 'Art and Architecture: Celtic and Norse', in F T Wainwright (ed), The Northern Isles, Studies in History and Archaeology, Nelson, Edinburgh, 163–187

Ralston, I and Inglis, J, 1984 Foul Hordes: the Picts in the North-East and their background, Anthropological Museum, University of Aberdeen

RCAHMS, 1946 Inventory of the ancient and historic monuments of Orkney and Shetland, 3 vols, HMSO, Edinburgh

RCAHMS, 1971 Argyll: an inventory of the monuments. 1 Kintyre, HMSO, Edinburgh

RCAHMS, 1994 South-East Perth: an archaeological landscape, HMSO, Edinburgh

RCAHMS, 2007 In the shadow of Bennachie: a field archaeology of Donside, Aberdeenshire, Edinburgh

RCAHMS, 1982 An inventory of the monuments, 4 (Iona), HMSO, Edinburgh

Reed, D, 1995 'The excavation of a cemetery and putative chapel site at Newhall Point, Balblair, Ross & Cromarty, 1985', Proceedings of the Society of Antiquaries Scotland 125, 779–791, fiche 3: G1–7

Reed, I, 1990 1000 years of pottery: an analysis of pottery trade and use, Riksantikvaren Utgravningskontoret for Trondheim, Trondheim

Reimer, P J, Brown, T A and Reimer, R W, 2004 'Discussion: reporting and calibration of post-bomb C-14 data', Radiocarbon 46(3), 1299–1304

Reimer, P J, Baillie, M G L, Bard, E, Bayliss, A, Beck, J W, Blackwell, P G, Bronk Ramsey, C, Buck, C E, Burr, G south, Edwards, R L, Friedrich, M, Grootes, P M, Guilderson, T P, Hajdas, I, Heaton, T J, Hogg, A G, Hughen, K A, Kaiser, K F, Kromer, B, McCormac, F G, Manning, S W, Reimer, R W, Richards, D A, Southon, J R, Talamo, south, Turney, C S M, van der Plicht, J, and Weyhenmeyer, C E, 2009 'IntCal09 and Marine09 radiocarbon age calibration curves, 0–50,000 years cal BP', Radiocarbon 51(4), 1111–50

Rhys, J, 1892 'The inscriptions and language of the northern Picts', Proceedings of the Society of Antiquaries Scotland 26, 263–351

Richards, M P and van Klinken, G J, 1997 'A survey of human bone stable carbon and nitrogen isotope values', in A Sinclair, E Slater, and J Gowlett (eds), Archaeological Sciences: proceedings of a conference on the application of scientific techniques to the study of archaeology, Liverpool, July 1995, Oxford, 365–367

Richards, M P and Mellars, P A, 1998 'Stable isotopes and the seasonality of the Oronsay middens', Antiquity 72, 178–184

Richards, M P, Fuller, B T and Molleson, T, 2006 'Stable isotope palaeodietary study of humans and fauna from the multiperiod (Iron Age, Viking and late medieval) site of Newark Bay, Orkney', Journal of Archaeological Science 33, 122–131

Ritchie, A, 1974 'Pict and Norseman in northern Scotland', Scottish Archaeological Forum 6 23–36

Ritchie, A, 1998 'Painted pebbles', in N Sharples, Scalloway. A broch, Late Iron Age settlement and medieval cemetery in Shetland, Cardiff Studies in Archaeology, Oxbow Monograph 82, Oxford, 176–178

Ritchie, A, 2003 'Paganism among the Picts and the conversion of Orkney', in J Downes and A Ritchie (eds), Sea change: Orkney and Northern Europe in the later Iron Age AD 300–800, Pinkfoot Press, Balgavies, 3–10

Roberts, C and Manchester, K, 1997 The archaeology of disease, Sutton Publishing Ltd, Cornell University Press, Ithaca, New York (2nd edition)

Sagar, P, 1969 Spondylosis cervicalis. A pathological and osteoarchaeo-logical study, Munksgaard, Copenhagen

Scheuer, L and Black, S, 2000 Developmental juvenile osteology, Academic Press, London

Schweingruber, F H, 1990 Anatomy of European woods, Haupt, Berne and Stuttgart

Scott, E, 1999 The archaeology of infancy and infant death, British Archaeological Reports, International Series 819, Oxford

Scott, E M, Harkness, D D and Cook, G T, 1998 'Inter-laboratory comparisons: lessons learned', Radiocarbon 40, 331–340

Scott, I G and Ritchie, A, 2010 Pictish and Viking-Age carvings from Shetland, RCAHMS, Edinburgh

Serjeantson, D, 1998 'Birds: a seasonal resource', Environmental Archaeology 3, 23–33

Sharman, P 1998a 'The steatite', in N Sharples, Scalloway. A broch, Late Iron Age settlement and medieval cemetery in Shetland, Cardiff Studies in Archaeology, Oxbow Monograph 82, Oxford, 119–121

Sharman, P, 1998b 'Lamp', in N Sharples, Scalloway. A broch, Late Iron Age settlement and medieval cemetery in Shetland, Cardiff Studies in Archaeology, Oxbow Monograph 82, Oxford, 149

Sharman, P, 1998c 'Whorls', in N Sharples, Scalloway. A broch, Late Iron Age settlement and medieval cemetery in Shetland, Cardiff Studies in Archaeology, Oxbow Monograph 82, Oxford, 150–152

Sharman, P, 1998d 'Steatite vessels', in N Sharples, Scalloway. A broch, Late Iron Age settlement and medieval cemetery in Shetland, Cardiff Studies in Archaeology, Oxbow Monograph 82, Oxford, 138–139

Sharman, P M, 1999 'The steatite', in O Owen and C Lowe, Kebister: the four-thousand-year-old story of one Shetland township, Society of Antiquaries of Scotland Monograph Series 14, Edinburgh, 168–178

Sharman, P M and Smith, A N, 1998 'Beads', in N Sharples, Scalloway. A broch, Late Iron Age settlement and medieval cemetery in Shetland, Cardiff Studies in Archaeology, Oxbow Monograph 82, Oxford, 171–172

Sharples, N, 1998 Scalloway. A broch, Late Iron Age settlement and medieval cemetery in Shetland, Cardiff Studies in Archaeology, Oxbow Monograph 82, Oxford

Shetland Museum, 1997a 'Breck of Hillwell', Discovery and Excavation in Scotland, 67

Shetland Museum, 1997b 'Ireland Wick', Discovery and Excavation in Scotland, 68

Sibbald, R, 1711 Description of the Islands of Orkney and Zetland T G Stevenson, Edinburgh

Silver, I A, 1969 'The ageing of domestic animals', in Brothwell, D and Higgs, E S (eds), Science in archaeology. A survey of progress and research, London, 283–302

Simpson, I, with Guttmann, E B, 2002 'Transitions in early arable land management in the Northern Isles: the papar as agricultural innovators', in B E Crawford (ed), The Papar in the North Atlantic: environment and history, St John's House Papers 10, St Andrews, 59–67

Simpson, W D, 1940 Saint Ninian and the origins of the Christian Church in Scotland, Oliver and Boyd, Edinburgh

Simpson, W D, 1944 The province of Mar (Rhind Lectures 1941), Aberdeen University Studies 121, Aberdeen University Press, Aberdeen

Simpson, W D, (ed) 1954 The Viking Congress, Lerwick, July 1950, Aberdeen University studies 132, Published for the University of Aberdeen, Edinburgh

Sims-Williams, P, 1992 'The additional letters of the ogam alphabet', Cambridge Medieval Celtic Studies 23, 29–75

Sims-Williams, P, 1993 'Some problems in deciphering the early Irish ogam alphabet', Transactions of the Philological Society 91.2, 133–180

Sims-Williams, P, 2003 The Celtic inscriptions of Britain: phonology and chronology, c. 400–1200, Blackwell, Oxford

Slota, P J, Jr, Jull, A J T, Linick, T W and Toolin, L J, 1987 'Preparation of small samples for ^{14}C accelerator targets by catalytic reduction of CO', *Radiocarbon* 29, 303–306

Small, A, 1973 'The site: it's history and excavation', in A Small, C Thomas and D M Wilson, *St Ninian's Isle and its treasure*, 2 vols, Aberdeen University Studies 152, Oxford University Press, Oxford, 1–7

Small, A, Thomas, C, and Wilson, D M, 1973 *St Ninian's Isle and its treasure*, 2 vols, Aberdeen University Studies 152, Oxford University Press, Oxford

Smith, A N, 1998 'Miscellaneous bone tools', in N Sharples, *Scalloway. A broch, Late Iron Age settlement and medieval cemetery in Shetland*, Cardiff Studies in Archaeology, Oxbow Monograph 82, Oxford, 152–158

Smith, B, 1984 'What is a Scattald? Rural communities in Shetland, 1400–1900', in B E Crawford (ed), *Essays in Shetland History*, Shetland Times, Lerwick, 99–124

Smith, B, 2000 *Toons and tenants. Settlement and society in Shetland 1299–1899*, Shetland Times, Lerwick

Smith, B, 2001 'The Picts and the martyrs or did Vikings kill the native population of Orkney and Shetland?', *Northern Studies* 36, 7–32

Smith, B, 2003 'Not welcome at all: Vikings and the native population in Orkney and Shetland', in J Downes and A Ritchie (eds), *Sea change: Orkney and Northern Europe in the later Iron Age AD 300–800*, Pinkfoot Press, Balgavies, 145–150

Smith, T B, 1973 'The law relating to the treasure', in A Small, C Thomas and D M Wilson, *St Ninian's Isle and its treasure*, 2 vols, Aberdeen University Studies 152, Oxford University Press, Oxford, 149–166

Southesk, Rt Hon Earl of, 1884 'The ogham inscriptions of Scotland', *Proceedings of the Society of Antiquaries of Scotland* 18, 180–206

Stace, C, 1997 *New flora of the British Isles*, Cambridge University Press, Cambridge (2nd edition)

Statistical Account of Scotland 1791–9 Number XXXIX: Parish of Dunrossness in Zetland, by the Reverend Mr John Mill

Statistical Account of Scotland 1845 Parish of Dunrossness, by the Rev David Thomson

Steier, P, and Rom, W, 2000 'The use of Bayesian statistics for ^{14}C dates of chronologically ordered samples: a critical analysis', *Radiocarbon* 42(2), 183–198

Steier, P, Rom, W, and Puchegger, S, 2001 'New methods and critical aspects in Bayesian mathematics for ^{14}C calibration', *Radiocarbon* 43(2A), 373–380

Stevenson, R B K, 1959 'The Inchyra Stone and some other unpublished early Christian monuments', *Proceedings of the Society of Antiquaries of Scotland* 92, 33–55

Stevenson, R B K, 1981 'Christian sculpture in Norse Shetland', *Fróðskaparrit (Heiðurscrit til Sverra Dahl)*, *Annales Societatis Scientiarum Faeroensis* 28/29, 283–292

Stevenson, R B K, 1986 'Votive coins deposited between 1600 and 1800 in Orkney and elsewhere', in C D Morris with N Emery, 'The chapel and enclosure on the Brough of Deerness, Orkney, survey and excavations 1975–7', *Proceedings of the Society of Antiquaries Scotland* 116, 343–345 (301–374)

Stewart, J, 1987 *Shetland place-names*, Shetland Library and Museum, Lerwick

Stuart Macadam, P, 1989 'Nutritional deficiency diseases: a survey of scurvy, rickets, and iron deficiency anaemia', *Reconstruction of life from the skeleton,* Alan R Liss Inc. 201–222

Stuiver, M and Kra, R S, 1986 'Editorial comment', *Radiocarbon* 28(2B), ii

Stuiver, M, and Polach, H A, 1977 'Reporting of ^{14}C data', *Radiocarbon* 19, 355–363

Stuiver, M, and Reimer, P J, 1986 'A computer program for radiocarbon age calculation', *Radiocarbon* 28, 1022–30

Stuiver, M, and Reimer, P J, 1993 'Extended ^{14}C data base and revised CALIB 3.0 ^{14}C age calibration program', *Radiocarbon* 35, 215–230

Stuiver, M, Reimer, P J, Bard, E, Beck, J W, Burr, G S, Hughen, K A, Kromer, B, McCormac, F G, van der Plicht, J and Spurk, M, 1998 'INTCAL98 radiocarbon age calibration, 24,000–0 cal BP', *Radiocarbon* 40, 1041–84

Thomas, A C, 1967 'An early Christian cemetery and chapel on Ardwall Isle, Kirkcudbright', *Medieval Archaeology* 11, 127–188

Thomas, A C, 1971 *The early Christian archaeology of north Britain*, the Hunter Marshall lectures delivered at the University of Glasgow in January and February 1968, London

Thomas, A C, 1973 'Sculptured stones and crosses from St Ninian's Isle and Papil', in A Small, C Thomas and D M Wilson, *St Ninian's Isle and its treasure*, 2 vols, Aberdeen University Studies 152, Oxford University Press, Oxford, 8–48

Thomas, C, 1983 'The Double Shrine "A" from St Ninian's Isle, Shetland', in A O'Connor and D V Clarke (eds), *From the Stone Age to the 'Forty Five': Studies presented to RBK Stevenson*, John Donald Publications, Edinburgh, 285–292

Thomas, C, 1998 'Form and function', in S M Foster (ed), *The St Andrew's Sarcophagus: a Pictish masterpiece and its international connection*s, Four Courts Press, Dublin, 84–96

Thomson, W P L, 2007 'The Orkney *Papar*-names', in B Ballin, S Smith and G Williams (eds), *West over the sea. Studies in Scandinavian sea-borne expansion and settlement before 1300: a festschrift in honour of Dr Barbara E Crawford*, Brill, Leiden, 515–538

Thurneysen, R, 1946 *A Grammar of old Irish* (Revised and enlarged edition with supplement), translated by D A Binchy and Osborn Bergin, reprinted 1980, Institute for Advanced Studies, Dublin

Toussaint, J, 1996 *Emaux de Limoges XIIe–XIXe siecle*, Namurois, Musee des arts anciennes du Namurois

Trotter, M, 1970 'Estimation of stature from intact long limb bones', in T D Stewart (ed), *Personal identification in mass disasters*, Smithsonian Institute, Washington DC, 71–83

Turner, V E, 1994 'Noss', *Discovery and Excavation in Scotland*, 93

Turner, V, 1998 *Ancient Shetland*, Batsford, London

Turner, V, forthcoming 'The partial excavation of the cemetery and "steeple kirk" at Gungstie, Noss'

Tweddle, D, (ed) 1992 *The Anglian helmet from Coppergate*, The Archaeology of York 17/8, London

Ubelaker, D H, 1989 *Human skeletal remains excavation, analysis, interpretation*, Taraxacum, Washington (2nd edition)

Uhlich, J, 1993 *Die Morphologie der komponierten Personnamen des Altirischen* (Beiträge zu Sprachwissenschaften 1), Wehle, Witterschlick/Bonn

VC: Adomnán's *Vita Columbae* 1961 *Adomnán's Life of Columba* (edited with translation and notes by A O Anderson and by M O Anderson), Thomas Nelson, Edinburgh

Verhaeghe, F, 1983 'Low Countries pottery imported into Scotland: note on a minor trade', *Medieval Ceramics* 7, 95–99

Wainwright, F T, 1961 *The Inchyra Ogam*, Dundee Archaeological Studies 1 [first published in *Ogam* 11 (1959), 269–278]

Ward, G K and Wilson, S R, 1978 'Procedures for comparing and combining radiocarbon age determinations: a critique', *Archaeometry* 20, 19–31

Watson, W J, 1926 *The history of the Celtic place-names of Scotland: being the Rhind Lectures on Archaeology (expanded) delivered in 1916*, William Blackwood, Edinburgh

Webster, L E and Blackhouse, J (eds), 1991 *The making of England: Anglo-Saxon art and culture, AD 600–900*, British Museum, London

Welander, R, Batey, œast and Cowie, T, 1987 'A Viking burial from Kneep, Uig, Isle of Lewis', *Proceedings of the Society of Antiquaries of Scotland* 117, 149–174

Whitehead, P J P, Bauchot, M L, Hureau, J C, Nielsen, J and Tortonese, E (eds), 1986 *Fishes of the North-eastern Atlantic and the Mediterranean, Volume 3*, United Nations Educational, Scientific and Cultural Organization, Paris

Whittle, A R W, 1986 *Scord of Brouster: an early agricultural settlement on Shetland*, Oxford University Committee for Archaeology, Monograph 9, Oxford

Will, R and Haggarty, G, 1996 'The pottery', in J Lewis, 'Excavations at St Andrews Castle, Castlecliff, 1988-90', *Proceedings of the Society of Antiquaries of Scotland* 126, 648-669 (605–688)

Wilson, D M, 1970 *Reflections on the St Ninian's Isle treasure*, the Rector of Jarrow, Jarrow

Wilson, D M, 1973 'The treasure', in A Small, C Thomas and D M Wilson, *St Ninian's Isle and its treasure*, 2 vols, Aberdeen University Studies 152, Oxford University Press, Oxford, 45–148

Wilson, G, 1998 'Counters', in N Sharples, *Scalloway. A broch, Late Iron Age settlement and medieval cemetery in Shetland*, Cardiff Studies in Archaeology, Oxbow Monograph 82, Oxford, 180

Woolf, A, 2007 *From Pictland to Alba 789–1070*, The New Edinburgh History of Scotland 2, Edinburgh University Press, Edinburgh

Youngs, S (ed), 1989 *'The work of angels': masterpieces of Celtic metalwork, 6th–9th centuries AD*, British Museum, London

Zohary, D and Hopf, M, 2000 *Domestication of plants in the Old World*, Oxford University Press, Oxford (3rd edition)

INDEX

Louisa Gidney

(Page numbers in italics refer to illustrations and/or their captions)